# UNLOCKING MATRIMONIAL ASSETS ON DIVORCE

## Second Edition

# UNLOCKING MATRIMONIAL ASSETS ON DIVORCE

Second Edition

by

**Simon Sugar, LLB (Warwick)**
*Of the Middle Temple, Barrister*

**Andrzej Bojarski, LLB (Lond)**
*Of Gray's Inn, Barrister*

with contributions by

**David Liddell, BSc (Bristol), ACA**
*Forensic Services Partner at PKF (UK) LLP*

**David Lockett, MA (Oxon), FIA**
*Partner, Actuaries for Lawyers*

**Family Law**

Published by Family Law
A publishing imprint of Jordan Publishing Limited
21 St Thomas Street
Bristol BS1 6JS

**British Library Cataloguing-in-Publication Data**

A catalogue record for this book is available from the British Library.

ISBN 978 184661 158 2

Typeset by Letterpart Ltd, Reigate, Surrey

Printed in Great Britain by CPI Antony Rowe, Chippenham, Wiltshire

# PREFACE

The law and practice of ancillary relief is truly dynamic. Since the first edition of the book some of the implications of *Miller v Miller; McFarlane v McFarlane* have filtered their way down to the Court of Appeal and on to a number of big money High Court cases. The importance of the source and categorisation of an asset became an increasingly significant concern. The battle between greater predictability of outcome and unfettered discretion continues to rage. Yardsticks of equality have mutated. The consequences of the application of the principles of needs, compensation and sharing are yet to be fully explored. Economic concerns have also had a significant impact on the application of the section 25 exercise and the former readily found anticipation of gold at the end of a rainbow has now been replaced by a rush towards the copper-bottom. Finally, for the vast majority of needs based cases more and more sophisticated arguments are being raised within the parameters of the section 25 exercise. Against this backdrop our hope is that the second edition of this book will be of some assistance to practitioners in identifying appropriate arguments to employ in their cases.

We believe that our aspirations for the book are assisted enormously by the contributions made by David Liddell and David Lockett, to whom we owe a debt of gratitude. Our clerks at 1 Garden Court and 36 Bedford Row have given the second edition of this book their wholehearted support. We thank them all for the sympathetic and skilful way in which they have assisted us in both running a practice and trying to keep to publishing deadlines. It is to be hoped that the entry 'keep free working on book' will not need to be made in our diaries for some time. Once again we would like to express our thanks for the help, encouragement and commitment given to us from all at Jordan Publishing, but especially Greg Woodgate, our commissioning editor. We would also like to thank Bobbi and John Whitcombe for their work turning our words into a book. Most of all, however, we would like to thank the contribution made to the welfare of our families by our spouses, who have tirelessly and stoically dealt with our absences from family life whilst working on this book; their conduct has been truly inequitable to ignore!

We have endeavoured to set out the law as at 1 July 2009.

*Simon Sugar*

*Andrzej Bojarski*

# CONTENTS

## Part II
## Disclosure

## Part VII
## Inherited Assets, Gifts and Non-Matrimonial Property

### Chapter 16
### Non-Matrimonial Property

### Chapter 17
### Property Already Acquired through an Inheritance

### Chapter 18
### Future Inheritance Prospects

## Part X
## Dealing with Ancillary Relief in Uncertain Economic Conditions

# BIOGRAPHICAL DETAILS

**Simon Sugar** was called to the Bar in 1990 after taking a law degree at Warwick University. He is a tenant at 1 Garden Court, Temple. His practice focuses on ancillary relief, co-habitation disputes and probate and Inheritance Act claims. With a background in Chancery law, Simon is particularly interested in ancillary relief cases involving companies, partnerships, trusts and farms. Simon contributes regular Finance Case Digests for Resolution's 'The Review'. He is a member of the Family Law Bar Association, the Chancery Bar and an affiliate member of Resolution.

**Andrzej Bojarski** studied law at the London School of Economics and was called to the Bar in 1995. He is a tenant of 36 Bedford Row. After obtaining wide experience in general common law practice in his early years at the Bar he is now a family law specialist, although he continues to conduct civil litigation linked to the financial aspects of relationship breakdown. He is regularly engaged in ancillary relief cases where the married couple's affairs have become intertwined with the affairs of a third party, such as a company, partnership or trust, or where there are disputes over the ownership of property or other related contractual or commercial disputes.

**David Liddell** is a Forensic Services partner at PKF (UK) LLP with over 15 years' experience of acting as an expert witness or in an advisory capacity in a variety of commercial and personal disputes and fraud investigations. He regularly assists in matrimonial cases when there are businesses to value, complex resources to divide, tax issues relating to the settlement, or allegations of fraud or non-disclosure of assets by one of the parties.

**David Lockett** was an Open Scholar at Oxford University, reading Mathematics with Philosophy. He is a Fellow of the Institute of Actuaries, having qualified in 1997 and has worked with Actuaries for Lawyers Ltd since it was formed. David now has 17 years' experience in pensions, of which 14 years have been in occupational pensions, and has been working exclusively on pensions advice for solicitors for 5 years; he has considerable experience acting as an expert witness. 'Actuaries for Lawyers' is consulted in over 1,000 matrimonial cases per year. David is a member of the Expert Witness Institute and an affiliate member of Resolution.

# TABLE OF CASES

References are to paragraph numbers.

# TABLE OF STATUTES

References are to paragraph numbers.

# TABLE OF STATUTORY INSTRUMENTS

**References are to paragraph numbers.**

# Chapter 1

# INTRODUCTION

**1.1**    Ancillary relief practice is challenging. Married couples often have complex financial affairs. Often those affairs are fully understood by only one of the parties to the marriage: frequently, but no longer exclusively, the husband. Sometimes the family finances are such that neither party to the marriage really has a grasp of their detail, particularly where there has been hopeless mismanagement and accumulation of debt upon debt. The family finances may also be inextricably enmeshed with the affairs of a third party, most commonly a new partner, other members of the extended family or business associates. These complexities, combined with the heightened emotional atmosphere which often surrounds a divorce and the far from uncommon desire of the parties to each become the 'winner' of the proceedings, create problems for any lawyer instructed to deal with the case. It falls to the ancillary relief lawyer to make sense of the whole picture and to chart an approach to 'unlock' assets and income so that they can be divided in a fair way.

## THE SCOPE OF THIS BOOK

**1.2**    This book attempts to provide the practitioner with a useful reference work when faced with the task of 'unlocking' the matrimonial assets. It aims to provide both a comprehensible and detailed overview of the law for the practitioner who only occasionally conducts ancillary relief litigation and also a useful reference work for the seasoned ancillary relief specialist. Although the book is written from the perspective of divorce proceedings, much of the content is equally likely to be applicable to cases concerning the dissolution of civil partnerships.

**1.3**    Relatively little is said in this book about the general principles and procedure applied in ancillary relief proceedings. The focus is principally on specific and more difficult areas of ancillary relief practice and the practicalities of finding the assets, protecting them and ultimately 'unlocking' their value for the parties. Those seeking guidance on matters of general procedure and practice should consult one of the more general texts on ancillary relief.[1] 'Legal ideas and phenomena are nearly always best viewed in some broader context rather than studied in isolation as if they were things in

---

[1]    For example, Roger Bird *Ancillary Relief Handbook* (Jordan Publishing Limited, 7th edn,

themselves'.[2] By analogy, an understanding of ss 22–25 of the Matrimonial Causes Act 1973 is clearly essential, but it is hoped that the contextual approach to the application of these sections adopted in this book will be of assistance.

**1.4**    The substantive content of this book begins in Part I with a detailed look at the law of evidence in the context of ancillary relief proceedings. This is an important but often forgotten area of practice. The lawyer who can authoritatively address the court on the relevant law of evidence is likely to place his or her client at a substantial advantage.

**1.5**    Part II considers the foundation of any ancillary relief case: disclosure. First, in Chapter 4, there is a detailed discussion of the duty of full and frank disclosure between the parties and the means by which further disclosure can and should be obtained. Secondly, the various methods by which disclosure can be obtained from non-parties are considered in Chapter 5 together with an exploration of the extent to which disclosure from non-parties can be or should be pursued.

**1.6**    Asset protection is at the heart of Part III. The important topic of protecting the assets from dissipation is explained in Chapter 6, while Chapter 7 sets out the means by which assets might be recovered even after they have been disposed of.

**1.7**    Part IV is devoted to the various forms of property commonly encountered in ancillary relief proceedings. Issues surrounding the ownership of property and third party interests are dealt with in Chapter 8. Chapter 9 is devoted to real property with a particular emphasis on the matrimonial home, which is so often the most important asset within any marriage, in terms of both financial and emotional value. Various problem areas such as reversionary interests and development potential are given specific attention. Chapter 10 considers some of the special issues which arise in respect of other forms of property, such as endowment policies, shares, options, intellectual property and offshore assets.

**1.8**    The spotlight is turned in Part V upon a difficult area of ancillary relief practice: business assets. Chapters 11, 12 and 13 explain in turn how companies, partnerships and farms are dealt with in a divorce context. Each chapter contains a clear summary of the legal nature and structure of each type of business enterprise, including an overview of company law in Chapter 11 and an explanation of farm subsidies in Chapter 13. Guides to reading business accounts are also included in those chapters, along with detailed explanation of

---

2009), *Duckworth's Matrimonial Property and Finance* (Jordan Publishing Limited (looseleaf)), *Rayden & Jackson on Divorce and Family Matters* (18th edn) and *Jackson's Matrimonial Finance and Taxation* (8th edn).

[2]    Twining and Miers *How To Do Things With Rules* (Butterworths, 4th edn), p 113.

the different methods of share valuation. Chapter 14 goes on to consider how finance can be raised from businesses in order to achieve a fair ancillary relief settlement.

**1.9** Parts VI and VII examine the interlinked topics of trusts and inherited assets. Chapter 15 provides a detailed exploration of trust law concepts and their relevance to ancillary relief practice. Chapter 16 reviews the extensive and often confusing case law dealing with the distinction between 'matrimonial' and 'non-matrimonial' property and how this distinction may affect the division of assets on divorce. The application of those principles to the specific case of assets which have already been inherited is the subject-matter of Chapter 17. Chapter 18 considers when the prospect of a future inheritance may be relevant to ancillary relief proceedings and how this might be dealt with in an order.

**1.10** Part VIII contains an explanation of one of the most complicated and frequently misunderstood family assets, namely pension funds. Chapter 20 describes the commonly encountered different types of pension scheme and the nature of the benefits paid under them. Chapter 21 looks at the types of order the court can make in relation to pensions and suggests when each type of order may be appropriate. Finally, Chapter 22 attempts to unravel the mysteries of the Cash Equivalent Transfer Value (CETV), assisting the practitioner in understanding when the pension scheme's own CETV will suffice for ancillary relief proceedings and when an independent valuation should be sought.

**1.11** Part IX provides an outline of the main forms of direct taxation to which a family is subject, so that the practitioner can understand the tax implications of various methods of dealing with the assets and so that those cases where the involvement of an accountant or tax consultant becomes essential are more readily identified.

**1.12** Finally, Part X contains a topical overview dealing with the practice of ancillary relief in uncertain economic times. Chapter 24 introduces the issues that potentially arise when divorcing in an economic downturn. Chapter 25 deals with insolvency and its impact on ancillary relief. Chapter 26 touches upon the vexed question of asset valuation in a volatile and fluctuating market. The creative use of ancillary relief orders in an uncertain financial climate is covered in Chapter 27.

## GENERAL PRINCIPLES AND THE USE OF CASE LAW IN ANCILLARY RELIEF PROCEEDINGS

**1.13** As every case falls to be decided on its own individual facts, it can be difficult to identify general guiding principles from the case law which will assist the parties in accurately predicting how a court will deal with their particular case. The House of Lords has endeavoured to provide some guidance by way of broad statements of principle in the landmark cases of

*White v White*[3] and *Miller v Miller; McFarlane v McFarlane*,[4] but always under the shadow of the legislation's direction to the court to consider 'all the circumstances of the case'.[5] Although the decisions of the House of Lords in *White* and *Miller/McFarlane* have sought to provide a greater degree of coherence to the driving principles the courts should apply, the judicial discretion exercised in ancillary relief proceedings remains extremely broad and, in practice, often difficult to predict with any precision. Although there have been judicial cries for a more predictable system,[6] any system which limits judicial discretion too far is likely to result in complaints of injustice in 'hard cases'.[7] The next few years are likely to see considerable debate, both inside and outside the courts, as to how the current system should develop and whether it requires wholesale legislative reform.[8] The tension between 'predictability' and 'fairness' is likely to be at the heart of this debate.

**1.14** In this book reference has been made to a great deal of the reported authority on each topic so that the reader has a detailed reference work which will be useful both in the office and at court. The relevant passages from the leading judgments are quoted in full in the text for more ready reference, especially when a law library is not to hand. Despite the generous reference to previous authority, the reader must remember that ancillary relief proceedings are no place for slavish adherence to reported case law. The reported cases[9] merely provide examples of the approaches which the courts have adopted to particular problems in the context of particular cases. As Thorpe LJ stated in *Atkinson v Atkinson*:[10] 'The function of the Family Division judge is not so much to state principles as to reflect the relevant circumstances of the particular case in the discretionary conclusion.'[11] Reported cases may provide examples of an approach which can be creatively fashioned into a form which

---

3   [2001] 1 AC 596, [2000] 2 FLR 981.
4   [2006] 1 FLR 1186.
5   Matrimonial Causes Act 1973, s 25(1).
6   For example, the suggestion of a 'tariff' based approach in 'very big/huge money' cases proposed by Coleridge J in *Charman v Charman* [2007] 1 FLR 593 (Fam) at [132]–[136].
7   See the commentary by Lord Hope of Craighead in *Miller v Miller; McFarlane v McFarlane* [2006] 1 FLR 1186 at [103]–[121] on the Scottish system enacted in 1985 and the unfairness it can create.
8   See *Charman v Charman (No 4)* [2007] 1 FLR 1246 at [106]–[126], where the Court of Appeal called for a Law Commission review.
9   Especially those concerning first instance decisions rather than appeals. Even at appellate level it is worth noting the comment of Wall LJ in *B v B* [2008] 2 FLR 1627 at [57] that the case contained no new point of principle and that the profession should resist the temptation to treat it as a precedent. Wall LJ went on to state that the only value of the case was as 'a demonstration of the manner in which this court has exercised its judgment in relation to particular facts'.
10  [1995] 2 FLR 356 at 361.
11  See also the words of Butler-Sloss LJ when *White v White* [1998] 2 FLR 310 at 322G was in the Court of Appeal: 'There is a danger that practitioners in the field of family law attempt to apply too rigidly the decisions of this court and of the Family Division, without sufficiently recognising that each case involving a family has to be decided upon broad principles adapted to the facts of the individual case'; and see *Calderbank v Calderbank* [1976] Fam 93 at 103 per Scarman LJ: 'Every case will be different and no case may be decided except upon its particular facts.'

achieves a fair outcome in another case, but each case needs to be approached on its own unique facts. As stated by Wall LJ:

'One of the frustrations of family law, as well as one of its fascinations, is that no two cases are ever the same. Since the essence of any judicial discretion lies in its application to particular facts, and since each case requires its own particular resolution, the concept of fairness becomes, essentially, a matter of judgment.'[12]

**1.15** Even where parallels can be drawn between a reported case and the case at hand, it should not be forgotten that, as Lord Nicholls of Birkenhead pointed out in *Miller v Miller; McFarlane v McFarlane*:

'Fairness is an elusive concept. It is an instinctive response to a given set of facts. Ultimately it is grounded in social and moral values. These values, or attitudes, can be stated. But they cannot be justified, or refuted, by any objective process of logical reasoning. Moreover they change from one generation to the next.'[13]

**1.16** So, whilst a reported case from the early years of application of the Matrimonial Causes Act 1973 may appear to have identical facts to the case at hand, what may have been considered a fair outcome then may no longer be considered fair more than 30 years later. When reading the older cases the reader should also be alert to the changes made to the legislation in 1984 and the effect this had on the court's exercise of discretion.[14] None of this makes the ancillary relief lawyer's task any simpler. This book cannot promise to provide the solution to every difficult case, but it is hoped that it will make the process of finding the solution slightly less difficult.

---

[12]  *B v B* [2008] 2 FLR 1627, CA at [54].
[13]  [2006] 1 FLR 1186 at [4].
[14]  The Matrimonial and Family Proceedings Act 1984 introduced s 25A to the Matrimonial Causes Act 1973 (imposing the duty on the court to consider a clean break) and removed the 'tailpiece' from s 25 which had required the court to try to put the parties in the financial positions in which they would have been had the marriage not broken down and each had discharged their financial obligations to the other. See also the discussion about removal of the 'tailpiece' from the statute in *White v White* [2000] 2 FLR 981 at 988G.

# Part I
# **EVIDENCE**

# Chapter 2

# THE LAW OF EVIDENCE IN ANCILLARY RELIEF PROCEEDINGS

## INTRODUCTION

**2.1**    Criminal lawyers and civil practitioners are regularly required to address the law of evidence and the burden and standard of proof, yet these are topics which rarely appear consciously to concern the ancillary relief practitioner. Indeed, these topics are hardly mentioned in the reported cases or in the textbooks.

**2.2**    Neither the Matrimonial Causes Act 1973 nor the Family Proceedings Rules 1991 offers much assistance as to the burden and standard of proof in ancillary relief proceedings. Section 25 of the Act merely sets out the factors the court should have regard to, all under the considerable shadow of the command to have regard to 'all the circumstances of the case'. FPR 1991, r 2.62(4) simply directs the judge to:

> 'investigate the allegations made in support of and in answer to the application, and may take evidence orally and may at any stage of the proceedings, whether before or during the hearing, order the attendance of any person for the purpose of being examined or cross-examined and order the disclosure and inspection of any document or require further statements.'[1]

**2.3**    The duty to 'investigate' indicates that the court has a quasi-inquisitorial function in ancillary relief proceedings. In other civil and criminal proceedings the court is asked to adjudicate on a specific dispute brought before it by the parties for resolution. In such proceedings the questions of who bears the burden of proving an allegation and the standard to which the allegation must be proved are often critical to the outcome. The family lawyer undertaking ancillary relief cases instinctively knows that the court hearing an ancillary relief application will approach such questions somewhat differently from the court in any other civil dispute. Nevertheless, it will often be necessary to consider questions of evidence and proof in ancillary relief proceedings, both when preparing a case and when having to answer one.

---

[1]    FPR 1991, r 2.59 is entitled 'Evidence on application for property adjustment of avoidance of disposition order', but is limited to procedural requirements relating to service of applications on interested third parties and their right to file a statement in answer to the application.

**2.4**    This chapter considers the law of evidence as it applies in the context of ancillary relief proceedings. It is not intended to provide a comprehensive reference work on the law of evidence. Where questions of the law of evidence arise, the practitioner should consult the specialist works on that topic.[2] The intention here is to give the reader some insight into the relevance of the law of evidence in ancillary relief proceedings and the manner in which the normal rules of evidence are adapted within the quasi-inquisitorial forum of ancillary relief cases. This chapter does not deal with the duty upon the parties to make full and frank disclosure, or the process of disclosure generally. That related and important topic is considered in Chapter 4.

## EVIDENCE AND PROOF IN ANCILLARY RELIEF

**2.5**    Broadly speaking, the evidence in an ancillary relief case will be advanced to prove that assets or income exist or do not exist, or to prove that a person has done or not done a particular act. As well as looking at the events of the past and the position at present, it is often critical to the outcome of an ancillary relief application to form a view as to what may or may not happen in the future.[3] Indeed, whereas in most civil litigation the focus is on what happened in the past, in ancillary relief cases there is often as much, if not more, focus on what the future holds for the parties. This should not be mere speculation but a conclusion reached upon an assessment of the available evidence.

**2.6**    Sometimes evidence will go to nothing more than the credibility of witnesses, but this is also of particular importance in ancillary relief cases, as we will see when the court's ability to raise inferences against a party is considered. Indeed, in many ancillary relief cases, the pursuit of disclosure during the early stages of an application will build up an arsenal of evidence which goes to a party's credit as much as it identifies his or her assets and income. The importance of the duty to make full and frank disclosure and the consequences of failing to comply with that duty, including loss of credibility, are considered in detail in Chapter 4.

**2.7**    Any particular piece of evidence will fit into a broader factual matrix and may go to prove more than one fact. Ultimately, to be useful the evidence must be admissible and it must be sufficient to prove the allegation to the required standard.

---

[2]    For example, *Phipson on Evidence* (Sweet & Maxwell, 15th edn).
[3]    See the comment of Baroness Hale in *Miller v Miller; McFarlane v McFarlane* [2006] 1 FLR 1186 at [129] on the importance of the foreseeable and on occasions more distant future in the context of the s 25 criteria.

## RELEVANCE AND PROPORTIONALITY – IDENTIFYING THE ISSUES AND PREPARING THE EVIDENCE

**2.8**    It is trite to say that evidence must be relevant to the issues to be decided in order for it to be admissible. But where do the boundaries of relevance lie in an ancillary relief case?

**2.9**    Ancillary relief proceedings are a species of civil proceedings.[4] They share with normal civil disputes many common rules of procedure in the form of the old Rules of the Supreme Court 1965 and the County Court Rules 1981, except where the Family Proceedings Rules 1991 provide otherwise.[5] But there is an approach to the conduct of ancillary relief proceedings which makes lawyers trained solely in other civil litigation or criminal law somewhat uncomfortable if they venture into this jurisdiction. Even though the rules of evidence (in particular in relation to the admission of hearsay evidence) have become much more relaxed in both civil and criminal proceedings over the last half century, there is an even more relaxed approach to such matters in family disputes generally. This is a natural result of key features of ancillary relief practice which mark it out from normal civil litigation.

**2.10**    In a normal civil dispute the court is asked to adjudicate on areas of disagreement which are clearly defined in a series of statements of case.[6] These are prepared by the parties sequentially so that as each allegation is raised by one party it is answered by the other. Perusal of the pleadings should allow the live issues to be clearly identified. The civil court is then usually limited to deciding the case on the basis of those pleadings. In such proceedings the court's role is as adjudicator in an adversarial dispute which the respective parties have brought before the court for resolution. In an ancillary relief case there is no similar system of setting out a case by way of statements of case.[7] This is a natural result of the court's function being much wider than its

---

[4]    In the High Court such proceedings are allocated to the Family Division by s 61 and Sch 1 of the Supreme Court Act 1981 and Part V of the Matrimonial and Family Proceedings Act 1984, which also provides for the designation of 'divorce county courts' and for the transfer of proceedings between the county court and High Court.

[5]    FPR 1991, r 1.3(1). The Civil Procedure Rules 1998 also apply in certain areas such as the instruction of experts and in relation to appeals.

[6]    See CPR Part 16. Known as 'pleadings' before the introduction of CPR 1998 and, despite the new terminology of the rules, still commonly so called by practitioners.

[7]    The closest the rules come to providing something in the form of a formal pleading is the requirement to file 'a concise statement of the issues between the parties' before the first appointment (see FPR, r 2.61B(7)(a)). The court may in some circumstances require the parties to set out their cases on a particular issue by way of some form of sequential statements of case: see e g *TL v ML and Others (Ancillary Relief: Claim Against Assets of Extended Family)* [2005] EWHC 2860 (Fam) in the context of claims against assets registered in the name of a third party; *A v A* [2007] 2 FLR 467 in the context of an allegation that a trust was a sham; and *NA v MA* [2007] 1 FLR 1760 in the context of allegations involving professional misconduct on the part of solicitors. In *W v W (Ancillary Relief: Practice)* (2000) The Times, March 15, Wilson J encouraged the use of affidavits from the parties in advance of a full ancillary relief hearing. See also *S v S (Ancillary Relief: Importance of FDR)* [2008] 1 FLR 944 on the importance of such statements in cases which are not run of the mill.

function in a normal civil dispute. The issues in an ancillary relief case are very wide ranging: they encompass almost every aspect of the parties' lives, in both a personal and an economic sense. The court is acting as more than a simple adjudicator in an adversarial dispute – it is acting in a paternal capacity and the judge's function is quasi-inquisitorial. Ultimately the court has very broad discretion as to the orders it makes. Although the parties to ancillary relief proceedings should endeavour to identify the issues between them, they are unable to limit the scope of the enquiry which the court is bound to undertake. In *Parra v Parra*[8] Thorpe LJ explained the court's function as follows:

> 'But the outcome of ancillary relief cases depends upon the exercise of a singularly broad judgment that obviates the need for the investigation of minute detail and equally the need to make findings on minor issues in dispute. The judicial task is very different from the task of the judge in the civil justice system whose obligation is to make findings on all issues in dispute relevant to outcome. The quasi-inquisitorial role of the judge in ancillary relief litigation obliges him to investigate issues which he considers relevant to outcome even if not advanced by either party. Equally, he is not bound to adopt a conclusion upon which the parties have agreed.'[9]

**2.11**   Despite the absence of a formal series of 'pleadings' in ancillary relief cases, the parties are invited by the Form E to provide some indication of the allegations they wish to make.[10] They are also required to file a concise statement of the issues between them in advance of the first appointment.[11] The parties should at an early stage identify any significant allegations which they seek to pursue to avoid adverse consequences in costs if those allegations only become apparent at a later stage in the proceedings. Where substantial allegations are raised and pursued, the court will usually direct the filing of narrative statements before the final hearing to enable the issues to be put before the court with clarity.[12] A failure to take this procedural step is often likely to result in a final hearing taking much longer, because the parties will need to give lengthy evidence in chief and issues may arise which require further investigations or an adjournment. Where very serious allegations are to be made, for example an allegation of fraud, and particularly if the allegations are made to impugn the professional integrity of a witness called in the proceedings, those allegations should be set out in advance in writing, rather

---

[8]   [2003] 1 FLR 942. The trial judge was criticised in that case for an over-elaborate and lengthy judgment which the Court of Appeal felt provided both parties with so much detail that it was easy for them to find points to criticise on appeal!

[9]   [2003] 1 FLR 942 at 949. This is consistent with the inability of the parties to settle ancillary relief proceedings without the scrutiny and final approval of the court: *Livesey v Jenkins* [1985] AC 424, HL. Although the judge is entitled to 'play the detective' and investigate matters behind an apparently unfair consent order, the duty to do so in the context of an order presented to the court by consent is limited: *L v L* [2008] 1 FLR 26.

[10]  See section 4 of the Form E dealing with standard of living, contributions, conduct etc.

[11]  FPR 1991, r 2.61B(7)(a).

[12]  *W v W (Ancillary Relief: Practice)* (2000) The Times, March 15. In *S v S (Ancillary Relief: Importance of FDR )* [2008] 1 FLR 944 at 948 Baron J recommended that in every case which was not 'simple or run of the mill' there should be detailed statements from the parties setting out their cases on the s 25 factors.

than simply made for the first time in cross-examination of the witness.[13] Counsel in such cases must remember that the Bar Council's Code of Conduct requires prima facie evidence in support before such serious allegations are made. It is common for parties in ancillary relief proceedings to raise a multiplicity of allegations and accusations. It is only natural that individuals in the throes of a relationship breakdown will feel a degree of antagonism towards their former partner. This tactic is also often born out of the belief that if enough 'mud' is thrown, some will stick and raise suspicions and, with luck, adverse inferences against the other party. When can the lawyer tell the client that the allegations they wish to raise are clearly irrelevant? When can the other side successfully argue that the matter should simply not be considered by the court because it is irrelevant? These are difficult questions to answer. The following paragraphs explain the difficulties.

**2.12** In a non-matrimonial context such issues of relevance can usually be fairly easily resolved by reference to the issues raised on the statements of case. The quasi-inquisitorial nature of ancillary relief proceedings and the broad-ranging enquiry required of the court by s 25 of the Matrimonial Causes Act 1973 means that the boundaries of relevance are far less distinct than in other kinds of litigation. In a civil case, largely unsubstantiated allegations and accusations may well result in early dismissal by a summary judgment application. There is no such procedure for summary adjudication in an ancillary relief application.[14] The court in ancillary relief proceedings will frequently embark on an investigation of an issue without there necessarily being clear prima facie evidence that that allegation can be made out. This will be considered further in Chapter 4 in the context of disclosure and the extent to which the court will permit a party to go on a 'fishing' expedition to build his or her case.

**2.13** In reality it is difficult to assess the relevance of some of the evidence capable of being produced until a relatively late stage of proceedings. There will always be evidence which is clearly relevant or clearly irrelevant. There will also be a very large amount of material which may be relevant, although its relevance or irrelevance may not become apparent until all disclosure has been pursued and obtained or until after all the evidence in the case has been heard

---

13  *NA v MA* [2007] 1 FLR 1760 at [135]. In what was described as 'brutal litigation' Baron J expressed concerns about the manner in which leading counsel for the husband had sought to impugn the wife's solicitor's professional integrity on the basis of relatively limited evidence. The learned judge also gave guidance as to the manner in which she expected counsel in ancillary relief litigation to co-operate in the interests of the smooth running of the trial (at [4]).

14  Other than in limited circumstances following the making of a final order: for example, the High Court has an inherent power to strike out an application to set aside a consent order: *Rose v Rose (No 2)* [2003] EWHC Fam 505; there is also a discretion to deal with an application in a more summary or abbreviated manner upon an application to show cause why a compromise agreement made between the parties should not be made an order of the court: *Dean v Dean* [1978] Fam 161; *Xydias v Xydias* [1999] 1 FLR 683; *X v X* [2002] 1 FLR 508; *Crossley v Crossley* [2007] EWCA Civ 1491, [2008] 1 FLR 1467; *W v H* [2008] EWHC 2038 (Fam).

and tested by cross-examination.[15] This does not justify the lawyer simply burdening the court with every allegation which the client can think of.[16] If no discrimination is shown by the parties and their lawyers, such an approach is likely to result in adverse consequences in terms of costs.

**2.14** The court retains a general discretion to regulate its procedure and to control the evidence which the parties are permitted to place before it.[17] Indeed, the overriding objective set out in FPR, r 2.51B includes a duty on the court to take a proactive approach in order to ensure that the costs and time spent on the case are proportionate to the value and importance of the issues in dispute. Inevitably this means that a more detailed and thorough investigation will be permitted where the assets are of very high value than in a case where the assets are modest. Litigants may perceive this as unfair in some cases because, self-evidently, the smaller the available pool of assets the more important it is to identify every last pound, whereas the very rich can afford to adopt a more broad-brush approach. Ultimately, in nearly every case, the costs of the proceedings will have to be borne out of the parties' own pool of assets. This fact is often forgotten by the parties and should be the real disincentive to them raising issues in a disproportionate fashion.

**2.15** It may be helpful to consider the following factors when dealing with questions of the relevance and proportionality of pursuing allegations in ancillary relief proceedings, and in terms of how such allegations are presented:

–   Will the allegation assist the court in considering any of the matters listed in s 25(2) or the requirement to give first consideration to the welfare of any child who is a minor?

–   Even if not, will the allegation be likely to influence the court's discretion as part of 'all the circumstances of the case'?[18]

---

[15]   See, for example, *P v P (Financial Relief: Non-disclosure)* [1994] 2 FLR 381, where the case developed during cross-examination of the applicant wife so that the husband's counsel was able 'to develop through the right to cross-examine what became a fully-fledged financial conduct case' (at 383 per Thorpe J).

[16]   The practitioner must at all times have regard to the 'overriding objective' set out at FPR 1991, r 2.51B and, in this particular context, especially the need to ensure that there is proportionality between the issues raised and the amount of money involved.

[17]   See, for example, *Krywald v Krywald* [1988] 2 FLR 401.

[18]   See *Miller v Miller; McFarlane v McFarlane* [2006] 1 FLR 1186 at [59]–[65] and [145], which points out that it is wrong to have regard to 'conduct' as part of all the circumstances of the case where it could not be brought into consideration under s 25(2)(g) as conduct which it would be inequitable to disregard. See also *S v S (Non-Matrimonial Property: Conduct)* [2006] EWHC 2793 (Fam), where Burton J, a Queen's Bench Division judge drafted in to hear the case due to its special features, surveyed the case law on 'conduct' and applied an interesting test for bringing conduct into the court's considerations. Burton J tested the relevance of the conduct by its 'gasp factor', holding that conduct which only had a 'gulp factor' should not affect the exercise of his discretion. In *Zeiderman v Zeiderman* [2008] EWCA Civ 760, unreported, the Court of Appeal expressed disapproval of the district judge making findings on a variety of issues of matrimonial misconduct which went only to credibility and had no bearing on financial matters.

– Consider the costs involved in obtaining and adducing the evidence required to deal with the allegation and weigh up the proportionality of those costs to the likely effect of the allegation, if proved, on the overall outcome of the proceedings.

– Emotive allegations which are only peripherally relevant to the issues in dispute should be avoided.[19] As well as raising the costs of the case unnecessarily, emotive allegations may raise the emotional temperature of the case and harden attitudes. Settlement of the proceedings may prove to be much more difficult after making allegations which are likely to further embitter the parties and polarise their respective positions. The risk of a 'tit for tat' escalation of the issues also becomes high. The parties need to be strongly dissuaded from including such allegations as part of their case unless they are genuinely relevant to the court's exercise of discretion. Where the allegation is genuinely relevant to the financial issues, it should be put carefully, avoiding unnecessarily emotive language, if possible.

– The temptation to overstate a case or to engage in hyperbole must be cautioned against. Once a court concludes that evidence has been presented in an exaggerated or extravagant manner, the court is likely to lose confidence in the evidence given.[20] The litigants need to reflect on the fact that whatever they say in their written evidence is likely to be intensely scrutinised as part of the trial process, and statements made in the comfort of the solicitor's office may come back to haunt them once they are giving evidence at the hearing.

– Consider whether the court is able to give directions which define the scope of the issues of fact to be determined and the evidence which the parties are permitted to adduce (considered further below).

**2.16** The court's discretion to control the evidence before it may well be exercised prior to the final hearing by the court giving directions as to the evidence which the parties may put forward at the final hearing.[21] Most commonly this discretion is exercised by the court granting or refusing permission for the instruction of an expert witness. The power may also be used

---

[19] *Evans v Evans (Practice Note)* [1990] 1 WLR 575.
[20] For example, *H v H* [2008] 2 FLR 2092 at [29].
[21] In *Crossley v Crossley* [2008] 1 FLR 1467 the Court of Appeal stressed the need for flexible and proactive judicial case management, Thorpe LJ saying (at [15]): 'I would particularly stress the overriding objectives that govern all these rules, carefully and fully drafted in r 2.51D. It is easy to attach this case on its facts to a number of the objectives there articulated. It is very important that the judge in dealing with the case should seek to save expense. It is very important that he should seek to deal with the case in ways proportionate to the financial position of the parties. It is very important, more so today than it was when these rules were drafted, that he should allot to each case an appropriate share of the court's resources, taking into account the need to allot resources to other cases. In his general duty of case management he is required to identify the issues at an early date and particularly to regulate the extent of the disclosure of documents and expert evidence so that they are proportionate to the issues in question.'

to control other evidence, although this is seldom done in practice. Where the irrelevance of an allegation can be clearly shown at an early stage, one of the parties may wish to ask the court to rule on this matter at a directions hearing so that the parties only need to address the relevant issues at the final hearing and so that the time estimate for that hearing can be set appropriately. Alternatively, a party may agree that it will not seek to rely on an allegation as part of its case.[22] Often it will not be possible to make such a ruling on a preliminary basis and the court will need to hear all the evidence before deciding on relevance in the context of all the circumstances of the case. The court may still penalise the party in costs if, at the conclusion of the case, it is clear that that issue was not ultimately relevant, or if the manner in which the evidence was adduced was disproportionate to the importance of the issue. Indeed, the party answering an allegation may choose to deal with the matter by way of an application for costs at the end of the case rather than by way of a preliminary ruling, especially where the relevance of the allegation may be unclear or where the costs of dealing with the allegation are not excessive.

## BURDEN OF PROOF

**2.17**  Even if the evidence is relevant and proportionate to the issues, it remains important to consider the question of where the burden of proving an allegation lies and what standard of proof will be required. It is self-evidently unwise to raise allegations and issues which are not capable of being substantiated at the final hearing.

**2.18**  The purpose of ancillary relief proceedings is to identify, value and divide the family assets in a fair manner.[23] The court's primary task in considering an ancillary relief application is to ensure it has as clear and complete a picture of the parties' finances as the circumstances allow.[24] Often one party, sometimes both parties, will be determined to ensure that the full extent of their assets and income is not disclosed to the other party and, therefore, to the court. Almost inevitably, where such conduct is suspected, the other party will allege that there has been non-disclosure of assets. This particular situation is considered in detail at **2.20–2.27**.

**2.19**  Ordinarily, it is for the person who makes an allegation to prove it. In the case of some allegations there may be a presumption of law which shifts the evidential burden of proof to the other party.[25] Generally, when allegations are

---

[22]  Although such an agreement may not ultimately preclude the court from hearing evidence on the matter and placing weight on it as part of 'all the circumstances of the case' if it is relevant to the s 25 exercise. See *Parra v Parra*, cited at **2.10** above.

[23]  *Charman v Charman (No 4)* [2007] 1 FLR 1246.

[24]  Bearing in mind the requirement of proportionality set by FPR, r 2. Thus, a broad-brush balance sheet valuation of a small family company which will not be sold may be appropriate in a case with modest assets, but a full forensic examination of company accounts may be justified in a case with very high value business assets.

[25]  For example, the presumption as to intention to defeat the applicant's claim by disposing of

made it will be a fairly simple exercise to identify the person making the allegation and the person who faces it. In such cases it will be obvious to all where the burden and standard of proof lies. There is no real distinction between proving allegations as to a party's conduct in an ancillary relief case and any other civil case. If a party alleges that the other party has performed a certain act, the normal principles of evidence will apply notwithstanding the quasi-inquisitorial nature of the proceedings: the accuser will have to prove the allegation on the balance of probabilities. Where the allegation is one of non-disclosure by the other party, however, there are special features in ancillary relief cases which distinguish the approach from other forms of litigation. This type of allegation deserves separate consideration.

## The burden of proof in cases of non-disclosure

**2.20** Identifying the party who bears the burden of proof is not straightforward where the allegation is one of non-disclosure of assets by the other party. The difficulty on this issue arises as a result of the obligation on the parties to ancillary relief proceedings to give 'full and frank' disclosure of their means.[26] Does the person alleging the non-disclosure need to prove that an asset exists but has not been disclosed, or is the burden on the other party to prove that they have complied with their duty to make full and frank disclosure?

**2.21** The answer to this question is not an entirely clear one and it has received surprisingly little direct examination in the reported case law. It does, however, appear that the approach in ancillary relief proceedings is slightly different from that which would be adopted in other civil proceedings. The burden of proving the existence of non-disclosed assets remains with the person making the allegation. That burden can be satisfied by adducing relevant and admissible evidence. This evidence is likely to include consideration of the respondent's conduct during the proceedings in terms of compliance with the court's orders for disclosure. Mere suspicion or assertion will not do. The totality of the evidence before the court may be sufficient to permit the court to infer that there are assets which have not been disclosed. The evidential burden of rebutting that inference then falls on the respondent.

**2.22** In *Baker v Baker*[27] the wife alleged that there had been non-disclosure by the husband of substantial assets. The trial judge found the husband's evidence wholly unreliable and found that, although the husband said he had virtually no assets, he did have substantial assets which he had not disclosed but which were sufficient to entitle the wife to a lump sum and periodical payments. The actual assets were not precisely identified, but the judge felt justified in inferring that they did exist and had not been disclosed. The husband appealed squarely on the basis that the judge had misdirected himself by failing to place the

---

assets contained in MCA 1973, s 37(5). There are also various common law presumptions which might arise in certain cases with varying degrees of force.

[26]   The meaning of 'full and frank' is considered further at **4.1–4.12**.

[27]   [1995] 2 FLR 829.

burden of proving the non-disclosure on the wife. The Court of Appeal rejected the appeal. Butler-Sloss LJ reminded herself of the duties of full and frank disclosure which lie upon the parties and the court's duty to exercise its discretion in the light of all the circumstances of the case and noted that:

> 'Special considerations apply to the exercise of this discretionary jurisdiction. Although the burden of proof is upon the applicant to prove his or her case, it is for the respondent to the application to provide to the applicant and to the court all the relevant information.'

The learned judge went on to consider the basis upon which the court is able to draw adverse inferences against a party who fails in his or her duty to make full and frank disclosure. She noted that the practice of drawing such inferences had been followed for over 40 years without criticism.[28] She went on to approve the first instance judge's approach, which he had explained as follows:

> 'In directing myself as to the proper approach I am of the view that a petitioner who brings a claim for ancillary relief assumes the burden of proving that there are the resources available to meet her claim. In my judgment the extravagant lifestyle that was adopted during the marriage … and, not unimportantly, after the breakdown of the marriage leads me to infer that this respondent who had gone to elaborate lengths to preserve his wealth, had the means to support that lifestyle. The evidential burden now falls on him. This is not ordinary civil litigation.'

**2.23**　On the facts of *Baker v Baker* the Court of Appeal was satisfied that the inference of undisclosed assets was justified based on the findings as to the husband's dishonesty and lifestyle:[29]

> '[The wife's counsel] pointed to an utterly false case and asked us to consider why the husband was lying and what did he have to hide. If the cupboard was bare, it was in his interests to open it and display its meagre contents. But on the contrary, the husband, despite his protestations to the contrary, continued to live the life of an affluent man. I agree with the submissions from [counsel] that if a court finds that the husband has lied about his means, lied about other material issues, withheld documents, and failed to give full and frank disclosure, it is open to the court to find that beneath the false presentation, and the reasons for it, are undisclosed assets.'

**2.24**　In *Al-Khatib v Masry*[30] Munby J followed the *Baker v Baker* approach and said, stressing the need to ensure that the inferences are drawn only on the basis of proper evidence, that:[31]

> 'I can properly draw adverse inferences only if there is some proper basis for them in findings of fact correctly arrived at in the light of admissible evidence.[32] I reject, however, [the] submission that, even if there is proven non-disclosure, inferences as

---

[28]　Referring in particular to *J v J* [1955] P 215, considered further at **2.53**.
[29]　[1995] 2 FLR 829 at 835.
[30]　[2002] 1 FLR 1053.
[31]　[2002] 1 FLR 1053 at 1075.
[32]　See also **2.44** as to the use of hearsay and anecdotal evidence.

to the existence of assets "must be based on credible evidence as to the existence of such assets". That submission, if I have correctly understood it, seems to be in reality but a repetition of the submission from Mr Holman (as he then was) which Butler-Sloss LJ was at such pains to reject. Indeed, put in these terms [the] submission seems to me ... to fly in the face of the Lady Justice's acceptance in the passage quoted that "it is open to the court to find that beneath the false presentation, and the reasons for it, are *undisclosed assets*" (my emphasis).'

**2.25**  At first blush, *Baker v Baker* appears effectively to reverse the burden of proving that there has been full disclosure upon the party answering the allegation. The process is not as simple as that. It remains necessary to do more than simply allege non-disclosure to throw the burden of proof on the other party. There must be sufficient admissible evidence placed before the court to establish, on the balance of probabilities, that there has been incomplete and inadequate disclosure. The court will not, however, require the party making the allegation of non-disclosure to prove that an identifiable asset actually exists as a prerequisite to making such a finding. So long as the evidence is such as to raise a prima facie case that there are assets in existence which have not been disclosed, the evidential burden of rebutting the inference will shift to the other party to prove that they do not exist.

**2.26**  The allegation of non-disclosure will often be built on inference rather than direct evidence and the party bringing the allegation will be permitted to carry out an investigation and develop the case through cross-examination of the other party.[33] In an appropriate case, this may be enough to impugn the other party's credibility to the point that inferences can be drawn as to the existence of undisclosed assets, and the finding of non-disclosure can then properly be made if the party facing the allegation is not able to produce credible evidence to rebut the allegation. In essence, the allegation of non-disclosure may begin as nothing more than an assertion with no evidence to support it. By the end of a lengthy process, in which disclosure is sought by way of questionnaires and other means and after cross-examination of the other party at the final hearing, that bare allegation may have attained real substance.

**2.27**  There is a certain element of circularity in this approach which could be criticised as a departure from the normal principle which places the burden of proving an allegation upon the person who makes it. There is good reason for this approach in the context and circumstances of ancillary relief. If a prerequisite to a finding of non-disclosure of an asset was proof that the undisclosed asset actually existed, the court's task in unravelling the financial affairs of those reluctant to provide full and frank disclosure would become impossible in many cases. For the same reasons, the courts have used the duty of full and frank disclosure to justify raising strong inferences against parties who have been found to be less than honest. The use of such inferences is considered further at **2.51–2.57**.

---

[33]  As in *P v P (Financial Relief: Non-Disclosure)* [1994] 2 FLR 381 (and see the passage set out at **4.36**).

# STANDARD OF PROOF

**2.28**  As already noted, ancillary relief proceedings are civil proceedings by their nature. The normal civil standard of proof applies, namely on the balance of probabilities.[34] The standard of proof is the ordinary civil standard. 'It must carry a reasonable degree of probability … If the tribunal can say: "we think it more probable than not", the burden is discharged, but if the probabilities are equal it is not.'[35] It was previously thought that the standard was a flexible one which adapted itself to the gravity of the allegation, so that the more serious the allegation the less likely it was assumed to have happened and the better the quality of the evidence required to prove it.[36] It has now been made clear by the House of Lords in *Re B ( Care Proceedings: Standard of Proof)*[37] that 'there is only one civil standard of proof and that is proof that the fact in issue more probably occurred than not'.[38]

**2.29**  Inherent probabilities still have a part in the process, as a matter of common sense. Lord Hoffman said:[39]

> 'I should say something about the notion of inherent probabilities. Lord Nicholls of Birkenhead said[40] … that:
>
>> "the court will have in mind as a factor, *to whatever extent is appropriate in the particular case*, that the more serious the allegation the less likely it is that the event occurred and, hence, the stronger should be the evidence before the court concludes that the allegation is established on the balance of probability."
>
> I wish to lay some stress upon the words I have italicised. Lord Nicholls of Birkenhead was not laying down any rule of law. There is only one rule of law, namely that the occurrence of the fact in issue must be proved to have been more probable than not. Common sense, not law, requires that in deciding this question, regard should be had, to whatever extent appropriate, to inherent probabilities. If a child alleges sexual abuse by a parent, it is common sense to start with the assumption that most parents do not abuse their children. But this assumption may be swiftly dispelled by other compelling evidence of the relationship between parent and child or parent and other children. It would be absurd to suggest that the tribunal must in all cases assume that serious conduct is unlikely to have occurred. In many cases, the other evidence will show that it was all too likely. If, for example, it is clear that a child was assaulted by one or other of two people, it would make no sense to start one's reasoning by saying that assaulting children is a serious matter and therefore neither of them is likely to have done so. The fact is

---

[34]  Although where a penal sanction is sought for breach of an order the criminal standard will apply in order to prove the breach.

[35]  *Miller v Minister of Pensions* [1947] 2 All ER 372 at 373–4, per Denning J.

[36]  See *Re H and R ( Child Sexual Abuse: Standard of Proof)* [1996] 1 FLR 80.

[37]  [2008] UKHL 35, [2008] 2 FLR 141.

[38]  Per Lord Hoffman at [13].

[39]  At [14] and [15].

[40]  In *Re H and R ( Child Sexual Abuse: Standard of Proof)* [1996] 1 FLR 80.

that one of them did and the question for the tribunal is simply whether it is more probable that one rather than the other was the perpetrator.'

Baroness Hale said,[41] 'The inherent probabilities are simply something to be taken into account, where relevant, in deciding where the truth lies.' The learned judge went on to say:[42]

'As to the seriousness of the allegation, there is no logical or necessary connection between seriousness and probability. Some seriously harmful behaviour, such as murder, is sufficiently rare to be inherently improbable in most circumstances. Even then there are circumstances, such as a body with its throat cut and no weapon to hand, where it is not at all improbable. Other seriously harmful behaviour, such as alcohol or drug abuse, is regrettably all too common and not at all improbable. Nor are serious allegations made in a vacuum. Consider the famous example of the animal seen in Regent's Park. If it is seen outside the zoo on a stretch of greensward regularly used for walking dogs, then of course it is more likely to be a dog than a lion. If it is seen in the zoo next to the lions' enclosure when the door is open, then it may well be more likely to be a lion than a dog.

In the context of care proceedings, this point applies with particular force to the identification of the perpetrator. It may be unlikely that any person looking after a baby would take him by the wrist and swing him against the wall, causing multiple fractures and other injuries. But once the evidence is clear that that is indeed what has happened to the child, it ceases to be improbable. Someone looking after the child at the relevant time must have done it. The inherent improbability of the event has no relevance to deciding who that was. The simple balance of probabilities test should be applied.'

**2.30**　Inherent probabilities may also affect the court's assessment of a witness's credibility. For example, the honesty of a solicitor giving evidence on oath to the court may be more difficult to challenge than the honesty of a witness who is not an officer of the court and for whom misleading the court may have less serious personal consequences. However, the circumstances of each case will determine the extent to which this factor is relevant. Anyone is capable of giving inaccurate or untruthful evidence.

**2.31**　Although it has been suggested that the criminal standard of proof may be appropriate to prove that a husband has obtained a bankruptcy order against himself on the basis of a false presentation of his assets,[43] it would

---

[41] At [70].
[42] At [72] and [73].
[43] See *F v F (Divorce: Insolvency)* [1994] 1 FLR 359 at 367, where Thorpe J was invited to decide the matter to the criminal standard and indicated he found that standard met, although he did not decide whether that was the necessary standard he should apply. It is doubtful that the criminal standard would be required to prove this allegation in the light of the House of Lords decision in *Re B* (above).

appear that in such proceedings the test always remains the balance of probabilities, and the civil standard of proof remains distinct from the criminal standard.[44]

**2.32** It has been argued that to infer that an asset exists which has not been disclosed is, in effect, a finding that one party has dishonestly concealed it and, being an allegation tantamount to one of fraud, it requires proof to a higher standard. If that principle applied in ancillary relief proceedings, it would be very difficult for the courts ever to find a way of piercing the cloak of secrecy many parties to such proceedings attempt to throw over their assets. Not surprisingly, the argument was rejected in *Baker v Baker*.[45] In that case, the Court of Appeal approached the question of whether undisclosed assets existed on the normal civil standard. Butler-Sloss LJ said:[46]

> 'The husband in this appeal was not accused of fraud and Ward J evaluated his assets on a balance of probabilities and cannot be faulted for so doing.'

Thus, an allegation of non-disclosure of assets is not regarded as an allegation of fraud, even though a party putting forward his or her Form E, having omitted to disclose significant assets, is knowingly misleading the court and the other party by implicitly representing that the Form E contains full and frank disclosure.

**2.33** By extension of the same principles, the court does not require credible evidence of the existence of assets before being able to infer that such assets exist.[47] This matter will be considered in greater detail in due course, when the use of inferences is examined.[48]

## INTERIM HEARINGS

**2.34** The court is likely to adopt a less formal approach to matters of proof at interim hearings relating to maintenance pending suit or interim periodical payments.[49] By their very nature such hearings do not make a final determination of the issues but are intended to maintain matters until the final hearing. Often there will be less than complete disclosure at the time of the interim hearing. Frequently the application for ancillary relief will only just

---

[44] *Re U (Serious Injury: Standard of Proof); Re B* [2004] 2 FLR 263 expressly rejected the suggestion by Bodey J in Note: *Re ET (Serious Injuries: Standard of Proof)* [2003] 2 FLR 1205 that where serious allegations were made, the difference between the civil and criminal standards of proof was 'largely illusory'. The decision in *Re U* was approved by the House of Lords in *Re B*. See also **25.10–25.12**.

[45] [1995] 2 FLR 829 at 833–4.

[46] [1995] 2 FLR 829 at 834.

[47] *Al-Khatib v Masry* [2002] 1 FLR 1053 at 1075 per Munby J. See also **2.24**.

[48] See **2.51–2.57**.

[49] Until determination of the suit by a decree the application is for maintenance pending suit (MCA 1973, s 22) and thereafter the payments are interim periodical payments until the final order is made.

have been issued and Forms E will not yet have been disclosed. The rules require a party to file only 'a short sworn statement about his means' for the interim hearing where Forms E have not yet been exchanged.[50] There is no requirement in the rules for the production of supporting documentation, although many solicitors ensure that at least some basic documentary evidence of income and outgoings is provided for an interim hearing. Even though the rules require only limited disclosure in the form of the sworn statement, the duty of full and frank disclosure applies even at an interim hearing. Indeed, a failure to provide full and frank disclosure may seriously work to the party's disadvantage, as demonstrated below.

**2.35**   The court will not embark on an extensive financial investigation at an interim hearing. The court will not ordinarily be in a position to determine disputes of fact at that stage. The courts adopt a pragmatic approach to such situations. The court is unlikely to accept an assertion of impecuniosity by the respondent if he or she does not provide full disclosure which supports that assertion. In *G v G (Maintenance Pending Suit: Costs)*[51] a husband submitted an affidavit indicating that his means would not allow him to afford the payments sought by the wife. He sought to argue that, although the wife did not accept his evidence, the court was bound to deal with the interim application on the basis that his evidence was accurate, because he had not yet been cross-examined and the court could not yet make any finding as to his credibility, and could not, therefore, find on the balance of probabilities that his evidence was not true. Charles J rejected those submissions and indicated that the appropriate approach at a hearing as to interim maintenance was as follows:

'I accept the submissions made on behalf of the wife that:

(a)   just as is the case when making a final award (see *White v White* [2001] 1 AC 596, [2000] 2 FLR 981) in awarding maintenance pending suit the overriding consideration for the court is to arrive at a fair result; and

(b)   *Baker v Baker* [1995] 2 FLR 829, *F v F (Divorce: Insolvency: Annulment of Bankruptcy Order)* [1994] 1 FLR 359 and, in particular, *F v F (Maintenance Pending Suit)* (1983) 4 FLR 382 are cases which support the view that in awarding maintenance pending suit a court does not have to accept the assertions of the paying party as to his or her means.

The reports of *Baker* and *F v F (Divorce: Insolvency: Annulment of Bankruptcy Order)* deal with the final hearings but it appears that in both of them maintenance pending suit was awarded at levels that did not accept the husband's assertions as to his means ...

In my judgment, important points to consider in respect of the dilemma posed when there is a dispute as to the means of the paying party are:

---

[50]   FPR 1991, r 2.69F.
[51]   [2003] 2 FLR 71.

(a)    the extent of the compliance by the paying party with his or her duty to make full and frank disclosure; and

(b)    the force of the points made by the applicant in the light of the disclosure made by the paying party and the other evidence as to, for example, the lifestyle and spending of that party.

If a paying party asserts that he or she does not have the means to meet the maintenance pending suit claimed, it is trite to point out that he or she has, or should normally have, the ability to provide full and compelling disclosure to demonstrate that this is the case and thus that the assertions of the applicant that he or she is more wealthy are based on sand and have little or no reasonable prospect of success. Thus, full and frank disclosure by the paying party can avoid or minimise the unfairness or oppression to that party which would result from a court not accepting his or her assertions as to means.

It is well established that parties to ancillary relief proceedings have a duty to make full and frank disclosure and that if they do not do so at the final hearing the court can make findings based on inferences against them (see for example *Jenkins v Livesey (Formerly Jenkins)* [1985] AC 424, *sub nom Livesey (Formerly Jenkins) v Jenkins* [1985] FLR 813; *Baker v Baker* [1995] 2 FLR 829 at 835F–G and 836G; and *F v F (Divorce: Insolvency: Annulment of Bankruptcy Order)* [1994] 1 FLR 359 at 367B–E).

In some cases of claims for maintenance pending suit it may be that a lesser degree of disclosure to one giving full particulars of property and income is acceptable (see, for example, *Jackson's Matrimonial Finance and Taxation* (Butterworths, 6th edn, 2002) para 2.19) on the basis that the disclosure given is sufficient for the purposes of an application which is being dealt with urgently and full disclosure will be given before the final hearing. But as that paragraph makes clear, there is no general rule that full disclosure should not be made for the purposes of such an application and full disclosure will often be ordered where allegations of concealment of assets are made. Again, as that paragraph makes clear, and I agree, the duty (as on the final hearing) is frankly to furnish to the court all the necessary materials to enable it to decide the issues that it has to decide.

If the paying party does not perform that duty and thus does not provide such disclosure, then, in my judgment, and without hearing oral evidence, the court on an application for maintenance pending suit does not have to accept and proceed on the basis of his or her assertions as to means and an inability to pay. In my judgment, this is so notwithstanding the point that because the court has not heard oral evidence it is not in a position to make findings as to credibility, or to make findings (which can be based on adverse inferences) as to the extent of the means of each party.

In my judgment, if the paying party does not perform his or her duty as to disclosure on an application for maintenance pending suit, the court, on an application for maintenance pending suit, can take a broad and robust view of disputes as to means which it is not then in a position to decide. This conclusion accords with the views expressed by Balcombe J in *F v F (Maintenance Pending Suit)* (1983) 4 FLR 382 at 385B.

In my judgment, this is an aspect of fairness in ancillary relief proceedings both in respect of procedure and result. As to procedure it would often be unfair and onerous (as well as expensive and of limited use) to hear oral evidence in the light of what is considered to be limited disclosure. As to result, and more generally as to an application for maintenance pending suit, a paying party who has in breach of duty failed to provide proper disclosure can take the practical remedy to the unfairness he or she alleges of remedying that breach of duty. In my view, this point and an examination of the degree and nature of the failure to provide proper disclosure addresses the point made by Balcombe J in *F v F (Maintenance Pending Suit)* at 385C, which I naturally accept, that administrative expediency even if it promotes justice for the great bulk of litigants cannot be allowed to work injustice in an individual case.'

**2.36** The principles to be applied to an application for maintenance pending suit were usefully summarised in the case of *TL v ML (Ancillary Relief: Claim Against Assets of Extended Family)*[52] as follows:

(i) The sole criterion to be applied in determining the application is 'reasonableness' (s 22 of the Matrimonial Causes Act 1973), which is synonymous with 'fairness'.

(ii) A very important factor in determining fairness is the marital standard of living. This is not to say that the exercise is merely to replicate that standard.

(iii) In every maintenance pending suit application there should be a specific maintenance pending suit budget which excludes capital or long term expenditure more aptly to be considered on a final hearing. That budget should be examined critically in every case to exclude forensic exaggeration.

(iv) Where the affidavit or Form E disclosure by the payer is obviously deficient, the court should not hesitate to make robust assumptions about his ability to pay. The court is not confined to the mere say-so of the payer as to the extent of his income or resources. In such a situation the court should err in favour of the payee.

(v) Where the paying party has historically been supported through the bounty of an outsider, and where the payer is asserting that the bounty had been curtailed but where the position of the outsider is ambiguous or unclear, then the court is justified in assuming that the third party will continue to supply the bounty, at least until final trial.

**2.37** A salutary example of the consequences for a litigant who embarks on an interim hearing, having made less than full and frank disclosure, can be found in *Re G (Maintenance Pending Suit)*[53] where Munby J felt able to make

---

[52] [2006] 1 FLR 1263.
[53] [2007] 1 FLR 1674. The case is also interesting for the court's robust rejection of the suggestion

'and, I emphasise, for interlocutory purposes – appropriately robust assumptions' about the husband's ability to meet a periodical payments order.[54]

## HEARSAY EVIDENCE

**2.38**  Hearsay evidence is admissible in ancillary relief proceedings. Although the strict rules of evidence appear to apply in such proceedings as in other civil proceedings, those rules are generally applied in a more relaxed manner than in proceedings outside the family context.[55] As a matter of formality, hearsay evidence is admissible by reason of s 1 of the Civil Evidence Act 1995 and when it is 'evidence given in connection with the upbringing, maintenance or welfare of a child' pursuant to the Children (Admissibility of Hearsay Evidence) Order 1993.[56] The 1995 Act provides a series of safeguards relating to the use of hearsay evidence (see ss 2–6). Foremost of these is the requirement to give notice of the use of hearsay evidence. Such notices are seldom given in practice in ancillary relief proceedings. The hearsay is commonly simply reported in a witness's statement, or it is contained in a document exhibited with such a statement. It is common for evidence to be produced from third parties by way of a letter written by that person.

**2.39**  Where hearsay is relied upon, it is useful to have regard to the provisions of s 4 of the Civil Evidence Act 1995. This provides a handy checklist of the factors the court ought to consider in evaluating such evidence:

> '(1) In estimating the weight (if any) to be given to hearsay evidence in civil proceedings the court shall have regard to any circumstances from which any inference can reasonably be drawn as to the reliability or otherwise of the evidence.
>
> (2) Regard may be had, in particular, to the following—
>
> (a)  whether it would have been reasonable and practicable for the party by whom the evidence was adduced to have produced the maker of the original statement as a witness;

---

by the husband that the court had no jurisdiction to make an interim lump sum order – see [8] at 1678. In *Wicks v Wicks* [1998] 1 FLR 470 the Court of Appeal did not decide the question of whether an interim lump sum order was available pursuant to the Matrimonial Causes Act 1973, but Ward LJ rehearsed the arguments on each side, and the court strongly hinted that such an order was not available to the court (see 484–486). However, the court's powers to make an award for the benefit of a child pursuant to Sch 1 of the Children Act 1989 were not considered in *Wicks v Wicks*.

[54]  [2007] 1 FLR 1674 at 1682.

[55]  There is authority to the effect that wardship proceedings in the High Court are not subject to the normal strict rules of evidence (see *Official Solicitor v K* [1965] AC 201) and so the provisions of the Civil Evidence Act 1995 would not apply to such proceedings (s 11 of the 1995 Act), but this principle does not appear to extend to ancillary relief proceedings, which in their modern form are the creature of statute.

[56]  SI 1993/621.

(b) whether the original statement was made contemporaneously with the occurrence or existence of the matters stated;

(c) whether the evidence involves multiple hearsay;

(d) whether any person involved had any motive to conceal or misrepresent matters;

(e) whether the original statement was an edited account, or was made in collaboration with another or for a particular purpose;

(f) whether the circumstances in which the evidence is adduced as hearsay are such as to suggest an attempt to prevent proper evaluation of its weight.'

**2.40** By s 3 of the Civil Evidence Act 1995 the author of the hearsay statement can be ordered to attend for cross-examination:

'Rules of court may provide that where a party to civil proceedings adduces hearsay evidence of a statement made by a person and does not call that person as a witness, any other party to the proceedings may, with the leave of the court, call that person as a witness and cross-examine him on the statement as if he had been called by the first-mentioned party and as if the hearsay statement were his evidence in chief.'[57]

**2.41** The credibility of the author of a statement admitted as hearsay may also be challenged by the same evidence which could have been used to impugn his credibility had he been called as a witness.[58]

**2.42** The rules for calling the author of a hearsay statement for cross-examination or adducing evidence as to his credibility are to be found in the Rules of the Supreme Court 1965 and the County Court Rules 1981[59] and are in the same terms whether the proceedings are in the county court or the High Court. Where a party wishes to have the author of a hearsay statement brought before the court for cross-examination, the application must be made on notice to the other parties not later than 28 days after service of the hearsay notice.[60] Where a party intends to adduce evidence to challenge the credibility of the author of a hearsay statement, that intention must be notified to the other party within 28 days of the service of the hearsay notice.[61] It should be borne in mind, however, that, even if the rules have not been complied with, the court may admit the evidence and give it such weight as is justified. These rules are rarely referred to (or indeed honoured) in ancillary relief proceedings, but where the hearsay evidence is of central importance, reference to them may provide some assistance to one of the parties.

---

[57] It should be noted that this power is limited to a situation where a hearsay statement has been tendered in evidence by one party. It does not overcome the court's inability to require a witness who has provided no statement to attend court solely for the purpose of cross-examination.

[58] CEA 1995, s 5(2).

[59] In the form in which those rules stood immediately before the Civil Procedure Rules 1998 came into force on 26 April 1999.

[60] RSC Ord 38, r 22 and CCR Ord 20, r 16. Where there has been no formal hearsay notice, the time limit would not appear to apply, but it would still be prudent to apply for the order as soon as it becomes clear that the author of the statement will not be called by the other side.

[61] RSC Ord 38, r 23 and CCR Ord 20, r 17.

**2.43**   Thus, where a hearsay statement is produced, the other side to the case has a choice: to require the witness's attendance for cross-examination or simply to attack the evidence in his or her absence. Which route is chosen will be a tactical one based on the particular circumstances of the case. In some cases, the evidence will be so vague or weak that it will be enough to comment on it and persuade the court that it is effectively worthless. In other cases, it may be that requiring the attendance of the author of the hearsay statement for cross-examination may allow an opportunity for a wide-ranging enquiry into their evidence through cross-examination. Parties should bear this risk in mind when tendering written evidence from a third party whom they have no desire to call as a witness, lest the witness is compelled to attend and submit to cross-examination, under which he may give evidence which is ultimately unhelpful or damaging to the case of the party who initially adduced the witness's evidence. Until a statement is served containing the hearsay evidence, the other party will not be able to compel the attendance of that person merely to be cross-examined.[62] Once the statement is presented as evidence, the witness can be compelled to attend and can be extensively cross-examined. The same obviously applies where the witness attends voluntarily or under a summons and gives evidence in chief.

**2.44**   It is important to be clear as to what amounts to evidence, hearsay or otherwise, and what is inadmissible material because it does not constitute hard evidence. The court may make its findings on evidence, not on the basis of anecdotes, beliefs, opinions[63] or rumours:

> 'In the circumstances I propose to concentrate on that which can be demonstrated in the light of the *evidence* before me. As [the husband's counsel] correctly says, referring to *Phipson on Evidence* (Sweet and Maxwell, 15th edn, 1999), para 37-01, general reputation prevailing in the community, and the opinions, inferences or beliefs of individuals (whether witnesses or not) are inadmissible in proof of material facts. Properly he counsels me against allowing an accumulation of anecdotal or equally insubstantial material to be elevated in status to hard evidence. I agree. That is why, as I have said, I propose to concentrate on that which can be demonstrated by *evidence*.'[64]

**2.45**   Often the parties to ancillary relief proceedings find it difficult to separate what they believe to be the case (often influenced by their feelings about the other party) and what they can substantiate by way of properly admissible evidence. In preparing a client's statement the lawyer must strive to get to the source of the client's beliefs and assertions and identify the evidence which gives rise to the belief, rather than simply state the belief itself.

---

[62]   See *W v W (Disclosure by Third Party)* (1981) 2 FLR 291 and also **5.17–5.18**; but see *Charman v Charman* [2006] 2 FLR 422, [2006] 1 WLR 1053 for an illustration of how some degree of oral examination of a witness who has not provided a witness statement can be compelled through an inspection appointment or issue of letters of request.

[63]   Other than expert opinion, which is admissible.

[64]   *Al Khatib v Masry* [2002] 1 FLR 1053 at 1058 per Munby J.

**2.46** This task often becomes confused by the more relaxed approach to the admission of evidence adopted by the family courts. The judge hearing an ancillary relief application is charged with actively investigating the matter.[65] This quasi-inquisitorial role means that his obligations extend beyond merely adjudicating on a dispute between adversarial parties. With such a statutory obligation upon the court it is much more difficult to exclude evidence from consideration on procedural grounds when the evidence is relevant to 'all the circumstances of the case'.[66] In general, relevant evidence is admitted in ancillary relief proceedings more readily than it might be in civil proceedings, where the procedural rules as to the admission of evidence are more strictly applied. With that said, of course, the court in an ancillary relief case must always have regard to the need to ensure that both parties have a fair hearing and are not disadvantaged by the admission of late evidence. There is also the obligation to further the overriding objective and ensure that the case is dealt with in a proportionate manner.

**2.47** There is no provision within the rules relating to ancillary relief proceedings requiring a party to serve a witness statement before calling a witness to give oral evidence. Nevertheless, it is usual to file a witness statement or affidavit before the witness is called.[67] This puts the other side on notice as to what the witness will say and saves time, because the statement will stand as that witness's evidence in chief. There may be circumstances where issues arise during the hearing which require evidence to be called from a witness whom no party had any prior intention to call. The court may admit that evidence.[68] Where the need for that evidence could have been reasonably foreseen, the court may penalise the party at fault by an order for costs where the admission of that evidence requires an adjournment or other delay in the proceedings.

## EVIDENCE OBTAINED FROM THE INTERNET

**2.48** The internet has created an enormous yet easily accessible library of information. It is now very common for material downloaded from the internet to be placed before the court in proceedings. Normally such material causes no problems in the proceedings, because the substantive facts it seeks to prove are unlikely to be contentious. For example, it is common for parties to produce sales particulars of properties they suggest are suitable for their rehousing, having downloaded the information from an estate agent's website. There is usually no dispute that those properties are indeed on the market for the prices indicated and, although the parties will comment on the suitability of the suggested properties, the court does not usually need to consider the status of the evidence itself.

---

[65]  See FPR 1991, r 2.62(4) and r 2.64(1).
[66]  Matrimonial Causes Act 1973, s 25(1).
[67]  See **2.11** above for a discussion of circumstances when the parties themselves will be required to file witness statements or some other form of statement of case.
[68]  See *Krywald v Krywald* [1988] 2 FLR 401.

**2.49**   Sometimes, however, the material obtained from the internet is more contentious. For example, in a case where the health of one party and his or her consequent ability to work is in issue, a party may produce various articles from the internet which seek to provide information about the relevant medical condition, its effects, and its treatment. This material is then relied upon at trial to seek to persuade the court that the medical condition will take one course or another. Another example may occur in a case where the value of a business is in issue. It is not uncommon in such a case for parties to seek to adduce material from the internet which sheds some light on the future prospects for the sector of industry in which the business trades. Such material is then used to challenge assumptions used about the future trading prospects of the company for the purposes of valuing it. What is the status of such evidence and how should the court deal with it?

**2.50**   There is, as yet, very little direct consideration of this issue in the case law. In *CR v CR*[69] Bodey J was asked to look at a variety of material sourced from the internet which provided opinions on the future prospects for the sector of industry in which the husband's business traded. This information, it was said, would assist the court in determining how profitable a business would be in the future. This material was put into evidence during the course of the hearing and it appears that there was no detailed argument as to its status as evidence. Nevertheless, Bodey J said:[70]

> 'This is not the place for a discourse on the admissibility of openly available internet material; nor did I receive any submissions on the point. Such material is often "put in" on a variety of topics, frequently without demur from the other side. However, except where it purports to go in some way to the facts, the material remains in the nature of expert evidence emanating from a purported fund of expertise possessed on the topic by whoever posted it on the net. If it is contentious material, then it must require leave to introduce it. The other side can then put in contrary expert evidence (if so advised) and the issue can be properly case-managed to a fair resolution.'

This analysis is, it is submitted, correct. A further point which can be made is that such evidence is also, by its very nature, a form of hearsay evidence. This is the case whether it is evidence of opinion, and therefore a form of expert evidence, or evidence of fact. In either case, the weight to be given to the evidence will have to be assessed in accordance with the principles applicable to hearsay evidence, as discussed in the previous section of this chapter. A very important factor to bear in mind is that very often the identity and status of the person posting material on the internet is difficult to ascertain. Consequently, the reliability of the material may often also be very difficult to judge.

---

[69]   [2008] 1 FLR 323.
[70]   [2008] 1 FLR 323 at 337.

# THE USE OF INFERENCES

**2.51** Often, in ancillary relief proceedings, one party will suggest that the other party has access to assets or income which have not been disclosed. Where there is direct evidence of the existence of such assets or income, this can be placed before the court and a finding can be made that those assets exist. More often, however, there is no such evidence in the possession of the party making the allegation of non-disclosure. In such circumstances that party will have to rely on the court making an inference that the asset or income exists.

**2.52** The use of inferences from the evidence is common in all forms of litigation. Inferences are particularly useful in ancillary relief proceedings and, in some respects, the court may be more willing to make inferences in such proceedings than in other forms of litigation. There is a duty of full and frank disclosure placed upon the parties to ancillary relief proceedings. The extent of this duty is discussed in detail in Chapter 4. Where a party can be shown to have breached this duty of full and frank disclosure, the court's suspicions will be aroused and it may be able to infer that the party who has failed to make full disclosure of his assets and income is actually in possession of further substantial assets, even though there is no direct evidence of the existence of those assets.

**2.53** The classic statement of the approach to inferences in ancillary relief proceedings was made as long ago as 1955 by Sachs J in *J v J*:[71]

'In cases of this kind, where the duty of disclosure comes to lie upon the husband; where a husband has – and his wife has not – detailed knowledge of his complex affairs; where a husband is fully capable of explaining, and has the opportunity to explain, those affairs, and where he seeks to minimise the wife's claim, that husband can hardly complain if, when he leaves gaps in the court's knowledge, the court does not draw inferences in his favour. On the contrary, when he leaves a gap in such a state that two alternative inferences may be drawn, the court will normally draw the less favourable inference – especially where it seems likely that his able legal advisers would have hastened to put forward affirmatively any facts, had they existed, establishing the more favourable alternative.'

And he went on to say:[72]

'... it is as well to state expressly something which underlies the procedure by which husbands are required in such proceedings to disclose their means to the court. Whether that disclosure is by affidavit of facts, by affidavit of documents or by evidence on oath (not least when that evidence is led by those representing the husband) the obligation of the husband is to be full, frank and clear in that disclosure. Any shortcomings of the husband from the requisite standard can and normally should be visited at least by the court drawing inferences against the husband on matters the subject of the shortcomings – insofar as such inferences can properly be drawn.'

---

[71]   [1955] P 215 at 227.
[72]   [1955] P 215 at 229.

**2.54** This approach, applied to wives in the same way as it is to husbands, has been regularly adopted by the courts and has been approved in various reported judgments.[73] It should be noted that the courts are seldom able to make a precise inference as to the extent of the undisclosed assets. More commonly, the court simply infers that the undisclosed assets are sufficient to meet the order it proposes to make.

**2.55** It is important that parties should not allow themselves to become carried away by evidence of non-disclosure by the other side. It is wrong to think that once a party is shown to be dishonest and in breach of the duty of full and frank disclosure, the court is free to make any inferences it chooses. The effect of the burden and standard of proof must be borne in mind. These topics are considered in detail above. Furthermore, although it will often be possible to raise a suspicion that there are other undisclosed assets, a mere suspicion is not enough to make a finding.[74] The court must still be satisfied on the basis of all the evidence that it is proper to make a finding that on the balance of probabilities there are other assets or income available. The fact that the respondent has been guilty of some non-disclosure is merely one important part of the evidence to be considered. The failure to make full disclosure, accompanied as it almost always is by a finding that the party in question is not a reliable or credible witness, may enable the court to reject all other explanations and make the adverse inference. Equally, in such a case, where the possible outcomes may cause some unfairness to one party or the other, the court is more likely to make an order which favours the innocent party more than the guilty party.[75] Non-disclosure will force the court to take a rather rough and ready approach to assessing the extent of the parties' assets, but is ultimately unlikely to benefit the person engaging in the non-disclosure.[76]

**2.56** Where an assessment of all the evidence indicates that on the balance of probabilities there are no other assets of substance, the court cannot infer that there are such assets simply because there has been a breach of the duty of full and frank disclosure. In such a case the non-disclosure is likely to result in a costs order against the guilty party. It is not usually appropriate to penalise non-disclosure or dishonesty by a reduction in the appropriate share of the available assets.[77]

---

[73]  For examples see *Payne v Payne* [1968] 1 WLR; *F v F (Divorce: Insolvency)* [1994] 1 FLR 359; *Baker v Baker* [1995] 2 FLR 829; *Al-Khatib v Masry* [2002] 1 FLR 1053; *Minwalla v Minwalla* [2005] 1 FLR 771. See also the cases referred to above in the context of interim hearings.

[74]  For example, *Zeiderman v Zeiderman* [2008] EWCA Civ 760, unreported, where the Court of Appeal ordered a rehearing on the basis that the first instance judge, having formed an unfavourable perception of the husband, made a very favourable order in favour of the wife on the 'assumption and belief', rather than on evidence, that the husband owned another property, which he denied.

[75]  See *F v F (Divorce: Insolvency)* [1994] 1 FLR 359 at 367.

[76]  See *Al-Khatib v Masry* [2002] 1 FLR 1053, where, despite the complete absence of financial disclosure by the husband, the court was able to conclude that he was worth at least £50 million.

[77]  *P v P (Financial Relief: Non-Disclosure)* [1994] 2 FLR 381. But sometimes conduct is taken

**2.57**   It is important to note that, even at a late stage, a party who has failed to make full disclosure can 'repent' and avoid having adverse inferences drawn against him or her. If a party accepts that 'the game is up' and gives frank evidence from the witness box, the court may find that party's credibility restored.[78] At the very least, such a frank acceptance of the past failings in disclosure may prevent the court being able to make adverse inferences. Where a party appears to have been in breach of the duty of disclosure, his or her lawyers should make the consequences of this plain when advising him or her. The guilty party must understand that it may be preferable to own up to the dishonesty rather than to continue to pretend that there are no shortcomings in the disclosure.

## UNLAWFULLY OBTAINED EVIDENCE – SELF-HELP AND 'DIY DISCLOSURE'

**2.58**   Frequently, the levels of bitterness and distrust between separating husband and wife result in one of them seeking covertly to obtain confidential information about the other's affairs for use in the proceedings. There is a place in appropriate circumstances for the use of enquiry agents and other means of discovering information which a party has been unwilling to volunteer.[79] There is also a public interest in litigants who present a false picture to the court in the course of proceedings being exposed. Nevertheless, caution has to be exercised in pursuing such enquiries and activities.

**2.59**   The ancillary relief lawyer is regularly presented with documentation or information about an opposing party's affairs which a client has secretly obtained. As a marriage breaks down, it is not uncommon for one party to secretly examine the other's private documents in order to learn more about their financial situation. Evidence gathered in this 'DIY' fashion presents the lawyer with a dilemma. Such activities usually amount to an infringement of the other party's rights to privacy and confidentiality, and so they need to be justified. Sometimes, the conduct also amounts to a criminal offence. Nevertheless, the documents so obtained are likely to be relevant to the proceedings. Such documentation is commonly admitted as evidence in the ensuing ancillary relief proceedings. It is rare that the court is asked to question the means by which the material was obtained. The introduction of the Human Rights Act 1998 and greater regulation by way of data protection and computer legislation suggest that greater scrutiny of disclosure obtained by such self-help methods may now be necessary.

---

into account in this way: e g *M v M (Third Party Subpoena: Financial Conduct)* [2006] 2 FLR 1253 and *M v M (Financial Provision: Party Incurring Excessive Costs)* [1999] 2 FLR 498.
[78]   *P v P (Financial Relief: Non-Disclosure)* [1994] 2 FLR 381.
[79]   For example, see *Al-Khatib v Masry* [2002] 1 FLR 1053 at 1065 (enquiry agents were able to find Swiss bank accounts the husband had failed to disclose).

**2.60**  The established approach to covertly obtained evidence in ancillary relief cases stems from the case of *Hildebrand v Hildebrand*.[80] Mr Hildebrand felt that his wife had concealed the full extent of her wealth from him. When he sensed the marriage was coming to an end he began to take photocopies of his wife's personal papers. Following their separation he secretly entered her home on five occasions and copied more of her papers. Eventually Mrs Hildebrand caught him in her flat and realised what he was up to. It was said that he had copied so much material that the copies would 'fill a crate'. Mr Hildebrand's lawyers composed a long questionnaire based on the documents he had obtained. They did not disclose the documents prior to presenting the questionnaire, obviously hoping to ensnare the wife in her deceit. Waite J refused to require the wife to answer the questions because (a) Mr Hildebrand's conduct was such that it was an abuse of process for him to require his wife to answer the questions he posed to her, and (b) he already knew the answers to the questions from the material he had taken. The judge went on to require Mr Hildebrand to disclose all the documents to Mrs Hildebrand's lawyers in line with his duty to make full and frank disclosure of all material documents in his possession. He was not permitted to 'keep them up his sleeve' to be used in cross-examination but, so long as he disclosed them, he could use them within the proceedings.

**2.61**  Following that decision, it became important to ensure that all such '*Hildebrand* documents' were disclosed prior to questionnaires being answered by the parties.[81] Many specialist practitioners seek an express assurance that there are no such documents being retained by the other party before answers to a questionnaire are supplied. There was no suggestion in the *Hildebrand* case or in subsequent cases that the manner in which the documents had been obtained rendered them inadmissible or that the husband should deliver up to the wife copies of all the documents he had obtained unlawfully. The introduction of the Human Rights Act 1998 and the development of the law of privacy seem to have passed relatively unnoticed in this area of practice. For example, in *K v K (Financial Capital Relief: Management of Difficult Cases)*[82] Baron J spoke with resignation of how a husband who was somewhat recalcitrant in making disclosure brought upon himself the wife's resort to secretly taking documents, taping telephone calls and the like. In *D v D & B Ltd*[83] Charles J did not seek to criticise a wife who carried out an extensive examination of the records of the husband's companies which he kept in an unlocked basement in the matrimonial home. Even in *T v T (Interception of Documents)*,[84] where the wife's conduct in breaking into the husband's office and taking his mail was described by Wilson J as 'reprehensible', there was no suggestion that she should return any of the material she had taken or that she

---

[80]  [1992] 1 FLR 244.
[81]  In *Klamer v Klamer* [2008] 1 FLR 238 Baron J reminded practitioners of the need to make prompt disclosure of documents which evidenced non-disclosure rather than drip-feeding them into the proceedings in an attempt to catch the other party out.
[82]  [2005] 2 FLR 1137.
[83]  [2007] EWHC 278.
[84]  [1994] 2 FLR 1083.

could not rely on it at the final hearing, although her conduct was such that it might be relevant to the question of costs.

**2.62** Judges sitting outside the Family Division have also been required to consider these matters. In *L v L and Anor*[85] Tugendhat J, sitting in the Queens Bench Division, was asked to make interim orders in civil proceedings by a husband against his wife and her solicitors. The husband had issued a claim requiring the wife and her solicitors to deliver up all copies of the hard drive of his laptop computer which she had removed from the family home and had copied by a computer expert. Interestingly, underlining that the *Hildebrand* approach described above had become commonly accepted in ancillary relief litigation, the wife said that she had been advised by leading counsel to act as she did. The application for an interim injunction came to be issued as a civil claim in the Queen's Bench Division because no matrimonial proceedings had yet been commenced. The computer hard drive contained various information concerning the husband and his business interests. The wife did not have a chance to examine the contents of the hard drive before the husband discovered what she had done and sought to recover the copies. The husband argued that he was entitled to have the copies returned to him because (a) they were his private and confidential documents and he was entitled to have his right to privacy under Art 8 of the ECHR respected, (b) some of the material stored on the computer was subject to legal professional privilege, (c) some of the material related to the confidential affairs of third parties who were not relevant to the divorce, and (d) the wife had acted unlawfully by contravening the provisions of the Data Protection Act 1998 and the Computer Misuse Act 1990. The wife in turn said that her actions had been necessary and justified because there was reason to believe that the husband would take steps to destroy or conceal evidence and thereby frustrate the proper administration of justice in the proposed financial proceedings between them.

**2.63** Hearing the husband's contested application for an interim injunction for the return of copies of the hard drive pending trial, Tugendhat J had no difficulty in finding that the husband had a real prospect of succeeding in establishing that the wife had acted unlawfully. He made an order requiring the wife to deliver up the copies of the hard drive to the husband's solicitors to be held by them pending the resolution of the case. Importantly, this being an application for interim orders, he was not required to decide whether the wife had in fact acted unlawfully, but he was clearly satisfied that she may have done.

**2.64** The most interesting observations by Tugendhat J are the following:

- He was deeply concerned about the implications of the court endorsing the self-help approach adopted by Mrs L by allowing her to retain and use the material she had taken. If she were permitted to do so, it meant that any litigant could obtain and use material without having to meet the stringent test for the grant of a search order (formerly an *Anton Piller*

---

[85]   [2007] 2 FLR 171.

order)[86] and without offering to the respondent the various safeguards to protect his rights which are usually built into a search order. It seemed to be common ground that the facts of Mr and Mrs L's case fell short of what was required for the making of a search order. It was a strong argument in the husband's favour that the wife should not be put in a better position as a result of her potentially unlawful conduct than she would have been in had she made an appropriate application to the court prior to taking the computer.

- He noted that the wife did not need to take matters into her own hands. She could have applied for an order pursuant to CPR Part 25.1(1)(c)(i),[87] preserving the laptop so that none of the information it contained could be destroyed. She would then have been protected by the order of the court and her actions in pursuance of the order would not have been unlawful.

- He was not impressed by the wife's submission that to require any spouse in her position to apply to the court for an order before attempting to seize or copy documents would result in the court lists becoming clogged with the volume of applications for interim order that would result.

- He expressed doubts as to the propriety of the admission of evidence by the family courts regardless of the manner in which it had been obtained. That approach differed from the approach in both the criminal law and in general civil litigation, where the courts were developing an increasing discretion to exclude such evidence.[88] He suggested that the time was ripe for the approach in the family courts to be considered further.[89]

**2.65**   The decision in *L v L* should not be elevated to the level of a binding precedent in ancillary relief proceedings. The court was dealing with an application for interim injunctions in a civil action for delivery up of goods. No findings of fact and no rulings on the law were made. A slightly different view of a similar situation was adopted by Eady J when striking out a husband's claim against his wife's solicitors for damages as a result of their alleged complicity in his wife's actions in taking various documents belonging to the husband and giving them to her solicitors for use in ancillary relief proceedings.[90] Eady J agreed that:

> 'the law regarding interference with personal property may have application notwithstanding a marital relationship. It is recognised in the *Hildebrand* line of cases that a document "left lying around" can be copied and used in the proceedings, but it would not seem to be right to take and keep an original,

---

[86]   See **4.43–4.49** for an explanation of the basis upon which such an order may be obtained.
[87]   See **6.89–6.91** below for a discussion of these powers.
[88]   For example, *Jones v Warwick University* [2003] EWCA Civ 151, [2003] 1 WLR 954.
[89]   As that was not a question falling to be decided in the interim application before him, these comments are, of course, wholly obiter.
[90]   *White v Withers LLP* [2008] EWHC 2821 (QB). It is the authors' understanding that the husband has appealed.

especially perhaps when that involves concealing the document's existence altogether from the intended recipient.'[91]

The learned judge went on to dismiss the husband's claims against the solicitors[92] on the basis that they disclosed no cause of action on any of the grounds advanced:

- There was no tort of conversion committed by the solicitors because the husband could not show that they ever had possession of the original documents or, if they did hold originals, that they had refused to return them to him. The fact that they had asked the wife to send them copies of the documents once she informed them that she had them did not amount to a tort. However, it appears to be implicit in the judgment that the solicitors might have been liable if they had advised or encouraged the wife to act in a way which unlawfully interfered with the husband's property.

- Although English law now recognised a right of protection against the misuse of private information,[93] it was not a misuse of such information if it has been 'received, noted and retained purely for use in connection with court proceedings and the protection of their client's interest in that context' because the *Hildebrand* line of cases permitted such a practice.

- There was no evidence that the solicitors had committed a criminal offence of theft or contrary to s 1 of the Regulation of Investigatory Powers Act 2000, and such allegations should not have been raised.

**2.66**   The decisions in *L v L* and *White v Withers LLP* highlight ambiguities in the current law and the potential for conflict between established practices in family litigation and the wider civil and criminal law. Both cases were interlocutory applications in civil proceedings. The decision to strike out the claim in *White v Withers LLP* was principally founded on the evidential difficulties the husband faced in proving his claims. Until these issues have been considered in a final, rather than an interlocutory, judgment, there must be doubt as to the exact scope of the law. Furthermore, the law of confidence and privacy continues to develop, and family lawyers cannot simply ignore it and assume that the family courts are governed by entirely different rules from those applied to the general civil and criminal courts. It appears that many litigants and their representatives are becoming aware of wider remedies for the wrongs they perceive they have suffered. The primary lesson for practitioners from *L v L* and *White v Withers LLP* is to be aware of the pitfalls of self-help methods of obtaining information or preserving documents (including those recorded digitally on a computer or other form of data storage). Careful

---

[91]   Ibid at [11].
[92]   It is important to note that the claim against the wife was not pursued by the husband, and the judgment did not need to comment on the potential merits as a matter of law if there had been a claim against the wife rather than the solicitors.
[93]   For example, *Campbell v MGN Ltd* [2004] AC 457.

thought needs to be given before any client is advised to take matters into his or her own hands. Such self-help remedies may be unlawful in a number of ways, examples being:

- Unlawful entry to another person's premises and the removal of property may amount to commission of the offence of burglary or theft.

- A course of such conduct may also amount to criminal harassment for the purposes of the Protection from Harassment Act 1997.

- The obtaining and 'processing' of another person's personal data may be in contravention of the detailed regulatory provisions of the Data Protection Act 1998.

- Unauthorised access to data stored on a computer may amount to a criminal offence under the provisions of the Computer Misuse Act 1990.

- The interception of a person's post, telephone or fax communications and their electronic communications by e-mail or otherwise may, unless done with their consent or under the authority of a warrant, constitute a criminal offence pursuant to s 1 of the Regulation of Investigatory Powers Act 2000 ('RIPA 2000') punishable by imprisonment for up to 2 years. By s 17 of the 2000 Act information obtained in breach of s 1 is wholly inadmissible in any legal proceedings. There is no discretion to admit such unlawfully obtained evidence. Some covert interceptions from a 'private communications system' will be lawful if made by a person who has the right to control that system.[94] So a homeowner attaching a 'bug' to his own domestic telephone and recording the conversations on that phone is unlikely to be guilty of the offence, and the evidence obtained by those means will not be automatically inadmissible.[95] Similarly, the obtaining of information belonging to another person by taking it from their personal records is unlikely to be an interception within the meaning of the 2000 Act, although it may constitute theft. Although interception of mail whilst 'in the course of its transmission by means of a public postal service' would be an offence pursuant to s 1 of RIPA 2000, no such offence is committed if the mail is intercepted or taken once it has been delivered.[96]

- Even if no criminal offence has been committed, the unauthorised accessing of another person's personal information may amount to an infringement of the 'right to respect for his private and family life, his home and his correspondence' under Art 8 of the European Convention on Human Rights or to a breach of confidence. Whether the Art 8 right is

---

[94] RIPA 2000, s 1(6).
[95] On the basis of the distinction between the public telecommunications system and a private communications system set out in *R v Effick* [1995] 1 AC 309 and apparently confirmed by the House of Lords in the context of RIPA 2000 by *Attorney-General's Reference (No 5 of 2002)*.
[96] *White v Withers LLP* [2008] EWHC 2821 (QB), unreported decision of Eady J.

infringed in any case will depend on the exact circumstances.[97] Notably, this right is not an absolute right to privacy, but is a right to 'respect' for privacy. It is a flexible concept judged according to the circumstances of the case and general societal attitudes.[98] Thus, it is submitted that a court may find the right infringed less quickly in a case where husband and wife are still living together in the same household than where they have separated and established separate lives and homes. The court should not allow evidence obtained in contravention of the Art 8 rights to be admitted in evidence unless it falls within Art 8(2), in that the interference was 'in accordance with law' and was 'necessary in a democratic society ... for the protection of health or morals, or for the protection of the rights and freedoms of others'. It is submitted that the use of such material as evidence within ancillary relief proceedings is likely to be considered to be justified on the basis that it is necessary to protect the rights and freedoms of the party who obtained the information.[99]

**2.67** There may be problems where evidence is obtained illegally and its admission in the proceedings would be contrary to Art 8(2), but that evidence is highly relevant to the issues the court is asked to decide within the ancillary relief proceedings. There appears to be no reported authority dealing with this situation. Neither is there any guidance as to how the duty of full and frank disclosure applies in the context of a party who has come into possession of information through circumstances which, if revealed, would lead him to be at risk of prosecution for a criminal offence. Which principle has priority: the right against potential self-incrimination or the duty to make full and frank disclosure? The answer appears to lie in s 14 of the Civil Evidence Act 1968, which enshrines the right against self-incrimination in statute.

## EXPERT EVIDENCE

**2.68** Expert evidence is commonly used in ancillary relief cases. Such evidence usually goes to the question of the value of the assets in question. The scope of the issues to be considered in ancillary relief proceedings is so broad that there may be a need for expert evidence on diverse issues. Ultimately, the principles in relation to the instruction of an expert, regardless of his or her discipline, are the same and are governed by the provisions of CPR Part 35[100] and the application of the 'overriding objective'.

---

[97] For examples of how the courts have sought to balance the competing rights of parties in personal injury proceedings where covert surveillance evidence has been adduced, see *Jones v Warwick University* [2003] 1 WLR 954, and in an employment law context in *Amwell View School Governors v Dogherty* [2007] ICR 135.

[98] *Re F* [2000] UKHRR 712 at 732.

[99] See *White v Withers LLP* [2008] EWHC 2821 (QB) at [16].

[100] CPR Part 35 is applied to ancillary relief proceedings, in appropriately modified form, by FPR, r 2.61C.

**2.69** Most readers of this book will already be fully familiar with these principles. They are already considered in detail in other textbooks. For this reason there is no further consideration of the general principles and practice here. The use of expert evidence in the context of particular types of assets is considered in the sections of this book dealing with property, business assets, trust and pensions.

# EVIDENCE FROM OVERSEAS OR FROM WITNESSES OTHERWISE UNABLE TO ATTEND COURT

**2.70** In the modern age there are a growing number of 'international marriages' involving parties with connections to more than one state. The assets owned by families are often spread around the globe. In many cases it will be necessary to obtain information and evidence from overseas. The practicalities of obtaining disclosure of information or documentation from overseas is considered at **5.43–5.48**. The discussion in this section concentrates on obtaining the evidence of witnesses located overseas rather than seeking disclosure from them.

**2.71** Where a witness is willing and able to travel from abroad to give evidence at a hearing, there is unlikely to be any significant procedural difficulty. He or she will simply arrive at court and give evidence in the normal way. Of course, there may need to be consideration given in advance to the listing of the case to enable the witness to give his or her evidence conveniently. There may also need to be an interpreter arranged. With the provision of frequent and affordable air travel around the world it is now much easier for witnesses to attend hearings in person than was the case even a few years ago.

**2.72** If an overseas witness is unable or unwilling to travel to a hearing, he or she cannot normally be compelled to do so. The court's power to summons a witness to appear before it does not extend beyond the borders of the jurisdiction. A party faced with this difficulty of calling evidence from a witness who is unable or unwilling to enter the jurisdiction and give evidence has a number of options.

## Adducing the evidence as hearsay

**2.73** An affidavit or witness statement may be taken from the witness and placed before the court.[101] Where the evidence is contentious and the other side is, due to the absence of the witness, unable to cross-examine him, the court will have to decide what, if any, weight should be given to the evidence. Clearly, the reasons for the witness's absence and the efforts which have been made to put

---

[101] The affidavit may be taken abroad. It may be necessary to prove that the affidavit was validly sworn in accordance with the law of the jurisdiction in which it was sworn.

his evidence before the court in a more open manner will weigh heavily in the court's consideration. This issue is dealt with in more detail in the section dealing with hearsay evidence above.

## Notice to admit

**2.74**  The party seeking to rely on the overseas witness to prove certain facts or documents may seek to have those facts or documents admitted by the other party by means of a notice to admit.[102] Plainly, where those facts or documents are contentious and at the heart of the dispute, it is unlikely that such admissions will be forthcoming. The service of such a notice will, however, focus both sides' minds on the actual facts in dispute and may be highly relevant to the question of costs in due course.

## Proof by alternative means

**2.75**  If the facts can be proved by some means other than the oral evidence of a witness, it may be possible to obtain an order from the court that the fact may be proved in a specified manner.[103] This may allow a fact to be proved by the use of material which would not normally be regarded as evidence (eg newspaper reports). Such an order is unlikely to be granted where the fact in issue is contested and at the heart of the dispute.[104] Nevertheless, with the more relaxed approach to evidence taken in family proceedings, the court may be willing to explore various ways in which disputed issues can be determined in a cost-effective manner.

## Evidence by deposition taken in England or Wales

**2.76**  Where the witness will not be available in the jurisdiction at the time of the final hearing but he will be available in the jurisdiction at an earlier date, his evidence may be taken at that point. This may be by listing the final hearing to commence at that point for the evidence to be taken before the trial judge in the normal way and, once the witness's evidence has been heard, adjourning the hearing to be concluded on another day. It will not always be practicable to proceed in this way. If it is not possible, the evidence may be taken by way of a deposition. Although this method of taking evidence is now clearly set out in the Civil Procedure Rules 1998, Part 34, those provisions do not apply in family proceedings, and so the procedure remains governed by RSC, Ord 39 and CCR, Ord 20, r 13. A deposition is taken following an order of the court made on application by one of the parties to the proceedings. The deposition will be conducted before an examiner appointed by the court. This may be a judge of the court (possibly even the trial judge), another officer of the court, or some other person appointed by the court (a practising lawyer may be appointed, which may well save both time and costs). The manner of the examination will

---

[102]  See RSC Ord 27 and CCR Ord 20.
[103]  See RSC Ord 38, r 3 and CCR Ord 20, r 8.
[104]  *H v Schering Chemicals Ltd* [1983] 1 WLR 143.

depend on the circumstances. It need not take place at the court (indeed, this procedure is sometimes used in the case of witnesses who are unable to attend court due to illness by way of examination at their hospital bedside). Arrangements will need to be taken for the evidence to be recorded, wherever it is taken. If the evidence is not too contentious, the parties may choose simply to submit written questions to be answered by the witness on oath. In a more contentious case, the parties will attend to examine the witness. The witness can be compelled to take the oath and to answer questions in the same way as he would at the final hearing itself.

## Evidence by deposition taken outside England or Wales

**2.77**   The county court may only take a deposition from a witness in England and Wales.[105] Where the deposition is to be taken abroad, the county court will require an order from the High Court, which the High Court can make without requiring transfer of the whole proceedings to it.[106] In reality, however, the high costs involved in the process of obtaining a deposition overseas are likely to ensure that the procedure will only be used in the highest value and most complex cases, which are unlikely to be proceeding in the county court in any event.

**2.78**   The examination of witnesses in foreign jurisdictions for the purposes of English proceedings requires respect for the comity of nations. The English court cannot assume jurisdiction over individuals within a sovereign foreign state. Not every state permits the examination of its residents for use in foreign courts. In fact, in some countries it would be unlawful to do so. Hence, the High Court issues a 'letter of request' to the appropriate judicial authority in the foreign state.[107] The letter of request will either request the judicial authority in the foreign state to take the evidence of the named person or to allow a person appointed by the High Court ('a special examiner') to take the evidence. If the foreign government indicates that there is no objection to an examination being conducted by the High Court on its territory, a formal letter of request may not be required.[108] It is likely that liaison between the parties, the court and the Foreign and Commonwealth Office will be required prior to the issue of a letter of request, or the making of an order for examination of a witness abroad. Reference may also need to be made to any special arrangements which exist by way of treaty or convention with another state.

**2.79**   A slightly different procedure applies where the deposition is to be taken from a person in one of the other states of the European Union (except Denmark). The 'Taking Evidence Regulation'[109] appears to apply to

---

[105]   CCR Ord 20, r 3(1).
[106]   See County Courts Act 1984, s 56.
[107]   See also **5.43–5.48** for consideration of the use of letters of request to obtain evidence and documents from non-parties based overseas.
[108]   *Peer International Corporation v Termidor Music Publishers Ltd* [2005] EWHC 1048.
[109]   Council Regulation (EC)1206/2001 of 28 May 2001 on co-operation between the courts of member states in the taking of evidence in civil and commercial matters.

matrimonial proceedings on the basis that they are 'civil' proceedings. A more harmonised system for the taking of evidence abroad applies as a result. As the Regulation came into effect after the RSC and CCR were replaced for other civil proceedings by the CPR, the only procedural rules dealing with applications under the Regulation appear in CPR Part 34.23. If an application pursuant to the Regulation is made in ancillary relief proceedings and the court finds that the Regulation applies to such proceedings, it seems that the procedure outlined in the CPR will be adopted by the court.

**2.80** Neither the High Court nor the county court may sit outside the jurisdiction.[110] However, there appears to be nothing preventing a High Court judge appointing himself as the special examiner to take a deposition abroad.[111] He would carry out that task not as a judge of the High Court but as the examiner, and the High Court would not be sitting outside the jurisdiction, even though the examination will, in effect, be part of the trial of the proceedings. Similarly, the court may use these provisions to deal with the evidence of a person in England and Wales who is physically unable to attend the hearing at the court building.

**2.81** The record of the deposition may be adduced as evidence in the proceedings. Although it remains a form of hearsay statement, the fact that it was given on oath and following questioning from all interested parties means that it is likely to be accorded more authority by the court than a unilaterally prepared affidavit or statement. Where, however, there is no good explanation as to why the witness could not actually give live evidence at the hearing, the court may still choose to give the deposition little weight, or even, in an appropriate case, refuse to admit it as evidence at all.

**2.82** In view of the relatively rapid and affordable international transport system and the availability of video links in appropriate cases, there will be relatively few cases where the use of a deposition taken overseas will be desirable or necessary. The high costs involved in obtaining a deposition overseas compared to the alternative means of taking evidence 'live' during the hearing indicate that this is a procedure which will only be used in rare and unusual cases. There does, however, remain a role for the use of letters of request in dealing with disclosure from overseas, and this is considered in more detail in Chapter 5.

## Video link

**2.83** The court's ability to take evidence by a video link arises by virtue of RSC Ord 38, r 3 and CCR Ord 20, r 8, which give the court a broad power to direct how evidence should be given.[112] Guidance as to the use of video conferencing in family proceedings in the RCJ or Principal Registry was given

---

[110] Supreme Court Act 1981, s 71(1) and County Courts Act 1984, ss 1–3.

[111] *Peer International Corporation v Termidor Music Publishers Ltd* [2005] EWHC 1048.

[112] See *Garcin v Amerindo Investment Advisors Ltd* [1991] 1 WLR 1140; *R v Horseferry Road Magistrates' Court ex parte Bennett (No 3)* (1994) The Times, January 14.

by way of a President's Practice Direction dated 14 January 2002. Recent investment in video conferencing equipment means that facilities for video conferencing are now extensively available in courts around the country. Its use is becoming increasingly familiar. Any party to proceedings considering applying to the court for a direction permitting evidence to be given by a video link would be well advised to first read the Video Conferencing Guidance published as Annex 3 to the Practice Direction to CPR Part 32. Although not strictly binding on the parties or the court in ancillary relief proceedings, this guidance is likely to be given considerable weight in such proceedings. It is often overlooked that a witness giving evidence by video link will require a copy of the court bundle (or at least the most relevant documents) whilst giving evidence. Practitioners should have in mind the criticism by Baron J in *K v K (Financial Relief: Management of Difficult Cases)*[113] of lawyers who had arranged a video link with the husband in Cuba without first checking that the link would actually work. The result was a huge waste of costs. The evidence had to be given over the telephone, leaving the court to be 'treated to the unedifying sight of experienced Silks standing by a "squawk box" in order to enable the call to be made'.

**2.84** Parties should be aware that a video link is still a poor substitute for a witness being physically present in the courtroom to give his or her evidence. Where the witness's evidence is of critical importance to the outcome of the case, it may be preferable to obtain his attendance at the hearing even if a video link could be arranged. This will be even more important if the examination of the witness is to involve substantial reference to documentation or if the witness requires an interpreter to give evidence. Nevertheless, if a witness or party is unwilling to come to England to give evidence and the only option is the use of a video link, then the party's right to a fair trial may require permission to be given for its use.[114]

---

[113] [2005] 2 FLR 1137 at 1144–5.
[114] *Polanski v Condé Nast Publications Ltd* [2004] 1 WLR 387; and see *K v K (Financial Relief: Management of Difficult Cases)* [2005] 2 FLR 1137 at 1144–5.

# Part II

# DISCLOSURE

# Chapter 3

# DISCLOSURE IN ANCILLARY RELIEF PROCEEDINGS

**3.1**   The process of disclosure lies at the heart of ancillary relief proceedings. The first stage of any ancillary relief application is ascertaining the extent of the assets available to the parties.[1] Much of the time and cost spent in contested ancillary relief proceedings is engaged in preparing material for disclosure, seeking further disclosure from the other side or from third parties and, ultimately, testing the accuracy and completeness of the disclosure.

**3.2**   Although the parties to the case will have been married to each other, the extent to which they already know about each other's financial affairs is often limited. Limited knowledge of the other party's financial affairs commonly arises in cases of substantial means where the assets and dominant economic power lie with one party, often, but not exclusively, the husband. Even in cases with modest assets it is not unusual for one party to have ceded control of the family finances to the other. In this context, inequality of knowledge is at the heart of any temptation to conceal assets. Even if there is no actual concealment, the other party may suspect it has occurred. Furthermore, since the decision of the House of Lords in *White v White*[2] established an approach which renders something close to equal division of assets more likely, the temptation to conceal the true extent of wealth in a case, especially in a case with substantial assets, is perhaps even greater than it was.[3]

**3.3**   The ancillary relief lawyer is well aware of the duty on the parties to make full and frank disclosure. The concept is at the heart of the process of disclosure. It militates against any temptation to conceal assets and operates to ensure that the court has sufficient knowledge of the assets of the parties to enable a fair division to take place. At the same time, practitioners are aware of the need to comply with the terms of the Family Proceedings Rules 1991 as to the time when disclosure should be made and when further disclosure can be sought. They are also all too conscious of the need to retain proportionality between the costs of the proceedings and the issues and assets in the case. However, many issues arise in the context of disclosure that are far from straightforward. Often difficult decisions need to be made as to what should be disclosed and in what form. Equally difficult decisions have to be made as to

---

[1]   *Charman v Charman (No 4)* [2007] 1 FLR 1246.
[2]   [2000] 2 FLR 981.
[3]   Although there may still be some scope for use of the 'millionaire's defence' to avoid the need for detailed disclosure in some cases – see **4.14**.

the extent to which further disclosure should be sought from the other side and
when a case can validly be pursued on the basis of non-disclosure.

**3.4**    This section considers the topic of disclosure in detail, beginning in
Chapter 4 with a consideration of the duty of full and frank disclosure,
particularly in the context of the Form E. Attention is then turned to the
question of obtaining further disclosure from the parties themselves, including
an examination of the consequences of non-disclosure. Chapter 5 deals with
the often difficult area of seeking disclosure from non-parties.

# Chapter 4

# DISCLOSURE FROM THE PARTIES

## THE DUTY OF FULL AND FRANK DISCLOSURE AND THE FORM E

**4.1**　Under the current procedural framework formal disclosure begins with the Form E.[1] This has proved to be a useful innovation by providing a standardised framework for parties to use when collating and presenting their disclosure. Prior to the introduction of the current procedure the parties were free to present their financial information as they saw fit, doing so by way of an affidavit they or their lawyers prepared. Although the Form E sets out, in a series of numbered boxes, the types of information which ought to be included, it is inevitable that a 'one size fits all' standard form such as Form E is unlikely to cope conveniently with every situation which may arise. Inevitably the parties and their lawyers need to decide precisely what appears on the Form E, how the information is presented and what supporting documents are attached.

**4.2**　Importantly, the rules provide that the Form E must not only include the information and documents required by that form but also 'any documents necessary to explain or clarify any of the information contained in Form E'.[2] This latter requirement is often overlooked by parties. In an ideal case the Forms E will be all that is required by way of disclosure:

> 'The theory behind the new procedure is that it should be possible, if the Forms E are filled in truthfully, carefully and fully, and are accompanied by all the prescribed essential documents, for the case to be tried without further inquiry or disclosure. Of course, it is idealistic to think that this actually happens in practice and in the majority of cases further inquiry is authorised. But that does not mean that the ideal is not something to be striven for. For this reason the Form E has an almost numinous status, and where it is found that a party has deliberately filled in a Form E falsely or has misrepresented facts then he must expect judicial censure and penalties in costs.'[3]

No doubt every practitioner in this field can think of numerous cases in their own personal experience where enormous cost, delay and acrimony could have been avoided if such an approach had been conscientiously applied by the parties when the Forms E were prepared.

---

[1]　This is the case whether disclosure is taking place pursuant to para 3.5 of the Pre-Application Protocol or within proceedings (see FPR 1991, r 2.61B).

[2]　FPR 1991, r 2.61B(3)(b).

[3]　*W v W (Financial Provision: Form E)* [2004] 1 FLR 494 at 496–7.

**4.3**     Many litigants come to ancillary relief proceedings ready for gladiatorial combat. They approach the case as they would a commercial dispute. They may well wish to obtain advantage, and a favourable outcome for themselves, by providing limited disclosure or by exploiting the misunderstandings or ignorance their former spouse has in relation to the financial affairs. Such an approach is incompatible with the duty of full and frank disclosure and rarely achieves the desired objective. The result of such conduct is almost certainly hugely inflated costs being incurred in the proceedings, a loss of credibility, the risk of adverse inferences being drawn and, even if a final order is obtained, the risk of the order being set aside subsequently on the basis of the non-disclosure.[4]

**4.4**     It is easy to state that there is a 'duty of full and frank disclosure', but what does that amount to in practical terms? As usual in ancillary relief practice, the answer depends on the circumstances of each case, but some useful guidance is to be found in the case law.

**4.5**     The classic statement of the duty imposed by the Matrimonial Causes Act 1973 is usually cited as Lord Brandon's judgment in *Livesey (formerly Jenkins) v Jenkins*:[5]

> 'In contested cases relating to the exercise of the court's powers under ss 23 and 24, the requirement that it should have the prescribed information is met by rules of court with which both parties must comply ... One party may be compelled to give further information to the other on any material matter; orders may be made for lists or affidavits of documents and for the inspection and production of documents referred to in them for the hearing of oral evidence; for the cross-examination of deponents upon their affidavits; and for the filing of further affidavits. Only when the registrar has before him all the material which he considers to be necessary for the exercise of his discretion under s 25(1) – and there may have to be more than one hearing before him in order that this should be achieved – does he go on to make such orders, if any, as he thinks right under ss 23 and 24. If the contested claims come before a judge instead of a registrar, as often happens in more difficult cases, the procedure is the same. Any changes in the situation of either party occurring between the filing of the original affidavits and the final disposition of the claims by the court must be brought to the notice of the other party and the court by further affidavits or otherwise. In this way, so far as contested claims are concerned, the court should normally be provided directly with adequate information on all the matters to which it is bound to have regard under s 25(1).'

Later in the same judgment Lord Brandon said:

---

[4]     See, for example, *Robinson v Robinson (Disclosure)* (1983) 4 FLR 102. See also *I v I* [2009] EWCA Civ 412. It will be no defence to such an application to say that the other side could have discovered the information by asking the right questions. See **4.50** for further examples of the consequences of non-disclosure.

[5]     [1985] FLR 813 at 822–3. The general thrust of the rules in force at the time of the decision of the House of Lords is preserved in the current FPR 1991.

'I stated earlier that, unless a court is provided with correct, complete and up-to-date information on the matters to which, under s 25(1), it is required to have regard, it cannot lawfully or properly exercise its discretion in the manner ordained by that subsection. It follows necessarily from this that each party concerned in claims for financial provision and property adjustment (or other forms of ancillary relief not material in the present case) owes a duty to the court to make full and frank disclosure of all material facts to the other party and the court. This principle of full and frank disclosure in proceedings of this kind has long been recognised and enforced as a matter of practice. The legal basis of that principle, and the justification for it, are to be found in the statutory provisions to which I have referred.'

**4.6** Therefore, if the party has any material which is relevant to the factors the court must consider pursuant to s 25(1) of the Matrimonial Causes Act 1973 (and by implication this must also include the specific matters referred to in s 25(2), (3) and (4)), it must be disclosed, whether it is helpful or detrimental to his or her case. As s 25(1) requires the court to have regard to 'all the circumstances of the case', this does not assist the lawyer in narrowing the scope of the required disclosure. Indeed, the broad scope of the court's inquiry in an ancillary relief case means that parties need to err on the side of caution and disclose anything which may be relevant. The statement of issues, along with any witness statements or statements of case filed by the parties,[6] are particularly important in terms of highlighting the particularly important areas where detailed and clear disclosure is required. It is sometimes thought that, as the proceedings are in relation to financial matters, the duty is limited to the existence of assets or income. However, it extends to other matters which have a financial effect, such as an intention to remarry.[7] Often, new issues and facts become relevant as a case develops. The relevance may often only become apparent during the final hearing. The parties and their lawyers must remain alert to the continuing duty to make disclosure. It is wrong for the parties to breathe a sigh of relief when the last questionnaire is answered and to assume that the duty of disclosure is at an end. The duty does not end until judgment is given.

**4.7** The (perhaps natural) instinct of parties to reveal the bare minimum must be advised against and resisted. Similarly, it is not acceptable to say 'I would disclose it if I was asked to, but as I have not been asked I do not need to.' Sachs J put it this way in the case of *J v J*:

'For a husband in maintenance proceedings simply to wait and hope that certain questions may not be asked in cross-examination is wholly wrong.'[8]

Those who attempt to treat an ancillary relief application as a game of 'cat and mouse' by limiting their disclosure to that which the other side requests are not

---

[6]   See **2.10–2.11** for examples of when such statements may be required by the court.
[7]   *Prow v Brown* (1983) 4 FLR 352, where Ormrod LJ stated, 'this court has always insisted, back to early days, on full and frank disclosure of assets in ancillary proceedings and, of course, with assets goes intention to remarry.'
[8]   *J v J* [1955] P 215 at 228.

complying with the duty of full and frank disclosure. In the same case Sachs J pointed out that where one party has knowledge of the financial affairs and the other does not, the onus on that party to make full disclosure is a strong one and failings will be met both in costs and by adverse inferences being drawn.[9] This does appear to leave some scope to argue that where the other side has detailed knowledge of the financial affairs, the duty to disclose is somewhat easier to satisfy. Even in such a case, however, the duty continues and it is not enough to assume that the other side knows about assets and to wait to be asked about them.

**4.8**   In *Bokor-Ingram v Bokor-Ingram*[10] the Court of Appeal approved the dicta of Sachs J in *J v J* and underlined the importance of disclosure being 'full, frank and clear'.[11] In that case the court criticised a husband who at the time the proceedings were compromised had failed to disclose to his wife or to the court that he was engaged in incomplete negotiations to change his employment and move to a better paid job. The court held that 'the duty to disclose extends beyond what is certain on the date that the order is made to any fact relevant to the court's review of the foreseeable future.'[12]

**4.9**   Those with complicated affairs have an even greater duty to make them transparent. Complex investment vehicles and tax-efficient trusts are, by their very nature, difficult to penetrate. A bald disclosure of an interest in such a complex financial structure within the Form E without a proper explanation or attempt to place an accurate and transparent value on the asset will result in mistrust, loss of credibility and increased costs. The heightened duty to present the material in transparent form was explained as follows in *GW v RW*:[13]

> 'Moreover, when a person's financial affairs are complicated it is incumbent on him, as part of the duty of full, frank and clear disclosure to give a presentation that is immediately understandable by a solicitor of average financial sophistication. It is no good to present very complex material in such a way that only an accountant of enormous financial acumen can understand it. As it happens, in this case, H did make such a clear presentation, but only in response to W's accountants' preliminary report. It would have been altogether better had that presentation formed part of his Form E. From that point onwards I am satisfied that H co-operated fully and clearly with W both in the disclosures made between solicitors and in his direct meetings with W's accountants. It is a pity that he should have sullied that impression of clear and honest co-operation by suppressing the draft severance terms which I am clear he should have produced as part of his continuing duty of full and frank disclosure. It cannot be emphasised often enough in these cases that a party's obligations of disclosure are not confined to providing the information and documents prescribed by Form E and as ordered by the court in response to a questionnaire. There is a continuing duty

---

[9]   *J v J* [1955] P 215 at 227, and see **4.50**.
[10]   [2009] EWCA Civ 412.
[11]   [2009] EWCA Civ 412 at [12]–[13]. The third aspect of the duty, namely that the disclosure should be clear, is often overlooked. The need for clarity is considered at **4.9–4.10.**
[12]   [2009] EWCA Civ 412 at [18].
[13]   [2003] 2 FLR 108 at 115.

to provide, without being asked, new information and documents that may affect the exercise of the statutory discretion.'[14]

In that case the husband had disclosed various share options in his Form E but had attributed a nil value to those interests on the basis that they were not currently realisable. That approach led to the instruction of forensic accountants by the wife at a cost of over £90,000. After much confusion the options were valued at £640,000. The judge criticised the husband's approach as one which set the parties on an expensive and prolonged course of litigation:

'In my judgment, it was a mistake for H to have presented his assets in his Form E in the way that he did. He accepted that the representation that he was only worth £3.6m was unfair. The very point of Form E is to give an honest and conscientious estimation of the true net worth of the party at the time of swearing it. For these purposes sensible and fair figures have to be attributed to unrealisable or deferred assets. The maker of the Form E is fully entitled to qualify those figures in the narrative part of the section. But a proper figure has to be put in. It is unacceptable, in my view, that simply because an asset is not realisable on the day that the Form E is sworn, but is assuredly realisable, or likely to be realisable, at some future date, for a zero figure to be inserted.'[15]

**4.10** Similar observations were made by Coleridge J in relation to offshore tax-efficient investments in *J v V (Disclosure: Offshore Corporations)*.[16] The family's affairs were arranged through a highly sophisticated and complex network of offshore corporations, behind which the husband sought to hide the extent of his wealth. A lengthy hearing inevitably ensued. At its conclusion Coleridge J made the following comments:[17]

'Nothing is more calculated to set the bells ringing in a specialist lawyer's mind than to be faced by such wealth contained within such a structure. It is designed and intended to be impenetrable and when it supports a lavish standard of living it is invariably like a red rag to a bull.

In order to prevent the instigation of an exhaustively searching enquiry, respondents to such applications are required to be from the outset perhaps even fuller and franker in the exposure and explanation of their assets than in conventional onshore cases. Otherwise skullduggery is instantly presumed. Applicants justifiably believe that advantage is being taken to hide assets from view amongst complex corporate undergrowth. To begin the process of disclosure, as here, by, without more, denying legal and beneficial ownership of all-important assets in the case by virtue of such arrangements is, quite simply, foolish and unhelpful. And once applications of this kind get off on the wrong foot they never regain equilibrium.'

---

[14] It should be noted that although FPR 1991, rr 2.61B(6) and 2.61D(3) limit the parties' rights to seek disclosure from the other party to that which the Form E requires or which the court otherwise permits, the case law indicates that the duty of full and frank disclosure continues to the point of judgment and no litigant in ancillary relief has sought to use these rules as a defence to an allegation of non-disclosure.

[15] [2003] 2 FLR 108 at 114–5.

[16] [2004] 1 FLR 1042.

[17] [2004] 1 FLR 1042 at 1047.

The following warning was also sent out to those who seek to hide behind complex offshore structures of this nature:[18]

> 'Clients whose cases fall into this category do need to be reminded by their advisers that these sophisticated offshore structures are very familiar nowadays to the judiciary who have to try them. They neither impress, intimidate, nor fool anyone. The courts have lived with them for years. If clients "duck and weave" over months or years to avoid coming clean they cannot expect much sympathy when it comes to the question of paying the costs of the enquiry which inevitably follows. And that is so whatever the outcome eventually is and whatever offers have been made before final determination. Applicants cannot be properly and fully advised about the merits of offers by their lawyers unless the disclosure is full (even if in *Thyssen*[19] defence form) and frank; all the cards must be put on the table face up at the earliest stage if huge costs bills are to be avoided.'

**4.11** It would appear that the duty to ensure that the disclosure which is made is complete, accurate and not misleading extends beyond the parties to their representatives as well. Solicitors and counsel must be careful, in their zeal to promote their clients' interests to their best ability, not to present information in a misleading way. Indeed, this duty may extend to ensuring that the assertions made in the Form E are capable of proof by credible evidence. A solicitor cannot simply rely on the client's willingness to attest to the truthfulness of the contents of the Form E. In *W v W (Financial Provision: Form E)*[20] a husband had failed to list certain assets on his Form E. These included some funds held in a joint account with his new wife but which he had transferred to her sole name shortly before the Form E was sworn. Furthermore, the Form E listed two contingent liabilities amounting to £2.5 million. At trial the husband and his solicitor were criticised for the presentation of the Form E. The husband's solicitor had advised the client that the joint account with his new wife did not need to be listed on the Form E. That resulted in a misleading presentation of the husband's assets in the Form E. It was wrong to use the new spouse's inchoate claims against the husband's in the event of them divorcing to reduce his assets in the ongoing ancillary relief. As to the contingent liabilities, the judge found there to be no realistic prospect of them arising and said:[21]

> 'Where there exists in a case a contingent liability it should certainly be mentioned in the Form E, as part of the narrative. But a figure should only be inserted in the computational box that forms part of the calculation of overall net worth if the deponent and his legal advisers are satisfied by credible evidence that on the balance of probabilities the liability is more likely than not to eventuate. Solicitors advising the makers of Forms E have, as Officers of the Court, an important responsibility to ensure that true and realistic figures are inserted in a Form E. And deponents have a greater responsibility to ensure that their Forms E are

---

[18] [2004] 1 FLR 1042 at 1064.
[19] *Thyssen-Bornemisza v Thyssen-Bornemisza (No 2)* [1985] FLR 1069. As to which see **4.13–4.16**.
[20] [2004] 1 FLR 494.
[21] [2004] 1 FLR 494 at 504.

truthful and honest. The rubric at the beginning of the form, warning of the consequences of falsehood, is not mere window-dressing.'

**4.12** This duty on the lawyer to ensure that the Form E is submitted with figures which are accurate and which reflect the true position verified by 'credible evidence' indicates the care which the lawyer must exercise in preparing this vital part of the case. The Form E is not simply the first form of disclosure: it is intended to provide in comprehensive form the full and frank disclosure which the party is obliged to make. So it should carry such documents and explanatory riders as necessary to ensure it is not misleading.

## IS FULL AND FRANK DISCLOSURE ALWAYS REQUIRED?

**4.13** Prior to the decision in *White v White*[22] the courts' primary focus in most cases of substantial assets was the reasonable needs of the party seeking ancillary relief. It was common in high value cases for the paying spouse to seek to avoid making disclosure by invoking the 'millionaire's defence' on the basis of an assurance given to the court that the assets available were more than ample to satisfy any order the court might make.[23] Following the decisions in *White v White*, *Miller v Miller; McFarlane v McFarlane*[24] and *Charman v Charman (No 4)*,[25] the 'sharing principle'[26] has made it essential for the court to have a clear indication of the total wealth of the parties in most cases where the assets exceed the parties' needs.

**4.14** The decisions in *White v White* and *Miller v Miller; McFarlane v McFarlane* suggest that the scope of the 'millionaire's defence' is no longer as broad as it once was. As Singer J observed in a slightly different context, 'It is not easy to undertake any evaluation [of fairness] by reference to equality of division, for the totality of the whole is unknown.'[27] There may, however, still be cases where the 'millionaire's defence' may be appropriate and a method by which the costs of the case can be very substantially reduced. The potential scope of this approach was explained in *J v V (Disclosure: Offshore Corporations)*:[28]

'The so-called *Thyssen* defence. That was a very useful mechanism employed regularly in the 1980s and 1990s for avoiding huge financial enquiries in

---

[22] [2000] 2 FLR 981.

[23] The *Thyssen* defence, after *Thyssen-Bornemisza v Thyssen-Bornemisza (No 2)* [1985] FLR 1069.

[24] [2006] 1 FLR 1186.

[25] [2007] 1 FLR 1246.

[26] In *Miller v Miller; McFarlane v McFarlane* [2006] 1 FLR 1186 the House of Lords explained that the importance of 'equality' to the concept of 'fairness' in ancillary relief proceedings, as initially explained in *White v White*, is only one part of the three interdependent ingredients of fairness: meeting the needs of the parties, compensation and sharing.

[27] *Minwalla v Minwalla* [2005] 1 FLR 771 at [95].

[28] [2004] 1 FLR 1042 at 1064 per Coleridge J.

circumstances where wealth was very considerable and where a respondent was prepared to make an admission as to the overall value of the available wealth and the broad categories into which it fell. It is sometimes said that nowadays, with the greater emphasis placed on fractions and "contribution" since *White v White*, that this mechanism is no longer apt or useful. I do not agree. I agree with the editors of *Essential Family Practice 2002* (Butterworths) in this regard (see p 2166). Especially where cases involve marriages of short/medium length and the wealth has largely come from sources other than the efforts of the respondent during the course of the marriage, *Thyssen* defences could still be usefully deployed. An application at the First Appointment stage to the High Court judge allocated to hear such a case might save enormous time and money by adjudicating on this as a preliminary issue.'

**4.15** Clearly, such an approach will not be appropriate in the case of a long marriage where the bulk of the family wealth has been built up during the marriage.[29] Where, however, one party has married an already very wealthy and successful person and the marriage ends after only a few years without children, the claims for ancillary relief may be limited to an extent which allows the defence to be permitted without unfairness. The facts of *Miller v Miller*, however, indicate that even in such circumstances the court will wish to look at the whole picture before reaching its decision. Although the *Miller* case concerned very large assets (in excess of £17m), it seems that this was not a case where the assets were of the sort of magnitude which Coleridge J had in mind when he made the comments in *J v V* set out above. It seems unlikely that the *Thyssen* approach will be appropriate in anything other than those exceptional cases concerning the very largest assets and other special factors.[30] The authors venture to suggest that the approach will usually only be adopted where both parties are to some degree prepared to agree to it or the facts justifying the approach are particularly stark (e g an exceptionally short marriage with little or no detrimental change of position by the applicant spouse as a result of the marriage). The application to limit the scope of disclosure in a case ought to be made at an early stage, most obviously at the First Appointment. In order to determine this issue at this preliminary stage there will need to be a reasonably thorough examination of the general approach which the court should adopt at the final hearing and, in all but the clearest cases, it is difficult to see how this preliminary issue can be resolved without resolving the substance of the entire application. Clearly, in most cases, such a decision cannot be made at the First Appointment. Examples of situations where the court may place limits on the scope of disclosure to be given are where a pre-nuptial agreement is likely to be a decisive factor in the s 25 exercise,[31] where a notice to show cause is issued following the parties making a separation agreement compromising their

---

[29] It was not adopted in *Miller v Miller* [2006] UKHL 24, a short marriage where the assets exceeded £17 million, in *Charman v Charman* [2006] 1 WLR 1053, where the assets exceeded £130 million, or in *McCartney v Mills McCartney* [2008] 1 FLR 1508, with assets of about £400 million, although in that case the court did set limits upon the extent to which the inquiry into the husband's wealth should go (see [118]).

[30] Although see *Lauder v Lauder* [2007] 2 FLR 802, where on an application for variation of maintenance the court did not seek to value the husband's assets with precision but adopted a 'not less than' value for his assets.

[31] *K v K (Ancillary Relief: Prenuptial Agreement)* [2003] 1 FLR 120; *Crossley v Crossley* [2008]

ancillary relief claims,[32] or where the application is limited to a variation of maintenance, capital issues having been resolved at an earlier time.[33] The court's case management powers are very broad and should be exercised flexibly in the interests of justice. In *Crossley v Crossley* Thorpe LJ said:[34]

> 'I would particularly stress the overriding objectives that govern all these rules, carefully and fully drafted in r 2.51D. It is easy to attach this case on its facts to a number of the objectives there articulated. It is very important that the judge in dealing with the case should seek to save expense. It is very important that he should seek to deal with the case in ways proportionate to the financial position of the parties. It is very important, more so today than it was when these rules were drafted, that he should allot to each case an appropriate share of the court's resources, taking into account the need to allot resources to other cases. In his general duty of case management he is required to identify the issues at an early date and particularly to regulate the extent of the disclosure of documents and expert evidence so that they are proportionate to the issues in question.'

**4.16** In a suitable case the parties may be able to reach some broad agreement about the extent of the assets available. Where there is no real basis for suspicion about the other party's honesty but the financial affairs are very complex and extensive, the parties may well be wise 'to compromise over precision providing sensible admissions at a high figure were made, in order to avoid acrimonious, lengthy and very expensive proceedings'.[35] The consequent savings in costs, time and acrimony may well prove to be worth far more than anything which may have been lost by such approximation of the assets. Practitioners well know that this approach is regularly taken by the parties, even in cases where the assets are far more modest. Of course, where such agreements are reached, the case is usually settled and does not trouble the law reporters. It should not be forgotten, however, that in the exercise of its paternal and quasi-inquisitorial role the court may refuse to accept the figures the parties have agreed if it appears to be unfair or unrealistic to do so.[36]

## THE QUESTIONNAIRE

**4.17** Any perceived deficiencies in the disclosure provided within the Form E will initially be addressed by way of a questionnaire served on the other side before the first appointment.[37] It is notable that the rules require this questionnaire to be set out 'by reference to the concise statement of issues' which the parties must file at the same time. This gives a hint of the approach

---

1 FLR 1467. See also *Vaughan v Vaughan* [2008] 1 FLR 1108 and *Behzadi v Behzadi* [2008] EWCA Civ 1070, where judges were advised to draw up a balance sheet demonstrating the overall effect of their proposed orders.

[32]   *W v H* [2001] 1 All ER 300; *S v S (Ancillary Relief)* [2009] 1 FLR 254.

[33]   *Lauder v Lauder* [2007] 2 FLR 802.

[34]   [2008] 1 FLR 1467 at 1472.

[35]   *Minwalla v Minwalla* [2005] 1 FLR 771 at 1064.

[36]   See *Parra v Parra* [2003] 1 FLR 942 and **2.10** above.

[37]   FPR 1991, r 2.61B(7)(c).

the court is obliged to take to the questionnaire. It is not for the parties to decide what disclosure should be given in addition to the 'full and frank' disclosure they should already have provided in the Form E. Indeed, the rules prohibit any disclosure being sought *or given* between the filing of a party's Form E and the first appointment, unless they are documents which should have been filed with the Form E but were not available at the time the Form was filed.[38] The parties may, therefore, provide information which explains the contents of the Form E before the first appointment, but new avenues of enquiry are not to be opened up without the court's approval.

**4.18**   At the first appointment the court will determine which parts of the questionnaire should be answered and which should not. The overriding objective[39] will be applied and, in this context, proportionality takes centre stage. Despite the need to ensure that the costs and time to be spent in dealing with the questionnaire should be proportionate to the nature of the issues in the case, it may sometimes be necessary to remind the court that the overriding objective requires more than financial proportionality. The overriding objective is to ensure that the case is dealt with justly. Financial proportionality is an important part of that exercise, but it is not the overriding objective itself. Importantly, the court must also ensure that the parties are on an equal footing[40] and that the case is dealt with expeditiously and fairly.[41]

**4.19**   Each case is unique and there can be no specific guidance as to the extent to which enquiries raised by a questionnaire will be permitted or disallowed. The judicial discretion at this case management stage is very broad and it will be very rare that a decision relating to a questionnaire will give rise to a viable appeal. The following points should be kept in mind when preparing a questionnaire which should be resistant to heavy judicial 'pruning' at the first appointment.

**4.20**   The questions should go to the issues in the case. When preparing the documents for the first appointment, great care must be taken in ensuring that there is a correlation between the concise statement of issues which is filed and the questionnaire. Without such a correlation it may be difficult to persuade the court that the question is relevant to any issue in the case. Quite often the issues can be flagged early on in the narrative sections of the Form E.

**4.21**   It is trite but important to remember that irrelevant issues should not be raised. In relation to each question, consider whether the information, when provided, will actually assist the court in reaching its conclusions. Sometimes, as already discussed in Chapter 2, relevance is difficult to determine until a late stage of the proceedings. Nevertheless, it is worth bearing in mind that in very many ancillary relief proceedings the process of disclosure produces a massive amount of documentation which is never even looked at during the final

---

[38]   FPR 1991, r 2.61B(5) and (6).
[39]   FPR 1991, r 2.51B.
[40]   FPR 1991, r 2.51B(2)(a).
[41]   FPR 1991, r 2.51B(2)(d).

hearing. That of itself does not mean that it was not necessary to have obtained it in the first place, but sometimes material is sought which will never be useful. Sometimes the parties may find it difficult to recognise what disclosure may be relevant to the issues in their case, and it is important for their lawyers to provide them with firm and clear advice on the consequences of pursuing irrelevant or disproportionate enquiries.

**4.22** It is equally trite to say, although often ignored, that the questions should not address issues where the answer is already contained in the disclosure provided. Often a particular transaction on a bank statement is questioned even though it is clear from other bank statements that this was simply a transfer to another account in that party's name. Unless something turns on the reason for that transaction itself, there is no point in asking the question simply to identify the destination of the funds. Such questions indicate the absence of proper scrutiny of the papers and will lead to the party's lawyers losing credibility before the court, with the potential result that other, more reasonable questions may be disallowed.

**4.23** Identify the most important areas where disclosure is required. Petty and minor enquiries which will have no real bearing on the outcome of the case might be better omitted. It may be easier to convince the court that the enquiries which are being raised are truly necessary and proportionate where the questionnaire is not lengthened by a large number of largely insubstantial enquiries which will take time and expense to answer but which will not ultimately have any real bearing on the outcome of the case.

**4.24** Ensure that the questions are specific. General or unparticularised enquiries are often more difficult to justify. A good example is to identify particular transactions shown on bank statements which call for an explanation rather than a blanket request to explain 'all transactions in excess of £500'.

**4.25** Identify the most effective way of obtaining the required information. There is often more than one way of discovering the facts. A good example often arises in relation to businesses. Where the true turnover and nature of a business is under scrutiny, parties often ask for copies of the business bank account statements. Such statements often show thousands of transactions but provide little useful information without further disclosure or expensive analysis by an accountant. Quite often the information which is really required will be found in a more useful and concise format within the management accounts, cash books or some other document.

**4.26** Bear in mind that the questionnaire prepared for the first appointment may not be the last questionnaire required in the case. The disclosure provided by the first questionnaire may throw up fresh issues which require further investigation by way of supplementary questionnaires.[42] This is particularly so where the matter under consideration is something which was not dealt with in

---

[42] See **4.30–4.36**.

the Form E at all (ie an asset which the other party alleges has not been disclosed) and so there may be little on which to base the initial question. Sometimes the further enquiries can be anticipated and can be mentioned in the first questionnaire. More often, however, it will be necessary to see the answer to the first enquiry before it is clear whether further enquiry is required. If it is anticipated that such further enquires will be required, this should be made clear to the court at the first appointment, and the directions ought to make provision for the possibility that an application for permission to raise a further questionnaire may be made.

**4.27** Also bear in mind that there are some matters which are simply better left to cross-examination at the final hearing rather than by way of paper disclosure. This will be considered further below in the context of oral disclosure hearings[43] and the use of inferences in cases of non-disclosure.[44] It has been noted that under the old rules the use of extensive interrogatories 'will not be allowed to provide a party with the means of some form of roving cross-examination before trial; and that a party who has been guilty of seeking to interrogate on that improperly broad basis is not entitled to come before the court and seek to rescue his position by going through an exercise of sifting and excluding the irrelevant or oppressive material.'[45] Nevertheless, applying the modern approach to litigation summarised by the overriding objective, it may be possible to persuade a court to allow extensive questions where it is clear that significant costs will be saved by proceeding in that manner rather than by way of cross-examination at trial. Where the answers to the questions are unlikely to produce much in the way of further documentation, but merely answers which state the other party's case, there may be little sense in allowing such questions to be posed in written form.

**4.28** The party presented with a questionnaire will seek to reduce the scope of the questionnaire as much as possible at the First Appointment. The key bases of challenge are likely to be that the questions are irrelevant or disproportionate. Failure to take into account the factors set out in the previous paragraphs can be used to undermine the questions posed. Importantly, however, that party must ensure that he or she has not included questions in their own questionnaire which are similar to those which are objected to. Where there are such questions, there must be a good justification as to why it is appropriate for one party to have to answer them but not the other.

**4.29** It is notable that the scope of a questionnaire in ancillary relief proceedings is likely to be much broader than any request for specific disclosure in other civil proceedings. This is a result of the court's quasi-inquisitorial function in such proceedings and the duty of full and frank disclosure on the parties. Consequently, questions which would be dismissed as impermissible 'fishing'[46] in other civil cases will be permitted against the other party to

---

[43] See **4.37–4.41**.

[44] Considered in detail at **2.51–2.57**.

[45] *Hildebrand v Hildebrand* [1992] 1 FLR 244 at 253.

[46] Defined in the context of civil proceedings as a situation 'where what is sought is not evidence

ancillary relief proceedings. In *B v B (Matrimonial Proceedings: Discovery)*[47] Dunn J observed that 'The wife is entitled to go fishing in the Family Division within the limits of the law and practice'. 'Fishing' is necessary in order to test whether the other party has indeed complied with the duty to make full and frank disclosure.

## SUPPLEMENTAL QUESTIONNAIRES

**4.30** The rules provide for only one questionnaire to be prepared by each party in each case. In a perfect world the answers to that questionnaire will deal with all issues and no further questions will be required. There are many cases where that happens. There are, however, many others where the disclosure is still not felt to be complete after answers have been given to the first questionnaire. Those answers may give rise to wholly new issues and enquiries. A distinction must be drawn between the situation where the truthfulness of an answer is simply not accepted and those cases where the answer is considered to be incomplete. In the latter case it will often be possible to identify further information which ought to be produced, and this can be set out in a fresh request for information. In the former case it may be necessary to seek disclosure of evidence which confirms or refutes the answer which is put forward. It may, on the other hand, be more appropriate to leave the matter for cross-examination at trial. Normally, where a party asserts a fact, he or she bears the burden of proving it. If that party does not produce evidence which the court would expect to see corroborating or confirming the assertion, it will be relatively easy to infer that he or she has not done so because there is no such evidence. It is not necessary to ask a party to produce the evidence to prove a fact they assert in order to criticise them for failing to provide the evidence required to prove their case at the final hearing. Sometimes the request will be made in order to call the other party's bluff, but sometimes it will be tactically better not to spell out to the other side what evidence they ought to put forward to prove their case. Nevertheless, it should be made clear that the answer is not accepted, so as to ensure that the other party is aware that he or she is being put to proof as to the truth of the answer. Otherwise they may explain the absence of any corroborative evidence at the final hearing on the basis that they did not realise that their reply was being challenged or that any such evidence was required.

---

as such, but information which may lead to a line of enquiry which would disclose evidence. It is the search for material in the hope of being able to raise allegations of fact, as opposed to the elicitation of evidence to support allegations of fact, which have been raised bona fide with adequate particularisation' (per Kerr LJ in *Re State of Norway's Application* [1987] QB 433 at 482C).

[47]   [1978] Fam 181 at 191. But see also the comments of Wilson LJ referring to Dunn J's observations as to 'fishing' in *Charman v Charman* [2006] 1 WLR 1053 at [38] and [47]–[49]. 'Fishing' to the extent that a party probes to ensure that the duty of full and frank disclosure has been complied with by the other party is acceptable, but 'fishing' is not to be permitted when seeking disclosure from third parties.

**4.31**   No further disclosure can be sought without the court's permission.[48] In the event that further information is required, an application to the court may be necessary. Where the concern is simply that the other party has not provided a proper and complete answer to a question in the court-approved questionnaire, the deficiencies can be requested of the other side by way of letter without contravening the rules. That is not a request for further disclosure, but a request for the disclosure which the court has already ordered. If the material is not produced, an application to the court for a specific disclosure order, with or without a penal notice endorsed on it, will be appropriate. Where the replies to the questionnaire disclose new issues about which questions have not previously been raised, the party seeking further disclosure will need to prepare a supplemental questionnaire and apply to the court for an order that it be answered.[49] There is nothing to prevent the party first requesting voluntary disclosure by way of correspondence and, in the interests of saving costs, it would be wise to do so before an application to the court is made. It may be that the other party accepts that the further disclosure is required by reason of the duty of full and frank disclosure. If the disclosure is not forthcoming, however, an application to the court will be required.

**4.32**   Where an application for an order that the other party answer supplemental questions is made, the court will apply the same test as at the first appointment. An additional feature in the consideration at that stage will be whether the questions should have been raised in the first questionnaire. In most cases that factor should not, it is submitted, finally determine whether the further questions should be permitted, but it may sound in costs against the questioning party. There will be some cases where a second questionnaire presented as a result of a wholly inadequate first questionnaire will be rejected because to compel it to be answered would offend the overriding objective. An obvious example could be where the questionnaire comes so late that to require it to be answered would jeopardise the final hearing date. It must be noted, however, that normally such situations will simply result in the questionnaire being allowed but the party responsible for making it necessary being required to pay the costs thrown away. This is an inevitable result of the court's quasi-inquisitorial function and the need to ensure that it has all relevant material before it when it comes to making its decision.

**4.33**   It is sometimes thought that the questionnaire can be used to ensnare the other party in his or her own deceit. Most commonly this arises when the questioning party has some document in his or her possession without the other party's knowledge, and that is a document which discloses information about the other party's financial affairs. Such documents are often referred to as '*Hildebrand* documents'.[50] The temptation is to ask a question about one of the issues referred to in that documentation prior to disclosing that the

---

[48]   FPR 1991, r 2.61D(3).

[49]   FPR 1991, r 2.61D(3) and (4).

[50]   After *Hildebrand v Hildebrand* [1992] 1 FLR 244. See **2.58–2.67** for a discussion as to the admissibility of evidence which may have been obtained in breach of another's rights to privacy.

documents are already in the questioning party's possession. This is done in the hope that the other party will give an answer which can then be shown to be a lie by production of the secret document. This approach is improper for several reasons.[51] First, each party is under a duty to make full and frank disclosure and, under that duty, such documents as they hold which are relevant to the issues the court is being asked to consider must be disclosed to the other party and to the court.[52] Secondly, the questionnaire is a device by which one party genuinely seeks information which he or she does not yet have. It is wrong to use it in the hope of obtaining answers which could be shown to be lies in order to attack the other party's credibility. Furthermore, where the documents have been obtained by improper means and in breach of a person's rights under Art 8[53] and Art 1 of the First Protocol[54] of the European Convention on Human Rights, the court may be compelled to apply its discretion against that party and refuse to allow their use in the proceedings.[55]

## EFFECTIVE CASE MANAGEMENT – JUDICIAL CONTINUITY

**4.34**  In cases of alleged non-disclosure it is common for the discovery stage of the proceedings to be very protracted. Each set of replies to specific questions may give rise to further enquiries. The more complex the financial affairs under scrutiny, the lengthier this process is likely to be. Given the complexities of such cases, it is important that there is a high degree of judicial continuity to ensure that there is consistency of approach and so that the court has a good and detailed grasp of the issues in the case each time the matter returns before it. In the High Court, guidance has been given for the management of such cases, including the allocation of the case to a nominated High Court judge from the outset.[56] Even in less complex cases in the county court concerning smaller assets than the astronomical wealth contemplated by the High Court guidance, it may be helpful to explain to the court at the first appointment the nature of the disclosure issues likely to arise in the case and to endeavour, where possible, to have all applications in the case referred to a particular judge, if available, to ensure that there is the judicial continuity necessary to deal with the case effectively.

---

[51]  *Hildebrand v Hildebrand* [1992] 1 FLR 244.
[52]  See *Klamer v Klamer* [2008] 1 FLR 238 on the need to make prompt disclosure of *Hildebrand* documents and not to 'drip-feed' them into the proceedings. It follows from these principles that it would be equally inappropriate to ambush a witness at trial with material which had not been previously disclosed. Where there has been a manifest breach of the party's duty to make full and frank disclosure in this way, the court may refuse to allow the evidence to be admitted, even though it may be highly relevant.
[53]  The right to respect for a person's private and family life, his home and his correspondence.
[54]  Rights to the protection of property.
[55]  See Chapter 2 for a further discussion on this topic.
[56]  *K v K (Financial Relief: Management of Difficult Cases)* [2005] 2 FLR 1137.

# THE CONSEQUENCES OF GOING TOO FAR IN PURSUIT OF DISCLOSURE

**4.35** Above all, any party pursuing the other for disclosure must remember that preparing and answering lengthy questionnaires is a laborious and expensive task. Those costs will inevitably reduce the assets available for distribution. The court may also criticise a party for pursuing enquiries unreasonably and this may result in an order for the costs incurred being made against that party at the end of the case. It will often be possible to justify a wide-ranging enquiry on the basis that there is good evidence of lack of frankness or full disclosure by the other party. But even in a clear case of such non-disclosure there is an obligation on the questioning party to retain a sense of balance and proportionality. In *E v E (Financial Provision)*[57] Ewbank J said:

> 'There are many loose ends in the husband's evidence. It has been established that he has made misleading assertions; assets have been forgotten; there has been a lack of frankness on his part and there has been non-disclosure on his part. At the end of the day, however, the court has to decide what has been achieved by the rigorous investigation of these aspects. The husband, by the non-disclosure and lack of frankness, has asked for such an investigation. One can understand the view that a failure on the part of the wife's legal advisers to investigate everything that needs investigating may lead to an action for negligence. At the same time, a balance has to be struck and the lay client needs to be informed of the dangers of continuing a case in order to investigate matters which in the end may not be relevant. If the investigation is justified then the exercise will have been worthwhile but, if not, ... the question of costs has to be carefully considered.'[58]

**4.36** Lawyers acting for a party in ancillary relief proceedings have a duty to pursue their client's case with reasonable skill and competence. A failure to make reasonable investigations of the other party's means will clearly be negligent.[59] Nevertheless, there is a point in many cases where it is not unreasonable to decide that it is no longer justifiable to seek to turn over every stone in pursuit of the full disclosure which the other party is clearly intent on making every possible effort to avoid providing. The comments of Ewbank J in

---

[57] [1990] 2 FLR 233 at 237. Examples of costs penalties being applied to an unreasonable litigant are: *S v H* [2005] EWHC 247 (Fam) (wife only awarded 20% of her costs notwithstanding gross failures by the husband to provide disclosure); *A v A* [2008] 1 FLR 1428 (costs awarded against a wife who ran an unrealistic and unreasonable case); *S v B (Ancillary Relief: Costs)* [2005] 1 FLR 474 (the wife was penalised in costs for pursuing an enquiry into loan repayments the husband had made to his parents. Although her initial desire to investigate these had been reasonable, she had allowed the investigation to incur costs entirely out of proportion to the amounts at stake and, in any event, the judge finally found that the loan repayments were genuine); and *RH v RH* [2008] 2 FLR 2142 (husband failed to recover all his costs due to his 'obsessional' approach to the litigation).

[58] The introduction of FPR, r 2.71, which dictates that the parties should bear their own costs unless unreasonable conduct is shown on the part of the other party, is likely to result in scrutiny during final hearings of the reasonableness of a protracted pursuit of disclosure during the proceedings.

[59] For an example of a wholly inadequate investigation of a husband's affairs see *Dickinson v Jones Alexander & Co* [1993] 2 FLR 521.

*E v E (Financial Provision)*[60] need to be borne in mind. The point is often reached where further questions could be asked but in reality there can be little reasonable prospect of further disclosure being made as a result of them. In *P v P (Financial Relief: Non-Disclosure)*[61] Thorpe J made an observation which many practitioners in this field will find rings true:

> 'The husband's solicitors had appropriately used their right to seek discovery generally and specifically by two questionnaires and by further questions addressed in correspondence. In one or two respects they did not press the right to specified discovery as far as it should have been pressed with hindsight view, but at the time their acquiescence in the wife's failure or refusal to answer specific questions was not unreasonable and I think that this case illustrates how the process of discovery is ineffective on its own to achieve complete disclosure. Accordingly, particular importance attaches to the oral evidence.'

## ORAL DISCLOSURE HEARINGS

**4.37** There comes a point in most proceedings when further questionnaires or orders for disclosure produce no new information. At that point the other party's vehement denials of non-disclosure of assets will stand or fall depending on that party's credibility. Experienced practitioners are able to judge when there is enough material to impugn the other party's credibility to the point that a finding of non-disclosure will be made. At that point it will probably be disproportionate to continue the quest for further disclosure which is highly unlikely to be forthcoming. Often that point is more clearly identified with the benefit of hindsight after the conclusion of the final hearing.[62] Nevertheless, once that point is reached, it is likely to be most cost-effective simply to request the court to list the matter for final hearing. In some cases the extent of the alleged non-disclosure may be so substantial that the court may even dispense with FDR appointment on the basis that it is wholly unrealistic to expect any agreement to be reached at such an appointment.

**4.38** In some cases, simply to proceed to the final hearing may be unrealistic. The parties and the court may feel that, whatever the outcome of the dispute about disclosure, further work will need to be done once the extent of the assets is known before final orders can be made. Without knowing the outcome of the disclosure dispute until the parties have given evidence and been cross-examined, the parties would find it difficult to be clear about the likely final outcome of the case and may well have to prepare the case on the basis of a number of hypothetical scenarios dependent upon the extent of the assets found to exist. In such a case, the court may decide that there should be a

---

[60] [1990] 2 FLR 233 at 237, set out above.
[61] [1994] 2 FLR 381 at 383.
[62] See, for example, *P v P (Financial Relief: Non-Disclosure)* and the quote from Thorpe J set out at **4.36**.

preliminary oral discovery hearing. This approach was adopted by Coleridge J in *OS v DS (Oral Disclosure: Preliminary Hearing)*.[63]

**4.39** In that case, which concerned substantial assets (which were not quantified in the brief reported judgment), the husband's wealth was contained within a complex group of corporate structures based in offshore tax havens. The wife felt there were very many questions left unanswered by the husband's disclosure. Coleridge J felt that, if the husband was able to give credible explanations for many of the transactions the wife was concerned about, the case could proceed without the need for joinder of the multifarious third party companies in which he had interests. Enormous costs and time would be saved. At an early directions stage, therefore, the judge suggested there should be a 3-day 'preliminary/oral discovery' hearing and gave directions as follows:

> 'There be a hearing, fixed for 4 October 2004 for 3 days, before Coleridge J, for the purpose of taking oral evidence from the respondent and resolving the issue of joinder of: (i) Mr A; (ii) B Ltd; (iii) C Ltd; and (iv) D Ltd (BVI), for the purposes of which hearing the following directions shall apply:
>
> (a)    Counsel for the petitioner and respondent do agree a statement of issues on or before 16 July 2004.
> (b)    The parties' solicitors do agree any further bundles on or before 30 July 2004.
> (c)    The parties' solicitors do agree a re-designation and full pagination of all bundles to be used at the hearing on or before 30 July 2004 (the existing bundles to be re-designated A–E etc).
> (d)    Counsel for the parties do exchange skeleton arguments on or before 1 October 2004, such skeletons to take the place of an oral opening of the case at the hearing.
> (e)    4 October 2004 shall be a reading day.
> (f)    On 5 and 6 October 2004 the following timetable shall apply:
> > (i)    there shall be no oral opening;
> > (ii)    the respondent's counsel shall have one hour to examine the respondent-in-chief;
> > (iii)    the petitioner's counsel shall have until 1 pm on 6 October 2004 to cross-examine the respondent;
> > (iv)    the respondent's counsel shall have one further hour to re-examine the respondent;
> > (v)    the remainder of the hearing shall be used for further legal argument, directions and provisional findings.'

**4.40** The hearing proceeded according to the directions. The wife's counsel cross-examined the husband on the crucial issues and documents. By lunchtime on the first day the parties were able to begin negotiations and the case was settled by the end of the day. A likely 10-day final hearing had thereby been saved. Despite the apparent attractiveness of this procedure, there are likely to be relatively few cases where it is really appropriate. The power to have a 'split trial' is used quite often in civil proceedings where there is often a very clear

---

[63]   [2005] 1 FLR 675.

division between the liability part of the claim and the assessment of damages. Even so, experience from civil proceedings and from child care proceedings indicates that over-enthusiasm to use the 'split trial' approach often has the opposite effect in terms of costs and time saving to that which was intended. In ancillary relief proceedings there is a need to have a complete overview of all the circumstances of a case so that the court can apply its discretion in a fair manner.[64] Separation of the issues into different hearings may actually involve greater expense than would be incurred at a single hearing where all issues could be heard at once. Before a preliminary oral disclosure hearing is directed to occur, the issues to be considered must be very clearly identified and it must be clear that some real benefit in terms of costs and time saved will be achieved. It will also be necessary to ensure that the hearing retains a proper focus and that all parties remember that it is a preliminary hearing which occurs before the normal process of full paper discovery has been exhausted and, as in *OS v DS*, before all relevant interested parties are before the court. Practitioners need to be wary and ensure that the preliminary hearing does not turn into a rehearsal for the final hearing.

**4.41** It is helpful to note some of Coleridge J's general observations in *OS v DS*:[65]

> 'I would not seek to suggest that this is the ideal procedure in all, or even the majority of, complex ancillary relief cases. Further, any judge considering this course, or conducting such a hearing, must be astute to ensure that both parties' right to a fair hearing is not jeopardised. But, where the financial substratum of the resources is bound to require considerable elucidation, I consider that this procedure has many advantages, including those set out in the previous paragraph.
>
> I have no doubt that the court has the power within the rules to order a hearing of this type. Whether it is designated as a trial of a preliminary issue or oral discovery or the first part of a split final hearing (cf public law children cases), the court has the necessary tools to case-manage in this way. After all, the court is primarily conducting an inquiry, not an adversarial trial. The procedure is, in my view, concordant with the overriding objective applicable to ancillary relief proceedings set out in the Family Proceedings Rules 1991, r 2.51B.
>
> In the recent and not dissimilar case of *J v V (Disclosure: Offshore Corporations)*[66] (involving serious non-disclosure) I commented, not for the first time, on the obvious desirability of putting "the cards on the table face up at the earliest stage if huge costs bills are to be avoided" in these cases. The court should always be vigilant to discover new and better ways of encouraging and assisting parties to that end so that they can resolve their litigation in as cost-efficient a manner as possible. I commend this as a procedure worthy of employment in the right case.'

---

[64]    In *Charman v Charman* [2006] 1 WLR 1053 Wilson LJ observed (at [24]) that it is generally undesirable to hear evidence from a witness in advance of a substantive hearing, since the judge and the parties 'are likely to lack the requisite overview necessary for their focused questioning and his focused listening'.

[65]    [2005] 1 FLR 675 at 678.

[66]    [2003] EWHC 3110 (Fam), [2004] 1 FLR 1042.

Perhaps the most important feature of these comments is the emphasis upon the flexibility the courts have to regulate their own procedure and to further the overriding objective in the most effective way.[67] Practitioners should, in every case, think about what the real issues in the case are and try to find the most appropriate and efficient way of resolving those issues. Sometimes those issues can be resolved more effectively outside court (by the use of mediators or other means of alternative dispute resolution) rather than in the courtroom. Practice in this field often requires a high degree of imaginative and creative thinking. All too often practitioners forget that such creativity does not need to be confined to the formulation of a compromised settlement, but that it is required even in the procedural stages of the case.

## OTHER MEANS OF OBTAINING DISCLOSURE

**4.42** The above-mentioned procedures are the most commonly used means of obtaining disclosure. There are other powers available to the court which might be used in an appropriate case:

- An *Anton Piller* or search order (considered in detail below).

- A disclosure requirement within a *Mareva* injunction.[68]

- An order for pre-action disclosure or production of property by a likely party to the proceedings. The general procedural provisions of the Supreme Court Act 1981 and the County Courts Act 1984 apply to ancillary relief proceedings to the extent that the FPR 1991 do not exclude them. So the power to make an order for 'the inspection, photographing, preservation, custody and detention of property which may become the subject-matter of subsequent proceedings in the ... court, or as to which any question may arise in such proceedings' pursuant to SCA 1981, s 33(1) and CCA 1984, s 52(1) is available for use in a suitable case. There are similar powers to order pre-action disclosure (SCA 1981, s 33(2) and CCA 1984, s 53(2)) (see **6.90–6.92**).[69]

- An order for disclosure or production of documents or property by a third party (see Chapter 5).

---

[67] This need for flexible and effective case management was emphasised by the Court of Appeal in *Crossley v Crossley* [2008] 1 FLR 1467.

[68] Such orders are considered in more detail in Chapter 6.

[69] In *L v L* [2007] 2 FLR 171 these civil disclosure orders were suggested as being a more appropriate remedy than the wife's resort to covertly copying her husband's computer hard drive. These orders are also less Draconian, and therefore easier to obtain, than an *Anton Piller* or search order.

# *ANTON PILLER* ORDERS

**4.43** The *Anton Piller* order[70] (known in civil proceedings as a 'search order' since the introduction of the CPR)[71] is the most Draconian form of disclosure order available to the courts. Rather than simply requiring a party to provide disclosure, the order actually requires the respondent to permit the applicant to enter the respondent's premises in order to search for the required material and to seize it. The origins of the order lie in the High Court's inherent jurisdiction, but it now has statutory recognition in s 7 of the Civil Procedure Act 1997.[72] This section usefully summarises the extent of such an order:

'(1) The court may make an order under this section for the purpose of securing, in the case of any existing or proposed proceedings in the court—

(a)   the preservation of evidence which is or may be relevant, or

(b)   the preservation of property which is or may be the subject-matter of the proceedings or as to which any question arises or may arise in the proceedings.

(2) A person who is, or appears to the court likely to be, a party to proceedings in the court may make an application for such an order.

(3) Such an order may direct any person to permit any person described in the order, or secure that any person so described is permitted—

(a)   to enter premises in England and Wales, and

(b)   while on the premises, to take in accordance with the terms of the order any of the following steps.

(4) Those steps are—

(a)   to carry out a search for or inspection of anything described in the order, and

(b)   to make or obtain a copy, photograph, sample or other record of anything so described.

(5) The order may also direct the person concerned—

(a)   to provide any person described in the order, or secure that any person so described is provided, with any information or article described in the order, and

---

[70]   Named after the case of *Anton Piller KG v Manufacturing Processes Ltd* [1976] Ch 55, when the Court of Appeal approved this form of order in the modern era. Its origin can be traced back at least to the early nineteenth century.

[71]   CPR Part 25.1(1)(h).

[72]   No doubt to mark the Draconian nature of the order and to ensure that the order is compliant with the European Convention on Human Rights by providing proper lawful authority for the making of such orders.

(b)    to allow any person described in the order, or secure that any person so described is allowed, to retain for safe keeping anything described in the order.

(6) An order under this section is to have effect subject to such conditions as are specified in the order.

(7) This section does not affect any right of a person to refuse to do anything on the ground that to do so might tend to expose him or his spouse to proceedings for an offence or for the recovery of a penalty.

(8) In this section—
    "court" means the High Court, and
    "premises" includes any vehicle;

and an order under this section may describe anything generally, whether by reference to a class or otherwise.'

**4.44**   Several important features of the *Anton Piller* order need to be borne in mind:

• It is an order at the extreme of the court's jurisdictional power and will be used sparingly and only in exceptional circumstances.

• It is not a form of search warrant. It does not permit the applicant to forcibly enter the respondent's premises. It requires the respondent to permit the applicant to enter and search the premises. If the respondent refuses to allow the applicant to do so, he is likely to be found to be in contempt of court, but his refusal will not permit the applicant to enter forcibly.[73] If the applicant did enter forcibly, the order would, it must be assumed, provide him with no defence to an action for trespass or to a prosecution for burglary.

• If the respondent refuses to comply with the order, not only may he be guilty of a contempt of court, but the court is likely to draw adverse inferences as to the reasons for non-compliance. A respondent acting in good faith and not contumaciously, on the other hand, may avoid punishment by the court, even if in breach of the order.[74]

• Only the High Court may make this type of order.[75]

• In the context of ancillary relief proceedings the *Anton Piller* order 'remains a rare weapon for use only in extreme or exceptional cases'.[76]

---

[73]  See *Anton Piller KG v Manufacturing Processes Ltd* [1976] Ch 55 at 60.
[74]  *Bhimji v Chatwani* [1991] 1 WLR 989.
[75]  Civil Procedure Act 1997, s 7(8). See **6.49** as to the use of orders of the High Court in proceedings pending in the county court.
[76]  *Burgess v Burgess* [1996] 2 FLR 34 at 41.

- It is very important that the order is made in the correct form and that all the necessary safeguards as to performance of the order are put in place.[77] If the order is in the incorrect form, it is likely to be set aside subsequently, with consequences in costs. The order must be executed by a 'Supervising Solicitor' with experience of such orders. It is not appropriate for the party applying for the order to participate in the search.

- The implementation of such an order is likely to be costly and, in the event that the order turns out to have been unjustified or unnecessary, there is also the risk of incurring a substantial liability to the other side in terms of their costs and potential losses as a result of the order.[78] This is not a remedy for the run-of-the-mill case.

- The order is made ex parte and this places a heavy onus on the applicant to be candid and frank in the presentation of the case. Failure to do so may have heavy consequences (see the procedural requirements for ex parte applications at **6.70–6.73**).

- The order can in appropriate circumstances require the respondent to permit a search of premises outside the jurisdiction.[79] But where the respondent is outside the jurisdiction, the order will only be made if it is clear that the court will have jurisdiction to entertain the main proceedings.[80]

## What are the criteria for making an *Anton Piller* order?

**4.45** The clearest presentation of the required elements for obtaining the order was set out by Ormrod LJ in his judgment in *Anton Piller* itself:[81]

> 'There are three essential pre-conditions for the making of such an order, in my judgment. First, there must be an extremely strong prima facie case. Secondly, the damage, potential or actual, must be very serious for the applicant. Thirdly, there must be clear evidence that the defendants have in their possession incriminating documents or things, and that there is a real possibility that they may destroy such material before any application inter partes can be made.'

If the preconditions for the making of the order are met, the court acting in matrimonial proceedings should, it seems, balance the potential harm to the applicant of the order not being made against the potential harm to the

---

[77] See the sample order annexed to the Practice Direction to CPR Part 25 and paras 7.1–7.11 of the Practice Direction.

[78] *Burgess v Burgess* [1996] 2 FLR 34. See also *Universal Thermosensors Ltd v Hibben* [1992] 1 WLR 840, although an undertaking in damages will not normally be required in ancillary relief proceedings unless a third party is affected by the order (see **6.82**). Nevertheless, the court may reflect any loss caused to the respondent by reason of an unjustified interlocutory injunction within the final order it makes.

[79] *Cook Industries v Galiher* [1979] Ch 439.

[80] *Altertext Inc v Advanced Data Ltd* [1985] 1 WLR 457.

[81] *Anton Piller KG v Manufacturing Processes Ltd* [1976] Ch 55 at 62.

respondent caused by the making of the order,[82] bearing in mind that the order is Draconian and to be used exceptionally.

**4.46** The *Anton Piller* case concerned an action for the recovery of confidential information which the claimant alleged the defendant was unlawfully in possession of. The interlocutory order was sought in order to recover the information from the defendant's premises. In other words, the subject matter of the interlocutory search order was essentially the subject matter of the whole proceedings. It was somewhat later that the courts were asked to make such orders simply to obtain documents to be used as evidence in the proceedings.[83] This is most likely to be the purpose of such an order in ancillary relief cases.[84] In such cases, the court will pay particular regard to the fact that a respondent's deliberate destruction or concealment of evidence is 'the grossest possible contempt of the court and ... that should he do so the whole processes of justice will be frustrated because the plaintiff will be left without any evidence to enable him to put forward his claim'.[85]

**4.47** This latter factor has clear resonance in the case of a party to ancillary relief proceedings who is hampered in the attempt to obtain proper financial relief as a result of a complete unwillingness on the respondent's part to provide any meaningful financial disclosure. Unlike in general civil litigation, where there is a real risk that the order may result in the applicant obtaining access to documents he would not normally be permitted to see, in ancillary relief proceedings the documents obtained by execution of the order are likely to be documents the respondent should have produced to the applicant under the duty of full and frank disclosure in any event. So, in *Emanuel v Emanuel*[86] a broad-ranging *Anton Piller* order was granted to a wife after the husband had shown himself to be in flagrant breach of the court's orders. In *Kepa v Kepa*[87] a wife was able to provide convincing evidence that her husband had lied about his means and that he was actually carrying on a successful business trading jewellery. The court made an *Anton Piller* order requiring the husband to permit the wife's solicitors and a named jeweller to enter the former matrimonial home to search for documents and to value the jewellery therein. The court noted that the harm to the wife if the order were not made far outweighed the inconvenience to the husband resulting from the order being made.

**4.48** In a more routine case with less extreme conduct by a party, an *Anton Piller* order is less likely and there is a real risk that if such an order is obtained ex parte the court may on later consideration find it to have been unjustified

---

[82] *Kepa v Kepa* (1983) 4 FLR 515.

[83] *Yousif v Salama* [1980] 1 WLR 1540.

[84] Although in exceptional circumstances it may be used either to seize or value an important asset (see *Kepa v Kepa* (1983) 4 FLR 515). The use of other less Draconian forms of order to achieve the same end may be more appropriate in most cases. See, for example, the orders discussed at **6.90–6.92**.

[85] *Yousif v Salama* [1980] 1 WLR 1540 at 1543 per Donaldson LJ.

[86] (1982) 3 FLR 319.

[87] (1983) 4 FLR 515.

and oppressive and penalise the applicant by an order for indemnity costs.[88] Even if the applicant is able to show that the other party is 'a devious and dishonest husband, who shows himself to have no respect for his family, nor for the orders of the court', if there is no convincing evidence that he will actually destroy or dispose of incriminating evidence, the order will not be granted.[89] Indeed, the very fact that the court is able to make adverse inferences upon proof of non-disclosure by a party may make the granting of an *Anton Piller* order less necessary than in other forms of proceedings. Ward LJ has indicated that 'an *Anton Piller* order should only be made where there is a paramount need to prevent a denial of justice which cannot be met otherwise than by launching this expensive pre-emptive strike'.[90] That comment predated the judgment of the House of Lords in *White v White*,[91] which appears to have made it more important for the court to have a more precise idea of a party's assets in order to do justice between them, although use of *Anton Piller* orders is likely to remain exceptional and a remedy of last resort.

## What is the procedure for applying for an *Anton Piller* order?

**4.49** The court is likely to adopt the CPR procedure set down for civil proceedings, in the absence of detailed provisions as to the exercise of the *Anton Piller* jurisdiction in ancillary relief proceedings. The general requirements for applying for injunctions are set out at **6.53–6.54** and **6.64–6.74**. Specific provisions relating to *Anton Piller* orders are set out at paras 7.1–7.11 of the Practice Direction supplementing CPR Part 25.

## THE CONSEQUENCES OF NON-DISCLOSURE

**4.50** It should be clear from the foregoing sections of this chapter that attempts at non-disclosure of financial resources are often sniffed out by experienced ancillary relief practitioners. The results of non-disclosure are clear:

- Increased costs. Almost as soon as a party to ancillary relief proceedings produces disclosure which is either incomplete or in an impenetrable form, the other side's suspicions will be aroused and a complex, tenacious and expensive process of forcing fuller disclosure will commence. This has been likened to 'Newton's Third Law of Motion, namely that every action produces an equal and opposite reaction.'[92] The party responsible for causing this process to commence by virtue of their less than frank disclosure is likely to bear the penalty in costs, even if at the end of the process the full extent of the assets is discovered. The costs penalty is

---

[88] *Burgess v Burgess* [1996] 2 FLR 34.
[89] *Araghchinchi v Araghchinchi* [1997] 2 FLR 142 at 145–6.
[90] *Araghchinchi v Araghchinchi* [1997] 2 FLR 142 at 146.
[91] [2001] 1 AC 596, [2000] 2 FLR 981.
[92] *W v W (Financial Provision: Form E)* [2004] 1 FLR 494 per Nicholas Mostyn QC sitting as a deputy High Court judge.

likely to be applied regardless of any offers which have been made in the
proceedings, because such offers cannot be properly considered by the
parties or approved by the court without proper financial disclosure.[93]
However, evidence of non-disclosure by one party does not provide the
other party with a blank cheque to pursue the proceedings without regard
to the resulting costs.[94] A disproportionate pursuit of disclosure by one
party may result in an adverse costs order against that party,
notwithstanding the initial non-disclosure by the other.[95]

- The court is more likely to make orders for broad-ranging disclosure from
  non-parties.[96]

- Adverse inferences are likely to be made about the true extent of the
  non-disclosing party's assets. That party's credibility is likely to have been
  destroyed, or at least heavily damaged, and the court's discretion is more
  likely to be used in the other party's favour. Inferences are considered in
  detail at **2.51–2.57**.[97]

- Although 'litigation conduct' of this nature is usually penalised in costs
  rather than by a reduction in that party's share of the available assets,[98]
  sometimes the litigation conduct is combined with other conduct to the
  extent that it does reduce the dishonest party's share in the assets.[99] The
  consequences of non-disclosure may not end with the making of a final
  order. A party with a track record of non-disclosure and dishonesty may
  be treated less favourably when the court comes to consider any
  consequential enforcement proceedings under the 'liberty to apply'.[100]

- The 'guilty party' and, if implicated in the non-disclosure, his lawyers or
  advisors are likely to be publicly named.[101] The consequences of such
  public condemnation could be very severe for individuals in positions of
  authority or trust.

---

[93] *J v V (Disclosure: Offshore Corporations)* [2004] 1 FLR 1042 at 1064. The same is likely to
hold true under the new costs scheme.

[94] See **4.35** above.

[95] See footnote 57 above.

[96] *D v D (Production Appointment)* [1995] 2 FLR 497.

[97] See also the greater willingness to make such inference at interim hearings, discussed at
**2.34–2.37**.

[98] See *P v P (Financial Disclosure: Non-Disclosure)* [1994] 2 FLR 381, although the penalty in
costs is not invariable and the court will weigh the dishonest party's conduct in the exercise of
the broad discretion as to costs. In *P v P* the court decided that the fairest order was no order
as to costs.

[99] *M v M (Financial Provision: Party Incurring Excessive Costs)* [1999] 2 FLR 498; *M v M (Third
Party Subpoena: Financial Conduct)* [2006] 2 FLR 1253; and *Behzadi v Behzadi* [2008] EWCA
Civ 1070. However, a recalcitrant litigant could not be subjected to an unfair order as a means
of forcing him or her to engage with the court process: *Hall v Hall* [2008] 2 FLR 575.

[100] For example, *Morgan v Morgan* [2007] EWCA Civ 1852.

[101] *W v W (Financial Provision: Form E)* [2004] 1 FLR 494.

- *Hadkinson* orders may be made. Where a party fails to comply with orders of the court, the strict rule used to be that the party who was in contempt was not entitled to be heard on any application he or she made to the court until the contempt of court was purged.[102] It now seems that this rule will not be applied so strictly. The court also has power to refuse to hear that party at the final hearing of the other party's application or otherwise limit the participation of the party in contempt in the proceedings. These are Draconian powers which must be applied with respect to the importance of ensuring that all parties have procedural justice. It is likely that use of such powers will be appropriate in only the grossest cases of contemptuous disregard for the court's orders. Even then, the court will need to be sensitive in ensuring that any restriction on the affected party's right to a fair trial enshrined in Art 6 of the European Convention on Human Rights is fully justified and proportionate. In *Al-Khatib v Masry*,[103] a case where the husband's litigation misconduct was probably as bad as could be imagined, the husband's lawyers were allowed to appear at the final hearing, but they were barred from questioning the wife. Notably, that ruling was never challenged by the husband and, presumably, the court did not have the benefit of full argument as to the legality of the order it made. There was full argument in *Mubarak v Mubarak*,[104] where the husband applied for variation of an order, and the court held that it was not inconsistent with the Human Rights Act 1998 to impose conditions on a contemnor before hearing him on his application. In *Laing v Laing*[105] conditions were also imposed on a husband who was in breach of a periodical payments order before he was permitted to pursue his application to vary the order. In both those cases, the court imposed conditions on the husband's right to bring the application rather than restrictions on his ability to respond to and defend an application made by the wife, as in *Al-Khatib v Masry*. The wife in *Mubarak v Mubarak* made subsequent applications in relation to the enforcement of the ancillary relief order. In the course of those applications she sought orders to prevent the husband from participating in the proceedings or, in the alternative, to make his participation conditional upon him satisfying strict terms set by the court. The application came before Bodey J,[106] who considered that the court had a broad discretion whether or not to hear a party in contempt, or to impose terms upon such a party. Such orders would not violate Art 6 of the European Convention for the Protection of Human Rights and Fundamental Freedoms 1950 so long as the restrictions were proportionate and so long as they were used to achieve procedural justice rather than to punish or penalise the husband, which would be an improper use of these powers. Bodey J imposed terms on the husband which he found were proportionate to the legitimate aims of creating a

---

[102]  *Hadkinson v Hadkinson* [1952] P 285.
[103]  [2002] 1 FLR 1053.
[104]  [2004] 2 FLR 932.
[105]  [2007] 2 FLR 199.
[106]  [2007] 1 FLR 722.

fair hearing and facilitating the enforcement of the court's orders. The husband would be able to comply with the terms and then fully participate in the hearing. The use of these restrictive powers against respondents rather than applicants in *Al-Khatib v Masry* and the most recent round of the *Mubarak v Mubarak* litigation is novel and cries out for a definitive ruling at appellate level.

- Even if the non-disclosure is successful to the extent that a favourable order is obtained, that order is liable to be set aside in the event that the non-disclosure is discovered at a later date.[107] The resulting application to set aside the order and the rehearing which ensues is likely to generate large additional costs which the guilty party is likely to be made to bear. There will also be the risk that the fresh order will be significantly more beneficial to the 'innocent' party than the order which would have been made originally if there had been no non-disclosure, particularly if the guilty party's means have improved in the intervening period. Nevertheless, not every breach of the duty to give full and frank disclosure amounts to 'material non-disclosure' justifying the setting aside of the order. It must be shown that, had the full disclosure been provided, there would have been a significantly different result.[108] In *Livesey (formerly Jenkins) v Jenkins*[109] Lord Brandon of Oakbrook said:

  > 'It is not every failure of frank and full disclosure which would justify a court in setting aside an order of the kind concerned in this appeal. On the contrary, it will only be in cases when the absence of full and frank disclosure has led to the court making, either in contested proceedings or by consent, an order which is substantially different from the order which it would have made if such disclosure had taken place that a case for setting aside can possibly be made good. Parties who apply to set aside orders on the ground of failure to disclose some relatively minor matter or matters, the disclosure of which would not have made any substantial difference to the order which the court would have made or approved, are likely to find their applications being summarily dismissed, with costs against them, or, if they are legally aided, against the legal aid fund.'

- It now also appears to be the case that failure to provide full disclosure in ancillary relief proceedings may amount to the commission of a criminal offence. Section 3 of the Fraud Act 2006 creates an offence of fraud which includes the dishonest failure to disclose to another person information which he is under a legal duty to disclose with the intention to make a gain for himself or cause loss to another. Arguably, a willful and dishonest

---

[107] See e g *Prow v Brown* (1983) 4 FLR 352. See *Harrison v Harrison* [2008] 2 FLR 35 for an example where alleged non-disclosure was said to amount to a fraud and an attempt was made to set aside the order in the ancillary relief proceedings by way of a fresh action in the Queen's Bench Division.

[108] See *Judge v Judge* [2008] EWCA Civ 1458; cf *I v I* [2009] EWCA Civ 412.

[109] [1985] AC 424, [1985] FLR 813.

breach of the duty to make full and frank disclosure in ancillary relief proceedings would contravene this provision. The offence is punishable by up to 10 years' imprisonment.

## THE IMPLIED UNDERTAKING IN RELATION TO DISCLOSURE

**4.51** It is important to remember, and to remind the parties, that disclosure provided for purposes of proceedings is given subject to an implied undertaking not to disclose the documents to any third party (other than legal advisers acting in the proceedings) without the court's permission. So disclosure of a Form E to a child support advice company without such permission is a contempt of court.[110] The position in respect of information disclosed voluntarily prior to proceedings being commenced is less clear. If there are no court proceedings in progress at that stage, it is difficult to argue that any duty to the court has yet arisen. Nevertheless, disclosure to some third party could amount to a breach of confidence, which could be prevented by an injunction or result in an action for damages.[111]

---

[110] *Gelber v Griffin* [2006] EWHC 3666 (Fam) (unreported).
[111] Under the principles arising from cases such as *Campbell v MGN Ltd* [2004] AC 457 and *McKennitt v Ash* [2008] QB 73.

# Chapter 5

# DISCLOSURE FROM NON-PARTIES

## INTRODUCTION

**5.1**   Thus far, the focus has been on obtaining disclosure from the parties to the proceedings themselves. Frequently, however, there will need to be disclosure from a third party who is in some way involved with the financial affairs of one or both of the parties to the marriage. The most common examples of such parties are companies partially or wholly owned by a party, business partners, or trustees of a trust fund of which a party is a beneficiary. There may also be circumstances where it is necessary to obtain disclosure directly from a new wife or partner, from a party's accountants or, exceptionally, from a party's lawyers. This section will look at the general principles of disclosure from non-parties. More detailed treatment of the issues which may arise in the context of companies, partnerships, trusts and jointly owned property appears additionally in the relevant chapters dealing with those topics. The specific categories of non-party considered separately in this section are new partners or wives, accountants and lawyers.

## WHO ARE THE PARTIES TO THE PROCEEDINGS?

**5.2**   Although this chapter is concerned with obtaining disclosure from third parties to the marriage, it is more accurate and helpful to make a distinction between seeking disclosure from parties to the proceedings, including any parties other than the spouses themselves and persons who are not parties to the proceedings at all. In this chapter the term 'non-parties' is used to describe the latter category of persons. Before turning to the specific procedural means by which disclosure may be obtained from non-parties, it is useful to be clear as to when someone is a party to the proceedings. Clearly, the husband and wife are parties to the proceedings and the court has power within its normal case-management powers to direct that they each provide such disclosure as is deemed necessary. The relevant rules relating to ancillary relief proceedings[1] proceed on the assumption that there will only be two parties, ie the husband

---

[1]   FPR 1991, rr 2.51A to 2.70. Although it should be noted that there may be a co-respondent to the main cause or a 'party cited' who appears not to be a 'respondent' to the ancillary relief application (see FPR, r 2.51A(2)) but who is entitled to file a statement in answer to any allegations made against him or her (r 2.60). Given that adultery is not normally relevant conduct within ancillary relief proceedings, this provision is rarely, if ever, now used. Under the Matrimonial Causes Rules 1977 it seems that such a person was not a party to the ancillary relief application: *Wynne v Wynne* [1981] 1 WLR 69 – although the opposite view seems to

and the wife. FPR 1991, r 2.59 does, however, require the application for a property adjustment order or an avoidance of disposition order to be served on any relevant interested parties as specified by the rule[2] or as directed by the court. Such persons do not become parties merely by virtue of being served.[3] Once served with notice of the proceedings, any such person may file evidence in response to the application and may apply to be joined to the proceedings. It appears that such a person may, however, be heard by the court on the issue in which they have an interest without formally being joined to the proceedings and becoming a party.[4] Such an approach may be more attractive than full joinder in many cases, particularly for the third party, because not being joined as a party makes it more difficult for the other parties to seek a costs order against the non-party, and the court's powers to obtain disclosure from the non-party are also more limited.

**5.3**   Curiously, there is nothing in the rules relating to ancillary relief proceedings that mentions joinder of interveners. It would appear to be unquestioned that the power of joinder exists and arises from the court's general case management powers or the provisions of the County Court Rules or Rules of the Supreme Court, as appropriate.[5] Once joined, an intervener appears to be a party to the proceedings and the court may make disclosure orders directly against him or her. When ordering an intervener to provide disclosure, the court needs to remain mindful of the relevance of the disclosure sought to the issues in which the intervener is concerned in order to ensure that disclosure orders are neither oppressive nor unfair. Nevertheless, there is no general reason why such a party should not be required to produce any material in his possession which is relevant to the issues in the proceedings as a whole, and this seems consistent with the court's broad quasi-inquisitorial role in ancillary relief proceedings. There appears to be no authority directly dealing with the duties of disclosure upon interveners. As a matter of principle it seems unlikely that the duty of full and frank disclosure applies to interveners in the same way as it does to the parties to the divorce. It seems more probable that interveners are subject to the normal disclosure requirements applying in civil

---

have been expressed obiter so far as co-respondents are concerned in *Re T (Divorce: Interim Maintenance: Discovery)* [1990] 1 FLR 1 at 9. There is no reason to suppose the position under the FPR 1991 is different.

2   In the case of an application to vary a settlement, the trustees of the settlement and the settlor, if living, are required to be served with the Form A and Form E completed by the applicant. On an application for avoidance of a disposition, the same documents are required to be served on the person in whose favour the disposition is alleged to have been made. Where an application for a property adjustment order or an avoidance of disposition order is made in respect of land, the mortgagees must be served with the Form A. The mortgagees have the right to apply to the court within 14 days after service for a copy of the Form E.

3   *Re T (Divorce: Interim Maintenance: Discovery)* [1990] 1 FLR 1.

4   *Re T (Divorce: Interim Maintenance: Discovery)* [1990] 1 FLR 1 at 15.

5   *Rossi v Rossi* [2007] 1 FLR 790. Sometimes the ancillary relief application is heard alongside an application made by a third party under the Trusts of Land and Appointment of Trustees Act 1996. In those cases the court will have power within those related civil proceedings to make orders against the parties to them. See also **8.9–8.14** for consideration of the joinder of third parties to resolve issues of property ownership.

litigation.[6] Nevertheless, the issue remains undecided and open to argument. In any event, such matters are always subject to the flexible approach of the family courts and its quasi-inquisitorial function in such proceedings.

**5.4**    Where in ancillary relief proceedings a potential claim is made on an asset in which a third party may have an interest, the rules of natural justice and, where a sale is contemplated, s 24A(6) of the Matrimonial Causes Act 1973 require notice to be given to the third party.[7] Having been served with notice, it is then for the third party to decide whether they wish to be heard on the issue and be joined to the proceedings for that purpose. If they do not wish to participate, the court has a discretion to join them on the application of one of the other parties. This discretion is exercised on the application of a 'balance of justice and convenience'.[8] Where the *only* purpose in the joinder is to seek disclosure from that party, it will not be allowed.[9]

## ALTERNATIVES TO DISCLOSURE ORDERS AGAINST NON-PARTIES

**5.5**    Before embarking on an application for disclosure from a non-party, consideration should be given to whether the information required may be obtained from the other party to the proceedings. Indeed, the court will need to be satisfied that all alternative methods of obtaining the information have been exhausted before requiring a 'stranger to the litigation' to provide the material sought.[10] It is important to note that the duty to disclose which attaches to the parties to ancillary relief proceedings relates not only to disclosure of actual documents which they have in their custody and control, but extends to full and frank disclosure of all information which is relevant to the determination of the case. Accordingly, the court can require them to disclose matters which are within their knowledge even if that information is not included in any document within their possession or control. Such information will often include their knowledge of the affairs of relevant non-parties. The

---

[6]    CPR 1998, r 31.6 defines 'standard disclosure' which a party to civil proceedings must provide as '(a) the documents on which he relies; and (b) the documents which (i) adversely affect his own case; (ii) adversely affect another party's case; or support another party's case'.

[7]    See **8.9–8.13** for more detailed consideration of the need for and effect of joinder of third parties.

[8]    *Re T* [1990] 1 FLR 1 at 16.

[9]    *Re T* [1990] 1 FLR 1. See also *KSO v MJO* [2008] EWHC 3031 (Fam) at [47]–[48]. One exception to this general rule is under the principle in *Norwich Pharmacal Co v Customs & Excise Commissioners* [1974] AC 133, where a party who has become involved (albeit innocently) in a tortious act may be joined to proceedings solely to provide information to the court and the wronged party about the act and the identity of the wrongdoers. There may be circumstances where this procedure may be appropriately used in ancillary relief proceedings, particularly where a party has been involved in fraud or contumacious conduct. It should be noted that in the normal civil jurisdiction this is a power of limited application. It is unclear whether the court in its quasi-inquisitorial function in family proceedings may apply the principle more broadly. Joinder may also be necessary to facilitate ultimate enforcement of the court's orders – see **15.78–15.85** for further discussion in the context of trustees.

[10]    *M v M (Third Party Subpoena: Financial Conduct)* [2006] 2 FLR 1253 at [116].

questionnaire will, therefore, be the first means by which the required information will be sought. It may be possible to obtain all the information which is required by a simple request addressed to the other party to the proceedings without recourse to applications against non-parties.

**5.6**    The other party will only be compelled to disclose a document if it is shown to be in his custody or control. This means that a party can be compelled to obtain documents which he or she does not actually have in their possession but which it is within their power to obtain (the most common example is a copy of an historical bank statement, even if paper copies of such statements have not been provided to him or her in the past). Problems arise where the request is made in relation to documents which the party to the proceedings may have access to in some capacity other than his personal capacity and those documents relate to the affairs of a third party. Most commonly this arises in the context of parties who are directors of companies. As a director of the company the party may have a right to inspect the company's books and other documents, but those documents are not necessarily in the party's custody or power. The same applies in relation to a company secretary.[11]

**5.7**    Where the company is the party's alter ego because he or she owns an overwhelming controlling interest in the company, the court is likely to be able to conclude that the company documents are indeed in that party's control. Indeed, this is usually conceded by the party concerned. Otherwise the court will only be able to compel production of such company documents which the party has actually had in his physical possession or custody, and even then any such order should be made subject to the company's right to object to the order.[12] The company may have a valid objection to the production of the documents, for example, on the basis of privilege, confidentiality or protection of technical secrets. The court may require detailed undertakings from the parties as to the manner in which the material is to be disclosed and used prior to making such an order for disclosure.

**5.8**    The court cannot compel the other party to produce documents which do not yet exist. So, although a wife was able to ask her solicitor husband for information about the terms of his partnership in a firm of solicitors (the partnership agreement not yet having been drawn up), she could not seek an order compelling him to produce a letter from the firm confirming the information he had given.[13]

---

[11]    *H v H (Disclosure by Third Party)* (1981) 2 FLR 303.
[12]    *B v B (Matrimonial Proceedings: Discovery)* [1978] Fam 181.
[13]    *G v G (Financial Provision: Discovery)* [1992] 1 FLR 40. Although the court said he could be ordered to use his best endeavours to obtain such a letter.

# HOW IS DISCLOSURE OBTAINED FROM NON-PARTIES?

**5.9** There are a number of methods by which disclosure may be sought from a non-party, the most commonly used being:

- by an 'inspection appointment' pursuant to FPR, r 2.62(7);[14]

- by a writ of subpoena duces tecum pursuant to RSC Ord 38, r 14 (the equivalent procedure in the county court being the issue of a witness summons pursuant to CCR Ord 20, r 12);

- by the court's power, arising from s 34(2) of the Supreme Court Act 1981 and s 53(2) of the County Courts Act 1984, on the application of a party to the proceedings to order a non-party to produce documents to the applicant or to his or her lawyers.

## The inspection appointment

**5.10** In modern ancillary relief practice the most frequently used method of obtaining third party disclosure has been the inspection appointment. The court must be asked to make an order for the inspection appointment to take place. The court will only allow the inspection appointment to occur if satisfied that inspection of the document is necessary for disposing fairly of the application or for saving costs. Accordingly, the court will consider the overriding objective and, in particular, the financial proportionality of allowing an inspection appointment to go ahead. Additionally, by virtue of FPR, r 2.62(8):

> 'no person can be compelled under para (7) to produce a document which he could not be compelled to produce at the substantive hearing. It is clear, therefore, that, while the court has to be satisfied that inspection of the document is necessary for disposing fairly of the application or for saving costs, the court should nevertheless exercise its discretion to refuse production if application of the general principles for setting aside a writ of subpoena to produce documents (as unfortunately the continuing link with the Rules of 1965 requires such a summons to be described) leads to that result.'[15]

It should be noted that where a party has been obstructive in producing full and frank disclosure, the court is more likely to set the scope of an order for inspection broadly rather than narrowly.[16]

**5.11** Usually the application for an inspection appointment will be made on notice to the other party, but not to the third party. The application should be

---

[14] Prior to the introduction of this rule there was a similar procedure available pursuant to RSC Ord 38, r 13, which rule remains in force for family proceedings but now seems to serve no purpose in ancillary relief proceedings.

[15] *Charman v Charman* [2006] 1 WLR 1053 at [23].

[16] *D v D (Production Appointment)* [1995] 2 FLR 497.

supported by an affidavit. An application made without notice is likely to be considered oppressive unless there is a legitimate concern that the document might be destroyed if notice were given.[17] If there are concerns which merit the application being made without notice to the other party, it is likely to be necessary to seek an injunction preventing any steps being taken to destroy or otherwise dispose of the documents in question.[18] The use of the more general 'civil' disclosure orders (considered below and at **6.89–6.92**) may be more appropriate in such circumstances.

## The subpoena duces tecum or witness summons

**5.12** Despite the routine use of the inspection appointment, there is still scope for using the subpoena procedure in certain circumstances.[19] The main difference between the two procedures is that an inspection appointment requires the applicant for disclosure to persuade the court that the order should be made compelling the third party to attend and produce the documents. In contrast, a subpoena or witness summons is issued by the court as an administrative act and, once served, the third party must attend the hearing, and the onus is thrown on him to persuade the court that the disclosure requested should not be permitted. In practice, especially in the High Court, this distinction between the subpoena and inspection appointment procedures is a slim one. In the High Court the subpoena will only be issued in family proceedings in chambers if supported by a note authorising it from the district judge.[20] In the county court the rules appear to be more relaxed and the leave of the district judge is only required if the witness's attendance is sought at a hearing in chambers for directions,[21] and even this restriction could be argued not to apply to a witness summons for the production of a document rather than a summons to give oral evidence. A party may feel that the subpoena procedure is more tactically advantageous and it may also require one hearing fewer than an application for an inspection appointment would, especially in the county court. Where a subpoena or witness summons is obtained after the refusal of the court to allow an inspection appointment, it seems likely that the court will need to be persuaded why the issue of the subpoena or witness summons is not an abuse of process.

---

[17]  *B v B (Production Appointment: Procedure)* [1995] 1 FLR 913.

[18]  See Chapter 6.

[19]  In proceedings for financial provision following a foreign divorce the rules do not provide for an inspection appointment, and the subpoena procedure or the use of the 'civil' disclosure order would appear to be necessary. Such proceedings are not included within the definition of 'ancillary relief' in the FPR 1991.

[20]  RSC Ord 32, r 7. The rules do not make it clear how such a 'note' is to be obtained. Presumably, a without notice application to the district judge of the day would be appropriate, although the judge may require an application to be made on notice before the matter is decided.

[21]  CCR Ord 20, r 12(8).

## Disclosure pursuant to the 'civil' disclosure powers

**5.13** By s 34(2) of the Supreme Court Act 1981 and s 53(2) of the County Courts Act 1984[22] the court has the power, on the application of a party to the proceedings, to order a non-party to produce documents to the applicant or to his or her lawyers.[23] These powers have not routinely been used in ancillary relief proceedings by name, although many practitioners have experience of the court making disclosure orders which could only have been founded on the powers provided by these provisions. In *L v L*[24] Tugenhat J suggested that the wife should have tried to use the powers provided by these provisions in preference to taking matters of disclosure into her own hands. In view of the various shortcomings in the inspection appointment procedure and the use of a subpoena duces tecum, discussed in the paragraphs below, these broader and more flexible powers are worthy of more regular use. The powers under the Supreme Court Act 1981 and the County Courts Act 1984 permit the court to require a non-party to produce the documents directly to the parties, or more likely to their lawyers, rather than to the court. They also permit the making of orders for the preservation of such documents. These powers may be a useful alternative to, or complementary to, the more traditional use of inspection appointments, a subpoena or a witness summons. The procedural aspects of applying for such 'civil' disclosure orders are considered further at **6.89–6.92**.

## THE NON-PARTY'S RIGHTS

**5.14** Whichever procedure is adopted, the person required to attend court and produce documents is entitled to be legally represented and to apply to the court to vary or discharge the order. It may be prudent to advise the non-party of this right when the order, subpoena or witness summons is served, so that costs are not wasted in the event the non-party arrives at the hearing in ignorance of the right to have legal representation to argue the case. It may be that the non-party raises some argument against disclosure, such as privilege attaching to the documents.[25] It may simply be said that no such documents exist and, if this assertion is not accepted, the court may need to hear evidence on the issue and make further orders as appropriate. It may be argued that the

---

[22] Although the title of these sections refers to their use only in actions for personal injuries or fatal accidents, this is misleading. Since 25 April 1999 the powers have been generally available in all forms of civil litigation – see **6.90** below.

[23] Supreme Court Act 1981, s 34(3) and County Courts Act 1984, s 53(3) contain further broad powers relating to the 'inspection, photographing, preservation, custody and detention of property which is not the property of, or in the possession of, any party to the proceedings but which is the subject matter of the proceedings or as to which any question arises in the proceedings.'

[24] [2007] 2 FLR 199. See Chapter 2.

[25] Frequently, the Data Protection Act 1998 is raised as a reason against disclosure being provided, usually on the basis that the material includes personal data referring to another. In *R (Davies) v Commissioners Office* [2008] 1 FLR 1651 it was made clear that a court order for disclosure overrides the non-disclosure provisions of the Act.

scope of the order is oppressive or irrelevant.[26] The court may also choose to refuse the order for production of documents on the basis that the information can be obtained by some other, less oppressive, means.[27]

**5.15** A subpoena or witness summons may specify attendance at the final hearing or an earlier hearing may be fixed to deal with that evidence. This is known as a '*Khanna*' hearing.[28] Clearly a request must be made to the court for a date to be fixed for such a hearing to take place before the final hearing. In effect, therefore, where such a hearing is sought, aside from the difference in the process by which the order is obtained, there is no real distinction between this procedure and the use of an inspection appointment. It will generally be undesirable to leave the production of important documents until the final hearing because there will be a high risk that the new information may cause the final hearing to be adjourned with unnecessary waste of costs. However, in circumstances where the existence of documents in the possession of a third party only comes to light at a late stage, there may be no option but to require their production at the final hearing.

## WHICH METHOD OF OBTAINING NON-PARTY DISCLOSURE SHOULD BE EMPLOYED?

**5.16** In practice, the authors suggest that an application for disclosure from a non-party should rely on each of these various alternative methods of disclosure to ensure that the court has the breadth of powers to allow it to make the most appropriate combination of orders in that case. The circumstances of each case will be different and the objectives of a non-party disclosure application will not be the same. Although the 'civil' orders pursuant to the Supreme Court Act 1981 and the County Courts Act 1984 provide a wide variety of flexible orders which can be tailored to provide a cost-effective means of disclosure, it should not be overlooked that a person required to attend court to produce documents at an inspection appointment or pursuant to a subpoena or witness summons can be cross-examined as to the existence or whereabouts of documents.[29] Although the court will be careful to keep such examination within reasonable limits, it is potentially of enormous utility in a case where disclosure of a party's documents is proving to be very difficult to obtain.

---

[26] See e g *H v H (Disclosure by Third Party)* (1981) 2 FLR 303; *Morgan v Morgan* [1977] Fam 122.

[27] In *Morgan v Morgan* [1977] Fam 122 the fact that a valuation of the wife's father's home could be made from the road without involving him in the proceedings seems to have been a factor which featured in the court's exercise of discretion.

[28] After *Khanna v Lovell White Durrant (A Firm)* [1995] 1 WLR 121.

[29] *Frary v Frary* [1993] 2 FLR 696. *Charman v Charman* [2006] 1 WLR 1053 at [23]. See also **5.17** below.

# THE PROPER SCOPE OF DISCLOSURE FROM NON-PARTIES

**5.17** It is important to note the limitations in the court's powers to order discovery from third parties by way of a subpoena, witness summons or inspection appointment. Both the inspection appointment procedure and the subpoena duces tecum are limited to the production of documents by a witness. Neither procedure can be used to require a third party to provide evidence or information to the court where that information is not in documentary form.[30] It is now clear that some limited oral questioning of a person required to attend an inspection appointment is permissible, but such questions should be limited to those which are necessary to enable the appointment to proceed effectively, e g to identify the source of a document, or how it relates to another document, or whether a document is missing and, if so, why.[31] It may be that this process of clarification as to the existence of documents can broaden into a slightly wider enquiry in an appropriate case.[32] On any basis, 'fishing' is not permitted in relation to requests for information sought from non-parties.[33] In *M v M (Third Party Subpoena: Financial Conduct)*[34] Peter Hughes QC, sitting as a deputy High Court judge, found that the following considerations were relevant when considering an application for disclosure against a third party:[35]

(a)   How important is the information to the issues in the proceedings?

(b)   Has the applicant taken appropriate steps to obtain the information within the proceedings and to enforce orders for disclosure, without success, before applying for third party disclosure?

(c)   Would it be sufficient for the court to draw inferences adverse to the respondent from the refusal to supply the information and comply with court orders?

(d)   What is the relationship between the respondent and the third party?

---

[30]   Note that oral evidence can be compelled at the substantive hearing by way of a writ of subpoena pursuant to RSC Ord 38, r 14, and witness summons pursuant to CCR Ord 20, r 12. Nevertheless, there are exceptional cases in which it will be appropriate to require oral evidence in advance of the final hearing, either by way of subpoena to attend and give oral evidence prior to the final hearing or by way of an order for a deposition to be taken before an examiner under RSC Ord 39, r 1: see *Charman v Charman* [2006] 1 WLR 1053 at [24].

[31]   *Frary v Frary* [1993] 2 FLR 696 and *Charman v Charman* [2006] 1 WLR 1053 at [23].

[32]   See the extent of the questioning permitted in *Charman v Charman* [2006] 1 WLR 1053 at [20]. But note the restrictions on cross-examining a person who has not provided an affidavit or witness's statement considered at **5.18**.

[33]   See **4.29** and *Charman v Charman* [2006] 1 WLR 1053 per Wilson LJ at [38] and [47]–[49].

[34]   [2006] 2 FLR 1253 at [116].

[35]   Although that case was concerned with a subpoena duces tecum, it would appear that the principles apply to an inspection appointment too.

(e)    If disclosure is necessary and proportionate,[36] do the documents contain private information that can be protected by editing?

**5.18**    The relatively limited scope of the enquiry permitted of non-parties contrasts with the court's power to require a party to the case to provide answers to wide-ranging enquiries within the questionnaire submitted during the proceedings. Such questions of a party can even extend to such amorphous matters as enquiries as to a party's future intentions. If a third party has chosen to provide an affidavit or witness statement in the proceedings, the situation is different and he or she can then be compelled to attend court and be cross-examined.[37] During cross-examination the third party can be asked about all manner of information which is within his or her knowledge, even if not recorded in documentary form, in the same way as any witness can be questioned. No person can be compelled to provide such an affidavit or statement if they do not wish to do so voluntarily.[38] In *Wynne v Wynne*[39] Bridge LJ said that, notwithstanding the absence of an affidavit or witness statement, a third party could still be 'ordered to attend and to give evidence, to be examined or cross-examined', thereby suggesting that such a person could be required to attend solely to be cross-examined. However, in *W v W (Disclosure by Third Party)* Balcombe J held in the clearest terms that a person who has not provided an affidavit or statement may not be summonsed to court simply to be cross-examined, summarising the position under the rule which now appears as FPR, r 2.62(4):[40]

> 'A witness who has already given an affidavit may be ordered to attend for cross-examination, because he has already given his evidence in chief by the affidavit. A witness may be ordered to attend for examination and, by the same order, be available for cross-examination by the other side. I am not prepared to allow the wife to call a witness for cross-examination only, as Mr Jackson made it quite clear that she seeks to do in this case. That would allow, in effect, a procedure – almost an interrogation – which, with certain statutory exceptions, is unknown to our courts, and I do not consider that litigation between husband and wife, although it bears certain special qualifications of its own, is so different from ordinary civil litigation that it should have a completely different procedure.'

**5.19**    The definition of 'document' in the context of the rules on disclosure is a broad one. Until the late twentieth century information was generally recorded in some written or printed form. The courts have remained flexible in the definition of the term to match developments in technology. So it is clear that

---

[36]    It seems that the words 'necessary and proportionate' here refer to the interference with the third party's rights under Art 8 of the European Convention on Human Rights, although it is submitted that proportionality in the context of the 'overriding' objective is also relevant.

[37]    See **2.38–2.47** as to the use of hearsay evidence and the power to compel the attendance at court for cross-examination of the author of a statement adduced as a hearsay statement.

[38]    *Wynne v Wynne* [1981] 1 WLR 69, CA.

[39]    [1981] 1 WLR 69 at 73.

[40]    *W v W (Disclosure by Third Party)* (1981) 2 FLR 291, a decision cited with apparent approval (albeit by reference to a slightly different point) by the Court of Appeal in *Frary v Frary* [1993] 2 FLR 696 at 702.

tape-recordings,[41] films,[42] and information stored electronically in a computer or other device[43] all qualify as documents. The Civil Evidence Act 1995 defines the term 'document' very broadly at s 13 as 'anything in which information of any description is recorded', and this definition, although strictly limited to the Act itself, is likely to have a strong influence on the definition of the word adopted within the Family Proceedings Rules 1991.

**5.20** Importantly, in ancillary relief proceedings there is no requirement upon the party seeking production of documents from a non-party to prove that the documents sought are in existence before the order is made.[44] However, this does not permit a party to embark on a 'fishing' expedition. The disclosure sought must be evidence relevant to one of the likely issues at the trial. Inevitably, owing to the breadth of the relevant issues at an ancillary relief final hearing, the limits of the disclosure which can be sought will also be very broad compared to the limits of disclosure usually permitted in civil proceedings.

**5.21** The inspection appointment[45] is an important and sometimes overlooked weapon in the ancillary relief litigant's arsenal. Where the other party seems to be unwilling or unable to provide full disclosure of his or her means, the information required may well be available from third parties. Even if those other parties do not provide sufficient information to establish the full extent of the other party's assets, their evidence may show the other party to have been dishonest or less than frank. It is important to note that when it comes to the production of documents there is no distinction between evidence which is relevant to a material issue in the proceedings and evidence which is relevant only to credit.[46] The case of *C v C (Financial Provision: Non-disclosure)*[47] provides a very good example of the use of a series of inspection appointments (or 'production appointments' as they were known under the rules at the time) to expose the husband's breach of his duty to make full and frank disclosure.

## THE RISKS INVOLVED IN SEEKING NON-PARTY DISCLOSURE

**5.22** The inspection appointment procedure has many shortcomings and comes with a number of 'health warnings'. The costs involved in this method of disclosure may be significant. In the first instance, the party seeking the disclosure will be responsible for the costs of any person required to attend court and comply with the order.[48] In the event that the non-party avails

---

[41]  *Grant v South Western and County Properties* [1975] Ch 185.

[42]  *Senior v Holdsworth ex parte Independent Television News Ltd* [1976] QB 23.

[43]  *Derby v Weldon (No 9)* [1991] 2 All ER 901.

[44]  *Charman v Charman* [2006] 2 FLR 422, [2006] 1 WLR 1053.

[45]  The comments in this paragraph and **5.20** are generally also applicable to a subpoena duces tecum or a witness summons to produce documents.

[46]  *W v W (Disclosure by Third Party)* (1981) 2 FLR 291 at 298 per Balcombe J.

[47]  [1994] 2 FLR 272.

[48]  See *JH Shannon v Country Casuals Holdings plc* (1997) The Times, June 16; *D v D (Production*

himself of his right to his own legal representation and challenges the order for disclosure, protracted and costly litigation on issue can result. Even once the disclosure is provided, the costs of processing it may prove to be substantial.[49] The third party often has no real interest in assisting the parties to the litigation, and the material requested will often be presented in an unsorted and difficult to digest form. The process of considering the voluminous boxes of papers which, for example, an accountant may produce is likely to be time-consuming and costly. In the first instance the documents will be presented to the court rather than to the parties and their inspection may need to take place in the court building. This is usually less convenient than having them available in the lawyers' office.[50] Furthermore, in some cases the other party's financial affairs will be complex, perhaps involving a large number of third party advisers and institutions. One inspection appointment may produce information which leads to the need for a further appointment and so on. Proportionality between the costs of the enquiry and the importance of the issue in question must be maintained.

## DISCLOSURE FROM BANKS

**5.23** Access to a party's bank account statements is often crucial in order to investigate their means. Usually such statements are produced by the other party as required by the court. Sometimes, however, such disclosure is not forthcoming. The situation is even worse where the relevant party has put him or herself beyond the jurisdiction of the court overseas. In such circumstances it may be appropriate to use the power contained within the Bankers' Books Evidence Act 1879 to compel the relevant bank itself to produce the bank ledgers relating to a named individual. Section 6 of the Act states that, unless the court finds a special reason for doing so, a banker or officer of a bank cannot be compelled to produce any bankers' books or to attend court as a witness to prove the contents of the books where those contents can be proved in one of the other ways specified by the Act. This means that an inspection appointment or subpoena duces tecum cannot usually be sought against a banker. The means of inspection of bank records set out in the Act must be

---

*Appointment)* [1995] 2 FLR 497 at 500; *Totalise plc v The Motley Fool Limited and Another* [2001] 1 WLR 1233; *Charman v Charman* [2006] 1 WLR 1053; *M v M (Third Party Subpoena: Financial Conduct)* [2006] 2 FLR 1253; *C v C (Costs: Leave to Appeal)* [2008] 1 FLR 136; and *KSO v MJO* [2008] EWHC 3031 (Fam).

[49] For example, *C v C (Costs: Leave to Appeal)* [2008 1 FLR 136, where costs of nearly £400,000 were incurred in the space of 3 months, including a sum of some £68,500 by the non-party for which the wife was in the first instance liable. See also *KSO v MJO* [2008] EWHC 3031 (Fam).

[50] If the third party will not agree to the release of the documents to the applicant or the applicant's solicitors, it may be possible to obtain an order for the production of the documents to the applicant or the applicant's lawyers and for the detention of the documents by the applicant pursuant to s 34 of the Supreme Court Act 1981 or s 53 of the County Courts Act 1984. These powers are discussed at **6.89–6.92**. It is not clear whether the court may permit the photocopying of the documents if the third party does not agree to this, but it would be surprising if the court were unable to make a direction to this effect, subject to the other parties providing appropriate undertakings as to the use to which the documents may be put.

used instead. Section 7 permits the court to grant an order permitting a party to inspect and take copies of any entries in a banker's book for any of the purposes of the proceedings. Such an order can be made with or without notice to the bank, but the bank must be served with the order not less than 3 clear days before the time it is to be obeyed, unless the court otherwise directs. Section 8 gives the court a broad discretion for dealing with the costs of applying for and complying with any such order, including the power to make the bank pay any costs occasioned by any default or delay on its part.[51] Section 9(2) defines 'bankers' books' broadly to include those records kept on microfilm or in some form of 'electronic data retrieval mechanism'. Building societies and the Post Office in its banking function are included within the definition of 'bank' and 'banker'. The provisions would appear not to extend to correspondence sent to or from the bank. Cheques and paying-in slips are not within the provision.[52] Where the material sought is as mentioned in the previous two sentences, it would appear that its production can be compelled by an order for an inspection appointment or by a subpoena or witness summons.

**5.24**  This provision is relatively rarely used in ancillary relief proceedings. In the right case it can be potentially very useful as a means of obtaining the complete disclosure which the other party is unwilling to produce.

## COMMONLY ENCOUNTERED THIRD PARTY DISCLOSURE PROBLEMS

### New partners or spouses

**5.25**  Where one of the parties to the proceedings has formed a new relationship or remarried, the other party will often be interested in that new partner's means. Although the new partner's assets and income are not available for redistribution in the ancillary relief proceedings, they plainly are relevant as part of all the circumstances of the case, particularly where maintenance is an issue.[53] The Form E invites the parties to volunteer such information as they have about their new partner's income and assets. Often this section is left blank and the resulting enquiry in a questionnaire is answered with a bald assertion that nothing is known. Although when it comes to the final hearing the court may reject that assertion as implausible, the other party remains in a position where little is known about the details of the new partner's resources.

---

[51]  It is submitted that, absent any culpable failure by the bank, the normal order will be for the bank's costs to be borne in the first instance by the party applying for disclosure, in the same way as the costs of a person who is complying with an order to attend an inspection appointment is entitled to his costs (see above).

[52]  *Williams v Williams* [1988] QB 161.

[53]  See *Roberts v Roberts* [1968] 3 WLR 1181; *Macey v Macey* (1982) 3 FLR 7; *Slater v Slater* (1982) 3 FLR 364; *Atkinson v Atkinson* [1988] 2 FLR 353; *Atkinson v Atkinson* [1995] 2 FLR 356, [1996] 1 FLR 51; *Fleming v Fleming* [2004] 1 FLR 667; and *K v K (Periodical Payments:Cohabitation)* [2006] 2 FLR 468 and *G v G* [2009] EWHC 494 (Fam).

**5.26**   In many cases little further enquiry will be necessary or justified. It may be possible to make broad inferences about the new partner's means from facts which can be readily discovered without the need for an inspection appointment.[54] Indeed, the failure of the other party and the new partner or spouse to produce the readily available material which would rebut any inference as to means is likely to strengthen the court's satisfaction that the inference is to be properly drawn. In most cases this will be the most cost-effective and tactically sound basis upon which to deal with this issue.

**5.27**   Certainly the court has no power to require a new partner or spouse to provide an affidavit of means, even where that person is named in the proceedings as a co-respondent.[55] It follows that there is also no power to compel that person to attend court and be cross-examined as to their means.[56] The power to require such a person to attend an inspection appointment and produce relevant documents such as wage slips, bank statements etc does exist. Nevertheless, the court will require considerable persuasion to find that such an interference with a person's privacy is necessary and not oppressive to them.[57] Since the incorporation of the European Convention on Human Rights into English law by the Human Rights Act 1998 the court must be careful to ensure that the interference with the third party's right to respect privacy is proportionate to the necessary protection of the applicant's rights.[58] There may well be cases where, rather than seeking wide-ranging disclosure of the new partner's financial affairs, an application for production of documents relates to a specific and important issue which will make disclosure just and necessary. For example, in *M v M (Third Party Subpoena: Financial Conduct)*[59] disclosure from the husband's new partner was permitted on the grounds that there was evidence that she had become involved in the concealment of assets from the wife. There is also some indication that judicial attitudes to disclosure being ordered from cohabitees is beginning to change. In *K v K (Periodical Payments: Cohabitation)*[60] Coleridge J underlined the importance of the court having an overall view of the financial situation in a household and he said that there was 'no room for shyness' on the part of the cohabiting partner when such requests for disclosure were made.

## Companies

**5.28**   Most of the documentation required to assess the worth of a company, at least in general terms, is freely available to the public at Companies House. The nature of the documents filed and retained at Companies House is

---

[54]   The value of a home can be assessed from the road, its ownership by a search of the Land Register; the partner's earnings can be inferred from the type of work they do etc.

[55]   *Wynne v Wynne* [1981] 1 WLR 69.

[56]   See **5.18**.

[57]   *Frary v Frary* [1993] 2 FLR 696.

[58]   *M v M (Third Party Subpoena: Financial Conduct)* [2006] 2 FLR 1253, Peter Hughes QC. See also **5.17** for the judge's guidance as to the relevant factors to consider on such an application.

[59]   [2006] 2 FLR 1253.

[60]   [2006] 2 FLR 468. See also the criticism of Coleridge J's 'heretical observations' on cohabitation by Singer J in *G v G* [2009] EWHC 494 (Fam).

considered at **11.29–11.34**. There may be other documents which are required over and above those filed at Companies House, especially in the case of a smaller company which is subject to the abbreviated filing requirements under the Companies Acts. For example, a detailed profit and loss account and balance sheet are likely to have been prepared for the shareholders and directors of such a company even if the rules do not require such detailed documents to be filed at Companies House.

**5.29** A court in ancillary relief proceedings must respect the separate legal personality of a company. There is no greater power vested in a judge in family proceedings to pierce the corporate veil than a judge in the Queen's Bench Division or the Chancery Division possesses.[61] With that said, the court in its matrimonial jurisdiction is always prepared to look at the reality of the financial situation as well as its strict legal form, and this may allow it to make an order which indirectly achieves the required aim.[62] Where the other party to proceedings is an officer of the company, it is likely that many of the company documents will be in his custody and control and the court can order them to be produced, subject to limitations and safeguards for the company and other affected third parties which have been considered at **5.7**. Where it cannot be shown that the other party has it in his or her power to produce the documents requested, an application against the company will be necessary and the company can be heard as to whether the order should be set aside or varied. In such a case it may be helpful to require the other party to first swear an affidavit confirming that the documents in question are not in his or her power.[63]

**5.30** Mere shareholders in companies have much more limited rights of access to most of the company's management documents. Usually they have access to little more than the general public is able to access at Companies House, save for documents which the company chooses to send to its shareholders, such as annual reports. Where the company is effectively the alter ego of the other party, the court will readily pierce the corporate veil and require him or her to produce company documents. Where other third parties also have a significant interest in the company, it is more likely to be necessary to allow the company to be heard on the question of disclosure or to apply for disclosure directly from the company, as appropriate. It may also be necessary for the party seeking the disclosure to provide undertakings to the company in relation to the confidentiality of the information disclosed, particularly where that information is commercially sensitive. The difficult issues raised by the separate legal personality of companies are considered in more detail in Chapter 11.

---

[61] *Ben Hashem v Al Shayif* [2009] 1 FLR 115, Munby J.
[62] *Mubarak v Mubarak* [2001] 1 FLR 673. See also Chapter 11 for a more detailed discussion of how the court deals with companies owned wholly or partially by the parties.
[63] *H v H (Disclosure by Third Party)* (1981) 2 FLR 303.

## Accountants

**5.31**   An obvious target for production of financial documentation is the accountant who acts for a party or for a business in which that party has an interest. Of course, many of the documents held by a party's accountant will have been provided to the accountant by the party himself, and so those documents will have been in the custody or control of that party and he can be directly ordered to produce them. There will be other documents which will not be within that category or, even if they are, the husband may be wholly unwilling to comply with orders for their production. In such cases the accountant may be ordered to produce the documents to the court. Such an order can prove to be very difficult, and therefore expensive, to implement in practical terms. The accountant's documentation is likely to be extensive and not necessarily easy to analyse. If possible, the order should specify the actual categories of documents to be produced with as much particularity as possible in order to avoid unnecessary documentation being produced. Where a party's affairs have been less than frankly disclosed, however, it may be difficult to limit the production order in that way, because the whole purpose of the production order in such a case will be to attempt to get to the truth.

**5.32**   As with all production orders, the party to whom it is addressed may argue that the order is too widely drawn or is otherwise oppressive. Generally, however, an accountant, as a professional, will find it difficult to argue that an order for production of documents at an inspection appointment is oppressive.[64] It may be possible to show that some of the documents which have been requested are irrelevant to the issues before the court. The court may also be persuaded that the scope of the enquiry being conducted is disproportionate and prevent or limit it accordingly. There also needs to be sensitivity to the fact that some documents may contain information which is confidential to other persons who are unconnected to the case. If it seems that such information must be disclosed to deal with the case, it seems likely that the affected person should be allowed to be heard on the issue before an order is made. Confidentiality of itself is not a reason for otherwise relevant documents not being produced if they are required for the purposes of disposing of the proceedings justly. Once an order for disclosure is made, the non-disclosure requirements contained within the Data Protection Act 1998 are overridden.[65]

**5.33**   Where the accountant has become complicit in the client's attempts to prevent full financial disclosure, the court is more likely to take a broad approach to disclosure.[66] The high costs incurred by such an approach are one of the inevitable results of non-disclosure. Although the court is likely to make the party who has made the process necessary by reason of his or her non-disclosure liable for the costs of the exercise at the end of the case, parties should be conscious of the fact that, in the first instance, the party applying for the production of documents will be responsible for the accountant's costs of

---

64   *Charman v Charman* [2006] 1 WLR 1053.
65   *R (Davies) v Commissioners Office* [2008] 1 FLR 1651.
66   *D v D (Production Appointment)* [1995] 2 FLR 497.

complying with the order.[67] This should discourage a speculative 'fishing expedition'. Only if efforts to obtain disclosure from the other party directly demonstrate that the full picture has not been disclosed will it be justifiable to incur the costs of obtaining third party disclosure from professional advisors.

## Solicitors

**5.34** Disclosure may be sought from a solicitor who has been previously involved in the parties' affairs. A solicitor owes a duty of confidence to his or her client in the conduct of their affairs. Coterminous with that duty of confidence, much of the information and documentation which the solicitor holds in relation to the client is also protected by a form of privilege. The duty of confidence will not prevent disclosure being ordered if the court feels disclosure is necessary.[68] However, where disclosure affects a third party who is not otherwise involved in the case (eg a business partner who uses the same solicitor), the court may conclude that to order the disclosure would be oppressive.[69] There may be means by which the papers sought to be disclosed can be redacted in a form which balances the interests of all affected parties.

**5.35** A greater obstacle to seeking disclosure from a solicitor is legal privilege. Legal professional privilege in its various forms is quite different from confidentiality and will usually be a complete bar to disclosure being ordered without the consent of the party who holds the privilege. Legal professional privilege is not limited to advice given for the purposes of proceedings. Even the file relating to a straightforward conveyancing transaction will be covered by the privilege against disclosure.[70]

**5.36** A party can, of course, elect to waive the privilege and allow the otherwise privileged material to be disclosed. Waiver can also be implied from the circumstances, but the scope of the doctrine of implied waiver is quite complex, and its application fact sensitive. Specialist texts on the law of evidence should be consulted on the topic. It is well established that where a client embarks on litigation with a former solicitor, the privilege which attached to their communications is implicitly waived.[71] It has been suggested that implied waiver of privilege occurred whenever a state of mind became an issue

---

[67] See *JH Shannon v Country Casuals Holdings plc* (1997) The Times, June 16; *D v D (Production Appointment)* [1995] 2 FLR 497 at 500; *Totalise plc v The Motley Fool Limited and Another* [2001] 1 WLR 1233; *Charman v Charman* [2006] 1 WLR 1053; *M v M (Third Party Subpoena: Financial Conduct)* [2006] 2 FLR 1253; *C v C (Costs: Leave to Appeal)* [2008] 1 FLR 136; and *KSO v MJO* [2008] EWHC 3031 (Fam). However, it is submitted that an accountant who is shown to have been complicit in efforts to hide the true financial picture may find it significantly more difficult to recover his or her costs of complying with the order.

[68] The order of the court requiring production of documents would also appear to ensure that disclosure of documents does not place the third party in breach of the Data Protection Act 1998.

[69] Although it is difficult to argue that complying with the order would be oppressive on the solicitor himself: *Charman v Charman* [2006] 1 WLR 1053.

[70] *C v C (Privilege)* [2008] 1 FLR 115.

[71] *Paragon Finance plc v Freshfields* [1999] 1 WLR 1183, CA.

in the proceedings and the legal advice was material to the question of what that state of mind was.[72] However, it now seems that implied waiver by raising an issue in the course of litigation is limited to the situation where there is litigation between the client and the lawyer.[73] It is not clear whether the same principle extends to the common situation in ancillary relief litigation where one of the parties seeks to resile from an earlier separation agreement on the basis that his or her solicitors failed to provide adequate advice. It is common for the solicitors' file to be disclosed in such cases, presumably on the basis that it would be evidentially more damaging not to do so.[74] It is less clear whether such disclosure can be compelled if privilege is not expressly waived.

**5.37** It has been suggested that in the special atmosphere of ancillary relief proceedings even this otherwise absolute privilege can be overridden if the party who asserts it has failed to make full and frank disclosure and has shown himself to be in contemptuous breach of orders of the court. In *Kimber v Brookman Solicitors*[75] the husband had indicated to the wife and her lawyers that he would take no part in the ancillary relief proceedings and he was, in Coleridge J's words '"cocking a snook" at the court'.[76] He had also managed to disappear with the bulk of the family assets. In an effort to advance the case the wife had obtained production orders against various persons who could be expected to have some information about the husband's whereabouts or affairs. One such order was made against a solicitor who had acted for the husband for a short period within the divorce proceedings. The solicitor attended before the court for guidance as to what he should disclose, in view of the fact that at least some of the material he was being ordered to produce was privileged. Coleridge J found that the husband had by his conduct lost any right to assert privilege. He had lost the protection of legal privilege for the following reasons:[77]

> 'The situation in this case is that this is an application by a wife under the Matrimonial Causes Act 1973 for ancillary relief. As such, the court has a statutory duty to inquire into the parties' means. It is not just a question as between two clients. It is a question between the court and the parties. The court has an inquisitorial function, not merely an arbitration function as between the two parties. That puts the court, it seems to me, in a different position to that more conventionally found in civil litigation generally.
>
> Secondly, there is a clear duty in this type of proceedings, as set out in the rules, on both parties to make full, complete and frank disclosure to the court of their means. In this case the husband has failed to abide by the rules and also is in

---

[72]   *Hayes v Dowding* [1996] PNLR 578.
[73]   *Farm Assist Ltd (in Liquidation) v Secretary of State for Environment, Food and Rural Affairs* [2008] EWHC 3079, [2009] PNLR 16; *Digicel Ltd v Cable & Wireless plc* [2009] EWHC 1437 (Ch).
[74]   For example, *NA v MA* [2007] 1 FLR 1760.
[75]   [2004] 2 FLR 221.
[76]   [2004] 2 FLR 221 at 223.
[77]   [2004] 2 FLR 221 at 224.

breach of orders of the court. He therefore forfeits, in my judgment, any entitlement in relation to retaining the usual cloak of legal privilege.

Thirdly, of course and importantly, he is, it is clear, taking every conceivable step he can to defeat his wife's legitimate claim. Whether or not she is claiming too much, I know not. All I know is that the actions which he has taken, on the face of it, appear to be designed to defeat her proper claim. That is underlined by the attitude which he set out in the recent letter.

Accordingly, even if the husband is not in contempt of court, the public interest is fully engaged in this application and it is in the public interest to get to the bottom of where this man is and what he has done with the parties' resources.'

**5.38** The decision in *Kimber v Brookman Solicitors* is a somewhat surprising one. Neither the solicitor nor the husband sought to challenge the ruling by an appeal, presumably because, once the disclosure had been made, such an appeal would have been somewhat academic. The doctrine of legal professional privilege has generally been strongly defended by English law, and the incorporation of the European Convention on Human Rights by the Human Rights Act 1998 appears to have reinforced it.[78] The decision in *Kimber v Brookman Solicitors* has not yet been directly addressed in any other case. However, in the course of giving a judgment in an appeal in the same litigation on a different point, Wilson LJ described Coleridge J's decision as 'controversial'[79] and in *C v C (Costs)*[80] Munby J said that if the decision in *Kimber v Brookman Solicitors* was to the effect that slightly different rules as to privilege apply in ancillary proceedings by virtue of their quasi-inquisitorial nature, he disagreed with that proposition.[81] Nevertheless, where a party is able to produce evidence which establishes a prima facie case that the transaction was a fraudulent one, the privilege will be set aside, but the burden of proving that the exception to the right to privilege applies is a heavy one and parties would not be permitted to embark on a fishing expedition.[82] As in all cases where a serious allegation such as fraud is being made, the party making the allegation should set out the allegation clearly in writing.[83]

**5.39** Frequently, the reason for the other party failing to provide the documents held by his or her solicitor is because the solicitor refuses to release the documents, as a lien is exercised over them whilst the solicitor's fees remain unpaid. Whilst such a lien may prevent the party in question from obtaining the release of papers from the solicitor, it does not absolve the solicitor from producing the documents to the court if an order for their production is made against the solicitor.[84]

---

[78]   *C v C (Privilege)* [2008] 1 FLR 115 at [25].
[79]   *Kimber v Kimber* [2006] EWCA Civ 706 at [8].
[80]   [2008] 1 FLR 136.
[81]   Ibid at [17].
[82]   *C v C (Privilege)* [2008] 1 FLR 115.
[83]   *C v C (Privilege)* [2008] 1 FLR 115. See also **2.11** above.
[84]   *Frogmore Estates v Berger* (1992) *The Independent*, May 8.

## Trusts

**5.40**  Where a trust can be shown to be effectively controlled by the other party, the court can require that party to produce documents relating to the trust. Otherwise the trustees must be compelled to produce the documents. In many cases the trustees will be joined to the proceedings, because the trust will have an important role to play in the outcome of the case beyond mere disclosure.[85] Once joined, the scope to make orders for disclosure will be broadened. Trusts and their treatment in ancillary relief cases are considered in more detail in Chapter 15.

## Inheritance prospects

**5.41**  Attempts are sometimes made to persuade the court to require non-parties to provide information as to their testamentary intentions. Such applications are usually dismissed as being irrelevant, speculative or oppressive.[86] It may be that there are cases where the inheritance prospects are of such importance that some order against the non-party may be justified. Such cases will be highly exceptional. The various difficulties arising for the litigant seeking to raise inheritance prospects as an issue in a case are considered in more detail in Chapter 18.

## Criminal proceedings

**5.42**  It is increasingly common to have ancillary relief proceedings before a family court at the same time as one of the parties is involved in criminal confiscation proceedings before a criminal court pursuant to the Proceeds of Crime Act 2002. The evidence in the criminal proceedings may well contain financial material which is relevant to the ancillary relief proceedings. Although the court has the power to require the prosecutor to disclose such evidence, that power should not normally be invoked. Instead, the application for disclosure should be made to the criminal court where the proceedings are pending and the judge in that court should normally approach such an application favourably, unless there was evidence of some improper motive on the part of the person seeking the disclosure.[87]

## DISCLOSURE FROM OVERSEAS – PERSONS BEYOND THE JURISDICTION

**5.43**  An inspection appointment is of little purpose where the non-party from whom disclosure is sought is not within the jurisdiction of the court. Different approaches are required depending on where the non-party happens to be based.

---

[85]  For example, *T v T (Joinder of Third Parties)* [1996] 2 FLR 357.
[86]  See eg *Morgan v Morgan* [1977] Fam 122.
[87]  *T v B* [2008] EWHC 3000 (Fam), [2009] 1 FLR 1231.

**5.44**   A person in another part of the United Kingdom[88] can be made subject to the subpoena of the High Court in the same way as a person in England and Wales.[89] It appears that the county court has no equivalent power, although the High Court may issue a subpoena in support of county court proceedings without the need to transfer the whole proceedings.[90]

**5.45**   A person in another member state of the European Union (except Denmark, which has an opt-out in this respect) can be required to give evidence or provide disclosure pursuant to the 'Taking Evidence Regulation'. The rules for its use are contained in Part 34.22 of the Civil Procedure Rules 1998. The Regulation allows the court to make an order which is addressed directly to the court in the other member state, which is obliged to give effect to the order. Of course, there are variations between nations as to how effectively the foreign court deals with the request. The advice of local lawyers in that jurisdiction is likely to be required to judge how effective the remedy might be in any case.

**5.46**   Where documents are required to be produced by a person outside the United Kingdom and the European Union, the appropriate form of order is for the issue, pursuant to RSC Ord 39, rr 1 and 2, of a letter of request to the relevant judicial authorities to cause the person to be required to produce documents.[91] Where it is sought to obtain oral evidence from a person abroad, since such a person cannot be compelled by subpoena to attend the hearing and give oral evidence, the appropriate form of order is for the issue pursuant to the same rules of a letter of request to cause the person to be required to answer written questions under RSC Ord 39, r 3(3) and/or oral questions.[92] There are similarities with the principles and procedure adopted when a deposition is sought to be taken from a person outside the jurisdiction (as to which see **2.77–2.82**). Some countries have bilateral conventions with the United Kingdom as to the taking of evidence to assist proceedings in another country. Other countries are signatories to the Hague Convention on the Taking of Evidence Abroad in Civil and Commercial Matters. Some countries have legislation equivalent to the Evidence (Proceedings in Other Jurisdictions) Act 1975 which provides a mechanism for the taking of evidence in support of proceedings in a foreign jurisdiction. The advice of local lawyers will be required to ascertain whether the remedy is worth pursuing.

**5.47**   The principles applicable to the determination of an application for an order for the issue of letters of request requiring documents to be produced by a person abroad will be the same as those determinative of an application for an order for an inspection appointment. Likewise, the principles applicable to the determination of an application to set aside a writ of subpoena are

---

[88]   That is, Scotland and Northern Ireland, but not the Channel Islands or the Isle of Man: Limitation Act 1978, s 5 and Sch 1.
[89]   Supreme Court Act 1981, s 36.
[90]   County Courts Act 1984, s 56.
[91]   The equivalent provision in the Civil Procedure Rules 1998 is Part 34.13.
[92]   *Charman v Charman* [2006] 1 WLR 1053 at [25]–[26].

determinative of an application for letters of request requiring oral evidence to be given by a person abroad.[93] Reference should be made to the sections above dealing with such orders.

**5.48** These procedures are likely to be used only in cases concerning very substantial assets. The costs of obtaining and then implementing letters of request are likely to be very substantial. The effectiveness of the request will ultimately depend on the approach taken by the judicial authority to whom they are submitted. In *Charman v Charman* letters of request were issued to the courts of Bermuda after expensive contested applications in England, only for the judge in Bermuda to refuse to compel witnesses to produce the disclosure which had been requested.[94] In *Minwalla v Minwalla*,[95] however, letters of request were used to great effect in relation to a trust held in Jersey. Indeed, in that case the effective use of the letters of request proved to be more cost-effective than most of the alternative methods of obtaining the required information.

---

[93]    *Charman v Charman* [2006] 1 WLR 1053 at [27].
[94]    A response which Coleridge J described as 'somewhat churlish': [2007] 1 FLR 593.
[95]    [2005] 1 FLR 771. See **15.71.**

# Part III

# DISSIPATION OF ASSETS

# Chapter 6

# PREVENTING DISSIPATION OF MATRIMONIAL ASSETS

**6.1**    The factors which motivate some divorcing spouses to resist providing each other with full and frank disclosure of their financial affairs often also create a strong temptation to dissipate assets in an effort to keep those assets out of the reach of the other spouse and the court. The whole purpose of an application for ancillary relief may be frustrated by such dissipation. Accordingly, it is of the utmost importance to ensure that all reasonable steps are taken to prevent assets disappearing out of reach.

## WHAT CONSTITUTES DISSIPATION OF ASSETS?

**6.2**    There are many and various ways in which assets can be dissipated. It is probably impossible to list them comprehensively because human ingenuity will constantly find new and more ingenious methods. Some examples of the types of dissipation of assets which occur in the context of ancillary relief proceedings are:

- spending funds, particularly when the spending is on intangible items such as holidays or expensive dining or entertainment;

- disposing of assets to third parties, perhaps under the guise of repayment of a debt or pursuant to some other, possibly bona fide, arrangement;

- moving assets out of reach, e g by transferring them overseas or by hiding a chattel;

- putting assets into a less realisable or less valuable form, e g by tying up cash in some form of bond for a defined period of time, by placing money in a trust or a pension arrangement, or by granting a long lease over a previously vacant and readily saleable property;

- mortgaging or charging an asset to a third party.[1]

**6.3**    Of course, there will be dissipation of assets in every case. Every person needs to spend money to live and to function on an everyday basis. No one can

---

[1]    As occurred in *Kemmis v Kemmis* [1988] 1 WLR 1307 and *Perez-Adamson v Perez Rivas* [1987] 2 FLR 472.

be expected to stop spending completely whilst ancillary relief proceedings are pending. A difficult judgment for practitioners in many cases is to determine the point at which one party's use of the assets available to him becomes unreasonable and needs to be restrained. This judgment may be particularly difficult in a case where there is an apparently legitimate call upon one party's assets, for example to support their business, but the consequence of allowing them to act as they please may be significantly to reduce the assets available for distribution in the proceedings. On the other hand, in some cases restraining the proposed dealings could cause a viable business to fail, taking the family's main source of income with it. Similar problems may arise where the parties are in a position where they have to live entirely off their capital rather than from income. It is also very difficult to judge the point at which some protective measures need to be taken. In some cases there will be sufficient other assets to ensure that appropriate and fair financial provision can be made, even if some of the assets have been dissipated by the other party.[2] Often only hindsight shows whether the decision to seek injunctive or other protection was reasonable or necessary. In any case where there is a significant concern that dissipation of assets may occur, consideration must be given to taking protective steps.

## BANKRUPTCY[3]

**6.4**    A further form of 'dissipation' worthy of mention is one which is usually out of the parties' own hands. Bankruptcy is normally forced upon one of the parties by his or her creditors, although a person may petition for his or her own bankruptcy.[4] A bankruptcy order has the effect of vesting ownership of all the bankrupt's assets to his trustee in bankruptcy. Once a bankruptcy order has been made, the court cannot make property adjustment orders against the assets which have been vested in the trustee in bankruptcy.[5] In fact, even if a property adjustment order is made by the court between the presentation of a bankruptcy petition and the making of the bankruptcy order, s 284 of the Insolvency Act 1986 renders the property adjustment order void upon the making of the bankruptcy order.[6] Nevertheless, where a potential bankruptcy against one party is looming, it may still be in the interests of the parties to conclude their ancillary relief proceedings as soon as possible. Where the final order is made before the presentation of a bankruptcy petition, any property adjustment order remains effective unless the case was exceptional and it could

---

[2]    See **7.5–7.6** for consideration of how the court might add back to a party's share of the assets such funds as he or she has unreasonably dissipated.

[3]    This subject is dealt with in more detail in Chapter 25.

[4]    See e g *Re Holliday (a bankrupt)* [1981] Ch 405 and *Woodley v Woodley (No 2)* [1993] 2 FLR 477.

[5]    *McGladdery v McGladdery* [1999] 2 FLR 1102. But see below as to the effect of an order pursuant to s 37(2)(a) of the MCA 1973 requiring money to be paid into court pending the final order. Such an order has the effect of making the applicant for the order a secured creditor of the respondent, thus avoiding the money in court vesting in the trustee in bankruptcy for general distribution to the respondent's other creditors.

[6]    *Flint (A Bankrupt)* [1993] 1 FLR 763; *Treharne & Sand v Forrester* [2004] 1 FLR 1173.

be established that the property adjustment order had been obtained by fraud or some broadly similar exceptional circumstance.[7] Even before a final order is made, it may be possible to protect some of the assets from the immediate effects of a bankruptcy order by having funds paid into court pursuant to an order made under s 37(2)(a) of the Matrimonial Causes Act 1973,[8] although it is likely that seeking such an order for no reason other than to avoid the claims of creditors through the bankruptcy would be an abuse of process.

**6.5**    Where a person seeks to arrange for his own bankruptcy purely to defeat the claims of his spouse, ie where there is no genuine inability on his part to meet his debts as they fall due, the other spouse may need to intervene in the bankruptcy proceedings to prevent the making of a bankruptcy order, or subsequently apply to annul such an order which has been improperly made to her prejudice.[9]

## CAN ASSETS BE PROTECTED WITHOUT RECOURSE TO THE COURT?

**6.6**    Where an effective self-help remedy is available to the parties, they would be well advised to use that before incurring the costs of an application to the court. Indeed, failure to do so may leave a party open to criticism for making a needless application to the court, and there may be a penalty in costs. Furthermore, failure to register an appropriate notice, restriction or charge against the title to land which is the subject matter of proceedings may make it difficult to set aside a subsequent sale or mortgage of that land pursuant to s 37(2)(b) or (c) of the Matrimonial Causes Act 1973.[10]

**6.7**    The most useful forms of unilateral protection of assets arise in the context of real estate. The system of land registration which applies to English land law makes it relatively easy to protect against dispositions of land. Where land is registered in the joint names of the parties, a disposition by one party acting alone is not possible, unless that party is prepared to go to the length of forging the necessary signature of the co-owner.

**6.8**    Where the land is held in the sole name of one of the parties, more formal steps are required to prevent the land being disposed of. If the property in question is, or was at some time, intended by the parties to be the matrimonial home, the non-owning spouse has statutory 'home rights' to

---

[7]    Insolvency Act 1986, ss 339 and 340 and Matrimonial Causes Act 1973, s 39. For an example of an order being set aside on the basis that it was made for no consideration see *Re Kumar (A Bankrupt)* [1993] 2 FLR 382. See also *Mountney v Treharne* [2002] 2 FLR 930; *Hill v Haines* [2008] 1 FLR 1192; *Papanicola v Fagan* [2008] EWHC 3348 (Ch); and *Re Jones (A Bankrupt)* [2008] 2 FLR 1969. See **25.31–25.34** for a more detailed discussion of this issue.

[8]    As to which see **6.31**.

[9]    *F v F (Divorce: Insolvency: Annulment of Bankruptcy Order)* [1994] 1 FLR 359; *Couvaras v Wolf* [2002] 2 FLR 107.

[10]    *Whittingham v Whittingham & National Westminster Bank* [1978] 3 All ER 805.

occupy the property so long as the marriage continues.[11] These rights are a charge on the owning spouse's interest in the property[12] and may be registered as a restriction in the case of registered land, or as a Class F land charge in the case of unregistered land. In either case, once registered the charge takes priority over any other interest subsequently taken in the land. The 'home rights' only protect the *right of occupation* of the matrimonial home rather than any beneficial interest in the proceeds of sale of the land. Consequently, the protection such a registration provides is very limited from a financial perspective. The existence of a home rights charge or notice on the Land Register does not by itself provide notice to a lender or purchaser of property that a dealing in the land by the other spouse is made with an intention to defeat the other party's claim to financial relief.[13] Furthermore, such home rights do not provide protection in respect of a property which was never intended to be a matrimonial home. The registration of such a charge is not appropriate where the party seeking to register the charge has no intention of occupying the property. In such circumstances the other party may successfully apply to have the charge removed.[14] There is a danger that where a spouse has left the former matrimonial home and found accommodation elsewhere, a simple Class F land charge may fail to fix any mortgage lender with constructive notice of the wife's beneficial or statutory claims against the property. For example, in *B v B (P Limited Intervening) (No 2)*[15] a wife failed to set aside a mortgage of the former matrimonial home taken by the husband following their separation. The property had been transferred into the husband's sole name following an earlier agreement with the wife, but she applied for ancillary relief. Although the lender became aware of the wife's Class F land charge, the husband managed to have it removed on the basis that the wife had now secured herself a new home. The wife argued that the lender had constructive notice of her claims against the property by reason of the charge. However, the Court of Appeal took the view that the husband's removal of the land charge meant that the lender was not required to make further enquiries of the wife's ancillary claims against the property, and no constructive notice arose.[16]

**6.9**    Land which is not a dwelling house or which was not intended to be the matrimonial home cannot be subject to statutory 'home rights'. Such property

---

[11]  Family Law Act 1996, s 30. The rights were formerly termed 'matrimonial home rights' until amendment by the Civil Partnership Act 2004. The right of occupation can be extended beyond dissolution of the marriage by an order pursuant to s 33(5) of the 1996 Act (see *Ansari v Ansari* [2008] EWCA Civ 1456, where it was anticipated that the wife would seek to have her rights so extended as to give her security of accommodation notwithstanding the sale of the property to third parties and the taking of a mortgage against the property).

[12]  Family Law Act 1996, s 31.

[13]  *Ansari v Ansari* [2008] EWCA Civ 1456, [2009] 1 FLR 1121 at [16].

[14]  *Barnett v Hassett* [1981] 1 WLR 1385.

[15]  [1995] 1 FLR 374.

[16]  The court specifically avoided deciding whether registration of a caution or notice of the ancillary relief claim as a pending land action would have protected the wife; Hoffman LJ described that question as a 'difficult one', and cast some doubt on the decision in *Perez-Adamson v Perez-Rivas* [1987] Fam 89 (as to which see **6.9**).

may form the largest part of the family assets if the parties have substantial interests in investment property, business premises or farmland. Alternatively, the other spouse may simply be interested in other land by way of a charge held over the land rather than being in possession of the land. An application for a property adjustment order, even made in general terms in the divorce petition without identifying any particular property, is a pending land action within s 5 of the Land Charges Act 1972.[17] The pending action is capable of being registered against the title to the property as a notice under Part 4 of the Land Registration Act 2002.[18] The effect of the notice is to ensure that a person taking a subsequent interest in the land takes that interest subject to the interest protected by the charge.[19] This protects the spouse registering the charge to the full extent of the interest in the property given to him or her in the final ancillary relief order, even though that spouse had no subsisting interest in the land at the time of the notice being entered on the register.[20]

**6.10** Sometimes the non-owning spouse may have an equitable claim to a beneficial interest in such a property by reason of a resulting or constructive trust, by way of proprietary estoppel, or pursuant to s 37 of the Matrimonial Proceedings and Property Act 1970. Such a claim could be advanced by proceedings pursuant to s 17 of the Married Women's Property Act 1882 or s 14 of the Trusts of Land and Appointment of Trustees Act 1996,[21] and could also be protected by registration of a notice of the pending land action.

**6.11** Assets other than real estate may be more difficult to protect unilaterally. Moveable chattels can be protected by retaining possession of them or by placing them in the custody of some independent party who will undertake not to release them. The parties may, if each is suspicious of the other's intentions, possibly agree to such an arrangement. The funds in joint bank accounts can often be frozen by asking the bank to require joint signatures for any future transactions, so long as the mandate under which the bank account was opened allows for such a unilateral instruction. Most high street banks are well accustomed to divorcing customers and deal with this situation as a matter of routine. Similarly, other investments held or managed on the parties' joint behalf by some third party may be capable of protection by an instruction to the third party to permit no transactions with those assets without the signatures of both parties.

---

[17] *Whittingham v Whittingham* [1978] 3 All ER 805, CA.
[18] Land Registration Act 2002, s 87(1).
[19] Land Registration Act 2002, ss 29, 30 and 32(3).
[20] *Perez-Adamson v Perez-Rivas* [1987] 2 FLR 472. But see *B v B ( P Limited Intervening) ( No 2)* [1995] 1 FLR 374, where some doubt was cast on this decision.
[21] Although such proceedings are unlikely to be justified if the matter can be resolved fully within ancillary relief proceedings. See *Tebbutt v Haynes* [1981] 2 All ER 238 and *TL v ML* [2005] EWHC 2860 (Fam), [2006] 1 FCR 465.

## UNDERTAKINGS

**6.12** Where there are concerns that one or other party may seek to dispose of assets or deal with them in a way which could frustrate the ancillary relief application, but the risk of this happening is not immediate, a request may be made for an undertaking that such steps will not be taken. Often such a request is backed by the threat of an immediate application to the court for an injunctive order if the undertaking is not proffered. Indeed, where the circumstances allow for such a request to be made, it will usually be desirable to do so. Not only will this strengthen a claim for costs against the unco-operative party if an application to the court is necessary and an order granted, but the refusal to offer the undertaking will also form part of the evidence presented to the court to support the assertion that there is a real risk of a disposition occurring if the order is not granted, although the refusal need not, taken by itself, justify an order being made by the court.[22]

**6.13** In the context of ancillary relief proceedings, undertakings take two forms. The first form is an informal undertaking given in correspondence. Such an undertaking carries no penal sanction by the court in the event of its breach. It may provide very useful future evidence of a party's lack of good faith if he subsequently fails to abide by it. It may also form a contractual obligation which, if not complied with, may found a civil action for damages, although this is unlikely to provide any benefit to the wronged party over and above the orders the court is able to make in the ancillary relief proceedings. Where, however, a third party such as a solicitor also gives an undertaking to guard some asset, a breach of that undertaking may provide a useful remedy in damages.

**6.14** The second form of undertaking is a formal undertaking given to the court. Commonly this is simply set out in the preamble to an order of the court. It may result from a compromise in relation to an application for an injunctive order or as a result of negotiations at a directions hearing. If it is not intended to impose a penal sanction for breach of the undertaking, it will be preferable to refer to the party's 'agreement' rather than 'undertaking', so as to avoid uncertainty. Such an undertaking is likely to be of contractual effect between the parties[23] and may also be capable of enforcement by way of proceedings for committal for contempt of court.

**6.15** Where a penal sanction for breach of an undertaking is intended, good practice suggests that the undertaking should be given on the appropriate court

[22] See, for example, *Shipman v Shipman* [1991] 1 FLR 250.
[23] *Atkinson v Castan* (1991) The Times, April 17. An undertaking which has contractual effect between the parties can usually be enforced by way of an application in the existing proceedings, rather than by requiring the issue of a fresh action. The remedy may be an order for specific performance of the agreement or an award of damages. Even if the undertaking is expressed to be to the court rather than to the other party, it may still be possible to construe it as having contractual effect between the parties: *Independiente Ltd v Music Trading Online (HK) Ltd* (unreported) 26 January 2007, CA.

form,[24] which sets out the penal consequences for breach and requires the signature of the party giving the undertaking to indicate his or her agreement and understanding of its terms. The use of this form avoids any possibility of the party giving the undertaking subsequently arguing that he or she did not agree to its terms or that the consequences of breach were not explained.[25] An undertaking appearing in clear and unambiguous terms on the face of a court order can potentially be enforced in the event of breach by committal proceedings, even if the undertaking is in terms which the court could not have ordered. It has been held in the context of public law children proceedings that the county court cannot accept binding undertakings in a form which the court could not have ordered.[26] However, that decision was in the context of the very limited coercive powers which the county court had when making a supervision order under s 31 of the Children Act 1989. That decision is certainly not directly binding on a court in ancillary relief proceedings. In the context of ancillary relief proceedings, Lord Brandon of Oakbrook in *Livesey (formerly Jenkins) v Jenkins*[27] had no hesitation in stating that undertakings given in terms which could not have been ordered by the court could be enforced by committal proceedings as if they were orders of the court, albeit that these comments were made obiter.[28] In *L v L*[29] Munby J confirmed that public policy means that the court can and will enforce undertakings voluntarily given to the court, even if the undertaking relates to something which the court could not have ordered.

**6.16** Although undertakings to safeguard assets are usually given in absolute terms, it should be noted that undertakings to use 'best endeavours' may, in an appropriate case, be enforced by an order for specific performance.[30] Such an undertaking, if validly given to the court and in sufficiently clear terms, may also justify committal proceedings being taken for its breach. In many cases, however, the difficulty will be in proving beyond reasonable doubt that the person who gave the undertaking has not used their best endeavours.

**6.17** If, subsequent to an undertaking being given and accepted by the court, there is reason to doubt the enforceability of the undertaking (e g where it is intended that third parties should be bound or there is some doubt as to whether the other party properly gave the undertaking), it may be necessary to

---

[24] Form N117 in the county court.
[25] Note that as long these requirements are met it is not necessary for a copy of the order complete with penal notice to be served on the party giving the undertaking: see commentary in White Book to RSC Ord 45, r 5(3).
[26] *Re B (A Minor) (Supervision Order: Parental Undertaking)* [1996] 1 FLR 676.
[27] [1985] FLR 813 at 829.
[28] See also *Gandolfo v Gandolfo* [1981] QB 359 and *Symmons v Symmons* [1993] 1 FLR 317. Outside the matrimonial context see *Kensington Housing Trust v Oliver* (1997) 30 HLR 608 at 611, where Butler-Sloss LJ said, 'Undertakings are convenient since a party can promise to do or abstain from that which a court would be unable to order. In that way an undertaking may cover a situation not capable of being the subject of a court order.'
[29] [2008] 1 FLR 26.
[30] *Bluzwed Metals Ltd v Trans-World Metals SA* [2006] EWHC 143 (Civ), unreported decision of Sir Andrew Morritt V-C on 26 January 2006.

apply to the court to convert the undertaking into an injunction bearing a penal notice, although the court is likely to require evidence to persuade it that this step is necessary.

## PROTECTION BY WAY OF INJUNCTIVE ORDER

**6.18** There are various forms of order which may be used to prevent dissipation of assets. Those which are usually encountered in ancillary relief proceedings, and are the subject matter of this chapter, are:

- an order restraining dispositions or dealings with property pursuant to s 37(2)(a) of the Matrimonial Causes Act 1973;

- a general civil injunction;

- a specialist form of injunction or order such as a *Mareva* or freezing order, or a writ ne exeat regno.

**6.19** It is generally open to a party to proceedings to choose the type of order to seek. In appropriate circumstances the application will seek more than one type of order. The grounds for making the different types of order are different and this may dictate which is considered most appropriate in a particular case. Similarly, the effect of each type of order is different and one may suit the circumstances of a particular case better than another.

## A RESTRAINING ORDER PURSUANT TO S 37(2)(A) OF THE MATRIMONIAL CAUSES ACT 1973[31]

**6.20** The parts of s 37 relevant to restraining orders read as follows:

'(1) For the purposes of this section "financial relief" means relief under any of the provisions of sections 22, 23, 24, 24B, 27, 31 (except subsection (6)) and 35 above, and any reference in this section to defeating a person's claim for financial relief is a reference to preventing financial relief from being granted to that person, or to that person for the benefit of a child of the family, or reducing the amount of any financial relief which might be so granted, or frustrating or impeding the enforcement of any order which might be … made at his instance under any of those provisions.

(2) Where proceedings for financial relief are brought by one person against another, the court may, on the application of the first-mentioned person—

---

[31]   MCA 1973, s 37 also contains provisions (at s 37(2)(b) and (c)) empowering the court to set aside certain dispositions which have already been made. These provisions are considered in Chapter 7.

(a)   if it is satisfied that the other party to the proceedings is, with the intention of defeating the claim for financial relief, about to make any disposition or to transfer out of the jurisdiction or otherwise deal with any property, make such order as it thinks fit for restraining the other party from so doing or otherwise for protecting the claim;

...

(5) Where an application is made under this section with respect to ... a disposition or other dealing with property which is about to take place and the court is satisfied—

(a)   in a case falling within subsection (2)(a) ... above, that the disposition or other dealing would (apart from this section) have the consequence ...

...

of defeating the applicant's claim for financial relief, it shall be presumed, unless the contrary is shown, that the person who ... is about to dispose of or deal with the property ... is about to do so, with the intention of defeating the applicant's claim for financial relief.

(6) In this section "disposition" does not include any provision contained in a will or codicil but, with that exception, includes any conveyance, assurance or gift of property of any description, whether made by an instrument or otherwise.'

## What is the nature and extent of an order made pursuant to s 37(2)(a)?

**6.21**   The order is a form of injunction, but made under a specific statutory provision, so the form of order must be one which the court is empowered to make strictly within the terms of the statute.

**6.22**   The section is addressed to preventing dealings with an asset. Any order made under the section should be prohibitory and not mandatory. An order pursuant to MCA 1973, s 37(2)(a) may prevent a person doing something he wishes to do, but it cannot be used to compel a person to do something he would not otherwise do, even if the failure to act may result in the loss of an asset or a reduction in its value. In *Crittenden v Crittenden*[32] the wife sought an order pursuant to s 37(2)(a) requiring the husband to sign a letter of intent agreeing to sell the family business. The Court of Appeal held that there was no power under that provision to make such an order.[33] Similarly, in *Field v Field*[34] a wife was rebuffed in her attempt to use s 37(2)(a) to force the husband to draw

---

[32]   [1990] 2 FLR 361, CA.
[33]   The court left open the question of whether a similar requirement could be forced upon the husband upon the making of the final order by way of the provisions of s 24A of the Act; see [1990] 2 FLR 361 at 367. That question does not yet appear to have been answered in the reported case law.
[34]   [2003] 1 FLR 376.

the maximum lump sum under his pension so that she could enforce a lump sum order against the funds so produced.[35] By analogy with those cases, the section could not be used, for example, to require a party to renew a lease over a property, to take up a lucrative option to acquire shares or land, or to take steps to preserve an asset from the legitimate claims of third parties, no matter how financially beneficial for both parties it would be if that step were to be taken.

**6.23** The provision is not limited to restraining disposals of property to a third party. It applies to any form of dealing with the asset. It includes mortgaging or charging a property. In *Shipman v Shipman*[36] a husband sought to place a limited interpretation on the section by arguing that his reasonable use of a lump sum paid to him as severance pay for a deposit on a house, to maintain himself or to pay existing debts would not amount to a disposition within the meaning of the section. The court rejected that argument and noted that not only would such transactions be 'dispositions', but they would also amount to the husband seeking to 'deal' with the property within the meaning of the section.

**6.24** The order may only be addressed to the other party to the proceedings and his property. It cannot be used directly against third parties.[37] Where an order is required against a third party, e g a bank, this would more properly be by way of an injunction or *Mareva* order addressed to the third party (see below).[38]

**6.25** Although the section refers to disposals or dispositions of 'any property', this cannot be read as referring to any property generally. It is limited to the property in which either or both of the parties to the marriage has a beneficial interest, either in possession or reversion.[39] Section 37(2)(a) is an aid to giving effect to the powers contained in ss 23–24 of the Act and, as the references to 'property' in those sections clearly refer to the property of the parties to the marriage, the word must bear the same meaning in s 37. An order cannot be

---

[35] The wife also sought a general injunction pursuant to s 37 of the Supreme Court Act 1981. This was also held to be inapt as a means of enforcement on the basis that 'Injunctions can be granted thereunder only for the purposes of protecting legal or equitable rights' and citing dicta of Lord Brandon of Oakbrook in *Richards v Richards* [1984] FLR 11 at 35 in support. On this basis it seems that a general civil injunction may also be limited to prohibitory rather than mandatory use in such interlocutory circumstances, although the width of the words used in s 37 of the Supreme Court Act 1981 (see **6.48**) does not apparently limit the court's discretion in this way.

[36] [1991] 1 FLR 250.

[37] MCA 1973, s 37(2)(a) refers only to 'the other party to the proceedings'. Where a third party is a company being the other party's alter ego, the court may pierce the corporate veil and treat the company's assets as the assets of the other party (see **6.22**). An order will bind third parties to the same extent as a *Mareva* injunction, preventing them from taking steps which assist the other party in breaching the order: see **6.83–6.88**.

[38] In *Graham v Graham* [1992] 2 FLR 406 at 409 Purchas LJ described an order preventing a building society from allowing withdrawals to be made from an account as a 'very ordinary precaution'.

[39] *Crittenden v Crittenden* [1990] 2 FLR 361 at 365.

made under this section which prevents dealings with the assets of a company, even if the parties own all the shares in that company.[40] Where there is concern about the manner in which the assets of a family company are being dealt with by a spouse who controls that company, a general civil injunction restraining his actions may be appropriate.

**6.26**  An order may be made in relation to property situated abroad. Although the English courts generally have no jurisdiction over property abroad, an order under s 37(2)(a) does not act against the property but against the other party. The order applies in personam rather than in rem.[41] Nevertheless, the court will not make an order which will be ineffective, either because the law in the jurisdiction where the property is situated so provides or for some other reason.[42] It should be noted that the effectiveness of an order goes to the question of the court's discretion in making an order rather than to the jurisdiction to make the order. As the burden of proving that foreign law differs from English law lies on the person making that assertion,[43] it will usually be the respondent to the application who will be required to produce the evidence that the order will be ineffective abroad. Nevertheless, the court may well look to the applicant for reassurance through evidence that the order will be effective, particularly where the case concerns a foreign jurisdiction of which the English courts have little experience and judicial notice cannot be taken of the law in that country.

**6.27**  Certain types of dealing with property fall outside the scope of protection offered by s 37(2)(a). The most commonly encountered exceptions are considered at **6.28–6.30**.

## *Surrender of a statutory tenancy*

**6.28**  The surrender of a statutory tenancy is not a *disposition* of property within the meaning of the section, although the statutory tenancy is 'property' for the purposes of the Matrimonial Causes Act 1973.[44] A statutory 'right to buy' under a secure tenancy is not property within the meaning of the section and cannot be protected independently of the tenancy which gives rise to the

---

[40]  *Crittenden v Crittenden* [1990] 2 FLR 361; *Harrison v Harrison* [2008] 2 FLR 35. Although it may be that where the company is wholly owned by one of the parties to the marriage and is his or her alter ego, the court may take the view that the assets of the company are effectively the assets of the party and make the order accordingly. See also *McGladdery v McGladdery* [1999] 2 FLR 1102. The circumstances in which the corporate veil can be pierced in this way are considered in detail in Chapter 11. Note that the court may make a *Mareva* order, which may indirectly bind a third party in some circumstances (see below).

[41]  But see the dicta of Munby J in *Re A* [2002] Fam 213 to the effect that there is a proprietary aspect to the rights created by an order pursuant to s 37(2)(a).

[42]  *Hamlin v Hamlin* [1986] 1 FLR 61.

[43]  This allocation of the burden of proof is sometimes elevated to the status of a legal presumption that the foreign law is the same as English law: see e g *Re W ( Ex Parte Orders)* [2000] 2 FLR 927 at 940; *University of Glasgow v The Economist* (1990) The Times, July 13 (in the context of the law of defamation).

[44]  *Newlon Housing Trust v Alsulaimen* [1998] 2 FLR 690, HL. See also avoidance of disposition orders at **7.15**.

right.[45] The question of whether the surrender of such a tenancy might be a 'dealing' with the property and therefore capable of being restrained by an order pursuant to s 37(2)(a) appears to remain open, although obiter dicta by Thorpe LJ in *Bater and Bater v Greenwich London Borough Council*[46] suggest that the broad language of s 37(2)(a) covers such a situation.[47] In any event, the threat of such a surrender appears to be capable of restraint by way of a specific civil injunction made under the powers contained in the Supreme Court Act 1981 and the County Courts Act 1984.

## Trusts

**6.29** In the case of a discretionary trust of which both spouses are beneficiaries, one party may have the power to remove the other as a beneficiary or in some other way to limit his or her rights to benefit from the trust. Such a step would appear not to amount to a 'disposition' of property.[48] It remains an open question as to whether such an act would amount to a 'dealing' with the property. The case law referred to at **6.28** suggests that the argument that it amounts to a 'dealing' with the property remains available, although there are clear difficulties in bringing the inchoate rights of a beneficiary of a discretionary trust within the definition of 'property'.

## Pension schemes

**6.30** A party's rights under most pension schemes do not amount to a beneficial interest in the funds or investments held in the pension scheme. It seems to follow that such a pension arrangement is not property which can be subject to an order pursuant to s 37(2)(a).[49] This may cause difficulties in the context of certain types of scheme where the beneficiary of the scheme is able to determine to some extent how the assets held by the scheme are to be managed, eg in a Self Invested Personal Pension (SIPP) or a Small Self-Administered Scheme (SSAS). A party to ancillary relief proceedings may be tempted to convert the investments in such a scheme into a form which will make a pension sharing order much more difficult to implement or less attractive to the other party. In such circumstances it may be necessary to apply for a general civil injunction restraining the other party from dealing with the pension fund in such a prejudicial fashion.

---

[45] *Bater and Bater v Greenwich London Borough Council* [1999] 2 FLR 993, CA.
[46] [1999] 2 FLR 993, CA.
[47] The authors are aware of anecdotal evidence of such orders regularly being made by county courts upon applications made ostensibly under s 37(2)(a), although it is not always clear whether the order was made pursuant to s 37(2)(a) of the MCA 1973 or as a general civil injunction.
[48] *Mubarak v Mubarak* [2007] 2 FLR 364 at [69]–[77].
[49] *Field v Field* [2003] 1 FLR 376 seems to imply this, without expressly deciding this particular point.

## Payment of money into court

**6.31** It appears to be within the court's power under s 37 to order the respondent to pay money into court or to his solicitor to be held to the order of the court.[50] Once this is done, the applicant becomes a secured creditor in relation to the monies. This is potentially very useful in the event that the respondent becomes bankrupt following the making of the restraining order, because the funds held under the order would not be part of the bankrupt estate. The authors suggest, however, that it is likely to be considered to be an abuse of process to seek such an order with the sole purpose of frustrating the claims of creditors pursued through a bankruptcy order. Where the order is justified under s 37 on bona fide grounds, on the other hand, the trustee in bankruptcy may have more difficulty in having it set aside.

## What needs to be established to obtain an order pursuant to s 37(2)(a)?

**6.32** If the disposition or dealing which is to be restrained falls within the scope of s 37(2)(a) (see preceding paragraphs of this chapter), the court has the jurisdiction to make an order so long as the other required criteria are met, as follows.

### Claim for 'financial relief'

**6.33** First, there must be a claim for 'financial relief', meaning an application for maintenance pending suit, periodical payment orders, a lump sum order, property adjustment orders, variation of settlement orders, or a maintenance order.[51] An application for variation of an order is also included in this definition.

### Disposition or dealing about to be made

**6.34** Secondly, the court must be satisfied that the other party to the proceedings is about to make a disposition or transfer out of the jurisdiction or otherwise deal with any property.[52] The statute does not indicate what level of proof is required to 'satisfy' the court. The word 'satisfied' in the context of an earlier matrimonial statute has been defined as requiring proof on the balance of probabilities.[53] This approach has been confirmed in the context of s 37.[54] It seems clear from the wording of the section and the case law that the burden of proving this lies on the applicant. It will not be enough to raise a suspicion alone. There must be evidence that the other party is, in fact, about to act.[55] In

---

[50] *Graham v Graham* [1992] 2 FLR 406; *Re Mordant* [1996] 1 FLR 334.
[51] MCA 1973, s 37(1).
[52] MCA 1973, s 37(2)(a).
[53] *Blyth v Blyth* [1966] AC 643.
[54] *K v K (avoidance of reviewable disposition)* (1983) 4 FLR 31; *Kemmis v Kemmis* [1988] 1 WLR 1307; *Trowbridge v Trowbridge* [2003] 2 FLR 231; and *Mubarak v Mubarak* [2007] 2 FLR 364.
[55] *Smith v Smith* (1974) 4 Fam Law 80.

some cases there will have been some preparatory act or direct threat by the other party which provides the evidence that a disposition or dealing is about to be made. More often, however, there will be no such direct evidence of the other party's intentions and the court will be asked to infer from circumstantial evidence that such a disposition or dealing is imminent. In such cases the evidence relied upon will be the same evidence which is used to prove that the other party is motivated to 'defeat the claim for financial relief', and so this is considered further in the next section. In simple terms, where an applicant is able to provide convincing evidence of an intention by the other party to frustrate the claim for financial relief, the court will in most cases be able to find that the other party also intends to make the disposition, transfer or dealing to put the intention into effect. The applicant may not, however, have any clear direct evidence of the respondent's intention and may need to rely on the statutory presumption contained in s 37(5). It is important to note that the statutory presumption of an intention to defeat the claim for financial relief in s 37(5) only arises once it has been proved both that a disposition is about to take place and that the disposition would have the consequence of defeating the applicant's claim for financial relief. It is important that the respondent who opposes such an application ensures that the applicant is fully put to proof of these preconditions to the statutory presumption arising.

## *Intention to defeat the claim*

**6.35**   Thirdly, it must be shown that the disposition, transfer or dealing is to be made with the intention of defeating the claim for financial relief. 'Defeating the claim' is broadly defined as preventing financial relief being granted to the other person for himself or for the benefit of a child of the family, reducing the amount of financial relief which might be granted, or frustrating or impeding the enforcement of any order.[56] It should be noted that this broad definition means that a restraining order may be granted at an early stage in the proceedings even if the threatened disposition, if made, could be set aside in due course pursuant to the powers contained in s 37(2)(b) or (c). The burden of proving that the intention exists falls on the applicant, although the applicant is assisted by the statutory presumption at s 37(5) that the person who is proved to be about to dispose of or deal with the property does so with the intention of defeating the applicant's claim. Unless the respondent is able to provide credible evidence to rebut the presumption, the applicant will have proved the required intention without needing to provide any other evidence. It is important to note, however, that the presumption only arises once the applicant has shown on the evidence that a disposition or other dealing with the property is about to take place (see above). The presumption will, therefore, be of considerable use at an ex parte application for an order so long as convincing evidence of an imminent dealing can be provided to the court. On an inter partes hearing, in the absence of any evidence as to intention apart from the respondent's own evidence, the presumption ought to be relatively easy to

---

[56]   MCA 1973, s 37(1).

rebut.[57] It will be rare that the applicant adduces no evidence of the respondent's intention and relies on the statutory presumption alone. The standard of proof remains the balance of probabilities.[58] It is now clear that there is only one standard of civil proof, being the 'more probably than not' test.[59] There is no longer scope for a respondent to argue that the allegation is that he is motivated by a dishonest or fraudulent intention to defeat the other party's lawful claims against him, with the consequence that more cogent evidence may be required to satisfy the court that he has the alleged intention.[60] The particular problems of proving a person's intention are considered further at **6.36**.

## *Proof of intention*

**6.36** It is important to remember that if a respondent seeks to rebut the presumption of intention to defeat the claim, his subjective intention will be in issue.[61] The consequences of his acts may assist in determining what the intentions behind the act may have been, but they cannot be determinative of the question of intention.[62] The intention to defeat the claims does not need to be the sole intention behind the other party's acts or even the dominant intention. It seems that it will suffice 'if it played a substantial part in his intentions as a whole'.[63] If the respondent is able to show a valid reason for the dealing he is about to carry out (eg the payment of a pressing debt, non-payment of which could have serious consequences), it may be that the court is persuaded that there is no substantial intention to defeat the applicant's claims. Where, on the other hand, there is no reasonable necessity in the proposed dealing and the effect of the transaction will be to make satisfaction of the applicant's claims more difficult, the court will, especially at the interim stage of proceedings when a s 37(2)(a) order is sought, probably have little difficulty in being satisfied of the required intention.

## *The discretion to make the order*

**6.37** Fourthly, if all the preconditions required by s 37(2)(a) are satisfied, the court still retains an overall discretion as to whether the order should be made

---

[57] See eg *Shipman v Shipman* [1991] 1 FLR 250, where the presumption was rebutted by a husband who showed he had made full disclosure of his assets, had maintained his wife without pressure from the court, and had kept his wife fully informed of his intentions as to the disputed assets.

[58] *Kemmis v Kemmis* [1988] 1 WLR 1307 and *Trowbridge v Trowbridge* [2003] 2 FLR 231.

[59] *Re B (Care Proceedings: Standard of Proof)* [2008] 2 FLR 141.

[60] This had been suggested in *Kemmis v Kemmis* [1988] 2 FLR 223 at 246 per Nourse LJ and *Trowbridge v Trowbridge* [2003] 2 FLR 231 at 248. Even before the decision in *Re B* by the House of Lords there had been doubts expressed that any higher level of proof was required in this context: *Mubarak v Mubarak* [2007] 2 FLR 364. See also the section on 'Standard of proof' at **2.28–2.33**.

[61] *Kemmis v Kemmis* [1988] 1 WLR 1307. See also Holman J's helpful summary of the law in *Mubarak v Mubarak* [2007] 2 FLR 364 at [53]–[55].

[62] *Kemmis v Kemmis* [1988] 1 WLR 1307 at 1326 per Lloyd LJ.

[63] *Kemmis v Kemmis* [1988] 1 WLR 1307 at 1330 1 per Nourse LJ.

or not and as to the extent and form of the order. In most cases, given that the court must be satisfied of an intention on the respondent's part to defeat the applicant's claim, it will be clear that the intended disposition or dealing must be prevented and the order should be made. Nevertheless, in exercising its discretion judicially, the court must look at the circumstances in the round before making the order. In an appropriate case there may be compelling reasons as to why the order should not be made, or why it should be made but in a narrower form than sought by the applicant.

## What is the procedure for applying for an order pursuant to s 37(2)(a)?

**6.38**　An application for a restraining order pursuant to s 37(2)(a) may also be accompanied by an application for a *Mareva* order or other general civil injunction, and reference should be made to the sections dealing with those forms of order below.

**6.39**　Jurisdiction to make the order only exists if there is an application for financial relief. Accordingly, there must be a petition for divorce, nullity or judicial separation with a claim for ancillary relief and, usually, an intention to proceed with that claim in Form A. So this remedy is not available where a party has not yet decided to seek a decree.

**6.40**　In a case of urgency, the need for an order may arise before the petition has been issued. In such a case the court may, if persuaded that the case is sufficiently urgent, permit the application to be heard upon the undertaking by the applicant or the applicant's solicitor to issue the petition and Form A within a very short time. It is essential that this is done, as the existence of the claim for financial relief is the basis for the court's jurisdiction.[64]

**6.41**　The application will be made by notice of application to the district judge,[65] although the district judge may (either of his own motion or at the request of a party) refer the matter to a judge for his decision.[66] In the county court such a referral is very unusual, as the district judges usually have far more experience of conducting ancillary relief applications than the circuit judge, but in a case where the application is combined with an application for a general civil injunction in the nature of a *Mareva* injunction, the matter may need to be heard by a judge.[67] It may be prudent to ensure at the time of listing that the district judge will accept jurisdiction.

---

[64]　See **6.64–6.74** for the analogous procedure for obtaining a *Mareva* order.
[65]　FPR, r 2.68(1). See also FPR, r 10.9, RSC Ord 32 and CCR Ord 13, r 1.
[66]　FPR, r 2.65.
[67]　See **6.66** for the apparently conflicting approaches of the CPR 1998 and the FPR as to the powers of district judges to make *Mareva* orders. The general weight of case law and guidance in practice directions suggest that, in most cases, orders in the form of a *Mareva* should be made by a judge rather than a district judge.

**6.42**   The court will require evidence to make the order. This should be given by sworn statement or affidavit, preferably from the applicant but, in a case of urgency, it may need to be a statement from the applicant's solicitor. Care must be taken to ensure that the statement contains sufficient detail to persuade the court that the criteria for making the order are met. Statements of suspicion alone are unlikely to persuade the court. The statement may need to exhibit correspondence and other documents to present the court with the circumstantial evidence from which the intention to make a disposition can be inferred. Ideally, the exhibits should be paginated for ease of reference. A draft order should also be prepared for the court.

**6.43**   The application will often need to be made without notice to the other party. Where this is so, the evidence should explain why the respondent should not have notice of the application. Court orders made after hearing from only one party carry clear risks of injustice, and parties should be aware of the heavy burden which lies on those who apply for ex parte orders: 'Such orders must not be made without thinking once, twice and three times about the effect they would have.'[68] Furthermore, on an ex parte application the evidence filed must present the case in a form which gives full disclosure of the facts, including those which are adverse to the applicant's case. Failure to do so, or presentation of the material in a potentially misleading fashion may have serious consequences, including a refusal to continue the order when it is reconsidered in the presence of the respondent. Reference should be made to the more detailed discussion of the appropriate procedure when applying ex parte in the context of *Mareva* orders at **6.68–6.74**.

**6.44**   Where the order is made ex parte, it must be served on the respondent promptly, together with the application notice and evidence placed before the court. Indeed, the court should obtain an undertaking from the applicant that this will be done. The order should state on its face that the respondent has the right to apply to vary or set the order aside. It should also set a date for an inter partes hearing. As a matter of good practice it should also set out the evidence and material the court had before it when making the order (see the guidance at **6.70**). It is also important that the applicant's lawyer keeps a note of the ex parte hearing so that this can be provided to the respondent on request.

**6.45**   Where an order was made ex parte, the respondent may apply to vary or set it aside. Where the order as made is likely to cause him immediate and serious prejudice, he may seek to vary it or set it aside by way of an urgent ex parte application to the court. For this reason it is important that the order makes clear what evidence the court had before it when the order was made, as the judge who hears the application to set the order aside may be a different judge from the one who made it. Such an application will be rare, and more commonly the respondent will apply on notice to the other party or simply await the inter partes hearing.

---

[68]   *Jackson v Jackson* (1979) 9 Fam Law 56 per Stamp LJ.

**6.46**  Where the hearing proceeds on an inter partes basis, it will normally be limited to a consideration of the written evidence produced by the parties. As this is an interim remedy, the court is generally reluctant to embark upon a detailed consideration and resolution of contested matters of fact. Nevertheless, the court is obliged by the statute to be 'satisfied' on the balance of probabilities and, in an appropriate case, it may need to hear oral evidence from the parties to determine the matter, although this would be very rare in the context of an interim order. A party may seek to avoid having adverse findings of fact made by offering an undertaking without making any admissions.

**6.47**  It is unusual to require an undertaking in damages from the applicant as a condition of the grant of an order pursuant to MCA 1973, s 37(2)(a), particularly as the order will normally only affect the parties to the proceedings, and the court has broad discretionary powers to do justice between them in the event that the restraining order causes the respondent harm.[69]

## CIVIL INJUNCTIONS

**6.48**  The High Court has a breathtakingly wide discretion to grant injunctions conferred upon it by s 37(1) of the Supreme Court Act 1981:

> 'The High Court may by order (whether interlocutory or final) grant an injunction ... in all cases in which it appears to the court to be just and convenient to do so.'

This statutory power is fortified, as necessary, by the High Court's inherent jurisdiction.

**6.49**  The county court has similar statutory powers conferred on it by s 38(1) of the County Courts Act 1984, although certain orders which may be made in the High Court are not permissible in the county court, including those which arise as a result of the High Court's inherent jurisdiction.[70] These include the administrative law orders of mandamus, certiorari and prohibition[71] and search orders (also known as '*Anton Piller* orders'). In general civil litigation the county court is not allowed to grant freezing or *Mareva* injunctions in respect of assets which are not the subject matter of the proceedings until judgment has been obtained,[72] but no such restriction applies to a county court engaged in family proceedings, including proceedings for financial relief ancillary to

---

[69]  *Practice Direction (Injunction: Undertaking as to Damages)* [1974] 1 WLR 576 and *Re W (Ex Parte Orders)* [2000] 2 FLR 927 at 948.

[70]  Unless the judge presiding in the county court happens to be a judge of the High Court or the Court of Appeal, or the county court is asked to vary an order of the High Court where all the parties are agreed as to the variation: County Court Remedies Regulations 1991, regs 3(2)(a) and 3(4)(b).

[71]  County Courts Act 1984, s 38(3)(a).

[72]  County Court Remedies Regulations 1991, regs 2(b) and 3(1), (3).

divorce.[73] In any event, a serious case requiring a wide-ranging *Mareva* injunction, particularly if it is worldwide in its terms, will be better dealt with by a judge of the High Court, who is likely to have greater experience of such matters than a judge of the county court. There is no need to transfer the whole proceedings to the High Court to achieve the remedy. The application may be made to the High Court directly and such an application is deemed to include an application for transfer of the proceedings to the High Court. Once the application is disposed of, the proceedings are automatically transferred back to the county court unless the High Court orders otherwise.[74]

**6.50** Despite the breadth of the wording of s 37 of the Supreme Court Act 1981, the court does not have freedom to make any form of order it sees fit. Injunctions may be granted only to protect legal or equitable rights, including those which arise under statute, such as the Matrimonial Causes Act 1973.[75] Any order made should not go so far as to create or protect rights which would not otherwise arise. In the same vein, an injunction can be used to protect assets to which an ancillary relief order applies, but it cannot be used as a form of enforcement of an ancillary relief order.[76] Nevertheless, there is likely to be somewhat greater flexibility in relation to the scope and effect of an interim injunction granted to protect assets which are the subject matter of the proceedings than might be shown in relation to an injunction made as a final order in a civil dispute. The court may make an order at an interim stage to preserve the status quo pending a full hearing which is wider in its scope than could be justified once the parties' rights have been conclusively determined after a full final hearing.

**6.51** It is clear that the broad injunctive powers apply within s 37 of the Supreme Court Act 1981 in ancillary relief proceedings, notwithstanding the specific power to make a restraining order contained in s 37 of the Matrimonial Causes Act 1973.[77] Thus, in each case the applicant has a choice of remedy. Which is selected will depend on the circumstances of the case. Often the court will be asked to use powers under s 37 of the Matrimonial Causes Act and under its general civil jurisdiction in unison to create the form of order which is required. The parties to the application need to be careful to ensure that the court approaches the matter on the correct basis.

**6.52** When considering the different jurisdictions there are several factors to be mindful of:

---

[73] County Court Remedies Regulations 1991, reg 3(3)(a).

[74] County Court Remedies Regulations 1991, regs 4 and 5.

[75] *North London Railway Co v Great Northern Railway Co* (1883) 11 QBD 30; *Mareva Compania Naviera SA v International Bulkcarriers SA* [1975] 2 Lloyd's Rep 509 at 510 per Lord Denning MR; *Field v Field* [2003] 1 FLR 376 at 381.

[76] *Field v Field* [2003] 1 FLR 376 at 381.

[77] *Roche v Roche* (1981) 1 Fam Law 243; *Walker v Walker* (1983) 4 FLR 455; *Shipman v Shipman* [1991] 1 FLR 250. See also dicta of Thorpe LJ in *Bater and Bater v Greenwich London Borough Council* [1999] 2 FLR 993.

- An order pursuant to s 37(2)(a) of the Matrimonial Causes Act 1973 may only be made if the statutory criteria for such an order are made out (see above). The applicant may be unable to establish the prerequisites for an order pursuant to s 37(2)(a) (ie that a disposition is about to be made or that the respondent has an intention to defeat the applicant's claims), but those factors are not prerequisites for the court making a general civil injunction in the interim period.[78]

- A general injunctive order on an interim basis under the court's general jurisdiction will be granted on the 'balance of convenience' test.[79] There is no such requirement in relation to s 37(2)(a), although the court still retains a discretion as to whether to make the order, even if all the grounds are established and a judicial exercise of discretion will require a balancing of the respective rights of the parties. Even in the context of a general civil injunction in family proceedings between divorcing spouses, the court is likely to adopt a more flexible approach than might be appropriate in commercial proceedings between business enterprises.[80]

- A general injunctive order made under the court's general jurisdiction may be much broader in scope than an order pursuant to s 37(2)(a). It may be useful in the sorts of circumstances when a s 37(2)(a) order is ineffective (see **6.21–6.30**). For example, a general injunction may be used to restrain one party from taking steps which would oust the other party from the board of a jointly owned company,[81] to prevent the other party from surrendering a joint tenancy,[82] or to preserve assets which are not yet in existence.[83] It will also be of use when it is necessary to restrain dealings by persons other than the other party to the ancillary relief proceedings.[84]

- It is unusual to require an undertaking in damages from the applicant as a condition of the grant of an injunction in family proceedings, because the court has broad discretionary powers to do justice between the parties in the event the restraining order causes the respondent harm.[85] Where a third party is likely to be affected by the order, however, justice may well demand that an undertaking be given.[86] In such a case the applicant for an

---

[78] *Shipman v Shipman* [1991] 1 FLR 250. But see the suggestion in *The Law Society v Shanks* [1988] 1 FLR 504 at 507, albeit in the context of an application for a *Mareva* order, that in the absence of evidence of an intention on the part of the respondent 'to defeat the due processes of the law' the injunction should not be granted.

[79] *American Cyanamid Co v Ethicon Ltd* [1975] AC 396, HL.

[80] *Shipman v Shipman* [1991] 1 FLR 250 at 253.

[81] *Poon v Poon* [1994] 2 FLR 857. See also **11.22**.

[82] Obiter dicta of Thorpe LJ in *Bater and Bater v Greenwich London Borough Council* [1999] 2 FLR 993.

[83] *Roche v Roche* (1981) 11 Fam Law 243.

[84] Section 37 of the Matrimonial Causes Act 1973 is limited by its terms to orders made in respect of the parties to the marriage alone.

[85] *Practice Direction (Injunction: Undertaking as to Damages)* [1974] 1 WLR 576 and *Re W (Ex Parte Orders)* [2000] 2 FLR 927 at 948.

[86] *Re W (Ex Parte Orders)* [2000] 2 FLR 927 at 949.

order must understand the potential liability he or she faces in respect of such an undertaking in the event that the court ultimately finds that the injunction was unjustified.

## General procedure for applying for a civil injunction

**6.53** As an order sought in family proceedings, the application for an injunction remains governed by the Family Proceedings Rules 1991 and the RSC and CCR as they stood prior to the introduction of the CPR 1998.[87] The practice and procedure will be similar to that set out for an application pursuant to MCA 1973, s 37(2)(a) at **6.41**. Strictly speaking, the rules require the filing of a notice of application in the county court[88] or a notice of motion or a summons in the High Court[89] with an affidavit in support. Unless the application is made ex parte or time for service has been abridged, the notice and supporting evidence should be served on the respondent not less than 2 clear days before the hearing.

**6.54** Nevertheless, in practice, the court is likely to be influenced by the procedures introduced for the grant of such injunctions in civil proceedings by the CPR 1998, particularly in the context of more Draconian orders, such as a *Mareva* injunction.[90] This may be even more so when the application is made by way of a freestanding application in the Family Division of the High Court in relation to proceedings pending in the county court.[91] Although the application remains 'quintessentially a matrimonial matter'[92] and the 'old' civil rules apply, the authors submit that the appropriate procedure to follow in most cases, and particularly those made in the High Court in pending county court proceedings, is as follows:

- Make the application by way of the form prescribed for interim applications by CPR Part 23,[93] although, because the CPR does not apply to such an application, a general notice of application will suffice in the county court or a summons in the High Court.[94] The application should

---

[87]    *Rhode v Rhode* [2007] 2 FLR 971.

[88]    CCR Ord 13, r 1.

[89]    RSC Ord 29, r 1.

[90]    *Re S (Ex Parte Orders)* [2001] 1 FLR 308 at 318. See also the procedural guide suggested by the editors of *The Family Court Practice* (Family Law, 2009). The Practice Direction to Part 25 of the CPR 1998 is particularly helpful.

[91]    See **6.49**. Guidance as to the conduct of such applications to the High Court incidental to county court proceedings, albeit in the context of non-matrimonial proceedings, was given in *Schmidt v Wong* [2006] 1 WLR 561, where the Court of Appeal held that the application should be made by a Part 23 application form in the Royal Courts of Justice or the appropriate district registry, and the application should contain an explanation that the application is being made in support of intended or pending county court proceedings pursuant to the County Court Remedies Regulations 1991. Such free-standing applications for an injunction may also be necessary in support of divorce proceedings in another jurisdiction (see *Rhode v Rhode* [2007] 2 FLR 971).

[92]    Per Baron J in *Rhode v Rhode* [2007] 2 FLR 971.

[93]    Form N244.

[94]    *Rhode v Rhode* [2007] 2 FLR 971.

state whether it is to be made to the judge or the district judge. In any event, the time estimate for the hearing should be stated on the application and a draft of the order sought should accompany it.[95]

- Support the application with a sworn statement or, if necessary in the circumstances of the case, statements containing the evidence relied upon. Where the application is made ex parte, this must contain a full, frank and candid account of the relevant circumstances of the case (see **6.70**) and explain why the application is made without notice.

- Where time permits, the court should also be provided with a chronology and a skeleton argument, unless the matter is very simple.

- Unless the application is being made ex parte or an order abridging time for service has been made, serve the application and supporting evidence on the respondent. As noted at **6.53**, the provisions of the RSC and CCR require service 2 clear days before the hearing.[96]

## FREEZING OR *MAREVA* INJUNCTIONS[97]

**6.55** A *Mareva* injunction[98] is a species of general civil injunction made pursuant to s 37 of the Supreme Court Act 1981. Since the introduction of the CPR in civil proceedings, the order has been renamed a 'freezing injunction',[99] although it is still commonly referred to as a *Mareva* injunction. Although a *Mareva* injunction is simply one form of injunction made under the court's broad injunctive powers, restraining a person from dealing freely with his property and possessions until a court has fully determined the rights between parties remains a serious infringement of that person's rights and freedoms and, accordingly, special safeguards have arisen around this potentially Draconian remedy. These special rules mean that *Mareva* injunctions merit separate consideration.

---

[95] It will often be helpful, especially in cases where the order is particularly long or complex, to provide the draft order to the court in electronic form at the hearing. This may be on a disk, on some form of removable memory device or, often most conveniently, by email.

[96] CPR Part 23.7 requires 3 clear days' notice to be given, except where another time limit is specified in the CPR or a practice direction. As the CPR does not apply to an application made in family proceedings, it would appear that 2 days' notice will suffice. Where an order is made ex parte it would be prudent to deal with the notice requirements prior to the inter partes hearing within that order to avoid future doubt.

[97] The *Mareva* injunction has become a specialised form of relief which has developed a substantial body of case law around it. This book provides a brief summary of the applicable principles for the matrimonial lawyer's easy reference. In complex cases, especially where the order is intended to have worldwide effect, the reader may need to refer to other specialist texts on the subject, eg the notes to Part 23 in the White Book (Sweet & Maxwell) or *Commercial Injunctions* by Steven Gee QC (Sweet & Maxwell, 5th edn).

[98] The name relates to the first case in which such an order was granted: *Mareva Compania Naviera SA v International Bulkcarriers SA* [1975] 2 Lloyd's Rep 509.

[99] CPR Part 25.1(f).

**6.56** In many respects it is surprising that it was as late as 1975 that the courts recognised the power to make an order restraining a party from disposing of assets pending a final hearing of the proceedings, particularly as the provisions now contained in s 37 of the Supreme Court Act 1981 have been in existence in a virtually identical form since the Supreme Court of Judicature Act 1875. Nevertheless, since the original *Mareva* injunction was granted, the parameters of the remedy and the procedure by which it is obtained have been refined, largely in response to the ever more sophisticated global financial systems now available. The power to make the order now has statutory recognition within s 37(3) of the Supreme Court Act 1981, which allows the court to make an order even if the other party is not domiciled, resident or present in the jurisdiction.

**6.57** This type of order is most commonly used in commercial litigation, where there is a concern that any judgment of the court may be frustrated by the defendant removing from the court's jurisdiction the assets against which any judgment might be levied. In a sense, it provides security for a judgment which might or might not be granted. The order can restrain dealings with assets which are in no way the subject matter of the proceedings and which the claimant would ordinarily have no claim to until a judgment was granted and steps were taken to enforce it. It is plain that a *Mareva* injunction can be of equal use in ancillary relief proceedings. It is particularly useful in the context of a case where one party is reluctant to make full disclosure of his assets and there is a concern that those assets will be put out of reach before their existence can be established through the process of disclosure. However, enforcement of such an order will prove difficult if the assets cannot be identified.

## What is the nature and extent of a *Mareva* injunction?

**6.58** There is no prescribed form for a *Mareva* or freezing order. A suggested draft order is set out in the annex to the Practice Direction to CPR Part 25, but this 'may be modified as appropriate to any particular case'.[100] Indeed, it is important to ensure that the order is carefully prepared so as properly to protect the applicant's interests, but also to ensure that the order does not restrict the respondent's freedom unnecessarily.[101] The proper scope of an order and some of the consequences of seeking an order which extends further than necessary are considered at **6.78–6.88**.

**6.59** The order can apply to assets within the jurisdiction and, if necessary, the assets worldwide. Worldwide orders are not routine, and special circumstances will be required to justify the order.[102] However, as with orders

---

[100]  Practice Direction to CPR Part 25, para 6.2.

[101]  It is generally impermissible to use the slip rule to correct errors in injunctive orders of this sort and so any failure to draft the order properly may make its enforcement difficult, if not impossible: *Langley v Langley* [1994] 1 FLR 383.

[102]  *Derby v Weldon (No 1)* [1989] 1 All ER 469, where it was held that such orders will only be made in exceptional cases. The fact that there was a good arguable case and a real risk of

pursuant to s 37(2)(a) of the Matrimonial Causes Act 1973 (see **6.26**), one eye needs to be kept on the enforceability of the order in relation to assets which are overseas, particularly where the respondent to the application is not within the jurisdiction either, making enforcement more difficult.[103] As with orders pursuant to s 37(2)(a), a *Mareva* injunction acts in personam rather than in rem, and is usually enforced by way of a committal application. Furthermore, where third parties are directly or indirectly bound by the order, the court needs to ensure that they are not unduly prejudiced by the order (see **6.83–6.88**). When deciding to make an order in respect of assets overseas, the court will consider whether there are reciprocal enforcement provisions with the state where the assets in question are located,[104] although this will not prevent the order being made where the evidence suggests that the respondent is likely to evade enforcement of any judgment notwithstanding the reciprocal enforcement provisions.

**6.60**  Although a *Mareva* injunction can restrain dealings with a person's assets even if those assets cannot be specified and set out in the order, there needs to be some realism when applying for such an order. For example, if it is known that the respondent must have funds in various bank accounts overseas but it is not known where those accounts are held or even which institution holds them, it will be enormously difficult to enforce the order and the court may decline to make it.[105] Similarly, if the assets sought to be restrained are only a small and perhaps insignificant part of the total assets under consideration in the case, the court may decline to make the order on the basis that the effect of the order would be disproportionate to the benefits it brings.[106]

**6.61**  The form of freezing order set out in the annex to the Practice Direction to CPR Part 25 includes a clause routinely added to *Mareva* injunctions requiring the respondent to provide full disclosure of all his assets in the form of a sworn statement. In a commercial case the parties are not usually obliged to provide each other with full financial disclosure as to their respective means, so this is an important provision to make the order effective. Such a provision may be unnecessary in an ancillary relief case where separate disclosure orders

---

disposal of assets within the jurisdiction did not justify the grant of a worldwide *Mareva* injunction. In that case a worldwide order was justified by the following factors: (1) insufficiency of assets within the jurisdiction; (2) substantial assets outside the jurisdiction; (3) D's ability to render assets untraceable; (4) D's unwillingness to reveal the present extent and location of assets; and (5) high risk of disposal of assets. Clearly, many similar factors will be present in ancillary relief litigation, but practitioners should not overlook the costs and complexities involved in making such orders.

[103]  It should also be noted that where the court makes a worldwide *Mareva* injunction, it is for the English court to determine whether and to what extent the applicant should be able to enforce it through foreign courts, and the court may require the applicant for such an injunction to undertake not to seek to enforce the order abroad without first obtaining the court's permission: *Dadourian Group International Inc v Simms* [2005] 2 All ER 651.

[104]  *Montecchi v Shemco Ltd* [1979] 1 WLR 1180.

[105]  *Araghchinchi v Araghchinchi* [1997] 2 FLR 142.

[106]  See eg *Rasu Maritima v Perushan Pertambangan* [1978] QB 644, CA, where the assets to be subjected to the order were a 'drop in the ocean' compared to the size of the claim being made.

may already have been made. Where the application for the order is made at a very early stage in proceedings, or even before proceedings have commenced, such a provision may be required. There is provision in RSC Ord 29, r 1A for the court to require the respondent to answer questions under cross-examination as to the sworn statement of means. Even in commercial proceedings, this step is considered exceptional[107] and it seems unlikely to be a favoured course in ancillary relief proceedings where there are ample alternative methods for obtaining disclosure of such matters (see Chapters 4 and 5).

**6.62**   A *Mareva* or freezing injunction offers some protection to third parties affected by the order. The effect of such orders on third parties is considered in detail at **6.83–6.88**.

**6.63**   An important shortcoming of *Mareva* injunctions ought to be borne in mind. The order will usually restrain dealings with property, and this will act to prevent that property being disposed of or charged in respect of borrowing. The order does not, in its conventional form, prevent a person from borrowing either by unsecured loans or by securing borrowing against assets which are not bound by the order.[108] In this way a respondent can still significantly reduce his net worth and remove assets from the jurisdiction without breaching the order. If such conduct is a concern, the court could be asked to grant a general injunctive order restraining the respondent from borrowing more than a specified amount, although there is no reported authority for such an order being sought or granted.

## What is the procedure for seeking a *Mareva* injunction?

**6.64**   The general procedure for making the application is set out at **6.53** and **6.54**. It is important also to have in mind the special requirements where the application is made ex parte (see **6.68–6.74**).

**6.65**   In family proceedings, the High Court and county court both have power to grant *Mareva* injunctions (see **6.49**). Where the order sought is a simple order freezing certain identified assets within the jurisdiction, there would appear to be no good reason why the order should not be made in the county court if the proceedings are pending there.[109] Where, on the other hand, the order sought is a wide-ranging order restraining dealings with undefined property, the application will be more appropriately dealt with by the High Court. Where the order sought is to be of worldwide effect, it seems that the application should only be considered by a High Court judge. Where the

---

[107]   *Yu Kong Line of Korea v Rendsburg Investment Corporation of Liberia* [1996] TLR 584.

[108]   *Cantor Index Ltd v Lister* (unreported) 22 November 2001 (Neuberger J).

[109]   See President's *Practice Direction (Family Division: Distribution of Business)* [1992] 2 FLR 87 of 5 June 1992 which indicates that *Mareva* injunctions or directions as to dealings with assets out of the jurisdiction should be dealt with by the High Court, 'unless the nature of the issues of fact or law raised in the case makes them more suitable for trial in the county court than in the High Court'.

proceedings are pending in the county court, the application may be made to the High Court without a transfer of the whole proceedings to that court (see **6.49** and **6.54**).

**6.66**   The CPR states that an application for a freezing order may only be heard by a judge, not by a district judge.[110] The CPR does not apply in general to ancillary relief proceedings and the old RSC and CCR, which do apply, do not appear to limit the application to being heard by a circuit judge.[111] Where the application for a simple freezing order in respect of a limited number of identified assets is made together with, or as an alternative to, an application pursuant to MCA 1973, s 37(2)(b), it is submitted that there appears to be little technical difficulty in the matter being determined by the district judge. As in the case of an application for an order pursuant to s 37(2)(a) (see **6.41**), it may be prudent to establish at the point of listing an application that the district judge will accept jurisdiction. Where, however, the matter concerns a full *Mareva* injunction of broad application, it would appear to be more appropriately dealt with by a judge, and probably by a judge of the High Court.

**6.67**   An application for relief by way of a *Mareva* injunction does not require pending proceedings, although there must be an intention on the part of the applicant to issue proceedings immediately, or almost immediately. In a civil claim the court should require a proper formulation of the claimant's substantive claim at the time of granting the order.[112] A *Mareva* injunction is not a remedy in its own right. The court should, in a case where an application is made for an order before proceedings are commenced, require an undertaking from the applicant to issue substantive proceedings within a very short time.

**6.68**   In a very urgent case the application may be made out of court hours over the telephone to the duty judge. If possible, the documents will be faxed to the judge in advance, but it may be that the hearing must proceed without time to prepare any significant documentation whatsoever.

**6.69**   By its very nature, a *Mareva* injunction anticipates a respondent acting in bad faith. Accordingly, the application is likely to be made ex parte. This carries heavy burdens for the applicant. The courts require more persuasion to grant an order ex parte, because there is such an inherent risk of injustice when only one of the parties is before the court.[113]

---

[110]   Practice Direction B to CPR Part 2.
[111]   RSC Ord 29. CCR Ord 13, r 6(2) specifically gives the district judge power to hear the application in a case where he has power to hear and determine the proceedings in which the application is made.
[112]   *Fourie v Le Roux* [2007] UKHL 1.
[113]   'Such orders must not be made without thinking once, twice and three times about the effect they would have' per Stamp LJ in *Jackson v Jackson* (1979) 9 Fam Law 56.

**6.70**   Helpful guidance as to the steps which ought to be taken by those presenting an ex parte application to the court was given by Munby J in *Re S (Ex Parte Orders)*:[114]

'(1) The circumstances in which ex parte relief is obtained in the Family Division vary very widely. What follows is not intended to be treated as a set of inflexible rules. In this area of practice, particularly in the Family Division, there can be no rigid rules. Circumstances alter cases and, in the final analysis, every case must be considered on its own facts.

(2) That said, generally speaking the following practice should be adopted both in ancillary relief cases and in cases relating to children, including cases where injunctive relief is sought against third parties or the world at large.

(3) This is subject to the need to recognise that in cases involving a child the court may have to act swiftly and decisively in order to safeguard the child's welfare.

(4) Those who seek relief ex parte are under a duty to make the fullest and most candid and frank disclosure of all the relevant circumstances known to them. This duty is not confined to the material facts: it extends to all relevant matters, whether of fact or of law. The principle is as applicable in the Family Division as elsewhere. Those who fail in this duty, and those who misrepresent matters to the court, expose themselves to the very real risk of being denied interlocutory relief whether or not they have a good arguable case or even a strong prima facie case.

(5) It is an elementary principle of natural justice that a judge cannot be shown evidence or other persuasive material in an ex parte application on the basis that it is not at a later stage to be revealed to the respondent. The respondent must have an opportunity to see the material which was deployed against him at the ex parte hearing and an opportunity, if he wishes to apply for the discharge or variation of the injunction either on the return day or earlier, to submit evidence in answer and, in any event, to make submissions about the applicant's evidence.

(6) It follows that those who obtain ex parte injunctive relief are under an obligation to bring to the attention of the respondent, and at the earliest practicable opportunity, the evidential and other persuasive materials on the basis of which the ex parte injunction was granted.

(7) Accordingly, generally speaking it is appropriate when granting ex parte injunctive relief in the Family Division for the court to require the applicant (and, where appropriate, the applicant's solicitors) to give the following undertakings:

(a)   where proceedings have not yet been issued, to issue and serve on the respondent either by some specified time or as soon as practicable proceedings either in the form of the draft produced to the court or otherwise as may be appropriate;

(b)   where the application has been made otherwise than on sworn evidence, to cause to be sworn, filed and served on the respondent as soon as practicable an affidavit or affidavits substantially in the terms of the draft affidavit(s)

---

[114]   [2001] 1 FLR 308. The judgment as a whole merits reading as a careful consideration of the practice surrounding making ex parte orders.

produced to the court or, as the case may be, confirming the substance of what was said to the court by the applicant's counsel or solicitors; and

(c)    subject to (a) and (b) above, to serve on the respondent as soon as practicable (i) the proceedings, (ii) a sealed copy of the order, (iii) copies of the affidavit(s) and exhibit(s) containing the evidence relied on by the applicant and (iv) notice of the return date including details of the application to be made on the return date.

(8) A person who has given an undertaking to the court is under a plain and unqualified obligation to comply to the letter with his undertaking. Where the undertaking is to do something by a specified time, then time is of the essence. A person who finds himself unable to comply timeously with his undertaking should either (i) apply for an extension of time before the time for compliance has expired or (ii) pass the task to someone who has available the time in which to do it.

(9) Whether or not express undertakings to this effect have been given, but subject to any order to the contrary, an applicant who obtains ex parte injunctive relief is under an obligation to the court, and the solicitor acting for the applicant is under an obligation both to the court and to his lay client, to carry out the various steps referred to in (7) above.

(10) Any ex parte order containing injunctions should set out on its face, either by way of recital or in a schedule, a list of all affidavits, witness statements and other evidential materials read by the judge. The applicant's legal representatives should whenever possible liaise with the associate with a view to ensuring that the order as drawn contains this information. On receipt of the order from the court the applicant's legal representatives should satisfy themselves that the order as drawn correctly sets out the relevant information and, if it does not, take urgent steps to have the order amended under the slip rule.

(11) Persons injuncted ex parte are entitled to be given, if they ask, proper information as to what happened at the hearing and to be told, if they ask, (i) exactly what documents, bundles or other evidential materials were lodged with the court either before or during the course of the hearing and (ii) what legal authorities were cited to the judge.

(12) The applicant's legal representatives should respond forthwith to any reasonable request from the respondent or his legal representatives either for copies of the materials read by the judge or for information about what took place at the hearing.

(13) Given this, it would be prudent for those acting for the applicant in such a case to keep a proper note of the proceedings, lest they otherwise find themselves embarrassed by a proper request for information which they are unable to provide.'

**6.71**    One of the most difficult aspects of a without notice application is for the applicant to put aside the natural partisan desire to present the case as forcibly as possible and comply with the duty to present the court with a full and frank account of all the relevant circumstances in the case, even those which are unfavourable to the applicant's case. Failure to do so may have very serious consequences. The party guilty of misrepresentation or non-disclosure may be publicly named and shamed. His lawyers, if implicated in the non-disclosure or misrepresentation may face similar embarrassment. Furthermore, the court may, as a form of penal sanction for the applicant's conduct, decide to discharge the order once the misrepresentation becomes known, even if there is a strong prima facie case on the merits for it continuing.[115] An order for indemnity costs may well be made.[116]

**6.72** Clearly, great care needs to be shown in preparing an ex parte application and in the conduct of the hearing. Often such applications have to be made in a hurry, causing the inexperienced to fall into the various pitfalls which can later be exploited by the respondent. The hearing of the application before the applications judge or by telephone to the duty judge is also likely to be short and summary in form. It is essential that the advocate considers carefully how the material, which may be complex, can best be presented to the court to ensure that there can be no later suggestion that the court was misled or that significant features of the case were not appreciated by the court.

**6.73** It is also important to ensure that the material which is placed before the court is recorded on the face of the order and served on the respondent with the order as soon after the hearing as possible. Once served with the order the respondent is entitled, in advance of any return date, to apply to the court to vary or discharge the order. This application may be made urgently and, in an exceptional case, even without notice to the applicant. A different judge may hear this application and, presented with an apparently credible version of events from the respondent, discharge the order because he knows little or nothing about the applicant's case. This is a foreseeable and avoidable risk, and an applicant's solicitor who fails to prepare and serve the evidence promptly may face a claim from the client if loss results.[117]

**6.74** The courts regard *Mareva* orders (and *Anton Piller* orders) as orders of great gravity and Draconian effect, almost akin to those which concern the liberty of the subject. Consequently, undertakings given to the court by an applicant or the applicant's solicitors as a precondition to the making of such an order are likely to be strictly enforced by the court.[118] A severe view may be taken of what may even be considered a minor breach of such an undertaking, for example filing an affidavit 21 minutes later than the time set in the undertaking.[119]

---

[115] *Behbehani v Salem* [1989] 1 WLR 723. But the court has a discretion how to proceed in such circumstances, and the rule itself should not be allowed to become an instrument of injustice: *Brink's Mat v Elcombe* [1988] 1 WLR 1350 and *Re W (Ex Parte Orders)* [2000] 2 FLR 927 at 943–5.

[116] *Harrison v Harrison* [2008] 2 FLR 35.

[117] *Re S (Ex Parte Orders)* [2001] 1 FLR 308 at 319.

[118] *Re S (Ex Parte Orders)* [2001] 1 FLR 308 at 320.

[119] *Re S (Ex Parte Orders)* [2001] 1 FLR 308 at 323.

## What needs to be established to obtain a *Mareva* injunction?

**6.75** Mere fear or suspicion that assets will be dissipated is not enough to justify the making of an order. The court is likely to require some clear evidence that there is a real risk of dissipation of assets,[120] although in the matrimonial context the court may simply apply a balance of convenience test and make the order on the basis that the harm to the applicant of the assets being moved out of the court's reach (even if there was no good evidence of a current intention on the respondent's part to do so) outweighs any prejudice to the respondent in making the order.[121]

**6.76** It also seems that the family courts dealing with parties who are closely involved with each other may permit a more flexible use of *Mareva*-type orders than might be appropriate in commercial litigation.[122] The authorities from commercial cases[123] are helpful when considering such applications, but are unlikely to be considered to be authoritatively binding on the family courts.

**6.77** The respondent may be able to persuade a court to discharge or vary a *Mareva* injunction by offering some alternative form of security to the other party. Whether this will be acceptable to the court is likely to depend on the nature of the security offered and the particular circumstances of the case, particularly the respondent's earlier conduct.

## What is the appropriate scope of a *Mareva* injunction in ancillary relief proceedings?

**6.78** A *Mareva* order can be in very broad terms. The form of order suggested within the CPR provides as follows:

> 'The Respondent must not remove from England and Wales or in any way dispose of, deal with or diminish the value of any of his assets which are in England and Wales up to the value of £ . . . . . .'[124]

**6.79** In a commercial case the amount inserted in the order will usually be the largest sum reasonably likely to be obtained by way of damages in the action. Where the assets held by the defendant are smaller than the amount claimed,

---

[120] *The Law Society v Shanks* [1988] 1 FLR 504. In the commercial context the risk of dissipation or removal of assets from the jurisdiction cannot be merely asserted but must be demonstrated by 'solid evidence': *Ninemia Maritime Corp v Trave Schiffahrtsgesellschaft mbH & Co KG* [1984] 1 All ER 398.

[121] *Shipman v Shipman* [1991] 1 FLR 250.

[122] *Shipman v Shipman* [1991] 1 FLR 250 at 253 and Munby J's comments, albeit in a procedural context, in *Re W (Ex Parte Orders)* [2000] 2 FLR 927 at 945–6.

[123] The reader will note that most of the important cases on *Mareva* injunctions cited in this book are within commercial rather than matrimonial disputes.

[124] There is an alternative form of wording to apply if the order is to have worldwide effect.

the order will not set a financial limit[125] and the order will then also cover any further assets obtained by the defendant between the date of the order and the trial.[126]

**6.80** In ancillary relief proceedings an order covering all the respondent's assets is unlikely to be appropriate, because it would be highly unusual for one party ever to come away with all the other's assets.[127] Where the concern is that the respondent has failed to make anything resembling full disclosure of his assets, it will be very difficult to set a limit, as the extent of the applicant's claims will be unknown. If the applicant provides a realistic estimate of the respondent's means, this could be used to set the limit. Similarly, if the applicant chooses to limit her claims to a certain level, this will also allow a limit to be set. It is likely, however, that where a respondent wholly fails to make any disclosure of his assets, the court will take the view that he only has himself to blame if a blanket unlimited worldwide *Mareva* order is made against him.[128] Assets held by a company should not be subject to a *Mareva* order unless the company is a party to the proceedings.[129] The same principle is likely to apply to a trust.

**6.81** Certain safeguards are built into most *Mareva* orders. The procedural safeguards following an ex parte application have been considered above. There should always be provision for a person subject to an order to be able to meet his living expenses, unless there is evidence that there are assets available for that purpose to which the order does not attach.[130] There should also be provision for payment of ordinary debts as they fall due, although this may be included in the sum allowed for living costs. Furthermore, the sum allowed should also provide an element for legal costs. A party should not be held to ransom by a *Mareva* order. The purpose of the order is to preserve the assets rather than to give either party an advantage in the proceedings or to punish the respondent. Where the respondent has a business, the order may also need to make allowance for him to use his assets for that purpose. There is a standard provision allowing transactions to permit a business to continue to trade.[131]

**6.82** In the commercial context the court will usually require an undertaking from the applicant to comply with any order the court makes to compensate the respondent for any loss sustained by reason of the order being made.

---

[125] *Z v A-Z* [1982] 1 QB 558.
[126] *TDK v Video Choice Limited* [1986] 1 WLR 141.
[127] *Ghoth v Ghoth* [1992] 2 FLR 300 at 301.
[128] For an analogous approach to the issue of adverse inferences in the event of non-disclosure see Chapter 2.
[129] *Harrison v Harrison* [2008] 2 FLR 35. See below for examples of situations where a company may be joined to the proceedings and be made subject to an order.
[130] *The Law Society v Shanks* [1988] 1 FLR 504 at 505.
[131] *Harrison v Harrison* [2008] 2 FLR 35.

Indeed, this is implied in such an order unless the contrary is stated.[132] In the family courts the practice is the exact inverse of that in the commercial context.[133] Generally, no such undertaking will be required where the order only affects the parties to the divorce. Where a third party is affected by the order, an undertaking may be required to protect their interest.[134] Otherwise that third party would have no remedy in the event of loss being sustained due to the order.

## How does a *Mareva* injunction affect third parties?

**6.83**   A *Mareva* injunction is granted to preserve the assets which are the likely subject matter of the proceedings. It follows that the order is addressed to the other party to the proceedings and concerns assets to which the other party is beneficially entitled. Nevertheless, a third party can become subject to a *Mareva* injunction in two principal ways.

**6.84**   First, a third party may be put forward as the owner of an asset in question. The courts recognise the sometimes devious means by which litigants arrange their affairs in order to put their assets beyond the reach of the courts, and the form of *Mareva* injunction suggested by the CPR includes a provision which extends the prohibition on dealing to:

> '... all the Respondent's assets whether or not they are in his own name and whether they are solely or jointly owned. For the purposes of this order the Respondent's assets include any asset which he has the power, directly or indirectly, to dispose of or deal with as if it were his own. The Respondent is to be regarded as having such a power if a third party holds or controls the asset in accordance with his direct or indirect instructions.'[135]

**6.85**   The court therefore has jurisdiction to restrain dealings in assets which ostensibly belong to someone else or to a company, but there is good reason to suppose that those assets are in fact the assets of the respondent, being held for him either on a bare trust or by the third party as the respondent's nominee. Similar principles apply where the assets are owned by a company which the respondent controls and which can be regarded as his alter ego.[136] As the words in the draft form of order above suggest, the order can also apply to any assets which are within the respondent's control, even if he is not legally or beneficially entitled to them.[137]

---

[132]   *Re W (Ex Parte Orders)* [2000] 2 FLR 927 at 946–7. The court may, in a suitable case, grant the order in the absence of a valuable undertaking: *Allen v Jambo Holdings Ltd* [1980] 2 All ER 502.

[133]   *Practice Direction (Injunction: Undertaking as to Damages)* [1974] 1 WLR 576 and *Re W (Ex Parte Orders)* [2000] 2 FLR 927 at 947–8.

[134]   *Re W (Ex Parte Orders)* [2000] 2 FLR 927 at 948–9.

[135]   Clause 6 of the sample order annexed to Practice Direction to CPR Part 25.

[136]   *TSB Private Bank International SA v Chabra* [1992] 1 WLR 231.

[137]   *Dadourian Group International Inc v Azuri Limited* [2005] EWHC 1768 (Ch), [2006] WTLR 239.

**6.86** In these circumstances the third party can be joined to the proceedings as a second respondent so as to be made subject to the order.[138] In any event, this joinder is likely simply to foreshadow that person's joinder to the proceedings in due course to decide the question of ownership of the disputed asset.[139] The joinder of the third party to the *Mareva* injunction does have an important consequence for the applicant. The applicant is likely to be required to give an undertaking to pay damages to the third party for any losses sustained as a result of the order in the event that the order proves to have been unjustified.[140] In the case of business assets or other assets of considerable value, the applicant must be aware that such compensation could be substantial. There is substantial risk in seeking such orders and they should not be sought on a speculative basis.

**6.87** The second way in which third parties may be affected by a *Mareva* injunction is in the event they become complicit in any conduct by the respondent which breaches the order. The court will not permit a third party to aid and abet a breach of an order which has come to the third party's knowledge.[141] The type of institution most often affected is a bank which holds funds on behalf of the respondent. Such parties do not usually need to be joined by the proceedings, but they ought to be served with a copy of the order, or at least notified of its terms. Having been served with or notified of the order, they must take no step which may assist the respondent in breaching the order by disposing of the assets, transferring them out of the jurisdiction or otherwise dissipating them. If they were to do so, they would be complicit in the respondent's breach of the order and in contempt of the court. Most banks treat the order as requiring them to freeze the relevant accounts until the order is discharged or varied.[142] Where the respondent has funds in banks overseas, the order should contain provisions which excuse any bank in the overseas jurisdiction from breaching the order if compliance with the order would put the bank in breach of any of its obligations under the law of that foreign jurisdiction.[143] It may be necessary to seek appropriate orders in that foreign jurisdiction to protect assets held there in the event that the English order cannot be effectively enforced.

**6.88** If a *Mareva* injunction is served on a third party who holds assets on behalf of the respondent, the third party will be in contempt of court in the event that it assists the respondent to breach the terms of the order. However,

---

[138] *TSB Private Bank International SA v Chabra* [1992] 1 WLR 231.

[139] See **8.9–8.16**.

[140] *Re W (Ex Parte Orders)* [2000] 2 FLR 927 at 949.

[141] *Z Ltd v A-Z* [1982] QB 558, where the court also held that a third party with knowledge of the order can be in contempt by acting in a way which caused a breach of the order even if the order had not yet come to the attention of the respondent who was enjoined by it.

[142] Notwithstanding that this probably breaches the terms of the banking mandate agreed with the respondent and the standard terms of the *Mareva* injunction would not, it seems, prevent them returning the assets to the respondent as the owner of the asset: *The Law Society v Shanks* [1988] 1 FLR 504 at 506.

[143] *Bank of China v NBM LLC* [2002] 1 WLR 844 applying *Baltic Shipping Co v Translink Shipping Ltd* [1995] 1 Lloyd's Rep 673.

that third party will not normally be required to compensate the applicant for any loss sustained as a result of failing to abide by the order. The existence of a *Mareva* injunction alone is insufficient to raise a duty of care towards the applicant.[144]

## OTHER FORMS OF INTERLOCUTORY ORDER

**6.89** An application pursuant to s 37(2)(a) of the Matrimonial Causes Act 1973 or for a general civil injunction (including a *Mareva* injunction) is likely to provide an adequate remedy in most ancillary relief cases. There are some further forms of interim order which can be used in the event that the general powers are felt to be insufficient, or to supplement those powers.

**6.90** Prior to the issue of proceedings, the court may make an order for:

'... the inspection, photographing, preservation, custody and detention of property which appears to the court to be property which may become the subject-matter of the subsequent proceedings in the ... court, or as to which any question may arise in such proceedings'.[145]

There are similar provisions dealing with the disclosure and production of relevant documents.[146] Until 25 April 1999 these provisions were limited to personal injury and fatal accident claims, but since that date they apply to all proceedings. These provisions could be extremely useful at the point of proceedings being commenced in a case where there are concerns about assets or documents being hidden or dissipated as soon as an ancillary relief application is made. The court may be more amenable to a specific order made under these provisions than making the more Draconian and exceptional *Anton Piller* order (see Chapter 4). Nevertheless, in ancillary relief proceedings the court is likely to require clear evidence that there is something exceptional about the facts of the case to justify such an order being made prior to proceedings being commenced. The justifications for an order for pre-action disclosure in normal civil litigation, such as the need to obtain evidence as to the merits and nature of the claim to be pursued, do not apply in the context of ancillary relief proceedings.

**6.91** Once proceedings have been issued, the court also has powers to order the production of documents or the inspection, photographing, preservation, custody and detention of property which is not the property of a party to the proceedings.[147] These powers also used to be limited to personal injury and fatal accident cases, but they now apply to 'any proceedings'. Such an order could be used as an alternative to, or as a useful order ancillary to, an

---

[144] *Customs & Excise Commissioners v Barclays Bank plc* [2006] UKHL 28, [2007] 1 AC 181, [2006] 3 WLR 1.

[145] Supreme Court Act 1981, s 33(1) and County Courts Act 1984, s 52(2).

[146] Supreme Court Act 1981, s 33(2) and County Courts Act 1984, s 52(2).

[147] Supreme Court Act 1981, s 34 and County Courts Act 1984, s 53.

application for an inspection appointment (see Chapter 5). These additional powers can be used to ensure that any documents sought at such an appointment are not destroyed before the inspection appointment occurs, or to deal with production to the parties and their use during the proceedings.

**6.92** The application of the powers mentioned in the preceding paragraphs are governed by the CPR in civil proceedings. In family proceedings the old RSC and CCR apply and the relevant rules refer to the provisions in their unamended form,[148] when they applied only to personal injury and fatal accident claims.[149] Nevertheless, the terms of those rules are sufficiently broad to suggest that they can be applied to the statutory powers in their current amended form. It would appear that these powers are rarely if ever used in ancillary relief proceedings, presumably because similar results can be achieved by the use of general civil injunctions or inspection appointments. Nevertheless, there will be cases where these powers provide the court with additional means of obtaining the information required for resolution of the proceedings.

**6.93** A further power worthy of mention is the ancient writ *ne exeat regno*. This order operates to prevent a litigant leaving the jurisdiction until he has satisfied a judgment or order of the court. It is rarely used.[150] It predates the *Mareva* injunction in origin by several centuries and was more appropriate to times when a litigant would carry his wealth on his person rather than move it from bank account to bank account by electronic transactions. In the modern age assets can usually be more effectively controlled by restricting a person's freedom to deal with his assets than by limiting his freedom of movement. There may be some doubt as to the availability of this common law remedy in ancillary relief claims, which are statutory in their nature.[151] Alimony was one of the forms of claim which the writ could be issued to support and the remedy has been used in a case where there were arrears of maintenance following an order made under the Matrimonial Causes Act 1973.[152]

**6.94** The use of the writ is limited to circumstances where the respondent could be imprisoned under s 6 of the Debtors Act 1869, which means that the order may only be made before final judgment and where the respondent's absence 'will materially prejudice the plaintiff in the prosecution of his action'.[153] It cannot, therefore, be used to hold the respondent to ransom as a means of enforcing the court's order. There may, however, be scope for its use at

---

[148] In the form which was in force prior to 25 April 1999.

[149] RSC Ord 29, r 7A and CCR Ord 13, r 7.

[150] See *Felton v Callis* [1968] 3 WLR 951 at 956–9 for a review of the history of the remedy and confirmation that it continues to exist as an available remedy.

[151] *Felton v Callis* [1968] 3 WLR 951 at 965, where Megarry J sets out the application of the remedy and notes that it was limited to equitable debts and claims, the only exceptions being alimony and a claim for an account.

[152] *Thaha v Thaha* [1987] 2 FLR 142, although in *B v B ( Restraint on Leaving Jurisdiction)* [1997] 2 FLR 148 at 154 that decision was said to be wrong in that the writ could not be used after judgment and the order in *Thaha* should be seen as an injunction under s 37(1) of the Supreme Court Act 1981.

[153] *B v B ( Restraint on Leaving Jurisdiction)* [1997] 2 FLR 148 at 151.

an earlier stage of proceedings to ensure that the respondent remains within the court's jurisdiction, where he is susceptible to the court's orders requiring him to provide disclosure of his affairs.[154] It must be noted that if the writ is obtained and it is later shown to be unjustified, the court may require the applicant to pay the respondent damages.[155]

**6.95**   The court has the power pursuant to s 37(1) of the Supreme Court Act 1981, quite independent of the writ ne exeat regno, to restrain a person from leaving the jurisdiction and requiring him to surrender his passport. Such orders are made on the same balance of convenience as other interlocutory injunctions, although with the added need to ensure that the order goes no further and lasts no longer than necessary, because it acts as a considerable interference with the liberty of the subject.[156] Such an order can be made to ensure that the court is able properly to carry through its procedures leading to a disposal of the proceedings, for example by compelling the respondent to provide disclosure or to answer questions.[157]

**6.96**   The most recent authorities on the writ ne exeat regno predate the incorporation into English law of the European Convention on Human Rights by the Human Rights Act 1998. It is not clear to what extent this common law power has been affected by the introduction of the ECHR. It is submitted that the effect of the Convention rights is minimal on the existing rules relating to the use of the writ ne exeat regno. The order does not cause the respondent to be imprisoned, and so the Art 5 right to liberty would not appear to be infringed. It may be that the facts of a particular case may permit a respondent to such an order to argue that the order infringes his Art 8 rights to respect for private and family life on the basis that it prevents contact with family overseas. In any event, it would appear that the use of the writ in accordance with the principles set out in the case law would ordinarily amount to a legitimate and proportionate means of securing compliance with orders of the court and obligations imposed by law,[158] or to protect the rights and freedoms of the applicant.[159] It is of interest that in *Kimber v Kimber*,[160] an appeal against an order preventing the husband leaving the jurisdiction, the appellant husband abandoned arguments based on the European Convention on Human Rights 1950 and relied instead upon his right as a citizen of a member state of the European Union to free movement around the states of the Union, and on the

---

[154]   *B v B (Restraint on Leaving Jurisdiction)* [1997] 2 FLR 148, although the same result may be achieved by an injunction pursuant to SCA 1981, s 37(1) requiring the respondent to surrender his passport and remain in the jurisdiction (see below).

[155]   *Allied Arab Bank Ltd v Hajjas* [1988] QB 2 FLR 145, although in ancillary relief proceedings, where the wronged individual is one of the parties, the court is likely to deal with the issue within its overall order on the ancillary relief application rather than by an assessment of damages.

[156]   *Bayer AG v Winter* [1986] 1 WLR 497.

[157]   *B v B (Restraint on Leaving Jurisdiction)* [1997] 2 FLR 148, cited with approval by Brooke LJ in *Kimber v Kimber* [2006] EWCA Civ 706 at [39].

[158]   See Art 5(1)(b) of the Convention.

[159]   See Art 8(2) of the Convention.

[160]   [2006] EWCA Civ 706.

basis of the established English authorities that the power to detain a person in England and Wales can be exercised only in the short term and as ancillary to a free-standing proceeding which his absence from England and Wales would otherwise frustrate.[161]

## COSTS OF AN APPLICATION FOR AN INTERIM INJUNCTION OR RESTRAINING ORDER

**6.97** Although FPR, r 2.71(4)(a) has established a general rule that the court will not make an order requiring one party to pay the costs of the other, frequently the applicant who successfully obtains an interim order (or who extracts at the door of the court an undertaking in the same terms as the order sought) will ask for the costs of the application to be paid by the respondent. The court retains the discretion to make a costs order on the basis of the parties' conduct in the course of the proceedings or before them.[162] In some cases it will be appropriate to make the order for costs because of the obviously bad conduct of the respondent. In other cases, however, the order will have been granted on the basis that 'it is better to be safe than sorry' and without any detailed investigation of the facts, which may be hotly contested. There is a strong argument in such circumstances for the costs to remain costs in the application, or to be reserved until the final hearing, when it will become more evident whether the application was justified or not.[163] On the other hand, where the application for the order is dismissed, there seems to be a strong argument for the applicant to pay the respondent's costs, on the basis that the application was wholly unnecessary and unjustified. There may, however, be circumstances where the consideration of costs is better left to the final hearing once the application can be seen in the context of the whole proceedings.

**6.98** Costs are usually reserved or left in the application at an ex parte hearing. There is no need to deal with the question of costs on an urgent basis and the court will want to hear both sides before making any order as to costs.

## BREACH OF AN ORDER

**6.99** Breach of an injunctive order or of a formal undertaking to the court amounts to a contempt of court and penal sanctions are available to the court. Accordingly, the court will require proof of the breach to the criminal standard of proof and the procedural safeguards for an alleged contemnor must be carefully applied.[164]

---

[161] The Court of Appeal declined to entertain the appeal or consider those arguments on the basis that the arguments had not been raised before the judge at first instance. The matter was remitted to the High Court for further consideration.
[162] FPR, r 2.71(4)(b).
[163] *Shipman v Shipman* [1991] 1 FLR 250 at 253.
[164] *Hammerton v Hammerton* [2007] 2 FLR 1133.

# Chapter 7

# SETTING ASIDE DISPOSITIONS

**7.1**   In an ideal world it would have been possible to anticipate the other party's intention to dissipate assets and obtain a suitable order or undertaking ensuring that such dissipation did not occur. In reality, of course, there will be many cases where the dissipation of assets has taken place before anything could be done to prevent it. It may only be after a lengthy process of extracting disclosure from a recalcitrant party that it becomes apparent that assets have been dissipated. In some cases the dissipation may have occurred in flagrant breach of an order restraining such conduct.

**7.2**   To deal with such situations, the courts have been given statutory powers to set aside, or 'avoid', transactions made with the intention of frustrating the other party's claims. In appropriate circumstances the court can salvage the applicant's claims even after 'the horse has bolted'. The main statutory provisions for use in ancillary relief proceedings appear in s 37(2)(b) and (c) of the Matrimonial Causes Act 1973. However, the court also has a broader general power pursuant to s 423 of the Insolvency Act 1986 to set aside transactions that are intended to put assets beyond the reach of persons who have a claim against the person disposing of the asset. In most cases it will suffice to rely only on the provisions of MCA 1973, s 37(2)(b) or (c), but there may be cases where it will be desirable to apply under the Insolvency Act 1986 as well. The court's jurisdiction under the two provisions is not identical, and one provision may be easier to apply on the particular facts of a case than the other.

**7.3**   Practitioners should bear in mind that these provisions apply to transactions concerning all forms of property, not merely real property.

## WHEN IS AN APPLICATION FOR AN AVOIDANCE OF DISPOSITION ORDER NECESSARY?

**7.4**   Not all transactions which have the apparent effect of transferring assets to another person will need to be set aside.

**7.5**   First, there will be cases where the dissipation of assets is not so extensive as to limit the court's power to make appropriate provision for the applicant. If the assets which have been disposed of are a relatively modest part of the overall family assets, there is unlikely to be any point in the court setting the transaction aside. So long as there are other remaining assets which are sufficient to meet the applicant's claims, the court can make orders to preserve those assets whilst proceedings are pending and then make appropriate orders at the final hearing. The court will apply the simple principle that 'a spouse cannot be allowed to fritter away the assets by extravagant living or reckless speculation and then to claim as great a share of what was left as he would have been entitled to if he had behaved reasonably.'[1]

**7.6**    The unjustified disposal of the other assets by the respondent can be taken into account by the court as part of the overall circumstances of the case or as conduct which it would be inequitable to disregard.[2] The court can proceed on the basis that the assets which the respondent has disposed of without good reason should be treated as part of his capital entitlement at the end of the marriage. In other words, the court will treat the respondent as if still in possession of the dissipated funds and 'add back' those funds to his share of the assets. Such an approach is likely to be more straightforward and less costly than an application to set aside transactions, which may require the addition of third parties to the proceedings. Nevertheless, there are risks and uncertainties in this approach. It is often difficult to predict how a judge will regard the expenditure which has occurred. There is often a risk that the judge will find that the expenditure was reasonable. Furthermore, the Court of Appeal has pointed out that 'a notional reattribution has to be conducted very cautiously, by reference only to clear evidence of dissipation (in which there is a wanton element) and that the fiction does not extend to treatment of the sums reattributed to a spouse as cash which he can deploy in meeting his needs, for example in the purchase of accommodation.'[3] There is also the risk that the party who has dissipated assets may be able to escape the allegation of wrongdoing by relying on mental illness or some other mitigating factor.[4]

**7.7**    Secondly, there are cases where it is possible to show that the transfer of assets to a third party is simply a sham designed to avoid the applicant's claims. 'Sham' in this context has been defined as meaning: 'Acts done or documents executed by parties to the "sham" which are intended by them to give to third parties or to the court the appearance of creating between the parties legal rights and obligations different from the actual legal rights and obligations (if any) which the parties intend to create',[5] or 'an agreement or series of agreements which are deliberately framed with the object of deceiving third parties as to the true nature and effect of the legal relations between the parties'.[6] For example, the respondent may have simply transferred funds from

---

[1]    *Martin v Martin* [1976] Fam 335 at 342H.
[2]    Matrimonial Causes Act 1973, s 25(2)(g). For an example of this approach being taken see *Norris v Norris* [2003] 1 FLR 1142 at 1167, *Vaughan v Vaughan* [2008] 1 FLR 1108; *Behzadi v Behzadi* [2008] EWCA Civ 1070 and *G v G* [2007] EWHC 494 (Fam) at [62].
[3]    *Vaughan v Vaughan* [2008] 1 FLR 1108 at [14]. In that case the husband had spent some £170,000 worth of assets, but only £100,000 was reattributed to him.
[4]    Ibid at [28].
[5]    *Snook v London and West Riding Investments Ltd* [1967] 2 QB 786 at 802 per Diplock LJ.
[6]    *Hadjiloucas v Crean* [1988] 1 WLR 1006 at 1019 per Mustill LJ. This definition and that from *Snook* (above) were both adopted by Munby J in the ancillary relief context in *Re W (Ex Parte Orders)* [2000] 2 FLR 927 at 939. See also the case law concerning sham trusts at **15.69–15.77**.

accounts in his own name to accounts in the names of relatives. Where such a transaction occurs with no justification or reasonable explanation, the court will readily be able to infer that the relatives hold the funds as bare trustees for the respondent and that the money remains his to do with as he will.[7] The court will be able to make orders in relation to those assets in the same way as it would if the assets remained held in the respondent's own name. In such a clear case there may be no need to embark on a complex application to set aside the transactions. Where the case is less straightforward and there have been greater formalities in the transaction, especially where the legal title to land has been transferred and registered in the third party's name, an application to set aside the transaction may be necessary alongside the application for the court to declare that the transaction was a sham.

**7.8**    Thirdly, where the ancillary relief proceedings have been registered against the title to property as a pending land action, any interest taken by a third party after registration of the notice ranks behind the interest in the property transferred to the applicant by a property adjustment order.[8] In such a case there is no need to set aside the transaction which granted the third party an interest, because that third party's interest already ranks behind the applicant's claim.

**7.9**    Fourthly, an application to set aside a transaction will not be appropriate where the asset which was disposed of did not belong to one of the parties to the proceedings in the first place. This scenario may arise where the asset was held by one of the parties on trust for some third party, leaving no beneficial interest for either of the parties to the marriage to enjoy. More commonly, however, the asset may be held by a company in which one of the parties has an interest. The company is a separate legal entity from the parties to the marriage and that asset could not be subject to a property adjustment order in the ancillary relief proceedings. Where the company is effectively the alter ego of one of the parties to the proceedings (in other words, where it is to all intents and purposes a 'one-man company' wholly controlled by one of the parties), the court may pierce the corporate veil and treat the assets of the company as the assets of the party.[9] In such a case the court could make an MCA 1973, s 37 order in respect of a disposal of assets nominally held by the company.[10] Where the corporate veil cannot be pierced in this way, however, the court will not be able to use the power to set aside a disposition and the court may need to reflect the conduct within the final order for financial provision. Alternatively, if both parties are shareholders in the company, they may need to resolve the matter in the Companies Court.[11]

---

[7]    *Purba v Purba* [2000] 1 FLR 444.

[8]    See *Perez-Adamson v Perez-Rivas* [1987] 2 FLR at 479.

[9]    *Nicholas v Nicholas* [1984] FLR 285; *Green v Green* [1993] 1 FLR 326. See also Chapter 11.

[10]    *Kemmis v Kemmis* [1988] 1 WLR 1307 at 1331.

[11]    *McGladdery v McGladdery* [1999] 2 FLR 1102, where the wife disposed of company assets after the making of final ancillary relief orders. Where disputes as to the governance and

# THE SCOPE OF MATRIMONIAL CAUSES ACT 1973, S 37(2)(B) AND (C)

**7.10**  Section 37(2)(a) deals with preventing dispositions which have not yet occurred. This provision has been considered in Chapter 6. Section 37(2)(b) permits the court to set aside dispositions made prior to the making of a final order, while s 37(2)(c) provides a similar power where the disposition is made after the making of a final ancillary relief order.

**7.11**  The relevant parts of s 37 relating to setting aside dispositions are as follows:

'(1) For the purposes of this section "financial relief" means relief under any of the provisions of sections 22, 23, 24, 24B, 27, 31 (except subsection (6)) and 35 above, and any reference in this section to defeating a person's claim for financial relief is a reference to preventing financial relief from being granted to that person, or to that person for the benefit of a child of the family, or reducing the amount of any financial relief which might be so granted, or frustrating or impeding the enforcement of any order which might be or has been made at his instance under any of those provisions.

(2) Where proceedings for financial relief are brought by one person against another, the court may, on the application of the first-mentioned person—

…

(b)    if it is satisfied that the other party has, with [the intention of defeating the claim for financial relief], made a reviewable disposition and that if the disposition were set aside financial relief or different financial relief would be granted to the applicant, make an order setting aside the disposition;

(c)    if it is satisfied, in a case where an order has been obtained under any of the provisions mentioned in subsection (1) above by the applicant against the other party, that the other party has, with that intention, made a reviewable disposition, make an order setting aside the disposition;

and an application for the purposes of paragraph (b) above shall be made in the proceedings for the financial relief in question.

(3) Where the court makes an order under subsection (2)(b) or (c) above setting aside a disposition it shall give such consequential directions as it thinks fit for giving effect to the order (including directions requiring the making of any payments or the disposal of any property).

(4) Any disposition made by the other party to the proceedings for financial relief in question (whether before or after the commencement of those proceedings) is a reviewable disposition for the purposes of subsection (2)(b) and (c) above unless it was made for valuable consideration (other than marriage) to a person who, at the

---

management of a company in which only the family have shares, the Family Division will be the appropriate venue to resolve them during the course of the ancillary relief proceedings: *Poon v Poon* [1994] 2 FLR 857.

time of the disposition, acted in relation to it in good faith and without notice of any intention on the part of the other party to defeat the applicant's claim for financial relief.

(5) Where an application is made under this section with respect to a disposition which took place less than three years before the date of the application ... and the court is satisfied—

(a)   in a case falling within subsection (2)(b) above, that the disposition or other dealing would (apart from this section) have the consequence, or

(b)   in a case falling within subsection (2)(c) above, that the disposition has had the consequence,

of defeating the applicant's claim for financial relief, it shall be presumed, unless the contrary is shown, that the person who disposed of ... the property did so ... with the intention of defeating the applicant's claim for financial relief.

(6) In this section "disposition" does not include any provision contained in a will or codicil but, with that exception, includes any conveyance, assurance or gift of property of any description, whether made by an instrument or otherwise.

(7) This section does not apply to a disposition made before 1 January 1968.'

**7.12**   There is no limit to the retrospective effect of this section, other than it not applying to dispositions which took place before 1 January 1968. It is difficult to conceive of circumstances where that limitation date could be relevant in proceedings before the court in the twenty-first century. It does not matter whether the disposition occurred before or after the commencement of proceedings. The disposition could have been made many years before, although clearly it will be more difficult to prove the necessary intention on the respondent's part where the disposition was made many years before the marriage broke down.

**7.13**   The section applies to all forms of property, including property abroad.[12] A 'disposition' is likely to be interpreted broadly as anything which reduces the party's interest in an asset.[13] Disposing of assets by a will or a codicil to a will is specifically excluded from the meaning of disposition. Presumably this is because the will has no effect on ownership of the asset until the death of the testator, and at that point any claims by the former spouse can be made against the deceased's estate pursuant to the Inheritance (Provision for Family and Dependants) Act 1975 rather than the Matrimonial Causes Act 1973.

**7.14**   An order made pursuant to this section acts in personam and not in rem. It requires the third party to the transaction and the respondent to ensure that the asset in question is conveyed or transferred back to the respondent. Despite the language of the section, it has been held that the making of the order does

---

[12]   *Hamlin v Hamlin* [1986] 1 FLR 61.
[13]   *Shipman v Shipman* [1991] 1 FLR 250 at 252.

not, of itself, set aside or avoid the transaction.[14] This may cause real difficulties where the third party who has obtained the asset is beyond the jurisdiction of the court and unwilling to comply with the order. It could also be problematic in the event that the third party becomes bankrupt before the order is complied with. In such circumstances the asset would, presumably, vest in the trustee in bankruptcy, making implementation of the order difficult. These difficulties underline the importance of trying to show that the transfer was a sham where possible (see **7.7**), as such a finding will mean that beneficial ownership of the asset always remained with the respondent to the application and never passed to the third party.

**7.15**　Certain types of disposal of an asset are not amenable to being set aside by an order. Classically, these are situations where the asset is simply destroyed rather than being disposed of to a third party. Some examples of such conduct are obvious (eg a farmer burning crops), but some are less obvious. The surrender of a secure tenancy of a local authority property is not a disposition of an asset which can be set aside.[15] Upon surrender, the secure tenancy simply ceases to exist and cannot be resurrected by the court. The same is true of any right to buy which is lost by reason of the surrender of such a tenancy.[16] The removal or exclusion of a spouse from potential benefits under a discretionary trust is not a disposition which can be set aside pursuant to s 37.[17] Where such assets are of importance in a case, it is important that they are preserved at an early stage by an injunctive order or undertaking. Failure to do so on a client's behalf may amount to negligence.

**7.16**　It should also be noted that the provisions under MCA 1973, s 37(2)(a) and (b) are drafted in a form which suggests that only the first disposition of property from the respondent to a third party is a reviewable disposition capable of being set aside. If the third party subsequently disposes of the property to another person, that second transaction appears not to be one which is susceptible to being set aside under this provision.[18] This is in contrast to the wider powers apparently available pursuant to s 423 of the Insolvency Act 1986, considered below. In *Ansari v Ansari*[19] the Court of Appeal expressed the view that s 37(3) was probably broad enough in its scope to permit the setting aside of subsequent dispositions of property so long as the first disposition was a reviewable disposition and so long as none of the parties to the later transfer were able to avail themselves of the defence pursuant to s 37(4). The court does, arguably, also have a broad power under s 37(3) to set aside the original disposition and in an appropriate case to direct that the third

---

[14]　*Hamlin v Hamlin* [1986] 1 FLR 61. This decision seems slightly in conflict with the dicta of Munby J in *Re A* [2002] Fam 213 to the effect that an order under s 37(2)(a) differs from a *Mareva* order in that the former has a proprietary aspect which is absent in the latter.
[15]　*Newlon Housing Trust v Alsulaimen* [1998] 2 FLR 690, HL.
[16]　*Bater v Greenwich London Borough Council* [1999] 2 FLR 993.
[17]　*Mubarak v Mubarak* [2007] 2 FLR 364.
[18]　*Green v Green* [1981] 1 WLR 391.
[19]　[2008] EWCA Civ 1456, [2009] 1 FLR 1121.

party to that initial transaction shall pay a sum equivalent to the value of the property he has subsequently disposed of again.

## What needs to be shown to obtain an order under s 37(2)(b) or (c)?

**7.17**  First, there must be an application for financial relief as defined in MCA 1973, s 37(1) which will be defeated by the disposition. 'Defeating the claim' in this context means in broad terms that:

(a)  in the case of an application under s 37(2)(b), the amount of financial relief which will be granted to the applicant will be reduced by the disposition or the disposition will make enforcement of the order for financial relief more difficult; or

(b)  in the case of s 37(2)(c), the disposition will frustrate or impede the enforcement of the order which has been made.

It should be noted that an order for costs made within the proceedings is not a form of financial relief that may be defeated by a disposition.

**7.18**  Secondly, if the application is under s 37(2)(b), the applicant for the order must prove on the balance of probabilities[20] the following matters:

•  That the other party has made a disposition of property.[21]

•  That the disposition was made with the intention of defeating the claim for financial relief. The applicant may be assisted in proving this by the statutory presumption set out in s 37(5), discussed at **7.22–7.23**.

•  That if the disposition were set aside, financial relief or different financial relief would be granted to the applicant. As the application to set aside under this provision is usually heard within the substantive ancillary relief proceedings, the court will have sufficient information available to judge the effect of the disposition upon the overall outcome of the case. Sometimes, however, an application under s 37(2)(b) is dealt with as a preliminary issue in proceedings, even before an FDR hearing takes place. This may be appropriate in cases where the effect of the disposition on the overall outcome of the case is obvious, but in other cases proper consideration of this requirement will mean that it will be more appropriate to hear the s 37(2)(b) application as part of the final hearing,

---

[20]  See Chapter 6 for discussion about the meaning of 'satisfied' and the burden and standard of proof in applications under MCA 1973, s 37.

[21]  If the disposition being challenged is made by a third party to a fourth party, it is not a reviewable disposition for the purposes of the section: *Ansari v Ansari* [2008] EWCA Civ 1456, [2009] 1 FLR 1121. In that case the husband sold a property to X, who in turn funded the purchase by mortgage from Y. The wife sought to set aside the charge against the property, but it was held that the transaction was not capable of being set aside under the section.

when the court is better able to judge whether an order setting aside the disposition is necessary in all the circumstances of the case.

**7.19** If the application is under s 37(2)(c), the requirements which the applicant for the order must fulfil are similar. The first two matters set out above must still be proved, but there is no need to consider the effect of the disposition on the overall outcome of the case. The applicant needs to show only that the effect of the disposition is to frustrate or impede enforcement of the order. Often this will be relatively easy to prove, as the asset in question is likely to have been the object of a property adjustment order or the intended source of a lump sum payment.

**7.20** Thirdly, the court must be satisfied that the disposition is 'reviewable' within the meaning of s 37(4). The transaction is reviewable unless:

(i)   made for valuable consideration to a person; and

(ii)  that person at that time acted in good faith and without notice of any intention on the part of the respondent to defeat the claim for relief.

The language of the section suggests that the onus of proving that the transaction is not reviewable lies on the respondent and the third party. This provision is considered in more detail at **7.24–7.31**.

**7.21** Fourthly, and this should not be overlooked, the court must be persuaded that it should exercise its discretion to make the order, even if all the technical requirements for the making of an order are met. The discharge of an injunction restraining the sale of an asset which was subsequently the subject of a disposition by the husband which the wife sought to set aside is a relevant factor to consider in deciding whether to set the transaction aside, but it does not prevent an avoidance order being made.[22]

## The presumption as to intention

**7.22**   Where the disposition took place within 3 years of the application under s 37(2)(a) or (b)[23] the applicant need only prove that the disposition would or did have the effect of defeating the claims. Once this is established, it will be presumed that the respondent acted with the intention of defeating the claims. This is a powerful tool which places the onus of proof on the respondent to prove that the disposition was not motivated by such an intention. This topic and its evidential consequences are discussed in the previous chapter[24] in the context of orders pursuant to s 37(2)(a).

---

[22]   *Sherry v Sherry* [1991] 1 FLR 307.
[23]   It seems clear from the language of the section that it is the application for the s 37 order rather than the application for financial relief which is the relevant date for this purpose. Logically this must be so, otherwise the presumption would not be available in many cases where the disposition is made after the making of a final ancillary relief order.
[24]   See **6.35–6.36**.

**7.23** Where the disposition took place more than 3 years before the application, there is no presumption of intention and the applicant must prove the relevant intention on the balance of probabilities. Frequently, in a case where the disposition took place before the making of a substantive ancillary relief application, the simple fact that the transaction took place more than 3 years before the making of an application to set aside a disposition will make this a difficult task, unless there is some evidence that the respondent had throughout the marriage arranged his affairs to ensure that his assets would be beyond the reach of the other party's claims for financial relief upon divorce. There is nothing on the face of the statute or in the case law to suggest that the intention to defeat the applicant's claims may only arise once the applicant decided to bring the claims. It seems open to argue that a respondent can have acted in anticipation of potential claims long before the marriage broke down, although it may be very difficult to prove this if at the time of the disposition the marriage was happy and settled, or there is some other credible explanation for the transfer.[25] Where there is evidence that the respondent has acted dishonestly in the proceedings and without making full or accurate disclosure, it may be somewhat simpler to infer the intention to defeat the claim if the transaction took place at a time when the applicant's intention to make ancillary relief claims was already apparent to the respondent.

## What protection do innocent parties to the transaction have?

**7.24** As already mentioned above, MCA 1973, s 37(4) imports the concept of 'equity's darling' to the disposition of assets. It is a general principle of fairness that a third party who innocently becomes mixed up in another person's dishonest conduct should not suffer financially if he honestly believed that he was entering into a bona fide transaction.

**7.25** It would appear that the burden of proving the matters required for this defence to the making of an avoidance order lies on the respondents to the application, although the reported cases suggest that the courts do not yet appear to have been required to determine where the burden of proof lies. There will usually be more than one respondent to the application, because the other party to the transaction which is sought to be impugned will usually have been joined as a party to the proceedings. To avail themselves of the defence the respondent and/or the other party to the transaction must show the following.

**7.26** First, that the disposition was for valuable consideration. Valuable consideration need not be equivalent to the value of the property in issue. So long as the consideration is not purely nominal, it can be 'valuable consideration', even if it is a transaction at a gross undervalue.[26] A simple gift of property to the third party cannot be for valuable consideration. There will need to be some evidence of the consideration changing hands. Otherwise the

---

[25] For example, *Mubarak v Mubarak* [2007] 1 FLR 722.

[26] *Trowbridge v Trowbridge* [2003] 2 FLR 231 at 249, although where the transaction is at a gross undervalue it may be very difficult for the respondent and the other party to the transaction to show good faith and a lack of knowledge of the circumstances.

court may simply conclude that the whole transaction was a sham. In *Trowbridge v Trowbridge*[27] the court compared the sums paid by the former husband to his new partner against their reasonable living costs and found that there was an excess of payments over expenses and this excess was paid for no valuable consideration and qualified as a reviewable disposition.

**7.27**   Secondly, the third party must have acted in good faith. This factor will usually be closely bound up with the third requirement, in that a person who is shown to act with actual knowledge of the respondent's intention to defeat the applicant's claims will find it very difficult to show that he acted in good faith. A stranger acting at arm's length from the respondent is more likely to be able to establish good faith than the respondent's best friend or a close relative. It may be similarly difficult for a person to show he acted in good faith if he has deliberately turned a 'blind eye' to the respondent's intentions so as to avoid having actual knowledge. Despite the close relationship which is likely to exist between the requirement for good faith and the requirement of acting without notice, they remain separate matters to be proved.

**7.28**   Thirdly, the third party must have acted without notice of any intention on the other party's behalf to defeat the claim for ancillary relief. The time for assessing the third party's good faith and notice is the time of the disposition. 'Notice' for this purpose can mean actual notice, in that the third party knew the respondent's intentions, or it can be constructive notice.[28]

**7.29**   Actual notice can be inferred from circumstantial evidence (eg the transaction being made with a close friend or relative who knew about the divorce and the applicant's claims, the transaction being for no consideration or at a gross undervalue and with no reasonable explanation for the transaction other than to avoid the applicant's claims). Inferring actual notice from the state of affairs is not the same as constructive notice, which is a different concept altogether.

**7.30**   Constructive notice has been defined as:[29]

> 'the knowledge which the courts impute to a person upon a presumption so strong of the existence of the knowledge that it cannot be allowed to be rebutted, either from his knowing something which ought to have put him to further enquiry or from his wilfully abstaining from inquiry, to avoid notice.'

The key ingredients of constructive notice are knowing something which ought to have prompted enquiry or wilfully abstaining from making the enquiry to avoid having actual notice. It is also necessary to show that the enquiry which ought to have been made would have actually revealed the respondent's intention. The need for this causative link is easy to overlook. Clearly, the more the third party knows or ought to know about the applicant's and respondent's

---

[27]   [2003] 2 FLR 231.

[28]   *Kemmis v Kemmis* [1988] 1 WLR 1307.

[29]   *Hunt v Luck* [1901] 1 Ch 45 at 52, approved by the Court of Appeal at [1902] 1 Ch 428.

relationship and affairs, the easier it will be to fix him with constructive notice of the respondent's intention. So where a mortgage is granted to a bank which knows nothing of the parties' private lives and there has been no registration of a pending land action by the applicant, it is unlikely that the bank will be fixed with constructive notice.[30] Where, on the other hand, a small private bank has very detailed knowledge of all relevant aspects of the respondent's affairs, even the absence of a notice of a pending land action registered against the land may not prevent the bank being fixed with constructive notice.[31] The actual registration of a pending land action would fix the third party to a transaction concerning land with actual notice of the claim,[32] but in such circumstances the third party's claims to the property would rank behind the applicant's interest obtained by the final ancillary relief order in any event, so there would be no necessity for an order setting the transaction aside.[33] The presence of a mere Class F land charge or restriction protecting matrimonial home rights[34] would not of itself fix a bona fide mortgage lender with knowledge of an intention to defeat a party's claims.[35]

**7.31**   If the requirements of MCA 1973, s 37(4) are satisfied, the transaction is not a reviewable transaction and the court may not set it aside, even if the respondent to the proceedings has acted very badly and the consequences for the applicant's claim for financial relief are serious. On the other hand, it should not be forgotten that, regardless of the formal requirements of s 37(4), the court retains a broad discretion to refuse to set the transaction aside if the circumstances as a whole make it unjust to do so. The order need not be made simply because the transaction is reviewable and made with the necessary intention by the respondent. So, where a third party did not act dishonestly and played a limited role as a conduit through whom the sale proceeds of a property had passed, an order against her pursuant to s 37 might be unjust.[36]

## What is the procedure for an avoidance of disposition order?

**7.32**   The application is made in Form A. Where the disposition that is sought to be impugned relates to land, the Form A is required to identify the land, stating whether it is registered or unregistered and, if registered, the Land Registry number. As far as they are known to the applicant, particulars of any

---

[30]   *Whittingham v Whittingham* [1979] Fam 19, [1978] 2 WLR 936, [1978] 3 All ER 805, CA.

[31]   *Kemmis v Kemmis* [1988] 1 WLR 1307; on the facts the Court of Appeal found that although the bank was put on inquiry by the facts it already knew, any reasonable enquiries it should have undertaken would not have revealed the husband's actual intention.

[32]   Law of Property Act 1925, s 198(1) and Land Registration Act 2002, ss 29, 30 and 32. Although see *B v B (P Limited Intervening) (No 2)* [1995] 1 FLR 374 at 377, where Hoffman LJ, without deciding the point, expressed some doubts as to whether decisions holding that a claim for ancillary relief could properly be characterised as a pending land action.

[33]   *Perez-Adamson v Perez-Rivas* [1987] 2 FLR 472.

[34]   See **6.8**.

[35]   *Ansari v Ansari* [2008] EWCA Civ 1456, [2009] 1 FLR 1121.

[36]   *Padley v Padley* (unreported) 12 June 2000, CA.

mortgage or other interest in the land should be provided.[37] The application and Form E should be served on the respondent and any person to whom the disposition has been made. Any person who is served with the application and the Form E may file a sworn statement in answer within 14 days of service.[38] A copy of the application is required to be served on any mortgagee identified in that document. Any mortgagee served may apply to the court in writing, within 14 days of service, for a copy of the Form E. A mortgagee may then file a statement in answer within 14 days of receipt of any requested Form E. It should be noted that the third party is not automatically joined to the proceedings, but it is likely that he or she will seek to be joined, and the court will almost inevitably allow the application. Joinder is most likely to be dealt with at the first directions appointment, unless an earlier hearing is sought to deal with the issue, although this is unlikely to be cost-effective. Ordinarily the third party will serve on the other parties an application seeking to be joined to the proceedings returnable at the first directions appointment and the court will deal with the question of joinder at the outset of the FDA.

**7.33** The application for an avoidance of disposition order under s 37(2)(b) will, if practicable, be heard at the same time as the related application for ancillary relief.[39] Sometimes the nature of the application is such that it is more appropriate to have it determined as a preliminary issue, either at a preliminary hearing some time before the final ancillary relief hearing or at the outset of the final hearing, so that the third parties are not required to sit through the hearing of all the other issues in the case, which may not be relevant to the s 37 application. Where the application is pursuant to s 37(2)(c), there may be a related application for variation of some part of the final order which ought to be heard at the same time. Alternatively, the application for the avoidance of disposition order may proceed as a freestanding application or there may be other related proceedings, such as an application pursuant to s 423 of the Insolvency Act 1986,[40] which should be dealt with at the same time.

**7.34** If an application is successful, any order obtained will usually require the third party to effect a transfer of the property back to the respondent's name. The court may also reinforce the order with a restraining order (either under s 37(2)(a) or by a general civil or *Mareva* injunction) preventing further dealings with the property or directing that money be paid into court or retained by solicitors to the order of the court. Furthermore, by s 37(3) the court may give whatever consequential directions appear to be necessary to give effect to the order.[41] Such an order might be restitutionary in nature, requiring the respondent to repay to the third party any sums which the third party had paid to the respondent as part of the transaction. Arguably the court could also

---

[37] FPR 1991, r 2.59(2).
[38] FPR 1991, r 2.59(5) and (6).
[39] FPR 1991, r 2.59(2).
[40] It will be rare that the circumstances will justify an application pursuant to the Insolvency Act 1986 as well as an application pursuant to s 37: *Mubarak v Mubarak* [2007] 2 FLR 364.
[41] The discretion granted by s 37(3) is a broad and flexible one. See *Ansari v Ansari* [2008] EWCA Civ 1456, [2009] 1 FLR 1121.

use this provision to require the third party to make a payment to the respondent or to the applicant in respect of any loss caused by reason of the third party's conduct in relation to the property. The wide nature of this provision may even allow the court to order a sale of any property and direct how the proceeds of sale should be applied, although the breadth of this power has not been fully explored in the reported authorities.

## AVOIDING TRANSACTIONS PURSUANT TO S 423 OF THE INSOLVENCY ACT 1986

**7.35** An application made under s 423 of the Insolvency Act 1986 is a potential alternative to using the avoidance procedures contained in s 37 of the Matrimonial Causes Act 1973. The two applications may even be made together in the alternative. The requirements for the two types of order are slightly different and one may be easier to obtain than the other on a particular set of facts. With that said, in most cases an application pursuant to the 1986 Act will add nothing to an application pursuant to s 37 of the 1973 Act.[42] The provisions of s 423 will be of particular relevance where a costs order made in ancillary relief proceedings needs to be enforced against assets which have been disposed of, because a costs order is not an order for 'financial relief' within the meaning of MCA 1973, s 37(1).

**7.36** So far as relevant, the provisions of s 423 read as follows:

'(1) This section relates to transactions entered into at an undervalue; and a person enters into such a transaction with another person if—

(a) he makes a gift to the other person or he otherwise enters into a transaction with the other on terms that provide for him to receive no consideration;

(b) he enters into a transaction with the other in consideration of marriage; or

(c) he enters into a transaction with the other for a consideration the value of which, in money or money's worth, is significantly less than the value, in money or money's worth, of the consideration provided by himself.

(2) Where a person has entered into such a transaction, the court may, if satisfied under the next subsection, make such order as it thinks fit for—

(a) restoring the position to what it would have been if the transaction had not been entered into, and

(b) protecting the interests of persons who are victims of the transaction.

(3) In the case of a person entering into such a transaction, an order shall only be made if the court is satisfied that it was entered into by him for the purpose—

(a) of putting assets beyond the reach of a person who is making, or may at some time make, a claim against him, or

---

[42] *Mubarak v Mubarak* [2007] 2 FLR 364.

(b) of otherwise prejudicing the interests of such a person in relation to the claim which he is making or may make.

...

(5) In relation to a transaction at an undervalue, references here and below to a victim of the transaction are to a person who is, or is capable of being, prejudiced by it; and in the following two sections the person entering into the transaction is referred to as "the debtor".'

**7.37** The application may be made to the High Court or a court which has bankruptcy jurisdiction over the defendant.[43] The application may be made by the victim of the transaction, being the beneficiary of the ancillary relief order which has been or will be frustrated by the transaction.[44] Although governed by the Insolvency Rules, the application is ultimately likely to be dealt with by the same court in which the ancillary relief proceedings are pending or where they were heard, although this need not necessarily be so.

**7.38** It is necessary to prove that the person who entered into the impugned transaction did so with the purpose of putting the asset out of the reach of the person making a claim against him or otherwise prejudicing the claim. The word 'purpose' in this context has been held to carry the same subjective meaning as the word 'intention' in s 37 of the Matrimonial Causes Act 1973.[45] There is no presumption of 'purpose' in the Insolvency Act 1986, unlike the presumption as to 'intention' in MCA 1973, s 37(5) and so the 'purpose' will need to be proved by the applicant on the balance of probabilities.[46]

**7.39** Section 423 requires the transaction to have been at an undervalue. A transfer of property at full market value will make the transaction immune from this provision. In contrast, MCA 1973, s 37(4) refers to 'valuable consideration', which need not be equivalent to the value of the property in issue. So long as the consideration is not purely nominal, it can be 'valuable consideration' even if it is a transaction at a gross undervalue.[47] There is, therefore, no requirement to show that the transaction was at an undervalue to invoke s 37.[48] There will be cases, therefore, where an application may only be pursued pursuant to s 37 of the MCA 1973 and not s 423 of the Insolvency Act 1986, because even though the intent to put the assets beyond the reach of the other spouse can be proved, it cannot be proved that the transaction was at

[43] IA 1986, s 423(4).

[44] IA 1986, s 424(1).

[45] *Trowbridge v Trowbridge* [2003] 2 FLR 231 at 247. *Mubarak v Mubarak* [2007] 2 FLR 364 at [47].

[46] *Trowbridge v Trowbridge* [2003] 2 FLR 231 at 248.

[47] *Trowbridge v Trowbridge* [2003] 2 FLR 231 at 249, although where the transaction is at a gross undervalue it may be very difficult for the respondent and the other party to the transaction to show good faith and a lack of knowledge of the circumstances.

[48] Although in most cases where MCA 1973, s 37(2)(b) or (c) is invoked it is likely that the disposal will have been at an undervalue and that fact will be relied upon as proof of the respondent's bad faith, whereas a transfer for full value to a third party acting in good faith may prove very difficult to challenge.

an undervalue. On the other hand, in many cases it will be easier to prove that the transaction was at an undervalue (for the purposes of s 423) than to show the absence of 'valuable consideration' (for the purposes of s 37(4)).[49]

**7.40** Further significant differences between the two provisions arise when consideration is turned to the treatment of the third parties who receive the property. First, whereas MCA 1973, s 37 appears to be limited to setting aside the first transaction from the respondent to a third party,[50] IA 1986, s 423 is capable of setting aside subsequent transactions so long as the statutory criteria are established.[51]

**7.41** Secondly, whereas MCA 1973, s 37(4) includes the concept of 'equity's darling', preventing the court from setting aside a transaction made for value to a person acting in good faith and without knowledge of the respondent's intention to defeat the applicant's claim (see **7.24–7.31**), there is no identical bar to setting aside a transaction pursuant to IA 1986, s 423. Section 425(2) of IA 1986 offers similar protection to that under MCA 1973, s 37(4) to a person who acquires the property from someone other than the respondent, but that protection does not extend to the person who received the property directly from the respondent. In other words, where a husband transfers property to his friend, X, who in turn sells it to a third party, Y, who has no knowledge of the husband or the origin of the property, then the transfer to Y cannot be set aside and Y will be able to retain full title to the property.[52] X, on the other hand, will not be able to prevent his transaction with the husband being set aside on this ground and may still be required to pay a sum to the husband even though the property can no longer be recovered by him. It is important to note that the section refers to 'notice' rather than actual knowledge. Constructive notice is likely to be implied to Y if he was put on notice of what lay behind the transaction but chose to close his eyes to the reasonably obvious.[53]

**7.42** Section 423 applies to a disposal of property both in the period before the making of a final order and the period after an order has been made and enforcement of that order is sought.[54] It is possible to apply for an order under this provision pending ancillary relief proceedings, if that is considered to be necessary, although the use of s 37 of the MCA 1973 is far more common in the later context.

---

[49]   It is important to remember that, notwithstanding this, the absence of 'valuable consideration' is only one of the three ingredients of the s 37(4) 'defence'.

[50]   In s 37(2)(b) and (c) 'the disposition' which may be set aside is in the singular and is limited to the disposition made by the 'other party' to the ancillary relief proceedings. Hence, a further disposition by the third party is arguably not within the scope of the section. In *Ansari v Ansari* [2008] EWCA Civ 1456, [2009] 1 FLR 1121 the Court of Appeal expressed the view, without formally deciding the point, that s 37(3) was broad enough in its scope to permit subsequent disposals made in bad faith also to be set aside.

[51]   IA 1986, s 425(2).

[52]   IA 1986, s 425(2)(a).

[53]   See the consideration of constructive notice in the context of MCA 1973, s 37(4) above.

[54]   *Trowbridge v Trowbridge* [2003] 2 FLR 231 at 248.

**7.43**    The court has broad powers to make whatever order it sees fit upon such an application, including vesting the property in any person, including the applicant for the order.[55] It is important to note that an order pursuant to IA 1986, s 423 cannot be used to put the applicant in a better position than he or she would have been in had the transaction at an undervalue not occurred. So, where a husband had disposed of property at an undervalue and subsequently became bankrupt, the wife could not seek to have the property re-vested in the husband's name so that she could obtain ancillary relief orders against it. Instead, the property would vest in the husband's trustee in bankruptcy.[56]

**7.44**    Any order obtained pursuant to s 423 is also likely to include restitutionary provisions to place the parties to the transaction, so far as is possible, in the position they would have been in had the transaction not occurred.[57]

---

[55]    IA 1986, s 425(1).
[56]    *Ram v Ram and Others* [2005] 2 FLR 63.
[57]    See IA 1986, s 423(2)(a).

# Part IV
# **PROPERTY**

# Chapter 8

# OWNERSHIP OF MATRIMONIAL PROPERTY

## INTRODUCTION

**8.1**    The parties to a marriage are likely to own many different types of property. In many cases ownership issues will be relatively straightforward and the court will have little difficulty in identifying the asset, placing a value upon it and then dealing with it as appropriate to the circumstances of the case. There are, however, many types of property where the situation is far less straightforward. Some of these are considered in the subsequent chapters, where companies, partnerships, farms, trusts and inheritances are explored in greater detail. This chapter deals with a fundamental general issue, namely when, if at all, it is necessary to identify ownership of property in the context of ancillary relief proceedings.

**8.2**    In most marriages the most important asset, and usually the most valuable, is the former matrimonial home. Particular issues relating to real property and the matrimonial home are considered in the next chapter, whilst other forms of property are looked at in Chapter 10.[1]

**8.3**    It is highly likely that practitioners will be faced by forms of property which are novel in their form and difficult to unravel. This is particularly likely in the context of those families of substantial wealth and greater financial sophistication where investments may be contained within complex and unusual arrangements. Such arrangements may use a combination of trusts, companies and contracts to hold the parties' funds in what is hoped to be a tax efficient and profitable fashion. Sometimes these arrangements are specifically constructed to protect them from claims by creditors or the other party to the marriage. The assets may also be spread across more than one jurisdiction. Plainly such arrangements are highly specialised in their form and expert advice is likely to be required to attempt to unravel and then value such assets.

---

[1]    For example, chattels including contents, choses in action, intellectual property rights, insurance policies, shares, options and other deferred assets. Pensions are dealt with in Chapters 19 to 22.

# OWNERSHIP OF PROPERTY – DOES IT MATTER?

**8.4**   Although the courts now habitually refer to 'matrimonial property',[2] it is important to understand what is meant by this term. During the 1960s there was a clear movement by the courts (led in the main by Lord Denning MR) to create a category of 'family assets', being those assets 'acquired by one or other or both of the parties, with the intention that there should be continuing provision for them and their children during their joint lives, and used for the benefit of the family as a whole'.[3] In such circumstances it was said that there was a presumption that the property in question was intended to be beneficially owned by the husband and wife in equal shares.[4] Indeed, many members of the public continue to believe that there is a high degree of joint ownership of assets as soon as two people are married. This concept of 'family assets' to which husband and wife became equally entitled as a matter of property law was firmly rejected by the House of Lords in the cases of *Pettit v Pettit*[5] and *Gissing v Gissing*.[6]

**8.5**   So, under English law, husband and wife may still own property in their own individual names and the other spouse may acquire a proprietary interest in such property only by the operation of the conventional law of property, applied between husband and wife in much the same way as it is applied between non-married persons. English law continues to resist any community of property regime between husband and wife, leaving them to decide between themselves how property is to be owned.[7] Indeed, they may decide to distribute property between themselves during the marriage to make the most efficient use of their respective tax allowances and other benefits.[8]

**8.6**   Nevertheless, it will only rarely be necessary or desirable to determine the precise shares the husband and wife own in any particular property. As Ormrod LJ pointed out in *Fielding v Fielding*,[9] 'It is nearly always a purely theoretical exercise to try to determine the strict property rights of each spouse'. The court is required by MCA 1973, s 25(2)(a) to have regard to all the property and financial resources of the parties.[10] Furthermore, the court has broad powers to redistribute the assets between the parties upon divorce. It seems to be of little relevance whether the property regarded as the

---

[2]   'Matrimonial property' and 'non-matrimonial property' per Lord Nicholls in *Miller v Miller; McFarlane v McFarlane* [2006] 1 FLR 1186 at [21]–[23] and 'matrimonial property' and 'family assets' per Baroness Hale at [149].

[3]   *Wachtel v Wachtel* [1973] Fam 72 at 90.

[4]   See, for example, the judgment of Lord Denning MR in the Court of Appeal in *Gissing v Gissing* [1969] 2 Ch 85 at 93.

[5]   [1970] AC 777.

[6]   [1971] AC 886.

[7]   *Miller v Miller; McFarlane v McFarlane* [2006] 1 FLR 1186.

[8]   See Chapter 23.

[9]   [1977] 1 WLR 1146 at 1148.

[10]   There can be no 'quarantining' of assets on the basis of their strict ownership by one party or by reason of their source from outside the parties' joint efforts in the marriage. See the cases on non-matrimonial property and contributions referred to in Chapter 16.

matrimonial home is owned in the parties' joint names or in the name of only one party.[11] In the vast majority of cases, therefore, no useful purpose will be served by determining the shares in which property is owned. Certainly the issue of separate proceedings pursuant to the Trusts of Land and Appointment of Trustees Act 1996 by one divorcing spouse against the other is likely to be criticised:

> 'I find it hard to conceive that where a married couple are engaged in contested ancillary relief proceedings, the application of a TOLATA claim by one against the other could possibly be justified. As the decision of the House of Lords in *White v White* [2000] 2 FLR 981 makes plain, issues between a husband and a wife are to be determined within the four corners of the Matrimonial Causes Act 1973 and on the application of the statutory criteria there set out. The issue of separate proceedings to establish relatively arcane questions as to equitable entitlement between them is deprecated.'[12]

**8.7**   Even in cases where a party seeks to argue that a distinction needs to be drawn between 'matrimonial property' and 'non-matrimonial property' to justify something other than an equal division of the assets, it seems unlikely that any strict determination of the parties' respective proprietary interests in property will be required. General practice in ancillary relief cases suggests that the court will take a 'broad brush' approach to the source of each asset and the purpose for which it was purchased. However, in *Rossi v Rossi*[13] Mr Nicholas Mostyn QC, sitting as a deputy High Court judge, stated the importance, since the case of *Miller v Miller; McFarlane v McFarlane*,[14] of identifying in every case the matrimonial and non-matrimonial property by reference to the time and manner of its acquisition by one of the parties. Similar sentiments have been expressed in several other authorities.[15] At the same time, a number of court judgments have deprecated the cost and complexity involved in what often becomes a laborious process of evidence gathering, historical valuations and difficult forensic fact-finding. Perhaps the most eloquent and powerful criticism of this technical approach was by Moylan J in *C v C*,[16] where he found it to be unhelpful and unnecessary when conducting the broad and flexible assessment required by s 25 of the MCA 1973. In most cases it seems that the process of analysing which party owns what will be subsumed within a wider analysis of the parties' respective contributions to the marriage and the general manner in which they have arranged their affairs, rather than as a strict analysis of their proprietary rights to the property as between each other. Where the parties have carefully planned the distribution of the property between them during the marriage, this may be a factor for the court to take into account

---

[11]   See *Miller v Miller; McFarlane v McFarlane* [2006] 1 FLR 1186 at [149] per Baroness Hale in the context of the broader discussion about the significance of the source and nature of assets.

[12]   *Prazic v Prazic* [2006] 2 FLR 1128 per Thorpe LJ at [25]. In *White v White* the House of Lords had been critical of attempts by the parties to draw up a strict partnership account in relation to their farming business.

[13]   See also *S v S (Non-Matrimonial Property: Conduct)* [2007] 1 FLR 790.

[14]   [2006] 1 FLR 1186.

[15]   Considered fully in Chapter 16.

[16]   [2009] 1 FLR 8.

when deciding how to divide the assets upon divorce, but it will be only one of many factors.[17] This is likely to remain a developing area in the case law, related as it is to the growing use and significance of pre-nuptial and post-nuptial agreements. The courts' approach to matrimonial and non-matrimonial assets is considered in considerably more depth in Chapter 17.

**8.8**     There are nevertheless two circumstances where the court will be required to determine the property interests of the husband and wife in a formal way:

• Where there are third party interests in the property.

• Where one spouse has become bankrupt or subject to a confiscation or recovery order pursuant to the Proceeds of Crime Act 2002.

## THIRD PARTY INTERESTS IN PROPERTY

**8.9**     The court in ancillary relief proceedings may only make orders in respect of the property of the parties to the marriage, not the property of third parties.[18] Where a third party claims to have an interest in property which is held by one or both parties to the marriage, it will be necessary to determine the extent of the third party's interest and how that interest should be dealt with within the proceedings. Where it is alleged by one of the parties to the proceedings that there is some third party interest in an asset, this should be made known to the court and to the other side at an early stage of the proceedings, in the Form A if the property in question is land,[19] or by correspondence in the case of other property. Steps can then be taken to serve the third party with notice of the proceedings so that they can seek to become involved in them. Where a third party asserts an interest in property which is the subject matter of the proceedings, he or she may apply to be joined to the proceedings as an intervenor to be heard on that issue.

**8.10**    It is not generally necessary to issue separate proceedings to deal with the disputed interests of third parties. The court conducting the ancillary relief proceedings is able definitively to settle any property claims made by an intervening third party.[20] To do so, however, it is essential that the third party has notice of the proceedings and the opportunity to be heard on the issue. So long as the third party is able to make his or her case to the court, the court's decision will be binding upon the third party, and he or she will be estopped from raising the issue again in any subsequent proceedings (other than in an appeal, of course). Lord Denning MR put it this way in *Tebbutt v Haynes*:[21]

---

[17]   See e g *Miller v Miller; McFarlane v McFarlane* [2006] 1 FLR 1186 at [153].
[18]   But regard may be had to property owned by third parties as a potential resource: *Thomas v Thomas* [1995] 2 FLR 668 and *TL v ML* [2006] 1 FLR 1263. See **15.25** et seq.
[19]   FPR 1991, r 2.59(2).
[20]   *Tebbutt v Haynes* [1981] 2 All ER 238.
[21]   [1981] 2 All ER 238 at 242. See also *Thrasyvoulou v Secretary of State for Environment* [1988]

'If there has been an issue raised and decided against a party in circumstances in which he has had a full and fair opportunity of dealing with the whole case, then that issue must be taken as being finally and conclusively decided against him. He is not at liberty to reopen it unless the circumstances are such as to make it fair and just that it should be reopened.'

**8.11**  It is important to remember that in dealing with the claim of a third party the court is not exercising discretionary powers pursuant to the Matrimonial Causes Act 1973. The court will be deciding property rights in accordance with the strict law of property and law of trusts. It should not be forgotten that it will be for the person asserting an interest in the land to prove the case on the balance of probabilities and that the liability for costs in respect of litigating the third party property issue will in general follow the event.

**8.12**  Useful guidance for the conduct of a hearing dealing with the property rights of a third party was given in *TL v ML*:[22]

- the third party should be joined to the proceedings at the earliest opportunity;

- directions should be given for the issue to be fully pleaded by points of claim and points of defence;

- separate witness statements should be directed in relation to the dispute; and

- the dispute should be directed to be heard separately as a preliminary issue, before the FDR.

**8.13**  The authors suggest that, notwithstanding the final point above, there may be cases where it will not be cost-effective to determine the issue as a preliminary issue ahead of the FDR.[23] However, in order for any FDR to be effective, the third party must be joined to the proceedings and/or in attendance at the FDR so that a binding settlement can be reached.

---

3 WLR 1. It remains unclear whether providing notice and an opportunity to the third party is enough to make the decision binding, or whether actual joinder as a party is required. *Tebbutt v Haynes* and *Thrasyvoulou* suggest that a fair opportunity to be heard and to participate in the proceedings will suffice, but in *Secretary of State for Trade & Industry v Bairstow* [2003] 3 WLR 841 at [39] the Court of Appeal appeared to suggest that findings would be binding only where the third party had party status in the proceedings. Dicta in *TL v ML* [2006] 1 FLR 1263 and *Rossi v Rossi* [2007] 1 FLR 790 also suggest that joinder is necessary to make declarations binding on interested third parties. On the uncertain state of the authorities it would seem prudent to join a third party with a potential interest in property at an early stage to ensure that all matters relating to particular property can be finally concluded within the ancillary relief proceedings.

22  [2006] 1 FLR 1263, echoing similar guidance given by Waite J in *Hammond v Mitchell* [1991] 1 WLR 1127. See also the comments in *A v A* [2007] 2 FLR 467 at [24] as to the benefits of 'the intellectual discipline which is one of the advantages of any system of pleading'.

23  For example, where the third party's interest in the proceedings extends beyond the discrete question of ownership of one asset and concerns the parties' financial affairs more broadly.

**8.14** Even where there is no dispute about the third party's interest in an asset, it may be necessary for the third party to be joined to the proceedings to be heard on the question of how that asset is to be dealt with. Before the court is able to make an order for the sale of a property in which a third party has an interest, the third party must be heard on the issue.[24] Fairness may also dictate that such a person should have a right to be heard before a property adjustment order is made which affects the ownership of property in which the third party has an interest. It may be that the costs of such an exercise can be avoided if the parties agree at an early stage in the proceedings that such an asset will not be sold or will not be subject to a property adjustment order. In those circumstances, the third party's interests are unlikely to be affected and it may not be necessary to join him or her to the proceedings. Where partition of land owned jointly with another person is sought (a not uncommon situation in the particular context of family farming cases), the affected third parties will also need to be joined to the proceedings, possibly following a formal application within the proceedings for orders pursuant to s 14 of the Trusts of Land and Appointment of Trustees Act 1996.[25]

**8.15** Where it cannot be shown that one of the parties to the marriage has a direct beneficial entitlement to property owned by a third party, that property may still be relevant to the resolution of the ancillary relief proceedings. Whilst the court has no power to provide relief from the assets of a third party, it can have regard to the assets of a third party as a potential resource from which one of the parties to the marriage may be able to satisfy the orders which the court proposes to make. This approach stems from the willingness of the matrimonial courts to look through strict legal entitlements to the reality of a person's financial resources.[26]

**8.16** In *Thomas v Thomas*,[27] for example, the Court of Appeal endorsed an order which provided 'judicious encouragement' to the husband's family to provide him with the means to satisfy the relief provided for the wife. Similar orders have been made in relation to parties who have some entitlement under a discretionary trust. Care must be exercised in adopting this approach.[28] First and foremost, the court should not normally make an order which exceeds the assets of the paying spouse, for such an order would in effect be an order in relation to the property of the third parties. Where, however, the property is effectively property to which the party has an entitlement, as under a discretionary trust, this property can be brought into account more readily than property belonging to third parties to which the spouse has no proprietary claim whatsoever. Secondly, a distinction should be drawn between, on the one

---

[24]  MCA 1973, s 24A(6).
[25]  See Chapter 9.
[26]  Historically, the ecclesiastical courts dealing with financial issues on marital breakdown 'showed a degree of practical wisdom ... they were not misled by appearances ... they looked at realities', per Lord Merriman in *N v N* (1928) 44 TLR 324 at 327 and see also *O'D v O'D* [1976] Fam 83 at 90. See **15.25** et seq for a detailed discussion of this topic.
[27]  [1995] 2 FLR 668.
[28]  See *TL v ML* [2006] 1 FLR 1263.

hand, the prospect of support from a professionally run discretionary trust, whose trustees would be expected to comply with the 'judicious encouragement' from the court and, on the other hand, hoped for support from members of the wider family, who would be quite entitled to reject the 'judicious encouragement' and refuse to provide the spouse with any support. In *TL v ML*[29] the position was summarised in this way:

> 'If the court is satisfied on the balance of probabilities that an outsider will provide money to meet an award that a party cannot meet from his absolute property then the court can, if it is fair to do so, make an award on that footing. But if it is clear that the outsider, being a person who has only historically supplied bounty, will not, reasonably or unreasonably, come to the aid of the payer then there is precious little the court can do about it.'

## BANKRUPTCY OR PROCEEDS OF CRIME PROCEEDINGS

**8.17** The husband or wife may need to prove a beneficial interest in property in the event that the other party to the marriage becomes bankrupt. A similar situation may arise where the other spouse faces a confiscation order following a criminal conviction or a civil recovery order of criminal property pursuant to the provisions of the Proceeds of Crime Act 2002.

**8.18** In the case of a bankruptcy order, all the property of the bankrupt spouse vests in the trustee in bankruptcy and ceases to be available to the other spouse to satisfy any ancillary relief order. In these circumstances the non-bankrupt spouse may have to prove that he or she beneficially owned some part of the bankrupt spouse's assets. Most commonly the asset in question will be the former matrimonial home, but the principles extend to all other forms of property. If the matter cannot be resolved by agreement, the non-bankrupt spouse will need to issue an application seeking a declaration as to his or her interests in the assets in question. This could be done in the ancillary relief proceedings (including joinder to the proceedings of the trustee in bankruptcy), in the bankruptcy proceedings, by freestanding application pursuant to s 17 of the Married Women's Property Act 1882 or, in the case of land, pursuant to s 14 of the Trusts of Land and Appointment of Trustees Act 1996.[30] Which option is most suitable will depend on the circumstances of the case and the progress of any particular set of proceedings. Clearly, the most appropriate option will be the one which incurs the least cost.

**8.19** On such an application the court will need to determine the non-bankrupt spouse's beneficial interest in the property in question in accordance with strict property law. The discretionary powers under the Matrimonial Causes Act 1973 may only be used against the other spouse to

---

[29] [2006] 1 FLR 1263 at [101].
[30] The proceedings may also be brought by the trustee in bankruptcy seeking an order for sale, as in *Re Citro* [1991] Ch 142 and *Avis v Turner* [2008] 1 FLR 1127.

alter existing property interests. They cannot be used against the trustee in bankruptcy once a bankruptcy order has been made. If a beneficial interest is established, it may become necessary to carry out an equitable accounting exercise in relation to mortgage payments, improvements and occupation rent since the separation.[31] Such an exercise may be important in increasing the non-bankrupt spouse's interest in the proceeds of sale of the property, particularly where a considerable period has elapsed since the bankrupt spouse left the property. The equitable accounting exercise may, on the other hand, reduce the non-bankrupt spouse's share. For example, where the bankrupt spouse has remained in occupation of the property following the making of a bankruptcy order, the non-bankrupt spouse may remain liable to the trustee in bankruptcy for occupation rent during that period.[32] Normally, equitable accounting should be delayed until after the property in question has been sold, because it is a discretionary exercise which is fact sensitive and so all the relevant information should be before the court before the process is undertaken.[33]

**8.20** Proceedings under the Proceeds of Crime Act 2002[34] raise particular problems. Confiscation proceedings following conviction of one spouse may require the other spouse to take steps to assert an interest in property held in the name of the convicted spouse. This will usually be at the stage that enforcement proceedings are taken in relation to a confiscation order.[35] Under the Drug Trafficking Act 1994 such enforcement proceedings took place in the High Court. Under the Proceeds of Crime Act 2002 they now take place within the Crown Court. This results in the criminal court being faced with having to resolve civil disputes as to the ownership of assets which would ordinarily be within the jurisdiction of the High Court or a county court. This also means that the former approach of having the confiscation proceedings and the ancillary relief proceedings listed together before a judge of the High Court is no longer possible.[36] The proceedings should, if possible, be timetabled to

---

[31] See e g *Re Pavlou* [1993] 1 WLR 1046. Since the enactment of the Trusts of Land and Appointment of Trustees Act 1996 the question of occupation rent is a matter of discretion to be determined by application of s 15 of that Act rather than by applying the old case law on equitable accounting: *Stack v Dowden* [2007] 2 AC 432. Notably, the interests of a minor occupying or who might reasonably be expected to occupy the property as a home is a factor which must be expressly considered.

[32] *Byford v Butler* [2004] 1 FLR 56. This decision needs to be read in the light of the decision in *Stack v Dowden* (above).

[33] *Wilcox v Tait* [2006] EWCA Civ 1867, [2007] 2 FLR 871. Although there may be cases where it can be done prior to sale, e g where a sale price has been agreed and a sale is imminent.

[34] This legislation effectively replaced the previous powers to make confiscation orders under the Criminal Justice Act 1988 and the Drug Trafficking Act 1994. To date there is a limited amount of case law dealing with the relationship between the 2002 Act and the Matrimonial Causes Act 1973. However, the similarities between the provisions of the parts of the 2002 Act dealing with confiscation orders and those of the 1988 and 1994 Acts mean that the authorities in relation to the earlier legislation remain relevant, subject to some procedural changes: *Webber v Webber* [2007] 2 FLR 116.

[35] For example, *Gibson v Revenue & Customs Prosecution Office* [2008] 2 FLR 1672.

[36] *Webber v Webber* [2007] 2 FLR 116, disapplying the practice which had been suggested in *W v H (HM Customs and Excise Intervening)* [2006] 2 FLR 258.

ensure that the matrimonial proceedings are completed before the confiscation enforcement proceedings are determined.[37] In *Webber v Webber*,[38] confiscation proceedings and ancillary relief proceedings were both in existence. In the interests of saving time and expense, it was held to be preferable for the ancillary relief proceedings to be heard first and, on the adjourned confiscation hearing, the criminal trial judge would then be in a position to know the extent of the guilty husband's interest in the former matrimonial home that was amenable to the confiscation proceedings.[39] The Crown Prosecution Service or other relevant prosecuting authority is likely to become a party to the ancillary relief proceedings.[40] Where the parties are not divorcing, the innocent spouse may need to seek a declaration of the interest within the confiscation proceedings in the same way as he or she would within bankruptcy proceedings.

**8.21** The court exercising its discretionary powers under the Matrimonial Causes Act 1973 in a case where there are also criminal confiscation proceedings must strike a balance between the matrimonial claims of the spouses and Parliament's clear intention that the parties should not benefit from the proceeds of crime. Neither the matrimonial legislation nor the criminal legislation has priority in this respect.[41] In a case where a wife was wholly ignorant of her husband's criminal activities and the matrimonial assets in relation to which she was making her claims were untainted by criminality, the wife obtained the relief she would have obtained had there been no confiscation proceedings, even though this reduced the amount against which the confiscation order against the husband could be enforced.[42] Where, on the other hand, the applicant spouse was aware of the tainted source of property, that was likely to weigh decisively in favour of the discretion being exercised in the direction of confiscation, unless there were compelling reasons to the contrary, such as the need of a severely disabled child for specially adapted accommodation.[43] Sometimes balancing all the relevant factors will still permit an order within the ancillary relief proceedings which relates to tainted assets.[44]

---

[37] *Webber v Webber* [2007] 2 FLR 116.

[38] [2007] 2 FLR 116.

[39] It should be noted that in *Webber* it was accepted that the wife's property was not tainted with knowledge of her husband's criminality.

[40] See e g *Grimes v Crown Prosecution Service* [2004] 1 FLR 910.

[41] *Re MCA; HM Customs and Excise Commissioners and Long v A and A; A v A (Long Intervening)* [2003] 1 FLR 164. The confiscation proceedings in that case were pursuant to the Drug Trafficking Act 1994 rather than the Proceeds of Crime Act 2002. The same principle applies to the relationship between the Matrimonial Causes Act 1973 and the Criminal Justice Act 1988: *Stodgell v Stodgell* [2008] EWHC 1926 (Admin). These principles also apply to the Proceeds of Crime Act 2002: *Webber v Webber* [2007] 2 FLR 116.

[42] *Re MCA; HM Customs and Excise Commissioners and Long v A and A; A v A (Long Intervening)* [2003] 1 FLR 164. See also *Revenue and Customs Prosecutions Office v S* [2008] EWHC 2214 (Admin).

[43] *Crown Prosecution Service v Richards* [2006] 2 FLR 1220. Although even the needs of children do not necessarily divert the statutory purpose of the confiscation legislation: *Stodgell v Stodgell* [2008] EWHC 1926 (Admin); see also the Court of Appeal judgment on refusal of permission to appeal this decision at [2009] EWCA Civ 243.

[44] *R v R (Financial Provision: Confiscation and Restraint)* [2006] 2 FLR 1137; *Revenue and Customs Prosecutions Office v S* [2008] EWHC 2214 (Admin).

**8.22**   Where the proceedings are brought under the civil recovery provisions of the Proceeds of Crime Act 2002, rather than following a criminal conviction, more complex issues may arise and the 'innocent' spouse will most probably need to intervene in the High Court recovery proceedings to protect his or her interest. As civil recovery proceedings take place in the High Court, it is possible to transfer the civil recovery proceedings to be heard by a judge of the Family Division alongside the ancillary relief proceedings. It seems that this would be the most appropriate means of resolving the interconnected issues, although the increase in the overall cost of both sets of proceedings is likely to be significant. Such cases can give rise to complex issues.[45]

---

[45]   For a more detailed consideration of the complex provisions of Part V of the Proceeds of Crime Act 2002 see Gumpert, Kirk and Bojarski *Proceeds of Crime Act: A Practical Guide* (Jordans, 2003).

# Chapter 9

# REAL PROPERTY AND THE FORMER MATRIMONIAL HOME

**9.1**    In many cases the most significant assets are likely to be the former matrimonial home and any other real property. The value of residential property has risen dramatically over the last part of the twentieth century and the first part of the twenty-first century. Recent years have seen many husbands and wives purchasing real property purely for investment purposes or with the combined purpose of providing a home for an elderly relative and investment. Sometimes such property is bought jointly with other investors or with contributions from family members. The ownership of such property may be a matter of dispute with third parties and this has been considered in the previous chapter. In this section some of the particular issues which arise in relation to real estate are considered.

## PROTECTING THE ASSET

**9.2**    The land registration system renders interests in land relatively easy to protect while proceedings are pending. This is considered in detail at **6.6–6.10**.

## REVERSIONARY INTERESTS

**9.3**    Sometimes land is owned subject to a trust which grants an interest in the property to a third party for a specified period. Such an interest may be a life interest permitting the third party to live at the property for as long as he or she wishes, or it may be a lesser interest of shorter duration. In either case the result is likely to be that the value of the property is affected by the third party's interest. The reversionary interest arising at the end of the life interest is a property right which can be transferred or sold. However, where the reversion is only likely to become available a long time in the future, it may be difficult to raise sums by sale of that reversionary right in in the short term. Reversionary interests can be valued and taken into account with the other assets. Clearly, if one party is to retain the reversionary interest, that party will be keen to stress that its value is unlikely to be realised for a long time and will argue for a discount when balancing that asset against more liquid assets which are retained by the other spouse.

**9.4**    Where the value of the reversion is likely to be a very substantial proportion of the overall assets, fairness may demand that one of three options be taken. First, a deferred lump sum order may be made, payable once the reversion falls in. The lump sum may specify an amount to be paid, if the value can be ascertained with some confidence, or it may be possible to specify that the lump sum shall be equivalent to an identified proportion of the value of the property at the time the reversion falls in.[1] Secondly, the lump sum application may be adjourned until the reversion falls in, at which time it can be restored and considered further. There are similarities here with adjourning a lump sum claim in expectation of an inheritance, and reference should be made to **18.33–18.41** where this issue is considered in detail. Thirdly, and this may be the preferred option in many cases,[2] the reversionary interest can be transferred into the parties' joint names with a direction that the property should be sold upon the reversion falling in, and the proceeds proportionally divided at that point. Of course, this approach may not suit all cases and it is not entirely consistent with a financial clean break between the parties.

## PROPERTIES SUBJECT TO A TENANCY

**9.5**    An investment property may be let to tenants. The tenancy may affect the value of the property. Whilst the freehold interest in the property can still be sold, property subject to a tenancy is not sold with vacant possession and its value may be lower. Whilst this is true of residential property, an existing lease of commercial property is less likely to affect the value of a property adversely. In fact, it may increase the value, because the lease provides a certain income stream from the property. The form of the lease may also affect the value of the property. An assured shorthold tenancy of residential property can be brought to an end by giving 2 months' notice once the original term of the tenancy has expired. An assured tenancy or older protected tenancy may be more difficult to bring to an end and the value of the property may be affected as a result.

**9.6**    These are all matters which must be addressed with the expert appointed in the proceedings to value the property. Not only should the property be valued subject to the tenancy, but the value with vacant possession should also be obtained for comparative purposes. The full market rent for the property should also be assessed to establish whether the current rent paid on the property by the existing tenants is appropriate. It will then be a matter of submissions as to what real value the court should attribute to the asset, and the parties will be better able to assess whether it is more beneficial to seek to sell the asset or to retain it.

---

[1]    It should be noted that the lump sum cannot be varied as to amount, save for the limited power to vary a lump sum by instalments (as to which see **27.48–27.51**), and interim lump sums are not permissible: *Bolsom v Bolsom* (1983) 4 FLR 21.

[2]    On the basis of the need to ensure that property of different types is distributed fairly between the parties: *Wells v Wells* [2002] 2 FLR 97.

# MORTGAGES

**9.7**    Most commonly a mortgage appears as a liability of the parties to the ancillary relief proceedings. Sometimes a mortgage may be an asset of one or both of the parties. A mortgage or charge over property is an interest in land. Where one of the parties holds a charge or mortgage over the property of a third party, the charge is in itself a form of property, which the court should take into account. The terms of the mortgage or charge will indicate what practical value should be attributed to it. Where the mortgage or charge cannot be realised for a considerable period, it must be considered in a similar way to reversionary interests referred to above. Where the charge is not for a fixed amount but for a percentage of the value of a property, the property against which it is charged may need to be valued. If the terms of the charge do not permit access to the property for the purposes of a valuation, which in all probability they will not, the valuation may have to be carried out from outside the property.[3]

**9.8**    Alternatively, a mortgage or charge may be held by a third party over one of the properties owned by the parties. Most probably this will be the loan from a commercial lender which allowed the parties to purchase the property. The court is unable to alter the rights of the third party lender against the parties within the ancillary relief proceedings. The only way in which the lender's rights against one or other of the parties may be altered is if agreement is reached with the lender (eg by an agreement to release one party from the personal covenants under the mortgage) or if the mortgage is successfully set aside on the basis of undue influence or fraud.

**9.9**    It must be noted that where there is a parallel dispute as to the validity of a mortgage, the parties are expected to be consistent between the two sets of proceedings. A wife cannot maintain in ancillary relief proceedings that a mortgage is valid against a property she seeks to obtain as part of the ancillary relief order (in order to reduce the apparent net value of the asset she is obtaining), but then claim in later proceedings against the mortgagee that the mortgage is unenforceable against the property. The inconsistency of the position adopted in the later proceedings is likely to be considered to amount to an abuse of process.[4]

**9.10**    Where an issue as to the validity of a mortgage arises, it would usually be appropriate to have that issue decided in appropriate proceedings before the ancillary relief proceedings are concluded. It is not generally appropriate for the court in ancillary relief proceedings to speculate as to the outcome of other

---

[3]    NB: There is a power (rarely utilised by practitioners in ancillary relief proceedings) for the court to order a non-party to permit property in his possession to be inspected – Supreme Court Act 1981, s 34 and County Courts Act 1984, s 53. This power may be used, if necessary, to obtain a valuation of property. In deciding whether to exercise its discretion to make such an order, the court will have regard to similar factors to those applied when considering an application for an order requiring production of documents from a third party (see Chapter 5).

[4]    *First National Bank plc v Walker* [2001] 1 FLR 495.

related civil proceedings when it is possible simply to adjourn the proceedings to await the outcome, or hear the two sets of proceedings together or sequentially.[5]

**9.11**   Where the mortgage remains charged against a property, any transfer of the land will be subject to the mortgage. Where there is a joint mortgage, both parties will almost certainly have given personal covenants guaranteeing the mortgage. The court will ordinarily require the transferee to undertake to use best endeavours to obtain the other spouse's release from the personal covenants under the mortgage. As a matter of good practice, parties should make enquiries of the mortgagee at an early stage to ascertain its position as to the personal covenants. If the mortgagee agrees to release one party from the mortgage upon a transfer of the property to the other party, this can be recorded in the order and, rather than undertaking to use 'best endeavours', the transferee may unconditionally agree to obtain the other's release. On any basis, there should also be an indemnity given by the transferee covering repayment of sums due under the mortgage. The court can extract this indemnity by refusing to make the property adjustment order unless the undertaking is given or by making the property adjustment order conditional upon the offer of such an indemnity.

**9.12**   Allowing one party to retain the former matrimonial home will in many cases require the other party to purchase a new home. Unless the other assets are sufficiently large and liquid to fund such a purchase, the outgoing spouse will need to borrow to buy. Sometimes the court is asked to find that a transfer of a property without the transferor's release from the mortgage covenants will not prevent the transferor from being able to obtain a further mortgage. In the absence of evidence from mortgage lenders to support this assertion, it is not an assumption which can be made in most cases. Such an assumption was made in *Thompson v Prater*.[6] It was proved to be incorrect and the order was set aside for consideration as to whether the property should be sold instead.

## DEVELOPMENT POTENTIAL

**9.13**   The value of land can be enhanced according to the use it may be put to. For example, land used as pasture may be worth much more if it could be used for residential development. On a lesser scale, part of a large garden attached to the former matrimonial home might be capable of being sold with permission to build a further property on it. The use of land is regulated by planning law. Where it can be shown that planning permission exists, or is very likely to be obtained for a change of use of land, that must be reflected in the valuations sought in relation to the land. Consideration should be given to asking suitable questions within the questionnaire to identify whether any attempts to obtain planning permission for development have been made.

---

[5]   *George v George* [2004] 1 FLR 421.
[6]   [2004] EWCA Civ 989, CA.

**9.14**  Where the development potential is less clear, a suitably qualified expert may need to be instructed to give a view as to the development potential of the land, the timescales for any possible permissions being granted, and the value of the land in the event that permission for development is granted. Such an expert may prove to be expensive, because his work will require careful scrutiny of the local, regional and national plans for development and knowledge of the policies of the local planning authorities. It may also be possible to say that, even without planning permission having been granted, there is a prospect of a purchaser for the land being found who is willing to pay a premium due to the 'hope value' of planning permission being granted in the future. Where the prospect of planning permission is likely to have a significant effect on the value of land, it may be in the interests of the parties to apply for 'outline' planning permission for development during the course of the proceedings, so that the reality of the planning potential can be assessed, rather than asking the court to speculate on such prospects.

**9.15**  Where the development potential of the land is not so proximate or clear as to affect the current value of the land, but it is not fanciful to believe that permission may be granted in the future and, if permission were to be given, the effect on the value of the land would be dramatic, fairness may demand that this is reflected in the order made. To divide the assets on the assumption that the land will obtain planning permission and increase in value may be unfair to the party retaining the land in the event that development is not permitted. To assume that the land will not be developed may be unfair to the party not retaining the land in the event that the property is developed in due course with a dramatic increase in its value. In such cases the parties may agree to provide for some form of 'claw-back' of the increase in value in the event that planning permission is given. The court may include such a provision in the order, although such an order (certainly if contested) is highly exceptional because of the costs involved in implementing it and the fact that it is inconsistent with the obligation on the court to achieve a clean break between the parties, if possible.[7] It is likely to be appropriate only in those cases where the grant of planning permission would have a very large effect on the value of the land when looked at in the context of all the assets in the case.

**9.16**  The form of the 'claw-back' will in most cases require specialist drafting by a conveyancer if it is to be recognised as a registrable charge against the land, rather than a personal obligation upon the parties. The parties will usually arrange for the charge to be professionally drafted by agreement, although the court retains the power to refer the matter to conveyancing counsel of the court if agreement cannot be reached.[8]

---

[7]  *Parra v Parra* [2003] 1 FLR 942. It may be that since the House of Lords decision in *Miller v Miller; McFarlane v McFarlane* [2006] 1 FLR 1186 the courts may be slightly easier to persuade of the justice of such an order, albeit that there may be a need to set some period over which the claw-back is to be effective so that the parties' claims over each other can be brought to an end at some identified point and prevent the potential for 'conflict beyond the grave' (per Thorpe LJ in *Parra* at 951).

[8]  MCA 1973, s 30.

# SALE

**9.17**   The court has flexible powers to order a sale of property upon making a secured periodical payments order, a lump sum order, or a property adjustment order.[9] As well as making an order for sale, the court is empowered to add such consequential or supplementary provisions as it thinks fit.[10] It is clear that such further provisions can be added when the main order is made or at any time thereafter pursuant to the liberty to apply.[11] The wording of these provisions suggests that the court may include directions for the payment out of the proceeds of sale to non-parties as well as the parties to the proceedings themselves. Where an order for sale is sought before the making of a final order, matters are more complicated.

**9.18**   If a property is held in one party's sole name, there is nothing to prevent that party selling it, unless an order has been made preventing such a sale (see Chapter 6). Equally, where a property is in joint names, the parties may agree a sale and the manner in which the proceeds of sale should be applied. Such an agreement may well be reached without prejudice to the manner in which the court will be asked to deal with the assets at any final hearing. Often it will be in both parties' interests to reach such an agreement, particularly in a case where it is obvious that the former matrimonial home must be sold.

**9.19**   Where there is no such agreement as to a sale at an interim stage, matters are more complex. There is no power under the Matrimonial Causes Act 1973 to order a sale of a property as an interim measure while proceedings are pending.[12] Neither is there any power available to the court to make an interim property adjustment or lump sum order.[13] The court may order a sale of a property pursuant to RSC Ord 31, r 1,[14] even at an interim stage, but once the sale has taken place, any redistribution of the proceeds of sale must await the making of final lump sum or property adjustment orders.[15] So this provision is

---

[9]    MCA 1973, s 24A.

[10]   MCA 1973, s 24A(2).

[11]   This is apparent from the wording of MCA 1973, s 24A(1); and see also *Brissett v Brissett* [2009] EWCA Civ 679 at [21].

[12]   *Wicks v Wicks* [1998] 1 FLR 470 disapproving a number of earlier authorities which suggested that the power did exist.

[13]   Although Ward LJ tentatively suggested in *Wicks v Wicks* [1998] 1 FLR 470 that the possibility existed that there was jurisdiction to make an interim lump sum order, this was doubted by the other members of the court and the suggestion appears to be contrary to the Court of Appeal's judgment in *Bolsom v Bolsom* (1983) 4 FLR 21, albeit that Ward LJ was looking to broader powers under the Supreme Court Act 1981, while in *Bolsom* the court looked only to the powers under the Matrimonial Causes Act 1973. See also *Re G (Maintenance Pending Suit)* [2007] 1 FLR 1674 at [8], where Munby J robustly rejected the suggestion that the court had no jurisdiction to make an interim lump sum order. It appears that Munby J had the powers available under Sch 1 of the Children Act 1989 in mind. It remains doubtful that the power to make an interim lump sum arises from the powers contained within the Matrimonial Causes Act 1973 alone.

[14]   Expressly applied to ancillary relief proceedings by FPR 1991, r 2.64(3).

[15]   Although, arguably, the court could specify a use for the proceeds of sale by way of directions consequential to the making of an injunction in relation to them – see Chapter 6.

of limited use where a party wishes to release equity from a property in the other party's sole name or where the property is in joint names and one party seeks more than half of the proceeds of sale. It may be of some use where the property is something of a millstone around both parties' necks, for example where the mortgage is large and neither party is able to meet the ongoing payments to it. It may also be useful where a property is held in joint names and the equity, if divided equally upon a sale, is sufficient to buy each a property.

**9.20** Where one party is able to assert some interest in a property held in the other's name or in joint names, an order for sale could be sought as an interim measure pursuant to an application under s 17 of the Married Women's Property Act 1882,[16] although where the other spouse is in possession of the property it may be difficult to obtain vacant possession of the property other than by an application for an occupation order pursuant to Part IV of the Family Law Act 1996. The court may decline to make such an order for possession of the property on the basis that the factors to be considered ought to be part of the general exercise of discretion at the final ancillary relief hearing.

**9.21** Where one party seeks a sale of a property at the final hearing and this is contested by the other, the court is likely to be asked to rule on the probable cost of rehousing the party in occupation of the property. Commonly this is achieved by both parties providing the court with bundles of estate agents' particulars of properties they deem to be suitable. Where this is likely to be necessary, it is unhelpful to produce the sales particulars shortly before the hearing. If the exercise is to be useful, there should be a proper opportunity for both parties to investigate, and even visit, at least some of the properties in question so as to be able to comment on their suitability. It would, therefore, be helpful to seek a direction for such property particulars to be exchanged by the parties well in advance of the final hearing or FDR, where they are to be considered. It is also important for the parties to ensure that the particulars submitted to the court are realistic. Often a bundle of sales particulars is put before the court without any discrimination as to the contents. This can prove to be something of an 'own goal' for the party concerned if the properties which are plainly unsuitable have not been sifted out. It is a gift to the cross-examining advocate to have particulars for properties submitted which are either extravagant or manifestly unsuitable.

**9.22** Where a property is required to be retained, a sale may be postponed to a future time. Most commonly this is under provisions in the form of a *Mesher*[17] order or a *Martin*[18] order. Usually this is achieved by transferring the property into the sole name of the occupying spouse and granting the other

---

[16]   See s 7(7) of the Matrimonial Causes (Property and Maintenance) Act 1958, which states, for the avoidance of doubt, that the court's power under s 17 of the 1882 Act includes the power to order a sale of the property.

[17]   *Mesher v Mesher & Hall* [1980] 1 All ER 126 – sale deferred until the children cease to be dependants.

spouse a deferred charge for a specified percentage of the net proceeds of sale.[19]
After the decision of the House of Lords in *White v White*[20] there was a
resurgence in the use of such orders on the basis that to give the party with care
of the children the full equity in the former matrimonial home would often be
too great a departure from equality of division.[21] In a case where the party
remaining in the property has care of the children and substantially lower
earnings than the other spouse, it may be justifiable to refuse to make a *Mesher*
order on the basis that to do so would fail to recognise the ability of the higher
earning party to accumulate savings and capital in the time until the property is
sold.[22] The deferral of a sale or a charge is not an order which is capable of
subsequent variation, and a court will be reluctant to do anything to change its
terms by delaying enforcement.[23] This can be problematic, given the lengthy
period such arrangements may remain in place. However, the parties may
themselves agree to vary the arrangement and enter into a binding agreement
to that effect. Such a variation may take effect by way of constructive trust or
equitable estoppel.[24] It might also be possible to vary the effect of an order
without directly varying the order itself by making an application for the
benefit of a child of the family either under the Matrimonial Causes Act 1973
or under Sch 1 of the Children Act 1989.[25] Although the spouse who will
benefit from the deferred interest in the property cannot apply to realise that
interest earlier than the terms of the order allow, on the basis that to do so
would be to vary the terms of the order, there would be nothing preventing that
spouse applying for such a sale pursuant to s 14 of the Trusts of Land and
Appointment of Trustees Act 1996. For that reason, where that spouse is made
bankrupt the trustee in bankruptcy may make such an application for a sale.
Upon such an application the court must exercise its discretion bearing in mind
the requirement that the interests of the bankrupt's creditors outweigh all other
considerations, unless the circumstances of the case are exceptional. This
requirement is imposed by s 335A of the Insolvency Act 1986.[26] Accordingly, a
spouse in occupation of a property under a *Mesher* or *Martin* order cannot
assume that such an order will protect him or her from the consequences of the
former spouse becoming a bankrupt.

---

[18]  *Martin v Martin* [1978] Fam 12 – sale deferred for as long as the wife required the property as
      a home.
[19]  See **23.69** for consideration of the potential tax implications of this option rather than simply
      deferring a sale.
[20]  [2001] 1 AC 596, [2000] 2 FLR 981.
[21]  See e g *Elliott v Elliott* [2001] 1 FCR 477; *Dorney-Kingdom v Dorney-Kingdom* [2000] 2 FLR
      855.
[22]  *B v B (Mesher Order)* [2003] 2 FLR 285 approved by Baroness Hale in *Miller v Miller;
      McFarlane v McFarlane* [2006] 1 FLR 1186 at [142].
[23]  *Swindale v Forder* [2007] 1 FLR 1905.
[24]  *S v S & M* [2007] 1 FLR 1123, where the wife agreed not to seek child maintenance from the
      husband on the understanding that he would waive his right to enforce his interest against the
      former matrimonial home. He was held to be bound by his agreement.
[25]  *MB v KB* [2007] 2 FLR 586.
[26]  *Avis v Turner* [2008] 1 FLR 1127.

# PARTITION OF LAND

**9.23**   An alternative to sale of property may be to order partition of jointly owned land. In practical terms this means dividing the land up between the owners of the land. Where the land is owned solely by the parties to the marriage, the court's broad property adjustment powers will be capable of achieving the desired result with relative ease.

**9.24**   Where the land is owned jointly with third parties, partition is likely to be more complex. The property rights of those third parties must be respected. The court has no power pursuant to the Matrimonial Causes Act 1973 to alter the nature of the strict property rights of a third party, other than to order a sale of the property in question.[27] Where land is held by beneficial joint tenants, any of the joint owners is able to sever the joint tenancy unilaterally by service of a notice in accordance with s 36 of the Law of Property Act 1925. The beneficial joint tenancy then becomes a tenancy in common. An application for ancillary relief does not, of itself, sever a joint tenancy.[28] Where all the beneficial owners of land agree to the partition of jointly owned land, the trustees of the trust of land can carry out such a partition[29] and, it seems to follow, the court can set out such an agreement within its order in ancillary relief proceedings. Where all the beneficial owners do not consent to the partition, the court may dispense with the need for consent and direct the trustees to partition the land as the court thinks fit.[30] Such an order can be made during the course of ancillary relief proceedings, so long as all relevant parties have been given notice of the proceedings and have had the opportunity of being heard on the issue. It is not entirely clear whether an application for an order for partition of land requires a specific application within the ancillary relief proceedings for an order pursuant to the Trusts of Land and Appointment of Trustees Act 1996. A general declaration as to the ownership of property can be made in ancillary relief proceedings without the need for an application pursuant to the 1996 Act.[31] Where an order for partition of land owned with other persons is sought, however, a formal application for such an order pursuant to the 1996 Act may be required, because s 14(2) specifically states that the court may make the order only 'on an application for an order under this section'. It would appear that the application can be made by way of a notice of application in the existing ancillary relief proceedings, rather than by the issue of separate civil proceedings under the 1996 Act.

**9.25**   Where the court orders partition of land, it can also provide for the payment of equality money between the affected parties,[32] and it may be

---

[27]   MCA 1973, s 24A, although the non-party has a right to be heard on the question before an order for sale is made (s 24A(6)).

[28]   *Harris v Goddard* [1983] 1 WLR 1203; *McDowell v Hirschfield Lipson & Rumney* [1992] 2 FLR 126.

[29]   Trusts of Land and Appointment of Trustees Act 1996, s 7.

[30]   Trusts of Land and Appointment of Trustees Act 1996, ss 14 and 15.

[31]   *Tebbutt v Haynes* [1981] 2 All ER 238. See also **8.9–8.16**.

[32]   Trusts of Land and Appointment of Trustees Act 1996, s 7(1).

necessary to carry out an equitable account between the parties. The power to order a sale of the land as an alternative to partition is always available as well. The parties may be well advised to agree to sale of the land rather than a contested hearing of a partition application. Such applications raise very complex issues of valuation and consideration of the practical effects of partition of the land in various ways. The costs involved in such a process tend to be large and the result is unlikely to be to any party's complete satisfaction. If partition cannot be agreed, it may be better to agree to sell the land at auction, with the parties being permitted to bid for it if they wish to do so.

## TENANCIES

**9.26** A tenancy of a property, be it residential, agricultural or commercial, is property for the purposes of the Matrimonial Causes Act 1973.[33] A statutory periodic tenancy pursuant to the Housing Act 1988 is also property for these purposes.[34] A long lease of property, or a tenancy having substantial statutory protection (as some agricultural or business tenancies have) is likely to have some saleable value and may need to be valued.[35] The court may order the tenancy to be transferred to the other party or, if necessary, sold.

**9.27** A statutory periodic tenancy of a dwelling will have no value on the market, but it may be of the utmost importance for the parties if it is their home and there is no other capital for them to share. Such cases are often the most intractable and difficult to resolve. Where there are dependent children who rely upon the property for a home, the tenancy is likely to be transferred to the party who is to have residence with them. Where there are no children, the court will need to balance all the MCA 1973, s 25 criteria on each side of the case and decide which party should have the tenancy. It is likely that neither party will be able to consent to an order transferring the tenancy to the other and removing them from the property, because doing so would render them 'voluntarily homeless', and the local authority would have no duty to rehouse them.

**9.28** Practitioners should be aware of the ease with which a tenant can unilaterally surrender a joint tenancy and, once this has been done, the impossibility of setting the surrender aside (see **6.28** and **7.15**). Where a joint tenancy is in issue between the parties, steps should be taken to protect this asset by means of an injunction or undertaking.

**9.29** Where the only asset is a statutory tenancy of a dwelling, the court may also order a transfer of the tenancy pursuant to powers contained in s 53 and Sch 7 of the Family Law Act 1996. In the context of a married couple it is

---

[33] *Newlon Housing Trust v Alsulaimen* [1998] 2 FLR 690 approving *Hale v Hale* [1975] 1 WLR 931 and *Thompson v Thompson* [1976] Fam 25.

[34] *Newlon Housing Trust v Alsulamein* [1998] 2 FLR 690.

[35] Some long tenancies include an entitlement to apply for enfranchisement by acquiring the freehold to the property, making them potentially more valuable.

difficult to see any general advantage in using those provisions rather than those contained in the Matrimonial Causes Act 1973. In an appropriate case there may be a benefit in an application for a tenancy transfer being made pursuant to the 1996 Act in that, unlike the MCA 1973, the 1996 Act allows the court to consider the parties' conduct in the round rather than being limited to conduct 'which it would be inequitable to disregard'.[36] Dealing with the issue under the 1996 Act would, however, leave any claims under the Matrimonial Causes Act 1973 open indefinitely, which would give either party the freedom to restore the proceedings at some future date. That might prove to be undesirable.

---

[36]  *Re H (A child)* (2006) The Times, August 16, CA (distinguishing *Miller v Miller; McFarlane v McFarlane* [2006] 1 FLR 1186).

# Chapter 10

# OTHER FORMS OF PROPERTY

## CHATTELS INCLUDING CONTENTS

**10.1** The parties' personal possessions are also property which the court should take into account. Where the possessions are of substantial value (motor cars, boats, aircraft etc) they will inevitably appear on a schedule of assets. The court will usually deal with such assets in a pragmatic way, recognising that they are usually, unless particularly rare and collectable, depreciating assets. Other items, such as works of art or antique furniture, may have genuine investment value and will require specialist valuation. Significant differences of opinion as to their value may arise. If the court cannot determine such disputes with any certainty, it may be that the only fair resolution is an order for the assets in question to be sold at public auction so that their true market value can be found. The parties can be allowed to bid for the items themselves.

**10.2** As with real property, issues may arise as to the interests of third parties in the chattels, particularly where the items are of substantial value. Such issues are resolved according to the same property law and trust concepts which apply to real property.[1] The third party may need to be joined to the proceedings to resolve such issues.[2] Where the asset in dispute is of low value it will generally be disproportionate to litigate ownership issues.

**10.3** The parties are often able to resolve most of the issues surrounding the valuation and distribution of the contents of the former matrimonial home upon their separation, but this is not always so and often, even if there is agreement about most things, disputes remain about others. Even though these disputes frequently raise the temperature of the proceedings more than other issues, they are often treated by the parties' representatives as an afterthought once all the other issues have been agreed. This approach can have unfortunate effects. Many practitioners will have experience of at least one case where a carefully engineered agreement as to the main parts of the order fell apart once the parties began to discuss the division of the chattels. This can be avoided by endeavouring to narrow the issues in relation to chattels in advance of the final hearing or FDR.

---

[1] For example, *The 'Up Yaws'* [2007] 2 FLR 444.
[2] See **8.9–8.16**. There should also be provision for the basis of the claim to be properly set out in writing: see **8.12**.

**10.4**　In *K v K (Financial Relief: Management of Difficult Cases)*[3] Baron J gave some helpful guidance as to how disputes about chattels should be resolved. Prior to the final hearing a Scott schedule should be prepared setting out the chattels about which there is disagreement. The schedule could summarise in the case of each item why that item is sought. How differences should be resolved will then be a matter for the court or the agreement of the parties. In *K v K* the parties agreed to make lists of favourite items in descending order of preference. They could then alternate in choosing items until their lists were exhausted. Any items remaining unclaimed would be sold and the proceeds divided equally. The merit of this approach is that no court time is required to resolve the matter. Other cases may require different approaches. The time spent on the chattels should, however, not be allowed to become disproportionate to the value or importance of the assets in dispute.

**10.5**　Where an item of property has been inherited or received as a gift by one party to the marriage from a third party, there will be a strong case for leaving the value of such property out of account when the other assets are divided. Where the financial value of the item is also substantial and realisable, however, the parties' needs may not permit such an approach. Where the parties to the marriage originate from a foreign cultural background, it may be appropriate for the court to have regard to their common cultural values in resolving the proceedings.[4] Where a dowry was paid upon marriage, issues often arise as to what is to happen to this upon divorce.[5] Cultural and religious factors should, it appears, have a bearing on how such disputes are to be resolved by the courts. This is likely to be a developing theme in the case law, given the multi-cultural and multi-faith society in which the law is now applied.

**10.6**　It may be that a final order is achieved in proceedings without the parties or their lawyers addressing the issue of chattels and their division. Once an order has been made dismissing their respective claims to property adjustment or lump sum orders, the court will be powerless to deal with outstanding issues as to contents in the ancillary relief proceedings. If a dispute as to the ownership of chattels comes to light at that stage, all is not lost. Either party may within 3 years of the decree being made absolute apply for an order pursuant to s 17 of the Married Women's Property Act 1882 for a declaration as to the ownership of the item in question.[6] It is important to remember that the court's powers pursuant to s 17 are limited to determining the parties' rights

---

[3]　[2005] 2 FLR 1137 at 1145–6.

[4]　*A v T (Ancillary Relief: Cultural Factors)* [2004] 1 FLR 977.

[5]　It would appear that a dowry may be claimed by way of civil action as a matter of contract law or property law: *Joseph v Joseph* [1909] P 217; *Kelner v Kelner* [1939] P 411; *Phrantzes v Argenti* [1960] 2 QB 19; *Shahnaz v Rizwan* [1965] 1 QB 390; and *Qureshi v Qureshi* [1972] Fam 173. There appears to have been no judicial consideration as to whether the abolition by s 1 of the Law Reform (Miscellaneous Provisions) Act 1970 of actions for breaches of an agreement to marry has affected the right to sue for a dowry as a matter of contract law.

[6]　The power to make such an application after divorce arises by s 39 of the Matrimonial Proceedings and Property Act 1970. The application will not be possible if the ancillary relief order included a clause and agreement dismissing the parties' rights to bring such claims against each other.

to property in accordance with strict property law. The court is not given any discretion to alter such rights of ownership. Nevertheless, to allow an orderly resolution of disputes as to how assets should be dealt with, the court may make an order for a lump sum to be paid to one party for the value of an asset, or his or her interest in an asset, in exchange for a transfer to the other party.[7] Clearly, before commencing such proceedings the parties should establish that the cost of the proceedings is proportionate to the value or importance of the chattels in dispute. It is quite conceivable that the court may penalise in costs a party who simply wishes unreasonably to continue pursuing issues which should have been dealt with in the ancillary relief proceedings.

## CHOSES IN ACTION

**10.7** Most property is a physical item which it is possible to take possession of. A chose in action is a form of intangible property. In essence, a chose in action is a right which can only be asserted by bringing an action rather than by taking possession. By their very nature choses in action are enormously wide-ranging in their scope. In its simplest form a chose in action may be a simple promise to repay a loan on demand. Much more complex forms of chose in action exist as forms of investment.

**10.8** As a general proposition, choses in action are a form of property and therefore susceptible to property adjustment orders and orders for sale in the same way as real property and chattels. Usually such assets will present no real practical problems during ancillary relief proceedings. Where the nature of the chose in action becomes more unusual or complex, however, practical problems of valuation and realisation do arise. The very breadth of the scope of choses in action makes a definitive discussion of these potential problems impossible. Some common examples of choses in action are considered below.

### Insurance policies

**10.9** An insurance policy is a contract by which the insurer agrees, in return for payment of premiums, to pay a sum of money upon the occurrence of a specified event. As such, it founds a chose in action which is property for the purposes of the Matrimonial Causes Act 1973 and the court can order the parties to transfer the benefits of the policy between each other as appropriate. The actual transfer will be carried out by the parties entering into an assignment of the benefits.[8]

---

[7] *Bothe v Amos* [1975] 2 WLR 838. This may prove to be a useful remedy where a sale of a jointly owned asset would appear to be unjust to one party, or where one party has retained property belonging to the other and either refuses to return it or has placed it somewhere beyond the court's jurisdiction.

[8] Pursuant to Law of Property Act 1925, s 136. It is not necessary to obtain the consent of the insurer to the assignment in most cases (see Policies of Assurance Act 1867), but it is likely to

**10.10** A distinction needs to be drawn between 'life assurance' and 'life insurance', even though the terms are often used interchangeably. The former assures the beneficiary of the benefits at a specified point, usually a specified date or the death of the person whose life is assured, if earlier. In other words, there is an event which is certain to occur within the life of the policy leading to benefits being paid out. The latter type of policy, life insurance, provides insurance against a contingency, usually the death of the insured before a certain date. The latter are often referred to as 'term life policies', because they have a fixed term during which benefits may arise. Often such policies also permit payment upon the diagnosis of a serious illness or other such contingencies. In general terms, life assurance policies usually carry a surrender value and a maturity value. Life insurance policies for a fixed term do not usually have a maturity or surrender value.

**10.11** Endowment policies are a particular form of life assurance policy taken out in connection with a mortgage. The benefits of such a policy are usually, but not always, assigned to the mortgagee, so that upon the death of any insured person the mortgage is discharged by the proceeds of the insurance policy. Any transfer of such a policy to the benefit of the other party will only be effective if the benefits under the endowment are first released by the mortgagee. A sale of the property, involving repayment of the mortgage, will usually free the endowment policy for assignment between the parties.

**10.12** Practitioners should be careful when drafting an order which envisages a transfer of endowment policies after a sale of a property. The intended effect of such an order can be radically changed by the death of one of the parties prior to the sale of the property. In *Bishop v Bishop*[9] a consent order provided for the immediate sale of the former matrimonial home and division of the proceeds in a manner which meant that the largest share of the proceeds of sale would go to the wife. Related endowment policies were to be transferred to the husband upon the sale of the property occurring. In the event, after the order was made but before the house was sold, the husband died. The insurer paid out on the endowment policies and the proceeds were paid directly to the mortgagee, discharging the mortgage. After the house sold, a dispute arose between the wife and the husband's estate as to how the proceeds of sale should be divided under the terms of the order. The estate argued that the sum raised by the endowments should be deducted from the proceeds of sale before they were divided, so that the estate would have the benefit of those funds. The Court of Appeal disagreed. On a proper construction of the order the proceeds of sale should be divided, with no deduction for the mortgage which had already been discharged. Although this situation is unusual, care must be taken

---

make the administration and effect of the assignment smoother if the insurer is party to the assignment and, if possible, it is carried out on the insurer's own standard forms for dealing with such matters.

[9]   [2004] EWCA Civ 738 (unreported) 26 April 2004, CA.

in drafting the order (and especially in defining the 'net proceeds of sale')[10] to avoid this potential difficulty, particularly where the value of endowment policies is considerable.

**10.13** Although the parties are usually interested in those policies which carry a capital value, practitioners should not overlook the fact that term policies of insurance without any surrender or maturity value may also be capable of transfer between the parties by way of a property adjustment order. A policy taken out many years ago when the parties were younger may have fixed premiums which are much lower than the parties could obtain on the insurance market at the time the order is made. Thus, the old policies have some real practical value. Not all such policies are capable of transfer, however, and the policy terms will have to be considered to ensure there is no clause which prohibits the transfer or assignment of the benefits of such a policy.

**10.14** A policy with a surrender value is simple to value. The insurer will, on request, provide a current surrender value for the policy. In some cases a higher value may be obtained for the policy by a sale of the policy to one of the various investment companies who buy such policies. The difference between the surrender value and the sale value is likely to be greater the closer to maturity the policy is. In any case, the parties will have to decide whether the best approach for them is to surrender the policy, sell it or to maintain the policy to maturity. Clearly, such decisions require careful investment consideration, and in anything but straightforward cases the advice of an independent financial advisor may be desirable. To that end, if the value of the policy is substantial, it may be useful to obtain various comparative valuations of the policy to include:

- the surrender value;

- the maturity value (bearing in mind that in the case of a 'with profits' or unit-linked policy this will be a projection estimated on the basis of average annual rates of return, which may, or may not, prove to be realistic);

- the paid up value (on the basis that payments to the policy are discontinued and the policy is effectively 'frozen' until maturity when a lower sum will be paid than would have been the case if premiums had continued – whether a policy can be treated as 'paid up' will depend on its terms and conditions and its age).

**10.15** Where one of the parties will remain dependent upon periodical payments from the other for a considerable time, the dependent party should be advised to consider obtaining some form of cover in respect of the paying party's life. Failure to do so may leave the dependent party without income in

---

[10]  For example, it may be possible to avoid this difficulty by defining the net proceeds of sale by reference to the mortgage redemption figure as at the date of the order.

the event of the other party's death and force the dependent party to make a claim against the deceased's estate pursuant to the Inheritance (Provision for Family and Dependants) Act 1975. Such a claim will provide little relief if the paying party had a good income but very little net capital value in his or her estate. In the context of ancillary relief proceedings, the court has no power to require a party to take out, or submit to, a policy on his or her own life.[11] Where a life policy is sought as security against the loss of periodical payments, this can only be achieved by agreement between the parties, unless such a policy can be obtained without the insurer requiring a medical examination of the insured.[12] It should be noted that an insurance policy will only be issued to a person who has an insurable interest at the time the policy is taken out. This may make it difficult for a former spouse to obtain insurance in respect of the other party's life if such a policy is applied for only after a final decree of divorce and a clean-break order.

**10.16** The transfer of a life policy, or an interest in a joint policy, from one spouse to the other may have tax implications. Following observations by Coleridge J in *G v G*[13] the Inland Revenue changed their approach to charging capital gains tax upon the transfer of a life policy from spouse to spouse pursuant to an ancillary relief order. Such transfers may have income tax consequences for the transferor, and specialist advice should be obtained where the transferor is a higher rate tax payer and the value of the policy is substantial.

## Shares

**10.17** A description of the rights attaching to shares and the problems raised by shareholdings in small private companies are considered in detail at **11.23–11.26**. The search for a fully comprehensive definition of a share is elusive even for company lawyers. For our purposes it is sufficient to describe a share as a chose in action.

**10.18** Shareholdings in public limited companies listed on a stock exchange, in this country or overseas, are usually straightforward to value. The value of the shares can be ascertained on a daily (or even up to the minute) basis from the index produced by the stock exchange on which the shares are traded.[14]

---

[11] But it may transfer the benefits under an existing policy – see above.
[12] It may be possible to obtain life cover in the absence of a medical examination, but the premiums on such a policy are likely to be significantly higher. If such a step becomes necessary due to the refusal of a party to submit to a medical examination, the court may be persuaded to add an element to the periodical payments to cover the premiums on such a policy.
[13] [2002] 2 FLR 1143.
[14] See **11.161–11.163**.

These indices, showing 'real time' prices are generally available on the internet. The shares are usually readily tradable and can be sold or transferred between the parties, as appropriate.[15]

**10.19** Three particular issues which can arise in relation to shares are worthy of mention, as follows.

**10.20** The value of the shares can be significantly affected by the date of dividend payments. Where a dividend is expected in the near future, the share price may be somewhat higher than just after a dividend has been paid.[16] In most cases the effect will not be significant. In cases where one party holds a large shareholding in a very profitable company, failure to recognise the unusually high value of shares due to an impending dividend payment may result in unfairness. In such a case the party holding the shares may face a degree of double counting in the value of the shares he holds and the fact that he has regular substantial dividends from the shares. In fairness, it may be more appropriate to look at the share price over a longer period to form a more realistic impression of the true capital value of the shares. Many of the internet-based share information sources now provide charts showing the historical share price movement. Most listed companies also have part of their website devoted to investors, with similar information available to the public at large.

**10.21** Where a party has a very substantial holding of shares in a company and those shares are to be sold, some regard must be had to the effect on the share price of 'dumping' a large number of shares on the market at once. Often the party in this position is also a key member of the company's management team and he or she will seek to compound this difficulty by saying that when word gets out that a key director is selling very large numbers of shares in the company investor confidence will plummet and the share price with it. These arguments now seem to cut little ice with the courts.[17] With a degree of careful public relations planning by the party concerned, together with appropriate announcements via the appropriate stock exchange and judicious phasing of the share sale, the effect of the sale of shares is unlikely to be large.

**10.22** Where the shares are not to be sold, consideration needs to be given to the nature of the asset in question. Shareholdings in companies are always, to a greater or lesser extent, 'risk laden'. This factor should be reflected in the

---

[15] See **14.5–14.9** for consideration of the problems which may arise where the shareholdings are very substantial, or where one of the parties is also involved in the management of the company.

[16] Stock market listings of share prices usually have annotations stating such prices as 'ex dividend'.

[17] *Sorrell v Sorrell* [2006] 1 FLR 497 at 506 and *Charman v Charman* [2006] EWHC 1879 (Fam) at [89], where Coleridge J described such arguments as 'old hat'.

division of the other assets, and fairness may demand that the risk-laden shareholdings are also divided between the parties so that they share in the risks.[18]

**10.23** Shareholdings in larger private companies may not throw up the difficulties of small family companies referred to in Chapter 11 but, nonetheless, it should be recognised that such shares may be more difficult to trade than those in listed companies, and the freedom to sell shares may be limited by pre-emption rights contained in the company's articles of association or any shareholder agreements.[19]

## Options and other deferred assets[20]

**10.24** Reversionary interests in real estate have been considered above. Similar issues can arise in relation to other assets which cannot be realised until some point in the future. Examples which regularly arise are shares in companies which cannot be sold until a future date[21] and options to purchase shares or other investments at some future date.[22] The key problems are likely to be (a) predicting what the value of the asset may be at the point in the future when it becomes realisable and (b) what, if any, discount should be applied to the value of that asset to take into account the delay until it becomes realisable and the degree of risk inherent in holding investments whose value can fall as well as rise.

**10.25** It is possible to instruct expert accountants to deal with all these issues and to provide a discounted value for the asset to place in the overall schedule of assets in the case. It should be noted, however, that this approach is likely to be costly and the outcome somewhat uncertain. The shortcomings in this approach were summarised in *GW v RW (Financial Provision: Departure from Equality)*[23] as follows:

> 'Discounts crop up in a number of areas when the valuation of assets is undertaken in ancillary relief proceedings. They arise in relation to the valuation of minority shareholdings in private companies; in the valuation of substantial blocks of publicly quoted shares, where it is said that a sale would drive down the price; and, as here, where it is said that the assets are illiquid, risky or deferred. Although the technique has a respectable pedigree it must be recognised that it is one that is devoid of any science and is never more than a guess by the expert valuer of what lesser price than face value a hypothetical purchaser would pay for the asset in question. And it is almost invariably the case that the expert will align his guess with his client's interests, so that the expert for the owning party will

---

[18]   *Wells v Wells* [2002] 2 FLR 97.
[19]   See **11.10, 11.116–11.122** and Chapter 14.
[20]   See **4.9** for a discussion as to how such deferred assets should be dealt with on the Form E.
[21]   As in *Miller v Miller; McFarlane v McFarlane* [2006] UKHL 24.
[22]   *GW v RW (Financial Provision: Departure from Equality)* [2003] 2 FLR 108 at 127, where both parties' accountants confirmed that the value of the options could only be ascertained by a 'wild guess'.
[23]   *GW v RW (Financial Provision: Departure from Equality)* [2003] 2 FLR 108 at 127.

almost always suggest a higher discount than the expert for the claiming party. So the court is asked to choose between less than disinterested guesses. Here H argues for a discount of 25%. W says it should be 15%. How and by reference to what considerations can I possibly decide this dispute? It is impossible, and any decision made by me would almost certainly be wrong. It is for this reason that I am clearly of the view that a *Wells* sharing is particularly appropriate where the asset in question is the subject of a dispute about discounts.'

In such a situation an approach based on the like-for-like sharing of the 'copper-bottomed assets' and the illiquid and risk-laden assets as suggested in *Wells v Wells*[24] is likely to commend itself.[25] To avoid such an approach, the parties will either need to agree upon a discounted value to attribute to the illiquid assets or produce compelling arguments as to why the *Wells v Wells* approach would be unfair in the particular circumstances of their case.

**10.26** In some cases it may be possible to await the actual event which will allow the value of the deferred asset to be realised and properly valued. Where there are pending proceedings which will resolve the value of a disputed asset, the ancillary relief proceedings can be adjourned to await their outcome.[26] Where the point at which the interest in the deferred asset crystallises and becomes realisable is sufficiently certain and proximate to justify the step, the relevant part of the claim may be adjourned until that point. Such adjournments are considered in more detail in the context of future inheritances at **18.25–18.41**.

## Intellectual property

**10.27** Very broadly, intellectual property rights exist to protect inventions and artistic works from being copied. As such, the rights are choses in action. Intellectual property rights can be divided into two categories: registered and unregistered. Registered intellectual property rights are usually used to protect industrial innovation. Unregistered rights tend to protect artistic works such as drawings, photographs and written work. Registered rights include patents, trade marks and registered design rights. Unregistered rights include copyright, confidential information and unregistered design right. Specialist valuation of intellectual property rights, as a business asset, may be required to be taken as part of the business valuation process.

**10.28** Where intellectual property rights are directly owned by parties to the proceedings, it will be necessary to identify them in the Form E. Difficult decisions will then arise as to whether the right will need to be the subject of a specialist valuation. It is relatively easy to decide this issue when a right is being exploited in the market place or one party has a history of successfully

[24] [2002] 2 FLR 97.
[25] By analogy, see *Martin-Dye v Martin-Dye* [2006] EWCA Civ 681, where the same approach was taken in relation to a pension in payment because of the difficulties of placing a capital value on the pension for the purpose of offsetting its value against the other assets.
[26] *George v George* [2004] 1 FLR 421.

exploiting intellectual property rights. Where a right has yet to be materially exploited and/or the party owning the right has no history of successful exploitation, the decision whether to seek a specialist valuation and how to deal with the asset will be difficult. Take the following as an example. A party to ancillary relief proceedings has completed the manuscript of a book. The rights to publish the book have not been sold. The intellectual property rights in the book could potentially be very valuable. On the other hand, they may be entirely worthless. It is submitted that the court should deal with this issue in the same way that it deals with any other form of property whose value is uncertain. Options include transferring the rights into joint names (highly unattractive as this is likely to be to at least one of the parties) either as joint tenants or tenants in common, the possibility of claw-backs and a *Wells v Wells* type of sharing order. A claim to periodical payments could be left open to ensure that the profits flowing from the intellectual property are shared. It is trite to note that, as with any other form of property, ownership and third party issues may also arise.

## FOREIGN PROPERTY – OFFSHORE ASSETS

**10.29** Property owned by the parties but held outside the jurisdiction remains property or a financial resource available to them which the court should take into account under s 25(2)(a) of the MCA 1973. Other than the practicalities of obtaining information about such assets and valuing them, there is usually no difficulty in bringing them into account in this way. The problems can begin at the point when it becomes necessary to make property adjustment orders in relation to such assets.

**10.30** Orders made pursuant to the Matrimonial Causes Act 1973 act in personam rather than in rem. So although the English courts do not usually have any jurisdiction to determine issues as to the ownership of property situated abroad, such property is relevant within ancillary relief proceedings and can be subject to a property adjustment order.[27] Similarly, a post-nuptial settlement in the form of a trust based overseas and governed by foreign law may also be varied by a property adjustment order.[28] Where the property is overseas, the parties should be alert to the potential difficulties of enforcing the order. Indeed, the court ought to consider the likely effectiveness of the order it proposes to make before it is made and the parties may need to put evidence before the court of the likely effect of the order in the foreign jurisdiction to dispel anxieties as to its enforceability.[29] It will probably be necessary for the party in whose favour the order is made to seek to have the property

---

[27] *Hamlin v Hamlin* [1986] 1 FLR 61.
[28] *Charalambous v Charalambous* [2004] 2 FLR 1093.
[29] *Hamlin v Hamlin* [1986] 1 FLR 61. In *Behzadi v Behzadi* [2008] EWCA Civ 1070 at [21] it was held that it is normally for the owner of property situated overseas to establish by evidence that the property's value cannot be realised or that there are restrictions on transferring its value outside the jurisdiction where it is located. Otherwise it will be presumed that there are no such restrictions.

adjustment order recognised and enforced by the courts in the jurisdiction in which the property is situated. This may be costly and the outcome uncertain. Consideration should be given as to whether such an approach is necessary or proportionate in the circumstances of the case.

**10.31**  Where the property overseas is owned only by the husband and wife, there are likely to be few difficulties in resolving issues as to its ownership, in the rare circumstances that it is necessary to do this in ancillary relief proceedings.[30] Where, on the other hand, the property is situated overseas and a third party who is resident in that foreign jurisdiction claims an interest in the property, it may prove to be impossible to resolve that issue in the ancillary relief proceedings. It may be that the issue of ownership will need to be resolved in the jurisdiction where the property is situated, depending on the nature of the claim being made and the domicile of the parties involved.[31] In a case where the court is not asked to make any order in relation to property overseas but to simply take it into account as property available to the party who owns it, but that party denies he has any beneficial entitlement to the property, there does not seem to be any reason why the English court cannot make findings as to whether there is such a beneficial entitlement or not. Such findings should be made in accordance with the law of property of the jurisdiction where the property is situated, but is unlikely to be binding upon anyone in the overseas jurisdiction, even if that person has notice of the proceedings.[32] There is then a risk of inconsistent findings as to ownership of the land arising in the two jurisdictions, to the prejudice of one of the parties. How such a problem should be resolved will depend on the circumstances of each case and the value and importance of the asset in issue. In some cases the issue of proceedings in the relevant jurisdiction to determine the issue may be possible and necessary. In other cases such a step will be wholly disproportionate and unnecessary.

**10.32**  Where one or both of the parties are not domiciled in the United Kingdom, they are likely to have assets kept offshore for reasons of tax efficiency. In such cases, particularly those where only one of the parties is non-domiciled, the tax consequences of any order which is made must be very carefully considered. Specialist advice is likely to be required to ensure that the

---

[30]  *Razelos v Razelos (No 2)* [1970] 1 WLR 392, in the context of a claim pursuant to s 17 of the Married Women's Property Act 1882.

[31]  Article 22 of Council Regulation (EC) No 44/2001 of 22 December 2000 on jurisdiction and the recognition and enforcement of judgments in civil and commercial matters (2001) OJ L 12/1 confers exclusive jurisdiction in the matter of rights in rem in immovable property on the courts of the contracting state in which the property is situated. But where the claim relates to beneficial entitlement in relation to the property, these are likely to be regarded as rights in personam, which can be litigated in the state where the respondent party is domiciled rather than in the state where the property is located: *Webb v Webb C-294/92* [1994] QB 696, [1994] ECR I-1717, [1994] 3 All ER 911, ECJ. See also *Prazic v Prazic* [2006] 2 FLR 1128.

[32]  Article 2 of the Council Regulation (EC) No 44/2001 indicates that any person should be sued in the state of the European Union in which he is domiciled, regardless of nationality, unless the Regulation specifically says that the proceedings are to be brought elsewhere. Where the property or the person is outside the EU, issues of jurisdiction will be decided according to principles of private international law and consideration of forum conveniens.

orders which are made do not have unintended effects to the prejudice of one of the parties. The court will need to know about the tax consequences of dealing with the offshore assets in particular ways, and the parties should be alert to the potential advantages of having property adjustment orders drafted in such a way that the transfer of property occurs offshore. These issues are considered further in Chapter 23.

# Part V

# BUSINESSES

# Chapter 11

# COMPANIES

## INTRODUCTION

**11.1**  Ancillary relief lawyers do not, of course, require a detailed knowledge of company law. However, some knowledge of the basic principles and concepts of company law will assist in fashioning arguments and effecting creative and sensitive[1] solutions to the division of assets. A creative and sensitive approach to achieving fairness in a case involving a company is frequently required because of the difficulty in valuing and then realising interests in a company. A detailed treatise on company law is beyond the remit of this book.[2] Nevertheless, this chapter begins with an introduction to some of the more relevant principles of company law, as a reminder to some, a point of reference to others and perhaps even a springboard, if necessary, for further research. The chapter subsequently deals with a number of specific topics that are relevant to an ancillary relief claim involving a company, including a guide to reading company accounts and share valuation, before concluding with a general discussion of some of the more frequently occurring themes that permeate the reported ancillary relief cases involving companies. Those readers with a passing interest in company law will be aware that the Companies Act 2006 received Royal Assent on 8 November 2006. The 2006 Act will replace nearly all the provisions in existing company legislation. However, the 2006 Act will not be fully in force until October 2009. With that caveat, references in this text will be to provisions of the 2006 Act, whether or not the relevant section is in force at the date of publication.

## PUBLIC AND PRIVATE COMPANIES

**11.2**  An incorporated company is formed when two or more persons subscribe their name to a memorandum of association and comply with the registration provisions of the Companies Act 2006.[3] An incorporated company will be given a registration number. The different types of company that exist are described in ss 3–6 of the Companies Act 2006.

---

[1]  The requirement of creativity and sensitivity in effecting an orderly redistribution of wealth was referred to by Coleridge J in *N v N (Financial Provision: Sale of Company)* [2001] 2 FLR 69.

[2]  See, for example, Gower and Davies *Principles of Modern Company Law* (Sweet & Maxwell, 8th edn, 2008) for a general text for students and practitioners alike and *Gore Browne on Companies* (Jordans, looseleaf) for a work directed more towards the company law practitioner.

[3]  Companies Act 2006, s 7.

**11.3** A company having the liability of its members limited by the memorandum of association to the amount, if any, unpaid on the shares respectively held by them is a company limited by shares. A company limited by shares is the company most frequently encountered by ancillary relief practitioners and will form the subject matter of the majority of this chapter.

**11.4** A company having the liability of its members limited by the memorandum to such amount as the members may respectively undertake to contribute to the assets of the company in the event of its being wound up is a company limited by guarantee. A company not having any limit on the liability of its members is an unlimited company. Both companies limited by guarantee and unlimited companies are rarely encountered in ancillary cases and nothing more will be said about them.

**11.5** A company limited by shares is either a private company or a public company. The memorandum of association of the company will state whether the company is a private or public company. A public company is better known as a 'plc'. Whilst there is no requirement to do so, many public companies are listed on a stock market. From the perspective of an ancillary relief practitioner this means that there are unlikely to be any valuation[4] issues that arise in respect of shares in a 'listed' or 'quoted' public company, since there is a readily available market for the shares with a price for the share determined by the market and quoted in the financial pages of newspapers. Since valuation and liquidity issues are less acute in a listed public company, most of the jurisprudence, and a fortiori most of this chapter, is concerned with private companies.

## CORPORATE CONSTITUTION

**11.6** There are two main documents that determine the constitution of a company: the memorandum of association and the articles of association. Both documents should be obtained when either of the parties to an ancillary relief application holds shares in a private company which appear to be a material asset in the context of the ancillary relief proceedings. Both are public documents and can be obtained from Companies House.

**11.7** The memorandum of association governs the relationship of the company with the world. Perhaps the most important provision in the memorandum from the perspective of an ancillary relief lawyer is the statement of the amount of share capital with which the company proposes to be registered and the division of the share capital into shares of a fixed amount. The fixed amount is the nominal, or par price, of the shares. The nominal value

---

[4]   For large shareholdings in listed companies any immediate realisation of the entire holding may depress the sale price. If appropriate, stockbrokers should be consulted to consider how best to dispose of the shares. Consideration ought also to be given to any restrictions on sale contained in either the memorandum and articles of association, any shareholders' agreements, placement documents or rules of the market. See also Chapter 14.

of the share is usually not indicative of the market value of the share after the company has begun to trade. The amount unpaid on the share is the maximum sum for which the shareholder would be liable in the event of an insolvent winding up.[5] The company may increase its share capital if there is provision to do so in the articles of association.

**11.8**   The articles of association deal with the internal aspect of running a company. Shareholders are bound by the articles of association. The Companies (Table A to F) Regulations 1985, SI 1985/805 provide model articles of association. Table A was in effect the default articles of association for a private company limited by shares. Upon incorporation Table A applied to govern the internal workings of the company unless or to the extent that it was modified or excluded. If a company was registered without articles of association, Table A would therefore apply.

**11.9**   A copy of Table A is set out in the appendices.[6] Although new model articles are prescribed for companies formed under the provisions of the 2006 Act, the vast majority of the private companies encountered in practice will still be companies incorporated under previous legislation to which Table A of the Companies (Table A to F) Regulations 1985 still applies.[7] Some of the articles within Table A still therefore warrant further consideration. Articles 12 to 22 deal with calls on shares and forfeiture. Broadly, the directors of the company have the right to make calls for the payment of any unpaid sums on shares and, in the event that those sums are unpaid, the shares may be forfeited. Any unpaid sums on shares held by a party to ancillary relief proceedings ought to be taken into account when a valuation is undertaken. If a call is made, the sums due under it are a liability attached to the ownership of the shares.

**11.10**   Articles 23 to 28 deal with the transfer of shares. One of the most frequent modifications to Table A is the addition of a right of pre-emption requiring the member, before transferring shares to an outsider, to first offer the shares to other members of the company. Such a provision is commonly designed to maintain family control over a company. It is also not uncommon for modified provisions on transfer to provide a mechanism and basis for the valuation of the shares under a right of pre-emption.[8] It is clearly therefore of the greatest importance when considering valuation issues to take into account the possible existence of rights of pre-emption.

**11.11**   Article 24 provides a general restriction enabling the directors to refuse to register the transfer of a share which is not fully paid to a person of whom they do not approve. They may also refuse to register the transfer of a share on

---

[5]   In appropriate cases the amount unpaid on a shareholding may therefore properly be considered to be a contingent liability of the shareholder.

[6]   See Appendix 1.

[7]   Companies Act 2006, s 20(2).

[8]   See *A v A* [2004] EWHC 2818 (Fam), [2006] 2 FLR 115, where different potential methods and brackets of valuation resulted in the trial judge having great difficulty in valuing the wife's minority interest. See also the section on miscellaneous valuation issues below.

which the company has a lien for an unpaid call. A modified Table A may provide a wider discretion to refuse to register a transfer. Provided the discretion to refuse the transfer is exercised bona fide and in the best interests of the company, it cannot be impeached. It follows that if a transfer of shares is sought, it would be well to consult the articles of association and, if necessary, the directors to see whether a transfer would be objected to.[9]

**11.12**   Article 35 deals with the power of a company to purchase its own shares. It provides that, subject to the provisions of the relevant companies legislation, a company may purchase its own shares (including any redeemable shares) and, if it is a private company, make a payment in respect of the redemption or purchase of its own shares otherwise than out of distributable profits of the company or the proceeds of a fresh issue of shares. Section 658 of the Companies Act 2006 contains restrictions on the ability of a company to purchase its own shares.

**11.13**   Table A deals with alterations to share capital in arts 32–34. These complex provisions, along with the purchase or redemption by a company of its own shares, are potential methods of capital generation. The complexity of raising capital by these methods means that their use will be extremely rare.

**11.14**   The remaining provisions of the articles deal with general meetings (arts 36–53), voting rights (arts 54–64) and detailed provisions relating to directors' powers, appointment, retirement, removal, remuneration and expenses (arts 64–98). The effect in broad terms of these articles is dealt with in the section on corporate governance.

**11.15**   Articles 102–108 deal with the payment of dividends to shareholders. The payment of a dividend is a source of income for a shareholder. As explained in the valuation methodology section of this chapter, one method of valuing a company is on the dividend yield basis. The payment of a dividend is also a method of withdrawing money from a company. There are detailed rules on the manner in which dividends are to be paid. The rules are set out in Part 23 of the Companies Act 2006. In essence, a company can only pay dividends out of accumulated, realised profits, so far as not previously utilised by distribution or capitalisation, less its accumulated, realised losses, so far as not previously written off in reduction or reorganisation of capital duly made.[10] Furthermore, any distribution made must not infringe the capital maintenance doctrine which requires the net assets of the company to be not less than the value of the share capital.

---

[9]   Such a step was taken in *C v C (Variation of Post-Nuptial Settlement: Company Shares)* [2003] 2 FLR 493.

[10]   Companies Act 2006, s 830(2). Problems can arise where, as sometimes happens in family run companies, payments have been made to a shareholder over the course of a year on account of an anticipated dividend which the company cannot declare at the year end because the profits were insufficient to do so. Such payments may then be repayable to the company.

**11.16** If a source of liquidity is being searched for, it may in an appropriate case be worth considering seeking to withdraw capital from a company by means of dividend payment. The right to withdraw capital from a company in ancillary relief proceedings is a matter of law.[11] The extent to which sums may be withdrawn is a matter usually requiring the assistance of an accountant. It should not be forgotten that dividends can essentially only be drawn out of a company's profits, thereby limiting the amount which can be withdrawn in each trading year.

**11.17** Although not traditionally part of the constitution of the company, a shareholders' agreement governing the control of voting rights and other matters impacts upon shareholders' rights within the company in much the same way as do the articles of association. In circumstances where a party is to maintain an interest in a company after final order, a properly drafted shareholders' agreement can provide effective regulation of the rights of a shareholder to interfere in the company affairs, whilst at the same time allowing that party to retain other benefits from the shareholding, such as the benefits of future dividends and capital growth arising from a potential takeover, buy out or flotation. *In P v P (Financial Relief: Illiquid Assets)*[12] the shares in the company were divided equally and the wife's concerns that her shareholding might be manipulated to her disadvantage were assuaged by Baron J, who stated that her position could be protected by a carefully drafted shareholders' agreement. It is suggested that corporate lawyers should be instructed to draft any shareholders' agreement where the rights enshrined in the articles are required to be modified. Given the potential costs of preparing such an agreement, it is important to ensure that those costs are proportionate to the value of the shareholding in question.

**11.18** An undertaking given to the court in respect of the exercise of shareholders' rights can also have a modifying effect on the rights granted to a shareholder under the articles of association. In *P v P (Financial Provision)*,[13] where the wife's continued holding of shares could have caused friction in the running of the company, the wife gave undertakings to the court, the effect of which was to reduce the risk of potential interference.

## GOVERNANCE

**11.19** In order to see how and by whom a company is to be run, it is necessary to consult the articles of association. In the absence of any modification to Table A, art 70 provides 'subject to the provisions of the Act, the memorandum and the articles and to any directions given by special resolution, the business of the company shall be managed by the directors who may exercise all the powers of the company'. Irrespective of any provision in the articles, a director

---

[11] See **11.76** et seq.
[12] [2005] 1 FLR 548 at [124] per Baron J.
[13] [1989] 2 FLR 241 at 245 per Anthony Lincoln J.

can be removed from the board under s 168 of the Companies Act 2006 by ordinary resolution. An ordinary resolution is usually required to elect a director to the board. An ordinary resolution requires a simple majority of those voting.[14] It follows that any shareholder with 51% or more of the voting shares of a company effectively controls the board and thus the business of the company. The existence of a majority shareholding clearly impacts upon valuation and realisation. An ordinary resolution is required for all decisions required to be taken under the Companies Act 2006, unless stated to the contrary.

**11.20** A special resolution is required to be passed by three-quarters of those voting. Special resolutions are usually required before alterations can be made to the constitution of the company. It follows that there is some value in having more than 25% of the voting shares in a company, because of the impact that such a shareholding can have on blocking special resolutions.[15] The corollary of this is that having 75% of the voting shares of a company amounts effectively to absolute control.

**11.21** The extent to which a party in ancillary relief proceedings has control over a company as a consequence of the extent of his or her shareholding has a clear impact on valuation. A more difficult question is whether and to what extent a court can require a majority shareholder to exercise their powers so as to achieve a particular outcome, such as the sale of company property, a distribution of dividends or a capital reduction scheme. It is submitted that if the corporate veil cannot be pierced and the concept of judicial encouragement cannot be employed, the court in ancillary relief proceedings does not have the power to order a majority shareholder to exercise his power over the company in any particular manner.[16]

**11.22** A party to ancillary relief proceedings who has a controlling interest in a company may be tempted to exercise their powers in order to effect a change to the structure of the board in an attempt to carry out a pre-emptive strike in advance of the ancillary relief proceedings. Any such attempt is likely to be restrained by the court. In *Poon v Poon*[17] the wife was the controlling shareholder and she sought to remove her husband from his position of managing director of a family company in what the court thought to be a strategic manoeuvre. The duty of the court was to preserve the status quo pending ancillary relief proceedings and to discourage or prevent either spouse from making pre-emptive strikes. On the facts of the case an injunction was granted restraining the wife from placing proposals or resolutions before an extraordinary meeting of the company, albeit upon terms that the husband,

---

[14] Companies Act 2006, Pt 13 and s 282.

[15] In *A v A* [2004] EWHC 2818 (Fam), [2006] 2 FLR 115, Charles J noted that it was unlikely that it was an accident that the wife held 25.37 per cent of the voting shares because with such a shareholding she would be able to block a special resolution.

[16] See *Nicholas v Nicholas* [1984] FLR 285, CA, where the power in question was the power to require the company to divest itself of assets. See **11.83**.

[17] [1994] 2 FLR 857, Thorpe J.

who had been accused of helping himself to company cash, agreed to the wife's proposals for the appointment of an independent director to join the board and the appointment of a professional company secretary.[18]

## SHARES[19]

**11.23** The search for a fully comprehensive definition of a share is elusive even for company lawyers. For our purposes, it is sufficient to describe a share as a chose in action. A share is therefore property that falls within s 25(2)(a) of the Matrimonial Causes Act 1973. A shareholder does not have a proprietary interest in company property, but does have an interest in the company as a consequence of the rights contained in the articles of association. Different classes of share can exist. The main types of share are the ordinary share, the preference share and the redeemable share.

**11.24** An ordinary share provides its owner with, amongst other things, the right to vote at shareholders' meetings.[20] It is the most commonly held share. A preference share provides an entitlement to a fixed dividend payment in priority to other shareholders. It is not usual to have voting rights attached to preference shares. A redeemable share is one that a company can redeem on terms. Any class of share may be made redeemable. The rights attached to shares will usually be made clear in the articles of association, sometimes the memorandum of association, and/or the resolution creating them. Identifying the type of share and the rights attached to it is of importance both when considering questions of control[21] and valuation.

**11.25** The shareholding in a private company limited by shares is identified in the annual return.[22] If further confirmation of shareholding is required, it should be noted that companies are required to keep a register of members.[23]

**11.26** As previously described, a shareholder has both the right to receive any dividend declared for distribution pari passu with other shareholders of the same class and an obligation to pay sums unpaid on any shares if called to do

---

[18] In the course of argument it was suggested that the Companies Court and not the Family Division had jurisdiction to hear the application. This argument was decisively rejected on the grounds that the company in question was a family business with no outsider interests and that all current disputes within the family should be litigated in the Family Division. The jurisdiction of the Family Division was contested in circumstances where allegations were made in ancillary relief proceedings in relation to misuse of the proceeds of sale of company assets. However, it was inappropriate to transfer even such a limited issue to the Companies Court in the course of ancillary relief proceedings: see *Taylor v Taylor* (2004) The Times, September 6.

[19] See also the general discussion of shareholdings in the context of quoted companies at **10.17–10.23**.

[20] It is possible, though, for non-voting ordinary shares to be created.

[21] See section on corporate governance.

[22] Companies Act 2006, s 856.

[23] Companies Act 2006, s 113.

so. An order frequently encountered in ancillary relief proceedings is a property adjustment order for one party to transfer shares to the other. If such an order is sought or likely to be made, thought must be given to any capital gains tax liability that may arise on transfer.

## DEBENTURES

**11.27**   A debenture is defined by s 738 of the Companies Act 2006 as including debenture stock, bonds and any other securities of a company, whether or not constituting a charge on the assets of the company. The definition is not particularly helpful. For our purposes, it is sufficient to say that a debenture is a document that evidences or creates a debt owed by the company to a creditor. A debenture holder is therefore a creditor of the company and his debenture a chose in action and thus an asset falling under s 25(2)(a) of the Matrimonial Causes Act 1973. The debenture needs to be obtained in order to determine the date for repayment of both the capital advanced under the debenture and the interest repayments that the company is required to make.

## PROTECTION OF MINORITY SHAREHOLDERS

**11.28**   As will be seen later in this chapter, a fair division of assets can result in both parties retaining shares in a company after final order. There is of course a risk in circumstances where the parties retain a financial relationship as shareholders that further disputes and disagreements will arise between them after the ancillary relief litigation has come to an end. Both parties retaining a shareholding in a company is plainly inconsistent with the general desire to achieve a clean break and it is not uncommon for the parties to strive to find some other fair basis upon which to deal with their shares. Where shares are retained in a company it is worth noting that s 994 of the Companies Act 2006 provides a general protection for a minority shareholder who has been unfairly prejudiced by the actions of the company. If unfair prejudice is established, a common order made is for the majority shareholder to buy out the minority shareholder's interest.

## ACCOUNTING REQUIREMENTS, AUDIT AND ANNUAL RETURNS

**11.29**   Every company is required to keep accounting records which are sufficient to show and explain the company's transactions and are such as to disclose with reasonable accuracy, at any time, the financial position of the company at the time.[24] The records that are kept form the basis of the accounts that are required to be prepared. The directors of the company are required to

---

[24]   Companies Act 2006, s 386.

prepare accounts for the company for each of its financial years.[25] The accounts are referred to as the company's 'statutory' or 'individual accounts'. Companies Act individual accounts must comprise a balance sheet and a profit and loss account. The balance sheet must give a true and fair view of the state of affairs of the company as at the end of the financial year; and the profit and loss account must give a true and fair view of the profit or loss of the company for the financial year.[26] The accounts are required to be approved by the board of directors and signed on behalf of the board by a director of the company.[27] The directors are required to prepare a directors' report complying with statutory requirements.[28] The directors' report is also required to be approved by the board and signed on its behalf by a director.

**11.30**  The company auditors are required to report on the company accounts unless the company is exempt from audit (see below). Amongst other requirements, the auditors' report must state whether the accounts have been properly prepared and whether they give a true and fair view of the balance sheet and profit and loss account. The auditors' report must be either unqualified or qualified and must include a reference to any matters to which the auditors wish to draw attention by way of emphasis without qualifying the report.[29] In a modest asset case, challenging audited accounts is unlikely to be a proportionate exercise. However, audited accounts are of course liable to challenge. Particular areas of challenge include the subjectivity and judgment used in accounting treatments, directors' remuneration and other expenditure, analysis of customers and suppliers, cash flow and contingent liabilities.

**11.31**  In general, in the case of a private limited company the directors are required to deliver the accounts, the directors' report and the auditors' report to the registrar of companies within 9 months after the end of the company's relevant accounting reference period.[30]

**11.32**  If a company qualifies as a small or medium sized company, different filing requirements apply. A company subject to the small companies regime is required to file a copy of a balance sheet, but filing a profit and loss account and a directors' report is optional.[31] The filed balance sheet may be prepared in less detail than would ordinarily be required and such accounts are described as 'abbreviated'. It should be noted that the accounts are required to state whether they have been prepared in accordance with the provisions applicable to companies subject to the small companies regime.[32] The filing obligations of qualifying medium sized companies are slightly different. The only difference from the usual filing obligations is that an abbreviated profit and loss account

---

25  Companies Act 2006, s 394.
26  CA 2006, s 396.
27  CA 2006, s 414.
28  CA 2006, ss 415–418.
29  CA 2006, s 495. Once filed, these documents are open to inspection by the public at Companies House.
30  CA 2006, s 442.
31  CA 2006, s 444.
32  CA 2006, s 444(5).

may be filed.[33] A qualifying small company may be exempt from the requirements in the Act relating to the auditing of accounts.[34]

**11.33**   The accounts of a company are clearly a source of important financial information. Form E requires disclosure of the last 2 years' accounts. Whether accounts are required for earlier years will depend on the facts of each case. Accounts are, of course, essential for valuation purposes. They are also helpful when seeking to examine whether benefits in kind have been received by directors and/or employees. An individual's personal tax returns and P11Ds are also helpful in this regard. The accounts assist the forensic accountant and the court in the search for liquidity and form the basis of all financial analysis relevant to capital and income streams deriving from the company.

**11.34**   Every company is required to file an annual return. The contents of the annual return are a source of much information for the ancillary relief lawyer. The annual return, amongst other information, is required[35] to provide details of the directors and shadow directors of the company. Helpfully, details of other directorships held by directors of the company are also required to be disclosed. The annual return will also provide evidence of the identity of shareholders, the number of shares that they hold and the type of shares held. Details of share transfers will also be set out in the return. Consideration should be given to obtaining the annual returns in every case involving a company. The period for which the returns are required will be case specific. However, it is submitted that in most cases it is proportionate to obtain the annual returns filed shortly before the breakdown of the marriage and for the period post-separation. These are a matter of public record and can be obtained from Companies House.

## READING COMPANY ACCOUNTS

### Types of accounts available

**11.35**   'Accounts' is a generic term which can cover many different formats. That accounts are prepared for varying reasons means that the end products can be very different in style, content and meaning.

**11.36**   Accounts may be prepared:

- by sole traders and partnerships to satisfy their need to provide details of their income to the taxation authorities. They may also be needed for submission to various others such as credit reference agencies, suppliers, landlords, bankers or other financiers. Such accounts are likely to have undergone little verification other than that which has been necessary to generate the information to be included.

---

[33]   CA 2006, s 445(3).
[34]   CA 2006, s 477.
[35]   CA 2006, s 856.

- for management purposes to help in decision-making. Management accounts range from the highly sophisticated to the remarkably simple. Typically they are produced on a periodic, eg monthly, basis. The information may be reported in customised fashion to highlight particular aspects of the operation, eg focusing on the difference between actual results and a budget, or 'variances'. Although such accounts may be released outside the management group, they are unlikely to be subjected to formal independent scrutiny.

- for proprietor information at intervals during the accounting year (typically quarterly), often called 'interim accounts'. These may or may not have been reviewed independently and may need to satisfy specified disciplines, such as the Stock Exchange Listing Agreement applying to listed entities. They will often be reviewed by reporting accountants, and carry a statement to that effect; this is not an 'audit opinion'.

- for statutory filing of abbreviated accounts by qualifying 'small' companies.[36] Increasingly, these will not have been audited. Where there has not been an audit, an accountant is required to report on whether the accounts are in agreement with the underlying records. In practice, the information in abbreviated accounts can be of relatively little value in ancillary relief proceedings. However, there should usually be fuller accounts prepared for the shareholders, which can be requested from the directors; again, these may not have been audited.

- for statutory and, where applicable, listing purposes by medium sized and larger companies. Such accounts can contain an abundance of information and are required to show a 'true and fair view'. Accountants often refer to these as 'financial statements', since much information is contained in textual form in addition to the tables of figures. Listed companies increasingly also produce a simpler 'shareholders' review', in which the directors set out to give a flavour of the activities and results of the review period but in simpler style than the formal financial statements. Note that the shareholders' review cannot take the place of the fuller information.

## Construction of accounts

**11.37** Company accounts usually contain a profit and loss account (or income statement) and a balance sheet, derived from the accounting records of the business. Full statutory accounts also contain at least:

- a cash flow statement, which re-analyses the information in the accounts to show the cash movements during the period;

---

[36] Broadly satisfying two out of three measures: turnover not more than £6.5m and/or balance sheet total not more than £3.26m and/or not more than 50 employees, as determined by the Companies Act 2006, s 382. These are the current figures. The first two are increased from time to time.

- a statement of recognised income and expense, which identifies amounts included in the profit and loss account which are also recognised directly in equity (via the note on the composition of capital and reserves) – formerly there was a statement of retained gains and losses (or 'STRGL') to bridge any difference between the profit or loss for the period and the change in shareholders' equity in the balance sheet;

- a description of significant accounting policies and various notes amplifying the information in the profit and loss account, the balance sheet, the cash flow statement and the statement of recognised income and expense;

- a directors' report; and

- an independent auditors' report.

Together the profit and loss account, the balance sheet, the cash flow statement and the statement of recognised income and expense supported by the respective notes are the four primary statements.

**11.38** Listed company accounts also include a chairman's statement, an operating and financial review (or similar), a statement on corporate and social responsibility, a statement on corporate governance, a statement on directors' responsibilities, a directors' remuneration report and, often, a table of salient figures over the previous 5 or 10 years.

**11.39** Companies may prepare a detailed trading profit and loss account for the shareholders. This provides a more detailed breakdown of the profit and loss account and is therefore a useful document. However, it does not form part of the statutory accounts and is therefore not available to the public through Companies House and must be requested from the directors, unless it is included in a shareholders' area of the company's website.

## The balance sheet

**11.40** The balance sheet is a table that lists the company's assets (but not contingent assets) and liabilities (again, not contingent)[37] and how they were arrived at. It provides a 'snapshot' of the affairs of the company at the accounts date. In statutory accounts this is the accounting reference date and there are rules as to what changes are permitted in this.

**11.41** Information in the balance sheet is grouped into categories such as fixed assets, current assets, current and non-current liabilities and shareholders' funds/equity.

---

[37]   Often, figures for liabilities are shown in brackets.

**11.42** An asset is something the company owns, or has constructive title to, including debts due from third parties. (Accounting theory has expanded in recent years beyond mere legal title.) Fixed assets are those assets which a company intends to retain for a number of years and use to produce and distribute its goods or services, or support its establishment. They are not bought with the intention of resale. Fixed assets include:

- tangible assets, such as buildings, machinery and motor vehicles;

- intangible assets, such as goodwill and trademarks; and

- certain (non-current) investments, e g shares in subsidiary companies.

**11.43** Current assets include cash and other assets that the company expects to sell or turn into cash within one year. They include amounts in bank accounts, items in stock and amounts due from customers.

**11.44** A liability is an amount the company owes to a third party or creditor. On a company balance sheet the liabilities are separated between those falling due within one year[38] (such as trade debts due to suppliers and sums due to the taxation authorities), and those falling due after more than one year, such as the non-current element of a mortgage. In the latter example, the amounts that the company is due to be paid in the next 12 months will be shown within liabilities falling due within one year, whilst the remainder will be shown as a liability falling due after more than one year.

**11.45** A third category of liabilities is contingent liabilities, which may never actually materialise. This includes possible liability under product guarantees, warrants and potential payments arising from legal claims against the company. Contingent liabilities are disclosed in notes to the accounts but not on the face of the balance sheet.

**11.46** The bottom half of the balance sheet usually comprises 'shareholders' funds' or 'shareholders' equity'. Broadly, this consists of the amounts invested into the company by shareholders and the profit the company has retained. The usual categories of shareholders' funds are as follows:

- Share capital – funds introduced by shareholders up to the nominal or face value of the shares allotted.

- Share premium reserve – funds introduced by shareholders over and above the nominal value of the shares allotted (if any).

- Profit and loss reserve – this comprises the profits (or losses) that the company has accumulated since its incorporation less sums distributed to shareholders, via dividends. The increase in this reserve from the start of

---

[38] Liabilities falling due within one year are referred to as 'current liabilities'.

the year (ie from the balance at the preceding year end) is generally the profit for the year shown in the profit and loss account less dividends paid. Only realised profits in the profit and loss account may be distributed to shareholders as dividends.[39]

- Revaluation reserve – this will be created when fixed assets are revalued upwards to reflect an increase in market value. The increase cannot be paid out to shareholders as dividends until realised by sale; hence the surplus is held separately from the profit and loss reserve.

**11.47**  The 'net assets', or sum of all the assets less the liabilities, will always equal the shareholders' funds; hence the two tables of figures balance. Looked at another way, somebody, either a third party or the shareholders, has a claim over every asset of the company.

**11.48**  Occasionally the balance sheet looks larger because long term finance is included after shareholders' equity rather than being treated as reducing assets. This is merely a matter of presentation, and once the style has been chosen it should be followed in subsequent years.

## *The profit and loss account*

**11.49**  The balance sheet and the profit and loss account are inextricably linked.

**11.50**  The profit and loss account shows the performance of the company for the year (or other accounting period). It describes the principal components of why the retained profit and loss reserve in the balance sheet changed over the year.

**11.51**  Categories that often feature in the profit and loss account are (in the order that they appear):

- Turnover (also known as sales) – this is the revenue earned during the year from normal operations and excludes customs duties and sales taxes.

- Cost of sales – these are the direct costs of producing goods or services for sale.

- Gross profit (or loss) – this is the surplus (or shortfall) of sales over cost of sales.

- Administration expenses and distribution costs ('overheads') – these are the other items of expenditure that the company incurs, such as rent, rates, depreciation and directors' remuneration.

---

[39]  Subject to rules in the Companies Act 2006, ss 829–853 regarding distributable reserves.

- Operating profit (or loss) – this is the trading profit or loss before taking into account interest and taxation. Note that, following a recent change, dividends when paid are usually charged in the note on capital and reserves rather than being shown as a deduction in arriving at retained profit of the previous year.

- Exceptional items – these are costs associated with the ordinary activities of the company but which, due to their size or nature, are disclosed separately.

- Interest – this is the cost of borrowing that the company has incurred, e g interest on bank loans and hire purchase agreements, netted off against any interest earned.

- Taxation – this is the Corporation Tax liability relating to the financial year (see below).

- Profit for the year – this is the resulting profit from continuing operations and any separately disclosed discontinued operations.

The above will be taken to the note on capital and reserves which will also include:

- Dividends – this is the portion of the accumulated profits (usually not the annual profit) that has been paid to shareholders during the year.

## The cash flow statement

**11.52** The cash flow statement sets out the movement of cash during the year and so, conceptually, is the easiest to understand. However, the cash flow statement is no longer a straightforward document but has become a complex analytical breakdown of cash movements.

**11.53** It is important to consider the cash position because, however profitable, more may be spent than is generated from the operations. Although this can often be managed for short periods (e g by using borrowings to set up a new manufacturing facility), in the longer run businesses must generate rather than consume funds. In the real world they tend to go out of business due to lack of cash rather than through being unprofitable, and this may happen despite a 'profitable' expansion, if it brings overtrading.

## The statement of total recognised gains and losses ('STRGL')

**11.54** In accordance with company law and accounting standards, certain gains and losses are specifically permitted or required to be taken directly to reserves without passing through the profit and loss account. Such gains and losses are shown in the STRGL, together with the profit or loss for the year, to give a complete picture of how shareholders' funds have increased or decreased in the period as a result of the company's activities apart from transactions with shareholders, such as share issues or redemptions, which are excluded.

**11.55**   Typically the STRGL will include:

- profit or loss for the year;

- unrealised surplus or deficit on the revaluation of fixed assets or investment properties (ie movements in the value of assets not sold);

- differences arising on the translation into sterling of net investments held in foreign currency;

- actuarial gains or losses on the assets and liabilities held in a defined benefit (final salary) pension scheme; and

- prior period adjustments (these are rare).

**11.56**   It should be noted that gains and losses recognised in the STRGL should not be recognised again in a later period. For example, a surplus arising on the revaluation of a fixed asset recognised in the STRGL should not be counted again through the profit and loss account when the asset is sold.

## How to review a set of accounts

**11.57**   When faced with reviewing a set of statutory accounts for a company it is important to know what information to seek from the accounts and how this can help to build up a picture of the business and its prospects. Although the latest set of accounts may be readily available, to assess the prospects of the company it can be useful to obtain copies of the accounts going back for several years, as these may help to identify trends. A tool accountants use is to assess a company by comparing identified trends in key measures over time and benchmarking these against other companies in the same industry.

**11.58**   Included in Appendix 2 is a listing of areas for consideration and of financial measures, which may be found within the accounts (or calculated from information in the accounts). It cannot be a definitive guide, as each company is different, but it is intended to provide a useful pointer in identifying trends. Additionally, a list of useful information to request when preparing a business valuation is set out in Appendix 10.

## Issues within accounts

### *Judgment and subjectivity*

**11.59**   It is important to remember that accounting has been described as an art and not a science. The interpretation of accounts requires an understanding of the figures and information disclosed, and different views can reasonably be reached on the same material. Except at the close of a business or at times when the balance sheet only comprises cash, accounts represent an interim view of the results, and there may be alternative ways in which costs and income can be allocated entirely properly to different accounting periods. The measurement of some items is subjective. Two separate authors of accounts may properly reach different results from the same transaction information due to:

- different, but appropriate, interpretation;

- careful use of the scope available within the adopted accounting policies to give a particular slant; or

- selection of new or different accounting policies to give a more favourable treatment.

**11.60** On the other hand, there may be deliberate manipulation of the figures so that the accounts do not represent the underlying economic reality.

**11.61** Subjectivity may affect the extent to which income or expenditure may be deferred to future periods, eg because of the need for bad debt provisions, and the appropriate evaluation of future liabilities.

**11.62** Some accounting areas are highly reliant on the knowledge of, and decisions made by, management. There may be little independent evidence to support the numbers. It is, therefore, important to look beyond the accounts themselves and to ascertain the source of the information used to compile them.

## *Self-serving presentation*

**11.63** When reviewing company accounts, especially for listed companies, be aware that those preparing the accounts seek to present the company in a favourable light to investors, analysts and other stakeholders. Bad news may be kept as brief as possible while positive events and statistics may be highlighted repeatedly. The chairman's statement and the financial review, for example, may draw attention to all the positive news, but place less stress on a negative issue or bury it within a paragraph that appears to be innocuous.

**11.64** When reviewing accounts try to 'read between the lines' and identify what the narrative statements do not say. Compare them with prior years' accounts and look for issues that were regularly mentioned that are omitted this year. This could be due to a deterioration in that area, or that nothing positive can be said.

**11.65** Check if the directors have been selling their own shares in the company, as that can be a bad sign.

**11.66** If a company has a qualified audit report, understand the qualification and the extent to which the identified matters permeate the information in the accounts.

## Creative accounting

**11.67** Self-serving presentation presents the facts in the most favourable way. 'Creative accounting' involves stretching, or even breaking, the requirements of accounting to show the figures that the company wants to show, rather than the true position. Depending on the size and nature of the transactions involved, this may involve deceiving the company's auditors.

**11.68** Always be suspicious of a change in accounting policy, as this may have been implemented to present the results in a more (or less) favourable way.

**11.69** Smaller, owner-managed companies may attempt to show lower profits, for instance to minimise their tax liability and particularly to reduce income and the value of the shares in a matrimonial dispute. Further investigation is required into a company that moves from a consistently profitable position to a loss-making one. This could include:

- reviewing external information about the company, including the company website, brochures and catalogues, industry-specific journals, local and national press coverage and that of trade associations.

- comparing the accounts to the company's competitors, particularly in respect of its accounting policies and whether these seem unduly tight or loose as against the peers.

- using a variety of parameters to get an overall picture. Do not rely on one financial parameter (such as net profit) to indicate the company's performance.

- applying common sense when analysing the parameters described in Appendix 2. For instance, is it likely that sales are decreasing if trade debtors are increasing? If so, why?

- linking the narrative statements in the chairman's statement, the directors' report and the financial review to the numbers in the profit and loss account and balance sheet and being aware that the directors may have put a 'spin' on the figures to serve their own objectives.

- focusing on the cash flow statement rather than the profit and loss account because, although cash can be massaged, the result will affect the cash flows into or out of other balance sheet items and leave clues.

- reviewing the management accounts, interim accounts, budgets, cash flow statements, tax returns, insurance records, shareholders' agreements and the memorandum and articles of association to form a broader understanding of the historical and prospective performance of the company, and to look for inconsistencies.

## Corporation tax

**11.70** Corporation tax is levied on the taxable worldwide profits of UK-resident companies and on the profits of non-resident companies attributable to permanent establishments located in the UK. A company will be tax resident if it is incorporated in the UK or if the central management and control of its business is in the UK. The latter may not be a straightforward concept.

**11.71** A company's taxable profits are based on its annual accounts where these are prepared in accordance with UK Generally Accepted Accounting Practice or, since 2005, where prepared in accordance with International Accounting Standards. However, despite the Government's stated aim of aligning taxable and accounting profit, a number of tax adjustments are still likely to be required to arrive at the taxable profits. Corporation tax is normally payable 9 months after the end of the period for which a company prepares its accounts, although larger companies are required to pay their tax liability by instalments during the course of the year.

**11.72** The UK corporation tax year runs from 1 April to 31 March and the top rate of corporation tax for the year to 31 March 2010 is 28%. 'Small companies' making annual profits up to £300,000 suffer tax at 21%. Note that this is a different definition of smallness from that which applies for accounts filing purposes, as set out above. The top rate of tax is currently charged on the whole of a company's taxable profit in a year once it reaches £1,500,000. For companies with annual taxable profits in between these levels, the tax calculation will effectively charge the first £300,000 of profit at 21% and the balance at a marginal rate of 29.75%. Together, these bands produce a charge of £420,000 once the profit level reaches £1,500,000 – the same as 28%. The profit limits are divided between 'associated companies' where the UK-resident company controls, or is under the same control as, other companies (in the UK or elsewhere). The definition of 'control' is complex and professional advice should be sought if it is thought this may be an issue.

## Deferred tax

**11.73** Deferred tax is a measure of the future tax effect of the difference between the accounts value and tax value of the company's assets and liabilities. For example, energy efficient plant and machinery costs £100,000; tax allowances of £100,000 are claimed based on the original cost; these reduce the company's tax liability for the year of acquisition and leave a 'tax written down value' for the plant of nil. In the meantime, the plant is recorded at a reducing value in the accounts, representing its useful life. If the plant were subsequently sold, part of the tax allowances would be reclaimed, creating a tax liability.

**11.74**   Deferred tax is shown as a liability in the accounts to account for the amount of tax payable on these differences. Other items with a deferred tax effect may include provisions and accrued liabilities. If the accounts are prepared on the basis of UK generally accepted accounting principles (rather than International Financial Reporting Standards), discounting may be applied to the liability to reflect the time value of money.

**11.75**   For financial measures for assessing accounts see Appendix 2 and for how to calculate key ratios see Appendix 3.

## SEPARATE LEGAL PERSONALITY AND LIFTING THE VEIL IN ANCILLARY RELIEF CASES

**11.76**   From an income perspective, the existence of a company in an ancillary relief case gives rise to relatively straightforward issues in respect of actual earnings and dividend payments. Evaluating future income, including increases in earning capacity, is of course altogether more difficult. However, from a capital perspective the issues are even more complex and frequently require an understanding of the concept of the separate legal personality of a company.

**11.77**   The general point on the separate personality of a company was spelt out by Lord Halsbury LC in *Salomon v A Salomon and Company*,[40] when he stated, 'Once the company is legally incorporated it must be treated like any other independent person with its rights and liabilities appropriate to itself, and that the motives of those who took part in the promotion of the company are absolutely irrelevant in discussing what those rights and liabilities are'.[41] Furthermore, it makes no difference that the company is a 'one man company', with the other shareholders mere dummies or nominees'.[42] The consequences of separate legal personality include the fact that a shareholder does not own any interest in company property. The company is a separate legal entity from its shareholders and is entitled to hold property and to sue and be sued in its own name.

**11.78**   The concept of separate corporate personality was described by Bodey J in *Mubarak v Mubarak*[43] in the following terms:

> 'Looking first at the authorities in the company/commercial sphere, the starting point is recognition of and respect for the juridical concept of the company as a separate legal entity. Upon this premise company law and practice is founded: *Aron Salomon (Pauper) v A Salomon and Company Limited; A Salomon and Company Limited v Aron Salomon* [1897] AC 22. It is as an incident of a company's separate legal persona that:

---

[40]   [1897] AC 22.
[41]   Cited in *Hashem v Shayif & Anor* [2009] 1 FLR 115 at [102] per Munby J.
[42]   *Hashem v Shayif & Anor* [2009] 1 FLR 115 at [103].
[43]   [2001] 1 FLR 673 at 678–9.

"… no shareholder has any right to any item of property owned by the company, for he has no legal or equitable interest therein. He is entitled to a share in the profits while the company continues to carry on business and a share in the distribution of the surplus assets when the company is wound up" *(Macaura v Northern Assurance Company, Limited, and Others* [1925] AC 619 at 626–627 per Lord Buckmaster).

In *Ord and Another v Belhaven Pubs Ltd* [1998] 2 BCLC 447, Hobhouse LJ (as he then was) stated at 457:

"The approach of the judge in the present case was simply to look at the economic unit, to disregard the distinction between the legal entities that were involved and then to say: since the company cannot pay, the shareholders who are the people financially interested should be made to pay instead. That of course is radically at odds with the whole concept of corporate personality and limited liability and the decision of the House of Lords in *Salomon* …"

The parent company in organising the group had there been entitled "… to expect that the court should apply the principles of *Salomon* … in the ordinary way" (458). Hobhouse LJ further noted that in *Adams and Others v Cape Industries plc and Another* [1990] Ch 433, the Court of Appeal had considered both the "single economic unit" and the "piercing the corporate veil" arguments for lifting the veil and had "… clearly recognised that the concepts were extremely limited indeed" (457).'

**11.79** From the viewpoint of an ancillary relief practitioner, the concept of separate legal personality brings into sharp focus a particular problem. Frequently, parties to ancillary relief proceedings hold shares in companies. In turn, those companies will own property. The question arises as to whether and in what circumstances the property of the company is available for redistribution by the court. Where the separate legal personality of a company is ignored, and company property is treated as if it is owned by a shareholder, the process is described as either 'lifting' or 'piercing the corporate veil'.

**11.80** The leading case on piercing the corporate veil in the context of ancillary relief proceedings is *Hashem v Shayif & Anor*.[44] In *Hashem* an offshore company was set up to hold English properties in a tax-efficient manner. The husband was a 30% shareholder. His children by previous marriages held the remaining 70%. The wife sought to pierce the corporate veil, alleging that the company was a small family company, that it was not a trading entity, that the directors were largely fee-paid professional company directors drawn from the corporate service providers in the Channel Islands rather than full-time employees, that there were no substantial creditors, that the company existed solely to hold property in a tax-efficient manner, that only the husband had contributed capital to the company and that no distinction was ever drawn by any of the directors or shareholders as between funds to which the company was entitled and funds to which the husband was entitled. It was argued on

---

[44]  [2009] 1 FLR 115.

behalf of the wife that the company was simply the husband's alter ego and the other shareholders simply his nominees.

**11.81** After noting that the same principles on piercing the corporate veil applied irrespective of the division of the High Court hearing the case, Munby J identified the principles justifying the lifting of the veil of incorporation as follows:[45]

> 'The starting point is the statement of principle by Lord Keith of Kinkel in *Woolfson v Strathclyde Regional Council 1978 SC(HL) 90* at page 96:
>
>> "it is appropriate to pierce the corporate veil only where special circumstances exist indicating that it is a mere façade concealing the true facts."
>
> That statement was treated by the Court of Appeal in *Adams v Cape Industries PLC* [1990] Ch 433 at page 539 as stating a "well-recognised exception" to the rule prohibiting the piercing of the corporate veil. It is, in my judgment, binding upon me and definitive.
>
> There is no particular magic in the word façade, which is here plainly being used in its secondary (and surprisingly recent) sense of "an outward appearance or front, especially a deceptive one". Down the years a variety of other epithets and metaphors have been used to express the same concept.
>
> ...
>
> I have been taken to a number of cases on the topic. In addition to those I have just mentioned I must also refer to *Nicholas v Nicholas* [1984] FLR 285, *Green v Green* [1993] 1 FLR 326, *Ord v Belhaven Pubs Ltd* [1998] 2 BCLC 447, *Wicks v Wicks* [1999] Fam 65, *Gencor ACP Ltd v Dalby* [2000] 2 BCLC 734, *Mubarak v Mubarak* [2001] 1 FLR 673, *Trustor AB v Smallbone (No 2)* [2001] 1 WLR 1177 and *Dadourian Groupinternational Inc v Simms* [2006] EWHC 2973 (Ch). I do not need to go through them all in turn, but the following principles can, in my judgment, properly be drawn from them.
>
> In the first place, ownership and control of a company are not of themselves sufficient to justify piercing the veil. This is, of course, the very essence of the principle in *Salomon v A Salomon & Co Ltd* [1897] AC 22, but clear statements to this effect are to be found in *Mubarak* at page 682 per Bodey J and *Dadourian* at para [679] per Warren J. Control may be a necessary but it is not a sufficient condition (see below). As Bodey J said in *Mubarak* at page 682 (and, dare I say it, this reference requires emphasis, particularly, perhaps, in this Division): "it is quite certain that company law does not recognise any exception to the separate entity principle based simply on a spouse's having sole ownership and control."
>
> Secondly, the court cannot pierce the corporate veil, even where there is no unconnected third party involved, merely because it is thought to be necessary in the interests of justice. In common with both Toulson J in *Yukong Line Ltd of*

---

45   [2009] 1 FLR 115 at [151]–[152] and [155]–[165].

*Korea v Rendsberg Investments Corporation of Liberia (No 2)* [1998] 1 WLR 294 at page 305 and Sir Andrew Morritt VC in *Trustor* at para [21], I take the view that the dicta to that effect of Cumming-Bruce LJ in *In re a Company* [1985] BCLC 333 at pages 337-338, have not survived what the Court of Appeal said in *Cape* at page 536:

> "[Counsel for Adams] described the theme of all these cases as being that where legal technicalities would produce injustice in cases involving members of a group of companies, such technicalities should not be allowed to prevail. We do not think that the cases relied on go nearly so far as this. As [counsel for Cape] submitted, save in cases which turn on the wording of particular statutes or contracts, the court is not free to disregard the principle of *Salomon v Salomon & Co Ltd* [1897] AC 22 merely because it considers that justice so requires. Our law, for better or worse, recognises the creation of subsidiary companies, which though in one sense the creatures of their parent companies, will nevertheless under the general law fall to be treated as separate legal entities with all the rights and liabilities which would normally attach to separate legal entities."

Thirdly, the corporate veil can be pierced only if there is some "impropriety": see *Cape* at page 544 and, more particularly, *Ord* at page 457 where Hobhouse LJ said:

> "it is clear ... that there must be some impropriety before the corporate veil can be pierced."

Fourthly, the court cannot, on the other hand, pierce the corporate veil merely because the company is involved in some impropriety. The impropriety must be linked to the use of the company structure to avoid or conceal liability. As Sir Andrew Morritt VC said in *Trustor* at para [22]:

> "Companies are often involved in improprieties. Indeed there was some suggestion to that effect in *Salomon v A Salomon & Co Ltd* [1897] AC 22. But it would make undue inroads into the principle of *Salomon*'s case if an impropriety not linked to the use of the company structure to avoid or conceal liability for that impropriety was enough."

Fifthly, it follows from all this that if the court is to pierce the veil it is necessary to show *both* control of the company by the wrongdoer(s) *and* impropriety, that is, (mis)use of the company by them as a device or façade to conceal their wrongdoing. As the Vice Chancellor said in *Trustor* at para [23]:

> "the court is entitled to 'pierce the corporate veil' and recognise the receipt of the company as that of the individual(s) in control of it if the company was used as a device or facade to conceal the true facts thereby avoiding or concealing any liability of those individual(s)."

And in this connection, as the Court of Appeal pointed out in *Cape* at page 542, the motive of the wrongdoer may be highly relevant.

Finally, and flowing from all this, a company can be a façade even though it was not originally incorporated with any deceptive intent. The question is whether it is being used as a façade at the time of the relevant transaction(s). And the court will pierce the veil only so far as is necessary to provide a remedy for the particular wrong which those controlling the company have done. In other words, the fact that the court pierces the veil for one purpose does not mean that it will necessarily be pierced for all purposes.

In *Trustor*, the defendant's plea (see para [16]) that Introcom had been formed in connection with an earlier scheme, having no connection with Trustor, and that it was a genuine company having its own separate existence, cut no ice with the Vice Chancellor, who nonetheless held that the corporate veil could be pierced. And as Warren J said in *Dadourian* at paras [682]–[683]:

> "[682] In all of the cases where the court has been willing to pierce the corporate veil, it has been necessary or convenient to do so to provide the claimant with an effective remedy to deal with the wrong which has been done to him and where the interposition of a company would, if effective, deprive him of that remedy against him. It seems to me that the veil, if it is to be lifted at all, is to be lifted for the purposes of the relevant transaction. It must surely be doubtful at least that the ex-employee in *Gilford Motor Co v Horne* would have been liable for the company's electricity bill simply because he was using the company as a device and sham to avoid a covenant binding on him personally; and the same goes for the vendor of the property in *Jones v Lipman*.
>
> [683] It is not permissible to lift the veil simply because a company has been involved in wrong-doing, in particular simply because it is in breach of contract. And whilst it is clear that the veil can be lifted where the company is a sham or façade or, to use different language, where it is a mask to conceal the true facts, it is, in my judgment, correct to do so only in order to provide a remedy for the wrong which those controlling the company have done.'"

**11.82**  The claim to pierce the corporate veil and to treat the assets of the company as being the assets of the husband failed. The wife had failed to establish the relevant degree of control over the company on the part of the husband. Perhaps more fundamentally, the wife had failed to establish any relevant impropriety.[46] The only impropriety relied upon by the wife was that the husband was purporting that the company was beneficially owned by the shareholders, when it was in fact, just like the properties owned by the company, his own. This argument elicited the following response from Munby J:

> 'The common theme running through all the cases in which the court has been willing to pierce the veil is that the company was being used by its controller in an attempt to immunise himself from liability for some wrongdoing which existed entirely *dehors* the company. It is therefore necessary to identify the relevant wrongdoing – in *Gilford* and *Jones v Lipman* it was a breach of contract which, itself, had nothing to do with the company, in *Gencor* and *Trustor* it was a

---

[46]  The wife's primary submission, based upon a reading of *Mubarak v Mubarak* [2001] 1 FLR 673, was that there was no requirement to establish impropriety. This argument was rejected by Munby J.

misappropriation of someone else's money which again, in itself, had nothing to do with the company – before proceeding to demonstrate the wrongful misuse or involvement of the corporate structure. But in the present case there is no anterior or independent wrongdoing. All that the husband is doing, in the circumstances with which he is now faced – the wife's claim for ancillary relief – is to take advantage, in my judgment legitimately to take advantage, of the existing corporate structure and, if one chooses to put it this way, to take advantage of the principle in *Salomon*.

That does not involve any impropriety. Indeed, to assert that it does is really to seek to resurrect the views expressed by Cumming-Bruce LJ in *In re a Company* [1985] BCLC 333 which were rejected in *Cape*. The circumstances of the present case are, of course, very different from the circumstances in either *Cape* or *Ord*, but the essential motivation of the protagonists in all three cases is the same, namely to obtain perceived financial advantage from insisting upon a proper distinction between personal liability and corporate liability. For better or worse, as the Court of Appeal put it in *Cape*, the *Salomon* principle is embedded in our law. And in my judgment, there is no more "impropriety" in the present case than there was in either *Cape* or *Ord*. Indeed, allowing for the very different circumstances, the passages from *Cape* which I have quoted in paragraphs [160] and [177] above, and the passage from *Ord* which I have quoted in paragraph [178] above, indicate clearly enough, even if only by analogy, why there is simply no relevant "impropriety" in the present case.'

**11.83** If on the facts of a case it is inappropriate to pierce the corporate veil, is the court able to use its powers, either under the Matrimonial Causes Act 1973 or the inherent jurisdiction, to require a party who is a controlling shareholder of a company to exercise his rights in such a way as to require the company to sell property to another spouse? In *Nicholas v Nicholas*[47] the Court of Appeal held that there was no such power vested in the court, either under statute or the inherent jurisdiction, to impose 'an obligation upon a respondent to procure that a third party in whom the property is beneficially vested to divest itself of that property by way of sale to a petitioning wife, whether the machinery be by exercise of the majority shareholder's voting powers or otherwise'. The rationale behind the decision was that a property adjustment order under MCA 1973, s 24(1)(a) can only be made against a party to ancillary relief proceedings in respect of property to which that party is entitled either in possession or reversion. As a shareholder does not have a proprietary interest in company property, no property adjustment order may be made in respect of such property.

**11.84** There are many reported cases in which courts have explored the possibility of raising money from assets of a company.[48] If the court has no

---

[47]   [1984] FLR 285, CA.
[48]   See, for example, *P v P (Financial Provision)* [1989] 2 FLR 241 at 244, where Lincoln J stated 'If there is liquidity in the company which could be realised to meet her requirements, then the final order will take that liquidity into account. If there is none, in the sense that the company (the source of the breadwinner's income) will be damaged, then the court must look elsewhere'; and *Evans v Evans* [1990] 1 FLR 319 at 325, where Booth J stated 'But in this case the parties seek a clean financial break and what is crucial to this enquiry is the liquidity of the company

power to order a party to ancillary relief proceedings to exercise a controlling interest in such a way as to realise company assets,[49] then the juridical basis for such an approach would appear to be either piercing the corporate veil, or the judicial encouragement of company directors or shareholders.[50] However, the usual basis for treating company assets as if they belonged to one of the parties is born of the pragmatic acceptance by the parties that the assets of the company are essentially inseparable from their own.[51]

**11.85** It is extremely difficult to pierce the corporate veil. In *Hashem v Shayif & Anor*[52] Munby J noted that the research of counsel had only identified one case in the Family Division where the veil of incorporation had been pierced.[53] Perhaps, from an ancillary relief perspective, that says it all. In the circumstances, commentary upon the applicable legal principles identified by Munby J is unnecessary.

## JUDICIAL ENCOURAGEMENT

**11.86** The judicial encouragement of fiduciaries to exercise their discretion in favour of a spouse involved in ancillary relief proceedings is dealt with in detail at **15.46–15.53**. The concept of judicial encouragement developed in the context of discretionary trusts. However, as was made clear by Glidewell LJ in *Thomas v Thomas*,[54] the principle applies in the context of a family company, with the family company treated as if it were the trust and the shareholders the trustees. On the facts of *Thomas* the judicial encouragement was directed at a husband, who was also a director and shareholder, to persuade his fellow shareholders to make changes in company policy in respect of the payment of dividends and/or the remuneration of management.

**11.87** By analogy with trusts, there will be a number of limitations to the concept. When making an order that encourages shareholders to act in such manner as will result in company resources being made available to a spouse,

---

since it is only through his ability to withdraw capital from the company that the husband has the capacity to provide the necessary funds ... The husband's accountant is of the opinion that the husband could properly withdraw £57,000 which will be subject to tax whether it was voted out by way of dividend or by way of remuneration'.

49    Including a company's ability to raise finance.
50    In *P v P (Financial Relief: Illiquid Assets)* [2005] 1 FLR 548 at [115] Baron J requested the accountants at trial to consider what sums could be withdrawn from the business over the next 20 months on the assumption that the company was going to continue to trade profitably, the sums to be withdrawn were not to damage the company's ability to trade or its plans for relocation and any funds were to be taken from cash flow. The accountants concluded that £430,000 net could be withdrawn from the company within the stated criteria and Baron J acknowledged that the moneys could only be extracted from the companies with the co-operation of a third party shareholder.
51    See *Mubarak v Mubarak* [2001] 1 FLR 673.
52    [2009] 1 FLR 115 at [221].
53    That case was *Green v Green* [1993] 1 FLR 326, a decision that Munby J had great difficulty with [173], as indeed did Peter Gibson LJ in *Wicks v Wicks* [1999] Fam 65.
54    [1995] 2 FLR 668 at 678.

improper pressure must not be exerted on the shareholders. Jurisprudentially improper pressure arises where an order is framed in terms that would leave the shareholders with no option but to act in such a manner as to advance company funds to a spouse who is either a shareholder and/or director and/or employee.[55] A fortiori, the award made by the court must also be capable of being met by assets and income that are in the parties' ownership as of right and not contingent upon the actions of the shareholders.[56] Furthermore, any judicial encouragement must have regard to other shareholders of the company, whose interests must not be appreciably damaged by compliance with a genuine request for funds.[57]

**11.88** It is submitted that the application of the concept of judicial encouragement in the context of companies is relatively limited. It is likely only to be applicable to a family company, otherwise there is likely to be a real risk of third party shareholders having their interests adversely affected. Where there are a number of different shareholders, all the shareholders will be entitled to receive any dividend declared pari passu with other shareholders of the same class. Making company funds available to a shareholder spouse by way of dividend payment may therefore result in 'leakage' of company assets to third parties. Withdrawing company resources by way of an increase in directors' emoluments and employees' salaries, whether on an ex gratia basis or otherwise, avoids any difficulties that may arise from shareholders requiring a dividend to be divided equally between shareholders of the same class. However, both methods of judicially encouraging payment to a spouse will be gross payments, which will be taxed as income in the hands of the recipients.

## THEMES IN COMPANY LAW CASES

**11.89** The ancillary relief jurisdiction is one where authorities are easily distinguishable on the facts and where the search for anything other than broad principle in the reported authorities can be counter-productive. A thematic approach to the manner in which courts have dealt with ancillary relief cases involving a company can, however, be of assistance in identifying some of the more frequently occurring factors to which the courts have had regard in the search for fairness. The extent to which these themes are determinative of outcome will vary from case to case. The themes identified below are of course neither a closed list nor mutually exclusive. Nevertheless, it is hoped that the themes identified will assist in the development of argument and the efficacious application of the MCA 1973, s 25 criteria to the facts of each case.

---

[55] See, for example, *Howard v Howard* [1945] P 1 and *B v B (Financial Provision)* (1982) 3 FLR 298.
[56] See *TL v ML and others* [2006] 1 FLR 1263.
[57] See *Thomas v Thomas* [1995] 2 FLR 668, CA.

## Protection of income-producing assets

**11.90**   In the search for liquidity it is all too often dangerous to lose sight of the fact that in many cases the shares in a private family company are a source of income for both parties as well as a capital asset. Historically, courts have shown a particular concern not to jeopardise the financial well-being of a company if it is the only income-producing asset of the family. Where the welfare of children of the family and a wife are dependent upon periodical payments from a husband, the company that provides the husband's income should not be damaged in order to additionally raise a lump sum to pay the wife. As Dunn LJ stated in *Smith v Smith*,[58] 'Where, as here, the only asset from which a lump sum could be raised are the shares in a private company, the court is always very cautious not to jeopardise the only income-producing asset, since to do so is of no benefit to either of the parties or the children'.

**11.91**   Similarly, a business should ordinarily not be put at risk merely to fund an immediate clean break[59] unless it is fair to do so, since a clean break should never be achieved at the expense of fairness.[60]

**11.92**   Whether it is permissible for the assets of a company to be used to raise capital lump sums or generate income streams is, it is submitted, dependent upon a concession by a shareholder spouse or the ability to pierce the corporate veil or judicial encouragement of those in control of the company. Piercing the corporate veil and judicial encouragement are questions for the judge. The extent to which sums can be raised without damaging the company will be determined by the trial judge, usually with the assistance of expert evidence.

**11.93**   Where prior to *White v White*[61] a wife was restricted to her reasonable requirements balanced against the husband's ability to pay, there was reluctance on the part of the courts to make an order for the sale of a company.[62] Since *White* it has been thought that the reluctance should not be so marked. As was stated by Coleridge J in *N v N (Financial Provision: Sale of Company)*:[63]

> 'I think it must now be taken that those old taboos against selling the goose that lays the golden egg have largely been laid to rest; some would say not before time. Nowadays the goose may well have to go to market for sale, but if it is necessary to sell her it is essential that her condition be such that her egg laying abilities are damaged as little as possible in the process. Otherwise there is a danger that the full value of the goose will not be achieved and the underlying basis of any order will turn out to be flawed.'

---

[58]   (1983) 4 FLR 154 at 157.
[59]   See *P v P (Financial Relief: Illiquid Assets)* [2005] 1 FLR 548 at [77] per Baron J.
[60]   See *Miller v Miller; McFarlane v McFarlane* [2006] 1 FLR 1186.
[61]   [2001] 1 AC 596, [2000] 2 FLR 981, HL.
[62]   See *Smith v Smith* (1983) 4 FLR 154, CA; *Potter v Potter* (1983) 4 FLR 331, CA; *P v P (Financial Provision)* [1989] 2 FLR 241, Lincoln J.
[63]   [2001] 2 FLR 69 at 80.

**11.94** In *N v N (Financial Provision: Sale of Company)* the husband was a partner in a successful accountancy practice and also the majority shareholder and chairman of a successful group of companies in the financial services industry. The accountancy practice generated earnings of £120,000 gross for the husband per annum. The companies provided a small income for the husband but had not contributed to the family's standard of living, since profits were not taken out of the business. The value of the husband's shareholding was assessed at £1.75 million after the deduction of capital gains tax. The total assets of the parties were approximately £2.6 million. Coleridge J found that fairness was reflected in a lump sum of £1 million to be paid to the wife and that the husband's shareholding would have to be sold in order to fund the lump sum. The husband was given more than 2 years to dispose of his shares in order to protect their value.

**11.95** In *N v N (Financial Provision: Sale of Company)* the shares in the financial services companies were primarily a source of capital. Selling the company did not impact materially upon the parties' income position, since the husband retained his interest in the accountancy partnership and the sale of the shareholding did not affect his ability to make periodical payments for the children of the marriage. By way of contrast, in *A v A*[64] Charles J viewed the wife's minority shareholding as primarily an income-generating asset whose value was so uncertain and liquidity so doubtful that the ownership of the shares would not be disturbed.

**11.96** Whilst an order for the sale of shares in a company is no longer unthinkable, the categorisation of the shares as a vital income-producing asset and the case being unsuitable for an income clean break strengthens arguments against sale. If sale is still sought, many questions will need to be asked,[65] including questions related to ease of valuation and realisation and whether, once capital gains tax and costs of sale are brought into account, dividend income is exceeded by the income generated by investment of the net proceeds of sale of the shares.

**11.97** Protecting the income-producing characteristics of shares in a family company whilst at the same time dividing assets fairly may be attained by an order for the transfer of shares, leading to both parties retaining an interest in the family company. Although such an order runs contrary to clean break principles, the retention and division of a shareholding in a family company can facilitate a fair division of assets and, as will be illustrated in the next section, is finding increasing popularity in the case law.

---

[64] [2004] EWHC 2818, Charles J.
[65] *A v A* [2004] EWHC 2818 (Fam), [2006] 2 FLR 115, discussed below in the section concerning miscellaneous valuation issues.

## Sharing the results of a company's performance – *Wells* sharing

**11.98**   The source of much jurisprudence on an approach to the reallocation of shareholding in a family company is found in *Wells v Wells*.[66] In a much cited passage[67] Thorpe LJ stated:

> 'In principle it seems to us that the separation of the family does not terminate the sharing of the results of the company's performance. That is easily achieved in any case in which the wife's dependency is met by continuing periodical payments. It is less easy to achieve in a clean-break case. In that situation, however, sharing is achieved by a fair division of both the copper-bottomed assets and the illiquid and risk-laden assets. After all, the wife was already a shareholder in Soundtracs and a substantial increase in her shareholding would at least have enabled her to participate in future prosperity by dividend receipts or capital receipts on sale or a cessation of trade. An increase in her share of the illiquid and risk-laden assets would have allowed a reduction in the *Duxbury* fund, if not in the housing fund. If profitability were not recovered then both parties would share the experience of a marked reduction in standards of living.'

**11.99**   In *Wells v Wells* the husband had a majority interest in a family company. The wife had a small minority shareholding. There were two teenage children and the parties sought a clean break. Additionally, neither party wished for there to be a transfer of shares. In those circumstances the court held that it would be inconceivable that it would impose an order against the wishes of the parties by transferring shares from the husband to the wife, especially since such an order would attract a capital gains tax liability. However, the court made it clear that had it been left to its own devices it would have increased the wife's shareholding to around 10% of the company.[68] However, the issue for the court was to determine the level of the lump sum to be paid by the husband to the wife, taking into account that the husband was to retain the illiquid and risk-laden assets represented by the shareholding in a company that was not successful at the time, was operating at a loss and which could not be valued with any reasonable precision. In allowing the husband's appeal and reducing the lump sum that he was required to pay, the Court of Appeal determined that insufficient regard had been had to the needs of the husband. The Court of Appeal also deferred absolute finality in the case by introducing a mechanism enabling the wife to apply to the court in the event of the husband's sale of his shareholding within 5 years.

**11.100**   The principle elucidated in *Wells v Wells*, albeit obiter, that post-separation the parties should share in the results of a company's performance in a clean break situation by a fair division of the copper-bottomed and the illiquid and risk-laden assets has been taken into account in a number of recent authorities.[69]

---

[66]   [2002] 2 FLR 97, CA.
[67]   [2002] 2 FLR 97, CA at [24].
[68]   [2002] 2 FLR 97 at [33].
[69]   In addition to those cases referred to in the text, see also, for example, *F v F (Clean Break:*

**11.101**  In *C v C (Variation of Post-Nuptial Settlement: Company Shares)*[70] the parties had agreed that there ought to be broad equality of outcome. The issue for the court was how this was to be achieved in relation to a Cayman Island settlement that held the husband's 48.1% interest in a company that both parties had established. The evidence before the court was that the company had received a very significant offer for its shares in 2000. The deal fell through and thereafter the value of the company went into decline. The intention was that the company would be sold within 5 years at a figure significantly more than the present and agreed valuation. It was clear that both parties recognised the potential for the shares to increase significantly in value on any future sale. The wife therefore sought a variation of the Cayman Island trust to enable her to hold half of the husband's shareholding. The husband sought to persuade the court to make a deferred lump sum order calculated at the date of future sale by reference to the value of the shares at that time, or alternatively that the wife should be able to vary and then subsequently capitalise any periodical payments order upon sale of the shares. The wife also adduced evidence that she wished to use the voting rights attached to any shares that she might obtain to influence the board of directors in policy decisions.

**11.102**  Coleridge J held that, almost as a matter of principle, where a wife has played a part and wishes to play a part in the future of a company, there would have to be a compelling reason why she should not be entitled to do so.[71] On the facts of the case, the wife was entitled to play a part in the future of the company, and fairness and broad equality of outcome would be achieved by an order transferring 30% of the husband's shares, which equated to 15% of the company, to the wife. A fair division of the copper-bottomed and illiquid and risk-laden assets in this case took into account that the wife received a significant copper-bottomed asset in the form of the former matrimonial home and the husband's far greater role in the creation and development of the company.

**11.103**  Similarly, in *P v P (Financial Relief: Illiquid Assets)*[72] Baron J took account of *Wells v Wells* when ordering that the husband's shares in the family company would be divided in order to effect broad equality of assets, taking into account the fact that the husband had a greater proportion of illiquid assets in the division.

**11.104**  A shareholding in a family company is frequently both illiquid and inherently risk-laden. If the company performs well, the shareholder may be rewarded by dividend. Additionally, if the company is to be sold against a backcloth of a successful trading history, the shareholder will be likely to achieve capital growth on the value of his shares. On the other hand, if the

---

*Balance of Fairness)* [2003] 1 FLR 847, *A v A* [2004] EWHC 2818, [2006] 2 FLR 115, Charles J, *Smith v Smith* [2007] 2 FLR 1103 and *S v S (Ancillary Relief after Lengthy Separation)* [2007] 1 FLR 2120.

[70]   [2003] 2 FLR 493.
[71]   [2003] 2 FLR 493 at [52].
[72]   [2005] 1 FLR 548 at [128].

company were to perform badly, the prospect of an income return on shares diminishes and the likelihood of realising any capital from the assets will seem an increasingly distant prospect. The retention and reallocation of shares between the parties as part of a fair division of the assets on a clean break enables part of both parties' fortunes to wax and wane with that of the company. There is obvious potential unfairness if there is not a fair division of copper-bottomed and illiquid and risk-laden assets. Furthermore, the solution adumbrated in *Wells v Wells* provides a mechanism to deal with a frequently occurring scenario where there is real belief that one spouse's interest in shares will in the future generate an uncertain and unfathomable increase in capital. A *Wells* sharing approach is also arguably the only way of achieving a fair division of assets in circumstances where there is a significant doubt as to the value to be attributed to deferred or risk-laden assets.[73]

**11.105**   Where there is no income clean break, an increase in the value of one party's shareholding could be compensated for on an application for variation and/or capitalisation of a periodical payment entitlement. Such a possibility was envisaged in *C v C (Variation of Post-Nuptial Settlement: Company Shares)*,[74] where Coleridge J stated:

> 'If there is need for further adjustment by way of further compensation to the wife in the event that the company achieves a very significantly greater sale price than that already achieved in 1999, there is ample power in the court to make such further adjustment. Principally, as Miss Stone has reminded me, this can be done by way of the final determination of the wife's claim for periodical payments which could be varied to a significant level and then capitalised in the usual way.'

**11.106**   Similarly, in *F v F (Clean Break: Balance of Fairness)*,[75] despite assets of over £4 million, a clean break was not possible. The husband held over 94% of the shares in the family company and the wife less than 0.5%. The wife did not want to force a sale upon the husband. Periodical payments of £75,000 per annum were ordered to be paid. The husband's shareholding was not divided between the parties. In so ordering, Singer J stated:

> 'If, however, as W proposes and I intend to order, H parts with less capital now and only 50% of the value of the self-administered pension fund, but pays W continuing maintenance, then each will share in the results of the company's performance until such time, if ever, as emerging liquidity enables a clean break to

---

[73]   See *GW v RW (Financial Provision: Departure from Equality)* [2003] 2 FLR 108, Nicholas Mostyn QC, where the same distribution ratio (60% to the husband and 40% to the wife) was applied to both the copper-bottomed and the illiquid and risk-laden assets. See also *S v S (Ancillary Relief after Lengthy Separation)* [2007] 1 FLR 2120 at [94], where Singer J noted that a *Wells* approach disposes of controversies over recent valuations of currently unrealisable assets, and indeed what is the right discount to apply to reflect deferred receipt and the element of risk.

[74]   [2003] 2 FLR 493 at [59]. See also *Smith v Smith* (1983) 4 FLR 154 at 157: '… and if, hopefully, the company resumes its profitability then the wife can be compensated through an increase in periodical payments.'

[75]   [2003] 1 FLR 847, Singer J.

be achieved upon a basis that is fair in the circumstances then prevailing. Such a result is indeed consistent with that passage in para [24] of the judgment in *Wells v Wells* where Thorpe LJ said:

> "In principle it seems to us that the separation of the family does not terminate the sharing of the results of the company's performance. That is easily achieved in any case in which the wife's dependency is met by continuing periodical payments. It is less easy to achieve in a clean break case."

Mr Moor furthermore makes the sound point, in my view, that if liquidity had been no object, and if broad equality would have been the outcome, W would have received far more (on my calculation £860,000 more than H proposes, and just over £1m more than will be the effect of my order). To the extent that she does not receive and may never receive that shortfall, H's continued trading through the company will take place with the benefit of funds in which W has a real interest. He will indeed be trading with and making profits from capital which, in changed circumstances, would fairly have been hers. It is difficult, therefore, to see upon that basis how an outcome is unjust which imposes upon him a maintenance obligation in return.'

**11.107** In highly exceptional cases the parties may benefit from the gain in value in an asset after ancillary relief proceedings have come to an end by way of a claw-back provision, usually in the form of a charge over assets in favour of one of the parties.[76] In *Parra v Parra*[77] there was a remote prospect of a very significant windfall if land jointly owned by the parties could be sold with the benefit of planning permission. The land was to be transferred to the husband but was subject to a charge in favour of the wife, giving her half of any increased value in the land in the event that planning permission was granted. The claw-back provision ran counter to the clean-break principle, but was fair as a consequence of the potential increase of at least £3.5 million in the value of the site if planning permission were to be granted and the fact that during evidence the husband admitted that it would be unfair if he were to receive all the benefit of the increase in value of the land. It is also worth recalling that in *Wells*, because the parties agreed that the husband was to walk away with the risk-laden shares, the wife was provided with a mechanism to come back to court in the event that the shares were sold within 5 years of the order.

## Sale

**11.108** The likelihood of an order for sale of a company, or more accurately an order for the shares in a company to be sold, has been touched upon under the section dealing with the protection of an income-producing asset. There are, of course, a whole variety of factors that a court will take into account when deciding whether to order the sale of a business. Some of these factors (eg difficulties in valuation and liquidity issues) are dealt with in the remaining sections of this chapter. Other factors are more case specific. For example, in *H*

---

[76] See **9.15**.
[77] [2003] 1 FLR 942, CA at [31].

*v H*[78] the court thought a sale would not be appropriate in circumstances where, amongst other matters, the business had been the focus of the husband's working life since 1974 and the husband intended to work in the business for many years in the future. Ultimately, however, the touchstone for determining whether an order for sale is required is fairness, and each case will turn on its own facts. That having been said, orders for sale are not commonly found in the reported case law, despite the perceived consequences of the decision in *White v White*.

**11.109**   A case in which a sale was envisaged was *Parra v Parra*.[79] The husband and wife were both 44. They had two children, aged 17 and 16. Together they set up and ran a successful family business in which they each held 50% of the shares. They also jointly owned property for future business purposes. Both sought a clean break. The Court of Appeal held that the assets of the parties ought to be divided equally. The husband was therefore required to pay the wife a lump sum of £818,641 in order to achieve the aim of equality of capital assets, and in return she was to transfer her shares in the company and the land to the husband. If the husband could not raise the funds to pay the lump sum, the company and land would have to be sold and the net proceeds of sale be divided equally.

**11.110**   In reaching his conclusion Thorpe LJ placed great store on the property holding arrangements made by the parties themselves during the course of their marriage and the virtue of simple equality over sophisticated and elaborate adjustments to the parties' respective interests in the capital assets. He put the matter as follows:

> 'In my appreciation the overwhelmingly obvious solution in this case was equal division of family assets. I would almost see more attraction in Mr Posnansky's submission that the full value of the wife's holding should be discounted for immediate cash realisation than in the judge's decision to discount the husband's share by 4.3%. However, the simple virtue of equality outweighs sophisticated arguments for adjustment one way or the other. If there is a principle it should, I think, be this: that in comparable cases the division of assets for which the parties have themselves elected should not be adjusted by judges on the grounds of speculation as to what each may achieve in the years of independence that lie ahead.

> The parties had, perhaps unusually, ordered their affairs during the marriage to achieve equality and to eliminate any potential for gender discrimination. They had in effect elected for a marital regime of community of property. In such circumstances what is the need for the court's discretionary adjustive powers? The introduction of the "no order" principle into s 25 of the Matrimonial Causes Act 1973 might contribute to the elimination of unnecessary litigation. As a matter of principle I am of the opinion that judges should give considerable weight to the property arrangements made during marriage and, in cases where

---

[78]   [2008] 2 FLR 2092 at [122].
[79]   [2003] 1 FLR 942, CA.

the parties have opted for equality, reserve the exercise of the adjustive powers to those cases where fairness obviously demands some reordering.'[80]

**11.111**  *Parra v Parra* was a case where both parties wanted a clean break and where the first instance judge found that the husband would have a gross income of £240,000 from the business, which was sufficient to raise a lump sum of just over £1 million. There was therefore sufficient liquidity to achieve a clean break and the order for sale was a default position.

## The generational family company

**11.112**  A successful family company can provide employment and income for successive generations of the same family. Where a shareholder of a long-established family company is caught up in ancillary relief proceedings, there is an understandable desire somehow to ring-fence the shareholding in the family company and to protect it for future generations. Despite this desire, where needs are required to be met, the shareholding in a generational family company will not be ring-fenced. Where needs can be met without recourse to the shares, then the fact that the shares are 'inherited' assets is a basis for a departure from equality within the sharing principle.

**11.113**  As Baroness Hale stated in *Miller v Miller; McFarlane v McFarlane*:[81]

> 'In *White*,[82] it was recognised that the source of the assets might be a reason for departing from the yardstick of equality ... In *White*, it was also recognised that the importance of the source of the assets will diminish over time (see 611B and 995 respectively). As the family's personal and financial inter-dependence grows, it becomes harder and harder to disentangle what came from where. But the fact that the family's wealth consists largely of a family business, such as a farm, may still be taken into account as a reason for departing from full equality: see *P v P (Inherited Property)* [2004] EWHC 1364 (Fam), [2005] 1 FLR 576.'

**11.114**  In *P v P (Financial Relief: Illiquid Assets)*[83] the husband sought to justify departure from the yardstick of equality in part on the basis that his father and uncle founded the business that he eventually took over and developed. Baron J held that this was a case where the needs of the parties meant that there would be no departure from equality to take into account the source of the husband's business assets. The learned judge went on to find that in any event it was the husband and not his father and uncle that were responsible for the creation of the wealth locked into the company. The matter was put succinctly as follows:

> 'During the marriage each party made equal but different contributions. The husband's father was (with his brother) the founder of the business. This factor merits consideration but it does not entitle the husband to a greater proportion of

80   *Parra v Parra* [2003] 1 FLR 942 at [26]–[27].
81   [2006] UKHL 24 at [148].
82   [2001] 1 AC 596, [2000] 2 FLR 981, HL.
83   [2005] 1 FLR 548, Baron J.

the assets in this case, given the parties' actual needs. Lord Nicholls of Birkenhead made it clear in *White v White* [2001] 1 AC 596, [2000] 2 FLR 981 that, whilst "inherited" assets might be placed in a special category, they might have to be invaded if there were a need to do so. In this case, Ps was in its infancy when the parties married. The real value of the company was founded on the XXX franchise which was obtained in 1977 after the date of the marriage. H was not started until 1990. As I find, it was the husband and his cousin who were really responsible for making these companies ultimately successful and valuable.'

**11.115** So, not only does the source of the shareholding have to be considered, but also the identity of the creator of the wealth in the company. It would appear insufficient merely to argue that there should be a departure from equality on the basis of 'inherited' shares in a family company if the value in the company was generated by the party that 'inherited' the shares.

## The search for liquidity

**11.116** Whether arising out of the sale or attempted sale of shareholdings or the traditional route of valuation of the shareholding and the payment of a balancing lump sum, the courts are frequently engaged in a search for liquidity. Liquidity has been described by Singer J in *F v F (Clean Break: Balance of Fairness)*[84] in the following terms:

'Liquidity, the ability to pay, finds no express reference amongst the s 25(2) "matters" to which the court is in particular directed to have regard, although clearly it is an element which can and often must be taken into account as one amongst "all the circumstances of the case". I do not for a moment suggest other than that it is a highly relevant consideration, nor indeed that the ease or difficulty with which any particular asset or class of asset can be realised should be disregarded when surveying the financial resources available to the parties. Liquidity can constitute an important element not only at the stage when the court considers the time for implementation of the order, but also at the earlier stage of arriving at a fair (albeit maybe only provisional) conclusion as to how the order should if practicable be fashioned.'

**11.117** The search for liquidity in *F v F (Clean Break: Balance of Fairness)* led to forensic accountants being instructed to establish the true extent of the husband's income from the company. In conducting their analysis the P11D benefits and any other expenditure which the company met for the husband but which salaried employees normally meet out of taxed income in their own pockets was taken into account. Determining the true extent of the husband's income can be aided by a combination of a careful reading of accounts and a sufficiently focused questionnaire. In an appropriate case the input of a forensic accountant at the questionnaire stage will satisfy any cost benefit analysis. Obviously, the higher the husband's income when properly assessed, the greater the prospect of his being able to fund a loan or increase the value of periodical payments.

---

[84]   [2003] 1 FLR 847 at [86].

**11.118** Ever since *N v N (Financial Provision: Sale of Company)*,[85] illiquidity has been a ground upon which to depart from equality. In *F v F (Clean Break: Balance of Fairness)* illiquidity of assets justified a departure from equality and militated against a clean break despite the fact that the assets in the case were in round terms assessed at over £4 million. As Singer J eloquently stated, 'illiquidity is an extremely relevant factor, not to be disregarded any more than the non-availability as free capital of the bulk of a pension fund'.[86]

**11.119** Selling shares in private limited companies is frequently not a straightforward task, and great care needs to be taken to ensure that shares are sold as close to their full value as possible. Setting unrealistic timetables for selling shares could result in their being sold for less than their true worth. In *N v N (Financial Provision: Sale of Company)*[87] Coleridge J recognised that 'the court ... must be creative and sensitive to achieve an orderly redistribution of wealth, particularly where this involves the realisation of assets owned by either of the parties'. In *N v N (Financial Provision: Sale of Company)* the inevitable consequence of the order for the husband to pay the wife a lump sum was the liquidation of his shareholding in a successful company. However, the husband was given over 2 years to sell his shares. In *R v R (Financial Relief: Company Valuation)*[88] the husband was given 5 years in which to raise money to buy out the wife's interest in a company and a discount for early repayment. Parties have therefore to be alive to the fact that immediate capital clean breaks can detrimentally affect the value of the assets in a marriage.

**11.120** It is clear that thought needs to be given in appropriate cases to the mechanics of asset realisation. How and when an asset is likely to be sold in order to achieve its maximum value needs to be considered as an inherent element of achieving a fair division of assets. Liquidity can improve, to the benefit of all parties, if a creative and sensitive approach is taken to asset realisation. Accountants and, where necessary, stockbrokers and merchant banks should be consulted. Consideration will also need to be given to the most tax-efficient manner of realisation.

**11.121** Where a party is looking to retain the benefit of a shareholding, the court will as part of its investigation look very carefully to see what remaining assets are available for distribution to the non-shareholding spouse. In a traditional case the shareholding spouse will be required to raise a lump sum to pay to the non-shareholding spouse. The capital-raising ability of the shareholding spouse will need to be investigated well in advance of trial. Converting taxed income into capital may be one way to raise a lump sum. A shareholder may be able to utilise dividends and/or income generated from employment to fund a loan. However, in *Smith v Smith*[89] the court concluded that the husband could not afford to raise a lump sum from his company

---

[85] [2001] 2 FLR 69.
[86] [2003] 1 FLR 847 at [79].
[87] [2001] 2 FLR 69 at 71.
[88] [2005] 2 FLR 365, Coleridge J.
[89] (1983) 4 FLR 154, CA.

drawings. Raising money for a lump sum is one thing: affording it is clearly another. Releasing equity in property is another frequently encountered method of raising a lump sum. It should be noted that borrowing against the security of shares in a private company is unlikely to be satisfactory to most commercial lenders. Commercial lenders would be likely to look at fixed and floating charges as a means of securing any capital advanced.

**11.122** In an appropriate case, a forensic accountant can be of valuable assistance in determining the ability of a party to raise money from his assets. For example, in *Evans v Evans*[90] a key issue for the court was the extent to which the husband could withdraw money from his business, either through dividend or remuneration, without damaging the family's income-producing asset. More recently, in *P v P (Financial Relief: Illiquid Assets)*[91] Baron J concluded that the company did not have the ability to raise further money and in the search for liquidity:

> 'asked the accountants to meet over an (extended) short adjournment to see whether they could agree what sums they considered could be withdrawn from the business over the next 20 months on the assumption that: (i) the companies were going to trade profitably; (ii) such moneys as were withdrawn would not damage Mr C's ability to trade; (iii) Ps was going to undertake the relocation project at a cost of £5m over the next 20 months and (iv) that the funds could not be derived by further borrowing from the bank or XXX Finance – in other words, moneys could only be extracted from cash flow/trading profit without being detrimental to the business.'

In the light of the evidence subsequently obtained, the learned judge was able to find that £430,000 net was able to be withdrawn from the company over 20 months. The said sum amounted to a further copper-bottomed asset of the parties and represents a marked illustration of the benefit that can be attained by the appropriate use of forensic accountants to search for liquidity in a case.

## Miscellaneous valuation issues

**11.123** An issue that screams out from the reported authorities is the consistent exhortation to avoid expending unnecessary costs on valuation issues when the costs could better be put to use for the benefit of the parties to the marriage. In *P v P (Financial Relief: Illiquid Assets)*[92] the parties incurred costs of around £360,000 against total assets of the marriage of around £2.8 million. Whilst the learned judge hoped that the wife would be able to remain in the former matrimonial home, the effect of any costs order would decide whether this would be possible. *P v P (Financial Relief: Illiquid Assets)* was not a big money case, since there was no great surplus of assets after needs had been

---

[90]  [1990] 1 FLR 319, Booth J.
[91]  [2005] 1 FLR 548.
[92]  [2005] 1 FLR 548, Baron J.

taken into account. It was also a case where the issues were relatively straightforward. In the circumstances of the case the learned judge was moved to state:[93]

> 'I have had the benefit of two expert accountants – Mr R on behalf of the wife, and Mr T on behalf of the husband. Each was loyal to their instructions and produced significantly different values for each business. I consider that it would have been of more assistance to me if there had been one jointly instructed expert. I so state because I consider that, in a case such as this where the issues are relatively simple, the court should be slow to permit each party to have their own expert. In this case, the experts have each produced a number of reports. In fact, the expert bundle was so large that it had to be divided.

> As each accountant was coming to the valuation from a different perspective (one seeking the highest possible value/liquidity and the other the lowest) their evidence was inevitably coloured. It would have been so much better (and significantly cheaper) if one expert had been instructed to report on an unbiased basis to the court. By that I am not suggesting that either expert was biased, merely that they had a specific cause to advance.'

**11.124** Of course, where the issues are more complex and the wealth of the parties greater, the court is more likely to accede to a request for each party to have their own expert. In most cases the court will be minded to follow the encouragement in the *President's Direction* dated 25 May 2000[94] and in the judgment in *P v P (Financial Relief: Illiquid Assets)* to appoint a single joint expert.[95] In a more modest asset case an obvious candidate for a single joint expert is the company auditor. However, sometimes a non-shareholding spouse may quite properly consider that the auditor is insufficiently independent to be appointed single joint expert.

**11.125** Whether it is necessary to instruct a forensic accountant, as a single joint expert or indeed at all, is in every case fact specific and is frequently a difficult decision to make. Where a party seeks the assistance of a forensic accountant on pre-trial matters (eg drafting questionnaires), the decision is frequently taken on a cost benefit analysis. It should be noted that an expert instructed to assist one party is unlikely to be appointed a single joint expert. When a direction for expert evidence is required, the court will determine the matter, having regard to the application of the overriding objective and the President's Direction for the Instruction of a Single Joint Expert.[96] It is worthwhile setting out the relevant provisions of the Ancillary Relief Rules,

---

[93]  [2005] 1 FLR 548 at [64]–[65].
[94]  [2000] 1 FLR 997, at para 4.1.
[95]  See 'At a Glance'; The President of the Family Division's Ancillary Relief Advisory Group *Best Practice Guide for Instructing a Single Joint Expert*, November 2002. Note the confirmations required to be put before the court contained in para 4(1) if there is no agreement on the appointment of an SJE before a directions appointment.
[96]  Ancillary Relief Rules, r 2.51D.

since they form the context in which the parties and the court will determine whether and the extent to which expert evidence is appropriate. Rule 2.51D provides as follows:

'(1) The ancillary relief rules are a procedural code with the overriding objective of enabling the court to deal with cases justly.

(2) Dealing with a case justly includes, so far as is practicable—

(a)   ensuring that the parties are on an equal footing;
(b)   saving expense;
(c)   dealing with the case in ways which are proportionate—
      (i)    to the amount of money involved;
      (ii)   to the importance of the case;
      (iii)  to the complexity of the issues; and
      (iv)   to the financial position of each party;
(d)   ensuring that it is dealt with expeditiously and fairly; and
(e)   allotting to it an appropriate share of the court's resources, while taking into account the need to allot resource to other cases.'

**11.126**   It is important to appreciate both the nature and the significance of a forensic accountant's task when valuing a company. These issues were concisely dealt with by Moylan J in *H v H*,[97] when he stated:

'The experts agree that the exercise they are engaged in is an art and not a science. As Lord Nicholls of Birkenhead said in *Miller v Miller; McFarlane v McFarlane* [2006] UKHL 24, [2006] 2 AC 618, [2006] 1 FLR 1186, at para [26]: "valuations are often a matter of opinion on which experts differ. A thorough investigation into these differences can be extremely expensive and of doubtful utility". I understand, of course, that the application of the sharing principle can be said to raise powerful forces in support of detailed accounting. Why, a party might ask, should my "share" be fixed by reference other than to the real values of the assets? However, this is to misinterpret the exercise in which the court is engaged. The court is engaged in a broad analysis in the application of its jurisdiction under the Matrimonial Causes Act 1973, not a detailed accounting exercise. As Lord Nicholls of Birkenhead said, detailed accounting is expensive, often of doubtful utility and, certainly in respect of business valuations, will often result in divergent opinions each of which may be based on sound reasoning. The purpose of valuations, when required, is to assist the court in testing the fairness of the proposed outcome. It is not to ensure mathematical/accounting accuracy, which is invariably no more than a chimera. Further, to seek to construct the whole edifice of an award on a business valuation which is no more than a broad, or even very broad, guide is to risk creating an edifice which is unsound and hence likely to be unfair. In my experience, valuations of shares in private companies are among the most fragile valuations which can be obtained.'

**11.127**   The judgment in *H v H* emphasises the broad as opposed to the particular approach of the court on an ancillary relief application to the quantification of assets (and also the categorisation of assets into either

---

[97]   [2008] 2 FLR 2092 at [5].

matrimonial or non-matrimonial property). The temptation to assess fairness of division by reference to precise asset value ought to be resisted. As the learned judge indicated, to take such an approach is likely to lead to an award that is unfair. It is submitted that the judgment also contains a powerful rationale towards the appointment of a single joint expert in all but the most exceptional of circumstances. Furthermore, on an assessment of fairness of asset division, the nature and purpose of any asset should perhaps be a primary consideration. It is submitted that if this approach is taken the mistaken desire to obtain precise asset valuation may be subdued.

**11.128** In addition to valuing shareholdings, forensic accountants are also frequently asked to quantify liquidity in a company, whether derived from existing company assets, future earnings or indirectly by way of borrowings that could be financed by the company. Another frequently asked question is to identify the available income which a party could reasonably draw from a business.

**11.129** The case of *A v A* [2004] EWHC 2818 (Fam)[98] contains perceptive judicial guidance on the process of deciding whether, and if so on what basis, to instruct an expert to value a company shareholding. In that case the wife held a 25.37% interest in her father's family company. She bought 7.64% of the shareholding herself. The remainder of her interest was a gift from her father. Both the husband and the wife called experts to value the wife's shareholding. The shareholding was a source of considerable income for the wife. As a minority shareholder in a family company her shareholding would not be easily realisable and it was difficult to put an accurate value on the shares. The primary value of the shares to the wife was therefore as an income-producing asset and not a capital asset. In these circumstances Charles J was moved to state:

> 'At the risk of being accused of seeking to revisit issues in *Parra v Parra*, I make the general comment that it seems to me that in ancillary relief proceedings it is important for the parties and their advisers to look at issues concerning private companies through the eyes of both: (a) persons with experience in and of matrimonial litigation; and (b) persons with experience in and of business and business litigation. For example, if this is done it may quickly become apparent: (a) that there is a wide bracket of valuation; and (b) that there may be a viable and pragmatic business solution which would avoid either or both of the uncertainties and difficulties of valuation and the raising of finance, albeit that it may not involve a clean break.'[99]

**11.130** After a detailed consideration of the issues that would be uncovered if a pragmatic approach by reference to the underlying commercial reality was adopted, the learned judge suggested that the consideration of the facts 'from the business perspective rather than from what seems to be a common approach in ancillary relief proceedings of seeing how a clean break on the

---

[98] [2006] 2 FLR 115.
[99] [2006] 2 FLR 115 at [60].

payment of a lump sum can be achieved by reference to snap shot valuations may in a number of cases point the way to more flexibility of thought and a fair solution'.[100] Parties in future litigation who were seeking a clean break by valuation of a shareholding and payment of a lump sum were exhorted to be 'clear why they are taking a course which involves the uncertainties and potential unfairness of a result dependent on valuation and the payment of a lump sum (which may have to be borrowed), or sale'.[101]

**11.131**  If a pragmatic approach had been taken to the issues before the court, the exercise would, therefore, at a very early stage have called into question whether it was appropriate to obtain valuations of the shares as a minority holding on a conventional basis rather than taking a broader approach which recognised that:

'(i)    in the hands of Mrs A the shares were producing a substantial income return by way of dividend and, therefore, had a dividend yield value, or a value based on the prospect of producing over the years an income by way of dividend and salary equivalent to that presently being paid;

(ii)    unless either (a) the company floated or was sold as a whole, or (b) another shareholder or the company was willing (and keen) and able to buy the shares, the price that could be obtained for them would almost inevitably be below their value as an income producing asset with the consequence that such a sale, or a division of assets between Mr and Mrs A on the basis of a valuation by reference to such a sale, may be not be fair;

(iii)   if Mrs A were to retain the shares in determining the orders to be made under the MCA 1973 the overall value and benefits (both as to income and capital) of the shares in her hands should probably be brought into account as opposed to only a capital valuation of the shares as a minority holding;

(iv)    if there were to be a division of the shares or a division of assets by reference to the capital value of the shares the possibility of a transfer of the shares, or the creation of a trust in respect of them, rather than the payment of a lump sum should be considered;

(v)     both parties needed to consider carefully whether either of them was asserting that there should, or could be, a lump sum payment by reference to a valuation of the shares and if so how the shares could fairly be compared to the other capital assets, whether there should be a transfer of (or trust created in respect of) the shares or whether the essential relevance of the shares was as to how their retention by Mrs A impacted upon the order to be made in respect of the matrimonial home;

(vi)    part of that consideration should relate to the relevance and effect of the point that the majority of the shares had been given to Mrs A by her father and X Ltd is a B family company;

(vii)   more generally it was likely that the parties would have to carefully define their contentions relating to the shares;

(viii)  the question of valuations being sought on a range of bases and specifically by reference to the articles and the issues as defined would probably have to be considered; and

---

[100]   [2006] 2 FLR 115 at [62].
[101]   [2006] 2 FLR 115 at [63].

(ix) even in the absence of differences between expert valuers the range of possibilities relating to income from the shares (and salary) and their sale would be likely to give rise to the result that (at least potentially) the shares had a wide range of capital value.'

**11.132** Charles J was of the view that the accountancy evidence could have been obtained in respect of the value of the shares in broad terms on the alternative bases mentioned above. The expert evidence would have been far less expensive and it was even postulated might not have been needed at all. The learned judge concluded his thoughts as follows:

'In the light of that broad approach decisions could be made as to whether an approach based on valuing all the relevant assets and making a division and capital award by reference to those snap shot figures was likely to be capable of founding a fair result. If that approach shows that even absent disagreement between valuers there is likely to be a wide range of value between, for example, a disposal of the company as a whole (or it being floated), and sales of the shares as a minority interest, either to the company or the other shareholders who were keen to buy, or at a valuation in accordance with the pre-emption rights, or to an outsider, this is likely to trigger: (i) the question whether and how a fair comparison based on snap shot valuations can be made between the shares and other assets for the purposes of an overall division of assets under the MCA 1973; and (ii) questions as to the bases upon which valuations should be made.'[102]

**11.133** Having regard to the source of the shares and the difficulty of valuing them as a capital asset, the court took the shares into account as part of the obligation to have regard to all the circumstances of the case under MCA 1973, s 25. The correct approach for the judge to take was to ask himself:

'the general question (against the backdrop that a crosscheck by reference to equality is appropriate in the context of this marriage): On a clean break basis (as sought by both parties) what is a fair distribution of the capital assets which represent the matrimonial property apart from the shares (ie the matrimonial home and the insurance policies) having regard in particular to the income prospects of the parties, their likely outgoings, the status quo as to the accommodation of the parties and their children, my findings and conclusions set out herein and the point that the wife will retain the shares in X Ltd the majority of which were given to her by her father? That is not a complete list of all the relevant circumstances but it seems to me that they are the magnetic factors in this case.'[103]

**11.134** Similar themes are echoed by Mr Justice Charles in his judgment in *D v D and B Limited*,[104] where the learned judge exhorted the parties to stand back and look at the range of possible options with the eyes of a commercial as well as a matrimonial litigator. The learned judge went so far as to say that:

---

[102] [2006] 2 FLR 115 at [71].
[103] [2006] 2 FLR 115 at [129].
[104] [2007] 2 FLR 653 at [103]–[104].

'parties and their advisers urging a clean break by reference to valuations of a private company as their primary case will generally, if not always, owe a duty (and in any event would be well advised) to consider commercial alternatives. This is particularly the case when there is, or is likely to be, a significant dispute or a significant uncertainty or a wide bracket on valuation and/or the ability to raise and pay a capital sum without unduly jeopardising or burdening the business or the paying party.

I therefore repeat my urging of those involved in ancillary relief cases involving private companies not to confine themselves to an approach based solely on valuation and liquidity (ie the ability to raise money to meet a lump sum payment) but to investigate and consider commercial alternatives and periodical payments. In my view it should be practical for this to be done without undue expense in particular with co-operation and the formulation of the correct type of questions. This is particularly so when it is remembered that rough and preliminary valuations on an earnings basis should be possible without incurring significant accountancy fees.'

**11.135** Furthermore, as emphasised in *D v D and B Limited*, in an appropriate case where creative solutions are being considered, it is necessary to take into account commercial, company and fiscal considerations to enable the court to be properly appraised as to the true or net effect of the order being sought and the practicalities involved in effecting the order. Such an approach in an appropriate case requires the likely instruction of experts in not only valuation, but taxation and company/commercial law matters.

**11.136** *A v A* and additionally *D v D and B Limited* contain encouragement to parties to consider the alternatives to the traditional ancillary relief approach of valuation of a shareholding and the payment of a lump sum. Avoiding detailed and unnecessary valuations of course saves costs. The case also reflects a theme that has permeated ancillary relief case law, namely that the inherent difficulties in valuing a minority shareholding in a family company mean that a fair division of assets is frequently achieved without the need to place a specific value on the shareholding. A number of seminal pre-*White v White* cases make it clear that where the business is not going to be sold, a precise valuation of a shareholding is unnecessary.[105] As was stated in *Evans v Evans*,[106] 'While it may be necessary to obtain a broad assessment of the value of a shareholding in a private company it is inappropriate to undertake an expensive and meaningless exercise to achieve a precise valuation of a private company which will not be sold'. In *N v N (Financial Provision: Sale of Company)*,[107] a post-*White* case, a value was placed on the husband's majority shareholding, which ultimately was required to be sold. However, apart from the husband's partnership capital, no particular figure was placed in the assets schedule in respect of the husband's

---

[105] See *Potter v Potter* (1983) 4 FLR 331, CA; *Nicholas v Nicholas* [1984] FLR 285; *P v P (Financial Provision)* [1989] 2 FLR 241.
[106] [1990] 1 FLR 319, Booth J.
[107] [2001] 2 FLR 69, Coleridge J. See **12.76**.

interest as senior partner in a highly successful group of partnerships, although the interest was taken into account in a more general way as part of the decision-making process.

**11.137** The inherent difficulty in valuing shares is one of the reasons why a fair division of assets is sometimes carried out without bringing into account the capital value of shares. In *A v A* Charles J described those difficulties in the following terms:[108]

> 'In an assessment of a fair division of assets under the MCA problems obviously arise in respect of "snap shot valuations". The greater the volatility in value, or the potential for a wide range of valuation, the greater the problem. In respect of private companies, and shareholdings therein, the difficulties and potential unfairness of a "snap shot valuation" clearly arise and can do so in a stark form. Such valuations turn in large part upon opinions as to prospects, and what multiple and discount should be used in the valuation method adopted. They suffer from the background difficulty that there is generally no open market for the shares. This can regularly give rise to large differences between highly reputable valuers even when they are using the same methodology and these can be compounded by differing views on prospects and methodology. All this, and other problems, flow from the nature of the asset.'

**11.138** The wide range of potential valuations in *A v A* meant that the learned judge felt that it was:

> 'very difficult to bring the value of the shares into account on a snap shot basis by the use of a mathematical crosscheck by reference to equality (or some other division) in which a valuation put on the shares is added to (or compared with) the valuations of the matrimonial home and the insurance policies'.

**11.139** Similar sentiments were expressed by Ormrod LJ in *Potter v Potter*[109] in the context of whether a one-third guideline should be applied to the division of capital assets. He stated:

> 'The problem when one comes to deal with capital, particularly in a case of this kind, is that one cannot use the one-third rule, as Dunn LJ has made clear, until the value of the assets of the parties have been ascertained. This is a highly speculative exercise in a great many cases particularly where a small business is concerned. Applying the one-third rule to this case would mean that the amount to be paid by the husband would depend on valuations by accountants and here, in this case, the unfortunate judge had before him no less than four different valuations by four different accountants. The spread of the valuations ranged between £10,000 and £40,000 for the goodwill; so that it is wholly illusory to think that, by using the one-third rule in relation to capital, any certainty is achieved. It simply exchanges one uncertainty for another. And there are no indications as to

---

[108]  [2006] 2 FLR 115 at [64].
[109]  (1983) 4 FLR 331 at 337. See also the similar comments, albeit in the context of valuing deferred assets, in *GW v RW ( Financial Provision: Departure from Equality)* [2003] 2 FLR 108 set out in Chapter 10.

which accountant is more likely to be right because the whole thing is an imaginary exercise from beginning to end.'

**11.140**   Post-*White* and *Miller/McFarlane* there is a tendency in some quarters to think that it is necessary to place a precise value on all capital assets. As illustrated above, this is not so. The purpose of valuations is to assist the court in testing the fairness of the proposed outcome. The MCA 1973, s 25 exercise requires a general consideration of sources of income and capital, not a detailed one.[110] In *White v White*[111] the House of Lords emphasised that a broad assessment of the parties' financial position and not a detailed partnership account was required. In some cases a broad consideration of the assets will mean that the fairness of a proposed outcome will be determined by having regard to an asset as one of the circumstances of the case without the need to ascribe to that asset a particular valuation. Furthermore, care needs to be taken to ensure that there is no double-counting,[112] particularly where there is no real value in a business other than as an income stream. As was stated by Coleridge J in *V v V* [2005] 2 FLR 697 at [28]:

> 'There can, of course, be no hard-and-fast rule in relation to the extent to which the capital value of businesses are or are not brought into account but where (as here) there is no real value except as an income stream, to include it in circumstances where there is no suggestion that there should be a clean break, runs the serious risk, in my judgment, of double-counting. I consider that the proper approach in a case of this kind is for the court to treat such business assets as primarily a secure income of the parties, from which there has to be a substantive and unlimited order for periodical payments.'

## Special contributions

**11.141**   In big money cases following *White v White*[113] the search was on to identify arguments justifying departure from the equal division of assets. One such justification was the stellar or special contribution of one of the parties to the marriage. A special contribution argument was raised in the House of Lords in *Miller v Miller; McFarlane v McFarlane*.[114] Baroness Hale dealt with the concept in the following terms:

> 'It had already been made clear in *White* that domestic and financial contributions should be treated equally. Section 25(2)(f) of the 1973 Act does not refer to the contributions which each has made to the parties' accumulated wealth, but to the contributions they have made (and will continue to make) to the welfare of the family. Each should be seen as doing their best in their own sphere. Only if there is

---

[110]   *B v B (Financial Provision)* [1989] 1 FLR 119 at 121.
[111]   [2000] 2 FLR 981 at 995.
[112]   See also *Smith v Smith* [2007] 2 FLR 1103, CA at [30], where an appeal was upheld, inter alia, on the ground that 'Having included the company at full value and allocated it to the husband, to award the wife the equivalent of half of the husband's income generated from the company by way of periodical payments for joint lives was also wrong. It amounted to double counting ...'.
[113]   [2000] 2 FLR 981.
[114]   [2006] 1 FLR 1186 at [146].

such a disparity in their respective contributions to the welfare of the family that it would be inequitable to disregard it should this be taken into account in determining their shares.'

**11.142** Further consideration of the special contribution argument and a detailed discussion on the approach to the subject taken by the House of Lords can be found in *Charman v Charman (No 4)*.[115] In respect of applicability, the Court of Appeal in *Charman* noted that the House of Lords took the view that a special contribution argument was a legitimate possibility, but only in exceptional circumstances. Equating special contribution with conduct, those exceptional circumstances would arise where it would be inequitable to disregard the contribution. As interpreted by analogy in *Wachtel v Wachtel*,[116] the special contribution would have to be 'obvious and gross' in order to be a relevant factor justifying a departure from equality.

**11.143** Helpful guidance on the nature of a special contribution can also be found in *Charman*, with the Court of Appeal stating:[117]

'The notion of a special contribution to the welfare of the family will not successfully have been purged of inherent gender discrimination unless it is accepted that such a contribution can, in principle, take a number of forms; that it can be non-financial as well as financial; and that it can thus be made by a party whose role has been exclusively that of a home-maker. Nevertheless in practice, and for a self-evident reason, the claim to have made a special contribution seems so far to have arisen only in cases of substantial wealth generated by a party's success in business during the marriage. The self-evident reason is that in such cases there is substantial property over the distribution of which it is worthwhile to argue. In such cases can the amount of the wealth alone make the contribution special? Or must the focus always be upon the manner of its generation? In *Lambert* Thorpe LJ said, at para [52]:

"There may be cases where the product alone justifies a conclusion of a special contribution but absent some exceptional and individual quality in the generator of the fortune a case for special contribution must be hard to establish."

In such cases, therefore, the court will no doubt have regard to the amount of the wealth; and in some cases, perhaps including the present, its amount will be so extraordinary as to make it easy for the party who generated it to claim an exceptional and individual quality which deserves special treatment. Often, however, he or she will need independently to establish such a quality, whether by genius in business or in some other field. Sometimes, by contrast, it will immediately be obvious that substantial wealth generated during the marriage is a windfall – the proceeds, for example, of an unanticipated sale of land for development or of an embattled take-over of a party's ailing company – which is not the product of a special contribution.'

---

[115] [2007] 1 FLR 1246, CA at [78]–[91].
[116] [1973] Fam 72.
[117] [2007] 1 FLR 1246 at [80].

**11.144** The Court of Appeal also noted, based on the previously quoted citation from the speech of Baroness Hale in *Miller v Miller; McFarlane v McFarlane*, that 'the generation of wealth should not always qualify as a contribution to the welfare of the family and, in particular, perhaps that in excess of a certain level its generation should not so qualify.'[118] However, it was held that the size of the assets in *Charman* did not compel departure from the usual conclusion that wealth generated by a party during a marriage is the product of a contribution to the welfare of the family. Bearing in mind that in *Charman* the total assets amounted to £131 million, the usual conclusion would appear to be extraordinarily difficult to displace.

**11.145** Finally, although the Court of Appeal refused to identify a threshold for the application of a special contribution argument, the court nevertheless felt able to provide guidance on the appropriate range of percentage adjustment to be made, although a fair adjustment might mean on the facts of any particular case that an adjustment outside the range might be appropriate. Where a special contribution was established, the Court of Appeal thought that it was hard to conceive that the percentages of division of matrimonial property should be nearer to equality than 55:45. Furthermore, fair allowance for a special contribution within the sharing principle would be most unlikely to give rise to percentages of division of matrimonial property further from equality than 66.6:33.3.

**11.146** In *Charman* the trial judge endorsed a 63.5:36.5 departure from equality, inter alia, on the basis that the husband had made a special contribution. The husband appealed against that decision and sought a greater departure from equality in his favour. His appeal was dismissed.

## SOURCE OF ASSETS – GENERAL

**11.147** In a case where there is a surplus over and above the needs of both parties generously assessed, the source of an asset is frequently used as a justification to depart from equality of division.[119] Despite the fact that this issue strays into general principles of ancillary relief and is dealt with in greater depth in Chapter 16, a brief summary is nevertheless provided in order to assist when the source of an asset becomes an issue in a business context.

**11.148** Assets brought into the marriage by gift or inheritance are categorised as non-matrimonial property, with the exception in general of any property brought into the marriage and subsequently used as a matrimonial home.[120]

---

[118] [2007] 1 FLR 1246 at [81].
[119] Where needs are not met, the source of an asset is still one of the circumstances of the case, although 'in the ordinary course, this factor can be expected to carry little weight, if any, in a case where the claimant's financial needs cannot be met without recourse to this property': *White v White* [2001] 1 AC 596 at 610 per Lord Nicholls.
[120] *Miller v Miller; McFarlane v McFarlane* [2006] 1 FLR 1186 at [22] per Lord Nicholls.

Property acquired during the marriage up until the date of separation[121] otherwise than by inheritance or gift is treated as matrimonial property,[122] with the exception that in a big money, short marriage case business or investment assets generated solely or mainly by the efforts of one party[123] may be treated as non-matrimonial property.[124]

**11.149** If property can be categorised as non-matrimonial, there is likely to be a better reason to depart from equal division.[125] In a short marriage, fairness may dictate that there should be a departure from equality in respect of non-matrimonial assets.[126] With longer marriages the issue is not so straightforward. Non-matrimonial property is not quarantined, and the court will decide the weight to be given to the contribution and the extent to which, if at all, the unmatched contribution will justify a departure from equality within the sharing principle. Factors to be taken into account include 'how important [the property] is in the particular case. The nature and value of the property, and the time when and the circumstances in which the property was acquired'.[127] Additionally, the court may wish to have regard to the way in which the parties organised their financial affairs.[128] As a general guiding principle the importance of the source of an asset will diminish over time. The duration of a marriage is clearly an important factor when seeking a departure from equality in respect of non-matrimonial assets. Note, however, that even in a long marriage case, such as *White v White*,[129] there may still be a departure from equality in recognition of the unmatched contribution of non-matrimonial property.

**11.150** As identified above, in a short marriage, big money case, any business or investment assets generated solely by one party will justify a departure from equality. It does not matter whether this is rationalised as a consequence of the assets having been generated by 'a developed career, existing high earnings and

---

[121] *Miller v Miller; McFarlane v McFarlane* [2006] 1 FLR 1186 at [175] per Lord Mance.
[122] Also known as 'the marital acquest'.
[123] Also known as 'unilateral assets': see *S v S (Non-Matrimonial Property: Conduct)* [2007] 1 FLR 1496 per Burton J. The treatment of unilateral assets as if they were non-matrimonial property arguably may in an appropriate case extend to a 'dual career' family 'where both parties worked throughout the marriage, had pooled some of the assets built up by their efforts but had chosen to keep other such assets under their separate control, the latter, although unequal in amount, were unilateral assets': see *Charman v Charman (No 4)* [2007] 1 FLR 1246 at [86].
[124] *Miller v Miller; McFarlane v McFarlane* [2006] 1 FLR 1186 at [149]–[153] and *Charman v Charman (No 4)* [2007] 1 FLR 1246 at [83].
[125] *Charman v Charman (No 4)* [2007] 1 FLR 1246 at [66].
[126] *Miller v Miller; McFarlane v McFarlane* [2006] 1 FLR 1186 at [24] per Lord Nicholls.
[127] *White v White* [2001] 1 AC 596 at 610 per Lord Nicholls.
[128] *Miller v Miller; McFarlane v McFarlane* [2006] 1 FLR 1186 at [25]. See also *C v C* [2007] EWHC 2033 (Fam) at [93]–[95] per Moylan J.
[129] [2001] 1 AC 596.

an established earning capacity'[130] having been brought into the marriage, or as a consequence of the nature and source of the assets generated[131] being treated as non-matrimonial.

**11.151** The yardstick of equality applies more readily to matrimonial property and departures from equality are less likely, although still possible. In *S v S (Non-Matrimonial Property: Conduct)*[132] the husband was aged 61 and the wife 41. The net assets in the case exceeded £7 million and needs were not a magnetic factor. The marriage was of 7 years. The husband brought significant assets into what was his second marriage. Burton J held that the husband was entitled to retain all the non-matrimonial assets. The husband was also entitled to 60% of the matrimonial property in circumstances where the source of the matrimonial property had been non-matrimonial assets that had been converted by sale and investment into matrimonial assets during the course of the marriage.

**11.152** In ancillary relief practice the understandable desire towards greater predictability of outcome can inadvertently transcend the flexibility inherent in the MCA 1973, s 25 exercise. The fashionable expression of this desire is currently manifested in a primary focus being placed on the categorisation of property as either matrimonial or non-matrimonial. The appropriateness of taking this approach and the extent of the investigation required is frequently a difficult judgment call. It is therefore worth setting out in full the words of Lord Nicholls in *Miller v Miller; McFarlane v McFarlane*[133] at [26]–[27]:

'This difference in treatment of matrimonial property and non-matrimonial property might suggest that in every case a clear and precise boundary should be drawn between these two categories of property. This is not so. Fairness has a broad horizon. Sometimes, in the case of a business, it can be artificial to attempt to draw a sharp dividing line as at the parties' wedding day. Similarly the "equal sharing" principle might suggest that each of the party's assets should be separately and exactly valued. But valuations are often a matter of opinion on which experts differ. A thorough investigation into these differences can be extremely expensive and of doubtful utility. The costs involved can quickly become disproportionate. The case of Mr and Mrs Miller illustrates this only too well.

Accordingly, where it becomes necessary to distinguish matrimonial property from non-matrimonial property the court may do so with the degree of particularity or generality appropriate in the case. The judge will then give to the contribution made by one party's non-matrimonial property the weight he considers just. He will do so with such generality or particularity as he considers appropriate in the circumstances of the case.'

---

[130] *GW v RW (Financial Provision: Departure from Equality)* [2003] 2 FLR 108, where the concept of fledged assets was considered.
[131] *Miller v Miller; McFarlane v McFarlane* [2006] 1 FLR 1186 at [158] per Baroness Hale. Although Lord Mance appeared to prefer the latter justification: see [169] and [172]
[132] [2007] 1 FLR 1496.
[133] [2006] 1 FLR 1186.

**11.153** Some assistance on the extent of any required investigation into the value of non-matrimonial assets can be derived from the judgment of Moylan J in *C v C*,[134] where a broad assessment of the position, rather than a precise view, was taken in respect of assets brought into the marriage approximately 23 years prior to final hearing. It was held on the facts of the case that it would be foolish after a long marriage to expect or require a party to produce a detailed account of their financial affairs at the commencement of the marriage. The quest for financial certainty was never going to be achieved and was, in any event, unnecessary. Instead, the learned judge concluded that the husband had introduced significant resources in the form of successful companies with a substantial asset base into the marriage, which justified a division of capital and pension assets, 60:40 in favour of the husband. By contrast, in a short marriage case it ought to be easier to ascertain the extent of the marital acquest, although the difficulty in valuing Mr Miller's New Star shares show that this is not necessarily always the case.

**11.154** *S v S (Ancillary Relief After Lengthy Separation)*[135] is an example of another case in which a broad as opposed to a precise approach to the valuation of matrimonial and non-matrimonial assets was followed. The final hearing took place 10 years after separation, during which time the husband developed his business without any matched contribution from the wife. H had owned shares in YD Limited at the date of separation. During the separation H had taken part in a management buyout, with company T Limited taking over part of YD's business. Singer J took the view that in principle independent endeavour after separation which was productive of money or property should be reflected in the division of assets.[136] He went on to state in broad terms:

'I regard the value which the T Ltd shares now represent as more akin to non-matrimonial property. But I have given the shares weight in the balancing exercise to what I regard as an appropriately constrained extent by having regard both to the approximate value of H's separation-date holding of YD shares, and to the fact that in my view what he has since built on the back of that asset has involved only incidental use of those shares and the business then conducted by that company which have been unmatched by any contribution on the part of W since the effective end of the marriage. I have also paid regard to what is described as the "passive economic growth" which might have been added over the relevant 10 years to those shares and to the underlying business conducted by H by reference to two published measures of economic growth in prices and share valuations.'[137]

---

[134] [2007] EWHC 2033.
[135] [2007] 1 FLR 2120, Singer J.
[136] [2007] 1 FLR 2120 at [87]–[88] and [109]. See also following section of this book.
[137] [2007] 1 FLR 2120 at [111].

## SOURCE OF ASSETS – POST-SEPARATION CATEGORISATION, FUTURE EARNINGS AND BONUSES

**11.155** The categorisation of an asset as matrimonial or non-matrimonial is not necessarily straightforward. How does one categorise any increase in value on an asset during the course of a marriage? Does it matter how the increase in value occurred and does the nature of the asset which has increased in value have any impact on categorisation? How are assets acquired or created after separation but prior to final hearing to be dealt with and categorised? These and other difficult issues were grappled with in the case of *Rossi v Rossi*,[138] where, following a divorce in 1992, there was a lengthy period of separation before the final hearing in ancillary relief proceedings came before the court in 2006. The following general propositions in respect of post-separation categorisation and subsequent distribution can be derived from *Rossi*:[139]

- Passive economic growth in respect of non-matrimonial assets is still treated as a non-matrimonial asset, even if the growth in value occurs during the marriage.

- Similarly, passive economic growth on matrimonial property occurring post-separation will not be classified as non-matrimonial property.

- An asset acquired or created by one party after or during a period of separation may qualify as non-matrimonial if it can be said that the property in question was acquired or created by a party by virtue of his personal industry and not by use (other than incidental) of an asset which had been created during the marriage and in respect of which the other party can validly assert an unascertained share.

- In deciding whether a non-matrimonial post-separation accrual should be shared and, if so, in what proportions, the court will consider, among

---

[138] [2007] 1 FLR 790, Nicholas Mostyn QC, whose approach was approved and followed in *S v S (Ancillary Relief after Lengthy Separation)* [2007] 1 FLR 2120 at [111] per Singer J and *S v S (Non-Matrimonial Property: Conduct)* [2007] 1 FLR 1496, Burton J. Note, however, that even pre-*Miller v Miller; McFarlane v McFarlane* post-separation accruals had been a 'live' issue: see *N v N (Financial Provision: Sale of Company)* [2001] 2 FLR 69, Coleridge J, where the learned judge took into account the increase in value of a business attributable to extra investment of time, effort and money by the husband post-separation. The learned judge, however, at [78] placed this contribution in context, in that the wife continued to play the part which she had done throughout the marriage in looking after the home and children. See also *M v M (Financial Relief: Substantial Earning Capacity)* [2004] 2 FLR 236 at [81] per Baron J, where bonuses earned during a period of 27 months' separation were taken into account in an equal division of assets, because the litigation had not been unduly delayed, the parties had been financially linked throughout and the husband had failed to make adequate interim provision. The learned judge did not consider the husband's future earnings to be a marital asset falling for division. Needs did not require the asset to be taken into account and the husband would have to work a punishing schedule to receive the future bonuses [78].

[139] The learned deputy also summarises at [24] more general principles in respect of the impact of the sharing principle on matrimonial and non-matrimonial property, to which reference is made in the previous section of this book.

other things, the diligence with which the applicant pursued the claim; whether the party with the accrual has treated the other party fairly during the period of separation; whether the money making party has the prospect of making further gains or earnings after the division of assets and, if so, whether the other party will be sharing in such future income or gains and, if so, in what proportions, for what period and by what means.

**11.156**  From a practitioner perspective the assets to which these issues most readily apply are post-separation earnings and bonuses. *Rossi* was the first case post-*Miller/McFarlane* that dealt with this issue. The conclusion reached was that if:

> 'the post-separation asset is a bonus or other earned income then it is obvious that if the payment relates to a period when the parties were cohabiting then the earner cannot claim it to be non-matrimonial. Even if the payment relates to a period immediately following separation I would myself say that it is too close to the marriage to justify categorisation as non-matrimonial. Moreover, I entirely agree with Coleridge J when he points out that during the period of separation the domestic party carries on making her non-financial contribution but cannot attribute a value thereto which justifies adjustment in her favour. Although there is an element of arbitrariness here, I myself would not allow a post-separation bonus to be classed as non-matrimonial unless it related to a period which commenced at least 12 months after the separation.'[140]

**11.157**  The approach of the courts to dealing with post-separation bonuses and a claim for an award including an element to reflect the loss of a share in future earnings and the enhanced income or earning capacity created by the contribution of the parties is developing incrementally at first instance. In *H v H*[141] the central issues argued by the parties were whether the post-separation bonuses should be classified as matrimonial and what award, if any, should be made in respect of future bonuses that were to be classified as non-matrimonial. The judgment of Charles J emphasised that there was no certainty or rigidity of division based on the categorisation of property as matrimonial; such an approach ignored the flexibility in the statutory provisions and the objectives of achieving a fair result.[142] The dicta in *Rossi* that post-separation bonuses ought not to be classified as non-matrimonial unless they related to a working period which commenced at least 12 months after separation was disapproved as too arbitrary and unnecessarily formulaic.[143] *H v H* was a big money, long marriage case. The assets of the parties at the date of separation were treated as matrimonial property, to which the yardstick of equality readily applied. However, the bonuses in issue which were earned by the husband in respect of working periods after separation[144] were not matrimonial property and would not be equally divided. Instead, the wife was entitled to a 'run-off' award to ease the transition to independent

---

[140]  *Rossi v Rossi* [2007] 1 FLR 790 at [24.4].
[141]  [2007] 2 FLR 548, Charles J.
[142]  [2007] 2 FLR 548 at [43].
[143]  [2007] 2 FLR 548 at [57]–[60].
[144]  [2007] 2 FLR 548 at [19].

living and which additionally reflected her contribution to the husband's increased earning capacity and the loss of her share in his future earnings, including bonuses post-separation. The award was capitalised taking into account one-third of the income earned in the first year following separation, one-sixth of the income earned in the following year and, finally, one-twelfth of the income earned in the third year following separation.

**11.158** In *CR v CR*,[145] Bodey J took a different approach to that adopted by Charles J in *H v H*. Again, the case was a big money, long marriage case. At separation the assets were valued at £8 million. At final hearing they were valued at £16 million, the rise being accounted for by the increase in the value and number of shares held by the husband in the company for which he worked. Although nearing retirement age, the husband could expect to earn £1 million net per annum until he chose to retire. The evidence before the court was that the wife had made significant contributions in supporting the husband and the family whilst he worked away from home. The wife was awarded £9 million, of which £1 million was to be paid in instalments over a three-year period. In respect of the post-separation accrual, Bodey J chose expressly not to cite from the various authorities on the topic, since the point was 'both discretionary and pre-eminently fact-specific'.[146] On the facts of the case the post-separation assets had accrued to the husband only by reason of the wife's sustained commitment to the family and the domestic infrastructure while the husband was making his way up the ladder of his chosen career.[147] This was a seed-corn case, where the husband's harvest post-separation only arose because of respective contributions during the course of the marriage. It was not a case where the post-separation accruals came from any new source of risk, endeavour or luck. It would not, therefore, be fair for the wife to exit the marriage with less than half of the assets. It was also held not to be fair to ignore the parties' future big income imbalance, since the wife with her contribution as homemaker must logically have contributed to the husband's future earning capacity and prosperity. The most straightforward way to quantify the imbalance was to assess the wife's needs generously. She was awarded a housing fund of £4 million and a £5 million investment fund to meet her income needs (not on a *Duxbury* basis). Looking at the case in the round and testing the outcome against the yardstick of equality, an award of £9 million to the wife was a fair outcome.[148]

**11.159** Both *H v H* and *CR v CR* were cited in *P v P (Post-Separation Accruals and Earning Capacity)*,[149] which was another big money, long marriage case with significant post-separation accruals. The two main legal issues in the case were (1) the effect of the fact that a significant part of the current wealth had been earned by the husband post-separation, and (2) the effect of the husband's future earning capacity. In answer to the first issue,

---

[145] [2008] 1 FLR 323.
[146] [2008] 1 FLR 323 at [40].
[147] [2008] 1 FLR 323 at [40].
[148] [2008] 1 FLR 323 at [103].
[149] [2008] 2 FLR 1135 at [111]–[112] per Moylan J.

Moylan J held that he was not, therefore, required to define what is and is not matrimonial property and that the weight to be given to the fact that some of the resources have accrued through the husband's earnings post-separation was a matter for his discretion. As to the second issue, future earning capacity is one of the express factors listed in s 25(2) of the Matrimonial Causes Act 1973 and could not be ignored. In reaching his decision on the facts of the case, the learned judge took into account both the fact that a significant part of the wealth has been earned by the husband since separation and the fact that he had a very significant earning capacity.[150] The learned judge awarded the wife just over half of the total assets, by reference to her needs, and this did not give her an unfair share, having regard to the husband's overall financial position, including future earnings and a prospective bonus.

**11.160** In big money, long marriage cases, which are almost by definition capable of resolution with a clean break, it is clear that the courts must and do take into account future earning capacity and the contribution made by a homemaking spouse to the future high earnings of the breadwinner.[151] As we have seen in both *CR v CR* and *P v P (Post Separation Accruals and Earning Capacity)*, there was a departure from equal division of capital assets in favour of the wife to take into account this factor. The courts will also, as part of the discretionary exercise, have regard to the accrual of assets post-separation. A seed corn argument will be effective to restrict or prevent departures from equality in respect of post-separation accruals, although new risk and endeavour might justify a departure. A generous assessment of a wife's needs would appear to be one means of factoring into an award a husband's future earning capacity and future earnings. Another approach is to provide the wife with a run-off award. Each case will of course turn on its own facts. It is submitted that the courts appear to be reluctant to embark upon particular identification and valuation of property as either matrimonial or non-matrimonial. A generalised approach to this issue appears likely to suffice, and the discretionary element inherent in the MCA 1973, s 25 exercise and the requirement to achieve a fair outcome are to override any formulaic distribution based upon asset categorisation.

# VALUING SHAREHOLDINGS

## Shares in quoted companies

**11.161** Establishing the value of shares in a quoted company is relatively straightforward, as share price information is usually readily available (subject to market suspension). Daily share prices of many companies listed on the London Stock Exchange and the Alternative Investment Market are quoted in the *Financial Times* 'Companies and Markets' pages. The price quoted is the

---

[150] [2008] 2 FLR 1135 at [123]–[125].
[151] In more modest asset cases these factors are also required to be taken into account, but reflection of these factors is less easy to achieve in an award where needs are the predominating distributive factor.

mid-point of the buying and selling prices quoted at the close of play on the previous day. It should be noted that there may or may not have been deals at this price, and this may be an issue when considering the value of less traded shares.

**11.162** Historical share prices at a given date can be found on websites such as FT.com, finance.yahoo.com and reuters.co.uk, and in the shareholder area of many companies' own websites.

**11.163** Take note of whether the price is:

- 'cum dividend', meaning the buyer is entitled to receive a dividend that has been declared but not paid; or

- 'ex-dividend', meaning the stock trades without the right to receive the next dividend and the price is consequently lower. In this case the forthcoming dividend represents further value in the holding.

## Shares in unquoted companies

**11.164** Valuing unquoted shares is more problematic, as there may be no real market for the shares, or only a restricted trading market and little if any published share price data. Also, a wide variety of factors can affect the valuation. Matrimonial lawyers will be familiar with 'At a Glance (Essential Court Tables for Ancillary Relief)', published annually by the Family Law Bar Association. This contains a one page summary for valuing shares in private companies. Although a useful starting point, it inevitably simplifies the valuation process, and a wider consideration is necessary if issues particular to the company and affecting its value are not to be missed. The opinion on value of an appropriately skilled accountant or other expert may well be invaluable.

**11.165** Given the variations between companies and their individual situations, there can be no standard valuation methodology. In these circumstances there is particular benefit in understanding the process a valuer might adopt, and some salient aspects are highlighted below. Paramount is that the company's individual circumstances are considered.

### *Actual share transactions*

**11.166** The first step is to check whether a relatively recent offer has been made for either the whole company or a shareholding, as this may give an initial indication of value. This should be a routine question asked in a questionnaire. However, it is important to establish that any such offer was genuine, was made at arm's length and to understand the circumstances that lay behind it. If negotiations on a possible deal are in progress, it may be appropriate to apply a discount to the offer price to reflect the inevitable uncertainty about whether a sale will go ahead. Where an offer has been made but refused, this is a suggestion that the management team of the company felt the company was worth considerably more, although in the context of a family run business other considerations, including pure sentiment, may have featured in the decision-making.

## *Basis of valuation*

**11.167**  In the absence of evidence of relevant actual transactions, the general valuation basis is of a hypothetical willing buyer and willing seller. This is, arguably, entirely artificial, as such a match is unlikely to be achieved and there will always be reasons behind a particular transaction, and the price achieved. The same business may have a different value to different people, depending on their circumstances. Nevertheless, it is a useful approach, particularly as in ancillary relief cases there may be no expectation that the shares in question will be sold. The court's aim is to establish the value so that there can be a fair division of the assets.

**11.168**  The valuer will take account of restrictions applying to the shares, and of the level of control that the shareholding conveys. Such restrictions may be expressed in a variety of documents, including a shareholders' agreement or the articles of association. The latter often include a requirement that available shares first be offered to the existing shareholders to see if they will buy them, and there may be a mechanism to determine the offer price in such circumstances. Then, only if the other shareholders decline to purchase may the shares be offered outside. In this context, the articles of association often refer to 'fair value', 'full value', 'market value' or 'arm's length value' of the shares, but each of these is to be regarded as a term of art which, absent further explanation, does not have a standard definition.

**11.169**  When the price description is clearly defined, this can guide the valuer as to how to proceed. However, when there is no definition or it is ambiguous, the valuer will need to exercise reasonable judgment to interpret how to proceed. This will include a direction to 'an independent accountant to establish a fair price for the shares'.

**11.170**  Ultimately, the value of shares depends on their entitlement to earnings, dividends and assets. The price paid for a shareholding will generally depend on the size of the shareholding and the rights attaching to it.

**11.171**  There are several bases for valuing shares, and part of the valuer's role is to identify the most appropriate basis in the circumstances. Common methods of valuation are outlined later in this chapter but, first, here are some of the factors to consider when determining the appropriate basis.

## *Size of shareholding*

*Majority holding*

**11.172**   When valuing a controlling shareholding, the nature of the company's operations may suggest the most suitable method for valuing the shares. For example, controlling interests in manufacturing, trading and commercial companies are usually valued on an 'earnings basis',[152] since the earnings stream provides the return on shares and the shareholder has the ability to distribute the profits as a dividend or to sell them to a third party. However, regard needs to be had to the value of the company assets and whether they might realise more on a break-up.

**11.173**   A majority shareholding in an investment company or property holding company is usually valued by reference to the value of the underlying assets.

*Minority holding*

**11.174**   As a rule of thumb, minority shareholdings in unquoted companies are valued on a historic dividend basis. This is because such holdings bring little or no influence over the company's affairs and the dividends paid are the only likely return on the investment. There is unlikely to be any, or only a very restricted, market for selling the shares and the directors may refuse to register the transfer even if a buyer could be found. Nevertheless, where there is no reliable dividend history, the valuer may be forced back on discounting the valuation of a controlling shareholding to reflect the lack of influence of the minority shareholder.

**11.175**   The inevitable exceptions to this rule include influential minority holdings (as described below), quasi-partnerships and companies which may be liquidated.

*Quasi-partnership*

**11.176**   Sometimes, the company is treated as a quasi-partnership and the shares are valued in direct proportion to the percentage shareholding interest without any discounting. The quasi-partnership basis of valuation often applies in divorce cases where the husband and wife are the only shareholders in a company. The value of the shares is determined on a pro rata basis of the company as a whole.

**11.177**   This basis may also be appropriate when the history of the shareholders' relationship is akin to that of individuals in a partnership. Thus, if the shares are owned in equal proportions by, say, three family or close-knit members, of whom the husband or wife is one, and historically these have acted

---

[152]   The various bases of valuation are described later in this chapter.

in concert, it is appropriate to value the individual one-third holding as one-third of the value of the company as a whole rather than on a discounted minority interest basis.

**11.178** Probably the majority of family-owned private companies operate as quasi-partnerships, but the concept is not just relevant to the valuation of family businesses. In *G v G (Financial Provisions: Equal Division)* [2002] 2 FLR 1143 the issue of a quasi-partnership was considered and found to apply to a private limited company where the four shareholders were not related to one another but would have acted in unison. Coleridge J stated (at 1151):

> 'I cannot seriously envisage a situation where the husband in this case will be forced to sell his interest in this company on the open market, in circumstances in which a discount would be forced upon him. It is just conceivable that he may sell to a friendly purchaser but in those circumstances I am sure he would get full value. Accordingly, I think it is artificial to apply any discount to the husband's shares in this company ...'

## Loss-making companies

**11.179** It is not uncommon in divorce proceedings for one spouse's owner-managed company to suffer an apparent nose-dive in profits and even to become loss-making. A valuer will investigate whether this is a genuine change in circumstances or the result of a change in accounting treatments, or whether it is a business strategy to depress the value of the business.

**11.180** The valuer will attempt to discover the cause of the poor results and identify whether the problem is within the company or caused by an external event, and whether it is reversible or not. If the losses are genuine and severe and there is no hope of recovery, then liquidation is a realistic prospect and the shares should be valued on a break-up basis.

**11.181** If the poor performance appears to be temporary and the business is likely to return to profitability in the foreseeable future, the value can be determined with reference to the potential future earnings, or a 'notional' dividend from these, and discounted back to the present value at an appropriate rate.

## Liquidation

**11.182** If the company is to be liquidated and the proceeds divided between the parties (a situation which is only likely to occur if the husband and wife own all, or the vast majority, of the shares and there is no real business which can be sold on), then the valuation should be prepared on a net asset break-up basis. There will be costs associated with the sale of the assets and the winding up of the business, such as redundancy costs. The liquidator's costs should also be taken into account in the valuation. A time window within which the assets need to be disposed of will have a further depreciatory effect. The shorter the period and the more forced the sale, the greater the discount.

**11.183** Subject to the rights of the shareholding class, in the event of liquidation a minority shareholder will be entitled to a pro rata share of the net asset value without a discount for lack of control, which would not usually be the case otherwise.

**11.184** If there is no intention that the shares should actually be sold to a third party, or for the company to be liquated, then valuation on a net asset or going concern basis is likely to be more appropriate.

## *Commercial factors affecting the value of unquoted shares*

**11.185** HM Revenue & Customs publishes a 'Shares Valuation Manual', which provides a useful diagram of commercial factors to consider when valuing shares in an unquoted company.

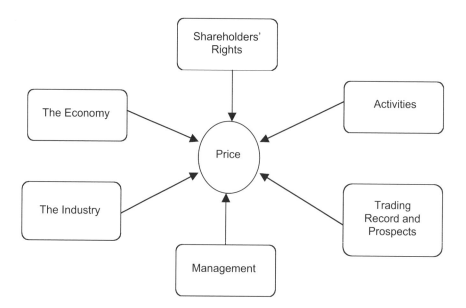

*Assessing the company's business activities*

**11.186** In considering the valuation of a company, it is essential to understand the business activities, to know about the products or services offered, to identify the customers, suppliers, competitors and employees, and to assess the business risks facing the company, including political and geographic risk. These will include issues such as:

- Is most of the income generated from one product or one customer?

- What are the competitive threats to the company?

Although it may not be formally produced, the aim is akin to a SWOT analysis (covering Strengths, Weaknesses, Opportunities and Threats).

*Assessing the company's trading record and prospects*

**11.187**　A purchaser of shares and, similarly, a valuer of shares will want to form a view of the likely profits the company may earn in the future. Some guidance on this can be provided by the company's historical performance and, in particular, its record of achieving budgets.

**11.188**　The level of profits is not the only consideration. Also to be taken into account are factors such as the ability to generate (or absorb) cash, the return on capital employed, the extent of borrowings and the cost of these, whether working capital is adequate or even excessive, the existence of surplus assets, and quantification of contingent liabilities or even, on occasion, contingent assets. When the company has a strong market presence or brand, or other forms of goodwill, this may also be relevant to the value of its shares, although care will be necessary to avoid double counting the effect of this both in the income stream and the asset base.

*Assessing the economy and its effect on the company*

**11.189**　Inevitably, companies cannot be wholly in control of their own destinies. They are susceptible to changes in the economic and political environment. Among these will be changes in particular measures of relevant inflation, interest rates or exchange rates. For example, are profits closely linked to externally determined prices such as crude oil, which may be subject to geo-political factors?

**11.190**　A valuer will try to establish whether the industry correlates with the business cycle, and whether the company is susceptible to political pressures.

**11.191**　This consideration may include whether:

- the company operates in a regulated industry or one that is likely to face more stringent controls in future;

- the workforce is highly organised or militant, or there is a present or foreseeable shortage of appropriately skilled workers; and

- the company is dependent on its ability to export or import and, if so, to assess the effect of changes in the political or economic climate of the relevant countries.

*Assessing the industry in which the company operates*

**11.192**　As well as considering the general political and economic situation, a valuer will also review the prospects for the industry in which the company operates and the company's position within that industry.

**11.193**   Key aspects include whether:

- the overall market is increasing, decreasing or remains fairly static;

- the company has a significant market share and whether that is increasing, decreasing or relatively stable;

- there are a few large firms or many small firms in the industry, and where the company fits;

- there is a trend for consolidation in the industry so that companies are merging; and

- the industry is currently popular with investors (eg in 2001 the 'dot.com' boom inflated the share prices of companies in the technology sector).

**11.194**   Information on these factors is available from what is said in the company's accounts and those of its competitors, particularly when there are listed companies in the same industry, and from reports of industry regulators and articles published in newspapers, trade journals and on the internet. Research companies such as ICC and LexisNexis can also provide wide-ranging industry analysis.

**11.195**   Importantly, however, particularly when valuing the company as a whole, the 'willing buyer' will be expected to have access to internal company information such as management accounts, budgets and projections, and these might have analyses and an understanding of the company's specific position with respect to the industry not available from purely publicly available information.

*Assessing the quality of management*

**11.196**   Evidence on the past performance of the directors and senior officials will be an important factor when projecting the future prospects of the company. In practice, there may be just one or two individuals whose skills determine the trading success, particularly for small companies, or there may be a larger team. Forming a judgment on their individual abilities and the way these mesh together is difficult. A valuer will have regard to:

- the historical financial performance of the company and whether there is firm financial control;

- the relationships between the directors, management and the staff;

- management's capacity to innovate, eg to lead the company into new markets or to introduce new products; and

- whether the directors and managers have shares in the company or performance-related bonuses to motivate them.

**11.197** The ability of the management is particularly important when valuing a minority interest, as the shareholder will have no opportunity to influence the stewardship of the company and is reliant on the management team. The quality of management succession will also be relevant if the existing management may be near to retiring.

*Assessing shareholders' rights*

**11.198** Initial steps when valuing a shareholding include:

- ascertaining the present share structure, including the classes of shares, the number issued in each and the individual holdings.

- establishing the rights of each class of share, including dividend rights and voting powers, e g on the appointment of directors and winding up of the company.

- noting the size of the shareholding that is to be valued. To reflect the reduced level of control, a discount is usually applied when valuing less than the entire share capital. Every valuation must be treated on its own merits, but it is useful that the HM Revenue & Customs' Shares Valuation Manual suggests the following in the case of larger holdings:
  - 50% holding in the absence of any casting vote (neither a majority nor a minority) – a discount of 20% to 30%;
  - over 50% and under 75% holding (giving day-to-day control) – a discount of 5% to 15%;
  - from 75% to below 90% holding (giving practical control, including power to wind up) – a discount of 0% to 5%;
  - over 90% (giving power to compulsorily acquire the remaining shares) – in practice likely to be the same discount as applying to a 75% to 90% holding.

**11.199** A vital step is to establish the relationships of the various shareholders in the company. For instance, are there groups of shareholders who are likely to act together, so that although there are individual holdings they are in practice to be treated as a block? There may be several such blocks, and reviewing past history may suggest how they should be treated. The holding being valued may benefit from being in such a block or suffer from being outside it. However, since in most cases there can be no presumption for a 'willing buyer, willing seller' valuation that the buyer will benefit from such a block, it is likely that only a disadvantage from an opposing block will have an effect on the value. The extreme case will be when there is a single dominant shareholder, so that the values of all the other holdings are to be heavily discounted.

**11.200**   Although some general guidance can be given, the level of discount appropriate to a minority shareholding is dependent on a wide variety of factors. Shareholdings of between 25% and 49% are potentially an 'influential minority', as they are able to block special resolutions.[153] For example, when the other holdings are widely spread, a holding of 33% may in practice give the holder effective control of the company. In contrast, a 49% holding may be entirely without influence if the remaining 51% is owned by one shareholder, and even a 50% holding may enjoy little influence when the remaining 50% is owned by a holder with a casting vote. In such cases a discount of at least 25% may be appropriate and even a much higher percentage discount, exceeding 50%, may be required. A shareholding of less than 25% is likely to bring no influence. The discount then will be even greater.

**11.201**   Investigation will include the effects of terms in the articles of association or a shareholders' agreement, as these can have a depreciatory effect on the value of the shares, even in a hypothetical sale situation. Relevant provisions may include restrictions on the transfer of shares, and also pre-emption rights. The shareholder may still be able to sell the shares to a third party despite issues in giving or registering title to the shares, but a further discount to reflect these difficulties would probably apply.

**11.202**   Care is necessary when determining the discounts to be applied to a single shareholding so that there is no element of duplication because of overlapping aspects. It is worth noting that a quoted company market capitalisation (which is based on quoted share values) will normally be less than the value of the whole company or of probable takeover values.

## Valuation methodologies

**11.203**   The key characteristics of some common valuation methodologies are set out below.

### *The earnings basis*

*The theory*

**11.204**   Trading companies are formed to operate a business profitably, and if the company being valued is succeeding in this objective and achieving a satisfactory return on the assets employed, it is advantageous to keep the company going. Therefore, when assessing a shareholding on a going concern basis the valuer will first look at the profit-generating potential of the company rather than the assets base. However, the valuer will consider whether all the assets are required for the business or whether some can be released without reducing the earnings.

---

[153] It is important to scrutinise the articles of association for these particular aspects. See **11.19–11.20**.

**11.205**  In the case of a majority shareholding, where the shareholder has influence over the direction and the distribution policy of the company, a valuer may seek to determine the maintainable future level of earnings available for distribution.

**11.206**  In this context, the usual definition of earnings is the residual profit after all business outgoings, including tax and preference dividends.

**11.207**  The overall worth of the company can be established by capitalising its maintainable earnings, often using a price–earnings ratio, and adjusting for factors such as growth and inflation.

*Assessing maintainable earnings*

**11.208**  Maintainable earnings are established by reference to the company's past profit record. However, estimates should be based on sound and rigorously challenged expectations for the future. A simple extrapolation of the historical level of the company's 'profit before tax' is unlikely to provide a reliable guide for estimating future profits.

**11.209**  The most up-to-date information regarding the company's current trading position should be collected, including the latest details of turnover, profits and future prospects. The company's statutory accounts, management accounts, budgets, forecasts and current business plans should be used to try to identify trends. Non-recurring items of income and expenditure should be removed before projecting future profits.

**11.210**  Various other adjustments may be required to assess the maintainable earnings figure. For example, in the case of a typical family company where the management team are also the controlling shareholders of the company, the valuer will need to consider whether the historical results reflect a 'commercial' cost of management, or if they include payments to directors (including salary, bonuses, and pension contributions) that are in excess of or below the amounts that would be paid to a third party for the stewardship of the company. The valuer should then adjust the cost of management figure accordingly. A similar adjustment may be necessary if other family members are employed by the company at a rate of pay in excess of or below the market level.

**11.211**  When projecting the future earnings of a company based on its historical performance, a valuer will also consider the appropriateness of the accounting policies employed in the past and consider the implications of changes to these before attempting to extrapolate a future trend.

*The capitalisation factor*

**11.212**  The next step in this methodology is to select a capitalisation factor, or 'multiple'. The price–earnings ratio ('P/E ratio') is a tool often used to capitalise earnings. A valuer will sometimes select a capitalisation factor based on a discounted P/E ratio from the relevant quoted sector (ie from an aggregation of public limited companies operating in the same sector).

**11.213**  The P/E ratio is the result of dividing the price of the share by the earnings per share for a year, and therefore represents the number of years' earnings (at a constant level of profitability) it would take to earn an amount equal to the current share price. The P/E ratio reflects what buyers will pay for the share and encompasses the market's view of the company's:

• maintainable earnings;

• growth potential; and

• level of risk.

**11.214**  The earnings, and the P/E ratio, may be either historic, the latest past record, or prospective – being the expectation for the current or coming trading period.

**11.215**  The choice of an appropriate P/E ratio is probably the most subjective decision made by the valuer. Almost never are comparable companies to be found with broadly similar profit records, earnings prospects and risk.

**11.216**  Furthermore, quoted P/E ratios are available for large public companies and are drawn from sales of usually very small minority holdings with negligible voting influence, typically less than one per cent. When more significant holdings come to the market, they may either have to be sold for a lower price or may realise more if they give a lever to gaining an influential holding. The valuation of the company as a whole is likely to entail consideration of a 'control premium' to recognise the control element not normally included in the valuation of small parcels of shares on the Stock Market.

*Selection of comparable companies*

**11.217**  The Stock Exchange Official Year Book provides a classification of quoted companies by subsector of the FTSE All-Share Index, and is a useful place to start searching for comparable companies. Subscriber services, such as Extel,[154] will make this process easier.

**11.218**  A valuer will aim to identify at least five or six comparable companies and to keep a note of companies in the industry that have been rejected and the reasons they are considered not comparable. Key information for each company when considering comparability includes:

---

[154] Extel Financial Ltd monitors the performance of thousands of UK and overseas companies and issues detailed annual reports to subscribers.

- company name and principal activities;

- turnover and profits figures;

- annual growth in turnover and in profits; and

- ratios of, for example, liquidity and gearing.

**11.219**  Benchmarking against only one company is not recommended.

**11.220**  P/E ratios for listed companies are readily available in the financial press, although, in order to ensure accuracy, consistency and comparability, most valuers prefer to calculate the P/E ratios themselves rather than rely on the published figures (at least not without understanding the underlying figures and any modification of these used). Nevertheless, where the comparator companies are making small profits or losses, the resulting P/E may be meaningless when applied to the company being valued.

*Calculating the P/E ratio*

**11.221**  This is an example of how to calculate the P/E ratio, using the following formula:

*Price per share / earnings per share = P/E ratio*

| | |
|---|---|
| Issued share capital | 100,000 £1 ordinary |
| Post-tax profits | £50,000 (derived from, say, the latest accounts) |
| Earnings per share | 50p (Post-tax profits / issued share capital) |
| Share price* | £2.50 per share |
| P/E ratio being £2.50 / £0.50 = | **5** |

\*   Source – the financial press.

*Discounts and adjustments to the quoted P/E ratio*

**11.222**  When considering unquoted companies, the P/E ratios of quoted companies must be adjusted (usually downwards) to reflect their different characteristics. In general, quoted as against unquoted companies enjoy the ability to raise finance more easily, have sophisticated management teams and greater diversification of income sources.

**11.223**  The key difference between quoted and unquoted shares is the lack of marketability of unquoted shares. Quoted shares can usually be disposed of readily, while unquoted shares may be difficult, if not impossible to sell. Inevitably this reduces the comparative value of the unquoted shares, although this would not in itself affect the valuation of the company as a whole.

**11.224**  The greater the financial risk to the capital and the greater the marketing difficulty as compared with the quoted company, the higher the discount for non-marketability.

**11.225**  The long-term trend is for the discount to be in the range of 20% to 40%, though this discount has fallen steadily over the past few years and is currently significantly lower than the long-term trend. The narrowing of the multiples paid for private companies as compared to their public peers is principally due to the increased liquidity in the private company arena.

**11.226**  Premiums are paid for controlling interests in listed companies; for example, when there is an announcement of a takeover bid for a listed company, the price of the shares often increases significantly. In the case of a shareholding that would give a controlling interest in the company, or where there may be a likelihood of a bid, it may be appropriate to include such a premium.

**11.227**  An alternative method of establishing a capitalisation factor can be to consider information about actual sales of unlisted companies that have recently taken place. Companies such as Extel, and CorpfinWorldwide.com calculate and publish the capitalisation factors for many transactions, and these can be used to assess typical capitalisation factors in the industry.

*Calculating the share price*

**11.228**  As an example, if we assume the company to be valued has maintainable earnings of £40,000 and has 100,000 ordinary shares in issue and the adjusted P/E ratio to be adopted is 4.5, then the value of each share would be:

   (£40,000/100,000) x 4.5 or £40,000 x 4.5/100,000 = £1.80 each.

# The dividend basis

*The theory*

**11.229**  A minority shareholder's return on his investment is the dividend declared by the company. This is usually expressed in relation to the nominal value of the shares. For example, a 5p dividend on a £1 ordinary share is 5%.

**11.230**  If a shareholder's only expectation from holding shares is to receive dividends and there is no impending liquidation, then a valuation of the shares can be prepared on the dividend basis.

**11.231**  The 'yield' is the current return on an investment in relation to its price. Using the example above, if the share was purchased at par, being £1, then the dividend yield would be 5%; but if the price of the share was £2, then the yield would be 2.5%.

**11.232**   The rate of return that an investor requires when buying shares in an unquoted company is to be assumed to be the same return that he would expect if he invested his capital in quoted shares or other assets with similar risk, growth prospects and ease of conversion into cash.

**11.233**   If the valuer cannot identify a comparable investment, the data for investments that are available (such as similar quoted companies) will be considered and the yield adjusted to compensate for the differences between the investments.

**11.234**   In a simple case, where dividends are expected to remain constant in the future, the formula for valuing the shareholding would be as follows:

*Share Value = the dividend per share / the required rate of return*

**11.235**   When applying the dividend basis it is therefore necessary to establish:

- the maintainable dividend per share (ie the level of dividends that the shareholder would reasonably expect to receive in future years);

- the rate of return on the investment that the (deemed) purchaser of the share would require if buying the shareholding.

*Calculating the maintainable dividend*

**11.236**   A valuer will need to establish whether, historically, the dividends paid by the company in question have been relatively constant or have either increased (or decreased) steadily or whether they have fluctuated from year to year. This information can be used, in conjunction with information regarding the company's likely future performance (such as budgets, forecasts, minutes of board meetings and press reportage), to assess the future maintainable dividend that the company could pay.

**11.237**   The following is an example of a company paying a relatively constant dividend:

**Dividends paid:**

| Year 1 | Year 2 | Year 3 | Year 4 | Year 5 | Total | Weighted Average* |
|--------|--------|--------|--------|--------|-------|-------------------|
| 12p | 9p | 11p | 8p | 10p | 50p | 9.6p |

The average dividend paid over recent years was 9.6p per share and there is no reason to suppose this will not continue in the foreseeable future. Assuming a dividend per share of 9.6p and a required rate of return of 10%, applying the formula above gives a share value of £0.96 (9.6p/10%). Note that the par value is irrelevant to this calculation.

\*   Weighted 1 for year one, 2 for year two and so on to 5 for year five.

**11.238**  A more sophisticated version of this method is the dividend growth model, which takes into account expected growth in dividends. The formula can be adapted to reflect dividends growing at a constant rate, or can be adjusted to reflect a temporary and abnormal increase or decrease in the dividend yield. The important thing here is to ensure consistency. For instance, if the required return in effect assumes a level of future inflation (say 2.5%), whilst the maintainable dividend is represented in constant money, then the valuation could materially understate the value of the company.

*Notional dividends*

**11.239**  A problem often encountered by valuers in divorce proceedings is that, although the company is profitable, it has not paid any dividends. In such cases it may be appropriate to calculate a 'notional dividend'. This involves determining an artificial dividend policy, although it has been the policy of the company not to declare dividends. However, a discount is necessary to reflect the uncertainty involved in assuming a notional dividend.

**11.240**  Determining the notional dividend requires an understanding of why no dividends have actually been paid and determining what level of dividend could be paid, based on the company's past and likely future performance. This can be complex.

**11.241**  Many valuers take the view that the degree of arbitrary judgmental assumptions needed using this approach rule it out as a reliable basis in its own right.

*The required rate of return*

**11.242**  Another problem faced by share valuers applying this method is selecting the required rate of return. A number of methods exist. We consider here the most usual, which is based on a quoted company comparison.

**11.243**  The starting point is to ascertain the quoted yields on a range of comparable listed companies. It can be difficult to identify quoted companies in the same industry that are similar in size, structure and characteristics and have a comparable profits record.

**11.244**  If suitable companies can be identified, the yields can be derived by dividing the dividends paid by the share price at the times of payment. Care must be taken to ensure that like-for-like figures are obtained. If comparable companies cannot be identified, an alternative source of quoted yields may be the *Financial Times* Actuaries Share Indices for the industry. If nothing else is available, use the FT 100 or 250 index.

**11.245** An adjustment should be made based on the liquidity of the company being valued, its size and diversification relative to the quoted shares, its level of dividend cover[155] and the absence of a market to trade the shares and any other restrictions on their transfer.

**11.246** A greater adjustment is required when using the quoted share index rather than individual companies. The uplift in the required rate of return compared to listed companies in a number of cases has been between 20% and 30%,[156] but could exceed 100%, depending on the circumstances.

**11.247** Valuers often prefer to apply a range of values as the required rate of return, reflecting the fact that share valuation is more of an art than a precise science. An alternative method is to build up a required rate from the risk-free rate available, for instance on government stock, plus the additional return required for the risk inherent in the specific company compared with the risk of the government defaulting.

## *The asset basis*

**11.248** The asset basis involves valuing the shares in a company by reference to the open market value of the assets belonging to the company. It will typically be used if:

- the company is loss-making with no prospect of future profits.

- the company is an investment company (including property investment companies).

- the assets are not used in the business and have a value in their own right. For example, if the company has considerable cash deposits that are not part of its normal working capital or set aside for a specific purpose (such as investment in machinery), then the cash effectively represents undistributed reserves which are not integral to the business and should be treated separately in the share valuation.

- the net realisable value of the assets is greater than the capitalised value of the dividends and earnings.

**11.249** To apply the asset basis it is necessary to establish the market value of each asset and liability, and an expert valuation should be sought. It is rarely possible to prepare such a valuation from the figures reported in the company's balance sheet. Accountants typically use the balance sheet as a starting point, or as a cross-check on the assets and liabilities to be considered, although there may be other items not recorded.

---

[155] That is, how many times over the dividend could have been paid out of the year's profits.
[156] *Re Holt* [1953] 1 WLR 1488; *Re Crossman* [1937] AC 26, HL; *Re Lynall* [1969] 3 WLR 771, CA. See HMRC Share Valuation Manual 14050.

**11.250** We comment below on some issues that commonly arise when applying the asset basis.

- Land and buildings often feature in valuations using the asset basis. Specialist valuers, such as chartered surveyors, may be needed for some or all of the assets. In general, the current use value will be relevant, but an alternative use basis may be appropriate if, say, there is planning permission in place.

- A surveyor may also be required to provide a market value for plant and machinery owned by the company if it is likely to be significant.

- If the company owns shares in an unquoted subsidiary company, shares in the subsidiary will need to be valued using an appropriate basis (which may be different from the basis used to value the parent company) and then reflected in the parent company's accounts. Care should be taken not to apply discounts twice.

- Another difficulty posed by the asset basis is the valuation of intangible assets, such as goodwill, patents and copyrights. Lord MacNaughton[157] described goodwill as 'the benefit and advantage of the good name, reputation and connection of a business. It is an attractive force which brings in custom ...'. Goodwill cannot exist separately from the business and hence has no value on a break-up basis. It is likely that if the goodwill is significant, then an earnings basis (or a combination of assets and earnings bases) may be a more appropriate method of valuing the shares, or valuing what the business can be sold for. Patents and copyrights can be sold.

**11.251** Once the value of the company's assets has been estimated, the valuer may make an adjustment for taxation in respect of the chargeable gains that would arise if the assets were sold.

## Other valuation methodologies

**11.252** In certain industries there may be 'rules of thumb' that provide a useful cross-check of the valuation. For example, small accountancy practices often change hands for a multiple of gross fees and insurance brokers for a multiple of annual commissions.

### Discounted cash flow method

**11.253** The discounted cash flow approach attempts to quantify the present day value of the future cash flows to the shareholders from their shares. This is generally achieved by 'modelling' the cash flows of the underlying business and then considering to what extent the business value is transposed to the

---

[157] *IRC v Muller & Co's Margarine Ltd* [1901] AC 217.

shareholding (clearly the link is greater for a majority shareholding than a minority one). This technique is highly mathematical and, owing to the difficulty in preparing long-term profit forecasts and selecting an appropriate discount rate, it is not widely used, although it can provide a useful cross-check of a calculation prepared on another basis. It is a technique much used in a private equity context.

## *Enterprise value method*

**11.254**  A company is sometimes measured in terms of the total funds being used to finance it. The enterprise value method is increasingly used to value shares in place of the earnings basis and is particularly suited to companies that have borrowed heavily to finance growth (such as telecoms companies) or to acquire subsidiaries or assets (such as management buy-outs, backed by venture capital equity and debt).

**11.255**  This method can be seen as an attempt to value the 'business' rather than the 'company', as it aims to quantify the cost of buying this business free of its debt and other liabilities.

**11.256**  The enterprise value is calculated by adding together the market capitalisation of the company, the value of its debt financing (such as bonds issued and bank loans, but excluding items regarded as part of working capital such as trade creditors) and other liabilities recognised in the accounts (such as a deficit in the company pension fund), and then subtracting the value of liquid assets such as cash and investments and dividing the result by the number of shares in issue. Often the value of assets that are non-core are excluded from the calculation. Where the company does not have a market value, an equivalent valuation will need to be assessed. In this context, care is necessary to ensure that the appropriate earnings basis is used: eg EBITDA comprises earnings before deducting interest payable, tax, depreciation and amortisation. Therefore, to also add back interest-bearing liabilities would be duplicative.

## *Hybrid method*

**11.257**  The hybrid basis refers to two valuation methodologies being applied in tandem. A full valuation is prepared on each basis, then a percentage of each value is used according to the relative importance accorded each approach. For example, 30% of the value is derived using the asset basis and 70% of the value is derived using the earnings basis.

## *Combination method*

**11.258**  The combination basis is used when the company owns investment assets which can be separated from the company's business assets and which stand alone as investments in their own right and their value is appreciating independently of the 'business' assets. Examples include a valuable piece of art displayed in the company's boardroom, or an investment property portfolio.

**11.259**   The business and non-business assets are valued independently and the total share value is the combined value. This is an example of excess assets.

## Valuation of non-equity shares

### *Preference shares*

**11.260**   A valuer will first check the rights attaching to the shares, which are usually, but not always, the entitlement to a fixed rate dividend, but with no voting rights. If there are voting rights, it may be appropriate to treat them as ordinary shares for valuation purposes. Other factors will be whether there are entitlements to surplus income or assets, and under what circumstances.

**11.261**   When the dividend is being paid regularly and the financial position of the company is secure, the valuer can use a similar methodology to value the preference shares as for a minority holding of ordinary shares in a dividend-paying company, using the following formula:

*Share Price = [Dividend % x Nominal value]*

*or*

*Share Price = [Dividend paid per share] / Required dividend yield*

**11.262**   Preference shares are generally easier to value than ordinary shares because the dividend percentage is fixed. Currently accepted practice for obtaining the required yield is to look at yields under the *Financial Times* Actuaries Fixed Interest Indices for Government Securities (5–15 years) and apply a suitable uplift. The uplift reflects the greater security of capital and interest provided by government securities. Care must be taken to match the life of the preference share to the valuation. For example, if the preference share is irredeemable, applying a yield based on 5–15 years is not appropriate. Also, some preference shares can be redeemable.

**11.263**   A further discount may be required if the company being valued compares unfavourably with quoted companies, or if there is doubt about the company's ability to pay the preference dividend.

### *Debentures and fixed interest securities*

**11.264**   The valuer's first step will be to determine the rate of interest (the 'coupon rate'), the redemption price (often par), and the date of redemption. The valuer will be aware that the interest may or may not be a fixed rate. It may float and be expressed by reference to something else, such as x percentage points above Bank of England rate or a particular government stock or index, which will affect how it is to be valued.

**11.265**   Debenture and loan stock can be compared with the yield available on comparable quoted securities. The *Financial Times* Actuaries Share Indices may be used as a guide. A valuer will need to consider increasing the yield to account for non-marketability and also for the lack of security compared with large quoted companies.

# Chapter 12

# PARTNERSHIP

## INTRODUCTION

**12.1** A general understanding of basic concepts of the law of partnership will be of great value to ancillary relief practitioners. If the basic mechanics of a partnership are understood, fashioning arguments to effect a fair division of assets ought to be made an easier task. This chapter aims to provide an introduction to some essential concepts in partnership law.[1] Following sections aimed at providing assistance with reading partnership accounts and valuing partnership interests, the chapter concludes by examining the manner in which partnerships are dealt with in ancillary relief proceedings. When carrying out this examination it is important to bear in mind that many of the broad themes encountered by the courts when dealing with company interests in the context of ancillary relief are also met in the partnership context and Chapter 11 should be consulted.[2]

## WHAT IS A PARTNERSHIP?

**12.2** Perhaps the most important of all the concepts of partnership law, is the idea that partnership, like a marriage, is a relationship. A partnership is defined by s 1(1) of the Partnership Act 1890 in the following terms:

> 'Partnership is the relation which subsists between persons carrying on a business in common with a view of profit.'[3]

**12.3** Flowing from the categorisation of a partnership as a relationship comes the necessary consequence that a partnership does not have a separate legal personality. This is in marked contrast to a company.

---

[1]   Where more detail is required, specialist texts, such as *Lindley & Banks on Partnership* (Sweet & Maxwell, 18th edn) ought to be consulted.

[2]   In particular, see the sections dealing with the protection of income-producing assets, sharing the results of the company's performance, sale, the generational family company, the search for liquidity, valuation issues and stellar contributions. Arguments will of course have to be adapted to take into account the different nature of an interest in a company and a partnership.

[3]   The effect of s 1(2) of the Partnership Act 1890 is to ensure that registered companies and limited liability partnerships are excluded from the definition of a partnership.

**12.4** The persons who carry on business in common with a view to profit are of course partners. The relationship between partners is fiduciary and based on principles of agency. When one partner enters into a contract on behalf of the business, he acts as agent on behalf of his fellow partners. Since a partnership does not have separate legal personality, there is no question of 'the partnership' entering into a contract. The absence of separate legal personality is sometimes confused when the partnership is referred to as 'a firm', with the implication being that a firm has legal personality.

**12.5** Another consequence of partnership as a relationship is that when the relationship comes to an end, so does the partnership. Bringing a partnership to an end is called dissolution. Dealing with the financial consequences of dissolution is the process known as winding up.

**12.6** There is no process of registration for an ordinary partnership. Whether a partnership exists is determined by establishing whether the relationship satisfies the general definition of a partnership set out above. This task is assisted by a number of rules set out in s 2 of the Partnership Act 1890. Perhaps the best known of the rules is contained in s 2(3), which provides that 'the receipt by a person of a share of the profits of a business is prima facie evidence that he is a partner in the business, but the receipt of such a share, or of a payment contingent on or varying with the profits of a business, does not of itself make him a partner in the business'. It is unnecessary to set out the rules in this text, since whether a partnership exists between spouses or between a spouse and third parties is unlikely to be an issue in ancillary relief proceedings. If it is, specialist texts will need to be consulted.

## PARTNERSHIP CLASSIFICATION

**12.7** Partnerships can broadly be classified as being either at will or for a fixed term. A partnership at will may be dissolved at any time by a partner giving notice to his other partners.[4] If the partnership is not one at will, the partnership can only be dissolved in accordance with the terms of any partnership deed, a provision of the Partnership Act 1890, court order or agreement between the partners. A partnership will be a partnership at will unless the terms of the agreement (whether express or implied) suggest that the partnership cannot be brought to an end at any time on notice.

**12.8** Limited Liability Partnerships ('LLPs') are rarely encountered in ancillary relief practice. However, there is a growth in the use of this business organisation amongst professional partnerships. An LLP does have separate legal personality and the liability of partners, as the name suggests, is limited. It is therefore arguable that LLPs probably have more in common with company than partnership law. LLPs are governed by the Limited Liability Partnerships Act 2000. An LLP is required to be registered and the fact of its incorporation

---

[4] Partnership Act 1890, s 26(1) and s 32(c).

should not therefore be a matter of doubt.[5] LLPs are required to file accounts and annual returns. However, any agreement equivalent to a deed of partnership between the members of the LLP is not required to be registered and is not therefore a matter of public record. Disclosure of filed accounts, annual returns and the members' agreement should clearly be obtained if an LLP is encountered in ancillary relief proceedings.

## THE DEED OF PARTNERSHIP

**12.9**  In essence, a partnership is a relationship supported by consideration and is thus a contract. The terms of a partnership contract are frequently embodied in a written partnership agreement or deed of partnership.[6] In all ancillary relief cases involving a partnership, it will be essential to see a copy of this document. Broadly, the partners are entitled to determine the terms upon which the partnership is to operate. The Partnership Act 1890 acts in effect as a default provision, providing a statutory basis for all or any terms of operation of a partnership in the absence of agreement, express or implied, between the partners. For example, a partnership agreement may be made orally. Inevitably the terms of such an agreement will not be fully comprehensive. In these circumstances the Partnership Act 1890 will provide by way of default those essential terms required for the operation of the partnership that have not been expressly or impliedly agreed between the partners. Finally, and perhaps to complicate matters, the terms of partnership, whether agreed in writing or orally, may be varied with the agreement of all the partners. The agreement to vary may be either express or inferred from a course of dealing.[7] However, in most cases encountered the deed of partnership will sufficiently define the relationship between partners.

**12.10**  The partnership deed should provide the practitioner with the following information:

- The identity of the partners.

- The proportion in which the partners are to share the profits and losses of the partnership. In the absence of agreement, the Partnership Act 1890 provides that the partners shall share the profits and losses equally.[8]

- Any agreement as to entitlement to any capital introduced into the partnership. In the absence of agreement, any capital contributed will be shared equally.[9]

---

[5]  The Registrar of Companies keeps an index of the names of LLPs.
[6]  Although it is usual for partnership agreements to be contained within a deed, it is unnecessary for a deed to be used unless, for example, it is intended that the document should convey land between the partners.
[7]  Partnership Act 1890, s 19.
[8]  Partnership Act 1890, s 24(1).
[9]  Partnership Act 1890, s 24(1).

- Any partnership property should be identified, as should the terms upon which the partnership is to use any property owned by a partner.

- The accounting periods for the partnership and details about the requirement to draw up partnership accounts.

- Information about the duration of the partnership and the powers of dissolution.

- Retirement provisions.

- Details of partner entitlement upon dissolution and winding up will usually be provided, including provisions giving the continuing partners rights to acquire the outgoing partner's interest in the partnership.

## PARTNERSHIP PROPERTY

**12.11** It is obviously essential for ancillary relief practitioners to identify whether property is owned by the partners within the partnership or whether it is owned by a party to the ancillary relief proceedings. If property is owned in a personal capacity, it is usually easier to realise in the context of ancillary relief proceedings. If there is an issue as to whether an asset is partnership or personal property and it is proportionate to warrant seeking the determination of the court on the issue, then the guidance for the conduct of such a hearing set out in *TL v ML and others*[10] should be followed. Establishing that property is not a partnership asset is not, however, the end of the matter, because a partner may allow his personal property to be used by the partnership on terms. For example, a partner may own business premises and lease them at a commercial rent to the partnership. The freehold interest would not be partnership property, whereas the leasehold interest would. The consequences of seeking to realise personal property allowed to be used by a partnership needs to be carefully considered.

**12.12** The first port of call in establishing whether an asset is a partnership asset is the partnership deed. Thereafter the partnership accounts will need to be consulted. If these documents or the existence of an agreement between the partners does not deal with ownership of any particular asset, it will be necessary to determine whether the asset in issue falls to be treated as partnership property by virtue of s 20(1) of the Partnership Act 1890, which provides that:

> 'All property and rights and interests in property originally brought into the partnership stock or acquired, whether by purchase or otherwise, on account of the firm, or for the purposes and in the course of the partnership business, are

---

[10]   [2006] 1 FLR 1263, and see **8.12**.

called in this Act partnership property, and must be held and applied by the partners exclusively for the purposes of the partnership and in accordance with the partnership agreement.'[11]

## WHAT IS A PARTNERSHIP SHARE?

**12.13**   The interest of a partner in a partnership is frequently referred to as a 'partnership share'. A partnership share is very different from a share in a company, which in broad terms may be transferred or sold for value. The nature of a partner's interest in a partnership was set out by Nourse LJ in *Popat v Schonchhatra*[12] as follows:

> 'Although it is both customary and convenient to speak of a partner's "share" of the partnership assets, that is not a truly accurate description of his interest in them, at all events so long as the partnership is a going concern. While each partner has a proprietary interest in each and every asset, he has no entitlement to any specific asset and, in consequence, no right, without the consent of the other partners or partner, to require the whole or even a share of any particular asset to be vested in him. On dissolution the position is in substance not much different, the partnership property falling to be applied, subject to ss 40 to 43 (if and so far as applicable), in accordance with ss 39 and 44 of the 1890 Act. As part of that process, each partner in a solvent partnership is presumptively entitled to payment of what is due from the firm to him in respect of capital before division of the ultimate residue in the shares in which profits are divisible; see s 44(b) 3 and 4. It is only at that stage that a partner can accurately be said to be entitled to a share of anything, which, in the absence of agreement to the contrary, will be a share of cash.'

**12.14**   A partnership interest is therefore broadly an interest in a 'proportion of the partnership assets after they have been realised and converted into money, and all the debts and liabilities have been paid and discharged'.[13] It is important to understand the distinction between partnership assets and capital.[14] Sections 39 and 44 of the Partnership Act 1890, referred to in the passage above, respectively identify the rights of partners in respect of the application of partnership property and the rules for distribution on a partnership dissolution account.

---

[11]   Section 21 of the Partnership Act 1890 provides that, unless there is a contrary intention, property bought with partnership money will be a partnership asset.

[12]   [1997] 1 WLR 1367 at 1372.

[13]   See *Lindley & Banks on Partnership* (Sweet & Maxwell, 18th edn), 19-05.

[14]   See *Popat v Schonchhatra* [1997] 1 WLR 1367 per Nourse LJ: 'I start with the distinction between the capital of a partnership and its assets. As I said at first instance in *Reed v Young* [1984] STC 38 at 57: "The capital of a partnership is the aggregate of the contributions made by the partners, either in cash or in kind, for the purpose of commencing or carrying on the partnership business and intended to be risked by them therein. Each contribution must be of a fixed amount. If it is in cash, it speaks for itself. If it is in kind, it must be valued at a stated amount. It is important to distinguish between the capital of a partnership, a fixed sum, on the one hand and its assets, which may vary from day to day and include everything belonging to the firm having any money value, on the other (see generally *Lindley on the Law of Partnership* (14th edn (1979)), p 442)".'

# GENERAL AND TECHNICAL DISSOLUTION

**12.15**   Since a partnership is a relationship, when the relationship comes to an end, then so does the partnership. However, when the relationship comes to an end and the remaining partners wish to carry on the partnership business, the dissolution of the partnership is described as 'technical'. The remaining partners, who will together constitute a new partnership, will be required to pay to the outgoing partner the value of his partnership share. In these circumstances there is no winding up. Partnership deeds frequently contain provisions dealing with the manner in which the outgoing partner's interest is to be calculated and paid. If the outgoing partner's share is not paid, he is entitled to press for a winding up of the partnership. A 'general dissolution' is one where the partnership comes to an end and the partnership is wound up.

**12.16**   It is important to recognise that in the event of a technical dissolution of partnership and prior to any final settlement of account, an outgoing partner is entitled to elect at his option to recover such share of post-dissolution profits as are attributable to his share of the partnership assets, or to interest at 5% per annum on the amount of his share of the partnership assets. It should be noted that this right may be excluded by agreement and will not apply where the continuing partners are given an option to purchase the interest of an outgoing partner, and the terms of the option are both duly exercised and in all material respects complied with.[15]

# READING PARTNERSHIP ACCOUNTS

**12.17**   Partnership accounts are akin to sole trader accounts and, in many respects, follow the same principles of preparation and presentation as company accounts. Therefore the guidance in Chapter 11 under the heading 'reading company accounts' will also be relevant to partnership accounts.

**12.18**   Some distinctive features of partnership accounts can, however, be identified.

## Features of partnership accounts

**12.19**   Partnership accounts are primarily prepared for the partners' own information and for taxation purposes. They may also be made available to outside lenders to the partnership. As a minimum they will comprise a balance sheet and profit and loss account, similar to those of a company. However, rather than share capital and reserves, the bottom half of the balance sheet will include a capital account for each partner and in some cases also a current account for each partner.

---

[15]   Partnership Act 1890, s 42.

**12.20** Although partnerships are required to compute their profits for tax purposes in accordance with generally accepted accounting policies, they are not required to prepare the accounts that the partners use for their dealings with each other on the same basis, although in practice many do.

**12.21** Where different accounting policies are adopted in the partnership accounts from those that are required for tax purposes, the correct figures of taxable profit will be produced by means of adjustments in the partnership tax return. A common area where divergent treatments are adopted is that of work in progress. Particular care needs to be taken to understand the accounting policies that are adopted in the preparation of partnership accounts.

**12.22** Unlike company accounts, partnership accounts do not follow a prescribed format. Sophisticated partnerships may well produce accounts that resemble company accounts, including detailed notes to describing the accounting policies and analysing items in a similar format to company accounts.

## Capital accounts

**12.23** Traditionally, the capital account records the introduction and withdrawal of long-term capital by partners. It shows how much money the partners have invested in the business and is sometimes referred to as 'fixed capital'.

## Current accounts

**12.24** During the year partners will withdraw cash for personal use, and any profits made during the year will be allocated between them at the year end. Traditionally these transactions are recorded in the partners' current accounts. The balance on the current account therefore shows each partner's accumulated share of profits, less any amounts withdrawn to date. At the year end any balance of undrawn profits may be transferred to the capital account (if it is intended to be retained in the business) or carried forward (if it is intended to be withdrawn in a later year).

**12.25** Some partnerships, particularly smaller ones, do not observe the distinction between capital and current accounts and all transactions with partners are recorded in a single 'capital' account.

**12.26** At any point in time, each partner's interest in the business is represented by the total of his or her capital account and current account.

## The appropriation of profit

**12.27** A feature of partnership accounts is that the profit and loss account includes an appropriation statement showing how the profit (or loss) for the year is divided between the partners.

**12.28**  The partners are free to decide between themselves how to allocate profit. Allocation can be done in several different ways. For instance:

- the profit may be shared in agreed proportions (equal or otherwise); or

- partners may be credited with a fixed amount ('salary') to reflect their input into the business; or

- partners may be credited with 'interest on capital' to allow for differences in the amounts of fixed capital they have contributed to the business; or

- a combination of the above.

**12.29**  The profit-sharing arrangements are usually described in the partnership agreement.

## Salaries

**12.30**  Only salaries paid to employees are charged to the partnership profit and loss account. This may include the wages of 'salaried partners'. Salaried partners are not partners in the business, but are effectively senior employees and have income tax and national insurance deducted at source from their salary.[16]

**12.31**  Unlike directors' or salaried partners' remuneration, partners' 'salaries' are not charged in the profit and loss account. Rather, they are part of the process of dividing up profit among the partners and often represent drawings or advances of profit share taken during a year. Many partnerships opt to include a 'salary' component in the profit-sharing arrangement in order to recompense full partners who contribute more to the business through time, effort or results.

## Interest on capital

**12.32**  If partners receive interest on the fixed capital they have invested in the business, the interest rate is usually specified in the partnership agreement, which may or may not reflect changes in the market rate of interest. This ensures that those partners who have invested more receive a greater profit share.

## Income tax provisions

**12.33**  As explained in more detail below, partnerships are not taxable entities as such, and each individual partner is responsible for paying tax on his or her share of the partnership profit.

---

[16]  See *Stekel v Ellice* [1973] 1 WLR 191.

**12.34** Nevertheless, it is a common practice for partners' tax liabilities to be discharged out of the partnership bank account. These payments can of course be accounted for as an immediate debit to the individual partners' drawings, but many firms find that it helps to ensure that partners' current accounts do not become overdrawn if impending tax liabilities are debited to drawings in advance (perhaps at the accounting year end immediately prior to the due date for the payment of the tax). This practice gives rise to income tax provisions in partnership balance sheets, which will usually be shown separately within creditors (and are to be distinguished from liabilities for income tax and national insurance deducted at source from staff salaries in the preceding month).

**12.35** The accounting policy determining the basis on which income tax provisions are calculated should be explained in the partnership accounts, but in any event will need to be ascertained by those advising partners in ancillary relief proceedings.

**12.36** An income tax provision computed on this basis is always (or at least should be) simply the sum of separate individual provisions for each partner. Although it may well not be apparent from the partnership accounts how much of the overall provision is attributable to each partner, a breakdown should always be readily available on request. The allocation of the provision is important to ensure that over-provisions (ie provisions in excess of what is in the event ultimately paid in tax) can be credited to the partner whose drawings were originally debited.

## *Deferred tax provisions*

**12.37** Sometimes described as 'future tax provisions', these may occasionally be found in partnership balance sheets, particularly those of larger and more complex partnerships.

**12.38** The reasons for including deferred tax provisions and the basis of accounting for them can vary widely. Typically they deal with cases where income is recognised for accounting purposes in one period but subject to tax in a later period. Where there are appointments or retirements of partners, or changes in profit-sharing arrangements, in the intervening period, to achieve equity between partners there needs to be an accounting adjustment to ensure that new partners do not suffer tax on income that they have not received.

**12.39** Unlike a general income tax provision, a deferred tax provision will not be the sum of separate individual provisions attributable to each partner. Indeed, the very reason for creating a deferred tax provision will usually be to create a mechanism for making transfers between different partners' capital and current accounts in different periods.

**12.40**   Needless to say, the basis of calculation of any deferred tax provision may be complex, but practitioners advising partners in ancillary relief proceedings will need to understand at least the general principles behind any provision that is encountered.

## *Reporting and regulation*

**12.41**   There are no rules or guidelines equivalent to the Companies Acts or Financial Reporting Standards governing unincorporated businesses. Partners choose the level of sophistication they wish to apply to their financial reporting.

**12.42**   There is no legal requirement for partnership accounts to be audited. It is open to partnerships to opt for their accounts to be audited, but very few choose to do so. Even accounts compiled by external accountants will not have been verified to ensure the accuracy and completeness of the accounting records. The accountants will not issue an opinion to state whether they show a true and fair view. However, it is rarely worthwhile to have the accounts verified in detail for the purposes of ancillary relief proceedings. Rather, the expert accountant or valuer may need to take a view on the reliability of the accounts, by considering whether they have been prepared by a reputable firm of accountants, whether suitable internal financial controls are in place and whether there are any indications that the results have been manipulated.

**12.43**   There is therefore less consistency and transparency in the way partnerships prepare their accounts compared to companies. As a result, the underlying profitability of the firm and its prospects are more difficult to assess, and it is hard to benchmark performance against competitors in the same industry.

**12.44**   As identified above, LLPs face more stringent regulations than ordinary partnerships. These are considered separately below.

## Access to accounts[17]

**12.45**   Partnership accounts are not a matter of public record and cannot be obtained without the permission of the partners. Partners are not obliged to file accounts with Companies House or to disclose any accounting information whatsoever, other than to the taxation authorities. Sole traders and partners are obliged to keep detailed accounting records of income and expenditure for taxation purposes and must file an annual self-assessment return to HMRC.

**12.46**   Similarly there are no annual returns for partnerships.

**12.47**   Any spouse who is a partner will be obliged as part of the usual process of disclosure to provide financial information about his or her partnership

---

[17]   As explained, the position in respect of LLPs is different.

interests. Furthermore, every spouse who is a partner has a right to inspect partnership books and accounts[18] and, in consequence, there ought to be little problem in obtaining disclosure in ancillary relief proceedings.

## Taxation

**12.48**  A partnership may trade as one business, but any tax liability that arises on profits, including profits of LLPs, is calculated under income tax rules. Each partner is taxed separately on his or her share of the profit earned in the accounting year as if they had started a separate business when joining the partnership or ceased a separate business when leaving the partnership. However, partners can become jointly and severally liable for other debts, including VAT, business rates, stamp duty, and land tax in connection with partnership property.

**12.49**  For each tax year, partners are taxed on their share of the total profit earned by the partnership in the 'accounting period' which ends in that tax year. For example, a partnership which makes up accounts to 30 June each year will have an accounting period from 1 July to the following 30 June. Those profits will be included as taxable income in the tax years which include that 30 June (there may be more than one, as illustrated below).

**12.50**  The table below shows the tax years in which profits are assessed. Although a partner may be taxed twice on the profits earned when first joining a partnership, an 'overlap relief' is given for this double taxation by deducting it from the partner's profits when leaving. In this way, tax is charged on the actual profits that the partner earns while with the partnership.

| Tax Year | Taxable profits |
|---|---|
| *Year 1* | The profits from the date of commencement with the partnership to 5 April following. |
| *Year 2* | The profits in the 12-month accounting period ending in year 2; <br><br> *or* <br><br> if the accounting period is less than 12 months, the profits of the first 12 months (apportioned from two sets of partnership accounts); <br><br> *or* <br><br> if the accounting period is greater than 12 months, the profits of the 12 months to the accounting date (apportioned from partnership accounts); <br><br> *or* <br><br> the profits of the tax year from 6 April to 5 April. |

---

[18]  Partnership Act 1890, s 24(9).

| Tax Year | Taxable profits |
|---|---|
| *Year 3 and later years* | The profits of the 12-month accounting period ending in the tax year. |
| *Final year* | The profits from the accounting date ending in the last tax year prior to the partner's leaving date, less any overlap relief due. |

**12.51** Each partner's tax liability is payable by two equal payments on account, one on 31 January in the tax year and one on 31 July following the tax year, with the final payment (if any is due) being made on 31 January following the end of the tax year. The amount of each payment on account will be 50 per cent of the partner's income tax liability (after tax deducted at source) for the previous tax year, subject to a partner's right to apply to reduce the payments on account if he or she can show that their tax liability has reduced since the previous tax year.

## LLPs

**12.52** LLPs are structured in the same way as ordinary partnerships, but, as the name suggests, the personal liability of each partner is restricted to the amount of capital he or she has invested (and to any personal guarantees he or she has given to raise finance).

**12.53** In exchange for this protection, LLPs must deliver an annual set of accounts to Companies House, which means there is public access to their financial statements.

**12.54** Furthermore, as an LLP is a separate legal entity, its accounts must present a true and fair view of the business and must be audited, unless it qualifies for an exemption. For accounting periods ending after 30 March 2004, an LLP can qualify for an audit exemption if it is 'small' (as defined by the Companies Act 2006) and its turnover is not more than £6.5 million, and it has a balance sheet of not more than £3.26 million.

**12.55** Unlike ordinary partnership accounts, the profit and loss account and balance sheet of an LLP follow a standard format. Detailed notes to the accounts, equivalent to limited company disclosures, must be included in accordance with accounting standards and the Statement of Recommended Practice for LLPs. The level of financial disclosure is much more extensive than an ordinary partnership typically produces.

# VALUING PARTNERSHIP INTERESTS

**12.56** Whether expert valuation of a partnership or a partnership interest is required will be case specific.[19] A valuation may be required if the partnership business is to be sold as a whole. If the intention is to realise a partnership share, the following should be noted. The continuing partners will frequently be entitled in accordance with the deed of partnership or subsequent agreement to pay to the outgoing partner the value of his partnership interest in order to forestall a general dissolution and subsequent winding up.[20] Since a partnership is a relationship based on contract, absent provision in a deed of partnership or agreement by the remaining partners, an outgoing partner cannot transfer his interest in the partnership to a third party, who would take the outgoing partner's place in a newly constituted partnership.

**12.57** An important factor to take into account in determining whether a partnership should be the subject of an independent valuation in ancillary relief proceedings is the fact that in many cases the true value of a partnership will be more than the net assets in its balance sheet, as unrealised gains, such as increases in the value of property and goodwill, do not always appear on the balance sheet. Goodwill, whether internally generated or purchased, is linked to a number of factors such as location, reputation, employees and the ability to earn profits. Furthermore, unless all the assets and liabilities (both tangible and intangible) are included at their market value in the financial records of the partnership, the partners' capital accounts total will not show the value of the partners' actual interest in the business.[21]

**12.58** In practice, if a partner leaves without the whole business being sold, he or she will as a consequence of the deed of partnership usually be given the balance on their current and capital accounts, not their share of the 'market value' of the business, unless the partnership deed says otherwise, or the partner can negotiate a larger amount.

## Valuation methodology

**12.59** The generally accepted approach for arriving at the value of a partnership interest is to establish the overall value of the business and deduct the net asset value recorded in the books to establish the surplus (or deficit), which is then divided between the partners into their capital accounts in the profit-sharing ratio. The value of the partner's interest is then the balance on his or her capital/current account.

---

[19] Care also needs to be taken to ensure that there is no double-counting (see **11.140** and *V v V* [2005] 2 FLR 697 at [28]), although it is submitted that in a partnership context, this will commonly be unlikely since the valuation of a partnership share is usually based on more than just capitalisation of an income stream.

[20] See **12.15–12.16**.

[21] See also Chapter 23 for tax consequences.

## Account balances

**12.60**   The capital account is the starting point of the valuation. The balance can be established from the most recent set of accounts, as can the net assets. These may need to be updated if the valuation date is not the year-end (or month-end, if monthly management accounts are prepared).

## Value of the overall business

**12.61**   The value of the overall business then needs to be assessed. A professional valuer may be needed. A valuer will approach this in the same way as valuing a company, by considering the income, profits and assets of the business and the factors affecting its future prospects, as well as industry-specific conventions (eg professional partnerships are often sold for a multiple of fees) and any comparable sales in the industry.

**12.62**   When arriving at the overall value, a valuer will seek to remove the impact of assets, liabilities and expenditure included in the partnership accounts that are personal, not business, items. This is particularly relevant in family partnerships. The value of the business may be depressed without the existing partners to manage it, and an adjustment may be required to take account of this.

**12.63**   There may be an income tax provision in the partnership accounts. Income tax is a personal liability, not a business one; hence, any liability for unpaid income tax for the partners should be added back to the partners' capital accounts for the purpose of valuing the partnership overall, although the individual's income tax liability should be taken into account in the Form E.

**12.64**   It can be difficult to attribute any goodwill to an outgoing partner, particularly one with a minority interest. The partnership agreement may provide explicit guidance on this point. For example, partnership agreements in large professional practices generally prohibit any payment of goodwill to an outgoing partner.

**12.65**   It is generally accepted that no discount should be applied for lack of control when valuing a minority interest in partnership because, under the Partnership Act 1890, any partner can broadly insist that the business be wound up. However, this is not always the commercial reality, and each case must be assessed on its own merits.

## Value of the partnership interest before tax

**12.66**   Deducting the net book value of the assets from the value of the business overall establishes the surplus or deficit. This is then allocated across the partners' capital accounts in the profit-sharing ratios to establish the share of each partner's interest in the business.

## *Capital gains tax*

**12.67** The value of the interest, for the purposes of dividing matrimonial assets, is the partner's share in the business less any capital gains tax that would arise on its disposal at that value. This is considered in more detail in Chapter 23.

# HUSBAND AND WIFE PARTNERSHIPS

**12.68** Where the only partners in a firm are a husband and wife, the issues that face a court in ancillary relief proceedings are relatively straightforward, mainly because the interests of third party partners do not need to be taken into account. It is unusual for a husband and wife to wish to continue to trade as partners after divorce. The more likely options for the parties are to sell the business as a whole as a going concern, dissolve the partnership and wind up the assets, or allow one of the parties to the marriage to take over the partnership business (as on a technical dissolution) and require, perhaps, either a compensating payment by way of lump sum or property adjustment order to be made in favour of the spouse leaving the partnership. Many similar issues arise in the context of a small family company. It follows that many of the themes developed in Chapter 11, to which regard should be had, will be applicable, albeit in the context of a partnership.

**12.69** In a case where needs and compensation are met, there is an argument to be made that fairness dictates that any surplus remaining, if it is represented by interests in a husband and wife trading partnership, be shared according to their respective interests in the partnership. As was stated in the Court of Appeal by Butler-Sloss LJ in *White v White*:[22]

> 'In a case where the spouses were in business together, the starting-point has to be their respective financial positions at the end of their business relationship. This may in many cases be achieved by a broad assessment of the financial position and I am not advocating a detailed partnership account. At this stage it is not a question of contribution to the family, which is to be found at subs (2)(f) but of entitlement. Of course, as Ormrod LJ said in *Browne (Formerly Pritchard) v Pritchard* [1975] 1 WLR 1366, subs (2)(a) should not be allowed to dominate the picture, but it has, in a suitable case, such as the present appeal, to be given its due weight in the balancing exercise.'

**12.70** *White v White* was a case where the parties were equal partners in the partnership business. In most husband and wife partnerships, this is likely to be the case. The interesting question that arises is whether, after needs and compensation are met, a partnership deed setting out unequal financial entitlements in the partnership may influence the ultimate division of the marital surplus. Clearly, such a provision in a deed of partnership must be

---

[22] [1998] 2 FLR 310 at 323. This approach was approved in the House of Lords: see [2000] 2 FLR 981 at 995F–G per Lord Nicholls.

given its due weight, but it is still just one of the factors to be taken into account in the exercise of discretion, along with the other s 25 factors.

**12.71**   The approach found in the speech of Baroness Hale in *Miller v Miller; McFarlane v McFarlane*, where family businesses or joint ventures in which both parties worked were viewed as family assets, to which the yardstick of equality might readily be applied,[23] would suggest that good reasons would have to be found to depart from equality in respect of a partnership in which both spouses worked. An agreed but unequal division of partnership profits and the reasons behind such an agreement may, in an appropriate case, justify a departure from equality.

**12.72**   As indicated by the passage from *White v White* cited above, the parties' partnership entitlements are to be broadly assessed. In general there is no need for a detailed partnership account.

## PARTNERSHIPS WITH THIRD PARTIES

**12.73**   Where a husband and/or wife are in partnership with a third party, the existence of a third party interest makes the fair division of assets a more challenging task. As we have seen,[24] sale of a partnership interest is not likely to be an option available to a court. Furthermore, raising money against the security of partnership property is likely to be difficult. Consent of the other partners would be required, and this would be unlikely to be forthcoming. A degree of judicial encouragement may be possible,[25] but it is likely to be efficacious only in circumstances where the third party partners are related to either of the divorcing spouses.

**12.74**   In many cases a partnership interest is essential to the generation of income for the benefit of the family. In these circumstances the courts will strive to protect the partnership interest,[26] and the spouse retaining the partnership interest will usually be required to make such balancing lump sum payment or property adjustment to the other spouse as fairness demands.

**12.75**   Where a partnership interest is to be left intact in order to provide the basis for periodical payments, a proportionate approach must be taken to the valuation of the partnership interest. By analogy with company cases, there would seem to be little reason for conducting a detailed valuation of a partnership interest where the interest is not to be realised.[27] For example, in *Evans v Evans*[28] it was stated that 'Whilst it may be necessary to obtain a broad assessment of the value of a shareholding in a private company it is

---

[23]   [2006] 1 FLR 1186 at [149], [168].
[24]   See **12.56** and **14.2**.
[25]   See **11.86**.
[26]   See the section in Chapter 11 on the protection of income-producing assets.
[27]   See the sections in Chapter 11 on miscellaneous valuation issues.
[28]   [1990] 1 FLR 319.

inappropriate to undertake an expensive and meaningless exercise to achieve a precise valuation of a private company which will not be sold'. In many cases, relying on the value of a partnership capital account may be sufficient. At the same time, however, regard should be had to those factors identified at **12.57**.

**12.76** The need to value partnership interests over and above the figure contained in a capital account was considered by Coleridge J in *N v N (Financial Provision: Sale of Company)*.[29] In that case, the husband was senior partner in a successful accountancy partnership. His capital account amounted to £345,000, but of that £282,000 was fixed capital 'which cannot in practical terms be withdrawn, certainly at present'.[30] The illiquidity of much of a capital account needs therefore to be considered and, as described in Chapter 11, illiquidity is of itself capable of justifying a departure from equality.[31] However, as far as the valuation of the husband's partnership interest was concerned, Coleridge J stated as follows:[32]

> 'It is to be noted that I have not included in the schedule any figure for the capital value of the husband's interest in his accountancy partnership, apart from his partnership capital. I have not been specifically invited to do so by the wife's counsel and, had he done so, I should have declined to in this particular case. However, that is not to say that this interest is in truth valueless.
>
> In the current climate now, where the court is engaged more in dividing up assets than in calculating a party's reasonable needs, there would be logic in trying to calculate and include a figure for any asset which generates a secure income. At its most extreme that might include the valuation of a party's earning capacity. However, in my judgment, the evaluation of such an ephemeral item would be pregnant with problems and lead to endless debate incapable of fair resolution. It would be even more problematic where there was ongoing provision for children.
>
> However, in this case this aspect of the husband's finances is much more than merely his own personal earning capacity. He is the senior partner of a highly successful group of partnerships with an ever-increasing turnover in the order of £7m. That represents, in my judgment, an asset which will go on producing a very secure income, quite apart from any actual earning capacity attaching to the husband, per se, as an accountant.
>
> Accordingly, although I do not include any particular figure in the assets schedule for this aspect of the husband's overall resources, I certainly bear it in mind in arriving at my decision and the overall result.'

It is submitted that, in most cases, the approach identified by Coleridge J will be suitable.

---

[29]   [2001] 2 FLR 69.
[30]   [2001] 2 FLR 69 at 74.
[31]   See the section in Chapter 11 on the search for liquidity. See also *Miller v Miller; McFarlane v McFarlane* [2006] 1 FLR 1186 at [148] per Baroness Hale.
[32]   [2001] 2 FLR 69 at 75.

**12.77**   It is less common for a court to make an order that will require the dissolution of a partnership. Such an outcome is likely only to arise if the needs of the non-partnership spouse can only be met by having recourse to the other spouse's partnership interest. In many respects this is the option of last resort. A potential source of income will be destroyed on dissolution, making the option more suitable to a case where the partnership produces little or insufficient income. Income returns on capital employed is likely to be an important factor to take into account. Another important factor to take into account is how the interests of third party partners will be affected by dissolution. The more adverse the consequences, the less likely it is that an order requiring dissolution will be made.

# Chapter 13

# FARMS

## INTRODUCTION

**13.1** Farmers are frequently asset rich and income poor.[1] Land farmed by a party to ancillary relief proceedings is commonly inherited and/or held jointly with other family members. The farm is habitually both a business and the location of the family home. Difficulties in liquidity are widespread and in all bar big money cases courts persistently toil to stretch resources to meet the needs of both parties. It is therefore not surprising to find judicial dicta to the effect that 'ancillary relief farming cases are notoriously difficult to resolve'.[2] The demanding task faced by courts in farming ancillary relief cases has, however, led to the creation of a rich seam of jurisprudence illustrating the 'creative ingenuity which may on occasions be necessary if a fair and just result is to be achieved'.[3] The case law dealing with ancillary relief farming cases will therefore be enlightening in both an agricultural context and in the more general ancillary relief cases. Finally, since a farm is a business and farmland will be held subject to trusts of varying degrees of complexity, the chapters on companies, partnerships and trusts may also need to be consulted.

## FARM ASSETS

**13.2** It is not hard to identify the traditional assets of a farm. Freehold farm land, tenanted farm land,[4] livestock, deadstock, crops and machinery all spring immediately to mind. Less immediately obvious, although of material significance, are the subsidies and quotas that farmers receive.

---

[1]  In some cases the low return on capital employed in the farming business may form the basis of an argument justifying an order for sale. As a generalisation, an order for sale of a farm is difficult to attain.

[2]  *R v R (Lump Sum Repayments)* [2004] 1 FLR 928 at [3] per Wilson J.

[3]  *P v P (Inherited Property)* [2005] 1 FLR 576 at 587.

[4]  The existence of tenancies within the Agricultural Holdings Act 1986 and the Agricultural Tenancies Act 1995 will in general depress the value of land, and the implications of selling or transferring land subject to an agricultural holding or farm business tenancy need to be considered with any agricultural valuer instructed to value the farm business and land. Where the farmland is itself held under a tenancy, one of the parties may have statutory rights to succession to that tenancy pursuant to the Agricultural Holdings Act 1986. This may be a resource to be taken into account in the proceedings, albeit one which will only become available in the future.

**13.3**   Wholesale and direct sales milk quotas exist.[5] The quotas are in general attached to the land and not to an individual. Milk producers are, however, able to transfer their milk quotas to another producer. A milk quota can also be leased. The price for the transfer or lease of a milk quota is driven by the market. A milk quota is therefore a resource of the farmer and can be utilised as a means of capital generation, especially where the quota is no longer used by the farmer. The existence of and the ability to raise money from a milk quota should, if uncertain, form the basis of an appropriately worded request for further information in the questionnaire. Trading milk quota entitlements is a specialist activity and questions about market rates and transfer and leasing should be referred to an agricultural valuer.

**13.4**   Prior to 2005, farmers were potentially entitled to receive a large number of direct subsidies under various schemes. From 2005 onwards, many of these schemes were replaced by the Single Payment Scheme. The entitlement to payment under the Single Payment Scheme can be transferred and leased. If it is to be leased, it may only be leased along with the land to which it is attached. Since the entitlement to the single farm payment may be traded and leased, it is, in theory at least, another means by which capital and income may be raised.

**13.5**   The trade in single farm payment entitlements is, however, new and currently low key. Although the trading of entitlement may well become more significant, the prospect of trading in order to generate liquidity whilst maintaining the business integrity of a farm is likely at present to be difficult. If the trading or leasing of entitlements is to be pursued, the advice of an agricultural valuer will be required.[6] In most cases however, the primary value of the single farm payment is that of an increasingly vital source of income for a farmer. The single payment scheme is dealt with in more depth at **13.64**, in the context of farm accounts and valuation issues.

## DUALITY OF PURPOSE – THE FARM AS A HOME AND A BUSINESS

**13.6**   Giving each party an equal start on the road to independent living can be particularly difficult in a farming case. Often the farmhouse will be both a home to the parties and an integral part of a working farm. The importance of living on the land being worked is sometimes reflected by the existence of an agricultural tie over the farmhouse, which can exist to restrict the occupancy of a farmhouse to those involved in working on the land. Consequently, as a matter of practicality and additionally sometimes as a matter of planning law, the option of transferring the former matrimonial home to the wife may not be available.

---

[5]   See www.rpa.gov.uk or www.defra.gov.uk for further information about milk quotas.
[6]   We are indebted to Mark Webb, an agricultural valuer at Webb Paton, for taking the time to explain some of the intricacies of the single farm payment scheme.

**13.7** The duality of purpose of the farmhouse is also reflected by the ability of the farm business to treat the living expenses referable to the farmhouse as legitimate deductible expenses of the business. The corollary of such an approach is that the expenses deducted must be added back to the farmer's income after being broadly assessed as benefits in kind.[7]

**13.8** Finally, it should not be forgotten that the contents of the farmhouse will usually need to be taken into account when reaching a settlement.

## HOW THE COURTS HAVE DEALT WITH FARMING CASES – GENERAL

**13.9** Ancillary relief authorities are primarily of use as sources of broad principle rather than as binding precedents. This approach has been emphasised by the courts on countless occasions.[8] One such warning, in the context of farming disputes, was given by Butler-Sloss LJ when *White v White* was in the Court of Appeal.[9] Her ladyship stated that 'There is a danger that practitioners in the field of family law attempt to apply too rigidly the decisions of this court and of the Family Division, without sufficiently recognising that each case involving a family has to be decided upon broad principles adapted to the facts of the individual case'. Whilst not ignoring those words of warning, it is valuable to see how courts have dealt with farming cases, not in order to attempt to formulate principle,[10] but as a guide to identify some of the more prevalent circumstances taken into account and by way of insight into the creative use of the ancillary relief orders available under the Matrimonial Causes Act 1973.

## EARLY CASES – PROTECTION OF INCOME-PRODUCING ASSETS AND SELLING PORTIONS OF LAND

**13.10** One of the earliest reported farming cases under the Matrimonial Causes Act 1973 was *Dixon v Dixon*,[11] where the size of the lump sum contended for by counsel for the wife was said to have been such that it would have necessitated the husband's farm being sold. The Court of Appeal refused

---

[7]  See **13.43** and *R v R (Lump Sum Repayments)* [2004] 1 FLR 928 at 931.

[8]  See, for example, *Calderbank v Calderbank* [1976] Fam 93 at 103 per Scarman LJ: 'Every case will be different and no case may be decided except upon its particular facts'. Perhaps the frequency of reminders from the bench indicates the insidious tendency of lawyers to seek to use precedents in ancillary relief in a rigid as opposed to a fluid manner. See also **1.13–1.16**.

[9]  [1998] 2 FLR 310 at 322G.

[10]  In *P v P (Inherited Property)* [2005] 1 FLR 576 at [44], Munby J made an order 'not ... because of any principle that this is the approach to be adopted in farming cases, but because in the particular circumstances of this case that is the approach which most closely accords with the over-arching requirement of fairness, having regard to all the circumstances ...'.

[11]  (1975) Fam Law 58, CA.

to make an order for such a large lump sum, in part on the basis of a passage from Lord Denning's judgment in *Wachtel v Wachtel*,[12] where he stated that 'One thing is however obvious. No order should be made for a lump sum unless the husband has capital assets out of which to pay it – without crippling [the farmer's] earning power'. In *Dixon*, Lord Salmon[13] stated that the lump sum contended for, requiring the sale of the farm, would 'not only be crippling his earning power, but it would deprive him of the earning ability to go on living the life he had led, which his father had led and in which he hoped his grandson would succeed him'.[14] The approach of the court in *Dixon* illustrates a familiar theme in ancillary relief cases, namely that where an asset is required to provide an income for the parties, a lump sum which damages the income-producing asset is unlikely to be ordered. Furthermore, when referring to generational interests Lord Salmon foreshadowed a theme developed in some depth by Munby J in *P v P (Inherited Property)*.[15]

**13.11**   In order to achieve a fair result, the Court of Appeal in *Dixon* fixed the lump sum at a level that could be met in part by the husband selling a portion of the farm. The effect of sale of the portion was such as to leave the husband with a farm 'from which he could just about make a living'. The Court of Appeal envisaged that the lump sum ordered to be paid would be invested to supplement the wife's periodical payments. It is also to be noted that the wife's housing needs had been met.

**13.12**   Selling a portion of the farm without affecting the overall integrity of the farm business is prima facie a simple concept.[16] From an evidential perspective the concept is more difficult. There is no discussion in *Dixon* as to how the court reached the conclusion that selling 6¾ acres of a 43-acre farm left the integrity of the farm business intact. Nor is there any indication as to how the trial judge was able to place a net value on the land to be sold. If selling a portion of the land to raise a lump sum is to be considered, as part of the process of valuation[17] conducted prior to final hearing (and ideally prior to FDR), figures for the price per acre of land and the potential income yield from the land ought to be obtained. It will also be necessary for the valuer to identify and value those portions of farm land that could be sold without affecting the integrity of the farm business. Where land is to be sold, liability to capital gains tax will need to be determined.

---

[12]   [1973] 1 All ER 829 at 840.
[13]   Who was sitting as a judge of the Court of Appeal.
[14]   (1975) Fam Law 58 at 59.
[15]   [2005] 1 FLR 576. See **13.47**.
[16]   This was also a factor taken into account by Ward J in *B v B (Financial Provision)* [1990] 1 FLR 20 at 32D, where a lump sum to cover reasonable housing needs and a *Duxbury* fund was ordered to be paid to the wife in circumstances where the husband would have to sell some farmland but would retain 'for himself, and I hope his children, a good deal of the family farms passed down to him'.
[17]   Carried out by a specialist agricultural valuer; see the Central Association of Agricultural Valuers website at www.caav.org.uk.

**13.13** The evidence of an expert agricultural valuer is frequently of critical importance in the creative resolution of farming ancillary relief cases. Of course, expert evidence from a valuer need not be limited to those issues addressed by the court in *Dixon*. Where farm income is low, the valuer could help both the court and the parties consider whether the assets of the farm could be put to better use, whether entitlements could be traded and whether there were any diversification schemes that might be suitable. If farm land and assets are to be sold, the advice of an agricultural valuer frequently assists in selecting the method of sale which will maximise value.

**13.14** In *Dawe v Dawe*[18] the Court of Appeal had to grapple with a relatively complex farm-holding structure. The husband had inherited, along with his two brothers, 136 acres from their great uncle. The land was jointly held by the husband and his brothers. The farming business was run through a limited company in which each of the brothers was a director and a shareholder. The company farmed the land as tenants of the husband and his brothers. The Court of Appeal upheld a lump sum order that resulted in the wife obtaining a fraction less than 25% of the husband's capital. In so doing Ormrod LJ sought to mitigate the discrepancy by explaining that 'it could not be right to get the husband to battle against his brothers, to convert the tenancy in common into a joint tenancy[19] and get an order for sale, unless that was the only way to provide for the wife. Such a course would destroy the livelihood of the husband and his brothers'.[20] The court was satisfied that the lump sum ordered would just about be sufficient for the wife's needs whilst at the same time not placing the husband into conflict with his brothers. On the facts of the case, a fair order limited the wife to her reasonable needs.[21]

**13.15** Furthermore, when comparing the parties' respective capital shares, Ormrod LJ commented that 'It was true that £18,000 was less than one-quarter of the husband's capital, but £18,000 cash was one thing and £73,000 unliquid capital was another'.[22] The distinction between liquid and illiquid capital is a feature of many farming ancillary relief cases.[23] This theme, along with many others, was considered in greater depth by the Court of Appeal in *P v P (Financial Provision: Lump Sum)*.[24]

---

[18]  (1976) Fam Law 51, CA.
[19]  *Quaere:* Did the learned judge intend to say 'convert the joint tenancy into a tenancy in common'?
[20]  (1976) Fam Law 51 at 52.
[21]  The case was decided before the now discarded concept of 'reasonable requirements' had begun its development in *O'D v O'D* [1976] Fam 83.
[22]  (1976) Fam Law 51 at 52.
[23]  See *Wells v Wells* [2002] 2 FLR 97, CA on the sharing between the parties of liquid and illiquid assets in a non-farming context.
[24]  [1978] 1 WLR 483, CA.

## *P V P* (FINANCIAL PROVISION: LUMP SUM) – VALUATION EVIDENCE, INHERITED ASSETS, BORROWING CAPACITY

**13.16**   *P v P* is a landmark case and it is worth considering in some depth. The wife was 34 and her husband 44. There were three children of the marriage, aged 11, 10 and 6 years. The marriage was dissolved after nearly 12 years. The only relevant asset was the farm. The farm had been conveyed into the wife's sole name by her father after the marriage. The farm business was carried out by the husband and wife in partnership. Both the parties to the marriage put hard work into the farm, which had as a consequence risen in value. The value of the farm, including the farm house, contents and stock was £102,000. Strangely, the partnership accounts were not in evidence and it was assumed that the income produced by the farm was 'sufficient to keep the wife and the three children and pay, at any rate something towards their private education'.[25] The wife's likely income position contrasted starkly with the husband's, whose earning capacity was accepted as being 'highly problematical at the moment. He is 44 years of age with no qualifications and I accept that he will have great difficulty finding a job'.[26] The financial obligations of the parties were 'equally but oppositely out of balance'. The husband had to look after himself, whilst the wife needed to provide a home, maintenance and education for the three children of the family as well as meeting her own needs.

**13.17**   The Court of Appeal upheld orders requiring a lump sum of £15,000 to be paid by the wife to the husband in three equal instalments.[27] This sum was considered to be sufficient to rehouse the husband and he was noted to have no practical proposals as to how he would use a larger sum.[28] The wife retained the farm on the basis that it was needed to provide her and the children with an income. The wife was also to make periodical payments to the husband until the instalments were paid. The husband was subject to nominal orders to make periodical payments.

**13.18**   The order effected an approximate 85% to 15% split of the marital assets in favour of the wife.[29] The court made it clear that merely comparing the value of the assets received by the parties after order was overly simplistic. As emphasised by Ormrod LJ, 'a sum of £100,000 in liquid assets is one thing; £100,000 invested in a small farm in the west country is something very

---

[25]   [1978] 1 WLR 483 at 488B.

[26]   [1978] 1 WLR 483 at 488D per Ormrod LJ.

[27]   One benefit of such an order is that it is variable. It also survives the death and remarriage limitation inherent in an order for periodical payments. This characteristic was referred to by Wilson J in *R v R (Lump Sum Repayments)* [2004] 1 FLR 928, when he carefully and creatively crafted an order to achieve fairness on the facts of the case before him.

[28]   See **13.25**.

[29]   Ormrod LJ stated (at 490D) that the words 'equality' and 'family assets' had no place in s 25 and it was a great mistake to approach these cases as if they were part of that section. The relevance of those terms has, of course, received considerable scrutiny by the House of Lords in *White v White* and *Miller v Miller; McFarlane v McFarlane*.

different'.[30] Of course, an asset which is illiquid has to be sold in order to realise value. Selling an asset can often take time and be inconvenient. There are also costs of sale to deduct. Additionally, liability to capital gains tax and potential inheritance tax considerations would need to be taken into account. All these factors reduce, sometimes considerably, the value of an asset. The valuation figures were not therefore accepted by the Court of Appeal as the equivalent of cash, leading Ormrod LJ to state that 'No one has any clear idea what the net value of this property is if it were sold. It is not likely to be anything near as much as £100,000'.[31] It is submitted that the key word in this passage is 'net'.[32]

**13.19** It is of course possible to place before the court valuation evidence (whether on a going concern and/or break up basis) and additionally the potential direct and indirect costs of sale so that the net value of the farm as an asset can be ascertained.[33] Obtaining the net value of a farm would make for a more accurate comparison between the value of liquid and illiquid assets. On the facts of *P v P* it seems unlikely that knowing the net value of the farm would in any event have resulted in a different order. Whether and the extent to which valuation evidence is required is clearly case specific. Due to the historic nature of accounts and the historic valuation and subsequent writing down of assets, it is likely that in most cases a valuation of the farmland and the farm business will be required to supplement any accounts. Identifying the net value of the assets, whether on sale or liquidation, is unlikely to be disproportionately expensive once the cost of valuation has already been incurred.

**13.20** In *P v P (Financial Provision: Lump Sum)* the husband had sought to establish both the value of his actual interests as a partner in the farming business and the increase to the value of the property resulting from his endeavours. Lord Justice Ormrod did not 'find it particularly helpful to try to ascertain and quantify his so-called interests. It is useful to ascertain these interests in a broad way so that one can see the justice of each side's case, but I would prefer to avoid quantifying or seeking to quantify these rights in terms of figures ...'.[34]

---

[30]   [1978] 1 WLR 483 at 487C.

[31]   [1978] 1 WLR 483 at 487F.

[32]   In *White v White* [1998] 2 FLR 310 at 319 Thorpe LJ makes reference to *P v P* stating, 'I would only say that the difference between a paper value of an interest in a farm partnership and cash in hand is dependent only upon the judgment of the valuer and future market fluctuations. Of course real value can only be established by signing a contract for the sale of land and by the fall of [the] hammer on the last lot of the farm sale. Of course there are substantial costs in turning farm assets into cash ... But there are few assets more stable, more predictably realisable and more proof against inflation than prime agricultural land.' In *White* it is recorded (at 313C) that a figure for the liquidation value of the farm was obtained for trial.

[33]   Of course, potential CGT implications on sale should be determined. It is frequently useful to instruct an expert to advise not only on CGT implications but options to mitigate the tax liabilities.

[34]   [1978] 1 WLR 483 at 489H. Note that this approach is echoed in *White v White* [2000] 2 FLR 981 at 995F–H.

**13.21**   Another factor that weighed heavily in the mind of the court was the very large contribution made by the wife to the welfare of the family that arose from her father having conveyed to her the freehold interest in the farm. Inherited or gifted assets are frequently encountered in farming ancillary relief cases, and the issue was considered in some detail in both *White v White*[35] and *P v P (Inherited Property)*.[36] The proper approach that a court should take to such assets was identified in a well-known passage in Lord Nicholls's speech in *White*:[37]

> 'Plainly, when present, this factor is one of the circumstances of the case. It represents a contribution made to the welfare of the family by one of the parties to the marriage. The judge should take it into account. He should decide how important it is in the particular case. The nature and value of the property, and the time when and circumstances in which the property was acquired, are among the relevant matters to be considered. However, in the ordinary course, this factor can be expected to carry little weight, if any, in a case where the claimant's financial needs cannot be met without recourse to this property.'

**13.22**   In *P v P (Financial Provision: Lump Sum)* the Court of Appeal determined the level of the lump sum to be paid, having regard to the need to avoid killing the goose that lays the golden egg. On the facts of the case, the lump sum ordered satisfied the husband's housing needs and did not destroy the business of the farm, which was required by the wife to provide income to maintain herself and the children. Interestingly, there was little apparent evidence or indeed apparent discussion before the court about how much could be raised by the wife against the security of the farm without destroying the integrity of the business. The evidence was that the farm was mortgage free, with a valuation of £102,000. Yet the lump sum required to be raised represented just less than 15% of the value of the farm. Could a larger sum have been raised? We of course will never know the answer to this question, but it is clearly of relevance to obtain evidence about borrowing capacity. In order to explore borrowing capacity, a specialist agricultural finance house, such as the Agricultural Mortgage Corporation,[38] for example, should be approached, as should any bank with which the farm business holds a bank account.

**13.23**   Another possible source of capital generation is the sale and lease back of farm land.[39] Such a scheme could in an appropriate case raise capital without unduly harming the income earning capacity of the farming business. Once again, it will be necessary to take advice from a specialist agricultural valuer if this option is to be pursued.

**13.24**   Raising capital is one thing, repaying it is frequently another. In *P v P* the trading accounts for the farm were not before the court and it is, with respect, difficult to see merely from reading the judgment how the court could

---

[35]   [2000] 2 FLR 981.
[36]   [2005] 1 FLR 576.
[37]   [2000] 2 FLR 981 at 994F.
[38]   www.amconline.co.uk.
[39]   As suggested by Munby J in *P v P (Inherited Property)* [2005] 1 FLR 576 at 582.

have reached the conclusion that any larger sum which might have been raised could not have been afforded. It will be necessary therefore to pay close attention to the trading accounts of any farm in order to evaluate whether the repayments on any loan can be afforded.

**13.25** There are two further aspects of the judgment in *P v P* that are of interest. Both stem from arguments made on behalf of the husband and both were rejected by the Court of Appeal. First, the husband argued in support of his claim for a larger lump sum that he required around £30,000 to set himself up as a tenant farmer so that he could begin to earn his living again. The court ignored the argument in the absence of 'positive evidence that a tenancy of a farm was available to him or would be likely to be available to him'.[40] Whether the provision of the evidence would have changed the outcome of the case is a matter of speculation. Nevertheless, the dictum indicates the importance of the provision of evidence to underpin arguments justifying quantum.

**13.26** Secondly, the husband sought to claim a deferred payment in the event of the farm being sold. This argument was rejected. Nevertheless, deferred payments ought to be considered as part of the creative settlement of farming cases. Where a spouse has worked hard to build up the capital in an asset over a number of years, there is certainly an argument to be made that fairness requires that spouse where possible to share in the capital gain.[41] An example of a charge over farm assets can be found in *Webber v Webber*,[42] where a charge was ordered equal to one-quarter of the net proceeds of sale of the farm after deducting the first £50,000 and excluding 32 acres.

## CONTRIBUTION

**13.27** Orders requiring the sale of part or parts of a farm business have been made not merely to meet needs but also to reflect contribution. In *S v S*[43] the lump sum awarded, which was considerably in excess of the wife's needs, was made to give some recognition to the wife's 'contribution in building up the husband's present assets, while not being of such an amount that to realise it would cripple the husband'.[44] Whilst the lump sum awarded was £375,000, a clear limiting factor on the size of the award was the effect of the order on the husband's farming enterprise and of any break up of the farm on the village in which farm workers lived.

---

[40]  [1978] 1 WLR 483 at 488G.
[41]  In the context of a non-farming case see *Elliot v Elliot* [2001] 1 FCR 477, CA.
[42]  (1982) Fam Law 179.
[43]  (1980) Fam Law 240, Balcombe J. The case was appealed (unreported) 16 July 1980, CA. It was also an authority cited in support of the wife in *White v White*.
[44]  (1980) Fam Law 240 at 241.

## ADJOURNING LUMP SUM APPLICATIONS

**13.28**   In rare and circumscribed cases a court may be prepared to adjourn an application for a lump sum.[45] This course was taken and subsequently approved by the Court of Appeal in *Davies v Davies*,[46] where the husband was in a farming partnership with a third party. The partnership was in difficulty, although not doomed. The decision not to force the husband to dissolve the partnership in order to raise money to provide the wife with a lump sum was coupled with a provision adjourning the wife's lump sum application. Such an approach was permissible because there was a real possibility that the partnership would be dissolved in the near future and that, if it was, there would be capital available which would fall to be considered in relation to an application for a lump sum order. The real possibility of sums being available in the near future, and not a mere remote hope or expectation, grounds the possibility of adjourning a lump sum application. Adjourning a lump sum application is a useful tool, albeit sparingly ordered.

## FINANCIAL MISCONDUCT

**13.29**   Many farming businesses encounter periods of difficulty. Sometimes the financial conduct of the farmer running the business is subject to scrutiny. To amount to conduct that it would be inequitable for the court to disregard is a high threshold to meet. The conduct required should be both obvious and gross. In *Moorish v Moorish*[47] financial misconduct was established. The court had evidence and accounts of the history of losses in recent years. The judge concluded that 'the husband had been managing the farm in an entirely wasteful way and that the continuation of the business under his management would lead to a progressive reduction of the assets and the farm would have to be sold'. This finding was upheld on appeal, the Court of Appeal going on to distinguish the case 'from those cases in which the court had been asked to make an order for a lump sum which would involve the closure and sale of the husband's viable business. Those principles could not be applied in the instant case since the husband had not been enhancing or preserving the capital but wasting it'.[48] The extent of the waste and mismanagement required before financial misconduct is made out is unclear from the report in *Moorish* and is in any event unlikely to be capable of definition. Whether waste and mismanagement are obvious and gross will depend upon the facts of each

---

[45]   See also Chapter 18, where the adjournment of lump sums is considered in the context of expectations of inheritance. Many of the principles are of general application.

[46]   [1986] 1 FLR 497.

[47]   (1984) Fam Law 26, CA. See also *Beach v Beach* [1995] 2 FLR 160 at 169 where the farmer/husband was found to have 'obstinately, unrealistically and selfishly trailed on to eventual disaster, dissipating in the process not only his money but his family's money, his friends' money, the money of commercial creditors unsecured and eventually his wife's money'. Not surprisingly, on his application for all forms of ancillary relief the husband was awarded merely such sum as would provide him with some basic accommodation.

[48]   (1984) Fam Law 26 at 27. Unfortunately, the short report of the case does not indicate the extent of the mismanagement, nor whether the farm was viable at the time of the order.

individual case. In *Dennis v Dennis*[49] financial misconduct was not established. The allegation against the husband in the case was that he had squandered assets. The husband's evidence was merely that he had lost money on renovation and purchases and in the carrying on of the business of the farm. In order to amount to financial misconduct, merely making a loss or incurring debt during the course of running a business is insufficient.

## WHITE V WHITE

**13.30**   *White v White*[50] is, of course, both a farming case and a landmark decision in ancillary relief. Mrs White was 62, her husband 61, and their marriage failed after 33 years. There were three adult children of the marriage. The history of their farming partnership was set out as follows by Lord Nicholls:[51]

> 'Throughout their marriage Mr and Mrs White carried on a dairy farming business in partnership. Farming was in their blood. They both came from farming families. The business was successful. At the outset each of them contributed, in cash or in kind, a more or less equal amount of capital, of about £2,000. A year after their marriage they bought a farm of their own, set in beautiful countryside in Somerset. Blagroves Farm comprised 160 acres of land. Blagroves itself, in which they made their home together, was a fine Jacobean house. The price was £32,000. Of this, £21,000 was borrowed on mortgage. Mr White's father made them an interest-free loan of £11,000, together with a further £3,000 used as working capital. Over time, they bought further land, substantially increasing the size of the farm. Eventually the farm comprised 337 acres. Throughout, Blagroves Farm and all the land were held by the two of them jointly. The whole was treated as property of the farming partnership. In 1974 Mr White's father released his loan. Initially this was reflected in an increase in Mr White's partnership capital account. Ten years later Mr and Mrs White's capital accounts were merged into a single joint capital account.
>
> Blagroves Farm, with its live and dead stock and machinery, together with milk quota, were Mr and Mrs White's principal assets. At the end of 1996, when the applications came before Holman J, these items were worth, in round figures, £3.5 million.
>
> Mr and Mrs White also farmed Rexton Farm as part of their partnership business. This farm also comprised over 300 acres. Rexton Farm was 10 miles from Blagroves Farm, but the two were run as a single unit. Rexton was part of the Willett estate. Mr White's father bought this estate in 1971 at an advantageous price, mainly with the assistance of borrowings. Later he transferred the estate into the joint names of himself and his three sons. The four of them held the estate in equal shares. Mr White's share of the cost of borrowing, in the form of interest

---

[49]   (1975) Fam Law 54.
[50]   [1998] 2 FLR 310, CA and [2000] 2 FLR 981, HL. This book is not intended to be a general guide to the principles of ancillary relief. Consequently, the broader consequences of *White* are not dealt with in any detail.
[51]   [2000] 2 FLR 981 at 984.

and endowment premiums, was met, through a tenancy agreement, by the Whites' farming partnership. In 1993 Mr White acquired Rexton Farm, subject to a mortgage debt of £137,000, as his partitioned share of the Willett estate. Rexton Farm, as distinct from the farming business carried on at the farm, was held in Mr White's sole name. Unlike Blagroves Farm, it was not in joint names, nor was it treated as belonging to the Whites' partnership. Rexton Farm was worth £1.25 million.

Mr and Mrs White had also made pension provision for themselves. A substantial mortgage was outstanding on both farms. After deduction of estimated liabilities for capital gains tax and costs of sale, the overall net worth of Mr and Mrs White's assets was, in round figures, £4.6 million. This comprised, on the figures found and used by the judge: Mrs White's sole property: £193,300 (mostly pension provision); her share of property owned jointly, either directly or through the partnership: £1,334,000; Mr White's share of jointly owned property: £1,334,000; and Mr White's sole property: £1,783,500 (mostly Rexton Farm).'

**13.31** At first instance, Holman J awarded Mrs White a lump sum payment of £800,000. The first issue decided by the learned judge was whether Mrs White should be entitled to fulfil her desire to continue to farm. It was held not to be justifiable to break up the existing farming enterprise to enable Mrs White to embark upon a speculative farming venture in her own right. The second issue determined by the judge was whether it was right to make a net transfer of assets from Mrs White to her husband. The judge assessed Mrs White's reasonable requirements by reference to the sum she needed to buy and equip a suitable alternative home coupled with an additional *Duxbury* fund to provide for her capitalised income needs. After deduction of a pension and minor investments in her sole name, the lump sum required to satisfy Mrs White's reasonable requirements was £800,000. The learned judge found that Mrs White had net assets to the value of £1.5m in her own name. Having so found, the judge then considered whether it would be fair to Mrs White to restrict her to her reasonable requirements if the effect of such an order would be a net transfer of assets from Mrs White to her husband. The learned judge held that such a restriction was justifiable on the facts of the case and that consequently Mrs White was to receive a lesser lump sum than the paper value of the assets in her name. In reaching this conclusion Holman J took into account the traditional distinction drawn between an interest in farm land and cash, the financial contribution from Mr White's father and finally an award of 1/5th of the total assets was thought not so low as to be unfair, since it met Mrs White's reasonable needs and because it reflected the well-known paradox that the longer the marriage and hence the older the wife, the lower the sum required for a *Duxbury* type fund. In restricting the wife to her reasonable requirements and seeking to maintain both the integrity and viability of Blagroves and Rexton farm, the judgment echoed many earlier farming authorities.

**13.32** Mrs White successfully appealed to the Court of Appeal. It was held to have been wrong for Holman J to have formulated the first fundamental issue in the case as he did. The dominant factor in the case was the fact that the parties chose to trade as equal partners and, by opting for equal partnership, the parties had introduced a legal mechanism for determining their resources. Mrs White was entitled to have the judge determine:

> 'what was hers in law and equity insofar as that was disputed. That share once determined was hers to deploy, to spend, or to invest as she thought fit. Her entitlement to farm with what was hers was absolute and the judge simply had no function to criticise her plan to farm independently with what was hers. Only insofar as she sought additional capital from the husband by way of lump sum or property adjustment was the judge entitled to evaluate critically the use to which such additional capital was proposed to be put.'[52]

**13.33** The Court of Appeal also found that it had been wrong to require a net transfer of assets from Mrs White to her husband. It was said to have been discriminatory on the facts of the case to assess the husband's but not the wife's reasonable requirements as including being able to farm in a worthwhile way. The fact that a greater contribution had come from the husband's family could be reflected in the extent of the share of the assets that each could take into independent farming. On the quite exceptional facts of the case there was 'no basis for an expectation that the husband should be protected against substantial realisations and that the quantification of the wife's share should be conversely restricted to what he could raise by borrowing and minor sales'.[53] Dicta from earlier cases would need to be re-examined in the light of social change, especially where a wife worked in partnership alongside her husband, a phenomenon rarely encountered in earlier authorities. Thorpe LJ rejected the distinction between an interest in farmland and cash. Any difference between the two was 'dependent only upon the judgment of the valuer and future market fluctuations'; additionally, 'there are few assets more stable, more predictably realisable and more proof against inflation than prime agricultural land'.[54] Finally, restricting a wife after a long marriage to a *Duxbury* award was unfair. *Duxbury* is a tool not a rule. In conclusion, it was not fair for a wife who worked as an equal partner for more than 30 years to be awarded less than her entitlement on dissolution of the partnership 'in the absence of extraordinary features'.[55]

**13.34** Having reached the conclusion that the decision of Holman J had been wrong, the Court of Appeal exercised its discretion afresh and awarded Mrs White a lump sum of £1.5 million. In arriving at that figure Thorpe LJ took into account the fact that there were evidential problems in determining Mrs White's absolute entitlement on dissolution. The value of the net assets had in all probability reduced due to problems in the dairy industry, and consequently there was real doubt whether the assets valued by Holman J at £4.5 million net would be valued at anything over £4 million. Mrs White's contribution under MCA 1973, s 25(2)(f) as wife and mother would also need

---

[52]  [1998] 2 FLR 310 at 318F per Thorpe LJ.
[53]  [1998] 2 FLR 310 at 319C per Thorpe LJ.
[54]  [1998] 2 FLR 310 at 319G.
[55]  [1998] 2 FLR 310 at 320C per Thorpe LJ.

to be taken into account, as would the significant contribution made by Mr White's father, without which Mr White's acquisition of the share of the Willett estate would not have occurred. Indeed, without that contribution, Thorpe LJ thought there would be a very strong case for the equal division of all the assets of the marriage. The lump sum ordered by the Court of Appeal was not thought likely to 'inhibit the husband from continuing to farm at least one of the farms. Whether the wife chooses to put the money in a farm or use it otherwise is entirely a matter for her'.[56]

**13.35**   Mr and Mrs White both appealed to the House of Lords. Both appeals were dismissed. The speeches in the House of Lords contain what are now well-known statements of general principle, such as the principles of equality, fairness and the yardstick of equality.[57] However, from the perspective of farming ancillary relief cases it is important to note that the fresh exercise of discretion carried out by the Court of Appeal was upheld. It is, however, worth considering some of the criticisms made of the Court of Appeal. Lord Nicholls stated that the statutory provisions of MCA 1973, s 25(2) 'lend no support to the idea that a claimant's financial needs, even interpreted generously and called reasonable requirements, are to be regarded as determinative'.[58] Consequently, Mr White's appeal to limit his wife's award to reasonable requirements was dismissed.

**13.36**   Mr White's counsel also criticised the members of the Court of Appeal for placing undue emphasis on the financial worth of each party on the dissolution of their partnership and also for purporting to decide the case on the basis that the court should not exercise its discretionary powers unless there was 'a manifest case for intervention'. Lord Nicholls doubted whether this approach was intended by either Thorpe LJ or Butler-Sloss LJ. In supporting this view, Lord Nicholls said:

> 'Indeed, Butler-Sloss LJ stated expressly that what she had in mind, where parties were in business together, was a broad assessment of the financial position and not a detailed partnership account. She rightly noted that, even in such a case, the parties' proprietorial interests should not be allowed to dominate the picture'.

**13.37**   Finally, Mrs White's counsel criticised the use of net values, arrived at after deducting estimates of the costs and capital gains tax likely to be incurred on sale of the farms. This criticism was rejected. When making comparisons it was important to compare like with like. Whilst Mrs White was to be awarded a lump sum, the equivalent comparison for Mr White was with the net value of the farms, because 'the farms would have to be sold before he can have money to invest or use in other ways'.[59]

---

[56]   [1998] 2 FLR 310 at 325C per Butler-Sloss LJ.
[57]   This book is not intended to deal with general principles of ancillary relief and detailed consideration of general points of principle is better discussed elsewhere.
[58]   [2000] 2 FLR 981 at 992D.
[59]   [2000] 2 FLR 981 at 996G.

**13.38**  *White v White* was a big money, long marriage case. One consequence of the decision in the case was to remove the upper ceiling on a wife's entitlement once her reasonable requirements had been met. Another was that departures from equality of division were required to be both justified and non-discriminatory. Where a husband and wife were in partnership together after a long marriage, there had to be good reason to depart from equality of division. Where needs were met, the existence of 'inherited' property was a sufficiently good factor to justify departure from equality even in a long marriage and business partnership case. Finally, with the emphasis of the court switching from the calculation of reasonable requirements to the calculation and division of assets, the old reticence against selling farms ought to have been devalued. It follows that in a big money farming case the effect of the decision in *White* was clearly enormous. However, in farming cases where the assets are more modest and where needs predominate, the impact of the case has been far less marked.

## POST-*WHITE*

**13.39**  The first significant reported farming case after *White* was *R v R (Lump Sum Repayments)*.[60] In that case the husband and wife had been married for 16 years and had two children who had left school and were working. The parties were in their early 40s. The husband was a farmer. The farming business was operated through a long-established family company. The husband owned 6.18% of the shares in the company. The executors of the estate of the husband's father held 53% of the shares of the company on trust for the husband's mother for life and thereafter as to 5/8ths of those shares for the husband. The husband's mother was 77 years of age. Upon the death of his mother, the husband would hold 39.5% of the shares of the company. The value of the shares in possession and in remainder on a pro rata basis was £1.5 million and, discounted for a minority interest, but not additionally for the mother's life interest, was £448,000.

**13.40**  The farm business was carried out on two sites. H lived in a cottage on one site and W lived in a farmhouse on the other site, surrounded by H's relatives. The 'grave conundrum' for the court was how to:

> 'contrive a raft of arrangements which enable the wife with the children to vacate the farmhouse at B Farm, to move to other accommodation and to live there at a reasonable level without disabling the husband from also living at a reasonable level. The bulk of the husband's shares are not yet in possession and, even when they fall into possession, they will represent a minority interest in a long-established family company which provides the husband with his livelihood.

---

[60]  [2004] 1 FLR 928, Wilson J.

Thus there are substantial question marks about the husband's ability to realise the proportionate value of the very substantial assets which may on paper be ascribed to the shares.'[61]

**13.41** The solution adopted by Wilson J was for the wife to buy a property in her name funded by way of a mortgage. The husband was required to pay a lump sum in monthly instalments, all but one of which would be equivalent to the wife's mortgage payments. The advantage of a lump sum payable in instalments was that the obligation would survive the re-marriage or death of the wife and, like periodical payments, could be varied.[62] The obligation would be secured by the wife holding a first charge over the husband's shares in the company. The charge was of value, since the wife could exercise all the rights of a minority shareholder and could take steps to squeeze cash value out of the shares, perhaps by seeking to persuade the company to buy them back. An order for periodical payments was made in favour of the wife. This left the husband ultimately with £13,007 net per annum, with the learned judge noting that the 'modesty of this residue seems unfair to the husband only until one remembers the astonishing width of the expenses met for him directly out of the company'.[63]

**13.42** When considering the husband's financial resources, Wilson J identified three areas where a careful analysis of the husband's financial position could increase the value of the assets that were available for distribution by the court. First, that whilst the balance sheet of the company showed assets of £851,000, the true real value of the assets was in fact much higher. Indeed the district judge found that the real value of the assets of the company amounted to about £3.8 million. The learned judge noted that the 'real property owned by the company is quite legitimately entered into the accounts at cost and indeed is depreciated year by year'.[64] In addition to real property, the balance sheet for a farm business will include other items of fixed assets, such as machinery and equipment, which will frequently be undervalued for the same reason. It is important to ensure that the true values of the assets of the farm business are placed before the court. In most cases the value of these assets and the direct and indirect (ie taxation) costs of sale should be obtained in advance of trial (and preferably before the FDR if a sale is being considered) from an agricultural valuer. When considering assets of the business, the single farm payment, milk quota and any other remaining subsidies ought also to be brought into account. These assets are frequently not identified in the accounts, since farm balance sheets fail to reflect a subsidy that is awarded and not purchased.

---

[61]  [2004] 1 FLR 928 at 934. It was also accepted both on the evidence and by way of judicial notice that the husband's shareholding was not acceptable security for mainstream lending institutions.

[62]  A lump sum by instalments order can be varied by suspending the payments or altering the time for payment rather than by variation of the overall quantum of the lump sum: see *Tilley v Tilley* (1979) 10 Fam Law 89 and *Penrose v Penrose* [1994] 2 FLR 621. However, variation of quantum is highly exceptional: see **27.48–27.61**.

[63]  [2004] 1 FLR 928 at 943. See **13.43**.

[64]  [2004] 1 FLR 928 at 931.

**13.43** The second point of interest in respect of resources relates to a farmer's income. The point was made by the learned judge as follows:[65]

'Before the district judge evidence was given that the husband's gross income from the company for the year most recently ended was £41,309 pa. It may now be seen that, for the year ended 31 October 2002, his income was the same. But, to use a well-worn cliché, that income is only the tip of the iceberg for, as the district judge found, this husband, like many other farmers, quite legitimately enjoys payment by the company directly on his behalf in the form of benefits-in-kind of very many expenses which the rest of us have to meet out of our net income. Thus, of course, he pays no rent for the farmhouse, and the company pays water rates, council tax, electricity bills, gas bills, telephone bills and property insurance referable to that house. It also pays his mobile telephone bills, pays for health insurance and supplies him with a car, although the husband implies in an affidavit that at least some of its running expenses, perhaps those not considered to relate to farm use, are met by himself. All these benefits-in-kind are taxable but only at a value identified by the district judge at £4,038 pa. The district judge accepted that the real value of the benefits-in-kind was much greater, indeed, as I would say, vastly greater. My experience would lead me to place a value of at least £20,000 pa gross upon all these benefits but their precise quantification is unnecessary and has not been the subject of submission.'

**13.44** It is clear that in order to unlock assets, in every case, close scrutiny will need to be had to the true income of a farmer. In most cases a strategically raised questionnaire, prepared sometimes with the help of a forensic accountant, will be of great assistance.

**13.45** A third and related point is that Wilson J found that, aside from the benefits in kind, the husband could increase the salary paid to him by the family company. It is worth setting out all the factors relied upon by the learned judge in reaching that conclusion as a foundation for similar arguments in future cases:[66]

'Exclusive of the benefits-in-kind, the husband's present income is £41,309 pa gross. I have promoted a considerable amount of debate as to whether that figure might reasonably be subject to substantial increase. Of course the level of directors' remuneration is fixed by the directors, no doubt usually following advice from the auditors, and is subject to the overall approval of the shareholders. Nevertheless the husband's voice – and the extent of his financial obligations under English law – would play a big part in any reasonable deliberation on the subject.

The husband explains that it is company policy for his remuneration to be linked to the results of the farming aspect of the business, while that of his cousin would be linked to the results referable to warehousing and potatoes. It seems to me that any decision about his future remuneration should reasonably have regard to the following factors among others:

---

[65]    [2004] 1 FLR 928 at 931.
[66]    [2004] 1 FLR 928 at [43]–[45].

(a) his remuneration has not been increased for at least 3 years;
(b) even when, following the separation, the wife ceased to be nominally employed by the company for tax purposes, there was no corresponding adjustment in his favour;
(c) in the year ended 31 October 2002 the farming business, after allowing for his remuneration, made a loss of £6,000 as opposed to a loss during the preceding year of £103,000;
(d) in the same year the consolidated figures for both strands of the company's business indicated a pre-tax profit of £80,000 as opposed to a loss in the preceding year of £72,000;
(e) as at 31 October 2002 the company held cash at the bank in the sum of £168,000 and felt able to leave outstanding a loan of £390,000 owed to it by a wholesaler of soft drinks, being a transaction not directly related to any aspect of the company's core business;
(f) the husband expects the farming results for the year 31 October 2003 to be broadly similar to those for the previous year;
(g) on vacation by the wife of the farmhouse at B Farm the husband will cease to be subject to any tax levy referable to that particular benefit-in-kind; and
(h) more importantly, upon her vacation of it, the company will be able to let the property and, to an extent that such is relevant, the rental income will be included in the farming side of the company's results. The district judge adopted a possible annual figure for rental of £15,000. In that the farmhouse was valued at about £600,000, a rental equivalent to 2.5% of value seems extraordinarily low. Perhaps, being situate in or near the middle of a working farm, its rental value would suffer but I take the suggested figure of £15,000 pa as an absolute minimum.

The combination of these eight factors leads me to the confident conclusion that, as the husband virtually conceded, he could probably secure a substantial increase in his remuneration. I believe that it could reasonably be increased to above £60,000 pa gross but, erring perhaps on the side of caution, I propose to work upon that gross figure, which amounts net to £38,350 pa, on top of which he will continue to enjoy the substantial benefits-in-kind.'

**13.46** Following *White v White* the learned judge found the wife's contribution 'as a wife, a mother and a homemaker was, however, no less valuable than if it had been directly, as opposed to indirectly, productive of income for the family'.[67] The importance of the fact that the vast bulk of the capital was represented by the shares in the company which the husband obtained by a combination of gift and inheritance was also of significance. This factor, coupled with the difficulties in realising the value of the husband's interests in the company, would have justified a departure from equality,[68] especially since the learned judge's creative order satisfied the wife's needs. It should be noted that the case was not a big money case and consequently *White* had little material impact on the outcome.[69]

---

[67] [2004] 1 FLR 928 at [23].
[68] See the speech of Baroness Hale in *Miller v Miller; McFarlane v McFarlane* [2006] 1 FLR 1186 at [148], where both the source and nature of the asset could justify departures from equality.
[69] Indeed, *White* was not even expressly cited in the judgment.

**13.47** The impact of *White v White* on a farming case was carefully considered by Munby J in *P v P (Inherited Property)*.[70] In *P v P* the husband and wife had been married 18 years to petition. There were two children of the family, aged 18 and 16. Both the husband and the wife were farmers. Throughout their marriage they farmed a hill farm that had been in the husband's family for some time. Indeed, the husband was the fourth generation of his family to farm the land. Whilst the land was vested in the husband's name, the farming business was a partnership between the husband and the wife. As in *White*, the wife played an active role in the partnership. The family assets, net of notional realisation costs and CGT, totalled £2,501,356. The assets were held as to £2,105,610 by the husband; £70,678 by the wife and the remaining £325,068 by the parties jointly. The vast bulk of the husband's assets were made up of the farm land and a mineral lease. Together these assets totalled over £1.8 million. The joint assets consisted of the value of the partnership assets. The wife sought a lump sum of some £930,000, representing 40% of the total value of the assets. Following *White*, the wife argued a departure from equality on the basis of the husband's inheritance. In the alternative, the wife sought a lump sum of £770,000 broken down between a housing fund of £422,000 and a *Duxbury* fund of £348,000 and a school fees order of £95,000. The husband offered the wife a lump sum of £340,000 (representing a housing fund of £400,000 less the value of the wife's liquid assets).

**13.48** Munby J rejected the wife's primary position that she should be entitled to a division of the assets on a percentage basis. Instead, he concluded that:

> 'in the particular circumstances of this case, the proper approach is to make an award based on the wife's reasonable needs for accommodation and income. I do that, applying the approach adopted by Bennett J in *Norris v Norris* [2002] EWHC 2996 (Fam), [2003] 1 FLR 1142, not (pace Mr Chamberlayne) because of any principle that this is the approach to be adopted in farming cases, but because in the particular circumstances of this case that is the approach which most closely accords with the over-arching requirement of fairness, having regard to all the circumstances but in particular to:
>
> (i) the fact that the bulk of the family's assets represent a farm which has been in the husband's family for generations and which was brought into the marriage with an expectation that it would be retained in specie;[71]
>
> (ii) the fact that although the farm business was put into the parties' joint names, the land and the other tangible assets were retained in the husband's sole name;[72]

---

[70] [2005] 1 FLR 576. Note that both Baroness Hale at [148] and Lord Nicholls at [20] in *Miller v Miller; McFarlane v McFarlane* [2006] 1 FLR 1186 approved Munby J's reasoning.

[71] [2005] 1 FLR 576: Munby J thought (at [37]) that inherited property ought clearly to be taken into account as a contribution made to the welfare of the family, although it was necessary per Lord Nicholls in *White* to 'decide how important it is in the particular case. The nature and value of the property, and the time when and circumstances in which the property was acquired'.

[72] Giving considerable weight to the property arrangements made by the parties during the course of the marriage: see *Parra v Parra* [2003] 1 FLR 942 at [27].

(iii) the fact that any other approach will compel a sale of the farm, with implications little short of devastating for the husband; and

(iv) the fact that this approach will meet the wife's reasonable needs.[73]

In short, because to give this wife more than she reasonably needs for accommodation and income would tip the balance unfairly in her favour and unfairly against the husband.'[74]

**13.49** The learned judge assessed the wife's reasonable needs (consisting of a housing and *Duxbury* fund) and awarded her a lump sum of £575,000. This sum together with the wife's existing assets resulted in her receiving 25% of the total family assets. It is fair to say that the outcome in *P v P (Inherited Property)* would not have been significantly different if it were decided prior to *White*. The outcomes in this case and *R v R (Lump Sum Repayments)* seem to confirm that in non-big money farming cases the impact of *White* on the outcome of a case may not be as significant as may have been first thought. The same is likely to be true of *Miller v Miller; McFarlane v McFarlane*,[75] although clearly the impact of these cases is in the process of filtering down through reported authorities.

## FARM ACCOUNTS AND VALUATION

**13.50** Farming businesses prepare accounts for the same reasons as other types of business, as described in Chapters 11 and 12. These include statutory accounts for farming companies, and partnership (or sole trader) accounts for partnerships and other unincorporated farming businesses. Just as for non-farming businesses, the format and content of these accounts will depend on the purpose for which they are prepared.

**13.51** A distinguishing feature of farming accounts is that they frequently append pages of supporting analysis of trading information, prepared for management purposes, showing details of trading results for different crops or farming activities. This analysis is not prescribed in any statute or accounting standard and therefore, for incorporated farming businesses, would not be placed on public record at Companies House. This additional information is of value to readers of the accounts, but would need to be requested from the directors or partners in the business.

**13.52** Farming businesses are often family-run. A principal asset in the business, the farmhouse, usually doubles up as the family home. Inevitably, domestic and business finances become mixed together and reported through the farming accounts. It can be difficult to identify and separate personal and

---

[73] Of course, the source of the asset will in the 'ordinary course ... carry little weight, if any, in a case where the claimant's financial needs cannot be met without recourse to this property', per Lord Nicholls in *White v White* [2000] 2 FLR 981 at 994G.

[74] *P v P (Inherited Property)* [2005] 1 FLR 576 at [44].

[75] [2006] 1 FLR 1186.

business transactions simply by reviewing the accounts. The corporate and personal tax returns submitted on behalf of the farming company and its proprietors may assist.

**13.53** A characteristic of farming businesses is a low return on the capital employed in the business caused by the ratio of significant assets (particularly land and buildings) to relatively low profits. The profits of farming businesses can be volatile and dependent on many unpredictable factors, including the vagaries of the weather and fluctuating market prices.

## Valuation of farming businesses

**13.54** Many of the principles of valuing unquoted shares and partnerships apply to farming businesses, and these are considered in detail elsewhere,[76] but there are some special features unique to farms that are set out below.

## Agricultural tenancy

**13.55** When valuing a shareholding in a farming business, the first issue to consider is the ownership of the land that is farmed, which may not be owned but held under an agricultural tenancy.

**13.56** Such tenancies can afford considerable protection to the tenant, which in turn adds to the value of the business. Any investigation of the value of the farming business would include consideration of the provisions in the tenancy and any other relevant written agreements. These may include rights to inherit the tenancy upon the retirement or death of the tenant.[77] A professional valuation should be sought.

**13.57** Conversely, if agricultural tenancies have been granted on land owned by the farming business to be valued, they will have a depreciating effect on the value of the land and consequently on the value of the business.

**13.58** It is important for the valuer to consider whether both the freeholder and tenant are within the family (or held by 'close' companies under the control of family members). In these circumstances, it may be appropriate to prepare an additional valuation based on the totality of the family interest, although in doing so it is important to ensure that proper respect is paid to the separate property rights of the various interested parties and also to the doctrine of separate corporate personality. When seeking to persuade a court to look at the totality of a family's interests in farmland it may also be useful to refer to the potentially related themes considered in the sections of this book which deal

---

[76] See Chapters 11 and 12.
[77] See the statutory rights of succession to certain tenancies under the Agricultural Holdings Act 1986 and also the consideration of future inheritance prospects in Chapter 18.

with lifting the corporate veil,[78] future inheritance prospects,[79] judicial encouragement,[80] and sham arrangements.[81]

## No land assets

**13.59**   If the farming business does not own any agricultural land, either freehold, leasehold or via an agricultural tenancy,[82] then a valuation of the business would generally follow the principles set out in Chapters 11 and 12, treating it as a normal, non-farming trading company or partnership. However, there are no quoted farming companies on the London Stock Exchange, so an exercise to compare an unquoted farming business with comparable quoted companies would not be possible.

## Land owned

**13.60**   If the farming business owns the land it farms (or has an agricultural tenancy), it is generally appropriate to value the shares on an assets basis rather than an earnings basis,[83] particularly for majority shareholdings.

**13.61**   A professional agricultural valuation of the land should be sought, as property is often held in the farm accounts at a fraction of its open market value, usually by adopting the acquisition value which is out of date and by applying notional depreciation to the value of the land.

**13.62**   It is worth considering alternative use valuations for the land too, particularly if the business has been making significant losses and the farm is located close to a residential area.

**13.63**   The farming business may own other assets requiring a professional valuation, including:

- subsidies under the Single Payment Scheme (see below);

- livestock (particularly if they are included in the accounts on the herd basis, which reflects historical costs);

- milk quotas after 1984; and

- specialised plant and machinery, such as combine harvesters and milking parlours.

---

[78]   See **11.76–11.85**.
[79]   Chapter 18.
[80]   See **15.46–15.53**.
[81]   See **15.69** and **7.7**.
[82]   It is not uncommon to find farming business operating in land subject to informal arrangements which do not amount to a lease and which provide very limited rights of tenure.
[83]   See **11.161** et seq for an explanation of different bases of valuation.

## The Single Payment Scheme

**13.64**  Under the CAP Reform package, the Single Payment Scheme (SPS) replaced 11 subsidy schemes with one new single payment. As a result, farmers should have greater freedom to farm to the demands of the market, as subsidies will be decoupled from production, and environmentally friendly farming practices will be better acknowledged and rewarded. The SPS took effect from 2005 and most existing production subsidies and quotas were replaced with the new single payment.

**13.65**  In broad terms, the SPS is based on a division of England into three areas: English moorland within the upland Severely Disadvantaged Areas (SDA); other English upland SDA; and England outside the upland SDA.

**13.66**  Every farmer who applied to the SPS in 2005 received an entitlement for each hectare of eligible land (including all arable and horticultural land as well as temporary grassland) that was declared in the application.

**13.67**  The single payment is taxable in the hands of the recipient. It is included in the trading income of individual farmers, partnerships or farming companies or taxed as 'income not otherwise charged' for others (eg landowners who have ceased farming).

**13.68**  If the recipient leases the entitlement to the payment with land he or she is letting, rents received will be taxable, but the element related to the single payment entitlement will remain taxable as 'income not otherwise charged'.

**13.69**  An entitlement to the payment is an asset in itself. Should the entitlement be sold with land, a separate capital gains tax calculation will be required. The entitlement will qualify for business property relief from inheritance tax on a transfer from the owner, provided it has been owned for 2 years and is transferred as part of the business.

**13.70**  The DEFRA website explains the impact of SPS on land values and rental prices:

'In order to claim the annual payment, those holding entitlements will need to farm, or at least keep in good agricultural and environmental condition, an equivalent number of hectares to that which established the entitlement.

This means that, depending on the method of allocation there are likely to be many farmers, including tenants, with an entitlement who would need to find land to attach it to in order to generate payments. Consequently, our initial assessment is that, while we might expect a greater equalisation of land values between land currently registered for arable area aid and that which is not, a marked change in average values seems unlikely.

It follows that landowners should continue to experience a benefit from the subsidy system in terms of land and rental values, although the nature of that benefit will probably vary according to individual circumstances.'

**13.71**   Clearly this is a specialised area and expert valuation advice should be sought.

## Minority interest[84]

**13.72**   When valuing a minority shareholding in a farming company, it is important to consider who owns the remaining shares. Most farming companies are family-owned. In such circumstances it is unusual for a minority interest to be sold outside of the family. An outside purchaser of even a significant minority interest could not guarantee that he or she would be allowed to contribute to the running of the company.

**13.73**   Furthermore, given that the farm is not only a source of income but the family home and a way of life, the prospects of realising any return on the investment may be more remote than investments in non-farming companies.

**13.74**   It is not uncommon for farming companies to make losses for several consecutive years. It is comparatively rare for dividends to be paid to shareholders and so the 'dividends basis' of valuation, which is often appropriate for minority shareholdings in non-farming companies, is not usually suitable.

**13.75**   Minority holdings in farming companies are not worthless, though, because the asset base is often substantial (principally in the form of the land owned) and the shares have a value to the other existing shareholders. A valuer may therefore treat a minority interest in a farming company in a similar way to one in a property investment company, albeit applying much larger discounts for lack of influence over the company's affairs and remoteness of dividends, as described above.

## RELEASING ASSETS FROM FARMS

**13.76**   Because the income from farming businesses is usually low in relation to the capital value of the business assets, it can be difficult for the departing spouse to demonstrate that the one remaining can afford maintenance payments or finance a loan taken out to make a capital payment.

**13.77**   Investigations should be made of surplus land, property or other assets within the farm that are not essential to ongoing business operations and whether these could be sold to raise a capital sum. Where the land is owned jointly with persons who are not parties to the marriage, many of the issues

---

[84]   See also **11.198–11.202**.

raised in Chapters 8 and 9 may arise,[85] and reference should be made to those sections as appropriate. Consideration will also need to be given to development potential of any of the land, both immediate and in the foreseeable future.[86]

## OTHER TAXATION ISSUES

**13.78**   Because of the volatility of agricultural profits, farmers have an option to average 2 consecutive years' results for income tax purposes in order to make best use of personal allowances and the basic rate tax band.

**13.79**   For inheritance tax purposes, Agricultural or Business Property Relief may be available on the transfer of farming assets.

**13.80**   The capital gains tax consequences of disposal of farm assets can prove to be very complex, and expert calculations of such liabilities will be required in most cases.

---

[85]   For example, dealing with third party interests (see **8.9–8.16**) and partition of land (see **9.23–9.25**).

[86]   See **9.13–9.16**.

# Chapter 14

# RAISING FINANCE FROM BUSINESS ASSETS

## INTRODUCTION

**14.1** Where a material part of one spouse's wealth or earnings is derived from business assets, careful consideration needs to be given to how the value of those assets can be realised, the cost of realisation (including tax consequences) and how the aggregate value may be shared.

**14.2** This chapter deals predominantly with incorporated businesses. Whilst a partnership may give rise to an income stream by way of a share of profits and a capital value attached to the capital account, it is nevertheless very difficult, short of dissolution and winding up, to raise finance from or against a partnership share. Subject to the terms of any deed of partnership, it is not usually open to sell a partnership interest without the consent of the other partners. In contrast, incorporated businesses are far more susceptible to creative schemes for raising finance in the context of divorce proceedings. The aim of this chapter is to identify some of the more common methods for raising finance from corporate assets.[1]

**14.3** It is important to bear in mind that forced sales generally achieve lower prices. Getting the timing and process right for realisation is crucial to protect the interests of both spouses. In the worst case scenario, a sale of shares at a reduced price owing to the timescales set by the parties in dispute (or the court) will reduce the combined wealth of both parties. When considering any distribution of business assets, advisers need to be mindful of the timescales necessary to achieve a sale at a full market price.[2] Furthermore, in contested proceedings evidence as to the effects of a forced sale on the value of the shares must be clearly presented to the court.

**14.4** Similarly, the effective execution of a corporate business plan generates value for a business. Any settlement that compromises the ability and incentives of operational management to achieve that plan will materially destroy value. For example, drawing substantial amounts of capital from a business in order to fund a divorce settlement may compromise the company's ability to develop and trade effectively.

---

[1]  This chapter should be read alongside Chapter 11, which deals with how corporate assets are dealt with in ancillary relief proceedings.

[2]  See **11.94**.

# QUOTED COMPANY SHARES

**14.5**  Quoted company shares are often readily marketable. Even a sizeable holding may be sold to generate finance. However, by no means are all quoted shares listed in markets with sufficient liquidity to permit the sale of a substantial block of shares. In these circumstances, it may be appropriate to aim for a settlement that involves an equitable apportionment of the shareholding itself, rather than attempt to sell the block of shares.

**14.6**  If shares are to be sold, it is prudent to determine a mechanism to ensure an orderly market in the securities. If, for example, one party sought to place a large block of shares in an illiquid market, the impact on the value of the other shareholders' holdings would in all probability be highly negative. This issue arises most often in relatively small companies, often trading on AIM or a similar market, where a large proportion of the shares are held by the employees and management. Occasionally, a similar situation will arise in larger companies, but the greater liquidity in the market for shares in larger companies makes a sale of such a shareholding significantly easier.

**14.7**  The London Stock Exchange has numerous restrictions on the sale of shares by employees and managers. Additionally, when considering the value of a particular shareholding, regard needs to be given to the impact of dividend payment dates and, in the event of a sale, the restrictions upon company 'insiders' trading securities during closed periods prior to company announcements.[3]

**14.8**  Similarly, advisers involved with clients holding shares in companies that are involved in significant transactions (typically mergers and acquisition transactions or profit warnings) need to be aware that legal requirements and Stock Exchange regulations may mean the other party or their advisers cannot be told about significant transactions in advance of a market announcement being made. The parties to a divorce may regard a delay in reaching a settlement as highly undesirable, but yet any apportionment of quoted shares prior to a price sensitive announcement (where only one party is aware of the imminent announcement) may be regarded as iniquitous and perhaps a ground for setting aside the settlement by the other party. Possible ways forward in such a situation are either to delay the valuation or adjourn the application until the significant transaction has been completed. The individual circumstances of each case will need to be considered in order to find the best approach.

**14.9**  Regard should also be given to the fact that the existence of the divorce settlement itself may have price implications for some smaller companies. It follows from the above that it cannot always be assumed that the value of shares in a quoted company can be realised without complications. In some instances the advice of a stockbroker may need to be taken.

---

[3]    See **11.161** et seq for sections on valuing shareholdings.

# UNQUOTED COMPANIES

**14.10** A spouse who has no commercial interest in a business after separation is generally unlikely to wish to continue to hold unquoted shares other than as part of a larger portfolio of investments. Where the business shareholding represents a substantial proportion of the wealth of the marriage, one or other spouse may wish to realise their proportion of that asset in cash. Realisation is frequently complicated where the spouse is not a controlling shareholder. In these circumstances an appropriate solution would be for professional advisers, recognising the non-marketability of the shares, to attempt to agree the valuation of the holding and to reach a solution which factors in the illiquidity of the shareholding.[4]

**14.11** When the shareholding represents a controlling interest in the business, matters are different. If the shares are not marketable, there are, as set out below, essentially five methods by which the value of the shareholding might be unlocked. In many of the cases identified below, attempts at creative solutions will necessitate the involvement of specialist corporate lawyers. In each case the cost of implementing a creative, but complex, solution to the problem will have to be balanced against the relative value of the shares and the circumstances of the case as a whole. It is important for the parties to understand the mutual benefits of adopting a creative solution, because a high degree of co-operation between the parties will usually make such arrangements easier to implement.

## Special dividend payments

**14.12** In cash rich companies with sufficient retained profits, a special dividend may be used to generate cash to achieve a settlement. In other companies, cash may be generated by external borrowings from a bank or the sale and leaseback of fixed assets (usually property) to generate funds to pay the dividend. This is generally not tax efficient, as the dividend will be taxed as income, but costs are not high and timescales are usually relatively short. The dividend would be payable on all shares entitled to receive it, unless the other shareholders can be persuaded to waive it, and therefore there may be material 'leakage' of capital if there is a wide shareholder base. This approach is likely to be appropriate only in the context of a company where the parties to the marriage own the vast majority of the shares.

**14.13** It may be possible to negotiate a staged settlement or a settlement based upon a dividend stream rather than a cash lump sum. For example, it might be agreed that one party is to receive a separate class of shares with preferential dividend rights (perhaps a percentage of all post-tax profits) to create an income stream to compensate for the loss of and/or non-marketability of the capital value of the shares. Creative solutions such as these often appear complex, especially to non-financially literate clients, but can, with goodwill on

---

[4]    See **11.116** et seq.

both sides, be effectively tailored to achieve what is often the best outcome for all concerned. The tax implications will also need to be borne in mind.

## Share buy-back

**14.14** It is possible to reduce the 'leakage' to other shareholders of a special dividend by the company offering to buy back the shareholding of the settling spouse and obtaining the agreement of other shareholders to forego any buy-back option. HM Revenue & Customs will generally regard this as a distribution of profits and will again tax it as income. In order to buy back the shares, sufficient distributable reserves need to be available in the group and passed up to the company. When there are insufficient reserves, a court-sanctioned scheme of arrangement could be sought. A court application is significantly more complicated and expensive than paying a dividend, particularly when external funds need to be raised from banks or similar lending businesses.

## Private placing

**14.15** Where the business prospects are good, it may be possible to place a parcel of shares with a private equity institution. Sourcing funds for minority stakes has become increasingly difficult over the past decade, especially at the smaller end of the market, but there are still funds willing to purchase shares in attractive, smaller companies. Timescales are long, a private equity transaction will typically take 3 to 6 months, and costs are high. However, a private placing may allow a wholesale reorganisation of the equity of the business and raise new capital. The possibilities are wide and again outside the scope of this chapter, but one would not usually use private equity simply to buy out a spouse unless all other courses had been examined. If this were the right solution, there would normally be other commercial considerations that justified the costs of the process.

## Public placing/flotation

**14.16** The flotation process is designed to transmit information about a company to potential investors in a consistent form. This means that it is very heavily document driven and expensive. This approach requires careful planning. Any company contemplating a flotation needs to begin planning the process and presentation of itself to the market at least a year ahead. Given the timescales of a matrimonial dispute, this lengthy process may not be a viable option for realising value. The process is prescribed and cannot be readily shortened, and this delay would need to be factored into any settlement agreement, eg by delaying the date for payment of a lump sum.

**14.17** There are a limited number of institutions which will invest in 'Pre IPO' stocks (the Initial Public Offering, or IPO, is the first sale of stock by a private company to the public). However, the sequence would be to sell a block of shares to an institution that would subsequently place the shares on flotation.

The institution wants a return from the investment and the risk and will buy at a (possibly sizeable) discount to the likely flotation price.

## Trade sale

**14.18**  In a number of cases, the divorce situation may precipitate the decision to sell the business outright. This typically occurs when either a trade sale was already likely or where neither individual is actively involved (or plans to be actively involved) in the business in the future. The value of a business is a function of many potentially contradictory factors, including the sustainable earnings, growth potential and strategic position in its market.

**14.19**  To realise the value of a business requires judicious use of the sale process to attract willing and, preferably, eager buyers. As noted above, where a vendor is perceived to 'have to sell', the sale value will be depressed.

**14.20**  The parties in dispute need to have regard to how the shares are held before sale. Part of the value a purchaser will place on the shares is his ability to recover compensation in the event that there is a claim upon warranties offered by the vendor at the time of the sale. If shares have been passed to a spouse prior to a sale, that party may have no involvement in the business and therefore will decline to give any warranty other than to title of the shares. This means that any purchaser will not be able to recover all the consideration if there is a warranty claim, which may be reflected in the price paid. Conversely, if the parties agree to apportion the consideration on an equitable basis, agreement will be necessary on how to apportion possible warranty claims, and the impact of that agreement on valuation before commencing a sale process.

**14.21**  The purchaser will often wish to make the recipients of any cash jointly and severally liable for any warranty claim. Given the circumstances of any divorce, this is rarely attractive to either spouse.

**14.22**  The process of selling a company is best handled by an independent third party adviser with experience in dealing with such transactions. The timescales are again longer than most spouses in dispute would care for, but compressing the process usually depresses the value achieved on the sale. A sale will normally take 6 to 18 months, depending on the business. Costs are high but may result in increasing the value received.

## OTHER CONSIDERATIONS

**14.23**  Consideration needs to be given to what happens if the business is not sold. In smaller companies, in particular, sale processes frequently fail to identify a buyer. The impact of a failed sale process on the morale and operations of the business should not be underestimated. There are examples of previously successful businesses which have either failed outright or been seriously affected by a failed sale process. Depending on the prospects of sale, the better solution may be to agree a settlement that takes into account the ability of the parties to share future capital gains rather than to force a business sale that destroys value.[5]

**14.24**  Finally, a word of caution: if one of the parties in dispute is key to driving the value of the business (usually the Chief Executive Officer or Managing Director), the other needs to consider both the impact on value of the inevitable strains of separation and divorce, and the incentive of the other party to temporarily 'manage down' the business's value to achieve a better settlement. Even successful business people may become irrational or cynically manipulate operations and consequent valuations when dealing with their businesses in a divorce scenario.

---

[5]  See **11.94** et seq.

# Part VI
# **TRUSTS**

# Chapter 15

# TRUSTS

## INTRODUCTION

**15.1** 'Legal ideas and phenomena are nearly always best viewed in some broader context rather than studied in isolation as if they were things in themselves'.[1] By analogy, an understanding of ss 22–25 of the Matrimonial Causes Act 1973 is clearly essential, but a contextual approach to the application of these sections will assist a practitioner enormously. Nowhere is this truer than in an ancillary relief case involving a trust. Fortunately a detailed knowledge of the law of trusts is not essential for an ancillary relief practitioner. If a difficult trust law issue arises in ancillary relief litigation, the question is frequently best resolved not by family practitioners but by a specialist trust lawyer.[2] A general knowledge of the subject is, however, necessary in order to assist the practitioner to marshal arguments and unlock assets for their client. By way of introduction, this chapter provides what can in the circumstances be no more than a flavour of the law of trusts.[3] The remainder of the chapter considers the jurisprudence on the treatment of trust assets in the context of ancillary relief.

## THE TRUST CONCEPT

**15.2**  A trust has been described as:

> 'the legal relationship created – inter vivos or on death – by a person, the settlor, when assets have been placed under the control of a trustee for the benefit of a beneficiary or for a specified purpose.
>
> A trust has the following characteristics—
>
> (a)  the assets constitute a separate fund and are not a part of the trustee's own estate;
> (b)  title to the trust assets stands in the name of the trustee or in the name of another person on behalf of the trustee;

---

[1]  Twining and Miers *How To Do Things With Rules* (Butterworths, 4th edn), p 113.
[2]  There is an increasing recognition that in an appropriate case a multi-disciplinary approach to the resolution of an ancillary relief dispute is essential: see *D v D and B Limited* [2007] 2 FLR 653, Charles J.
[3]  For detailed texts on the law of trusts see, for example, *Lewin on Trusts* (Sweet & Maxwell, 18th edn) and *Snell's Equity* (Thomson/Sweet & Maxwell, 31st edn).

(c)    the trustee has the power and the duty in respect of which he is accountable, to manage, employ or dispose of the assets in accordance with the terms of the trust and the special duties imposed upon him by law.

The reservation by the settlor of certain rights and powers, and the fact that the trustee may himself have rights as a beneficiary, are not necessarily inconsistent with the existence of a trust.'[4]

## DIFFERENT TYPES OF TRUST

**15.3**  There are many different types of trust. The broadest categorisation divides trusts into three: express, resulting and constructive. An express trust arises where a person expressly intends to create a trust relationship. Express trusts may be orally created, although trusts of land or any interest in land must be 'manifested and proved by some writing signed by some person who is able to declare such trust or by his will'.[5] A typical express trust encountered in an ancillary relief case is a family settlement, where the terms of the trust are encapsulated in a deed.

**15.4**  A resulting trust is imposed by law and is based on what is presumed to be the intention of the parties. A commonly encountered resulting trust is a purchase monies resulting trust. Such a trust arises where one party, A, buys property in his name with money provided by B. In these circumstances the law will presume a resulting trust of the beneficial interest in favour of B, unless there is evidence to establish a contrary intention.

**15.5**  Broadly, a constructive trust is imposed by law to enable a party to receive restitution after unconscionable conduct on behalf of a property owner. Constructive trusts of land are frequently encountered. There are three elements to be established before a constructive trust will be imposed. First, there must be a common intention that one party should have an interest in land owned by another. Second, the party without an interest in land must have acted to his or her detriment on the basis of the common intention. Finally, it must be shown to be unconscionable to allow the owner of land to act in a manner contrary to the common intention. There is no requirement that a resulting or constructive trust of land is required to be declared in or evidenced by writing.[6]

**15.6**  A claim to a beneficial interest in land (or any other property), whether by resulting or constructive trust or as a consequence of a claim for proprietary estoppel is sometimes made by a third party against a party to ancillary relief proceedings and sometimes by a party to ancillary relief proceedings against a third party. The effect of the former is potentially to reduce the assets available for distribution, and the effect of the latter potentially to increase the assets of

---

4    Article 2 of the Schedule to the Recognition of Trusts Act 1987.
5    Law of Property Act 1925, s 53(1)(b).
6    Law of Property Act 1925, s 53(1)(b)(2).

the marriage. The general procedure for dealing with these claims was set out by Nicholas Mostyn QC, whilst sitting as a deputy judge of the Family Division in *TL v ML and others*:[7]

'In my opinion, it is essential in every instance where a dispute arises about the ownership of property in ancillary relief proceedings between a spouse and a third party, that the following things should ordinarily happen:

(i)     The third party should be joined to the proceedings at the earliest opportunity;

(ii)    Directions should be given for the issue to be fully pleaded by points of claim and points of defence;

(iii)   Separate witness statements should be directed in relation to the dispute; and

(iv)    The dispute should be directed to be heard separately as a preliminary issue, before the financial dispute resolution (FDR).'

**15.7** A more refined classification of trusts divides trusts into bare trusts, special trusts, fixed trusts and discretionary trusts. A bare trust, which is also known as a simple trust, exists where property is vested in a trustee for the benefit of a beneficiary, without the trustee being subject to any express powers of management. By contrast, a special trust is one where the trustee holds property subject to express powers of management and control imposed upon him by the settlor. A special trust may be either fixed or discretionary.

**15.8** A fixed trust is a trust where the entitlement of beneficiaries is fixed or defined by the terms of the trust. A beneficiary will know his potential entitlement from reading the terms of the settlement. There is consequently usually little problem in ancillary relief proceedings in identifying and valuing assets to which a party is entitled under a fixed trust.[8]

**15.9** In contrast, it is of the very essence of a discretionary trust that a trustee commonly has discretion not only in the selection of a beneficiary from a defined class of potential beneficiaries but also as to the extent of any property to be made available to the chosen beneficiary. The relationship between a trustee and beneficiary under a discretionary trust has been described in the following terms:[9]

'A trust exists where a trustee holds property for the "benefit of one or more beneficiaries" (see Art 2 of the 1984 Law). The important point is that save to the

---

[7]   [2006] 1 FLR 1263 at [36]. See Chapter 8. But see *A v A* [2007] 2 FLR 467 [23]–[24], where Munby J stated that he was sympathetic to the approach identified in *TL v ML*, but would take a less prescriptive approach emphasising that directions were case-specific; however, directions for pleadings should normally be given.

[8]   Note that in *Re C (Divorce: Financial Relief)* [2008] 1 FLR 625 the wife's annual gross trust income had been capitalised by actuarial calculation. The capitalised figure was described as being uncontroversial but theoretical because the wife would not have sold her income stream (per Baron J at [20]). See also *C v C & Ors* [2009] EWHC 1491 at [21]–[22].

[9]   *Re The Esteem Settlement* [2004] WTLR 1 at 60, a decision of the Royal Court of Jersey, cited in *TL v ML and others* [2006] 1 FLR 1263 at [87] and referred to by Coleridge J in *Charman v Charman* [2007] 1 FLR 593 at [79] as 'a very useful description of general application'.

extent permitted by the trust deed (eg remuneration) the trustee may not benefit from the assets; they are held entirely for the benefit of the beneficiaries. As Lord Blackburn put it in the Privy Council decision in *Letterstedt v Broers* (1884) 9 AC 371 at 386: "It must always be borne in mind that trustees exist for the benefit of those to whom the creator of the trust has given the trust estate". In other words, trustees have no interest of their own in the trust property; their sole purpose is to deal with the trust assets for the benefit of the beneficiaries. All the powers of the trustees may be exercised only in the interests of the beneficiaries and in accordance with the terms of the trust deed.

What the exercise of such powers will involve will, of course, vary considerably according to the nature of the trust, the number of beneficiaries, the underlying purposes behind the establishment of the trust, the nature of the assets and many other factors ...

Furthermore, it is important that the relationship between trustee and beneficiary should be harmonious. Indeed, lack of harmony may be of itself a good reason for a trustee to resign or be dismissed (see *Letterstedt* at 386). This is not surprising because the trustee's sole duty is to act for the benefit of the beneficiaries. In our judgment there is nothing untoward in beneficiaries making requests of a trustee as to the investment of the trust fund, the acquisition of properties for them to live in or for the refurbishment of properties in which they already live. In our judgment many decisions of this nature are likely to arise because of a request by a beneficiary rather than because of an independent originating action on the part of a trustee. The approach that a trustee should adopt to a request will depend upon the nature of the request, the interests of other beneficiaries and all the surrounding circumstances. Certainly, if he is to be exercising his fiduciary powers in good faith, the trustee must be willing to reject a request if he thinks that this is the right course. But when a trustee concludes that the request is reasonable having regard to all the circumstances of the case and is in the interests of the beneficiary concerned, he should certainly not refuse the request simply in order to assert or prove his independence. His duty remains at all times to act in good faith in the interests of his beneficiaries, not to act against those interests for improper reasons.

In our judgment, where the requests made of trustees are reasonable in the context of all the circumstances, it would be the exception rather than the rule for trustees to refuse such requests. Indeed, as Mr Journeaux accepted, one would expect to find that in the majority of trusts, there had not been a refusal by the trustees of a request by a settlor. This would no doubt be because, in the majority of cases, a settlor would be acting reasonably in the interests of himself and his family. This would particularly be so where there was a small close-knit family and where the settlor could be expected to be fully aware of what was in the interests of his family. Indeed, in almost all discretionary trusts, the settlor provides a letter of wishes which expresses informally his desires in relation to the administration of the settlement. Furthermore he may change his wishes from time to time. In our judgment it is perfectly clear that trustees are entitled (see *Abacus Trust Company (Isle of Man) Ltd v Barr* [2003] 1 All ER 763) to take account of such wishes as the settlor may from time to time express provided, of course, that the trustees are not in any way bound by them. The trustees must reach their own independent conclusion having taken account of such wishes.

On numerous occasions during the course of the hearing, Mr Journeaux was driven to repeat that Abacus had not rejected any request of Sheikh Fahad. A lack of any refusal may of course be indicative of the fact that trustees have abdicated their fiduciary duties and are simply following the wishes of the settlor without further consideration. But, as mentioned above, a lack of any refusal may be equally consistent with a properly administered trust where the trustees have in good faith considered each request of the settlor, concluded that it is reasonable and concluded that it is proper to accede to such requests in the interests of one or more of the beneficiaries of the trust. But one does not start, as at times seems to have been the plaintiffs' case, with an attitude that it is very surprising and worthy of criticism that the trustee acceded to all Sheikh Fahad's requests. On the contrary, as the Privy Council said in *Letterstedt*, trustees exist for the benefit of beneficiaries and it is in our judgment very common that trustees will have perfectly properly acceded to all the requests of a settlor without in any way abdicating their fiduciary duties and responsibilities.'

## THE NATURE OF A BENEFICIAL INTEREST UNDER A DISCRETIONARY TRUST

**15.10**   A beneficiary under a discretionary trust does not have an equitable interest in trust property. He merely has the right to require trustees to act in accordance with the terms of the trust and to exercise their discretionary powers from time to time in accordance with the law. The inherent uncertainty of a beneficiary's financial expectation under a discretionary trust causes difficulty for ancillary relief practitioners, and parties commonly take diametrically opposing views of their expectation interest as a beneficiary. A spouse who is also a beneficiary under a discretionary trust will seek to argue that they have only a hope (and frequently not even that!) of benefiting from the trustees' discretion. The converse position will frequently be adopted by the spouse on the other side of the litigation, who will seek to argue that despite the legal characterisation of a beneficiary's rights, the reality of the case is that the beneficiary spouse expects to receive and will receive benefit from the exercise of the trustees' discretion. It is not surprising, then, that discretionary trusts are the subject of much ancillary relief jurisprudence.

**15.11**   As has been explained, there is usually little room for uncertainty when identifying the nature of a beneficiary's interest under a fixed trust. However, identifying whether the nature of the interest is a resource to be taken into account in the s 25 exercise is not always straightforward. In *C v C & Ors* [2009] EWHC 1491 the husband's mother had a life interest in a trust fund which on her death would pass to the husband as one of four tenants in common in equal shares. The trustees had power to advance capital at their discretion to the mother. Munby J found that there was a possibility verging on a probability that the trustees would have to exercise this power. The life expectancy of the mother was 15 years. The preliminary issue for determination was whether the husband's interest under the trust was a resource within s 25(2)(a). Munby J held that it was a financial resource that the husband was likely to have in the foreseeable future; albeit that the interest was only 'dimly visible'. Receipt of an interest under a fixed trust may be brought forward or indeed varied under the rule in *Saunders v Vautier*.[10] The rule enables adult and legally capable beneficiaries who are between them entitled to the whole of the property to vary or bring a trust to an end. A careful reading of the trust deed and the rules on varying and bringing trusts to an end should be considered in order to potentially increase liquidity in a case.[11] However, as in *C v C & Ors*, if the beneficiaries are not in express agreement to vary the terms of the trust, the court is likely to hold that any future agreed variation is speculative and no more than a vague contingency that would not amount to a resource.

## ENTITLEMENT TO TRUST DOCUMENTS

**15.12**   The law on a beneficiary's entitlement to see trust documents has recently undergone major change. It used to be thought that the right of inspection was based upon supposed proprietary rights attaching to trust documents.[12] Trust deeds, deeds of appointment made by the trustees under the terms of the trust, resolutions, trust accounts, details of investments, supporting vouchers, a trust minute book recording any administrative decisions, counsel's opinion where advice was taken on behalf of the trust and any other documents containing information about the assets of the trust and dealings with those assets were all trust documents that a beneficiary was entitled to see.[13] In contrast, a beneficiary had no free-standing entitlement to see documents or parts of documents that contained details of the motives and reasoning relied upon by trustees when exercising their discretion under the terms of a trust. Accordingly, for example, beneficiaries were not entitled to see agendas for trustees' meetings, minutes of those meetings, letters of wishes, correspondence between trustees and beneficiaries, correspondence between appointors/protectors and trustees and other documents disclosing the deliberations of trustees as to the manner in which they should exercise their discretionary powers, or the reasons for any particular exercise of such a power, or the materials upon which such reasons were or might have been based.[14] Perhaps the primary rationale for the restriction of information was the protection of a trustee's right not to give reasons for their decisions.

**15.13**   However, in *Schmidt v Rosewood Trust Limited*[15] the Privy Council expressed their view that a beneficiary's right to seek disclosure of trust documents was 'best approached as one aspect of the court's inherent

---

[10]   (1841) Cr & Ph 240.

[11]   See e g *Lewin on Trusts* (Sweet & Maxwell, 18th edn), ch 24.

[12]   *O'Rourke v Darbishire* [1920] AC 581.

[13]   In *Re Londonderry's Settlement* [1965] Ch 918 at 938, Salmon LJ stated 'the category of trust documents has never been comprehensively defined. Nor could it be – certainly not by me. Trust documents do, however, have these characteristics in common: (1) they are documents in the possession of the trustees as trustees; (2) they contain information about the trust which the beneficiaries are entitled to know; (3) the beneficiaries have a proprietary interest in the documents and, accordingly, are entitled to see them.

[14]   *Re Londonderry's Settlement* [1965] Ch 918, CA.

[15]   [2003] 2 AC 709, PC.

jurisdiction to supervise and where appropriate intervene in, the administration of trusts'.[16] Whether a beneficiary was entitled to see trust documents would therefore be decided by the exercise of the court's discretion. However, in the exercise of their discretion the courts will inevitably have regard to the previous types of documents that a beneficiary would have been entitled to see and the likelihood of the receipt of trust property by a beneficiary. The remoter the claim the potentially more restricted the right to information might become. For example, whilst a beneficiary under a fixed trust and a beneficiary under a family discretionary trust would have good grounds upon which to see documents relating to the assets of the trust and their administration, a remoter claimant (such as a person who was merely a potential beneficiary under a wide power of appointment) would have a lesser claim to inspect. Even documents that were previously thought to be protected from disclosure may, however, now be ordered to be disclosed. A letter of wishes is a document that trustees may take into account in their deliberations and accordingly pre-*Schmidt* would not be disclosed to a beneficiary. However in *Breakspear v Ackland*[17] Briggs J departed from the general position only because the trustees had indicated that they would be seeking a direction from the court approving a distribution and the letter of wishes would therefore have been disclosed in that litigation, and the trustees had given reasons for their refusal to disclose the document – which decision therefore became potentially reviewable. Upon being requested to disclose 'trust documents' by a beneficiary spouse who is a party to ancillary relief litigation, the trustees will have a discretion as to whether and the extent to which they comply with the request. In a difficult case the trustees may feel the need to seek guidance from the Chancery Division.[18] The right of a beneficiary to inspect documents relating to a trust is of course separate from the concept of disclosure in litigation. A trustee who is a party to litigation will be ordered to give disclosure of documents in accordance with at the very least the obligations of standard disclosure.

**15.14** In *Browne v Browne*[19] one of the issues before the court was whether the wife exercised effective control over two offshore discretionary trusts. Evidence of the motives and the reasoning of the trustees were before the court.[20] The documents were relevant to an issue being litigated and were presumably disclosed as part of the duty of disclosure in litigation. In ancillary relief litigation, where issues arise that require disclosure of trust documents and documents evidencing the motives relevant to the exercise of any discretion, trustees should be invited to disclose those documents. If they refuse and the trustees are not party to the litigation, consideration will need to be given to

---

[16]  [2003] 2 AC 709 at [66].

[17]  [2008] EWHC 220 (Ch) [2008] WLR (D) 52, Briggs J.

[18]  See, for example, the Jersey case of *Re Rabaiotti 1989 Settlement* [2000] WTLR 953, where the Royal Court exercised their discretion in favour of disclosure of letters of wishes because, amongst other reasons, one of the beneficiaries had been ordered to produce the documents in English divorce proceedings.

[19]  [1989] 1 FLR 291.

[20]  [1989] 1 FLR 291 at 294 per Butler-Sloss LJ: 'There can be little doubt from reading the correspondence of the trustees that they were looking very carefully to see what the wife really wanted'.

making an application for an inspection appointment or, if the trustee is outside of the jurisdiction, a letter of request.[21] If the trustees are party to the litigation, they will be under a duty to disclose the document in the usual course of the proceedings. It is submitted that the decision in *Schmidt* makes it unlikely that a beneficiary will be held to have trust documents and documentary evidence of discretionary motive under their control. An order for a beneficiary spouse in ancillary relief proceedings to use best endeavours to obtain documents from trustees would appear to be as far as any direction can extend in the absence of the trustees being joined to the proceedings. Such an order may be a relevant factor taken into account by the trustees when they are requested to disclose the documents and indeed by any court in the exercise of its supervisory jurisdiction to intervene in the administration of a trust if directions are sought.

**15.15** On rare occasions, a party to ancillary relief applications may know that they are beneficiaries under a settlement, but be unaware as to the identity of the trustees of the settlement. On application by a beneficiary, a court has a wide jurisdiction to order a third party to disclose the names and contact details of the trustees of a settlement.[22] Such an application is likely to be a rarity, because trustees are required to inform beneficiaries certainly of fixed trusts and presumably additionally of 'small' family discretionary trusts of the nature and extent of their interests.

## ACCOUNTING OBLIGATIONS AND VALUATION

**15.16** A trustee is required to keep trust accounts and to provide them upon request to a beneficiary. The duty to provide accounts extends to a beneficiary under a discretionary trust.[23] A trustee can be compelled to account. Trust accounts should contain sufficient detail to satisfy a litigant in ancillary relief proceedings. However, if there is any doubt, particularly about the basis and/or date of valuation of trust assets, inquiries should be raised by questionnaire before consideration is given to obtaining a valuation of trust assets in the ancillary relief proceedings. The valuation of life interests is, however, not entirely straightforward, and expert evidence may be necessary to assist the court if a capital value is required to be attached to a life interest.

**15.17** There is no requirement for trust accounts to be audited, although under s 22(4) of the Trustee Act 1925, a trustee has discretion to require an audit, albeit in general not more than once every 3 years. A beneficiary may seek an audit under s 13 of the Public Trustee Act 1906, although the beneficiary will be at risk of having to bear the costs of the audit if nothing untoward is discovered and sufficient information had already been provided to the beneficiary.

---

[21] See *Charman v Charman* [2006] 1 WLR 1053 and see Chapter 5.
[22] *Re Murphy's Settlements* [1999] 1 WLR 282.
[23] *Re Murphy's Settlements* [1999] 1 WLR 282.

# THE DUTY TO ACT IMPARTIALLY AND THE DUTY NOT TO FETTER DISCRETION

**15.18** A detailed exposition of the duties of trustees is beyond the scope of this book. Nevertheless there are two duties that are worth touching upon, since they are relevant to an argument that a beneficial interest under a discretionary trust is a potential resource of one of the parties. The two duties are the duty to act impartially and the duty of a trustee not to fetter his discretion. The duty to act impartially has been described in the following terms:

> 'Properly understood, the so called duty to act impartially is no more than the ordinary duty which the law imposes on a person who is entrusted with the exercise of a discretionary power: that he exercises the power for the purpose for which it is given giving proper consideration to the matters which are relevant and excluding from consideration matters which are irrelevant. If trustees do that, they cannot be criticised if they reach a decision which appears to prefer the claim of one interest over others. The preference will be the result of a proper exercise of the discretionary power.'[24]

**15.19** When a trustee is met with a request to advance capital or income from a trust to assist a beneficiary to meet an order of the court in ancillary relief proceedings, the trustee will have to act impartially when exercising his discretion. The relevant matters for a trustee to take into account will clearly be case-specific. However, as a general proposition, a trustee will be required to consider the settlor's wishes, the terms of the trust deed, the impact of any decision on other beneficiaries, the nature of the trust assets and the potential tax consequences of any distribution made.

**15.20** 'It is trite law that trustees cannot fetter the exercise by them at a future date of a discretion possessed by them as trustees'.[25] In other words, a trustee cannot say how they will exercise their discretion at a future date and then be bound by such expression. Any such fetter is of no effect. A trustee is required to take into account all relevant matters at the time they exercise their discretion. Obtaining evidence from a trustee as to how they might exercise their discretion in the future will not be binding. Furthermore, a change of circumstance of a third party beneficiary under a trust could dramatically affect the view which a trustee takes of any judicial encouragement. It follows that an attempt to judicially encourage a trustee at trial contains an element of speculation.

# THE POWERS OF MAINTENANCE AND ADVANCEMENT

**15.21** Ancillary relief practitioners need to be aware about the existence of powers of maintenance and advancement. Both concepts unlock trust assets.

---

[24] *Edge v Pensions Ombudsman* [2000] Ch 602 at 627.
[25] *Swales v IRC* [1984] 3 All ER 16 at 24 per Nicholls J.

Both powers are statutory and both apply subject to any contrary intention being expressed in the trust deed. Broadly, the power of maintenance enables income to be applied for the benefit of a minor, and the power of advancement enables capital to be advanced for the benefit of a minor or an adult.

**15.22** The power of maintenance is contained in s 31 of the Trustee Act 1925. In essence it enables trustees at their discretion to apply income towards the maintenance, education or benefit of a minor. When exercising their discretion, the trustees are required to have exclusive regard to the benefit of the child in question, irrespective of the fact that the effect of providing maintenance might reduce or extinguish, for example, the effect of a school fees order or a consent order for periodical payments in favour of children in ancillary relief proceedings.[26]

**15.23** The power of advancement is contained in s 32 of the Trustee Act 1925. In broad terms, trustees are given discretion to advance capital money to the benefit of any person entitled to the capital of the trust property or any share thereof, whether absolutely or contingently.

**15.24** Practitioners need to be alive to the potential for trustees to exercise their powers of maintenance and advancement in favour of a party to the marriage or a child of the marriage. The powers are bound up with an argument that trust assets ought to be treated as a resource. Furthermore, the effect of the exercise of the powers may be to reduce the burden of expenditure of a party to ancillary relief proceedings.

## INTERESTS UNDER DISCRETIONARY TRUSTS AS A RESOURCE AND JUDICIAL ENCOURAGEMENT OF TRUSTEES

### Introduction

**15.25** The nature of a beneficial interest under a discretionary trust frequently provides an incentive to a beneficiary spouse to argue that their interest does not amount to a valuable resource. Understandably, this stance is commonly challenged by the other spouse.[27] The resolution of these conflicting positions

---

[26] See *Fuller v Evans* [2000] 2 FLR 13, where there was the real possibility that the trustees of an accumulation and maintenance trust settled by the husband would discharge his obligations under a consent order in ancillary relief proceedings. An accumulation and maintenance trust is defined by s 71 of the Inheritance Tax Act 1984. It exists where beneficiaries are entitled to trust property only upon attaining a specified age not exceeding 25. Until that time the beneficiaries are not treated as having an interest in possession and the income generated by the trust fund is to be accumulated unless or to the extent that it is applied for the maintenance, education or benefit of a beneficiary.

[27] For an extreme example see *Charman v Charman (No 4)* [2007] 1 FLR 1246, where the husband unsuccessfully argued for the exclusion of the entirety of the assets of a Bermudan trust said to be worth around £68,125,000.

requires the court[28] to resolve the tension between respect for the integrity of the trust and the desire to ensure that the reality of the situation is taken into account, irrespective of legal characterisation.[29] The modern law on the resolution of this tension derives from *Howard v Howard*.[30]

**15.26** In *Howard* the settlor transferred money to trustees to be held during the life of the husband on protective trusts.[31] The trustees had discretion to apply the trust fund for the benefit of the husband, any wife of the husband and any children of a marriage of the husband. The wife obtained a decree absolute and a substantive order for maintenance. Thereafter the husband was declared bankrupt and then subsequently discharged from bankruptcy. The wife re-married. The trustees subsequently informed the husband that he would receive no payment from the trust fund for a considerable time, as the trustees had allocated income to the maintenance of the husband's son and the husband's medical and legal costs. Unsurprisingly, the husband applied for the maintenance to be reduced to a nominal sum.[32] The Registrar made an order reducing the maintenance to a shilling a week. On appeal, Barnard J ordered the husband to pay the wife £100 a year maintenance on the basis that pressure could be brought on the trustees to exercise their discretion to provide the husband with an allowance out of the settlement. The husband successfully appealed to the Court of Appeal and the order of the Registrar was reinstated.

**15.27** In *Howard* the trustees had already exercised their discretion. It was held to be wrong in principle to make an order that would 'leave the husband in a state of starvation (to use rather picturesque language) with a view to putting pressure on trustees to exercise their discretion in a way in which they would not have exercised it but for that pressure'.[33] The Court of Appeal also

---

[28] Note that in *Re C (Divorce: Financial Relief)* [2008] 1 FLR 625 at [17] Baron J appeared to indicate that where a case included the unusual and complex aspect of the entitlement of a party under a trust, it should be transferred to the High Court at the earliest opportunity. Whether the guidance is followed or thought too prescriptive remains to be seen. The guidance was followed in *C v C & Ors* [2009] EWHC 1491.

[29] See, for example, *Charman v Charman (No 4)* [2007] 1 FLR 1246 at [57], where the court stated in respect of an inquiry as to whether assets held under trust are a resource, 'whenever it is necessary to conduct such an inquiry, it is essential for the court to bring to it a judicious mixture of worldly realism and of respect for the legal effect of trusts, the legal duties of trustees and, in the case of off-shore trusts, the jurisdictions of off-shore courts'. Of course, treating an interest under a discretionary trust as a resource does not mean that the beneficiary has a proprietary interest in the trust assets.

[30] [1945] P 1 – and can be traced in its development through *B v B (Financial Provision)* (1982) 3 FLR 298, CA, *Browne v Browne* [1989] 1 FLR 291, CA, *Thomas v Thomas* [1995] 2 FLR 668, *TL v ML* [2006] 1 FLR 1263, *Charman v Charman* [2006] 2 FLR 422, CA, *Charman v Charman (No 4)* [2007] 1 FLR 1246, CA and *A v A and St George Trustees Limited* [2007] 2 FLR 467. The approach to treating interests under a discretionary trust as a resource can be traced back to the ecclesiastical courts.

[31] Broadly, a protective trust creates a life interest with provisions applying to transfer the life interest to trustees on a discretionary trust upon the happening of specified events – most commonly bankruptcy of the life tenant.

[32] There was at the time no provision preventing periodical payments extending beyond re-marriage: see s 28(1)(a) of the Matrimonial Causes Act 1973 as amended.

[33] [1945] P 1 at 4 per Lord Greene MR.

foreshadowed a theme developed in more recent authorities when they stated that, in relation to the husband's means, consideration should be given not only to what the husband was receiving but also to what he 'can fairly be assumed to be likely to get'.[34]

**15.28**  Unlocking assets held under a discretionary trust is not conceptually straightforward. In an example of lateral thinking, the Court of Appeal in *Howard* noted that the difficulties could potentially be reduced by orders varying the discretionary nature of the settlement to make a fixed sum payable to a beneficiary.[35] The sum payable to the beneficiary under the varied settlement could then be treated as a financial resource of the beneficiary spouse as of right.

## Interests under a discretionary trust as a resource

**15.29**  In *B v B (Financial Provision)*[36] the husband had no capital assets. The wife was a member of a wealthy family. She had a life interest in two settlements. Under a settlement made in 1951, the trustees had power at their absolute discretion to vest the whole or any part of the trust capital in the wife absolutely. The capital value of this fund was found to be £78,000. The wife settled the second fund on herself for life in 1965. She was entitled with the consent of the trustees to withdraw all or any part of the trust fund. The capital value of the second fund was £212,000. The wife had significant assets free of trust. One trustee, who was also the wife's solicitor in the ancillary relief litigation, gave evidence to the effect that no consent would be given to the further withdrawal of funds.[37] Booth J awarded the husband a lump sum of £50,000 and the wife appealed.

**15.30**  Following *Howard* the main ground of appeal argued by the wife was that the order put pressure on the trustees to exercise their discretion in a way that they would not have chosen to exercise it, namely by allowing the wife to raise a capital sum. This argument was rejected. In doing so, Ormrod LJ stated:

> 'The first question is whether the wife's interests under the settlements are "other financial resources", e g of a capital nature. Under the 1951 settlement the trustees have power to vest the trust-fund, or part of it, in the wife "in their absolute discretion"; under the 1965 settlement the wife, with the consent of the trustees, can revoke it in whole or in part. Both settlements are potential sources of capital for the wife and are, therefore "other financial resources", though not under her absolute control. Some assessment must be made of the worth of these potential sources of capital to her, not necessarily in valuers' terms, but in terms of the

---

[34]  [1945] P 1. Note also that benefits in kind (e g if the trustees were to directly meet any of the husband's income needs, such as 'paying his tailor's bills or his butcher's bills') would be treated as part of the husband's income. In order that the wife could see what, if any, benefits were received by the husband from the settlement, the husband undertook to provide half-yearly statements of all benefits (if any) received and their nature.

[35]  See **15.54–15.68** for variation of settlements.

[36]  (1982) 3 FLR 298.

[37]  The evidence was discounted on the grounds of professional embarrassment.

practical realities of life, or in terms of reasonable expectations. As Lord Merrivale said in *N v N* (1928) 44 TLR 324 at 327, the ecclesiastical courts "showed a degree of practical wisdom ... They were not misled by appearances ... they looked at realities". Much the same was said by this court in *O'D v O'D* [1976] Fam 83 at 90. Looked at in this way the potential of the 1951 settlement may be small, but that of the 1965 settlement is great. The wife herself was the settlor, settling her own money on herself for life, for her own purposes, and retaining a power of revocation subject only to the consent of the trustees. It is not to be supposed that the trustees would withhold their consent if the wife wished to free capital for any reasonable purpose, more especially when the other beneficiaries are already amply provided for.

Balancing the financial resources of each party and their respective needs, giving full weight to the wife's exceptional needs, particularly in the future, it is impossible to regard a lump sum of £50,000 as an unreasonable sum for the purposes of ss 23 and 25 of the 1973 Act.

The next question, and it is often the crucial question in these cases, is practicability. It is at this stage that the court has to consider such problems as liquidity, the cost of raising money on mortgage or overdraft, the effect on a business of withdrawing a substantial capital sum and so on. These are practical matters and must be approached realistically, "penetrating to the underlying realities" (*O'D v O'D* (above)), and "not being misled by appearances" (*N v N* (above)).

In this case the question is, "Is it practicable for the wife to raise the sum of £50,000?" To start with she has £28,300, plus accumulated interest, from the sale of 9 Clumber Crescent North on deposit or in cash. There remains a balance of £21,000. In a case such as this it is distasteful, and ought to be unnecessary, to look at the wife's personal possessions, but the attitude of her trustees makes it unavoidable. She could, undoubtedly, but painfully, raise such a lump sum from her stamps (which in this case are real assets, if not investments) and her jewellery, or she could borrow it (at great and unnecessary expense) by way of mortgage. Alternatively, she could withdraw a relatively small part of the 1965 settlement fund with the consent of her trustees. The consequent loss of income would not be significant, and could be made good by reinvesting part of the fund which will, or may, involve some capital gains tax.'[38]

**15.31** The Court of Appeal in *B v B (Financial Provision)* further distinguished *Howard* because the order did not leave the trustees with little option but to benefit the wife. The wife could have chosen to realise her free assets, including personal possessions and cash on deposit, to satisfy the lump sum order. She was not obliged to have recourse to the trust fund in order to meet the award. By contrast, in *Howard*, the order made would have 'left the husband with little or nothing to live on if the trustees did not apply the income of the trust fund by paying it to him'.[39] 'Moreover the wife was the principal

---

[38]  (1982) 3 FLR 298 at 303. Note, then, that when dealing with practicability the order was fashioned in such a way that the wife could meet it out of her own resources without putting pressure on the trustees.
[39]  (1982) 3 FLR 298 at 304.

beneficiary of the trust and the court plainly felt that a proper discharge of the trustees' fiduciary obligations was to help her meet the award'.[40]

**15.32** Interests under discretionary trusts are therefore potential sources of capital and income that fall to be considered as a resource under MCA 1973, s 25(2)(a). When assessing the worth of these interests as a resource, *B v B (Financial Provision)* identified the need to consider the practical reality or the reasonable expectation of the beneficiary. These considerations were recently refined in *Charman v Charman*,[41] when the Court of Appeal provided a detailed and helpful analysis of the essential question that is required to be answered by a court when there is an issue between the parties about whether to treat an interest under a discretionary trust as a resource. Wilson LJ encapsulated the issues as follows:

> 'There has been some debate at the hearing of this appeal as to the nature of the central question which, in this not unusual situation, the court hearing an application for ancillary relief should seek to determine. Superficially the question is easily framed as being whether the trust is a financial "resource" of the husband for the purpose of s 25(2)(a) of the Matrimonial Causes Act 1973, "the Act of 1973". But what does the word "resource" mean in this context? In my view, when properly focused, that central question is simply whether, if the husband were to request it to advance the whole (or part) of the capital of the trust to him, the trustee would be likely to do so. In other cases the question has been formulated in terms of whether the spouse has real or effective control over the trust. At times I have myself formulated it in that way. But, unless the situation is one in which there is ground for doubting whether the trustee is properly discharging its duties or would be likely to do so, it seems to me on reflection that such a formulation is not entirely apposite. On the evidence so far assembled in the present case, as in most cases, there seems no reason to doubt that the duties of the trustee are being, and will continue to be, discharged properly. In his written argument in this court Mr Pointer QC on behalf of the wife at one point referred to the possible "unity of interest" between the husband and Codan; and in his written argument before the judge he tentatively described Codan as "quasi-agents" of the husband. Both phrases imply that Codan is not asserting, or would not assert, the independence that its duties require of it; and in my view, on the present evidence, it was wise of Mr Pointer in oral argument to withdraw them. A trustee – in proper "control" of the trust – will usually be acting entirely properly if, after careful consideration of all relevant circumstances, he resolves in good faith to accede to a request by the settlor for the exercise of his power of advancement of capital, whether back to the settlor or to any other beneficiary.

> Thus in effect, albeit with one small qualification, I agree with the suggestion of Butler-Sloss LJ in this court in *Browne v Browne* [1989] 1 FLR 291 at 239d–e that, in this context, the question is more appropriately expressed as whether the spouse has "immediate access to the funds" of the trust than "effective control" over it.

---

[40] Per N Mostyn QC sitting as a deputy judge of the Family Division when commenting on *B v B* (1982) 3 FLR 298 in *TL v ML and others* [2006] 1 FLR 1263 at [91].

[41] [2006] 2 FLR 422, CA at 433. There are a number of reported authorities in the *Charman* litigation. In this authority the main issue for the Court of Appeal was the identification of the principles by reference to which the court should grant an application for the issue of a letter of request to the authorities of an overseas jurisdiction.

The qualification relates to the word "immediate". In that case the trial judge knew that, if he was to proceed also to order the wife to pay the husband's costs, she would be unable to comply with his orders for her swift payment of a lump sum and costs without recourse to the off-shore trusts over which he found her to have "effective control": see 295b–c. So the question in that case was whether her access to their funds was immediate. In principle, however, in the light of s 25(2)(a) of the Act of 1973, the question is surely whether the trustee would be likely to advance the capital immediately or in the foreseeable future.'[42]

## Evidence establishing whether a trustee is likely to advance trust funds

**15.33** An interest under a discretionary trust may then be treated as a resource if a trustee would be likely to advance capital or pay income immediately or in the foreseeable future to the beneficiary. In *Charman v Charman* the husband was the settlor of a Bermudan discretionary trust. Both the husband and the wife were, amongst others, potential beneficiaries. The wife sought during ancillary relief proceedings to have the capital assets of the trust, said to be worth some £68 million, taken into account as a resource under MCA 1973, s 25(2)(a). As set out above, more specifically defined, the issue was whether the Bermudan trust company would be likely immediately or in the foreseeable future to advance trust funds to the husband if he requested it to do so. In support of this issue the wife sought and obtained before Coleridge J an order for the issue of a letter of request to the Bermudan authorities to take evidence from Mr Anderson, a director of the Bermudan trust company and an order for an inspection appointment against the husband's English accountant, Mr Clay. The issue for determination by the Court of Appeal was whether the orders were correctly made.

**15.34** It is instructive to look at the terms of both orders made by Coleridge J as examples of the type of evidence that should be sought when seeking to determine whether a spouse is likely to have capital and or income advanced to them under the terms of a discretionary trust.[43] The orders were summarised by Wilson LJ in the following terms:[44]

'20 The letter of request ordered by the judge was that Mr Anderson should be asked specified written questions annexed to the letter and, where applicable, be required to produce documents specified in the annexe. In summary the request was for him to be required to:

(a) produce trust accounts for the two most recent completed years;
(b) produce any trust deeds, written resolutions and letters of wishes, other than identified documents of each class already disclosed by the husband;

---

[42] [2006] 2 FLR 422, CA at [12]–[13].
[43] It is worth noting that in *J v V (Disclosure: Offshore Corporations)* [2004] 1 FLR 1042 at [17–18] Mr Justice Coleridge stated that a party with offshore assets had perhaps to be even fuller and franker in the exposure and explanation of their assets than in a conventional on-shore case in order to prevent exhaustively searching enquiry.
[44] [2006] 2 FLR 422, CA at [20]–[21].

(c)    state whether it was the practice of the trustee to consult the husband, and/or to be guided by him, about prospective policy decisions, whether as to investment, distribution or otherwise, and, if so, give full details and produce all relevant documents;

(d)    state whether the trustee and the husband had discussed the possible collapse of the trust or change in the expression of his wishes and, if so, give full details and produce all relevant documents; and

(e)    state whether there had been any communications between Mr Clay and the trustee "regarding the trusts" and, if so, give full details and produce all relevant documents.

The letter also requested that the wife's representative be permitted orally to ask – and impliedly that Mr Anderson should be required to answer – supplementary questions in order to elicit the clearest possible account of the above matters.

21 The order for the inspection appointment obliged Mr Clay to produce to the court:

> "any documents … containing evidence of any advice given to, discussions with or communications from, [the husband], relating to the past, present and future treatment of the trust funds or which bear upon the conception, creation and possible ultimate dissolution of [Dragon] …".'

**15.35**    Before determining the appeal, Wilson LJ reflected on the pattern of orders available in ancillary relief proceedings for causing persons who are not parties to the proceedings to produce documents and/or to give oral evidence in advance of substantive hearings. In respect of persons within the jurisdiction of the court, inspection appointments may be made for the production of documents. Although an order for an inspection appointment is not an order for the person to give oral evidence, it is permissible to ask any questions necessary to enable the inspection to proceed effectively, 'for example, if it is not clear from the face of a document produced, to identify its source or how it relates to another document or whether a document is missing and, if so, why'.[45] It may also be the case that a subpoena to attend and give oral evidence can lawfully be made returnable prior to the substantive hearing. In respect of persons outside the jurisdiction a letter of request may be made to the appropriate judicial authorities to cause a person to be required to produce documents and answer written and/or oral questions. In respect of letters of request it would be wise to check with an overseas lawyer about the implementation and enforceability of letters of request ordered by the English courts.

**15.36**    Subject to a minor modification to the letter of request, the appeal was dismissed.[46] The modification made was to paragraph 20(e). That request was too wide, since it required the trustee to divulge communications between

---

[45]    [2006] 2 FLR 422, CA at [23].
[46]    The interim applications were ultimately of little use because a Bermudan judge declined to assist the English court when upholding a request by the trustees to reject the order for the production of documents: see *Charman v Charman (No 2)* [2007] 1 FLR 593 at [54].

himself and the accountant defined by reference to a formula wider than the formulae defining the communications to be divulged between the husband and the trustee.[47]

**15.37** The historical pattern of trustees' responses to requests by beneficiaries for distribution will of course be important evidence in determining whether trust funds are likely to be advanced to a beneficiary. In the Court of Appeal case of *Browne v Browne*[48] the evidence before the court was that every application for funds made by the wife up to separation was met. Bearing in mind the wife's ability to obtain immediate access to the funds held on trust, the reality was that the discretion of the trustees would be exercised in her favour if she made a reasonable request for payment. This was an unsurprising conclusion given that the wife was the sole beneficiary of at least one large offshore trust. Improper pressure was not therefore being placed on the trustees to exercise their discretion in favour of the wife. Furthermore, any argument on appeal that the wife did not have sufficient assets within the jurisdiction and free of trust to meet the original order was rendered academic by the receipt of funds by the wife post the first instance decision.

**15.38** Another relevant factor to consider when determining whether a trustee would advance capital or income on request to a beneficiary is the nature and liquidity of the trust assets.[49] The tax consequences of realisation also need to be considered. The more liquid the asset the easier it is to argue that the nature of the asset will not prevent a trustee exercising his discretion in favour of distribution. The converse position requires a creative approach to unlocking trust assets.

**15.39** In assessing whether trustees would comply with a request from a beneficiary to advance trust assets to assist with the burden of meeting a court order, it is submitted that the court is being asked effectively to stand in the shoes of the trustees and to reach a finding as to how the trustees' discretion would be exercised. Clearly such an assessment is fact-sensitive. When assessing how a trustee would be likely to exercise their discretion, a court is required to have regard to a trustee's duty to be impartial and the duty not to fetter their discretion. Furthermore, one of the key issues will be whether the interests of the trust or other beneficiaries would be appreciably damaged by a genuine request for an advance.[50] It is likely that in many cases this issue will be determinative of outcome.

---

[47] The Court of Appeal dismissed the suggestion that the wife's application was a fishing expedition. Neither was it oppressive, too wide (with one exception), unnecessary or disproportionate. Furthermore, due to the 'quasi-inquisitorial role' of the court, there was no restriction in ancillary relief proceedings requiring W to be able to prove the existence of particular documents before being entitled to an order. See Chapter 5 for more detailed consideration of the means by which such disclosure from third party trustees might be obtained.

[48] [1989] 1 FLR 291.

[49] See *A v A and St George Trustees Limited* [2007] 2 FLR 467 at [96].

[50] See *Thomas v Thomas* [1995] 2 FLR 668, CA, Glidewell LJ.

**15.40** A court is entitled to look critically at any expressions from the trustees that they would not accede to a request for an advance. For example, in *B v B (Financial Provision)*[51] a trustee gave evidence indicating that their policy was not to consent to the withdrawal of any more funds from the settlement. This evidence was discounted on the basis that the trustee in question was the wife's solicitor in the ancillary relief proceedings and was professionally embarrassed. Furthermore, the court expected the trustees to await the outcome of the proceedings before finally exercising their discretion.

**15.41** Although '... one would expect to find that in the majority of trusts, there had not been a refusal by the trustees of a request by a settlor'[52] and 'where the requests made of trustees are reasonable in the context of all the circumstances, it would be the exception rather than the rule for trustees to refuse such requests',[53] the courts should nevertheless 'be careful not to jump too readily to the conclusion that trustees will always accede to 'judicious encouragement'.[54]

**15.42** The judgment in the trial of the ancillary relief final hearing in the *Charman* litigation is reported in *Charman v Charman (No 2)*.[55] As will be recalled, the husband was the settlor of an offshore discretionary trust. The beneficiaries included the husband, the wife, the two sons of the husband and wife, future children and remoter issue of the husband. The wife sought during ancillary relief proceedings to have the capital assets of the trust, said to be worth some £68 million, taken into account as a resource under MCA 1973, s 25(2)(a). As set out above, more specifically defined, the issue was whether the trustee, which was by this time a Bermudan trust company, would be likely immediately or in the foreseeable future to advance trust funds to the husband if he requested it to do so.

**15.43** At final hearing, the husband in *Charman v Charman (No 2)* argued that since the intention behind the Bermudan trust was to benefit future generations of his family, it ought not to be considered a resource of the parties for the purpose of the ancillary relief proceedings. On the facts of the case the dynastic intention behind the trust was rejected. However, of more general interest, Mr Justice Coleridge held that even if the dynastic intention had been established, it would have been wrong to have ignored the existence of the assets held on trust. The Bermudan trust was a discretionary trust in conventional form and the trust funds could have been made available to the husband if he requested an advance. Mr Charman appealed.

**15.44** In *Charman v Charman (No 4)*[56] the husband argued on appeal that the judge fell into error in including within the assets of the marriage the sum of

---

[51] (1982) 3 FLR 298 at 304.
[52] *Charman v Charman (No 4)* [2007] 1 FLR 1246, CA at [50].
[53] *Re The Esteem Settlement* [2004] WTLR 1 at 60.
[54] *A v A and St George Trustees Limited* [2007] 2 FLR 467 at [97].
[55] [2007] 1 FLR 593, Coleridge J.
[56] [2007] 1 FLR 1246.

£68 million held in an offshore discretionary trust. It was argued that the judge failed to ask himself the necessary question, namely whether, if Mr Charman requested the trustees to advance to him the whole (or part) of the assets of the trust, the trustees were likely to do so. If the necessary question had been asked, it was argued that the judge would have concluded that the trustees would not have advanced the whole (or part) of the assets of the trust to the husband.

**15.45**  The appeal was dismissed. When determining whether the assets held by the discretionary trust were properly to be classified as a resource, the judge did ask himself the necessary question. Having applied the correct test, the judge was right on the facts of the case to have concluded that if a request was made, funds would be likely to be advanced. Significant factors taken into account by the Court of Appeal on this issue included the fact that the husband was the settlor of the trust, the fact that the wealth of the trust represented the fruits of investments made by the trust at the husband's request in business ventures in which he was involved, the contents of the husband's first letter of wishes which provided that he should 'have the fullest possible access to the capital and income of the Settlement', and the contents of the second letter of wishes which expressed the husband's wish to be treated as the primary beneficiary.[57]

## Judicial encouragement of trustees

**15.46**  Whilst not entirely free from doubt, it is submitted that the concept of judicial encouragement is the mechanism by which a court will seek to give effect to a finding that an interest under a discretionary trust is a resource. If an affirmative answer is given to the *Charman* question (namely would a trustee be likely in the immediate or foreseeable future to advance trust assets to a beneficiary), an order cannot be made forcing a trustee to advance funds to a beneficiary spouse. Such an order would be in wholesale disregard of the trust structure and the trustees' fiduciary obligations. Instead, an order can be made that takes the resource under the discretionary trust into account and which encourages trustees to exercise their discretion to advance trust funds. As was stated by Munby J in *A v A and St George Trustees Limited*:[58]

> 'In the first place, although the court can "encourage" it cannot compel. As Mr Wagstaffe put it, and I agree, although the court can encourage a third party to transfer an asset to a party to the marriage, if that third party disregards the court's encouragement, the court has no power under *Thomas v Thomas* to compel the transfer, for only property owned by a party to the marriage can be the subject of a property adjustment or other order under the Matrimonial Causes Act 1973.'

**15.47**  When making an order that encourages trustees to make funds available to a beneficiary spouse, the court must not place improper pressure on trustees to exercise their discretion in a particular manner. However, the boundary

---

[57]  [2007] 1 FLR 1246 at [52].
[58]  [2007] 2 FLR 467 at [95].

between acceptable judicious encouragement and improper pressure is a fine one and case-specific.[59] It is submitted that improper pressure arises where an order is framed in terms that leave the trustees with no option but to advance trust funds to a beneficiary.[60] A fortiori, the award made by the court must also be capable of being met by assets and income that are in the parties' ownership as of right and not contingent upon the exercise of discretion in their favour by a trustee.[61] Furthermore, any judicial encouragement must have regard to the interests of other beneficiaries under the trust, whose interests must not be appreciably damaged by compliance with a genuine request for payment.[62]

**15.48**   It is submitted that proper judicial encouragement of trustees does not directly swell the assets of the marriage available for distribution. Instead, it enables the court to assume that the beneficiary spouse will be provided with financial assistance from the trust to relieve the burden of meeting an order of the court.[63] If it were otherwise and if the court were entitled to make an order that could only be met if the trustees advanced funds to a beneficiary spouse, then an insoluble problem as identified in the following passage taken from *TL v ML*[64] would arise:

> 'What happens if the person being encouraged says very politely "Thank you for your encouragement, but I have decided not to assist"? Or, as here, "I am only prepared to assist to such and such an extent". Is the court supposed to ignore that stance and simply make an award on the basis that the assistance will be given? What happens if and when it is not? How is the court supposed to enforce its order? It could hardly be said that the payer is in wilful default justifying a penalty under the Debtors Act 1869. It is for this reason that I expressed the view during argument that often the so called "judicious encouragement" can turn out to be no more than mere empty rhetoric.'

---

[59]   *Thomas v Thomas* [1995] 2 FLR 668, CA at 671 per Waite LJ.

[60]   See, for example, *Howard v Howard* [1945] P 1 and *B v B (Financial Provision)* (1982) 3 FLR 298.

[61]   See *TL v ML and others* [2006] 1 FLR 1263.

[62]   See *Thomas v Thomas* [1995] 2 FLR 668, CA.

[63]   Counsel for the trustees in *A v A and St George Trustees Limited* [2007] 2 FLR 467 at [97]–[98] described with apparent approval from Munby J that the question for the trustees would be whether they would exercise their discretion in such a way as to enable the husband to live more comfortably with the consequence of the order. See also *Re C (Divorce: Financial Relief)* [2008] 1 FLR 625 at [25] per Baron J: 'I note that, in this particular case, the trustees would not be asked to make funds available for this husband. They would only be asked to make funds available to enable the wife to remain in a home that she loves, but which the district judge stated was not essential. That is a relevant factor, because the court would not be asking the trustees nor be putting improper pressure upon them; it would simply be giving the trustees an opportunity to react to a proper request to assist their beneficiary.' In *Charman v Charman (No 4)* the husband was required to pay his wife a lump sum of £40 million. His non-trust assets amounted to some £55 million. However, liquidity issues to one side, the order made was theoretically capable of being met from the husband's non-trust assets.

[64]   [2006] 1 FLR 1263 at [85]. In the context of the judgment the passage cited was referring to the judicial encouragement of a parent to make money available to a child. However, it is submitted that the passage has resonance in the context of a trust situation. If trustees carry out a bona fide exercise of their discretion and decide not to advance sums to a beneficiary, there would appear to be very little that the court could do about it.

The absence of a power of compulsion against a trustee being judicially encouraged justifies a practical approach to fashioning an order in a judicial encouragement case. It is submitted that to make an order in ancillary relief proceedings which exceeds in value the assets which are the parties' as of right crosses the line between judicial encouragement and improper pressure and from a practical perspective encourages the risks of non-compliance.

**15.49** Having analysed the concept of judicial encouragement in general terms, it is worthwhile considering the Court of Appeal case of *Thomas v Thomas*,[65] which is perhaps the seminal case on the judicial encouragement of third parties to provide a spouse with the means to meet an award made by the court in ancillary relief proceedings. Strictly speaking, *Thomas* is a case concerning a company rather than a trust. Nevertheless, Glidewell LJ distilled the principles to be applied from the trust authorities as follows:

> 'The judge also had, as we have, the guidance to be derived from the various authorities to which Waite LJ has referred. Those which are the most helpful in this case are, in my view, the decisions of this court in *O'D v O'D* [1976] Fam 83, *B v B* (1982) 3 FLR 298 and *Browne v Browne* [1989] 1 FLR 291. From these authorities I derive the following principles:
>
> (a) Where a husband can only raise further capital, or additional income, as the result of a decision made at the discretion of trustees, the court should not put improper pressure on the trustees to exercise that discretion for the benefit of the wife.
>
> (b) The court should not, however, be "misled by appearances"; it should "look at the reality of the situation".
>
> (c) If on the balance of probability the evidence shows that, if trustees exercised their discretion to release more capital or income to a husband, the interests of the trust or of other beneficiaries would not be appreciably damaged, the court can assume that a genuine request for the exercise of such discretion would probably be met by a favourable response. In that situation if the court decides that it would be reasonable for a husband to seek to persuade trustees to release more capital or income to him to enable him to make proper financial provision for his children and his former wife, the court would not in so deciding be putting improper pressure on the trustees.
>
> In relation to the facts of the present case, I would apply these principles to the family company as if it were a trust, and the shareholders (the husband, his mother and brother) the trustees.'[66]

**15.50** In *Thomas* the husband was joint managing director of a family company along with his brother. The husband and his brother owned 50.05% of the shares in the company, their mother owned 25.05 % and a family trust the balance. As a matter of policy the company paid relatively low salaries, instead ploughing back profits and providing generous pension provisions to the directors. The husband's shareholding was valued at £600,000 and his

---

[65]   [1995] 2 FLR 668, CA.
[66]   See also the judgment of Waite LJ.

pension fund £394,000. His income from the company was £2,791 per month plus an additional £172 per month from other sources. The matrimonial home was worth £250,000, but subject to a mortgage of £78,000 and securities covering contingent liabilities to Lloyd's of up to £100,000 and a loan in respect of Lloyd's losses of £43,000. The net assets excluding the contingent liabilities were £1.24 million.

**15.51**  The judge at first instance ordered the sale of the former matrimonial home and the payment of a lump sum to the wife of £158,000 and periodic payments for the benefit of the children of £1,500 per month and payment of the school fees of £1,000 per month. On appeal, the award was upheld. It was noted by the Court of Appeal that the first instance judge was confronted by a husband with immediate liquidity problems but possessing substantial means. There was a heavy onus on the husband to satisfy the court that he had explored all means of access to liquid funds to make suitable provision for the wife and that access to liquid funds was not possible. The husband had failed to discharge that burden and the court could properly infer that there were available funds to provide alternative security for the bank in respect of the guarantee and the Lloyd's losses loan, the effect of which was to increase the available equity in the former matrimonial home. In respect of income, the court found that outgoings exceeded income, but only as a consequence of the inclusion of private school fees. The school fees were a luxury that the parties would have to forego unless the husband's brother and mother agreed to change the company remuneration policy. It is to be noted that the ancillary relief award did not range over assets or income that were not the husband's as of right.[67] The judicious encouragement did not amount to improper pressure on the directors of the family company to exercise their discretion in favour of the husband. If company policy was not changed, the husband would still have got by, albeit in more straitened circumstances.

**15.52**  In *TL v ML and others*,[68] Nicholas Mostyn QC, sitting as a deputy judge of the Family Division, carried out a comprehensive review of judicial encouragement authorities. The learned deputy dealt with, amongst other issues, a claim from the wife that when assessing the resources of the husband, the court ought to include the 'bounty' that the husband would continue to receive from his parents. The wife then sought an order that could only be met if the husband's parents provided him with assistance. It was held that it would neither be proper, nor correct as a matter of principle, to make an award that ranged outside the assets or income that are the husband's as of right.[69] In the context of trusts and, indeed, wider fiduciary obligations, a clear distinction was drawn in the judgment between the position where the person sought to be encouraged was a trustee with a fiduciary obligation to consider a beneficiary's

---

[67]  See *TL v ML* [2006] 1 FLR 1263 at [82].

[68]  [2006] 1 FLR 1263. The case also provides valuable guidance on maintenance pending suit applications, especially in the context of a claim for an allowance for legal costs and the proper procedure to employ when determining a dispute about the ownership of property between a spouse involved in ancillary relief proceedings and a third party.

[69]  [2006] 1 FLR 1263 at [109].

interests and the relationship of donor and donee where there is no legal obligation to consider making a payment. 'The very reason for the existence of the trust is to provide benefit for the beneficiary'.[70] The learned deputy was driven to conclude:

'If the court makes a reasonable request of trustees to make funds available to meet an ancillary relief award then it can assume that ordinarily the trustees will accede to such a request. The same cannot be assumed of a request of a mere donor, for it is his prerogative to be unreasonable, if that is his inclination.'[71]

**15.53**   As was made clear in *TL v ML*, if a court is satisfied on the balance of probabilities that a non-fiduciary third party will provide money to meet an award that a party cannot meet from his absolute property, then the court can, if it is fair to do so, make an order on that footing. If the non-fiduciary third party, whether reasonably or otherwise declines to come to the aid of the payer, there is nothing that the court can do about it. In these circumstances a third party cannot be judicially encouraged: see *C v C & Ors* [2009] EWHC 1491 at [19].

## VARIATION OF MARRIAGE SETTLEMENTS

**15.54**   Marriage settlements are not inviolable. As part of its property adjustment arsenal, the court has power under the Matrimonial Causes Act 1973 to make an order varying for the benefit of the parties to the marriage and of the children of the family or either or any of them any ante-nuptial or post-nuptial settlement (including such a settlement made by will or codicil) made on the parties to the marriage, other than one in the form of a pension arrangement (within the meaning of s 25D).[72] The court also has power to make an order extinguishing or reducing the interests of either of the parties to the marriage under any such settlements, other than one in the form of a pension arrangement (within the meaning of s 25D).[73] On an application to vary a settlement, the trustees and settlor, if still living, are required to be served with the Form A and Form E: FPR 1991, r 2.59(3). Once served, there is an option to file a sworn statement in answer within 14 days after service or receipt, as the case may be: FPR 1991, r 2.59(5). No doubt such a provision is designed to ensure that the impact of a proposed variation on third party beneficial rights is brought to the attention of the court. Furthermore, unless it is clear that their interests and rights are not adversely affected by any proposed variation, a direction may be made requiring any children concerned to be separately represented: FPR 1991, r 2.57.

---

[70]   [2006] 1 FLR 1263 at [86].
[71]   [2006] 1 FLR 1263 at [88].
[72]   MCA 1973, s 24(1)(c).
[73]   MCA 1973, s 24(1)(d).

**15.55** The leading case on the variation of nuptial settlements is *Brooks v Brooks*.[74] The issue for determination by the House of Lords was whether the court had jurisdiction to make an order varying the terms of the husband's pension scheme.[75] Their Lordships concluded that they had power to vary the scheme. In reaching their conclusion they considered the proper interpretation of 'any ante-nuptial or post-nuptial settlement' within s 24(1) of the Matrimonial Causes Act 1973 and provided some general observations on the law applicable to variation applications.

**15.56** On matters of interpretation, their Lordships held that the expression 'any ante-nuptial or post-nuptial settlement' was not to be narrowly or restrictively construed. A broad and wide meaning ought to be given to settlement in this context in order to serve the objective for which the power was given, namely to promote the best interests of the parties and their children on divorce. Consequently, 'broadly stated, the disposition must be one which makes some form of continuing provision for both or either of the parties to a marriage, with or without provision for their children'.[76] Continuing provision was to be contrasted with absolute gifts. Lord Nicholls provided guidance as to the types of disposition that would fall within the section when a broad approach is taken to the meaning of a nuptial settlement:

> 'Applying this approach, there is no difficulty with a disposition which creates interests in succession in specified property. Nor is there difficulty where the interests are concurrent but discretionary. Concurrent joint interests are nearer the borderline, such as a case where parties to a marriage hold the matrimonial home as beneficial joint tenants or tenants in common. Even in such a case, however, given the restrictions which would impede any sale of the house while the marriage subsists, this type of case has rightly been held to fall within the scope of the section: see *Brown v Brown* [1959] P 86. Periodical payment provisions have also been controversial. But income provision from settled property would readily qualify, and it is only a short step from this to include income provision which takes the form of an obligation by one party to the marriage to make periodical payments to the other. This was held to be so from the earliest days of this statutory provision whose ancestry stretches back to the Matrimonial Causes Act 1859: see *Worsley v Worsley and Wignall* (1869) LR 1 P & D 648, a decision subsequently affirmed in *Bosworthick v Bosworthick* [1927] P 64.'[77]

**15.57** The House of Lords also made some general observations in respect of the power of the court to vary a nuptial settlement.[78] Those observations were stated by Lord Nicholls as follows:

---

[74] [1995] 2 FLR 13.

[75] It is to be noted that the case was decided prior to the introduction of pension sharing orders and that the jurisdiction to vary pensions under s 24(1)(c) cannot be made unless the petition was presented prior to 1 December 2000: see Welfare Reform and Pensions Act 1999, s 85(4) and Sch 3, para 3.

[76] [1995] 2 FLR 13 at 19. See also *N v N and F Trust* [2006] 1 FLR 856, where Coleridge J additionally noted that motive was irrelevant.

[77] [1995] 2 FLR 13 at 19.

[78] For more detail on the powers of the court when exercising its jurisdiction under MCA 1973, s 24(1)(c) see *Rayden & Jackson on Divorce and Family Matters* (18th edn), paras 21.142–21.159

'One feature of the power of the court under the section is to be noted. The section gives the court power to vary a settlement. Inherent in this provision is the notion that the court's jurisdiction extends to all the property comprised in the settlement. Thus it includes any interest the settlor himself thenceforth may have in the settled property by virtue of his own settlement.[79] Further, the court's power is not confined to varying the interests of the parties to the marriage under the settlement. The power includes, for instance, the interests in the settled property of the children or, more widely, of others under an old-fashioned protective trust. *Blood v Blood* [1902] P 78 is an example of the former, and *Marsh v Marsh* (1877) 47 LJP 34 of the latter. Conversely, it is also implicit in the section that the court's power does not extend to property which is not part of the settled property. In some cases, of which *Dormer v Ward* [1901] P 20 is an example, nice questions may arise over whether property is or is not property brought into the settlement.

A further preliminary point may also be noted. Where the settled property comprises a chose in action, it is possible for the creation of the chose and the making of the settlement to be telescoped into a single transaction. Perhaps the simplest example is an insurance policy, written on terms whereby the policy proceeds are payable to persons other than the person paying the premiums. As between the latter person and the insurance company there is an arm's length commercial contract. As between him and the persons beneficially interested in the policy proceeds, there may be a marriage settlement of the proceeds, as occurred in *Lort-Williams v Lort-Williams* (above). Thus, entitlement to payment of amounts of money in one capacity, for example, as an employee, is not inconsistent with the terms of payment arranged by the employee being a marriage settlement made by him.'

**15.58** Traditionally one thinks of a settlement as being contained formally in a deed of trust. However, it should be noted that an apparently informal agreement may be capable of being a settlement within the provisions of s 24(1)(c) of the Matrimonial Causes Act 1973.[80] In *N v N and F Trust*[81] after their engagement the husband and wife began looking for a matrimonial home. Once they had agreed on a property, the house was purchased for them by a Bahamian company, whose shares were owned by a Guernsey trust. The husband was a beneficiary of the trust. After a number of years in negotiation, the trustees eventually granted an assured shorthold tenancy to the husband and the wife. On her application for ancillary relief the wife argued that the purchase of the former matrimonial home by the Bahamian company amounted to a settlement on the husband and wife of a licence to occupy

---

and *Jackson's Matrimonial Finance and Taxation* (8th edn), ch 7. The power to vary is a general principle of ancillary relief and provision of anything more than a general outline is unnecessary in this text.

[79] See the arguments raised in *Ben Hashem v Al Shayif* [2009] 1 FLR 115, dealt with later in this section.

[80] 'Where the relevant transaction is embodied in a formal written document, the exercise involves the familiar process of construction of the document ... Where the transaction ... is not said to be embodied in any formal document, the process is essentially one of finding facts, a process which can legitimately involve the process of drawing inferences with a view to ascertaining what the terms of the transaction are': *Hashem v Al Shayif and others* [2009] 1 FLR 115 at [238].

[81] [2006] 1 FLR 856 at [22]–[30].

capable of variation and which relationship was undisturbed by the subsequent tenancy, which was a matter more of form than substance. Mr Justice Coleridge agreed and stated:[82]

> 'My task is to consider what the real substance of the arrangement was which governed this property. The authorities make it clear that I should consider the question broadly and ask myself whether or not it was an arrangement which made ongoing provision for the husband, wife and/or child in those capacities. Motive is irrelevant.
>
> This property was bought by the trust during the parties' engagement and prior to their marriage. I think there can be no doubt it was nuptial. In terms of the question of ongoing provision for them during their marriage; it is hard to think of any arrangement that is more ongoing than the provision of a matrimonial home'

**15.59** Establishing the existence of a settlement capable of variation is one thing; achieving a substantial variation of that settlement is another. As we shall see it is necessary, particularly in the context of an informal settlement, to consider the nature of the property contained within the settlement. Thereafter, and perhaps of prime importance, the extent to which the court may exercise its discretionary power needs to be evaluated.[83] In broad terms, the court has a potentially far-reaching and valuable discretion to vary the terms of a nuptial settlement. The power to vary is clearly one that enables a practitioner to unlock assets for his or her client. The possibility of variation should therefore be considered as a matter of course.

**15.60** In *Charalambous v Charalambous*[84] the Court of Appeal dealt with whether it was possible for the nuptial element of a settlement to be lost, thus removing the settlement from the jurisdiction of the court to vary. The relevant background was set out by Thorpe LJ as follows:[85]

> 'The deed of settlement of 18 September 1995 purports to have been made by the husband's mother (whether she was in reality the settlor is in issue). The original trustee, a Jersey trust company, was replaced ultimately by a company connected to a Mr and Mrs Tsirides on 27 January 2003. The sum originally settled was a token US$100, subsequently supplemented by substantial assets which the wife asserts were derived from the joint resources of the parties. The settlement created a discretionary trust for the benefit of the settlor, the parties, their then only child and such other persons as the trustees might subsequently add. The trustee's powers to add or remove persons from the beneficial class are subject to the consent in writing of the "trust's" protector. The parties were appointed joint protector of the trust during their joint lives. However, the husband received the power to remove and appoint trustees.'

---

[82]  [2006] 1 FLR 856 at [33]–[34].
[83]  *Hashem v Al Shayif and others* [2009] 1 FLR 115.
[84]  [2004] 2 FLR 1093.
[85]  [2004] 2 FLR 1093 at [16].

**15.61** By instrument dated 8 January 2001, the husband and wife were removed as beneficiaries of the settlement. The husband argued that the settlement ceased to be a post-nuptial settlement upon removal of the parties as beneficiaries. This argument was rejected by the Court of Appeal. It was a question of fact whether the nuptial element of a settlement had been removed. On the facts of the case, the nuptial element had not been removed and the court retained jurisdiction at trial to vary the settlement under s 24(1)(c). In reaching this conclusion the court relied upon a number of factors, including: the fact that the parties remained joint protectors with extensive powers effectively to veto any decision of the trustees to distribute or accumulate; the removal of the parties as beneficiaries was apparently driven by a desire to protect the parties against claims that might be brought against them by the spouses' creditors; the fact that the children remained in the class of beneficiaries; the fact that the husband had benefited from the trust; and that the parties could be reinstated to the beneficial class.

**15.62** A characteristically succinct but nevertheless encyclopaedic review of the case law on variation of marriage settlements is contained within the judgment of Munby J in *Ben Hashem v Al Shayif*.[86] In that case a company owned two properties which had been used by the husband and wife throughout the marriage when they were living in the United Kingdom. One of the properties had been occupied exclusively since 2000 by the wife and (for part of that time) the husband. No rent had been paid to the company. At final hearing the wife argued, amongst other things, that both properties had been settled upon the parties as husband and wife and were capable of variation.

**15.63** It was clear that as a matter of principle the simple provision of the matrimonial home as a home for the family was cable of being a settlement within the provisions of MCA 1973, s 24(1)(c).[87] However, a key issue in this case was the determination of the nature of the property comprised within the settlement. The wife sought to argue that the reversionary interest of the company after the grant of either a life interest or licence to occupy would form part of the settlement and thus be capable of variation. This argument was rejected. A settlor's interest in the fee simple existed before the settlement and continued to exist *dehors* the settlement, the settled property being merely carved out of it.[88] Munby J concluded his judgment on this issue in the following terms:[89]

> 'it is an extraordinary proposition that because the owner of Blackacre has granted a married couple some revocable licence or tenancy to occupy, this court should have power to deal with the fee simple (or, as here, a long leasehold). Everything will, of course, depend upon the facts of the particular case. In some cases the facts will show that what has been created is an interest analogous to a life interest (or even successive life interests) or to a term of years certain. In some

---

[86]  [2009] 1 FLR 115 at [222]–[301].
[87]  See *N v N and F Trust* [2006] 1 FLR 856.
[88]  [2009] 1 FLR 115 at [249].
[89]  [2009] 1 FLR 115 at [272].

cases (and the present is one such case, in my judgment) the interest created, although sufficiently enduring to satisfy the criterion of making "continuing provision", will be analogous to a licence or tenancy determinable either at will or on notice. It is all a matter of fact. In the present case, the facts, in my judgment, although establishing a sufficient degree of continuity to bring s 24(1)(c) into play, do not point in the direction of a life interest (let alone any greater interest); they point quite clearly, as it seems to me, in the direction of an interest analogous to a licence determinable on reasonable notice.'

**15.64** The court therefore concluded that there was a settlement of a licence to occupy granted to the wife determinable upon reasonable notice in respect of the property that she had occupied exclusively since 2000. The next question for the court was to consider the basis upon which it should exercise its discretion to vary that settlement. Surprisingly, there was little assistance in the few reported authorities on variation post-1973. The learned judge was compelled to consider elderly authorities which he wove together to produce the following summary of the approach that a court should take:[90]

'Surveying all this learning, identifying what is of enduring significance whilst ruthlessly jettisoning what has become more or less irrelevant in modern conditions, I can perhaps summarise matters as follows:

(i)     The court's discretion under s 24(1)(c) is both unfettered and, in theory, unlimited. As Miss Parker put it, no limit on the extent of the power to vary or on the form any variation can take is specified, so it is within the court's powers to vary (at one end of the scale) by wholly excluding a beneficiary from a settlement, to (at the other end) transferring some asset or other to a non-beneficiary free from all trusts. She points to *E v E (Financial Provision)* and *C v C (Variation of Post-Nuptial Settlement: Company Shares)* as illustrations of property held on trust being transferred free from any trusts to the applicant, in *E v E* a sum of £50,000 and in *C v C* shares in a Cayman company.

(ii)    That said, the starting point is s 25 of the 1973 Act, so the court must, in the usual way, have regard to all the circumstances of the case and, in particular, to the matters listed in s 25(2)(a)–(h).

(iii)   The objective to be achieved is a result which, as far as it is possible to make it, is one fair to both sides, looking to the effect of the order considered as a whole.

(iv)    The settlement ought not to be interfered with further than is necessary to achieve that purpose, in other words to do justice between the parties.

(v)     Specifically, the court ought to be very slow to deprive innocent third parties of their rights under the settlement. If their interests are to be adversely affected then the court, looking at the wider picture, will normally seek to ensure that they receive some benefit which, even if not pecuniary, is approximately equivalent, so that they do not suffer substantial injury. As Sheldon J put it in the passage in *Cartwright* which I have already quoted: "if and in so far as [the variation] would affect the interests of the child, it should be permitted only if, after taking into account all the terms of the

90    [2009] 1 FLR 115 at [290].

intended order, all monetary considerations and any other relevant factors, however intangible, it can be said, on the while, to be for their benefit or, at least, not to their disadvantage."'

The learned judge gave the wife not less than 6 months' notice to vacate the property that she had been occupying. In doing so he noted that the statutory jurisdiction was one of variation and not confiscation and there was no benefit to the company or its shareholders that could be identified in resettling the property on the wife free of any trust.

**15.65** In contrast, *E v E (Financial Provision)*[91] is an example of a case where the court exercised its powers of variation in sweeping terms, albeit bound by the confines that third party rights should not be invaded other than as fairness requires. In this case the wife sought to vary a post-nuptial settlement. The beneficiaries were the husband, the wife, the husband's children and remoter issue by any subsequent wife. The trust contained a protector clause, the effect of which was that the powers of the trustee were only exercisable with the consent of the protector, who in this case was the husband's father. On the facts of the case, the protector would not have given his consent to any exercise of discretion that would benefit the wife. The net value of the fund was just over £1 million. Ewbank J ordered £250,000 to be pulled out of the settlement and a separate fund created for the wife, in which £50,000 was to be given absolutely to the wife and the remaining £200,000 settled on the wife for life, with the remainder held for the children of the marriage. The remainder of the fund was to remain on trust for the husband and the children. The husband's father was removed as a protector of both the settlement created for the benefit of the wife and the settlement of the remaining funds. As a further example of the powers of the Family Division on the variation of a post-nuptial settlement, the learned judge ordered that the trustees of the discretionary trust be changed as well.

**15.66** When considering the exercise of his powers in respect of the post-nuptial settlement, Ewbank J stated that 'the first consideration is the welfare of the children, and the second consideration, in my judgment, is that I should not interfere with it more than is necessary for the purposes of s 25'.[92] Although each case will of course turn on its own facts, third party beneficial interests will not be lightly interfered with.

**15.67** It is important to note that offshore trusts can be penetrated by a court exercising its powers under the ancillary relief regime. In *Charalambous v Charalambous*[93] the Court of Appeal held that the courts of England and Wales have jurisdiction under MCA 1973, s 24 to vary a post-nuptial settlement of an overseas trust. The trust in question was a Jersey trust and contained an exclusive jurisdiction clause in favour of the Royal Courts of Jersey. This did not prevent the court having power to vary the settlement, because the power to

---

[91]   [1990] 2 FLR 233.
[92]   [1990] 2 FLR 233 at 249.
[93]   [2004] 2 FLR 1093, CA.

vary was 'derived not from the settlement but from the matrimonial regime of the state. Equally the right to seek variation derives not from the settlement but from the matrimonial regime of the jurisdiction that dissolves the marriage'.[94] The trust instrument also contained an express choice of law clause in favour of Jersey. But the Court of Appeal held that after the pronouncement of a decree on a divorce petition 'all ancillary issues must be determined in accordance with the relevant provisions of the Matrimonial Causes Act 1973'.[95] In so holding, the Court of Appeal rejected the husband's submissions that the Recognition of Trusts Act 1987 operated in such a manner that the provisions contained in the choice of law and exclusive jurisdiction clause ought to be followed.

**15.68**  Post-*Charalambous* English courts appear to be more receptive to requests, certainly of the Royal Court of Jersey,[96] to exercise judicial restraint in the exercise of their power to vary offshore trusts. The Royal Court has suggested that English courts should refrain from exercising their jurisdiction to vary Jersey trusts and that instead they ought to request the Jersey courts to act as an auxiliary with regard to any proposed variation. Such an approach would avoid the prospect of inconsistent judgments between the English courts making an order varying offshore trusts and the prospect of enforcement not being ordered. The approach outlined was described by the Court of Appeal in *Charman v Charman (No 4)*[97] as an 'important suggestion'. In much the same way in *Mubarak v Mubarak*[98] Holman J recognised that as a general rule it would be an exorbitant exercise of jurisdiction for an English court to purport to vary a Jersey settlement. Nevertheless, on the extraordinary facts of that case, which were said to take it outside of the general rule, variation of a Jersey trust was ordered. In so ordering, Holman J was of the view that the prospect of enforcement was not sufficiently low to warrant the order not being made in the first place. If it is sought to argue that a case falls outside the general rule and that the exercise of jurisdiction would not be exorbitant, consideration should be given at final hearing to obtaining evidence of the prospect of enforcement. It is beyond the scope of this book to provide a comprehensive description of the response to enforcement of variation orders outside of the jurisdiction. Clearly this is a matter for a foreign lawyer, both, as we have seen, in order to obtain the variation order in the first place, but also to avoid the prospect of a pyrrhic victory.

---

[94]  [2004] 2 FLR 1093 at [30].
[95]  [2004] 2 FLR 1093 at [31].
[96]  *Re B Trust* [2006] JLR 562 at [30]–[32].
[97]  [2007] 1 FLR 1246 at [58]; and see *P v P (Post-Separation Accruals and Earning Capacity)* [2008] 2 FLR 1135, Moylan J.
[98]  [2007] 2 FLR 364 at [159]. However, see *Mubarak v Mubarak* [2009] 1 FLR 664, where the Royal Court refused to enforce the order made by Holman J.

# SHAM TRUSTS AND THE CONSEQUENCES OF NON-DISCLOSURE

**15.69**   Perhaps the option of last resort for a spouse seeking to unlock trust funds is an argument that the trust is in fact a sham. A sham exists where acts or 'documents are not intended to create the legal rights and obligations which they give the appearance of creating'.[99] For acts or documents to be a sham, all the parties to the sham should have a common intention that the acts or documents, whether bilateral or unilateral, were not to create the legal rights and obligations which they give the appearance of creating. The establishment of the common intention is a key fact-finding exercise for the court to undertake. In an appropriate case reckless indifference would be taken to constitute the necessary intention: see *A v A and St Georges Trustees Limited*[100] and *Minwalla v Minwalla and others*.[101]

**15.70**   Establishing a sham is not an easy task, mainly because the bona fides of any trustee of the settlement would have to be impugned. As stated by Neuberger J in *National Westminster Bank v Jones*,[102] 'there is a strong and natural presumption against holding a provision or document a sham'. Running an argument of sham will in general be an expensive and difficult exercise. In *A v A and St George Trustees Limited* the wife failed to impugn the bona fides of the trustees and her claim accordingly failed. The litigation was a disaster for the wife, who ultimately bore a heavy costs order which served significantly to reduce her award.[103] In his judgment Munby J noted that a trust could not, as a matter of law, be a sham if either the original trustees or the current trustees were not, because they lacked the requisite knowledge and intention, parties to the sham at the time of their appointment. It followed that a trust that was initially a sham could become a valid trust if subsequently appointed trustees did not have the requisite knowledge and intention of the sham. Furthermore, as a matter of principle a trust which was not initially a sham could not subsequently become a sham unless the trustees and the beneficiaries, all of whom had to be ascertained, joined together for the purpose of a sham.

**15.71**   In *Minwalla v Minwalla*[104] Singer J adopted the following analysis of the law in relation to sham trusts:

> 'In order for a trust to be found to be a sham, both of the parties to the establishment of the trust (that is to say the settlor and the trustees in the usual case) must intend not to act on the terms of the trust deed. Alternatively in the case where one party intends not to act on the terms of the trust deed, the other

---

[99]   *Snook v London and West Riding Investments Ltd* [1967] 2 QB 786 per Diplock LJ. See also *Midland Bank v Wyatt* [1995] 1 FLR 696.

[100]   [2007] 2 FLR 467.

[101]   [2005] 1 FLR 771.

[102]   [2000] BPIR 1092 referred to in *A v A and St George Trustees Limited* [2007] 2 FLR 467 at [53].

[103]   *A v A (No 2)* [2007] EWHC 1810.

[104]   [2005] 1 FLR 771 at [53]–[55].

party must at least be prepared to go along with the intentions of the shammer neither knowing or caring about what they are signing or the transactions they are carrying out.'

**15.72**   In *Minwalla* the husband was a wealthy international businessman. He conducted a large part of his affairs through a Panamanian company. Another Panamanian company owned the former matrimonial home. The shares in both companies were owned by a Jersey trust. The husband claimed that he had no beneficial interest in either the Jersey trust or the two Panamanian companies. The husband failed to comply with his disclosure obligations, with the learned judge finding that it was 'no exaggeration to describe H's stance in relation to the court and to W's claim as wilfully contemptuous of his obligation to make full, frank and clear disclosure in these proceedings so that the overall objective of fairness to both parties can be facilitated'.[105] The wife was consequently compelled to conduct a costly investigation into the husband's affairs. The Jersey trust company along with the two Panamanian companies were joined as parties to the proceedings. Letters of request were issued and directed to the nominee directors of the two companies and the managers of the trust. Pursuant to the letters of request a 2-day hearing was conducted in Jersey and the transcript of the questions asked by the wife's counsel and the answers given was relied upon by Singer J in his judgment. Much of the information about the husband's affairs was obtained by the wife during this process, and the learned judge commented that:

'During this case there has been a series of three letters of request addressed to CI in Jersey. In each case the requests have attracted maximum co-operation from the Jersey courts. They have been dealt with with the utmost courtesy, speed and efficiency. I am given to understand that Deputy Judicial Greffier Matthews, who has had the management in Jersey of this case, has gone out of his way to accommodate the timetable laid down by this court for the progress of the case, and has fitted in hearings so as to enable the information to be produced speedily. I am informed that there is statutory provision in Jersey that, if there be an oral hearing on the letters of request, English counsel have a right of audience, so that they may investigate the matters arising on the letters of request with the respondent to the hearing; and, secondly, that no order as to costs is made by the court. (Although that is not to say that in an appropriate case the witness should not recover the expense, including professional time, incurred in meeting the request: in this case and understandably CI did not pursue the totality of their potential claim under this head.) This is, therefore, an efficacious and comparatively inexpensive method of extracting necessary information concerning off-shore trusts where the settlor or beneficiary is unwilling to provide relevant information.

It has, however, been courteously drawn to my attention in a letter from Mr Jowitt, the Senior Legal Adviser to the Law Officers' Department in Jersey, that it is important for English courts and lawyers to bear well in mind that such assistance as letters of request can provide must be sought in accordance with the formal requirements of the Hague Convention of 18 March 1970 on the Taking of

---

[105]   [2005] 1 FLR 771 at [16].

Evidence Abroad in Civil or Commercial Matters, which in the case of Jersey requires that they be sent to Her Majesty's Attorney-General for Jersey, and not direct to residents of the island or to public authorities there.'

**15.73** The evidence relied upon in support of the sham included two contradictory letters of wishes from the husband to the trustees in respect of the exercise of their discretion; periodic wealth statements in which the husband had included the assets of the trust as his own; the absence of trading accounts for the two companies; the fact that the husband treated the bank account of one of the Panamanian companies as his own; evidence from the hearing in Jersey that the trustees accepted that the husband had total investment control over one of the companies; and that the same company was in truth the husband's alter ego. It was also revealed during the hearing in Jersey that the trustee had not seen company bank statements, nor had knowledge of the existence of a consultancy agreement under which significant sums were to be paid to one of the Panamanian companies.

**15.74** Singer J stated:[106]

'The nature and structure of sophisticated off-shore arrangements such as have been deployed by H is well understood in this Division. No doubt the professional advisers and trustees of wealthy individuals wish honestly to strive to construct a network of interwoven trusts and companies able successfully to withstand the scrutiny of the internal revenue services of the parts of the world relevant to the interested parties. That shelter is dependent upon there being properly constituted corporate and trust structures in place; and there being a level of competence and of formality in the production of minutes of board meetings, powers of attorney and so on. There must also be supporting evidence (if and when questions arise which must be answered) for the proposition that proper consideration has been given by the trustees to the exercise of their discretionary powers.'

**15.75** In light of the evidence referred to and the finding that the trustees were 'certainly prepared to go along almost totally passively with the way in which H made plain he intended to manage and was managing this trust',[107] the learned judge concluded that the husband was not entitled to rely on the shelter of the offshore trust. The trust was found to be a sham and the assets of the trust, namely the shares in the two Panamanian companies, vested in the husband. As part of the order made, the learned judge ordered the shares in the companies to be transferred to the wife, thereby giving her the ability to realise assets held by the companies.

**15.76** *Minwalla* is a case that is also of interest in respect of the approach which a court should adopt in circumstances where one party has failed to meet their disclosure obligations and sought to hide their assets off-shore. The approach to be adopted was summarised by the learned judge as follows:

---

[106] [2005] 1 FLR 771 at [51].
[107] [2005] 1 FLR 771 at [58].

'As is already apparent from this judgment thus far, I am far from persuaded that H has made proper disclosure of his financial resources in this case. He has set out at every juncture to obstruct W's investigation of his financial affairs. He has, I find, concealed resources, and has been taking steps throughout the pendency of these proceedings to put them beyond the reach of this court and of any enforcement process that W may be minded to pursue against him, whether in this country or elsewhere. In *J v V (Disclosure: Offshore Corporations)* [2003] EWHC 3110 (Fam), [2004] 1 FLR 1042, to which I referred at the start of this judgment, Coleridge J condemned the all-too frequent practice of attempting to conceal resources behind the screen of off-shore structures and identified the costs consequences that would flow from such litigation conduct. I agree entirely with each of those observations. The suppression of assets is not of course behaviour that of itself enhances an award. But the non-disclosing spouse does make himself vulnerable to adverse inferences being drawn against him, in accordance with the well-established line of authorities recording that principle, of which *Baker v Baker* [1995] 2 FLR 829 was a useful example. In this case, given the relative modesty of the claim that is advanced by W in the context of the standard of living enjoyed by the parties during the marriage, I readily conclude that H has available to him ample resources with which to satisfy an award at or about that level.

Nevertheless, it is of course appropriate that I should examine (so far as I can despite his lies and obfuscations) what are the actual resources of H in order that the probable scale of his fortune may be understood, against which I can then measure the claim by W and the award that I have in mind to make.'[108]

Having undertaken that task, the wife was awarded a lump sum of £4,185,000 as against the husband's assets, which were found to be between £13m and £14m at least. The sum awarded was based upon a *Duxbury* fund, the wife's reasonable housing aspirations, a car, clearance of her debt and the costs of meeting litigation that the husband was likely to bring against her.

**15.77** In *Re Fountain Trust*[109] the Royal Court observed that an assumption of jurisdiction by a judge of the High Court to declare a Jersey trust to be a sham would generally be exorbitant. The Court of Appeal in *Charman v Charman (No 4)* agreed with this proposition.[110] The *Fountain Trust* case concerned an application to enforce the order in *Minwalla*. The Royal Court noted that where there was an exorbitant exercise of jurisdiction, the courts of Jersey would be reluctant to enforce an order of the High Court. However, on the facts of the case the order would be enforced as a matter of comity because the trustees submitted to the jurisdiction and because it was not contrary to public policy to enforce the order in circumstances where the husband had been obstructive and failed to disclose his assets. The Royal Court also noted that in relation to a trust governed by Jersey law and Jersey trustees, the Jersey law of sham and not the English law should have been applied. It may be the case, then, that in future cases where an offshore trust is sought to be declared a sham, the trial of

---

[108] [2005] 1 FLR 771 at [45]–[46]. See also **4.50** for further consideration of the consequences of non-disclosure.
[109] [2005] JLR 359.
[110] [2007] 1 FLR 1246 at [58].

a preliminary issue offshore may be the appropriate way to proceed. In other cases falling outside the general rule, careful consideration will need to be given to the enforceability of High Court orders declaring trusts to be shams.

## JOINING TRUSTEES

**15.78**  Practitioners will frequently have to consider whether it is necessary to join trustees to ancillary relief proceedings.[111] The reported cases dealing with this issue predominantly concern themselves with overseas trusts, where the issue of enforcement is one of the prime considerations.[112]

**15.79**  In *T v T and others (Joinder of Third Parties)*,[113] the husband was a successful businessman who transferred his business interests to be held by a Jersey trust. The value of the trust fund was said to be £25m. The husband was entitled to the interest from the fund for life and the trustees had a power to appoint income and capital to whichever beneficiary they chose. The power of appointment was subject to a protector clause, whereby the husband's consent to the appointment was required during his lifetime. The husband was a beneficiary, as were his children and any spouse of his for the time being. The wife obtained a freezing injunction[114] without notice that was subsequently upheld at a contested hearing. One of the reasons for extending the injunction was that there was a denial by the husband that he effectively controlled the interests under the Jersey trust. However, the issue in the reported case was whether the trustees for the Jersey trust ought to be joined as parties to the ancillary relief proceedings.

**15.80**  In the High Court the power to order a person to be added as a party in ancillary relief proceedings is, by virtue of r 1(3) of the Family Proceedings Rules 1991, contained in RSC Ord 15, r 6(2)(b)(i) and (ii). Ord 15, r 6(2)(b)(i) confers power on the court to order any person to be added as a party 'whose presence before the court is necessary to ensure that all matters in dispute in the cause or matter may be effectually and completely determined and adjudicated upon'. Ord 15, r 6(2)(b)(ii) provides the court with power to add as a party, 'any person between whom and any party to the cause or matter there may exist a question or issue arising out of or relating to or connected with any relief or remedy claimed in the cause or matter which in the opinion of the court it would be just and convenient to determine as between him and that party as well as between the parties to the cause or matter.'

---

[111]  See Chapter 5 as to joinder of parties. It appears that joinder of a third party is not appropriate if the only purpose for which joinder is sought is to seek disclosure from that person: *Re T (Divorce: Interim Maintenance: Discovery)* [1990] 1 FLR 1.

[112]  Enforcement of English court orders is beyond the scope of this book. Reference should, however, be made to Mark Harper *International Trust and Divorce Litigation* (Jordans, 2007).

[113]  [1996] 2 FLR 357.

[114]  See Chapter 6 for consideration of orders preventing the dissipation of assets.

**15.81**   In *T v T and others (Joinder of Third Parties)* it was held that the application to join the Jersey trustees fell within both limbs of r 6(2)(b).[115] Wilson J stated that:

> 'A crucial matter for my determination in March 1996 will be to evaluate the real control over the assets of this trust which forms so substantial a fund in relation to any other assets which the parties have. Are these funds, in terms of capital and not just of income, funds which, in effect although not in form, are able to be deployed by the husband? That is directly relevant to the duty of inquiry that I have under s 25(2)(a) of the Act. I have to have regard to the "... property and other financial resources which each of the parties to the marriage has ...". It seems to me that that question will, in addition to its relevance to any lump sum order, be of the greatest importance in the decision which I reach as to whether (and if so in what terms) to vary the settlement under s 24(1)(c).'

**15.82**   Another factor relied upon by the learned judge was his view that the enforcement of any order made would be more likely to be facilitated by the trustees being joined as parties to the proceedings. Enforcement of English ancillary relief orders overseas is a matter of foreign law and beyond the remit of this book. However, it makes sense when dealing with offshore assets to obtain advice from an overseas lawyer on the method and ease with which English ancillary relief orders may be enforced.

**15.83**   In *C v C (Variation of Post-Nuptial Settlement: Company Shares)*[116] the trustees were not joined. The offshore trust held the husband's former shareholding in an English company. The value of the shareholding was agreed at £313,246. The trial judge felt confident that the husband would co-operate 'to the fullest extent with any order that I make'. The underlying assets of the trust were effectively onshore, being assets in an English company. The learned judge was also satisfied that he was possessed of adequate powers to deal with enforcement of the variation of settlement order that he proposed to make. In these circumstances, the learned judge approved the entirely responsible decision not to join the trustees.

**15.84**   Another case where trustees were not joined was *Charalambous v Charalambous*.[117] On the facts of the case there was a clear issue as to whether the high legal costs incurred were proportionate to the sums at stake. Both parties asserted that they were either insolvent or in straitened financial circumstances. The sums targeted by the wife in her application under MCA 1973, s 24 amounted to £250,000. The said assets were held offshore, but neither party had joined the trustees at the time that the interim application was heard, and Arden LJ stated that if the wife were to obtain an order under s 24(1)(c) 'she will have to take separate proceedings against the trustees, probably in Jersey, in order that they too should be bound by the order'.[118]

---

[115]   The case is also authority for the proposition that service of a Form A on a trustee does not make the trustee a party to the proceedings.
[116]   [2003] 2 FLR 493, Coleridge J.
[117]   [2004] 2 FLR 1093.
[118]   [2004] 2 FLR 1093 at 1108.

**15.85** As the authorities indicate, whether trustees should be joined as parties to ancillary relief proceedings is case-specific.[119] However, in general where it is sought to vary a settlement and/or argue that the trust is a sham, it is submitted that joining trustees as parties to the ancillary relief proceedings is essential. Joining the trustees in theory minimises enforcement difficulties and subjects trustees to the duty of litigation disclosure,[120] as opposed to the more cumbersome inspection appointment regime. It is often sensible to make application to join the trustees at FDA and certainly prior to the FDR.[121] Helpful guidance on joinder was given by Munby J in *A v A (No 2)*,[122] when he commented that there was no need to join trustees where a judicial encouragement argument was being run, but joinder was necessary when a sham was being alleged.

## TAX CONSEQUENCES

**15.86** The jurisdiction of the court to take into account a beneficial interest in an offshore trust as a resource and the power to vary offshore settlements has been outlined. Where offshore assets are involved and where one of the parties may be a non-domicile, the tax consequences of any order sought needs to be carefully considered. The court will of course want to know the tax consequences of any proposed order, whether or not the assets are offshore. In a suitable case the early instruction of a joint expert to deal with the effect of the range of options available to the court and the parties may be a sensible way to proceed.

---

[119] Of course, trustees have to be served with the Applicant's Form A and Form E: see FPR 2.59(3).

[120] Although joinder purely for the purpose of obtaining disclosure would appear to be improper: *Re T (Divorce: Interim Maintenance: Discovery)* [1990] 1 FLR 1.

[121] In *Minwalla v Minwalla* [2005] 1 FLR 771, Singer J joined the trust company and offshore companies whose shares were said to be held by the trust as parties to the proceedings prior to the FDR.

[122] [2008] 1 FLR 1428.

# Part VII

# INHERITED ASSETS, GIFTS AND NON-MATRIMONIAL PROPERTY

# Chapter 16

# NON-MATRIMONIAL PROPERTY

**16.1**  One of the thorniest issues in modern ancillary relief practice is the question of how assets which have not been accumulated by the joint endeavours of the parties during the marriage should be divided. The methods by which such assets may have been acquired by the parties are varied and numerous. Most common in practice are inherited assets, gifts made to one of the parties, and assets which a party acquired before the relationship or marriage commenced. An understanding of how the courts approach the division of such assets is now a fundamental aspect of the ancillary relief practitioner's required knowledge.

## THE ORIGINS OF THE MATRIMONIAL/NON-MATRIMONIAL ASSET DISTINCTION

**16.2**  Prior to the introduction of the 'yardstick of equality' and then the 'sharing principle' the distinction between matrimonial and non-matrimonial assets was rarely of significance in most cases because the applicant's reasonable needs were usually the determining consideration. However, in *White v White*[1] Lord Nicholls said:

> 'This distinction [between inherited property and matrimonial property] is a recognition of the view, widely but not universally held, that property owned by one spouse before the marriage, and inherited property whenever acquired, stand on a different footing from what may be loosely called matrimonial property. According to this view, on a breakdown of the marriage these two classes of property should not necessarily be treated in the same way. Property acquired before marriage and inherited property acquired during marriage come from a source wholly external to the marriage. In fairness, where this property still exists, the spouse to whom it was given should be allowed to keep it. Conversely, the other spouse has a weaker claim to such property than he or she may have regarding matrimonial property.
>
> Plainly, when present, this factor is one of the circumstances of the case. It represents a contribution made to the welfare of the family by one of the parties to the marriage. The judge should take it into account. He should decide how important it is in the particular case. The nature and value of the property, and the time when and circumstances in which the property was acquired, are among the

---

[1]    [2001] 1 AC 596 at 610.

relevant matters to be considered. However, in the ordinary course, this factor can be expected to carry little weight, if any, in a case where the claimant's financial needs cannot be met without recourse to this property.'

**16.3**    Lord Nicholls returned to this theme in *Miller v Miller; McFarlane v McFarlane*:[2]

'This does not mean that, when exercising his discretion, a judge in this country must treat all property in the same way. The statute requires the court to have regard to all the circumstances of the case. One of the circumstances is that there is a real difference, a difference of source, between: (1) property acquired during the marriage otherwise than by inheritance or gift, sometimes called the marital acquest but more usually the matrimonial property; and (2) other property. The former is the financial product of the parties' common endeavour, the latter is not. The parties' matrimonial home, even if this was brought into the marriage at the outset by one of the parties, usually has a central place in any marriage. So it should normally be treated as matrimonial property for this purpose. As already noted, in principle the entitlement of each party to a share of the matrimonial property is the same however long or short the marriage may have been.

The matter stands differently regarding property ("non-matrimonial property") the parties bring with them into the marriage or acquire by inheritance or gift during the marriage. Then the duration of the marriage will be highly relevant. The position regarding non-matrimonial property was summarised in the *White* case, at 610 and 994 respectively:

> "In the case of a short marriage, fairness may well require that the claimant should not be entitled to a share of the other's non-matrimonial property. The source of the asset may be a good reason for departing from equality. This reflects the instinctive feeling that parties will generally have less call upon each other on the breakdown of a short marriage."

With longer marriages the position is not so straightforward. Non-matrimonial property represents a contribution made to the marriage by one of the parties. Sometimes, as the years pass, the weight fairly to be attributed to this contribution will diminish, sometimes it will not. After many years of marriage the continuing weight to be attributed to modest savings introduced by one party at the outset of the marriage may well be different from the weight attributable to a valuable heirloom intended to be retained in specie. Some of the matters to be taken into account in this regard were mentioned in the above citation from the *White* case. To this non-exhaustive list should be added, as a relevant matter, the way the parties organised their financial affairs.'

**16.4**    Baroness Hale (in the speech expressly supported by the majority of their Lordships in *Miller/McFarlane*) agreed that the significance of assets introduced from outside the marriage will diminish over time.[3] She also said that it is important to look at how the parties have run their lives in deciding

---

2    [2006] 1 FLR 1186 at [22]–[25].
3    [2006] 1 FLR 1186 at [152].

how any such assets should be shared.[4] She went on to state that in 'very big money cases' it might also be necessary to take into account assets acquired solely or mainly by the efforts of one party.[5] This further category of 'unilateral assets' may also justify inequality of division of the assets, even though those assets may have been acquired during the course of the marriage. However, this is a Pandora's box which the lower courts have, as yet, been reluctant to open. In *Charman v Charman (No 4)*[6] the Court of Appeal noted that Baroness Hale's comments were obiter, but still commanded great respect. Nevertheless, the court indicated that the concept of unilateral assets should remain 'closely confined'.[7] If the law was to move in that direction it was likely to be a 'no doubt cautious movement in the law towards a more frequent distribution of property upon divorce in accordance with what, by words or conduct, the parties appear previously to have agreed'. So, when considering the concept of unilateral property, the Court of Appeal appears to have changed the emphasis from the efforts of the party who acquired it (which Baroness Hale had used as the definition of such property in *Miller/McFarlane*) to the married couple's agreement to regard this property as different from matrimonial property.

**16.5** Lord Nicholls and Baroness Hale also stated that the former matrimonial home will always be regarded as matrimonial property, even if brought into the marriage by one of the parties. However, that does not necessarily mean that the matrimonial home should automatically be shared equally.[8]

## THE DEVELOPMENT OF GUIDANCE AND PRINCIPLES

**16.6** In *B v B (Ancillary Relief)*[9] the Court of Appeal stressed that the decisions in *White v White*, *Miller/McFarlane* and *Charman v Charman (No 4)* did not establish that the starting point in every case was equality of division. The objective in each case was fairness. The yardstick of equality was to be used as a cross-check to ensure that the division in each case was fair. Against this very general guidance it is clear that assets brought into the marriage by gift or inheritance are categorised as non-matrimonial property, with the exception in general of any property brought into the marriage and subsequently used as a matrimonial home.[10] Property acquired during the marriage up until the date of separation[11] otherwise than by inheritance or gift is treated as matrimonial property,[12] with the exception that in a big money short marriage case business or investment assets generated solely or mainly by

---

[4]   [2006] 1 FLR 1186 at [153].
[5]   [2006] 1 FLR 1186 at [150]–[153].
[6]   [2007] 1 FLR 1246.
[7]   [2007] 1 FLR 1246 at [86].
[8]   See Baron J in *NA v MA* [2007] 1 FLR 1760 at [175].
[9]   [2008] 2 FLR 1627.
[10]  *Miller v Miller; McFarlane v McFarlane* [2006] 1 FLR 1186 at [22] per Lord Nicholls.
[11]  *Miller v Miller; McFarlane v McFarlane* [2006] 1 FLR 1186 at [175] per Lord Mance.
[12]  Also known as 'the marital acquest'.

the efforts of one party[13] may be treated as non-matrimonial property.[14] Some further guidance on the question of how non-matrimonial property should be dealt with have arisen from the case law. The general principles are summarised in the following paragraphs. They do not appear in order of importance. The facts of each case will determine the relative importance of each principle.

**16.7**  First, when dividing up assets there is no scope for either ignoring non-matrimonial property or for leaving it off the 'balance sheet' of assets. This principle applies regardless of whether the property was acquired before the marriage, during the marriage, or after separation. As soon as *White v White* was reported, Lord Nicholls's words contained in the last two sentences of the second paragraph set out on the first page of this chapter were seized upon by lawyers seeking to persuade the court to move away from an equal division of assets. They sought to argue that such inherited assets should be left out of account when the other assets were divided. Some further support for this view appeared to be provided by the Court of Appeal when it had one of its first opportunities to consider the effect of *White v White*. In *Cowan v Cowan*[15] Thorpe LJ only quoted this selective passage from Lord Nicholls's guidance as to the relevance of an inheritance:[16]

> 'Property acquired before marriage and inherited property acquired during marriage come from a source wholly external to the marriage. In fairness, where this property still exists, the spouse to whom it was given should be allowed to keep it.'

This argument for wholly excluding the inherited assets from the assets to be divided between the parties was used with partial success in *H v H (Financial Provision: Special Contribution)*,[17] where the court disregarded from its calculations an inheritance the husband had received but always 'kept separate and apart' from the other family assets. However, in the same case the court included in the family balance sheet other inheritances which the parties had

---

[13]  Also known as 'unilateral assets': see *S v S (Non-Matrimonial Property: Conduct)* [2007] 1 FLR 1496 per Burton J. The treatment of unilateral assets as if they were non-matrimonial property arguably may in an appropriate case extend to a 'dual career' family 'where both parties worked throughout the marriage, had pooled some of the assets built up by their efforts but had chosen to keep other such assets under their separate control, the latter, although unequal in amount, were unilateral assets': see *Charman v Charman (No 4)* [2007] 1 FLR 1246 at [86].

[14]  *Miller v Miller; McFarlane v McFarlane* [2006] 1 FLR 1186 at [149]–[153] and *Charman v Charman (No 4)* [2007] 1 FLR 1246 at [83].

[15]  [2001] 2 FLR 192.

[16]  [2001] 2 FLR 192 at 212. See also Mance LJ at 240–1.

[17]  [2002] 2 FLR 1021. The decision was criticised by Bennett J in *Norris v Norris* [2003] 1 FLR 1142 at 1162 and he declined to follow it. It is fair to note that the decision in *H v H* to leave the inheritance out of account completely was wrong in principle, but the drawing of a distinction between an inheritance which has been kept separate and apart from the other assets and one which has been used by both parties for the joint family benefit is appropriate in the light of the speeches of Lord Nicholls and Baroness Hale in *Miller v Miller; McFarlane v McFarlane* [2006] 1 FLR 1186, and would justify the ultimate order made in *H v H*.

permitted to become more mixed in the 'family pool', or which they had both played a role in realising and managing.

**16.8** The argument that an inherited property or other non-matrimonial property could be 'quarantined' from the pool of assets upon which the discretion under the Matrimonial Causes Act 1973, s 25 operated was comprehensively demolished in *Norris v Norris* by Bennett J who, after considering the words of s 25, said:[18]

> 'applying the words of the statute, in my judgment, the court is required to take account of *all* property of each party. That must include property acquired during the marriage by gift or succession or as a beneficiary under a trust. Thus, what comes in by statute through the front door ought not, in my judgment, to be put out of the back door, and thus not remain within the court's discretionary exercise, without very good reason. In my judgment, merely because inherited property has not been touched or does not become part of the matrimonial pot is not necessarily, without more, a reason for excluding it from the court's discretionary exercise.'

Bennett J went on to confirm that an inheritance was one of the factors the court should consider under the heading 'contributions', as suggested in the third of Lord Nicholls's paragraphs set out above. This approach was confirmed in *GW v RW (Financial Provision: Departure from Equality)*[19] and *P v P (Inherited Property)*,[20] although in *Re G (Financial Provision: Liberty to Restore Application for Lump Sum)*[21] Singer J appears to have suggested that the inheritance could be 'ring-fenced' if the wife's claim could be satisfied without recourse to it.[22] The point was not required to be considered explicitly by the House of Lords in *Miller v Miller; McFarlane v McFarlane*,[23] but the approach which is implicit throughout their Lordships' speeches is consistent with the need to consider all the assets, whatever their origin. Indeed, Lord Nicholls[24] and Baroness Hale[25] both referred to *P v P (Inherited Property)* in the course of their speeches without criticism of that approach. Furthermore, Lord Nicholls indicated the need to distinguish 'matrimonial' and 'non-matrimonial' property flexibly, whilst underlining the need for the judge to 'give to the contribution made by one party's non-matrimonial property the weight he considers just',[26] thereby suggesting general agreement with the proposition that all the assets must be considered as part of the s 25 exercise of discretion. If any doubt remained following the *Miller/McFarlane* decision, it was firmly dispelled by the Court of Appeal in *Charman v Charman*

---

[18] [2003] 1 FLR 1142 at 1162.
[19] [2003] 2 FLR 108.
[20] [2005] 1 FLR 576, considered in more detail below.
[21] [2004] 1 FLR 997 at 1006.
[22] This was an unusual case where the inheritance was obtained long after the parties separated. It is considered in more detail at **18.45**.
[23] [2006] 1 FLR 1186.
[24] [2006] 1 FLR 1186 at [20].
[25] [2006] 1 FLR 1186 at [148].
[26] [2006] 1 FLR 1186 at [27].

*(No 4)*,[27] which held that the 'sharing principle' applies to all the parties' property but, to the extent that their property is non-matrimonial, there is likely to be better reason for departure from equality.[28]

**16.9** The second general principle, as already made clear by the foregoing paragraphs, is that non-matrimonial property is different in its nature from the other property acquired by the parties during the marriage, which is variously termed 'matrimonial property'[29] or 'family assets'.[30] Non-matrimonial property is usually taken into account as an unmatched contribution made to the welfare of the family by one party.[31] The weight to be given to this contribution will be determined by all the circumstances of the case, and Lord Nicholls identified some relevant factors in the third paragraph quoted from his speech in *White v White* above.

**16.10** Thirdly, the nature of the property inherited is also a relevant factor to consider when assessing how inherited property is to be dealt with. Greater weight may be given to arguments seeking to preserve the non-matrimonial property for one party where it is inherited property in the form of a family heirloom or an asset which has been retained in the same form within the family for many generations. In *P v P (Inherited Property)*[32] Munby J said:

'There is inherited property and inherited property. Sometimes, as in *White v White* itself, the fact that certain property was inherited will count for little ... On other occasions the fact may be of the greatest significance. Fairness may require quite a different approach if the inheritance is a pecuniary legacy that accrues during the marriage than if the inheritance is a landed estate that has been within one spouse's family for generations and has been brought into the marriage with an expectation that it will be retained in specie for future generations.

That said, the reluctance to realise landed property must be kept within limits. After all, there is, sentiment apart, little economic difference between a spouse's

---

[27] [2007] 1 FLR 1246.

[28] [2007] 1 FLR 1246 at [66]. See **16.18** et seq for a discussion as to the extent to which the Court of Appeal's words in *Charman v Charman (No 4)* require the matrimonial and non-matrimonial property to be accurately identified and valued.

[29] Lord Nicholls in *White v White* and *Miller v Miller; McFarlane v McFarlane*.

[30] Lord Denning in *Wachtel v Wachtel* [1973] Fam 72 and Baroness Hale in *Miller v Miller; McFarlane v McFarlane*. It should be noted that these terms are used as a matter of convenience in the modern ancillary relief cases to describe a category of assets. They should not, as Baroness Hale pointed out in *Miller v Miller; McFarlane v McFarlane* [2006] 1 FLR 1186 at [151], be used to create some sort of quasi-property rights leading to a system of community of property between spouses.

[31] Although it is difficult to see how it can be seen as a contribution to the welfare of the family if the inheritance is kept separate and apart and never used for the benefit of the family, as in *H v H (Financial Provision; Special Contribution)* [2002] 2 FLR 1021. In such a case the party with the inheritance is more likely to use it to justify a departure from equality on the basis of the source of the funds being outside the marriage and the fact that the parties always considered the property to be separate rather than part of the 'family assets' – see the comments on *Miller v Miller; McFarlane v McFarlane* below.

[32] [2005] 1 FLR 576.

inherited wealth tied up in the long-established family company and a spouse's inherited wealth tied up in the long-held family estates.'[33]

**16.11**  Fourthly, the manner in which the parties have organised their affairs and used an inheritance is an important factor to take into account. To a large degree this consideration goes hand in hand with the court striving to determine what is 'matrimonial' and 'non-matrimonial property' under the second general principle. In *Miller v Miller; McFarlane v McFarlane* Baroness Hale stressed the importance of paying due respect to the manner in which the parties managed their property and affairs during the marriage:[34]

> 'This is simply to recognise that in a matrimonial property regime which still starts with the premise of separate property, there is still some scope for one party to acquire and retain separate property which is not automatically to be shared equally between them. The nature and the source of the property and the way the couple have run their lives may be taken into account in deciding how it should be shared. There may be other examples.'

**16.12**  Lord Mance also agreed the importance of having regard to the manner in which the parties chose to organise their own affairs.[35] It is also important to note that in *Miller* Baroness Hale appeared to suggest that the use to which assets were put could cause them to be considered as family assets.[36] In *Charman v Charman (No 4)*[37] the Court of Appeal also identified a potential for the law to develop, albeit cautiously, an approach to dividing the assets upon divorce in accordance with the arrangements the parties have themselves previously sought to agree, either expressly or by their conduct in arranging their financial affairs during the marriage. The decision to leave out of account inherited property which had always been kept separate from the family assets in *H v H (Financial Provision: Special Contribution)*[38] can be justified on this basis.

**16.13**  It remains unclear to what extent the concept of 'merger' or 'amalgamation' of inherited assets with the matrimonial assets is to be developed by the courts.[39] In *Rossi v Rossi*[40] Mr Nicholas Mostyn QC, sitting

---

[33]  The second paragraph of the passage is particularly important from a socio-economic perspective if the courts are to ensure that the principles which govern cases involving very wealthy dynastic families are not dramatically different from those which apply in the majority of cases.

[34]  [2006] 1 FLR 1186 at 1224.

[35]  [2006] 1 FLR 1186 at 1229.

[36]  [2006] 1 FLR 1186 at [149]. See *S v S* [2006] EWHC 2793 (Fam), where Burton J interpreted Baroness Hale's words in this way. Although Lord Nicholls, technically in the minority in the *Miller* decision in the House of Lords, proceeded on the basis that it was the source of the assets which gave them their matrimonial or non-matrimonial character, so that property acquired by inheritance or gift would be considered to be non-matrimonial property (see [2006] 1 FLR 1186 at [22]–[23]).

[37]  [2007] 1 FLR 1246 at [86].

[38]  [2002] 2 FLR 1021.

[39]  See also the sixth consideration at **16.15** below.

[40]  [2007] 1 FLR 790.

as a deputy High Court judge, suggested that although an inheritance was automatically considered to be non-matrimonial property (unless it was the former matrimonial home), the degree to which it had 'become merged or entangled with matrimonial property'[41] would have a bearing on the extent to which such property should be shared. The use of inherited property to buy the matrimonial home and for other family purposes also seems to have been a factor in *L v L*,[42] diluting the force of the arguments in favour of a larger departure from equality. In *S v S (Ancillary Relief: Importance of FDR)*[43] Baron J ordered equal division of all the assets, including those which had been inherited, on the joint grounds that with assets of £2m the parties could only be met by recourse to the whole lot and also because:

> 'this case is typical of many and I consider that it would be unfair and discriminatory to ignore each of the parties' contributions, whenever made, including that made by bringing moneys in at the beginning of the relationship. As time goes by, all assets become amalgamated and it would seem to me to be inappropriate to omit them from overall consideration.'[44]

**16.14** Fifthly, with time a party may have contributed to the retention of an asset which was provided by the other party and thereby may have 'earned' a greater right to share in it. In *White v White* Lord Cooke of Thorndon cited with approval the comments of Lord Simon of Glaisdale in the Privy Council case of *Haldane v Haldane*,[45] which concerned New Zealand legislation providing for equality of division of family assets unless justice demands otherwise:

> 'Initially a gift or bequest to one spouse only is likely to fall outside the Act, because the other spouse will have made no contribution to it. But as time goes on, and depending on the nature of the property in question, the other spouse may well have made a direct or indirect contribution to its retention.'

It seems that a contribution to retaining and, implicitly, maintaining or improving an asset is a factor which can be considered separately from the general consideration that over the course of a long marriage the separation of property may become less significant or realistic, although it seems plain that in most cases the two arguments will simply be opposite sides of the same coin.

**16.15** Sixthly, the length of the marriage will have a very significant bearing on the court's approach. The strands of principle contained within the second, third, fourth and fifth factors set out above will all be considered in the light of this sixth factor. In *White v White* the husband's contribution to the assets through a gift from his father came at an early stage of the marriage, and 'the significance of this is diminished because over a long marriage the parties jointly made the most of that help and because it was apparently intended at

---

[41] At [24.6].
[42] [2008] 1 FLR 142 at [88].
[43] [2008] 1 FLR 944.
[44] [2008] 1 FLR 944 at [49].
[45] [1977] AC 673 at 697.

least partly for the benefit of both'.[46] In *Miller v Miller; McFarlane v McFarlane* Lord Nicholls, drawing together many of the themes already discussed above, said:[47]

'In the case of a short marriage, fairness may well require that the claimant should not be entitled to a share of the other's non-matrimonial property. The source of the asset may be a good reason for departing from equality. This reflects the instinctive feeling that parties will generally have less call upon each other on the breakdown of a short marriage.

With longer marriages the position is not so straightforward. Non-matrimonial property represents a contribution made to the marriage by one of the parties. Sometimes, as the years pass, the weight fairly to be attributed to this contribution will diminish, sometimes it will not. After many years of marriage the continuing weight to be attributed to modest savings introduced by one party at the outset of the marriage may well be different from the weight attributable to a valuable heirloom intended to be retained in specie. Some of the matters to be taken into account in this regard were mentioned in the above citation from the *White* case. To this non-exhaustive list should be added, as a relevant matter, the way the parties organised their financial affairs.'

Baroness Hale echoed those sentiments by saying:[48]

'In *White*, it was recognised that the source of the assets might be a reason for departing from the yardstick of equality (see 610C–G and 994 respectively). There, the reason was that property had been acquired from or with the help of the husband's father during the marriage, but the same would apply to property acquired before the marriage. In *White*, it was also recognised that the importance of the source of the assets will diminish over time (see 611B and 995 respectively). As the family's personal and financial inter-dependence grows, it becomes harder and harder to disentangle what came from where.'

**16.16** Finally, but most importantly, their Lordships in *Miller v Miller; McFarlane v McFarlane* were all clear that the luxury of making some special allowance for an inheritance is likely to arise only in cases where the parties' needs and the needs of the children of the family are met without recourse to the inherited property. Since needs are relative to available assets and standard of living arguments, it is only likely to be in cases of substantial assets that a special allowance can be afforded to an inheritance. This approach was adopted by Baron J in *S v S*,[49] in which she remarked that a case with assets of just over £2m was not a 'big money case', and it was wrong to 'ring-fence' inherited assets where 'all of the assets which came into this marriage have to be available to cover the parties' requirements'.

**16.17** Clearly, each case will require application of these principles to the particular facts and circumstances. There are no hard and fast rules. Indeed, it

---

[46]   [2000] 2 FLR 981 at 999 per Lord Cooke of Thorndon.
[47]   [2006] 1 FLR 1186 at 1194–5.
[48]   [2006] 1 FLR 1186 at 1222–3.
[49]   [2007] EWHC 1975 (Fam) at [47].

must be remembered that the court must ultimately apply the terms of MCA 1973, s 25 to each case and the words of guidance given by the House of Lords and other courts 'are explanations of and expansions upon the statute and not the statute itself'.[50] See also *B v B (Ancillary Relief)* [2008] 2 FLR 1627, where Ward LJ warned against the use of ancillary relief cases as precedents.

## IS THERE A NEED FOR PRECISION IN CALCULATING THE 'MARITAL ACQUEST'?

**16.18**   The comments in the two House of Lords cases of *White v White* and *Miller/McFarlane* have caused practical difficulties in application. Not only is it not always easy to draw a clear line of demarcation between matrimonial and non-matrimonial property, but disputes are likely to arise as to the actual value of assets introduced into the marriage by one party and the value of the assets acquired during the marriage. Identification of the 'non-matrimonial' property and the marital acquest has been dealt with in a variety of different ways. The two extremes of the range of approaches taken in the reported cases are:

- Cases where it has been argued that the 'marital acquest' needs to be precisely valued so that it can be divided equally, while the 'non-matrimonial property' is identified and dealt with separately.

- Cases where attempts at strict valuation of the 'marital acquest' have been deprecated, preference being given to a more broad-brush application of judicial discretion to the assets as a whole.

The former approach is demonstrated by the cases mentioned at **16.19–16.21**. The latter approach was adopted in the cases set out at **16.23–16.26**.

**16.19**   In *Rossi v Rossi*[51] Mr Mostyn QC, sitting as a deputy High Court judge held that:

> 'In all cases now a primary function of the court is to identify the matrimonial and non-matrimonial property. In relation to property owned before the marriage, or acquired during the marriage by inheritance or gift, there is little difficulty in characterising such property as non-matrimonial (provided it is not the former matrimonial home). The non-matrimonial property represents an unmatched contribution made by the party who brings it to the marriage justifying, particularly where the marriage is short, a denial of an entitlement to share equally in it by the other party.'

Likewise passive economic growth on such non-matrimonial property also qualified as non-matrimonial property.

---

50   Per Coleridge J in *Charman v Charman* [2006] EWHC 1879 (Fam) at [114].
51   [2007] 1 FLR 790.

**16.20** In *S v S (Non-Matrimonial Property: Conduct)*[52] Burton J held that the yardstick of equality should only be applied to the matrimonial property, and the non-matrimonial property should only be shared so far as needs required. This decision is, probably, the high water-mark of the approach of strictly distinguishing between matrimonial and non-matrimonial property and dividing each category differently.

**16.21** *McCartney v Mills McCartney*[53] involved assets of over £400m and a short, 4-year marriage. Even though the outcome of the case turned on the 'magnetic importance' of the wife's needs, the court did permit extensive (and it must be assumed also very expensive) expert evidence by both sides as to the value of the husband's assets at the outset of the marriage and, therefore, the extent of the marital acquest.[54] In the end, the 'active' marital acquest was held to be a tiny proportion of the overall assets.[55] It is questionable whether the extensive forensic exploration of this issue would have been permitted in a case involving a more 'normal' level of assets.

**16.22** There have been several cases where the precision and potential rigidity of the former approach have been rejected in favour of a much more fluid and generalised approach to the exercise of discretion.

**16.23** In *H v H*[56] Charles J said in the course of addressing the question of how to treat substantial bonuses paid to a husband following the parties' separation:

> 'Both sides correctly acknowledged that the task of the court was to apply the statutory test and thus to have regard to the s 25 criteria. Thus, for example, it was common ground that the husband's income and earning capacity were matters to which the court was directed to have particular regard.
>
> However, in my judgment, from that correct starting point both sides fell into error in arguing what were described as the "hot topics" by treating, or seeking to treat, the guidance given by the House of Lords as if it were a series of statutory tests and that a pass or a failure of those tests led to particular and set results.
>
> The arguments were, or came close to, an assertion that, given the length of this marriage and, because of that, the force of the application of the yardstick of equality to the fruits of the marital partnership, it was appropriate at the first stage of the court's reasoning for it: (1) to define the matrimonial property with precision; (2) to divide its value in half; and (3) to treat that result as an established and unalterable part of the award. For example, one progression in the argument advanced on behalf of the wife was that the matrimonial property included the 2006 and 2007 bonuses and therefore she was effectively entitled to half of them and then to a further award in respect of future earnings. The husband took a

---

[52] [2007] 1 FLR 1496.
[53] [2008] 1 FLR 1508.
[54] [2008] 1 FLR 1508 at [102]–[132].
[55] [2008] 1 FLR 1508 at 309.
[56] [2007] 2 FLR 548 at [40]–[49].

similar approach to exclude both those bonuses from a 50/50 division by an application of the yardstick to the matrimonial property.

In my judgment this is an incorrect approach because (i) it ignores the flexibility of the statutory provisions and the objective of achieving a fair result in the given case that was emphasised by the House of Lords, and (ii) it seeks to impose a certainty or rigidity of division on a foundation of the matrimonial property and thus on a concept that (a) is not expressly mentioned by the MCA, and (b) cannot always easily or precisely be identified and valued.

In my judgment I should not fall into similar error by reference to the phrases and concepts "matrimonial acquest" and "family assets" (and therefore matrimonial property) which can also be described as alluring judicial phrases. This is particularly so because:

(i)    they lead to an application of the yardstick of equality and thus to a quantification of an award (as did the phrase 'the wife's reasonable requirements' by reference to a *Duxbury* calculation when a clean break was ordered);
(ii)   even though the yardstick of equality applies readily and with force to such assets, it does not do so as a matter of course, and it does not necessarily lead to an equal division of the capital value of the matrimonial property;
(iii)  as Lord Mance points out, it is as to the extent and identification of this concept that Baroness Hale of Richmond (and the majority in the House of Lords) differ from Lord Nicholls of Birkenhead although, as I have mentioned, it is accepted that this difference is in most cases not going to produce a different result; and
(iv)   whichever approach is adopted to the concept of matrimonial property, it is not always easy to identify all of it precisely.

I appreciate that there are attractions in seeking to achieve clarity by applying judicial guidance, and the concepts set out therein, but it seems to me that particularly when such concepts themselves introduce uncertainties and value judgments the attraction is flawed and can lead to a flawed progression of analysis and argument in achieving the ultimate goal of an application of a statutory test to achieve a fair result.

I hasten to add that that does not mean that the process of reasoning identified by the guidance given by the House of Lords is not to be followed. Rather in my view it means that when following it, with a view to achieving the overall aim of a fair result, the court must take care not to create set or rigid stepping stones, or apply a formulaic approach, that is not set out in the statute.

So it seems to me to be more sensible, and in accordance with the statutory test and the guidance: (i) to have regard to the particular circumstances of a given case when considering concepts such as the matrimonial property and the application of the yardstick of equality and thus to the range of reasonable possibilities in their application; (ii) to stand back and take an overview of the circumstances of a given case by reference to those possibilities and the guidance and the flexibility built into it, and therefore; (iii) not to take a formulaic or progressive approach that introduces a set and unalterable ingredient of the award (eg half of the matrimonial property) particularly when an aspect of its evaluation is not clear or common ground.'

**16.24** On the issue of how to deal with an increase in the value of the husband's businesses after separation in *CR v CR*,[57] Bodey J also favoured a broad discretionary approach in most cases because of frequent difficulty in drawing a clear division between matrimonial and non-matrimonial property, particularly where the 'harvest' reaped by one party after the separation had its source in the 'seed corn' planted during the marriage and tended by the joint efforts of the parties:

'Without the wife's support, the husband would not have had that important role and status within the group by virtue of which he came by those assets for which he seeks differential and favourable treatment. In other words this was a financial continuum, the groundwork for which was laid and the seeds sown during the parties' married life together, through how they chose their respective marital roles. Attempted forensic distinction between the differing assets in the kitty creates issues which are in many (though not all) cases sterile. In my view, therefore, whilst the "matrimonial property" may nowadays need to be identified, the court should still strive to take as broad a view as possible, especially in cases such as this, where the husband's asset-accruing role has not changed in any way since the separation and where the accruals have not come from any new source of risk, endeavour, or luck.'

**16.25** In *P v P (Post Separation Accruals and Earning Capacity)*[58] the husband argued for a strict dividing line between the property earned during the marriage (matrimonial property) and that earned after separation (which should be non-matrimonial). He argued that £6.8m earned by him post-separation should not be shared with the wife. Moylan J expressed the view that such formulaic approaches were not consistent with s 25:[59]

'It might have been assumed, if the marital partnership is treated as coming to an end on separation, that this general proposition creates, in all cases, a clear dividing line as from that date. This is not so. It is plain from *Miller* that it is not necessary to draw a "clear and precise boundary" between matrimonial and non-matrimonial property. At para [26], Lord Nicholls of Birkenhead draws attention to the dangers and difficulties inherent if such an approach were to be adopted. Not only can it be an illusory search, but as he says, the greater the emphasis placed by the courts on the need to identify what is and is not marital property, the greater the amount that the parties will be willing, indeed encouraged, to spend on seeking to value assets at the start and at the end of a relationship.

---

[57] [2008] 1 FLR 323. This case and the other cases referred to in this section which dealt with assets which were accrued by one party after the breakdown of the marriage are considered further at **11.155–11.160**.

[58] [2008] 2 FLR 1135.

[59] [2008] 2 FLR 1135 at [115]–[119].

In a recent case before me,[60] the main focus was on: (a) the date on which the parties' relationship had started (between 15 and 20 years previously) for the purpose of identifying when marital property began to accrue; and (b) the extent to which the husband had a developed business at that date, again for the purpose of defining what was marital property. In *RP v RP* Coleridge J also referred to applications for costly valuations at different times during a relationship in pursuit of an alleged entitlement to a "share" of the "matrimonial property". I have no doubt that these sorts of inquiries were specifically not intended by the House of Lords.

To be fair to Mr Marks and Mr Pointer, they both recognise that we are engaged in the application of guidance to the exercise of the statutory discretion. We are not engaged in the rigid application of any specific formula with a requirement to find clear and precise boundaries. Apart from agreeing that any award must meet the wife's needs, neither submits that the issues referred to in para [105] above point to a particular result as a matter of principle. They agree that these issues are matters which should be taken into account as part of the discretionary exercise although they clearly differ as to the weight they should be given.

In *Charman v Charman (No 4)* the Court of Appeal, at [103] and [104], declined to address an argument belatedly advanced that the husband's post-separation bonus should have been treated differently. However, the decision makes plain, at para [66], that the sharing principle is not confined to matrimonial property. It applies to all the parties' property "but, to the extent that their property is non-matrimonial, there is likely to be better reason for departure from equality".

I mention, in passing, one concern as to a possible effect of this approach. I have referred to Mr Pointer's submission that all the wealth in this case "should be treated as subject to the presumption of equal division". In other cases I have heard the view expressed that, as all property at the date of a hearing is included within the (equal) sharing principle, it is in the interests of the applicant spouse to delay the determination of their application if in the meantime that property is likely to increase significantly. This is based on an expectation or belief that the property which exists at the date of the hearing is more likely than not to be divided equally. This is not in the interests of justice. Further, although an award might be differently constructed, the court's approach should be the same whenever the application happens to be determined.'

**16.26** In an admirably clear and helpful judgment in *C v C*[61] Moylan J criticised the parties for their endeavours to quantify the husband's value at the start of the relationship, some 20 years earlier:[62]

'I appreciate that certain passages in the speeches in *Miller v Miller; McFarlane v McFarlane* might seem to require almost an account of the sources of the family's wealth. However, these passages have to be put in context and, in particular, have to be applied in the framework of the Matrimonial Causes Act 1973. It would, in my view, be a very regrettable step if parties were obliged or even encouraged to

---

60   *C v C* [2009] 1 FLR 8, considered in more detail below.
61   [2009] 1 FLR 8.
62   [2009] 1 FLR 8 at [4] and [77]–[78].

conduct a financial account after a long marriage. I do not consider that this can be what the House of Lords intended ....

It would, in my judgment, be foolish after a long marriage or relationship either to expect or to require a party involved in ancillary relief proceedings to produce a detailed account of the state of their financial affairs at the commencement of the marriage or relationship. On several occasions in the course of his evidence the husband replied, to a question put to him in cross-examination, that he and his advisors had done the best they could after a lapse of some 20 years. Different cases will, of course, throw up different factual issues and different factual solutions to those issues. However, in the present case I do not accept the general assault mounted by the wife on the evidence produced by the husband. The quest for historical financial certainty was never going to be achieved and, in my view, was not a necessary quest in any event.

It would, therefore, be foolish for me to seek to undertake a task which only an accountant and valuer could undertake, namely to arrive at a precise view as to the extent of the husband's wealth at any point in the period from 1984–1988 (and I repeat that I am not suggesting that this was either necessary or even appropriate). I propose to make a broad assessment of the position, taking into account the points made, both during the evidence and in the parties' respective submissions.'

On that broad assessment the judge awarded the wife 40% of the assets.

**16.27**  Although the case law in this area continues to develop, the weight of judicial authority now appears to lie on the side of a more broadbrush and discretionary approach to the matrimonial/non-matrimonial property distinction. There appears to be little judicial appetite for a more formulaic approach based on a rigid distinction between the two types of property. Indeed, the authorities as a whole indicate that the formulaic approach would be likely to result in disproportionate costs and unjust results in all but the biggest of big-money cases.

## THE PARTICULAR PROBLEMS OF POST-SEPARATION ACCRUAL, INCLUDING FUTURE EARNINGS AND BONUSES

**16.28**  The particular issues raised by cases where substantial assets have been acquired or created after separation but prior to the final hearing are dealt with elsewhere in this book. The acquisition of wealth through business activities and employment is dealt with at **11.155–11.160**. The approach to property acquired by way of an inheritance in the period between separation and the final hearing is discussed at **17.16–17.22**.

# Chapter 17

# PROPERTY ALREADY ACQUIRED THROUGH AN INHERITANCE

**17.1**  Inheritance may be relevant as an issue in ancillary relief proceedings in two distinct circumstances. First, one or both of the parties to proceedings may have some expectation of an inheritance in the future, either under the will of a third party or by reason of intestacy. Secondly, one or both of the parties may have inherited property before the marriage, during the marriage or even in the period between the end of the marriage and the ancillary relief application being heard. Different, albeit related, considerations apply to both circumstances, and they are each considered in this part of the book. This chapter considers the relevance of property which has already been acquired through an inheritance. The next chapter looks at the relevance of some expectation of a future inheritance.

**17.2**  Inherited property often causes difficulties in ancillary relief cases. Such property is not generated by the joint efforts of the parties to the marriage and, understandably, the party who has obtained an inheritance will seek to argue that the other spouse should have no claim to it, particularly if the other spouse still has a potential expectation of an inheritance in the future.

**17.3**  As will be seen, there is a subtle difference in the relevance of an inheritance which one of the parties received before or during the marriage and an inheritance which has been received between the time of the parties' separation and the hearing of the ancillary relief application. There may also in some cases be a distinction in the treatment of an inheritance which was obtained before the marriage and one which was received after the parties married, although this distinction may arise more from the way in which the parties have dealt with the inherited property than from the time it was acquired. It will, therefore, be useful to consider the case law by reference to the time when the inheritance is acquired. However, before embarking on an examination of these distinctions it is first useful to consider the general principles under which the court considers the relevance of a past inheritance.

## THE RELEVANCE OF A PAST INHERITANCE – GENERAL PRINCIPLES

**17.4**  In stark contrast to the situations discussed in Chapter 18, where the inheritance has not yet been received and is merely a possible future resource, a vested inheritance amounts to property in the parties' hands that is available for their use. The relevance of an inheritance as a resource is therefore immediately obvious. Sometimes the inheritance will remain separated from the parties' other assets, most obviously when it is contained in a trust fund under which one of the parties is a beneficiary. More commonly, especially in modest asset cases, the inheritance will have become 'mixed' with the parties' other assets. For example, it may have been used to buy a larger house or to renovate an existing property. As we shall see, the manner in which the parties have dealt with the inheritance will be a significant consideration when determining what influence the inheritance should have on the division of assets.

**17.5**   Before any practitioner is able to provide advice in relation to inherited assets, he or she must have a grasp of the distinction which is made between matrimonial or family property on the one hand and non-matrimonial property on the other. Property inherited solely by one of the parties, whether obtained before the marriage, during the marriage, or after it has broken down, is likely to be non-matrimonial property. However, such property may become matrimonial property by being applied for the direct benefit of the family, eg by being used to buy or improve the family home. The relevance of this property's status as matrimonial property or non-matrimonial property will differ from case to case. Chapter 16 contains a detailed discussion of the principles which have begun to develop around the concepts of matrimonial and non-matrimonial property. That chapter should be consulted alongside this one whenever an inheritance is being considered within ancillary relief proceedings.

**17.6**   A number of general principles have developed through the case law. These principles were initially expressed in broad terms in *White v White*, although they have now seen considerable further clarification and development in subsequent cases. The general principles are summarised below. These principles are explained in much more detail in Chapter 16. They are not rules. These are broad considerations which the courts will take into account in the right circumstances. Ultimately, each case must turn on its own unique set of facts. These principles are not listed in order of importance:

(1)   When dividing up assets there is no scope for either ignoring inherited property or for leaving it off the 'balance sheet' of assets by 'quarantining' it. This principle applies regardless of whether the inheritance was received before the marriage, during the marriage, or after separation.

(2)   Inherited property is different in its nature from the other property acquired by the parties during the marriage, which is variously termed 'matrimonial property' or 'family assets'. Inherited property is usually taken into account as an unmatched contribution made to the welfare of the family by one party. The weight to be given to this contribution will be determined by all the circumstances of the case.

(3)  The nature of the property inherited is also a relevant factor to consider when assessing how inherited property is to be dealt with. Greater weight may be given to arguments seeking to preserve the inheritance for one party where the inherited property is a family heirloom or an asset which has been retained in the same form within the family for many generations.

(4)  The parties' agreement as to how their property affairs have been managed, whether that agreement is express or implied from conduct, may be relevant to the manner in which the court deals with that property.

(5)  A party may have contributed to the retention of an asset which was provided by the other party and thereby may have 'earned' a greater right to share in it.

(6)  The longer the marriage, the less likely the court will be to regard the inheritance to be of significance in the exercise of its discretion. This is particularly likely to be so where the inherited assets have become 'merged' or 'amalgamated' with matrimonial assets over time.

(7)  Finally, but most importantly, some special allowance for an inheritance is likely to be made only in cases where the parties' needs and the needs of the children of the family are adequately met without recourse to the inherited property.

The facts of each case will determine the relative importance of each principle. In most cases, the parties' respective needs will be by far the most important factor, and in some cases the parties' needs will make any debate about the relevance of inherited assets completely sterile.

## CHOOSING THE APPROPRIATE JURISDICTION

**17.7**  Consideration should also be given to whether the divorce proceedings might be more appropriately dealt with in a foreign jurisdiction with which the parties have a connection. In *Krenge v Krenge*[1] the husband was German and the wife English, but they had both spent most of their married life in Germany. Late in the marriage the husband had obtained an inheritance from his German aunt which made up the vast bulk of the assets the parties had available to them. Under German law this inheritance would be excluded from the assets to be divided between the parties and, not surprisingly, the husband wanted the financial issues resolved in Germany, while the wife wanted them to proceed in England where she had a reasonable prospect of obtaining a share in the inherited assets. The court stayed the English proceedings on the basis that Germany was the more appropriate forum. The practitioner must be highly alert to the possibility of the parties litigating the case in a jurisdiction

---

[1]  [1999] 1 FLR 969.

which separates inherited assets from the matrimonial assets, especially where the other jurisdiction is a contracting state for the purposes of Council Regulation (EC) 2201/2003 (known as 'Brussels IIA or II*bis*'). The prompt commencement of proceedings in the more beneficial jurisdiction or an application to stay proceedings in the less appropriate jurisdiction may pay dividends.

## INHERITANCE RECEIVED BEFORE THE MARRIAGE

**17.8** In *P v P (Inherited Property)*[2] Munby J had to consider a very difficult case where the husband and wife had spent their whole married life farming a hill farm. The farm had been in the husband's family for three previous generations. He had been born there and it was described as 'his way of life, indeed it is his whole life'. Essentially the vast majority of the assets available to the parties had been introduced to the marriage by the husband by inheritance, although the wife's role in contributing to the maintenance of the value of the assets by her work as an active farmer's wife was recognised (adopting the approach indicated by the Privy Council case of *Haldane v Haldane* (see **16.14**)). The learned judge indicated that a flexible approach must be taken to inheritances, depending on the circumstances of the case (see **16.8**). It was noted to be a significant feature that although the farm business had been put into the parties' joint names, the land and other tangible assets had always remained in the husband's name.[3] On the very particular facts of this case (described by the judge as 'excruciatingly difficult') the wife was awarded about 25% of the total assets on the basis that this was what she required for her housing and income needs. It is clear that the generational ownership of the farm was a very important factor in that case, justifying a substantially less than equal share of the assets for the wife, despite the length of the marriage.

**17.9** Although it was not a case concerning inherited assets, *Foster v Foster*[4] concerned a short, childless marriage of 4 years. The parties had each brought property to the marriage. During the marriage they invested in further property and increased the value of their assets. The Court of Appeal upheld the district judge's decision to (in broad terms) return to each party the assets they brought to the marriage and to divide the 'profits' of their investments during the marriage equally between them. Hale LJ noted that 'there are many different ways of approaching assets brought into the marriage and contributions made

---

[2] [2005] 1 FLR 576.

[3] This is perhaps an example of the development of an approach based on dividing the assets with some regard to the manner in which the parties themselves agreed to order their affairs, suggested in *Charman v Charman (No 4)* [2007] 1 FLR 1246 at [86] (see **16.11–16.13**). No doubt many wives presented with the argument that this retention of assets in the husband's sole name is an indication of the way they had agreed to arrange their financial affairs will respond with the argument that this was not an arrangement they chose, but one about which they had no option. How is a wife who wants assets transferred into joint names during the marriage to achieve that if her husband objects?

[4] [2003] 2 FLR 299.

after it',[5] and the district judge's approach was not unfair in the circumstances of that case. In *Foster* the key factors justifying this approach appear to have been the short duration of the marriage and the absence of any dependent children. It seems clear that, had the assets in question been inherited by one of the parties prior to the marriage, the same approach would have applied.

**17.10** The question of inherited assets was not directly at issue in *Miller v Miller*. There were, however, substantial assets which the husband owned prior to the marriage, and the court was required to consider how those assets should be dealt with. The approach adopted towards those assets is closely analogous to the situation where assets have been inherited prior to the marriage. The facts of that case were exceptional in various ways, not least because of the sums involved (the husband was worth some £16.7 million at the start of the marriage and perhaps £32 million by the time of the final hearing, although the valuation of the shares which made up the bulk of his assets was very difficult to perform accurately). The general observations about inherited assets made in that case have already been considered above. As to the decision in the *Miller* appeal itself, it was clear that the husband was given considerable credit for the substantial wealth he brought into the marriage but, even though the marriage lasted less than 3 years, his wealth had as much as doubled during that time. Precisely how the award of £5 million to the wife was settled upon by the judge remains difficult to fathom with certainty, but the House of Lords felt that it was within the range of fairness. It amounted to about one-third of a reasonable estimate of the amount by which the husband's fortune had increased during the marriage.

**17.11** Further examples of the courts' approach to inherited assets are:

- *NA v MA*[6] was a case where the assets of some £40m were nearly all brought to the marriage by the husband. There was virtually no matrimonial property. Baron J awarded the wife £9.127m, amounting to about 23% of the total assets.

- In *Smith v Smith*[7] the Court of Appeal held that a starting point of an equal division of the assets was wrong where the marriage had lasted 10 years and the husband had brought the main assets into the marriage (the matrimonial home and a company), although the court's decision involved a multitude of factors and it is not entirely clear what the court thought the appropriate starting point for division of the assets should be in such a case.

- *B v B (Ancillary Relief)*[8] is a useful Court of Appeal authority reviewing the law set out in *White v White*, *Miller/McFarlane* and *Charman v Charman (No 4)* in a case which did not concern 'big money'. The facts

---

[5]   [2003] 2 FLR 299 at 306.
[6]   [2007] 1 FLR 1760.
[7]   [2007] EWCA Civ 454.
[8]   [2008] 2 FLR 1627.

were unusual in that all the assets had been introduced by the wife's inheritances and the main asset was a car wash business which the husband now ran and relied upon for his income. The court emphatically rejected the suggestion that the starting point in such a case should be equal division. In the very unusual circumstances of this case the Court of Appeal gave the husband just under 30% of the total assets. It was also pointed out that the guidance from the 'big money' cases had limited assistance for a 'modest' asset case such as this (assets of about £1.35 million) and, more importantly, each case had to be approached on its own facts and this case, like others, should not be regarded as a precedent.

- Also worthy of consideration is the lucid and pragmatic judgment of Moylan J in *C v C*,[9] where the court departed from equality of division and awarded the wife 40% of the assets on the basis of the husband's 'substantial wealth' (which the court declined to attempt to value precisely) at the outset of the marriage.

These decisions all indicate that there are no hard and fast rules or a formula which can be applied to such cases. Whilst they provide examples of the sorts of arguments which can be used to influence the court's exercise of discretion, ultimately 'fairness' in any particular case will depend on consideration of all the circumstances.

# INHERITANCE RECEIVED DURING THE MARRIAGE

**17.12**   In *White v White*[10] the parties farmed in partnership. Part of the farm assets they owned had been funded or acquired from the husband's father during the marriage. Those contributions came at an early stage of the marriage and 'the significance of this is diminished because over a long marriage the parties jointly made the most of that help and because it was apparently intended at least partly for the benefit of both'.[11] Nevertheless, these contributions were significant enough for the House of Lords to decline to interfere with the Court of Appeal's decision to give the wife roughly 40% of the assets and the husband 60%, although Lord Cooke of Thorndon clearly felt that this was the very minimum the wife should have been awarded. Their Lordships appear to have been clear that, but for the contribution from the husband's father (which bears an obvious and close analogy to an inheritance), it would have been difficult to justify anything but an equal division of the assets.

**17.13**   In *H v H (Financial Provision: Special Contribution)*[12] the wife and husband had each received inheritances during the marriage, which had been drawn upon to support their family expenditure. The husband had a further

---

9    [2009] 1 FLR 8. See also **16.26.**
10   [2000] 2 FLR 981.
11   [2000] 2 FLR 981 at 999 per Lord Cooke of Thorndon.
12   [2002] 2 FLR 1021.

inheritance in the United States and this had remained separate and never drawn upon by the husband, on the basis that he was keeping it for their children's inheritance. The remaining parts of the first two inheritances were taken into account by the court and formed part of the pool of assets shared equally by the parties. The husband's US inheritance was left out of account on the basis that it did not form part of the family's resources. This reasoning was not followed in *Norris v Norris* (see **16.8** and **17.14**), and seems to be the wrong approach. It now seems possible to justify the same conclusion, however, on the basis of the House of Lords' speeches in *Miller v Miller; McFarlane v McFarlane* and the approach adopted in *P v P (Inherited Property)*, ie by giving substantial weight to the fact that the inheritance had remained separate and had not been mixed with the 'matrimonial' or 'family' assets. It is also explicable by placing weight on the significance of the arrangements the parties themselves made in relation to their property, as suggested in *Charman v Charman (No 4)* (above). In *Rossi v Rossi*[13] Mr Nicholas Mostyn QC, sitting as a deputy High Court judge, suggested that, although an inheritance was automatically considered to be non-matrimonial property (unless it was the former matrimonial home), the degree to which it had 'become merged or entangled with matrimonial property'[14] would have a bearing on the extent to which such property should be shared.

**17.14** One of the significant features in *Norris v Norris*[15] was that there were a number of substantial inheritances received by the wife in the course of a 23-year-long marriage. As already noted in Chapter 16, the judge declined to 'quarantine' these assets and leave them out of account. The inheritances, although substantial, remained a relatively small percentage of the overall wealth of the parties. Taking all matters into account in what was a complex case, the court's order left the parties with roughly an equal share of all the assets. The length of that marriage and the relatively small proportion of the assets derived from the inheritances justified that approach rather than one which resulted in an unequal division of the assets.

**17.15** In *S v S*[16] Baron J set aside a district judge's order on the basis that it was wrong to ring-fence assets inherited by the wife where the assets as a whole did not exceed the parties' joint needs. Baron J acknowledged the wife's capital contribution, but noted that the husband had also made a full contribution by working extremely hard during the marriage. The learned judge said:

> 'As time goes by, all assets become amalgamated and it would seem to me to be inappropriate to omit them from general consideration.'[17]

Taking all factors into account, she made an order for equal division of all the assets.

---

[13] [2006] EWHC 1482 (Fam).
[14] At [24.6].
[15] [2003] 1 FLR 1142.
[16] [2007] EWHC 1975 (Fam).
[17] [2007] EWHC 1975 (Fam) at [49].

# INHERITANCE RECEIVED AFTER SEPARATION BUT BEFORE FINAL HEARING

**17.16** The situation where an inheritance is received after separation but before a final hearing will normally only arise in those cases where there has been a substantial delay between the parties' separation and the hearing of the ancillary relief application. Such cases pose particular difficulties. Not only is the source of the fund outside the parties' joint endeavours, so it is not considered to be matrimonial or family property, it is also at a time after they have decided to live separate lives. Where there are minor dependent children, that separation will inevitably be less complete, but it must remain of significance that a separation has occurred. The principal effect of this will be that there will have been no opportunity for the inheritance to have become mixed or entangled with the matrimonial property, or for the other party to have contributed to the retention of the asset.[18] A further complication may be the fact that there has been a delay in the ancillary relief claim being brought.[19] Such a delay and the reasons for it may have a bearing on the court's discretion. The question of the relevance of such 'after-acquired assets' has arisen a number of times in the reported cases. Not all these cases concern inherited assets, but they are useful illustrations of the approaches the courts adopt to 'after-acquired assets'. As a general proposition, the applicant seeking to share in such after-acquired assets will have a more difficult task than where the assets were acquired before the marriage or at an early stage during the marriage.

**17.17** Although not concerned with an inheritance, the case of *Lombardi v Lombardi*[20] arose after a 5-year marriage which produced two children. After 3 years of separation the children went to live with the husband and he set up home with his new partner. He and his new partner also formed a business together. The wife obtained a decree of judicial separation and some periodical payments, but it was only some 12 years after the parties separated that the husband petitioned for divorce and the wife then applied for ancillary relief. In the time which had elapsed since the parties separated the husband, with the joint efforts of his new partner, had improved his situation significantly and had accumulated not insubstantial assets. The court declined to consider that in some way the position had 'crystallised' at the point of separation, and so assets obtained since the separation remained relevant to the court's exercise of discretion, but it was also relevant to look at the delay and the fact that the assets had been accrued largely through the efforts of the husband's new partner. The wife obtained no capital orders in the circumstances. Of course, a distinction between that case and any case where an inheritance has been

---

[18] See **16.13–16.14** and **17.13**.

[19] For a useful summary of the effect of delay in making the application upon the court's exercise of discretion see *Rossi v Rossi* [2007] 1 FLR 790 at [25]–[32], although the suggestion in that case that a prima facie limitation period of 6 years between the petition for divorce and the ancillary relief application appears to be unsupported by authority or by the terms of the statutory provisions themselves.

[20] [1973] 1 WLR 1276.

obtained following separation is that Mr Lombardi built up the assets by his own efforts. An inheritance is, by contrast, a windfall. It was also significant that his new partner had played a significant role in the acquisition of those new assets. It is not clear whether the result would have been different had he obtained the assets by way of an inheritance after separation instead of by his own hard work and the efforts of his partner.

**17.18** The parties in *Pearce v Pearce*[21] separated after a 10-year marriage. The husband was at that time an undischarged bankrupt and he left the wife with the children of the family and no financial support. The wife applied for and obtained a nominal periodical payments order at the time of the divorce. Some 9 years later the husband obtained an inheritance from his father, and the wife applied for a lump sum. She required leave because she had not made a prior application for a lump sum in the petition. She was given leave to make the application and obtained a £12,000 lump sum from the husband's inherited assets of some £34,000. Ormrod LJ indicated, as in *Lombardi*, that 'there is no justification in my judgment for trying to create, as it were, reserved funds, or reserved sources of money to which the court should not, in proper cases, have resort',[22] but he did acknowledge that the facts in this case were 'wholly extraordinary and … very exceptional indeed'[23] and even 'extreme'.[24] The implication of Ormrod LJ's comments appears to be that if the wife and the children had not been left in such a dire financial state by the husband, her claim to a share of the inheritance might have been much smaller. This case provides an illustration of how the needs of a party may take priority over any other arguments against sharing an inheritance.

**17.19** The term 'after-acquired assets' seems to have first been coined in *Schuller v Schuller*.[25] In that case the wife left the husband after an 11-year marriage. She went to work for an elderly friend as his housekeeper and upon his death she inherited his flat and the residuary estate. She argued that although this inheritance had to be taken into account, it should be considered in a different way from the assets accumulated during the parties' cohabitation, so that she should obtain well over 50% of all the capital assets. The district judge awarded the wife a lump sum, which brought her assets to about half of all the assets, including her inheritance. The Court of Appeal declined to interfere with that decision. It was a case where the assets certainly did not exceed the parties' needs, and Butler-Sloss LJ, referring to Ormrod LJ's judgment in *Pearce* (above), observed that:[26]

> 'Where there are no special circumstances in the way in which the money which is the after-acquired property has been achieved and where the resources of the parties are not particularly great, each living in quite an expensive house but if

---

[21]  (1980) 1 FLR 261.
[22]  (1980) 1 FLR 261 at 267.
[23]  (1980) 1 FLR 261 at 262.
[24]  (1980) 1 FLR 261 at 264.
[25]  [1990] 2 FLR 193 at 196.
[26]  [1990] 2 FLR 193 at 198.

they were to sell it and buy anywhere else they would not achieve very much money unless they went very much downmarket, and each of them has small amounts of savings, there is a considerable degree of parity and what has been criticised as a somewhat crude or indeed unsophisticated approach of the registrar in adding all the assets together and then dividing them does not appear to me in any way to be outside the contemplation of the observations of Ormrod LJ when he said in particular that one should look realistically at the figures.'

The assets in that case were not particularly large, which clearly had a bearing on the court's approach. It also seems to have been a significant factor in Butler-Sloss LJ's mind that the inheritance was not obtained in 'special circumstances'. This may be to distinguish the situation in a case such as *Lombardi*, where the 'after-acquired assets' arose by reason of the husband's labours with the support of his new partner. This does suggest that the court may be more willing to share a 'windfall' in the form of an inheritance than the proceeds of one party's work following separation.

**17.20** The case of *Lombardi* can be seen as special on its facts because of the delay and the change of position by the husband during that time by his and, more importantly, his new partner's efforts. Similar principles can be seen at work, albeit in a much larger asset case, in *N v N (Financial Provision: Sale of Company)*.[27] The parties were married for 14 years and during that time the husband built up a successful accountancy business. After the parties separated, but before the proceedings for ancillary relief were heard, the husband rapidly expanded his business enterprises. Four years after the separation, the ancillary relief application was heard, and the husband argued that there should be a discount to the wife's entitlement to the value of the businesses which had increased so markedly since separation. He said that this was just because she had made no contribution to that increase in value. Coleridge J agreed that this was a significant factor. He felt that the company should be valued as at the date of the hearing, but it was right to have an eye to the value at the date of separation where there had been a very significant change in value 'attributable to the extra investment of time, effort and money by the husband since separation'.[28] It remained important to balance that contribution against the wife's continued contribution in that time to looking after the home and the children. The wife was awarded £1 million out of assets of some £2.6 million. The special significance attached to a party acquiring assets after separation through his or her own industry has been identified in *Cowan v Cowan*,[29] *GW v RW*,[30] *M v M*[31] and *Rossi v Rossi*.[32] *S v S (Ancillary Relief After Long Separation)*[33] is an example of the husband being allowed to keep the fruits of his post-separation labours in his company where there was

---

[27] [2001] 2 FLR 69. For a different response to the same argument on different facts see *Cowan v Cowan* [2001] 2 FLR 192 at 217 and 234–5.
[28] [2001] 2 FLR 69 at 78.
[29] [2002] Fam 97 – see Mance LJ at [135].
[30] [2003] 2 FLR 108 at [52].
[31] [2004] 2 FLR 236 at [62]–[64].
[32] [2007] 1 FLR 790 at [23] and [24.3].
[33] [2007] 1 FLR 2120.

no matching contribution by the wife. By reason of his labours the value of the shares he held in the company was more appropriately to be viewed as akin to non-matrimonial property. However, it is not possible or desirable to draw a strict line between those assets earned before the separation and those after. There is often a continuum linking that which is earned after the marriage (the 'harvest') to the joint contributions of the parties before the marriage (the 'seed corn' planted and nurtured during the marriage).[34] The parties' needs may also dictate a different approach.[35]

**17.21** It is immediately apparent that an inheritance does not accrue, in most circumstances, as a result of the labours of the party who obtains it. There is, therefore, perhaps less unfairness in requiring it to be shared with the other party even when it accrues after the separation. Nevertheless, it is clear that when obtained after the parties have separated, it must be treated as non-matrimonial property and not automatically susceptible to being shared. The degree to which it should be shared will depend on weighing all the circumstances of the case. The parties' conduct in relation to their assets during the marriage may also be of some relevance. For example, it may be easier to seek to share in an inheritance obtained after separation if the spouse who is making the claim against the inheritance received an inheritance during the marriage and used it for the benefit of the family. The converse will apply where the earlier inheritance was kept separate from the other assets by agreement. On the other hand, where the parties have lived and made their joint financial plans in the expectation that they would both benefit from an inheritance which is ultimately only received after they have separated, the court may be more readily persuaded to share that inheritance.[36]

**17.22** As already noted, in cases where the parties' means are modest and not in excess of their needs, an inheritance is likely to be treated as a resource which must be used to meet the parties' needs. This factor seems to have been central to the outcome in the cases of *Pearce* and *Schuller*. The emphasis on meeting the needs of the parties and the children of the family in the judgments of Lord Nicholls and Baroness Hale in *Miller v Miller; McFarlane v McFarlane* suggests that this approach is likely to continue. Where the assets are more extensive, however, the inheritance may have a different effect. The court may then, as Lord Nicholls pointed out in *White v White*, have the luxury of treating the inheritance as property which justice dictates does not need to be shared between the parties. The judgments of the House of Lords in *White v White* and *Miller v Miller; McFarlane v McFarlane*, considered in more detail in Chapter 16, have confirmed that such inherited property can be treated differently from the property acquired during the marriage. If that is so in relation to property inherited during the marriage, there must be an even

---

[34]  See, for example, *CR v CR* [2008] 1 FLR 323; see also **11.158** and **16.24**.

[35]  For example, *P v P (Post-Separation Accruals and Earning Capacity)* [2008] 2 FLR 1135.

[36]  See, by way of analogy, the arguments successfully advanced by the wife in *MT v MT (Financial Provision: Lump Sum)* [1992] 1 FLR 362. She argued that the parties had planned their future in the expectation of obtaining an inheritance from the husband's father within about 5 years and, as a result, they had become heavily indebted. See also **18.31**.

stronger case for special treatment of an inheritance obtained after the parties separated, so long as doing so does not deprive one party of what is required to meet his or her needs. Additional support for this view can be found in the words of Baroness Hale, albeit apparently in the context of future claims against income rather than capital:

'In general, it can be assumed that the marital partnership does not stay alive for the purpose of sharing future resources unless this is justified by need or compensation.'[37]

## FUTURE DEVELOPMENTS

**17.23**  In *White v White* and *Miller v Miller; McFarlane v McFarlane* the House of Lords emphasised the need to decide ancillary relief cases by reference to the criteria laid down by Parliament in ss 25 and 25A of the Matrimonial Causes Act 1973. It was considered to be beyond the judicial role to place a gloss on the statutory provisions which could fetter the open discretion by the use of a presumption or starting point of equality of division. Similarly, the introduction of any form of regime providing for community of property between the parties to a marriage remains a question for Parliament. In the same way, it is clear that unless the Act is amended or replaced by different provisions, the courts cannot choose to leave out of account, or 'quarantine', any assets on the basis of their origin from an inheritance or other source outside the marriage.

**17.24**  At the present time, therefore, inheritances, whenever received, will continue to be considered by the courts as part of the fund of assets to be redistributed as necessary. The House of Lords has provided guidance as to the exercise of discretion but it is, consistent with the terms of MCA 1973, s 25, guidance in the broadest possible terms. An inheritance will be seen as a contribution made by one party for which they will receive a degree of credit as appropriate in all the circumstances of the case. Judicial discretion rules in this area and, inevitably, this makes it difficult for litigants and their lawyers to anticipate precisely how important a feature such as an inheritance will be in the judge's mind compared to all the other factors in the case.

**17.25**  Other legal systems have a more tightly constrained degree of judicial discretion. New Zealand has a statutory scheme which has a presumption of equality of sharing assets and where an inheritance is seen as a contribution to the marriage which may justify a departure from equal division. Australia has a similar statutory regime to the English one, but the courts there have been more

---

[37]  *Miller v Miller; McFarlane v McFarlane* [2006] 1 FLR 1186 at [144]. However, these words should not be taken too far. In a number of decisions the courts have declined to draw clear lines of demarcation between matrimonial property and non-matrimonial property based on the time when the property was acquired. See **16.18** et seq.

willing to lay down strong guidelines for the exercise of discretion.[38] Many civil law systems leave inherited assets entirely out of the matrimonial property to be shared by the parties. Some common law systems have a similar approach. Scottish law adopted a very different approach to that of the English system in 1985. It replaced a general discretionary system with a system in which judicial discretion is very closely fettered. Matrimonial property is clearly defined so that inherited assets are left out of account in the divorce and, until recently, the assets were valued at the date of separation rather than the date of making the order. As Lord Hope of Craighead pointed out in his opinion in *Miller v Miller; McFarlane v McFarlane*, such tightly drawn rules make the outcome of cases predictable, but they carry a risk of real injustice in many cases.

**17.26**  It remains to be seen to what extent some of the general approaches indicated by the House of Lords are developed into rules or presumptions in all but name by the lower courts, even though such an approach would fly in the face of the need to apply the s 25 criteria flexibly to the facts of each case. In *Charman v Charman*[39] Coleridge J lamented the lack of predictability in the current system and postulated the idea of 'tariffs' to act as guidance, at least in the 'very big/huge money cases', akin to the guidelines issued by the Judicial Studies Board to assist in the assessment of general damages in personal injury cases, or the sentencing guidelines laid down for the criminal courts. It seems likely that such developments are likely to require the input of Parliament rather than being left to the judges alone. However, to date the approach of the Court of Appeal and the specialist judges of the Family Division has remained the broad and flexible discretion based approach, deciding cases on the basis of what is fair after taking into account all the circumstances of the case and the specific considerations listed in s 25 of the Matrimonial Causes Act 1973.[40] That appears to be the approach which is likely to prevail for the foreseeable future. Development of further principles is likely to be highly incremental, at least until the Law Commission completes its report on marital property agreements,[41] which may provide fresh reasons for the courts to adapt their approach to these issues. Any wholesale reform of the Matrimonial Causes Act 1973 appears to be unlikely in the foreseeable future. More likely is a focus on the relevance of pre-nuptial and post-nuptial agreements which permit parties to a marriage to opt-out of the statutory scheme for asset redistribution on divorce to a greater or lesser extent.

---

[38]  A review of the antipodean approaches can be found in Lord Cooke of Thorndon's opinion in *White v White* [2000] 2 FLR 981.

[39]  [2006] EWHC 1879.

[40]  See **16.22** et seq.

[41]  Due to be completed in 2012.

# Chapter 18

# FUTURE INHERITANCE PROSPECTS

## INTRODUCTION

**18.1**  This chapter considers the situation where one or both parties to the proceedings are thought to have some inheritance prospects. This issue often arises where a party is known to have parents or relatives upon whose death it is thought that some significant inheritance will be received. Chapter 17 looks in detail at the treatment of assets which have already been inherited, drawing distinctions between cases where the inheritance was received before, during or after the breakdown of the marriage.

**18.2**  Frequently, cases which concern an 'inheritance' in the broadest sense will also raise questions of interests under trusts. This is particularly likely where the inheritance in question is large and liabilities under inheritance tax could be substantial. In such cases some degree of estate planning may have occurred prior to the death of the testator, tying the estate up in one or more discretionary trusts to the benefit of beneficiaries. The relevance of an interest under such a discretionary trust in a case will be guided by many of the principles considered in this chapter, but particular reference should also be made to Chapter 15, which considers trusts.

**18.3**  Litigants in ancillary relief proceedings frequently ask their lawyers whether their former partner's future inheritance prospects should be taken into account. As will be seen, the answer to this question is not entirely straightforward. However, before turning to consider the approach that the courts take to this question, it is useful to consider what an 'inheritance prospect' amounts to in terms of hard legal entitlement.

## WHAT IS THE NATURE OF AN EXPECTATION OF INHERITANCE?

**18.4**  Assets pass to a person upon the death of another person by way of inheritance. The inheritance can arise by the deceased's testamentary intentions contained in a will, by virtue of the law of intestacy if there is no will, or by a combination of the will and the law of intestacy in the case of a partial intestacy. These are potentially complex areas of law and this section merely sets out a general review of the law. More specialist texts on the subjects should be consulted in the event that more complex inheritance issues arise.[1]

**18.5**  In the absence of a valid will, the law of intestacy will determine entitlement to a deceased's estate. The detailed provisions on intestate succession are set out in the Administration of Estates Act 1925, as amended.[2] The provision made to surviving relatives following the death of an intestate depends on precisely which classes of relative survive.

**18.6**  Where a spouse survives the deceased by a period of 28 days, the following provision arises:

- the surviving spouse takes the deceased's personal chattels absolutely;

- the surviving spouse takes a fixed sum (net of inheritance tax and costs), which is set by statute and periodically reviewed.[3]

Any remaining estate after the above distributions have taken place is distributed or held on trust as follows (if there are relatives within any class, there is no need to proceed to the subsequent class):

- Where the deceased left issue,[4] one-half of the remaining estate goes to the surviving spouse for life and then to the issue absolutely on the death of the spouse, the other half goes directly to the issue on a statutory trust.

- Where the deceased left a surviving parent or parents, one-half of the remaining estate goes to the spouse absolutely and the other half to the parent or parents absolutely.

- Where the deceased left brothers or sisters of the whole blood (or the issue of any deceased brothers or sisters), one-half of the remaining estate goes to the spouse absolutely and the other half to the brothers and sisters (or, if deceased, their issue)[5] absolutely.

No other classes of relative are entitled to benefit from the estate and, in the absence of any of the above classes of relative, the spouse will take the whole estate absolutely.

---

[1]  See, for example, Williams, Mortimer and Sunnucks *Executors, Administrators and Probate* (Sweet & Maxwell, 19th edn, 2007).
[2]  Section 46 of the Administration of Estates Act 1925 as amended.
[3]  Currently £450,000 if the deceased left no children, or £250,000 where there were surviving children: Family Provision (Intestate Succession) Order 2009, SI 2009/135.
[4]  Where a person died after 4 April 1988 the law makes no distinction between a person's legitimate and illegitimate children when it comes to distributing an estate: see the Family Law Reform Act 1987.
[5]  See footnote 4.

**18.7**   Where there is no surviving spouse or the spouse survives the deceased for less than 28 days, the order for provision on intestacy of the entire estate is as follows (again, if there are surviving relatives within any class there is no need to go on to a subsequent class):

- Issue.[6]

- Parents or a parent.

- Brothers and sisters of the whole blood (or the issue[7] of any deceased brothers and sisters of the whole blood).

- Brothers and sisters of the half blood (or the issue of any deceased brothers and sisters of the half blood).

- Where grandparents survive, the whole estate passes to them equally or to the lone survivor.

- Uncles and aunts of the whole blood (or the issue of any deceased uncles and aunts of the whole blood).

- Uncles and aunts of the half blood (or the issue of any deceased uncles and aunts of the half blood).

Where there are no surviving relatives in any of the above classes, the estate will pass to the Crown, the Duchy of Lancaster or the Duke of Cornwall, as appropriate.

**18.8**   The rules of intestacy only apply if there is no valid will in existence at the date of the deceased's death, or if the gifts made by a will fail for some reason. Any person with testamentary capacity is free (subject to exceptions identified below) to determine how his estate is to be left by making a will which formally satisfies the requirements of the Wills Act 1837, s 9. A will may be added to, varied or revoked by subsequent codicils or wills. Ideally, the whole of a person's testamentary intention will be contained in a single document, but it is quite possible for the testamentary intention to be set out in a series of validly executed documents, which must be admitted to probate and construed together to identify the testamentary intention of the deceased.

**18.9**   A will differs from a declaration of trust or a deed making a gift in that the dispositions of property the will seeks to make only crystallise on a testator's death. Up to that point, subject to issues of formal and substantial validity,[8] a testator is free to change or revoke the terms of a will. As identified

---

[6]   See footnote 4.

[7]   See footnote 4.

[8]   Formal validity requires compliance with the provisions of the Wills Act 1837; substantial validity requires testamentary capacity, knowledge and approval and the absence of undue influence and fraud.

in the following section, there may be circumstances where the testator's freedom to dispose of his property upon his death has effectively been restricted. However, in these circumstances a testator remains at liberty to revoke a will, although the revocation may not have the desired effect.

**18.10** What becomes clear is that testamentary intentions expressed in a will or codicil or the rules of intestacy are usually, but not always, entirely variable or revocable by the testator. Herein lies one of the greatest problems in bringing future inheritance prospects into consideration in ancillary relief proceedings: generally there is no entitlement to an inheritance. There may be a hope of inheritance, or even an expectation, but until the death of the testator there is, save in special circumstances considered below, no right to an inheritance. Furthermore, even the hope or expectation of an inheritance in ancillary relief proceedings may be thwarted by a whole range of factors, some of the most common of which are set out below.

**18.11** A testator may change his or her mind and make a new will, or a codicil to an existing will, providing no or reduced provision for a party to the proceedings. Indeed, the very suggestion in ancillary relief proceedings that the potential inheritance may be taken into account in the proposed final order may actually prompt such a change of testamentary intention.[9] Alternatively, an elderly parent may remarry and choose to leave their estate, or a large part of it, to the new partner or to a loyal housekeeper or companion.

**18.12** There is always the risk that a testator may fall out with a potential beneficiary and delete him or her from the will. Those who have experience of probate practice or who choose to peruse the Chancery law reports will know that there are many elderly individuals with some wealth who revel in writing and re-writing their wills on an almost daily basis, benefiting those people who are in their favour at that particular time.[10]

**18.13** The testator may choose to bypass a generation of the family in favour of grandchildren entirely for tax avoidance purposes.[11] Similarly, the testator may choose to tie the assets up in some form of trust, which would give the party to proceedings very limited entitlements or perhaps only a life interest in the capital.

**18.14** There can be no guarantee that at the time of the testator's death the estate will be worth anything. The appearance of wealth does not always match the financial realities. There is nothing to prevent the testator spending and using his or her assets as they please. Lifetime gifts of assets can be made, even

---

[9] A concern identified by Nourse LJ in *Michael v Michael* [1986] 2 FLR 389 at 396, where he noted that adjourning a lump sum application to await a potential inheritance was often likely to be 'a self-defeating exercise'.

[10] 'It is notorious that some elderly persons of means derive enjoyment from the possession of testamentary power' per Robert Walker LJ in *Gillett v Holt* [2001] Ch 210 at 228.

[11] A concern identified by Thorpe J in *H v H (Financial Provision: Capital Allowance)* [1993] 2 FLR 335 at 343.

if the gifts are not to be effective until the person's death.[12] Where a gift has been made, the ownership of the asset no longer falls within the estate. As health fails in older age much of the estate could be depleted in nursing fees or other treatment costs.[13] Many individuals now choose to supplement their pension provision by taking out some form of lifetime mortgage to release the equity in their home for their own maintenance. Occasionally an estate may be insolvent.

**18.15**   A testator may by their words or conduct effectively limit their freedom to leave assets by their will, or they may already have done so (see the next section of this chapter).

**18.16**   Furthermore, any provision by way of will or intestacy may be subject to challenge by some other dependant under the Inheritance (Provision for Family and Dependants) Act 1975. Such a dependency may only arise after the ancillary relief proceedings are concluded, for example through a further marriage or some other relationship.

## CAN AN EXPECTATION OF INHERITANCE BECOME AN ENTITLEMENT?

**18.17**   In certain circumstances the law makes the intentions contained in a will irrevocable in effect, even if not in form, or otherwise gives a proprietary entitlement to assets within the estate to a third party. Thus, a will may not be all it seems to be. In some cases, it may be possible to show that there is more than a mere expectation or hope of inheritance and instead an absolute right to some property upon the testator's death, regardless of any subsequent attempt to alter a will. On the other hand, a party may be able to show that, notwithstanding a will in their favour, he or she will not actually obtain any financial benefit because there is already some prior proprietary claim on the estate by a third party.

**18.18**   There are essentially three broad methods by which a potential inheritance can either have been elevated to an absolute entitlement or irrevocably extinguished by a prior claim on the estate by a third party. As the reader will discern, there are very similar principles underlying all three categories of case, although they remain distinct legal doctrines.

**18.19**   First, a person can make a contract with another to leave certain property to them in their will. In the Australian case of *Schaefer v Schuhmann*[14] a man agreed to leave his house to his housekeeper by his will, so long as she

---

[12]   This will be some form of irrevocable gift of the asset during the testator's lifetime, but which was intended only to take effect upon the occurrence of a future event, such as his death. Examples are a donatio mortis causa or a deed making a gift conditional upon the donor's death.

[13]   A concern raised by Scott Baker J in *K v K (Conduct)* [1990] 2 FLR 225 at 227–8.

[14]   [1972] 2 WLR 481, PC.

remained his housekeeper at the time of his death. She, in reliance upon this promise, agreed to forego any further wages as his housekeeper and looked after him until his death. When he died, some of his children sought further provision from his will under the Australian equivalent of the Inheritance (Provision for Family and Dependants) Act 1975. The Privy Council confirmed that in the circumstances there was a contract between the man and his housekeeper to leave her the property and, upon his death, she was beneficially entitled to it. This entitlement arose from the contract and not the will, so even if the will had been changed the housekeeper would have been entitled to compel performance of the contract. If the man had tried to sell the property before his death, the housekeeper could have obtained an injunction restraining the sale[15] or, if the sale had been completed before it could be stopped, she could have sued the man for breach of contract and obtained damages.[16] Had the contract been a promise to leave a monetary legacy rather than a bequest of specific property, the housekeeper would have been able to enforce the contract by an action against the estate and, once again, this would have taken precedence over the claims of beneficiaries under a will or intestacy. In *Schaefer v Schuhmann* the court felt that the deceased's dependent children had not been properly provided for by the estate, but there was nothing the court could do about it in the light of the equitable rights to the estate which had arisen in the housekeeper's favour by reason of the contract.[17]

**18.20**    Secondly, a proprietary right to the estate or some part of it may have arisen by virtue of the doctrine of mutual wills or secret trusts. Mutual wills are usually made by a husband and wife who mutually agree[18] that they wish the same person or persons to have their property after they are both dead. The wills are made in mirror terms, leaving their property to each other, so that the survivor will benefit from all the property,[19] but specifying in both wills a remainder gift to the same agreed ultimate beneficiaries, usually children and/or grandchildren. This amounts to a contract between husband and wife, and if either sought to change their will during their lifetimes, this would constitute a breach of contract for which the other could sue. After the death of one party, however, the other party may seek to alter their will on the basis that an existing will is always revocable. Equity will not permit the survivor who has

---

[15]    [1972] 2 WLR 481 at 586 per Lord Cross of Chelsea and *Synge v Synge* [1894] 1 QB 466. The interest could also be registered against the title to the land, ensuring that any purchaser took subject to the housekeeper's interest.

[16]    [1972] 2 WLR 481 at 586.

[17]    This injustice was addressed by Parliament to some extent when the Inheritance (Provision for Family and Dependants) Act 1975 was enacted. By s 11 the court may set aside a contract to leave property by will, but only where the contract was made with the intention of defeating a claim for relief by dependants under that Act and where the contract was not made for 'full valuable consideration'. So, on the facts of *Schaefer v Schuhmann*, this provision would probably still not have assisted the dependent children.

[18]    This element of agreement and an intention to be bound by it is essential. It is not enough merely to show that the wills were made simultaneously – the agreement to be bound in this way must also be proved: *Re Cleaver (dec'd)* [1981] 2 All ER 1018.

[19]    Although this is the normal arrangement, it is not essential for the benefit of the property to have passed to the survivor for the doctrine of mutual wills to arise: *Re Dale (dec'd)* [1993] 3 WLR 652.

obtained the benefit of the other spouse's estate to deal with the property inconsistently with the mutual agreement.[20] Consequently, a constructive trust is imposed on the property which was the subject matter of the agreement, and the ultimate named beneficiary of the mutual wills has an equitable proprietary claim to the assets.

**18.21** Secret trusts and half-secret trusts are so called because they arise under a will but do not appear expressly, or in full terms in the case of a half-secret trust, on the face of the will. A secret trust arises where a testator leaves property by will absolutely and beneficially to another person but, while still alive, the testator has communicated to that person, either orally or in writing, that the property is to be held by him on trust for certain specified persons or purposes. If that person accepts the trust, it is binding on him and, despite the wording of the will giving him an absolute interest in the property, he actually has no beneficial interests in the property but holds it on trust for the beneficiaries identified by the testator. Clearly, the main difficulty in relation to a secret trust is proving its existence after the testator's death if he has not recorded it anywhere and the appointed trustee denies its existence. A half-secret trust is somewhat more straightforward to prove because the terms of the will set out that the property is given to the other person with a direction that it is to be held by him on trust on terms communicated to him before or at the time of the will,[21] albeit that those terms are not stated on the will itself. In such a case, the person taking the property under the will has no beneficial entitlement to it. Even if the terms of the secret trust cannot be proved, that person still holds the property on trust for the named residuary beneficiaries of the will.

**18.22** Thirdly, a person may have become beneficially entitled to an interest in a testator's property prior to his or her death. Most often this will be a partner or new spouse who acquires an interest in the testator's home by reason of a purchase money resulting trust or a constructive trust based on agreement or common intention as to ownership. A claim may also arise by way of proprietary estoppel where a person has been encouraged or permitted to believe that he or she will have some interest in the property of another in the future and has detrimentally relied on that expectation. Such an estoppel can arise not only in relation to a defined asset, such as a house, but it may extend to the whole of a person's estate in certain circumstances.[22]

**18.23** Any of the above-mentioned circumstances will result in the existence of a proprietary claim against assets which ostensibly appear to be part of a deceased's estate. If the beneficiary of that claim is one of the parties to the ancillary relief proceedings it can be argued that instead of an uncertain prospect of inheritance there exists a concrete property right which they will be able to realise in the future. On the other hand, where such rights are held or

---

[20]   *Re Cleaver (dec'd)* [1981] 2 All ER 1018.
[21]   A later communication of the trust will not do: *Re Bateman's Will Trusts* [1970] 3 All ER 817.
[22]   *Re Basham (dec'd)* [1986] 1 WLR 1498; see also *Gillett v Holt* [2001] Ch 210 and *Thorner v Major* [2009] UKHL 18.

may be obtained by persons who are not parties to the marriage, the
inheritance prospects of either of the latter may be limited or extinguished,
regardless of the evidence of any testamentary intention which may be
available.

**18.24**   Where a will has already been made in favour of one of the parties and
the testator has permanently lost the capacity to revoke or vary that will, it will
be possible to argue that the prospects of the inheritance are considerably more
certain than they would have been had that person retained testamentary
capacity and the ability to change the will. Nevertheless, in most circumstances
there will remain a significant doubt as to when the inheritance might be
received and what, if anything, it will be worth by that point.

## WHEN DOES THE PROSPECT OF A FUTURE INHERITANCE BECOME RELEVANT TO ANCILLARY RELIEF?

**18.25**   The prospect of a potential inheritance is not the 'property' of a party
because of the revocability of wills, as already discussed.[23] It may, nevertheless,
be one of the 'other financial resources which each of the parties to the
marriage ... is likely to have in the foreseeable future'.[24] It will be readily
apparent that the key words in this context appear to be 'likely to have' and 'in
the foreseeable future'.

**18.26**   'Likely' in the context of proceedings concerning the welfare of children
has been defined by the House of Lords in *Re H & R* as 'a real possibility'
rather than requiring proof that it is more likely than not.[25] It is not clear
whether this same definition is to be taken in the context of financial
proceedings. In *Priest v Priest*[26] (in the context of a future retirement gratuity)
the Court of Appeal clearly did not require proof of certainty of future receipt
but, notwithstanding a number of uncertainties, was satisfied 'on the balance of
probabilities' that the gratuity was likely. In *Davies v Davies*[27] the court spoke of
'the probability of that capital being available for payment to the wife, other
things being equal' and went on to say that the court should not be looking to
mere possibilities or vague contingencies.[28] In *Michael v Michael*[29] the court
declined to find that an inheritance was likely due to the 'considerable
uncertainty as to whether [the wife] will take any interest, even a life interest, in

---

[23]   But the prospect of an inheritance must be distinguished from property rights which may
        already have accrued in a party's favour (as discussed in the previous section) or by way of a
        trust which has been established prior to the testator's death for estate planning purposes.
[24]   MCA 1973, s 25(2)(a) and see *Michael v Michael* [1986] 2 FLR 389 at 395.
[25]   *Re H & R (Minors) (Sexual Abuse: Standard of Proof)* [1996] AC 563, HL.
[26]   (1980) 1 FLR 189 at 192.
[27]   [1986] 1 FLR 497 at 501.
[28]   Although the facts of the case suggest that the first instance judge had only considered a
        possibility of capital becoming available, rather than a firm probability.
[29]   [1986] 2 FLR 389 at 396.

the property'. These decisions all appear to have adopted the 'more likely than not' approach to determining likelihood. However, they all predated the House of Lords decision in *Re H & R*. There is then an argument to be made that the same definition of 'likely' ought to apply in both the Matrimonial Causes Act 1973 and the Children Act 1989. Currently it remains unclear whether it must be shown that there is a probability that is more likely than not (the higher test which the decisions in *Priest* and *Davies* suggest is necessary), or whether a real possibility will do.[30] The considerable uncertainties which surround any prospect of future inheritance (discussed above) compared to more definite interests (eg to a pension on retirement, a reversionary interest under a trust etc) will ensure that if the tougher test of likelihood apparent from *Davies* and *Priest* is to be applied, there will be relatively few cases where the future inheritance will be considered sufficiently likely to be relevant to the MCA 1973, s 25 exercise.[31] It may be that this is a sufficient justification for adopting the higher standard of required proof, although, inevitably, a more stringent test potentially reduces the flexibility of the court's approach and imports a greater risk of injustice for the party who had hoped to share in an inheritance expected by the other party.

**18.27** It is submitted that the period of time represented by the 'foreseeable future' is to be determined on the facts of each case. Foreseeability is also connected with the question of likelihood. If the court is able to say that certain property will almost certainly vest in a party at a fairly definite point in the future, the test of foreseeability may be satisfied even though that point is many years away. In *Michael v Michael*[32] Purchas LJ stated that he did 'not think that the foreseeable future is necessarily the same thing as the near future. If, as in *Milne v Milne*, it can be foreseen that the interest will vest on a certain future date, albeit a somewhat remote one, I can understand that the court might think that it will vest in the foreseeable future'.[33]

**18.28** The courts have sought to give some guidance in respect of the period of time over which the 'foreseeable future' could extend. However, in many of these cases the question of foreseeability was considered in the same breath as the separate although related question as to whether a lump sum claim should

---

[30]   In *D v D (Lump Sum: Adjournment of Application)* [2001] 1 FLR 633 Connell J justified a lump sum claim being adjourned on the basis that there was a 'real possibility of capital from a specific source becoming available in the near future', thereby apparently adopting the *Re H & R* test, although it is not clear whether this point was argued before him. Certainly *Re H & R* was not cited in the judgment and the authority for the proposition that a 'real possibility' will suffice was given as *Davies v Davies*.

[31]   In *MT v MT (Financial Provision: Lump Sum)* [1992] 1 FLR 362 Bracewell J took the future inheritance into account because it was an inheritance from the husband's father who lived in Germany, and German law ensured that at least one-eighth of the substantial estate would pass to the husband, so the inheritance could be seen as a certainty. In *K v K (Conduct)* [1990] 2 FLR 225 at 227–8 Scott Baker J declined to give inheritance prospects any weight, although he seems to have found some inheritance likely, but not in the sufficiently proximate future.

[32]   [1986] 2 FLR 389 at 397.

[33]   See also *C v C & Others* [2009] EWHC 1491 (Fam), Munby J.

be adjourned. In *Morris v Morris*[34] 2 or 3 years was within the foreseeable future. In *Priest v Priest*[35] 5 years was considered sufficiently proximate, although it was suggested that 15 years might be too long even though that was still 'dimly in the foreseeable future'. *Milne v Milne*[36] did not regard 10 or 11 years as being outside the 'foreseeable future'. In *Davies v Davies*[37] it was considered permissible to project forward, albeit for 'not a long period'. In *Roberts v Roberts*[38] Wood J commented that an application should not be adjourned for more than 4 or 5 years, although the question the judge was clearly addressing was specifically the use of the discretion to adjourn a claim to await a future event. This is plainly not the same as finding that the 'foreseeable future' is limited to only 4 or 5 years.[39] In *C v C & Others*[40] Munby J reviewed the reported case law and reached the conclusion that an inheritance likely to fall into possession in 15 years was only 'dimly visible' but it was to be considered a financial resource of the husband within the meaning of s 25(2)(a). Nevertheless, the learned judge took the view that an adjournment of the application for a lump sum for a period of 15 years was 'quite out of the question'.[41]

**18.29**  Most of the cases referred to concern the date of receipt of a gratuity or pension lump sum, which is a relatively predictable event. The particular difficulty in future inheritance cases is the need to predict how long the testator may live. Mortality tables may be of some assistance,[42] but they are based on statistical averages and take into account none of the particular genetic and lifestyle attributes of the potential testator in question. Reference to that person's health may assist in arguing that the inheritance is relatively proximate, but it may meet with the withering judicial riposte that 'the world is full of women in their eighties who had high blood pressure in their sixties.'[43] This uncertainty makes the courts generally reluctant to consider future inheritance prospects as of relevance in anything other than the most general way.

**18.30**  Examples of this reluctance are:

- *K v K (Conduct)*.[44] Thorpe J was unwilling to take into account in any significant manner the wife's prospects of inheriting from her mother, who

---

[34]  (1977) 7 Fam Law 244.
[35]  (1980) 1 FLR 189.
[36]  (1981) 2 FLR 286.
[37]  [1986] 1 FLR 497 at 502.
[38]  [1986] 2 FLR 152.
[39]  The decision was approved by the Court of Appeal in *Ranson v Ranson* [1988] 1 FLR 292, apparently on the basis that a claim should only be adjourned 'in the comparatively short term' (per Waterhouse J at 298).
[40]  [2009] EWHC 1491 (Fam).
[41]  [2009] EWHC 1491 (Fam) at [60].
[42]  *H v H (Financial Provision: Special Contribution)* [2002] 2 FLR 1021 at 1040 and *C v C and Others* [2009] EWHC 1491 (Fam).
[43]  Per Nourse LJ in *Michael v Michael* [1986] 2 FLR 389 at 397.
[44]  [1990] 2 FLR 225 at 227–8.

was aged 79 and in good health, because there was no likelihood of her inheritance falling in 'in the immediate future.'

- In *H v H (Financial Provision: Capital Allowance)*[45] the same judge took the same approach where the husband's mother was aged 67 and in good health, because the inheritance 'may lie many years forward' and 'to bring it in as though it were a vested interest, likely to fall into possession within the foreseeable future, is in my judgment to exaggerate its significance unreasonably'.[46]

- Similarly, in *H v H (Financial Provision: Special Contribution)*[47] a potential inheritance from the husband's mother with a life expectancy of about 6 years was left out of account with no view expressed as to whether 6 years was within the range of the foreseeable future. The main reason for leaving it out in that case seems to have been reliance on the approach to inherited property suggested by the decision in *White v White*[48] (as to which, see Chapter 16).

- In *L v L*[49] it was held that a wife's future prospects of inheritance were too remote to take into account, even though the husband had already inherited assets before the separation and regarded it as discriminatory that his inheritances should be taken into account whilst the wife's future prospects were to be disregarded.

- In *S v S (Ancillary Relief: Importance of FDR)*[50] Baron J held that a wife's inheritance prospects were too uncertain in terms of quantum and timing to form anything more than a background factor in the case.

**18.31** But where the parties to the marriage have themselves made assumptions about a future inheritance prospect and given it significance in their lives, the court is more likely to take it into account. So in *MT v MT (Financial Provision: Lump Sum)*[51] the husband's father was aged 83 and had a history of ill health, although there was no clear evidence as to his life expectancy. The potential inheritance was regarded as highly relevant in the case. However, there were two very unusual features of that case which gave the inheritance greater relevance than the norm: the father's estate would be governed by German law, which guaranteed the husband at least a one-eighth share of the estate and the parties to the marriage had jointly planned their future in the expectation of the inheritance falling in, on their own estimate, within about 5 years. In *Re G (Financial Provision: Liberty to Restore*

---

[45]   [1993] 2 FLR 335.
[46]   [1993] 2 FLR 335 at 343.
[47]   [2002] 2 FLR 1021 at 1040.
[48]   [2000] 2 FLR 981.
[49]   [2008] 1 FLR 142.
[50]   [2008] 1 FLR 944.
[51]   [1992] 1 FLR 362.

*Application for Lump Sum)*[52] the parties clearly regarded the husband's prospects of inheritance in the foreseeable future as likely and relevant because they agreed a consent order adjourning the wife's claim to a lump sum until after the inheritance became available. On hearing the restored application for a lump sum after the husband obtained the inheritance some 6 years after the consent order was agreed, Singer J indicated that this was clearly a case where that approach had been appropriate and necessary.[53] It should be noted that in that case the expected inheritance was large and the other assets were rather modest.[54]

**18.32** It should be clear from the foregoing that a future inheritance will be brought into account only in rare and unusual cases. Most cases will fall within the 'norm' referred to in *Michael v Michael*,[55] where the inheritance is neither sufficiently likely nor proximate to be relevant. Furthermore, the different treatment of inherited assets to 'family assets' or 'marital property' set out in the House of Lords decisions in *White v White* and *Miller v Miller; McFarlane v McFarlane*[56] further reduces the relevance of a potential asset which is to be obtained by one of the parties after their marriage has come to an end. Those House of Lords cases state important principles which need to be borne in mind when arguing about the significance of a future inheritance in any case. These principles are considered in detail in Chapter 16.[57] It is only where special circumstances exist (as in *MT v MT*) or the assets available at the time of the final hearing are significantly less than required justly to meet the parties needs and entitlements (as appears to have been the case in *Re G*) that future inheritance prospects are likely to become relevant.

## HOW SHOULD THE QUESTION OF FUTURE INHERITANCE BE DEALT WITH IF IT IS CONSIDERED A RELEVANT FINANCIAL RESOURCE OF THE PARTIES?

**18.33** There appear to be four potential options. First, the application for a lump sum may be made but adjourned to be considered if and when the inheritance is received. This approach will not be appropriate where there are other assets and an immediate lump sum payment is sought as part of the order, because only one lump sum may be made for a party to the marriage,[58] and if a lump sum is made by the same order there will be no claim remaining to be adjourned. Adjournment of a lump sum claim is rare. The general principle, particularly since the clean-break provisions of s 24A were added to MCA 1973 in 1984, is that the parties should have finality, particularly of their capital claims, once the marriage is over.

---

[52] [2004] 1 FLR 997.
[53] [2004] 1 FLR 997 at 999.
[54] See also *C v C and Others* [2009] EWHC 1491 (Fam).
[55] [1986] 2 FLR 389 at 396.
[56] [2006] 1 FLR 1186. Considered in detail in Chapter 16.
[57] In particular at **17.26–17.30**.
[58] *Coleman v Coleman* [1973] Fam 10 and *Banyard v Banyard* [1984] FLR 643.

**18.34** An unquantified claim for a lump sum should not be left hanging over one of the parties indefinitely unless fairness demands that this is the only way to do justice between the parties. There has been a general reluctance to adjourn claims for any significant period. Many of the cases in point have been considered above in the context of foreseeability of an inheritance being received:

- In *Roberts v Roberts* Wood J suggested that the longest a claim should be adjourned for is 4 or 5 years. There is no reported authority of an adjournment for longer than that.

- In *Ranson v Ranson* the Court of Appeal felt that an adjournment for 7 years was too long.

- Although in *Milne v Milne* the benefits under a pension were not expected for 10 or 11 years, the court did not adjourn the claim in that case, but made a deferred lump sum order to be paid when the pension vested.

- Even in *MT v MT*, where Bracewell J reviewed the case law and decided that she was not bound by any authority limiting an adjournment to any particular period,[59] the evidence was that the inheritance was expected within about 5 years.

- In *Re G*[60] the case report sheds no light on the period the parties anticipated would elapse before the inheritance was received when they agreed a consent order adjourning the claim. In the end, it was 6 years before the event occurred.

- In *C v C and Others*[61] Munby J unhesitatingly stated that an adjournment for what was likely to be 15 years was 'quite out of the question'.[62]

**18.35** Ultimately, the question of an adjournment is a matter for the court's broad discretion exercised on all the facts of the case. The general approach to adjourning a lump sum claim appears to be accurately summarised by Connell J in *D v D (Lump Sum: Adjournment of Application)*:[63]

'this step should only be taken in rare cases where, as Sir David Cairns said in *Davies v Davies*, there are circumstances in which justice to both parties can only be done if there is an adjournment. One of those circumstances in an appropriate case is likely to be the real possibility of capital from a specific source becoming available in the near future.'

---

[59] She found that the cases of *Roberts v Roberts* and *Ranson v Ranson* were decided on other grounds and the comments about the appropriate length of an adjournment were obiter.
[60] [2004] 1 FLR 997.
[61] [2009] EWHC 1491.
[62] [2009] EWHC 1491 at [60].
[63] [2001] 1 FLR 633.

In that case Connell J approved a decision to adjourn a wife's lump sum claim where the husband would receive some large bonus payments from his employer within about 2 years. The continued theme of treating inherited assets somewhat differently from the assets accumulated during the marriage, espoused in *White v White* and now *Miller v Miller; McFarlane v McFarlane*,[64] suggests that an adjournment of a lump sum claim to await an inheritance is likely to be limited to unusual facts or to cases where the available assets, excluding the expected inheritance, do not meet the needs of the parties.

**18.36**  A second option for the court is to order a lump sum which is to be payable only once the inheritance is received. The real difficulty with this approach is the uncertainty in most cases as to what the extent of any inheritance will be. It has already been noted that testamentary intentions can be changed or affected by many factors. Furthermore, it is unlikely that there will be any reliable estimate of the value of the testator's potential estate even at the date of the hearing (see the section on disclosure below). To set the amount of a deferred lump sum in monetary terms could work great injustice if the inheritance is worth much less than anyone had anticipated. The same may be true if the lump sum is set as a fixed proportion of the inheritance. If the inheritance is particularly large, the beneficiary of the lump sum may obtain far more than the court ever felt justice required. Although the courts have made a deferred lump sum order in anticipation of a future receipt of capital, in the reported cases this has never been in the context of inheritance, but only where the payment was from a pension and therefore more predictable as to both quantum and time for payment.[65] Even in *MT v MT*, where the court was able to be satisfied that the husband would receive an inheritance of one-eighth of his father's estate, it was not possible to do anything other than adjourn the lump sum claim.

**18.37**  A third option is to ask the court simply to take the inheritance prospects into account as part of the general circumstances of the case. In most cases the court will consider a potential inheritance to have little weight (see above). Where the inheritance is likely to be substantial enough to have a material effect on the proposed division of assets, it is likely to be appropriate to anticipate the level of the inheritance in this manner only where there is very clear evidence that it is likely to be received quite soon and there is a fairly accurate assessment of its scale (an example might be where it is known that one of the parties is the sole beneficiary of his or her father's will, the father's estate has been identified and valued and the father is very ill and therefore both incapable of changing his will and making any significant alteration to the extent of his estate). Where matters are more uncertain and the inheritance is likely to have a significant impact on the outcome of the case, an adjournment of the lump sum application may be preferable. It is, nevertheless, open to the court to adopt the third option if it achieves fairness between the parties.[66]

---

[64]  Considered in detail in Chapter 16.

[65]  See *Richardson v Richardson* (1979) 9 Fam Law 86; *Milne v Milne* (1981) 2 FLR 286; and *Priest v Priest* (1980) 1 FLR 189.

[66]  For a rare case where this seems to have had considerable influence see *Calder v Calder* (1976)

Where a judge is 'commuting'[67] between two figures which he has in mind as an appropriate award, taking the inheritance prospects into account in a general way may sway the judge to adopt the higher figure rather than the lower one.

**18.38** A fourth option potentially exists. However, the option is so fraught with complications and uncertainties that it will rarely be a party's option of first choice. The option involves making no application for a lump sum order in the petition, answer or Form A and then seeking to bring the claim at a later time once the inheritance is available. It must be noted that the efficacy of this approach remains untested and therefore carries a high degree of risk as well as potential complexity. Furthermore, it will be inappropriate in any case where an immediate lump sum is required as part of the financial provision sought, since it is not possible to obtain more than one lump sum order. The reasoning which suggests that this approach may be open to a party is as follows.

**18.39** Section 23(1) of MCA 1973 makes it clear that a court may make a lump sum order at any time, either before or after a decree is made absolute. It appears from the wording of s 23(1) that it may be open to the court to make a form of order provided by that section even without a formal application being made for it. However, the terms of FPR, r 2.53 speak of the need for the party seeking relief to apply for that relief, even if only orally at the trial, suggesting that the court has no power to make an order of its own motion.[68] It is generally the approach of the family courts to avoid over-technicality. It has been held that a claim for a lump sum can be implied to have been made where there has been an application for a property adjustment order,[69] although a more technical approach has also been taken, refusing to accept that a claim for periodical payments allowed the court to make a lump sum order.[70]

**18.40** The question which appears to remain open, and which is central to the efficacy of seeking to bring a lump sum application at a future date, is whether the court is able to dismiss an application which has not been formally made by a party.[71] Where the application is made in the prayer to the petition, this

---

6 Fam Law 242, CA. For a more recent example underlining the difficulty in bringing future inheritance prospects into account see the decision of Baron J in *S v S* [2008] 1 FLR 944.

[67] See Coleridge J in *Charman v Charman* [2006] 1 WLR 1053, quoting Wilson J in *Conran v Conran* [1997] 2 FLR 615 at 628.

[68] See also FPR 2.64(1) requiring the district judge to 'make such order as he thinks just', which could be read as providing a broad power to grant whichever form of relief seems appropriate, regardless of the applications formally before the court. But see the decision of Singer J in *E v E* [2008] 1 FLR 220 holding that a remarried wife could not seek relief in her favour on the basis of her former husband's application for orders. However, *Dart v Dart* [1996] 2 FLR 286 was not cited in that decision and, in particular, the Court of Appeal's reference in that case to the unreported decision in *Jagger v Jagger*.

[69] *Doherty v Doherty* [1976] Fam 71, although this decision concerned older procedural rules and a very broad interpretation of what the word 'maintenance' meant in the context of the law as it stood before the MCA 1973 was enacted. But see also *de Lasala v de Lasala* [1980] AC 546 at 559, where lump sum orders and property adjustment orders were considered to be related as 'the difference between providing money and money's worth'.

[70] *Wilson v Wilson* [1976] Fam 142.

[71] In *Dart v Dart* [1996] 2 FLR 286 at 292 the Court of Appeal held that it was open to a party to

application is before the court and may be dismissed even if there is no notice to proceed with the application for that form of order in the Form A.[72] In *Hardy v Hardy*,[73] on unusual facts, the Court of Appeal appears to have accepted that the wife, who was the respondent to the petition and had not made an application for ancillary relief therein, had the right to make her applications for relief any time she saw fit after decree absolute. It follows that she could keep her claim for a lump sum open indefinitely by not applying for such an order. However, this decision predated the introduction of the Family Proceedings Rules 1991 and, more importantly, the amendments to the Matrimonial Causes Act 1973 made by the Matrimonial and Family Proceedings Act 1984, which introduced the 'clean-break' provisions by inserting s 25A into the Act. It remains unclear whether s 25A is sufficiently broad in its scope as now to permit the court to dismiss an application for a lump sum in the interests of securing a clean break even if an application has not been made for such an order by the party concerned. It appears arguable, albeit not entirely clear, on a construction of s 23 and s 25A(1), (2) and (3) that this power does not exist and, in some circumstances, an application for a lump sum can be reserved for the future. It should be noted that where the party wishing to make the application has remarried before the lump sum application is made, no subsequent application will be possible.[74]

**18.41** Where the application for a lump sum was not made within the petition or answer, as the case may be, it may only later be made in Form A with leave of the court.[75] The court will have to be convinced that it is just to give leave to make the application at that stage.[76] Certainly, a case with reasonable prospects

---

[72] apply for a determination of the financial provision he should make, in other words to apply for orders against himself. It is unclear whether this can extend to making an application against oneself solely for the purpose of having that application dismissed. Considering the routine practice of making an application 'for the purpose of dismissal of claims' to obtain a clean break it seems likely that this principle does extend this far.

[72] *Sandford v Sandford* [1986] 1 FLR 412.

[73] (1981) 2 FLR 321 at 326.

[74] MCA 1973, s 28(3).

[75] FPR 1991, r 2.53(2).

[76] See *Pearce v Pearce* (1980) 1 FLR 261 for an example of a case where leave to apply for a lump sum was granted and a substantial lump sum awarded where the husband obtained an inheritance 9 years after a nominal periodical payments order had been made upon the divorce, although it should be noted that Ormrod LJ said (at 262) that 'The facts of the case are wholly extraordinary and must be very exceptional indeed' and, notwithstanding the jurisdiction to allow such a claim to be brought, 'That does not mean to say, however, that the court should give any encouragement to persons, wives or husbands, to make application for lump sum or property adjustment orders long after the divorce has taken place. At the same time it makes it clear that the court retains its jurisdiction to entertain such applications in cases where the circumstances are unusual, or where there are good reasons for thinking that the justice of the case requires the court to make a lump sum order, even though a long period of time has elapsed since the marriage was dissolved. In other words, lapse of time is an important factor to be taken into account in the exercise of discretion under s 25 of the 1973 Act. It is part of "all the circumstances of the case", and in some cases it will be a very important circumstance: it may be a decisive circumstance, but in this case the facts are so extreme' (at 264).

of success will have to be made out.[77] The delay in making the application is likely to be a significant factor in the exercise of the discretion to grant leave.[78] If there were earlier fully contested ancillary relief proceedings which appear to have finally resolved the parties' capital claims against each other, it may be difficult to bring the claim for a lump sum at a later stage unless it can be shown that this possibility had been a factor in the court's considerations at the earlier hearing. It is submitted that leave is unlikely to be granted if the possibility of the future claim was not made apparent to the court and the other side at the time of the original order, particularly if the other party is able to demonstrate a change of position in reliance upon the belief that all claims between the spouses had already been concluded.[79] If a party intends to reserve a lump sum claim to be made in the future, the court should be asked to declare on the face of the order that a future claim has been reserved to prevent future confusion and dispute.

## HOW WILL THE COURT DEAL WITH AN ADJOURNED APPLICATION FOR A LUMP SUM WHEN THAT APPLICATION IS RESTORED?

**18.42** If a lump sum application is adjourned, the applicant is entitled to restore the application when circumstances merit it. The rules do not envisage this situation and so it is not clear what procedural form the application to restore the application should take. In theory, a simple notice of application will suffice, but it is probably better to use Form A in most cases, as this will trigger the court's procedure of issuing the standard directions for preparation of Form E and listing the first appointment. As the court will need to review the s 25 factors when considering the restored application, it is likely that it will need proper disclosure of the parties' means by way of Form E. The parties may need to consider the breadth of the disclosure required to deal with the restored application and the court may be asked to assist with this at an early stage by giving appropriate directions. The court must still have regard to 'all the circumstances of the case' at the time the restored application is heard, but it may be possible to agree that the same extent and detail of disclosure as is necessary when all forms of financial provision are being considered will not be necessary or proportionate to deal with this discrete issue.[80]

**18.43** The court will once again need to apply the MCA 1973, s 25 criteria to the application. Plainly it will be relevant to look at the history of the matter and consider the financial relief which has already been granted at the earlier hearing when the application was initially adjourned. To that end, when an

---

[77] *Chaterjee v Chaterjee* [1976] Fam 199.
[78] See *Rossi v Rossi* [2006] EWHC 1482 (Fam) at [25]–[32] for a useful review of the way delay in making an application may affect the court's exercise of discretion and the interesting suggestion that the courts should apply a prima facie limitation period for the making of an application for ancillary relief of 6 years from the presentation of a petition.
[79] *Marsden v Marsden* [1973] 1 WLR 641.
[80] See **4.13–4.16**.

application for a lump sum is adjourned, it may be advisable to record, either in the preamble to the order or by some side-agreement or exchange of letter, why that step has been taken, what future change of circumstances was envisaged and precisely what provision was made at the time. The addition of a clear schedule of assets, liabilities and incomes as they were at the time of the original order may also be very useful. Without sufficient clarity as to which issues had been concluded by the original order and which left open it will be very difficult for the court to ascertain to what extent the restored application may amount to an impermissible 'second bite at the cherry'.

**18.44**  By their very nature, cases where a lump sum is adjourned to await an inheritance will be exceptional on their facts. It is difficult to provide general guidance as to how the application will be considered when it is restored, perhaps many years later. Suffice to say that there will be a variety of complex matters to weigh in the balance, including the fact that the lives of both parties are likely to have moved on considerably and their circumstances may be very different from those which existed at the time of the original hearing. The case law as to 'after-acquired assets', discussed in Chapter 17,[81] ought to be considered in this context.

**18.45**  In *Re G (Financial Provision: Liberty to Restore Application for Lump Sum)*[82] Singer J considered a restored application for a lump sum. The wife's application had been adjourned generally by consent in 1995. The parties had been married for about 4 years until they separated. In that time they had two daughters. The wife also suffered health problems. At the time of the ancillary relief hearing in 1995 the only asset of note was the former matrimonial home, which was already in the wife's sole name, the purchase having been funded by her mother. The only provision in 1995 was an order for the husband to pay maintenance for the wife and children and to adjourn her claim for a lump sum. The latter provision was agreed because the husband had an expectation of substantial inheritances from his father and uncle. In 2001 the husband inherited estate that took his worth to over £2 million. Between 1995 and 2001 the circumstances of both parties had changed in various ways: both had remarried; the wife was divorcing her second husband; the husband had also separated from his second wife; the wife had moved home; the husband had been made bankrupt and was subject to an individual voluntary arrangement at the time he received his inheritance. Singer J weighed all the factors and considered the wife's past and continuing contribution to the welfare of the family through her care of the children as particularly significant. It was acknowledged that all of the husband's wealth had been inherited rather than stemming from the parties' own efforts, and anything approaching equality of division would be unfair. The wife was awarded £460,000, which was intended to meet her housing needs, pay her debts and provide her with a new family car.

---

[81]  See also **11.155–11.160**.
[82]  [2004] 1 FLR 997.

# WHAT IF THE CLAIM FOR A LUMP SUM IS NOT ADJOURNED AND THE INHERITANCE IS OBTAINED SHORTLY AFTER THE FINAL HEARING? – INHERITANCE AS A *BARDER* EVENT

**18.46** It is reasonable to assume that a party who argued that the other party's inheritance prospects were sufficiently likely and proximate, but who failed to persuade the court to adjourn the lump sum claim or give those prospects any significant weight, will feel deeply aggrieved if the inheritance is obtained shortly after the final order was made. What, if anything, can be done?

**18.47** It is possible to seek to appeal an order out of time if there has been a significant event which has occurred since the order was made and which undermines a fundamental assumption upon which the order was made. The grounds required for disturbing an otherwise final order in this way were set out by the House of Lords in *Barder v Barder (Caluori Intervening)*[83] as:

(i)    the new events relied upon invalidated the fundamental assumption on which the order was made so that, if leave were given, the appeal would be certain or very likely to succeed;

(ii)   the new events had occurred within a relatively short time (probably less than a year) of the order being made;

(iii)  the application had been made promptly; and

(iv)   the grant of leave to appeal out of time did not prejudice third parties who had acquired in good faith and for valuable consideration interests in the property which was the subject of the order.

**18.48** In *Barder* itself, and in other cases,[84] the appeal was allowed where one of the parties to the proceedings died shortly after the final order was made. It certainly seems possible that receipt of the inheritance much sooner than anyone had foreseen at the time of the final hearing could be a *Barder* event and, if the other grounds set out in *Barder* can be satisfied, it may found a successful appeal out of time. Nevertheless, the fact of the inheritance being acquired sooner than expected will not justify an appeal by itself. It will have to be shown that the inheritance would have made a difference to the outcome of the case had it been acquired prior to the order being made. Where the parties' respective needs and entitlements have already been adequately met out of the other assets which were ample for that purpose, it may well be that the inheritance would have made no difference at all, given that it came after the

---

[83]    [1987] 2 FLR 480.

[84]    See e g *Reid v Reid* [2004] 1 FLR 736; *Benson v Benson* [1996] 1 FLR 692 (although in that case the husband did not apply for leave to appeal sufficiently promptly and permission was refused).

end of the marriage.[85] On the other hand, in a case with more modest assets which may have been distributed in a way which failed to fully meet the needs of either party, the inheritance may have made all the difference. Overall, however, it must be remembered that the court will generally be reluctant to reopen an order.[86]

## DISCLOSURE AND VALUATION OF INHERITANCE PROSPECTS

**18.49** The parties have no proprietary claim over any property they hope to inherit until the death of the testator, unless they have already acquired a proprietary interest in the property by one of the means previously discussed. Consequently, the court has no direct jurisdiction over those assets or over their owner, who is 'a stranger to the suit'.

**18.50** The court can compel the parties to disclose what they know of their inheritance prospects. Sometimes the party will have been told or shown the full extent of what he can expect to obtain. Indeed, he may have been named as the executor of the will and be in possession of the will. If so, production of the will and information as to its contents can be compelled, although fairness may require the testator, whose personal affairs this concerns, to have notice of the order and have the right to object to it on the basis that it delves too far into his personal affairs or is otherwise oppressive.[87]

**18.51** Theoretically, the testator could be required to attend an inspection appointment and produce his will and any other relevant documents.[88] However, the court is very unlikely to accede to such a request. In *Morgan v Morgan*[89] the husband sought to bring the wife's elderly father to court under a subpoena duces tecum to produce his will and various documents which would identify the extent of his estate which the wife was likely to inherit upon his death. It was held that the information he sought was both relevant and admissible, but the father should not be compelled to provide it because:

> 'it would be oppressive to cause [the father] to come under the duress of a subpoena to give evidence to the court about his assets and what he means to do with them ... In my opinion, the paramount consideration (though I bear in mind the importance of the evidence to the respondent) is the right of the individual. I do not see why a stranger to this suit should be forced to divulge evidence of this kind against his will.'

---

[85] See **11.155–11.160** and **17.16–17.22** for consideration of the treatment of 'after-acquired assets'.

[86] For example, *Myerson v Myerson* [2009] EWCA Civ 282.

[87] See Chapter 5 – alternatives to third party disclosure.

[88] See Chapter 5 for detailed consideration of the means by which information can be obtained from non-parties.

[89] [1977] Fam 122, (1976) FLR Rep 473.

In view of the wide variety of circumstances the family courts encounter and the flexibility of approach they reserve to themselves, it seems doubtful that this is an inflexible rule, but it seems that the court will require a heavy degree of persuasion before allowing such a request and, even then, the scope of the permitted enquiries is likely to be kept in the narrowest compass possible. Where unusual circumstances arise to make the fact of an imminent inheritance a virtual certainty, the court may permit a greater degree of enquiry than *Morgan* suggests will ever be permitted.

**18.52** Similar problems are likely to arise when it comes to attempting to value the potential inheritance. Very powerful reasons are likely to be required before a court will override the principle stated in *Morgan* and require a testator to permit valuations of his assets. Where the likely inheritance is several years ahead, the costs of a valuation are unlikely to be considered to be justified, especially considering that the future value of the inheritance is likely to be impossible to assess accurately.[90] There may be wholly exceptional cases where a valuation is necessary to do justice between the parties. In the correct circumstances the court has the jurisdiction to order inspection and valuation of such property which, although not strictly the subject matter of the proceedings, is property 'as to which any question arises in the proceedings'.[91] Often, however, there will be no need to go to such lengths. It may be possible to obtain reasonably accurate indications of the value of real property or chattels by inspection from a public place. So land can be valued from the road.[92] Valuations of cash and investments, on the other hand, cannot be valued in this way unless there is some clear information as to the nature and extent of the holdings.

## TAXATION ISSUES

**18.53** It is important also to bear in mind that an inheritance may come subject to an inheritance tax liability. The first £325,000 of the inheritance is exempt from tax, but sums above this level will be taxed at 40%. It should also be noted that any lifetime gifts to an individual made within 7 years of the donor's death may also be subject to tax, although at a lower rate. If the issue of a potential inheritance arises in a case and the likely value of the estate has been valued, it may be necessary to calculate the potential tax liabilities to provide a figure net of tax. Inevitably, any figure produced will be no more than an educated guess, because the actual tax consequences will depend on the circumstances at the date of death. Inheritance tax is considered in more detail in Chapter 23.

---

[90]   *C v C and Others* [2009] EWHC 1491 (Fam).
[91]   Supreme Court Act 1981, s 34(3) and County Courts Act 1984, s 53. See also 'further forms of interlocutory order' in Chapter 5.
[92]   As suggested in *Morgan v Morgan* [1977] Fam 122 at 124. Although this will not of itself establish the extent to which the property is charged by way of mortgage or otherwise and, therefore, the net equity available.

# Part VIII

# PENSIONS

# Chapter 19

# INTRODUCTION

**19.1**  Following the growth of occupational pension schemes during the latter half of the twentieth century it has become increasingly common for a significant portion of a family's assets to be tied up in a pension. The favourable tax treatment offered by the Government for contributions made to pension schemes has made a pension fund an efficient and attractive way of providing retirement provision. Despite the fact that pensions (unless already in payment) are essentially a form of deferred asset, they remain highly significant in many cases. Indeed, it is becoming more common to see cases where the funds accrued in a pension will be the most valuable asset available for division in a divorce settlement.

**19.2**  The importance of pension funds as a substantial part of a family's wealth began to be recognised during the 1970s and 1980s in reported cases where applications were made for lump sums to be paid from pensions when they were drawn. Many of these cases are referred to in Chapter 18 on the issue of adjourning a lump sum application or making a deferred lump sum order. In *Brooks v Brooks*[1] the House of Lords treated a small family company pension fund as a post-nuptial settlement which was capable of variation under a property adjustment order. Following this decision, a degree of 'pension sharing' became available, but only in those limited cases where the order could be made without prejudicing third parties. The remedy was at that time not available in the context of the vast majority of occupational or personal pension schemes.

**19.3**  The Pensions Act 1995 introduced 'earmarking orders' (later renamed 'attachment orders') permitting the courts to make orders directly against pension funds. Those powers were very limited in scope and, as discussed in Chapter 22, had many shortcomings, not least because they failed to provide any real sharing of the pension as an asset and did not offer security in retirement, but only until the member's death. They merely permitted a degree of sharing of the benefits under the existing pension. On the whole they were inconsistent with the clean break principle. With the passing of the Welfare Reform and Pensions Act 1999 the courts were finally given the power to make 'pension sharing' orders, so that the pension fund itself can now be divided between the parties in a similar way to any other capital asset.

---

[1]   [1996] 1 AC 375.

**19.4** Although pensions are frequently very important assets, they are also complex in their form. The parties often fail to understand fully the nature of the pensions they hold. A thorough understanding of pensions and their treatment in ancillary relief proceedings is an essential part of the ancillary relief practitioner's armoury.

**19.5** This section begins in Chapter 20 with an examination of the nature of a pension as an asset and the types of pensions most commonly encountered in practice. Chapter 21 considers the ways in which the courts are able to deal with pensions in ancillary relief proceedings. Finally, in Chapter 22 the complex subject of the valuation of pension funds through the use of the Capital Equivalent Transfer Value ('CETV') is discussed.

# Chapter 20

# TYPES OF PENSIONS

**20.1** Pension schemes as a generic concept cover a very broad number of different kinds of arrangement. They have a number of common features, the central concept being that they are designed to provide a form of income provision after retirement. So long as the relevant rules set by HM Revenue & Customs are met, pension schemes generally provide a tax efficient method of saving for retirement, in that contributions to a pension scheme, whether made by an employer or an individual are treated as if they were from tax-free income.

**20.2** In very broad terms, a pension will fall into one of the following categories:

- State pensions.

- Occupational salary related pensions.

- Occupational money purchase pensions.

- Personal pensions.

There are some hybrids of the above, but these cover the main categories. It is important to understand the differences and the way each form of scheme operates, because this will determine the way in which the pension should be considered as an asset and financial resource. The four categories are discussed below; the first two promise specific benefits in the form of income in retirement and the last two are funds of investments that can be used to purchase pension benefits at retirement.

## STATE PENSIONS

**20.3** State pensions are paid from state pension age and are based on National Insurance contributions.

**20.4** State pension age was originally 60 for women and 65 for men. The disparity between the retirement ages between men and women appears no longer to be capable of justification and provisions have been introduced to harmonise the retirement age regardless of gender. A later retirement age for women is being phased in as follows:

- Women born on or before 5 April 1950 will obtain their state pension from the age of 60.

- Women born on or after 6 April 1955 will obtain their state pension from the age of 65 or later (see **20.5**).

- Women born between 6 April 1950 and 5 April 1955 will obtain their state pension at between their 60th and 65th birthdays depending on their date of birth.

**20.5**   The Government is to revise state pensions and increase state pension age. The state pension age for men and women will increase to 66 in 2024, to 67 in 2034 and to 68 in 2044. Each rise will be phased in over 2 years.

**20.6**   The basic state pension is available to all who pay National Insurance contributions, whether self-employed or employed or those who receive credits as a result of home responsibilities or other reasons. On divorce a wife can substitute her husband's contribution record for her own up to the tax year before the divorce, to give her a greater basic state pension if his record is better. This substitution is lost if she re-marries before state pension age. If substitution is used, the husband's basic state pension rights are not reduced. The husband can likewise substitute the wife's contributions.

**20.7**   The full basic state pension is currently payable to anyone who has paid National Insurance contributions for 90% of their working life; working life being defined as the number of years from age 16 until state pension age. The Government have announced intentions to pay a full basic state pension to anyone with 30 years' contributions, to be effective from 6 April 2010. The rates for the basic state pension are set by the government and are, of course, liable to change in accordance with the political pressures operating at any particular time; the intention is that it will increase in line with average earnings in future.

**20.8**   In addition, for those in employment (as opposed to self-employed) there have been a series of 'top up' pensions:

- From 1961 to 1975, the State Graduated Retirement Benefit (this cannot be made subject to a pension sharing order).

- From 1978 to 2002, the State Earnings Related Pension Scheme ('SERPS').

- From 2002 the State Second Pension ('S2P').

The last two of these are collectively termed 'Additional State Pensions'. The original intention behind their creation was to provide a pension for those who did not have an employer's scheme to join. Final salary schemes may contract out of the Additional State Pensions (not the basic state pension) as long as they provide a certain level of benefits. Individuals have been able to contract out through a personal pension with effect from 6 April 1987, and in this case funds are paid into a personal pension.

**20.9** The State Earnings Related Pension Scheme ('SERPS') was set up in 1978 and the original intention was that it should provide a pension of 25% of 'middle band earnings'[1] at the end of the working life; this target was reduced to 20% of middle band earnings from 1988 until 2002. In 2002, this 'second tier' (as it is known) was reformed and named 'the State Second Pension'. The new design is better for those at the lower end of the earnings scale, in that it provides higher pensions, whilst for those earning at the top of the earnings scale it remains as it was between 1988 and 2002. In 2006, the Government announced an intention to make this a flat rate scheme in future, but has deferred consideration of this until the next Parliament.

# OCCUPATIONAL SALARY RELATED SCHEMES

**20.10** These are typically sponsored by an employer or the state. There will be a set formula for the benefits payable under the scheme and these will be contained in the scheme rules and summarised in the scheme booklet (the booklet is not a guaranteed entitlement to benefits).

**20.11** Such a scheme will usually promise:

- A pension at retirement linked to either pensionable salary near to the time of leaving the scheme (whether by resignation or retirement) or total accumulated earnings (usually revalued by inflation to retirement) as an employee.

    Typically a scheme might be '60ths' or '80ths'. A 60ths scheme will pay an individual 1/60th of their final salary for every year of service in the scheme. This is a contractual benefit. It does not depend on investment performance of the underlying fund. So long as the company is solvent when the benefits are payable, the member can enforce payment of the full agreed amount.

- Either a separate tax-free lump sum at retirement or the right to exchange some of the pension for a tax-free lump sum (known as commutation).

- Some provision for increasing the pension in line with the Retail Prices Index or other measure of the cost of living, either in payment or in the period before retirement if a member leaves before retirement age (since 1986 this latter has become a compulsory right). Very often, the rights will be protected against inflation both before and after retirement.

---

[1]  Currently (2009/10) any earnings between £4,940 per annum and £43,890 per annum.

- Spouses' (widows') pensions (usually as a percentage of the member's pension) on the member's death either before or after retirement. Sometimes the scheme may also provide some provision for other dependants.

- Lump sums on death before retirement, usually a multiple of the salary for those still in service.

- Ill health pensions on early retirement if unable to work.

**20.12**  The public sector schemes (the Principal Civil Service Pension Scheme, the Police Pension Scheme, the Teachers' Pension Scheme, the Armed Forces Pension Scheme, the Firemen's Pension Scheme and the NHS Pension Scheme) are all Defined Benefit Schemes. Unlike other occupational schemes which are created as a contractual arrangement between the employer and employee, the public sector schemes are usually governed by statutory material. Furthermore, unlike other occupational schemes they are 'unfunded' in the sense that no fund is put aside to meet future pension payments. Future pensions will rely on future tax revenues for payment. Nevertheless, these schemes provide inflation-proofing of the pensions in payment by way of index-linked increases in the pension when in payment.

**20.13**  The majority of public sector pension schemes traditionally promise 1/80th of final salary for every year of service plus a tax-free cash lump sum at retirement of three times this amount. The Police Pension Scheme and some sections of the Principal Civil Service Pension Scheme instead offer a better accrual rate, but tax-free cash by commutation. For example, 1/60th of final salary for every year of service, with a tax-free cash lump sum available by reducing the amount of the pension.

---

**Example: *Civil Servant, 60ths section***

*Details*

Husband is aged 48 and Wife aged 45. Husband joined the scheme at age 23 and his current salary is £60,000 per annum.

This is a '60ths' scheme.

His current accrued pension is 25/60 x £60,000      = £25,000 per annum
                                                     payable from age 60

He retires at age 60 (37 years' service) from active service on a salary of £120,000 per annum

His final pension is 37/60 x £120,000      = £74,000 per annum.

He will then be able to give up some of that pension for a tax-free cash lump sum.

Based on rates at the time of writing, he could receive £166,500 in cash and reduce the pension to £60,125 per annum.

---

**20.14**  In addition, the public sector schemes offer the right to transfer benefits from one public sector employment to another (the Public Sector Transfer

Club). Thus, many public sector workers have benefits on retirement fully linked to their final salary, regardless of how many different public sector employments they may have had.

**20.15** Many private sector employers used to provide final salary schemes and a good number still do, at least for existing employees. However, in recent times, many private sector employers have been withdrawing from providing final salary schemes. They are being withdrawn primarily due to the high cost of providing the benefits and running the schemes. The chief problem with such schemes has been the absence of a direct link between the contributions paid into the scheme and the value of the pension to be paid upon retirement. The pension is based on the final salary rather than the value of the fund built up through the payment of contributions. The ultimate cost of the pension for the scheme is affected by a member's final salary, life expectancy and the investment returns that are achieved. The last few years have seen these costs spiral as a result of increased life expectancy and poor investment performance.

**20.16** Most occupational schemes offer the opportunity to make additional voluntary contributions ('AVCs') to 'top up' the basic pension rights under the scheme. As an alternative to the scheme's AVC arrangement, a member has been able to pay free-standing additional voluntary contributions ('FSAVCs') instead of, or alongside, AVCs. AVCs are contributions into the occupational scheme, whereas FSAVCs, as the name suggests, allow the employee a degree of choice as to the scheme into which the contributions are paid and a degree of privacy, if, for example, they are trying to provide a fund for their early retirement.

**20.17** Recently, the liberalisation of pensions has meant most of these arrangements have been re-named personal pensions.

**20.18** Some highly paid senior executives or directors may also be offered an executive pension plan ('EPP') which is usually a money purchase scheme which tops up their basic pension. Such schemes can be funded in various ways and will usually form part of the individual's agreed remuneration package.

## OCCUPATIONAL MONEY PURCHASE SCHEMES

**20.19** These schemes could be considered as savings plans but with the tax advantages of a pension contract. Contributions are built up with investment returns to provide a fund of money at retirement or upon earlier death, which can then be used to purchase pension benefits, including a tax-free cash lump sum at retirement.

**20.20** The amount that a member receives at retirement depends on a number of factors:

- The amount of contributions paid (the employer must contribute, but the employer can require the employee/member to pay a further contribution as provided by the scheme's rules and as agreed by the employee/member at the time of joining).

- Investment performance over the period from the payment being made to retirement.

- The market cost of buying a pension at retirement – this can vary considerably, depending on economic factors and life expectancy; traditionally money purchase funds are used to purchase an annuity at retirement, although they can now be placed into Drawdown.[2]

- Administration and other expenses.

**20.21** From the point of view of employers, such defined contribution schemes are becoming more popular as the cost of funding the scheme is known in advance. However, the employee will not know how much pension they will receive until the time of actual retirement. This difference between defined contribution schemes and final salary schemes should not be overlooked, particularly when looking at the estimated benefits payable under a pension on retirement. In the case of a final salary scheme these estimates (so long as they are based on the member's current pensionable salary) provide a reasonably accurate indication of what the pension will be worth to them on retirement. In the case of a 'money purchase' scheme, however, the estimate of benefits upon retirement is based on expectations as to the performance of the investments upon which the fund is based. The estimate may prove to be far from accurate.

## PERSONAL PENSIONS

**20.22** Personal pensions (many of which are stakeholder pensions) are also defined contribution schemes with tax advantages but no guarantee of what will be payable at or during retirement. The ultimate value of the pension fund at retirement will be related to the contributions the employee has made and the performance of the underlying investments up to the point of retirement. It is even possible that a poorly invested personal pension could be worth less at retirement than the sum total of the contributions which have been paid into it. Similarly, a stock market crash can reduce drastically the value of a personal pension invested in equities. For example, a fund invested at the start of January 2000 may have halved in value by March 2003.

**20.23** The real difference between a personal pension and an occupational money purchase scheme is that the employer does not have to pay into the personal pension, and contributions can continue even if the policyholder

---

[2] Drawdown is explained at **20.29**.

changes job. The self-employed generally have no option but to have a personal pension scheme to provide for their retirement.

**20.24** Personal pension schemes can take various different forms. They are open to the employed or the self-employed. The most common type of personal pension is a form of investment purchased from a life assurance institution. These take various forms, but generally involve the purchase of units in an investment fund. The type of fund can often be chosen by the investor, but the management of that fund lies in the hands of a fund manager.

**20.25** In recent years Self-Invested Pension Plans ('SIPPs') have grown in popularity and use. Such schemes allow the investor to have some control over the way in which the funds in the scheme are invested. The SIPP can be used to invest in stocks, shares, unit trusts or commercial property (but not, as yet, residential property or personal chattels). From time to time the investor, or an investment manager appointed by the investor, can sell or buy the assets owned by the SIPP with a view to increasing the value of the fund. Such schemes can throw up real complexities and difficulties in the context of ancillary relief proceedings. Often the assets held by the SIPP will not have obvious and readily realisable values. For example, the SIPP may own shares in numerous, obscure unlisted companies. Careful thought should be given as to how to deal with the valuation of such schemes and the implementation of pension sharing orders in respect of them.

**20.26** Although not strictly personal pensions, some small family companies operate small self-administered schemes ('SSASs'). These are in essence a hybrid form of pension, with much in common with SIPPs on the one hand and an occupational pension scheme on the other. Such arrangements are usually very closely bound up with the family company in question, and dealing with such a scheme within ancillary relief proceedings will probably require the close involvement of the forensic accountant engaged to value the family company. Often they will own a property that is connected with the company and there may be liquidity problems when trying to share these in a divorce settlement.

## TYPES OF BENEFITS PAID BY A PENSION SCHEME

**20.27** A pension scheme can offer a variety of types of benefit payable to a member and their dependants. These can include:

- Periodical pension payable to the member from retirement age.

- Lump sum (usually tax-free) payable at retirement, either as part of the accruing pension or by reducing the pension in retirement.

- Periodical pension payable to a spouse (or a dependant, sometimes) following the member's death.

- Lump sum payable to spouse, dependant or estate on death.

## Periodical pension payable to the member

**20.28** Typically, in an occupational salary-related pension scheme the rules of the scheme will specify the amount of pension that is to be paid in respect of an individual and their salary. This has been explained above.

**20.29** In an occupational money purchase pension scheme or a personal pension, the benefits build up as a fund which can be used to provide benefits. Traditionally, the fund is then used to provide a lump sum and purchase an annuity payable for life. Options are available to provide other benefits. More recently, however, the right to 'drawdown' income from the fund without buying an annuity has been introduced, as has the option for alternatively secured annuities. These allow the member to retain the funds invested for growth whilst the member can draw income within set limits. This is particularly useful if the member wishes to take retirement at a time when the investments in the fund have a particularly depressed value or at a time when the cost of purchasing an annuity is unusually high. Some individuals who have taken this route have found themselves with a considerably lower income than they originally expected, due to the poor investment performance after they have started to draw their pension.

## Lump sums at retirement

**20.30** In an occupational salary related pension scheme, the rules of the scheme may specify the amount of lump sum that is to be paid in respect of an individual based on their salary and service. In other schemes, the rules will specify how some of the retirement pension can be exchanged for a lump sum by way of commutation.

**20.31** In an occupational money purchase pension scheme or a personal pension it is likely that the individual will be able to take a lump sum of up to one-quarter of the fund value. As this lump sum is usually drawn free of tax, it is often more beneficial to take the full lump sum rather than leave the funds in the scheme, where they can be drawn only as an income stream for life, and such income will be subject to income tax. Some executive pension plans exist where the lump sum available is greater than 25% of the value.

## Widows' pensions

**20.32** In an occupational salary-related pension scheme the rules of the scheme will usually specify the amount of pension that is to be paid in respect of an individual (related to their salary) on their death. It is particularly important for practitioners in on-going divorce cases to consider this. The benefit may or may not be payable if the parties are separated (either through judicial separation or even if they are living apart) or divorced and may or may not be payable to an ex-spouse if there are maintenance payments being made at the time of death. Practitioners should check in respect of each scheme.

**20.33** In an occupational money purchase pension scheme or a personal pension the whole fund will usually pay out as a lump sum on death prior to retirement, but it is unusual for a spouse's pension to be payable as of right. If the member chooses to take an annuity, then they will have the option at that time to purchase an annuity which provides a pension for a spouse, although this will reduce the amount of the pension payments payable to the member.

### Lump sum payable on death before retirement

**20.34** In an occupational salary-related pension scheme the rules of the scheme will often specify a lump sum payable on death, which is generally a multiple of the member's salary. This is only paid on death before retirement whilst still in service. If a member leaves service and does not take the benefits, the scheme can offer a lump sum payable before retirement, but more usually will only refund contributions.

**20.35** In a money purchase scheme or a personal pension policy, the fund will typically pay out in full on death before retirement and it may be that the employer or individual sets up further life assurance on top of the benefits.

## RIGHTS AND OBLIGATIONS ATTACHING TO A PENSION

**20.36** Any pension confers a promise to the member of pension rights in retirement from the scheme or pension provider. The rights that a member has are governed by the rules of the scheme, which are then subject to overriding legislation. The overriding legislation is that set by the governing country.

**20.37** In the UK, with a few exceptions, the majority of schemes are eligible for tax advantages, but have to act within certain limits. In April 2006, these limits were changed to allow higher tax-free cash sums (in many cases) and higher amounts of contributions (for all except the highest earners). With the exception of certain professions (professional sportsmen, for example), the earliest age at which benefits from a pension scheme can be taken is currently (in 2009) age 50. This applies to both occupational and personal pensions.

**20.38** The main changes to the rules that took place in April 2006 were:

- Inland Revenue restrictions on pension contribution levels have been removed. In future, up to 100% of earned income in any tax year[3] may be invested in pensions, with tax relief available.

---

[3] Currently in the tax year up to April 2010, up to £245,000 and this will increase to £255,000 the following year and remain at that level until 2016.

- A cap on the total that may be held in pension funds is £1.75 million for the tax year 2009/2010, increasing to 1.8 million for tax year 2010/2011 and then staying at that level for the following 5 years.

- 25% of the pension fund may be drawn as a tax-free lump sum – an option previously available under some but not all types of pension and still dependent on the scheme rules.

- Rules about working until later in life and buying an annuity no later than age 75 have been relaxed slightly and there is increased flexibility for purchasing annuities and continuing contributions.

- Retirement age will be increased from 50 to 55 by 2010.

**20.39** The benefits under occupational final salary pension schemes are defined by the scheme rules. Where the scheme receives all the tax advantages which exist for pension schemes, it must operate within the rules as set down by legislation. However, it is under no obligation to offer terms as generous as those rules and many schemes will not allow retirement as of right from age 50 or 55, and some still offer a tax-free lump sum that is significantly less than 25% of the total value.

## FUNDING OF PENSION SCHEMES

### Occupational salary-related schemes

**20.40** Where the scheme is sponsored by a private sector employer, the scheme will have to set up a fund with assets separate from that employer (with the exception of certain 'directors only' schemes). The intention is that the funds in the scheme should be sufficient to meet the liabilities (ie to pay the promised pensions) that the scheme has to the members of the scheme, which will include the employees, former employees, pensioners and spouses of employees and former employees. The scheme has to perform a valuation periodically to ensure the funds it holds are considered sufficient to meet the liabilities.

**20.41** Once a benefit has been earned by a member, regulations prevent the scheme from reducing the benefit while the scheme remains active. Where the scheme collapses through insolvency and the sponsoring employer cannot meet the shortfall, however, the benefits can be reduced to the extent that the funds are insufficient to meet the liabilities. However, it may be that the scheme would apply to be accepted into the Pensions Protection Fund.

**20.42** There are a number of public sector pension schemes (NHS Pension Scheme, Police Pension Scheme, Firefighters' Pension Scheme, Principal Civil Service Pension Scheme, Teachers' Pension Scheme and Armed Forces Pension Scheme) and these do not have funds to support them: they are paid from the Treasury. This means that they are effectively guaranteed out of future taxation, subject to any changes in legislation reducing or extinguishing the liability to pay the benefits, although changes which retrospectively affect the accrued benefits of the members of such schemes would no doubt be ferociously contested on public law and human rights grounds.

## Occupational money purchase schemes

**20.43** With these schemes, again the sponsoring employer will set rules for the benefits that can be taken. In this case, the rules may restrict retirement ages (it may be in the employer's interest to have some control over when staff can leave with retirement benefits); however, it is very unusual for the rules to restrict the type of benefit that can be paid. Therefore, it will be usual for up to 25% of the fund at retirement to be available as a tax-free lump sum and for the member to have some control over the decision whether to purchase a spouse's pension and whether to have the pension inflation-linked.

**20.44** The funds will be held either in insurance company funds or in specific managed funds, but are entirely separate from the employer.

## Personal pension plans

**20.45** Although the plan provider (usually an insurance company) could place restrictions on the rights under the plan, in practice they follow the limitations imposed by legislation. Therefore, in the UK, 25% of the fund will be available as a tax-free lump sum, and benefits can currently be taken at age 50 rising to age 55 by 2010. Clearly, the earlier a pension is drawn the greater reduction will be made to the annual income it produces to take into account the longer period over which the income will be paid.

## PROTECTION OF PENSION BENEFITS

**20.46** State scheme benefits and public sector pension benefits are paid out of taxation and are therefore secured by the public purse. Money purchase contributions are paid into specific funds and the benefits are dependent on the performance of the investments of those funds.

**20.47** Occupational final salary schemes are intended to be protected by the scheme's funds, and an actuarial valuation is done every 3 years to ensure the scheme holds sufficient funds. If the valuation reveals that the funds are insufficient to meet the promised benefits, then the employer should pay a sufficient additional contribution to meet the shortfall, either a one-off payment or a series of periodical payments.

**20.48**   There is now also the Pension Protection Fund ('PPF').[4] In the circumstance where an employer folds and there are insufficient funds in the scheme, the scheme can apply to join the PPF. The basic principles of the PPF are:

- For individuals who lose their final salary pension benefits after April 2005 the PPF will pay 100% of pensions currently being paid and 90% of pensions for those who have not yet reached retirement, subject to a £25,000 per annum cap at age 65, and less for lower retirement ages.

- Individuals whose employer became insolvent before April 2005 are not covered by the PPF. There is the Financial Assistance Scheme, which is not as generous as the Pension Protection Fund but does provide some benefits for those whose scheme became insolvent before April 2005.

**20.49**   The PPF does not cover money purchase pension schemes. It is still in its early days and we are yet to see how it will work, as it is funded by a levy on all the other schemes, but it does add an additional level of protection to final salary benefits. Furthermore, pursuant to MCA 1973, s 25E any compensation to which a party is or is likely to be entitled must be considered by the court as part of the s 25(2) matters as a future financial resource which one party is likely to have and which the other will lose the chance of acquiring an interest to. The PPF compensation must be taken into account by the court, even if it cannot be shown as something which will be available in the foreseeable future. Section 25E also makes provision for how assumption of responsibility for a pension scheme by the PPF affects any existing pension attachment or pension sharing orders.

## THE TAXATION OF PENSIONS

**20.50**   The different benefits available from a pension have been described above. Although there is usually a tax-free lump sum available upon retirement, the main part of a pension is an income stream. In an occupational final salary scheme this is paid by the scheme and, traditionally, the funds from money purchase schemes (after the tax-free cash is taken) were used to purchase an annuity. Each of these is liable to income tax at the same rate as earned income, although National Insurance contributions are not payable on pension income.

**20.51**   Likewise, if 'drawdown' or 'alternatively secured annuities' are used, any income taken is still liable to income tax. Drawdown policies and alternatively secured annuities allow individuals with pension funds to retain the funds in a chosen investment vehicle and draw income between prescribed limits to supply retirement income. The individual takes the risk that if the investments do not perform well in retirement, the retirement income will be much lower in the long term.

---

[4]   Established by the Pensions Act 2004.

**20.52** Where an individual makes excessive contributions to pension funds or the total of an individual's pension funds exceed the lifetime allowance,[5] tax penalties will arise and it will usually require specialist advice at the time to deal with issues surrounding this.

---

[5] £1.75 million in the year to April 2010 increasing to £1.8 million the following year and remaining at that level for an expected 5 years.

# Chapter 21

# PENSION ORDERS ON DIVORCE

**21.1** There are essentially three different methods of treating pension rights on divorce.[1] These are pension sharing orders, attachment orders and offsetting.

## PENSION SHARING

**21.2** Pension sharing orders were introduced by the Welfare Reform and Pensions Act 1999 and are available in cases where the petition for divorce was presented after 1 December 2000. New ss 21A, 24B, 24C and 24D were introduced into the Matrimonial Causes Act 1973 to provide the court with the powers to share pension rights between the parties. Where the petition for divorce or nullity predates 1 December 2000, the parties will have to rely on the alternative means of dealing with a pension, considered below. Where a petition was issued before 1 December 2000, but for some reason a decree absolute has not yet been pronounced, it may be possible to dismiss the petition and, in some cases set aside the decree nisi,[2] in order to allow a new petition to be presented after the date when pension sharing became permitted.

**21.3** Pension sharing has now become routine and there appears to be a growing trend to deal with assets on a 'like-for-like' basis in the interests of fairness.[3] Indeed, where the assets are adequate to meet the competing needs of the parties, the use of pension sharing orders to deal with the pensions and property adjustment orders to deal with the other assets usually makes a case simpler to conduct and easier to deal with than to embark on the more difficult exercise of pension offsetting (considered below).

**21.4** Pension sharing can only take place upon a decree of divorce or nullity and not upon judicial separation.[4] It should also be noted that the court may

---

[1] The *Brooks v Brooks* [1995] 2 FLR 13, HL variation of settlement approach is dealt with at **15.55**. Note that this approach is only available in respect of petitions presented before 1 December 2000. Such cases are unlikely now to be encountered in practice.

[2] See *S v S (Rescission of Decree Nisi: Pension Sharing Provision)* [2002] 1 FLR 457, where the court endorsed a consent order setting aside a decree nisi in order to allow a new petition to be presented to allow a pension sharing order to be made. Where the parties do not agree to rescission of the decree nisi, on the other hand, the court will not rescind the decree: *H v H (Pension Sharing: Rescission of Decree Nisi)* [2002] 2 FLR 116.

[3] *Wells v Wells* [1999] 1 AC 345; *Maskell v Maskell* [2003] 1 FLR 1138; *Martin-Dye v Martin-Dye* [2006] EWCA Civ 681, [2006] 2 FLR 901.

[4] Matrimonial Causes Act 1973, s 24(1).

make a pension sharing order upon an application to vary a periodical payments order, although the power to do so only exists in those cases where the divorce or nullity proceedings began after 1 December 2000.[5]

**21.5** Pension sharing orders are available against most forms of pension scheme, including the second state pension or the State Earnings Related Pension Scheme ('SERPS'), but not against the basic state pension. Furthermore, in principle, it appears to be possible for the court to make a pension sharing order against a foreign pension but, in common with all orders made in relation to property overseas, the court may need to be reassured that its order will be effective in a foreign jurisdiction.[6] Some jurisdictions (such as the United Kingdom itself) have 'anti-alienation' provisions which prevent pension funds being moved overseas. Such provision may therefore prevent a transfer out of a pension fund based overseas to a fund in England and Wales.

**21.6** When implemented, a pension sharing order results in the legal transfer of a specified proportion of the scheme member's pension rights to the other party. This results in a 'pension debit' being applied to the transferor's fund, reducing the value of the member's fund or the member's benefits, and the creation of a 'pension credit' for the transferee. Once implemented, it is an irreversible transfer and the parties will have separate pension rights in their own name completely independent of each other. The very detailed rules as to how the scheme managers are to implement a pension sharing order are set out in the Welfare Reform and Pensions Act 1999. They are complicated and it will be rare that the ancillary relief practitioner will need to concern himself or herself with the 'nuts and bolts' of how the order is implemented.

**21.7** In some cases the party obtaining the pension credit remains within the original pension scheme (known as an 'internal transfer') and in others the party obtaining the pension credit transfers the pension credit away from the scheme (an 'external transfer'). In the case of most pension schemes the scheme managers must offer an external transfer as an option (in the same way as in most circumstances they must permit the scheme member to transfer the pension into another scheme prior to benefits becoming payable). It must be noted that the non-contributory public sector schemes (eg the National Health Service Pension Scheme, Police Pension Scheme, Teachers' Pension Scheme, Principal Civil Service Pension Scheme, Armed Forces Pension Scheme and Firefighters' Pension Scheme) only allow an internal transfer. In other words, the party obtaining the benefit of the pension sharing order will have to become a member of that scheme and cannot seek to transfer the benefits into another scheme. So in such a case the transferee cannot use the pension credit to increase the value of another personal pension fund they already own, no matter how financially beneficial that step may appear to be.[7] Many private

---

[5]    MCA 1973, s 31(7B)(ba).

[6]    *Hamlin v Hamlin* [1986] 1 FLR 61.

[7]    This feature of the public sector schemes which keeps the party obtaining the pension credit within the scheme can pose practical problems in some cases, the most common being to create an 'income gap' (discussed at **21.21**).

sector schemes insist the ex-spouse transfers the 'pension credit' out of the scheme and to a personal pension policy, but a number do allow the ex-spouse to choose between remaining in the scheme and transferring out.

**21.8** Even if the ex-spouse remains within the scheme, the pension credit remains entirely separate from, and independent of, the original member's pension rights. The party obtaining the pension credit will become a member of the scheme in his or her own right and this new pension will have no further connection with the other party's pension. This is frequently misunderstood by the parties and they may resist a pension sharing order because of the erroneous belief that it will keep them bound together in some way through the pension fund. Quite the opposite is true, and practitioners should be careful to ensure that clients understand the practical effect of a pension sharing order.

**21.9** If the pension credit remains in the original scheme, it should retain the 'actuarial value' of the benefits as assessed before the pension sharing order was made. For example, if the pension sharing order specified a 50% share of the pension and an internal transfer is taken, then after the order is implemented both parties will have a new pension fund worth exactly half of the CETV of the original pension. This is not always the case when there is a transfer of the pension credit out of the scheme into a new scheme. The new scheme will apply its own scheme rules and principles to valuing the new pension and the value of the new pension rights could therefore be more or less than 50% of the value of the original pension. It is important to note that if a scheme member has a pension in payment of £20,000 per annum, then a 50% pension sharing order will reduce this to £10,000 per annum. The wife, however, will not necessarily receive (and in practice seldom does receive) £10,000 per annum. This is because the pension for the ex-spouse is based on her age, circumstances and gender. A female will usually require a larger fund than a male of the same age to produce the same income for life, simply because the female's statistical life expectancy is greater. In short, a woman's pension usually costs more than a man's pension if both are taken at the same age. Clearly, where a pension sharing order is made against a wife's pension in favour of the husband, the same principle will operate in reverse. This is an important feature of pension sharing, which is considered further in the context of valuing pensions in Chapter 22.

**21.10** Section 21A of the Matrimonial Causes Act 1973 provides that a pension sharing order is an order which specifies the percentage value to be transferred of one party's shareable rights. Despite the uniform requirement for a pension sharing order to specify the percentage of the member's CETV to be transferred,[8] there are a number of areas where scheme practice varies and which the practitioner should check before an order is made.

---

[8]   See also Form P1, the prescribed pension sharing annex form.

## Does the scheme accept only integer (whole number) percentages in the order?

**21.11**   At one extreme, situations have arisen where only an integral percentage would be accepted by the pension arrangement. That is, the arrangement would not accept an order for, say 46.2% of the member's CETV; it would only accept orders for whole number percentages (46%, 47% or any other whole percentage). The majority of arrangements will accept fractions of a percentage point.

## Will the scheme accept a percentage transfer to provide a specified monetary amount?

**21.12**   A significant number of arrangements are still prepared to accept wording in the order such as 'such percentage of the CETV as will provide a "pension credit" for the ex-spouse of £200,000'. Such an order is clearly conditional on the CETV being greater than or equal to the specified amount (£200,000 in our example), but it is also dependent on the rules and procedures of the pension arrangement itself. As the court would be asking the scheme to do something that, strictly, is not contained within the legislation, the scheme is entitled to say that it can only accept orders in the prescribed form. In some cases, the scheme does not have the ability within its system to accept such an order. However, other schemes will take the view that if the court orders this, they will comply with it. Practitioners are advised to check with the administrators of the pension arrangement regarding what they consider to be acceptable. As long as the 'person responsible for the arrangement' (usually the administrators on behalf of the Trustees of the Scheme) will accept the wording in an order, then there is no reason why it should not be used if all parties and the court are in agreement. Whether an order expressed in such terms is compliant with s 21A is, of course, another matter. If there is any uncertainty or potential problem, practitioners are advised to use a percentage or to ensure that an order is made only once it has been approved in principle by the pension arrangement in question. There are times when the parties would want an order termed in this way. This might be because the settlement is based on the recipient receiving a certain amount either as the best estimate to achieve a required level of income or because a proportion is required to be taken as a lump sum to meet certain financial commitments.

**21.13**   Even where there has been an independent actuarial valuation of a pension conducted within the proceedings which is found to be a fair valuation of pension rights,[9] it will continue to be the CETV which is used for the implementation of the order rather than the independent valuation. Care must be taken not to confuse the two valuations. The percentage inserted in the order is the proportion of the scheme's CETV required to produce the desired result,

---

[9]   See Chapter 21 for a discussion of the circumstances in which this may be appropriate.

even if the basis for the percentage inserted in the order is the information produced by the independent valuation.[10]

## Value of the pension at the date of implementation

**21.14**  It is also important to keep in mind that the percentage specified in a pension sharing order is applied to the CETV on the implementation date rather than the last CETV figure being produced. Parties to a divorce will often conduct the negotiations based on a CETV supplied at some point in the past. When the pension sharing order is implemented, it will be based on a different CETV and this may be more or less than the one used in the negotiations. Practitioners should warn their clients of this, as if the amount is less than expected, the recipient may complain, and if it is more than expected, the member may complain.

**21.15**  Where the pension is 'live' in the sense that contributions have continued to be made, or further employment service accrued, since the last CETV was obtained, it is likely that the CETV at the date of the pension sharing order being implemented will have increased. Many pensions are affected by fluctuations in the financial markets and these can significantly affect the CETV at any point in time. Pensions in the form of an SSAS or SIPP (see Chapter 20) may be even more volatile in terms of their value than larger unit-based schemes where the risk is spread over a wider range of investments. Where such unpredictable fluctuations in the value of a pension could have a serious effect on the implementation of the pension sharing order, it may be desirable, if possible, to use a form of words in the order similar to that suggested at the **21.12** above.

**21.16**  Where the pension is already in payment, the CEB[11] is likely (all other things being equal) to have decreased since the date of the valuation due to the payments made from the pension. The most dramatic difference will occur where the pension is brought into payment between the provision of the CETV and the implementation of the pension sharing order. If a lump sum was paid out of the pension upon the pension being taken, the CEB may be as much as 25% or more smaller than the CETV. Practitioners should be alert to this and, in appropriate circumstances, seek assurance from the party holding the pension that the pension has not been drawn and will not be drawn prior to implementation of the pension sharing order. Pensions in payment should, in any event, be considered as a financial resource available to the parties rather than as a capital asset.[12]

---

[10]  See **21.9**.
[11]  The Cash Equivalent of Benefits ('CEB') is used instead of the CETV when valuing a pension in payment.
[12]  *Martin-Dye v Martin-Dye* [2006] 2 FLR 901. See **21.44**.

# Health issues

**21.17**   One important point to bear in mind is that pension schemes are permitted to take a member's health into account when calculating a CETV on implementation of a pension sharing order. The scheme must disclose that they might do this if asked as part of their disclosure. Practitioners are always advised to check this point, particularly if the member has poor health.

**21.18**   The effect of poor health on the value of the pension can be dramatic. A man, in normal health, aged 62 years with a pension entitlement under a final salary pension scheme of £20,000 per annum might have a CETV of £320,000. If, however, this man has only a year to live (according to interpretations of his health), then the CETV, at implementation, will be dramatically different if his health is taken into account. The CETV might be £320,000 if the scheme does not take that into account, and approximately £20,000 if it does. This will make a significant difference if a pension sharing order is implemented subject to such a recalculation. If the risk of this occurring appears to be significant, the pension arrangement may need to be approached with a view to providing clarification or some assurance as to the approach likely to be taken. Alternatively, the rest of the order should be drafted in a way which allows some form of alternative provision if the pension sharing order turns out to be worth a great deal less than anticipated. Where the pension sharing order is not implemented in the way the parties and court expected it to be, this may constitute a *Barder*[13] event permitting an appeal out of time, but the pension sharing order itself may not be capable of being reopened and revised.

# Deferred pension sharing orders or adjourning pension sharing

**21.19**   It is not clear whether the possibility of the court making an order to take effect on a future date, thus deferring the pension sharing, was intended by those who drafted the legislation.

**21.20**   There are a number of pension arrangements which will not accept orders expressed to take effect at a future date. A principal reason for this seems to be that the pension administrators do not have the systems to cope with such orders. There has been a suggestion that further legislation will be enacted which will prohibit such orders being made but allowing those arrangements that have already accepted 'deferred orders' to be implemented at the due date. Until such orders are expressly barred, practitioners should check with the pension arrangement before a deferred order is made.

**21.21**   There are circumstances where making the order to take effect at a date in the future may be in the best interests of both parties. This is most likely in what are known as 'income gap' cases. This is where the member's pension comes into payment before the other party can receive the pension that is

---

[13]   *Barder v Barder ( Caluori intervening)* [1987] 2 FLR 480.

available from the pension sharing order. In other words, the effect of a pension sharing order is to reduce the pension in payment immediately to the spouse who holds the pension, but the other party will not obtain a pension from the pension credit until the age of eg 60 or 65 years because the scheme rules prevent the pension being paid earlier to the non-serving member of the scheme. Well-known examples of the above have traditionally been the uniformed services (Armed Forces Pension Scheme and Police Pension Scheme), where a full pension can be obtained by the member many years before he or she reaches the statutory retirement age. This has been alleviated to some extent, as some public sector schemes now allow pension credit members to retire at age 55, although it still has not resolved the problem. It is common for military personnel to complete sufficient service by the time they are age 40 or earlier to be able to retire at that point with an immediate pension. An example of the problem would be a naval officer being able to take his pension at the age of 45. Upon retiring from the Navy he may have a pension of, say, £30,000 per annum. If a pension sharing order for 50% of his pension were to be implemented at that point, his pension would immediately reduce to £15,000. Although it is now possible for his former wife to take the pension credit from age 55, there can still be a period when the husband is receiving his pension less the debit and the wife is not receiving anything. Thus, the income available to the couple would have reduced by £15,000 for some 20 years. The real beneficiary of the order in that 20-year period would be the Exchequer. The problem is not confined to these specific occupations and it can arise in various situations.

**21.22** One way around this problem would be a deferred order (discussed above), although this will not be possible in the context of the scheme in question and strictly is not allowable. The parties could consider whether they can adjourn the financial settlement in order to make an order at a date in the future when the pension credit can come into payment immediately.[14] It may even be that the parties are able to agree prospectively the terms of the order to be made in the future and state this in the preamble to the order which adjourns the application for a pension sharing order. Where the parties do not agree to such an adjournment, the court is likely to be reluctant to impose it upon the parties. It flies in the face of a clean break and complete determination of both parties' claims. The principles to be applied to adjourning applications to await future events is considered in more detail in Chapter 18 in the context of inheritance prospects. It should be noted, however, when considering the cases referred to in that section, that most predate the inclusion of s 25B(1) in the Matrimonial Causes Act 1973, which provides that, when considering a party's future benefits under a pension arrangement, the court does not have to be satisfied that those benefits will be available 'in the foreseeable future' and, accordingly, some of those cases might have been decided differently had they been cases where the asset in question was a pension and the petition had been presented after 1 July 1996.

---

[14] MCA 1973, s 24B(1) expressly permits the court to make the pension sharing order at any time after a decree of divorce or nullity.

**21.23** There are various pitfalls in this approach which make the prospect of adjourning a pension sharing application unattractive in all but exceptional cases.

## Pitfalls in adjourning the application

**21.24** If the intention is to make an order at a date in the future, then such order can only be made on the member's pension rights if he is still alive. To protect the ex-spouse against the husband dying before the order can be implemented, it is possible that a life assurance policy could be taken out on the member's life in favour of the ex-spouse. This requires the member to be in good health, and the parties should be aware that they may be required to disclose their medical records. If a life assurance policy is taken out and the life assured fails to disclose any medical condition, then the policy can be invalid on death. Similarly, most policies have exclusions for death caused by suicide (at least in the early years) or by certain hazardous occupations or pastimes. Therefore, it is not possible to be sure that this will always pay out on death.

**21.25** The court has to agree to adopt this approach and there is a risk that a different court at a date in the future may not be persuaded to make the order for pension sharing at that time.

**21.26** Potentially, pension sharing could be abolished or be replaced by future legislation before the adjourned application is restored.

**21.27** The rules surrounding 'pension credits' could change. The most obvious example of this was seen in the Armed Forces Pension Scheme, where orders made before April 2006 would pay the ex-spouse's pension from age 60; those made after that date would only pay from age 65, and therefore those adjourning an application to a date after 5 April 2006 then needed to wait longer than initially planned before the ex-spouse could obtain income from a 'pension credit'. This has, however, changed again as pension credits since 5 April 2009 are payable at age 55!

**21.28** The scheme member could remarry and subsequently undergo another divorce or judicial separation in which an attachment order is made in respect of the pension in favour of the later partner. This would preclude pension sharing in respect of the first spouse.[15]

**21.29** The parties should also note that although this solves a cash flow issue in the short term, the final pension income is likely to be lower as a result of the pension sharing order being made in the future. This has to be seen as a cash flow solution and does not add value to the pension rights.

---

[15]   MCA 1973, s 24B(5).

# ATTACHMENT ORDERS

**21.30**  Pension attachment orders (known as pension earmarking orders from their introduction for cases commenced after 1 July 1996 until they were renamed by the Welfare Reform and Pensions Act 1999 in relation to cases commenced after 1 December 2000) are available upon both a decree of divorce and a decree of judicial separation.

**21.31**  Attachment orders are not a new form of financial provision order. They are simply an extension of the court's powers to make periodical payments and lump sum orders pursuant to MCA 1973, s 23.[16] The pension rights remain entirely in the member's name, and a proportion of the pension payments are made directly to the former spouse at the time of payment. In other words, the order operates in the same way as an attachment of earnings order used to enforce a periodical payments order.

**21.32**  A court can order that:

- the pension scheme shall pay to the ex-spouse a percentage (which can be anywhere between 0% and 100%) of a payment that is due to the member;[17] this can be a percentage of –
  - the periodical pension payments, and/or
  - the lump sum available under the pension.

- the pension scheme member shall exercise his or her rights under the scheme rules to commute part of the pension for a lump sum.[18] This can be an order to commute anything between 0% and 100% of the maximum allowed under the scheme rules, so it can be used to maximise the lump sum produced by the pension (an order for commutation of 100%) or to maximise the income produced by the pension (an order preventing commutation or limiting it to a very low percentage of the maximum allowed).

- all or part of the lump sum on death in service shall be paid to the ex-spouse.[19]

**21.33**  An attachment order includes all pension rights accrued in that arrangement after the making of the order, as well as those accrued to the date of the order. Where a pension has been subjected to a pension attachment order, the spouse who holds the pension may well wonder why it is in his or her interest to make further contributions to the pension when up to 100% of the benefit of that pension will be paid to the other party under the attachment order. The court cannot compel further contributions to be made to the

---

[16]  MCA 1973, ss 25B(3), 25C(1) and 25D(1)(a). See also *T v T (Financial Relief: Pensions)* [1998] 1 FLR 1072 at 1085E–G.

[17]  MCA 1973, s 25B(4) and (5).

[18]  MCA 1973, s 25B(7).

[19]  MCA 1973, s 25C(2)(a).

pension in question. Similarly, if the pension is an occupational scheme and, subsequent to the making of the order, the party whose scheme has been made subject to the order leaves that employment to join a new employer with a new scheme, or if the employer closes the scheme to further accrual of benefits, the order will not attach to the benefits under the new scheme.

**21.34** Attachment orders may be varied if circumstances change.[20] Although the periodical payments element will be variable from time to time in the same way as any periodical payments order,[21] it may be more difficult to vary the quantum of the deferred lump sum element of a pension attachment order if the court applies the same principles as are applied to the variation of a lump sum payable by instalments.[22] Generally, the court is reluctant to interfere with the finality of capital orders.

**21.35** An important point to have in mind is that, following pension attachment orders, the pension rights remain entirely in the member's name. Therefore, the *member* is taxable on the total income. For this reason, attachment orders can be inefficient in terms of utilising the parties' respective tax allowances, particularly if one is a high rate tax payer and the other is not. The parties need to be alert to these tax implications. If a pension is paid gross of tax, then the ex-spouse will receive a proportion of the gross pension and the member will be left to account for all of the tax on the pension payments. Calculations of the tax implications must be made to ensure that the intended 'net effect' of the order is achieved and care also taken to find out whether the pension is paid net or gross of tax.

**21.36** The most important drawback of attachment orders is that, as a form of periodical payments order, they cease upon death of the member. Specifically, if the member dies, the ex-spouse has to live for the remainder of their life without income from this source. Where an attachment order is made in relation to any lump sum payable upon the member's death, this may provide some relief, although payments are unlikely to be available where the death takes place after the scheme member's retirement date. Pension attachment provides only limited financial security in retirement. Income attachment orders also cease upon the re-marriage of the receiving party.

**21.37** A further serious drawback with attachment orders is that any sums become payable only once the scheme member begins to draw benefits under the pension. The legislation contains no power for the court to order that the benefits be drawn at any particular date.[23] This does seem strange when the court can order the member to commute some of the pension for a lump sum

---

[20]   MCA 1973, s 31(1)(dd).
[21]   See *T v T (Financial Relief: Pensions)* [1998] 1 FLR 1072 at 1086–7, where Singer J identified various reasons as to why an attachment order directed to the regular periodical payments under a pension scheme made many years before retirement would be undesirable in most cases. See also *Burrow v Burrow* [1999] 1 FLR 508.
[22]   *Tilley v Tilley* (1980) Fam Law 89.
[23]   *T v T (Financial Relief: Pensions)* [1998] 1 FLR 1072.

but not order the member to take benefits at a certain time. A party can, therefore, choose to defer drawing on a pension so as to avoid the pension attachment orders being effective. So, unless an undertaking is voluntarily given to take the pension at a particular date, the order could be rendered utterly useless.

**21.38** Furthermore, pension attachment orders generally prevent a clean break between the parties. There cannot be a dismissal of a party's claims to periodical payments if it is anticipated that there will be attachment of the other party's pension payments upon retirement. The periodical payments claim must be kept alive in order to keep the attachment order alive.

**21.39** Pension attachment orders are rarely used and are unlikely to be useful unless the petition in the proceedings predates 1 December 2000, so that pension sharing orders are unavailable, or in the exceptional cases (such as the Armed Forces Pension Scheme) where there is an 'income gap'. Even where there is an 'income gap' there may be other solutions that are better suited to the needs of the particular case. Indeed, even before the introduction of pension sharing orders, pension attachment orders were usually only made in relation to the lump sum benefits and death benefits available under a pension, there being few cases where any real purpose was served by an attachment of the periodical payments arising under a pension scheme.

## OFFSETTING

**21.40** 'Offsetting' is not a form of pension order. It is a means by which the pension benefits of one party are taken into account in the court's order without any form of order being made which affects the pensions. Offsetting works by taking a value for one party's pension provision and setting this off against the value of the other assets, so that the pension is left intact and a larger proportion of the other assets is received by the other party to compensate him or her for leaving the marriage without a share of the other's pension funds. If offsetting is used against the full value of the pension, ie as a complete alternative to a pension sharing order, the parties will retain all of their own pensions and the rest of the settlement will be adjusted to reflect the fact that one party has greater pension rights than another. In some cases it will be appropriate to mix the offsetting approach with a degree of pension sharing in order to achieve the most appropriate outcome for the parties.

**21.41** Difficulties always arise in determining the value to place on the pension rights because pension funds are not directly comparable with other assets.[24] There are various reasons for this, the most significant being:

---

[24]  *T v T (Financial Relief: Pensions)* [1998] 1 FLR 1072; *Burrow v Burrow* [1999] 1 FLR 508; *Maskell v Maskell* [2003] 1 FLR 1138; *Martin-Dye v Martin-Dye* [2006] 2 FLR 901.

| Attributes of a pension | Attributes of non-pension assets |
|---|---|
| The rules of a pension scheme tightly control how the benefits are paid under the member's pension fund. The fund cannot be used in the same way as cash savings. There will be a minimum age at which the benefits can be drawn. Usually this is at the age of 50 years (55 years after 2010); often it is later.* | Other capital assets can be cashed in at will and used at any time. The benefits of such assets are available immediately rather than at some point in the future. In other words, there is a marked difference in liquidity. |
| The value of a pension fund may be dependent on the performance of the investment markets. Unless the pension is an SSAS or an SIPP the member may have very little control over how the pension fund is invested. | Other assets can be invested or used as the owner desires with a view to minimising risks. |
| At the retirement date a maximum of (in most cases) 25% of the pension fund can be drawn as a tax-free lump sum. In some schemes this may be less than 25%. The remaining fund cannot be drawn as capital, but must paid as a pension or used to buy an annuity or secure an income in another way. | Other assets can be used for whatever purpose the owner desires. |
| If an annuity is purchased, the real value of the annuity depends on how long the pension holder lives and is able to enjoy it. If the member dies within a year or two of retirement, the pension will prove to have been worth very little. If the member lives to over 100 years of age, the benefit is very substantial. | The same uncertainties as to life expectancy exist, but if a short life expectancy becomes apparent (eg diagnosis of a terminal illness) the flexibility to use the assets as desired exists. |
| Pension annuity payments are taxable. | Periodical payments from a former spouse are not taxable and drawing on capital savings is also free of tax (unless assets have to be sold, in which case CGT may arise and any income produced by capital will be taxed). |
| Upon the member's death in retirement the pension would normally cease, leaving no benefits in the member's estate if an annuity has been purchased. Even where some benefits are payable upon death in retirement, these are usually very modest. | Other capital can be preserved and left as an inheritance if not used during the owner's lifetime. |

*   Some occupations, most famously professional sportsmen, are permitted to draw pensions at an earlier age due to the short nature of their careers.

**21.42** Although in general a pension should not be equated with capital, it should be noted that in the case of a few pension schemes the value of the fund can be 'cashed in' and drawn as capital. Such a step will often have very heavy tax consequences, potentially leaving the fund decimated by tax penalties.

**21.43** There is no formula for 'converting' pension rights into an equivalent capital value, and neither is there guidance in the case law detailing how an offset should be calculated.[25] In *Maskell v Maskell*[26] the Court of Appeal noted that to add the pension CETVs to the other assets before dividing them up was potentially unfair because of the different nature of pensions and other assets. In *Norris v Norris*[27] the court in a big money case felt it was appropriate simply to add the CETVs of the husband's pensions, which were already vested and available for payment, to the other assets for the purposes of dividing up the assets. The difference between the two approaches may be explained by the fact that in the *Norris* case there was no significant delay before the pension benefits could be obtained.

**21.44** More recently, in *Martin-Dye v Martin-Dye*[28] the Court of Appeal considered the treatment of pensions in payment. The overall assets in that case amounted to approximately £6.3 million and included in that sum were pensions in the wife's name worth some £100,000 and in the husband's name of some £940,000. The court felt that it was wrong to add the parties' pensions to the other assets and then divide the whole lot without distinguishing the difference between the nature of the pensions and the other realisable assets. In particular, a pension in payment was no more than a whole life income stream which could not be sold, commuted for cash, or offered as security for a loan. Furthermore, once a pension was in payment it had no capacity for capital appreciation and, upon the member's death, it would leave no benefit in the member's estate. As the nature of the value of a pension in payment differed so markedly from the other realisable assets, the court felt that the only fair approach was to deal with the assets on a like-for-like basis. So pension orders were made, rather than offsetting orders. It should be noted, however, that the case is not authority for the proposition that one can never aggregate a pension in payment to existing capital assets for offsetting purposes, as Dyson LJ made clear in the following passage:[29]

> 'The question for the court was how to distribute the parties' assets fairly having regard to the matters specified in s 25(2) of the 1973 Act: see *White v White* [2001] 1 AC 596, at 604H. Fairness requires the court to take account of all the circumstances of the case. In my view, it may be appropriate in some circumstances to aggregate the value of pensions in payment with all the other assets of the parties and make a distribution of the resultant value that is fair in all

---

[25] See *T v T (Financial Relief: Pensions)* [1998] 1 FLR 1072 at 1077–9 for an example as to how the lost pension benefits were valued in that particular case and for comment as to the shortcomings of any such assessment.

[26] [2003] 1 FLR 1138.

[27] [2003] 1 FLR 1142.

[28] [2006] 2 FLR 901.

[29] [2006] 2 FLR 901 at [83].

the circumstances. There is no rule of law that prohibits such an approach. Our attention was drawn to *Maskell v Maskell* [2001] EWCA Civ 858, [2003] 1 FLR 1138. In that case, Thorpe LJ had said, at 1139, para [5]:

> "If one looks at this as a comparatively long marriage ... one could then see £26,000 and the £6,000 endowment policies, £32,000, going to the mother. The father has his £40,000 pension fund, plus the £4,000 endowment, so £44,000, less the debts of about £8,000, so that brings him to £36,000. So there is a rough equivalent."

At 1140, para [6], Thorpe LJ said:

> "That passage seems to be fundamentally flawed, for the judge is making the seemingly somewhat elementary mistake of confusing present capital with a right to financial benefits on retirement, only 25% of which maximum could be taken in capital terms, the other 75% being taken as an annuity stream. He simply failed to compare like with like. I have a grave anxiety that the district judge made the same mistake ..."

But I do not read Thorpe LJ as saying that, as a matter of law, it is never open to the court to aggregate the value of pensions with that of other assets and distribute the resultant total value between the parties. Examples of where such an approach might be appropriate could be where the parties have pensions in payment which are of approximately equal value and/or where the value of the pensions is small in comparison with that of the other assets. It will all depend in the particular circumstances of the case.'

**21.45** Actuarial calculations can attempt to place a value on pension funds which is intended to give a more accurate comparison between the real value of the pensions compared to other realisable assets. The basis upon which such calculations are carried out will depend on whether the pension is in payment or whether the benefits remain deferred until a point in the future. Inevitably, the calculations will contain so many variable and subjective assumptions that different actuaries will produce different figures. The costs of this valuation exercise are likely to be substantial. Judges are likely to have in mind the dissatisfaction with expert valuation evidence in relation to deferred assets, as was expressed in *GW v RW (Financial Provision: Departure from Equality)*.[30] It seems likely that in those cases where the assets are adequate for the purpose, the courts will adopt the *Martin-Dye* approach and avoid the complexities of trying to compare pensions with other realisable assets (a comparison of 'apples with pears'). There will, however, be cases where such an approach does not meet the circumstances of the case or the parties' priorities. An example would be where a husband is anxious to preserve his pension funds while the wife is desperate to retain the former matrimonial home. It may be possible to achieve this by permitting the husband to keep his pensions intact in return for taking a smaller lump sum from the wife in respect of his share of the equity in the former matrimonial home. As ever in ancillary relief proceedings, the court's powers are sufficiently broad and flexible to cover an infinite variety of

---

[30]  [2003] 2 FLR 108.

situations, and firm rules or guidelines in this area are likely to be considered inappropriate. What is clear, however, is that the offsetting process as a tool to achieve a fair division of assets is more akin to the meat cleaver than the salami slicer.

**21.46** Practitioners considering advising a client to engage in offsetting pensions against other assets should not overlook the fact that investments in the form of real estate and investments in stocks and shares through a pension do not usually perform at the same rate, or with any degree of synchronicity. Share prices may rise sharply over a period when house prices fall. Alternatively, a sustained period of growth in house prices can occur at the same time as a depression in the performance of the stock market. Whilst an order which leaves one party with all the equity in a property and the other with the pensions intact may leave them both satisfied at the time of the order, in the long term one may feel that the outcome was unjust.

## COMBINING METHODS

**21.47** Offsetting can be used with pension sharing or attachment orders, but attachment orders and pension sharing cannot be used in respect of the same pension in the same divorce settlement.[31] Pension sharing cannot be used in respect of a pension which is already the subject of an attachment order.[32] This is clearly to ensure that the benefits under the pension to be taken under the attachment order cannot be reduced by a subsequent pension sharing order in a subsequent divorce.

## WHICH METHOD TO USE?

### Pension sharing

**21.48** Use:

- Where proceedings commenced after 1 December 2000.

- To provide incomes in retirement for both parties when one party has all or most of the pension assets.

- To provide a clean break.

- To provide the ability to have an income in retirement that pays out, in principle, until the recipient's death.

- To avoid the expense and uncertainty of 'discounting' the value of pensions for the purposes of offsetting.

---

[31]   MCA 1973, s 25B(7B).
[32]   MCA 1973, s 24B(5).

**21.49**  Not useful:

- Where pension sharing means a significant loss in value of the pension.

- Where the pensions are very small and the cost of implementing sharing is disproportionate to the value of the pension funds.

- Where the pension is payable soon, or is already in payment, and the pensions arising under the 'pension credit' are not payable for many years and income is needed in the short term (income gap cases).

- Where the parties' priorities are focused on other issues, such as one party retaining the bulk of the other assets to provide a home and a clean break being sought, so that offsetting the pensions may be preferable.

## Attachment orders

**21.50**  Use:

- Where the proceedings commenced after 1 July 1996 but before 1 December 2000.

- Where (eg uniformed services) the member's pension is payable a long time before a pension credit would be and income, in particular for the ex-spouse, in the short term is more important (a simple periodical payments order will have the same effect without the expense of implementing the order, although the attachment order means the payments are made direct from the scheme).

- Where pension sharing is poor value for money and the ex-spouse has other means of security in retirement.

- Where pension in payment is to be used for periodical payments.

- Where other capital assets are low, an attachment of the deferred lump sum payment might provide a spouse with a lump sum when there were no other means of doing so.

- Where one spouse is financially dependent on the other for periodical payments (spousal or in respect of children) and needs protection if the payer were to die, then attach death in service benefit.

**21.51**  Not useful:

- For providing the only or main source of financial security in retirement.

- Where a clean break is sought.

- Liable to variation in the event of change of circumstances and (excluding death in service benefit) terminable upon death of beneficiary of pension rights.

## Offsetting

**21.52** Use:

- Where pension sharing orders or attachment orders are unavailable.

- Where pension rights are small (or comparatively small) so as to make the costs of pension sharing or attachment orders disproportionate.

- Where one party wants to retain the matrimonial home and there are insufficient assets to 'buy out' the other's share without offsetting the pension.

- Where pension sharing is poor value for money.

- Where there are significant other assets.

- Where the parties are relatively young, leaving sufficient time in the circumstances of the case to build up pension rights.

**21.53** Not useful:

- If the amount paid by way of offsetting is then needed to purchase pension income, it is likely that this will be insufficient to provide the non-member spouse with a lump sum to purchase the additional pension rights to provide that level of benefits.

- If the value of the pensions to be used for offsetting cannot be agreed without expensive actuarial evidence.

- Where the pensions amount to a very substantial part of the total assets.

- Where the pension is in payment, unless the parties have broadly equivalent pension provision, the pension in payment is small compared to the other assets or there are other special features of the case which make offsetting appropriate.

**21.54** Identifying the appropriate manner in which to deal with pension rights in ancillary relief proceedings is not always a straightforward task. The suggestions outlined above are not intended to be prescriptive, nor could they ever be fully comprehensive. The touchstone in each and every case is a fair division of assets. The new pensions procedure introduced by the Family

Proceedings (Amendment) (No 5) Rules 2005,[33] and in particular the Form P (the new pensions inquiry form), is designed to provide the practitioner with sufficient information to assist in the decision-making process. A completed Form P should be available in advance of any FDR for each pension.[34] The parties should ensure that suitable directions are made at the FDA to enable this to be achieved. A thorough and careful reading of FPR 1991, r 2.70 should be carried out to ensure compliance with other essential procedural obligations. The importance of the rule is such that the practitioner is directed to the Appendix of this book rather than a paraphrase of the rule.

## PENSION ORDERS IN THE LIGHT OF *MILLER V MILLER; MCFARLANE V MCFARLANE* – PENSIONS ACCRUED PRIOR TO THE MARRIAGE OR AFTER SEPARATION

**21.55**  Pension sharing is now commonly used as the appropriate method of dealing with pension rights. Guidance as to how courts should approach pension sharing is sparse. Furthermore, it is not entirely clear how the holy trinity of needs, compensation and sharing apply to the adjustment of pension rights. It is submitted that the most difficult of the concepts is that of need. How is the court to meaningfully calibrate the adjustment of pension rights having regard to a party's income needs many years into the future? It is only once needs are met that the sharing principle comes into play. Satisfying needs is also a requirement before the categorisation of an asset as either matrimonial or non-matrimonial can have any significance in the ability to depart from equal division of assets within the sharing principle. If identifying future needs is difficult or so speculative as to be meaningless, how can the court meaningfully divide pension rights on the basis of need, let alone move into the application of the sharing principle? Even on an application of the sharing principle, when if at all, will pension rights brought into a marriage become converted into matrimonial property?

**21.56**  Perhaps these conceptual difficulties explain the absence of explanation for the approach to be taken to pension sharing in the light of *Miller v Miller; McFarlane v McFarlane*, particularly in cases where a significant portion of the pension was earned prior to the marriage or in the period after separation. A traditional argument found in support of departures from equal division of pension rights is found in the case of *H v H*,[35] where Thorpe J suggested the division of the number of years of cohabitation by the number of years of pension contribution would identify the proportion of the CETV attributable to the relationship. The argument which is then advanced is that only the pension rights attributable to the relationship ought to be shared, the contributions made prior to the relationship being non-matrimonial property.

---

[33]  SI 2005/2922.
[34]  *Martin-Dye v Martin-Dye* [2006] 2 FLR 901, CA at [71].
[35]  [1993] 2 FLR 335.

But for such an argument based on pre-marital contributions to succeed, needs have to be met first; and in most cases which do not involve 'big money' this is a difficult or impossible task for a court to undertake, even if the court paints with its broad brush. Before some tribunals the *H v H* approach can find favour. In other tribunals an acceptable approach to pension sharing for other than short marriages is to seek to equalise pension income on retirement.[36] Sometimes pension rights are divided in the same proportion as capital.

---

[36] The calculation of the percentage sharing of a pension CETV to achieve equality of retirement income is likely to require expert actuarial evidence – see **22.42–22.45**.

# Chapter 22

# VALUATION OF PENSIONS

## THE CETV

**22.1**  A Cash Equivalent Transfer Value ('CETV') has been available for an individual's pension rights for many years, and at least since 1985 for all UK pensions. It was created to enable individuals to move ('transfer') their pension rights from one pension provider to another. This was originally used for employer's schemes so that, on leaving one employer, an individual could choose to transfer the pension rights into a new employer's scheme and receive pension rights from that scheme. The CETV is the value (of the fund) to be transferred from one scheme to another.

**22.2**  The valuation of a pension in payment is by way of the cash equivalent of benefits ('CEB')[1] rather than CETV. Although the CETV is mentioned throughout this chapter, much of what is said applies to a CEB as much as to a CETV.

**22.3**  The CETV was not therefore designed specifically for use in divorce calculations, although it was adopted as the standard basis for providing a value for pensions for use in ancillary relief proceedings when pension attachment and pension sharing orders were introduced. There are, however, circumstances in ancillary relief proceedings where adopting the CETV does not place a fair value on the pension rights of the member. For example, in the case of money purchase schemes, the CETV is often more than the true value of the benefits that the fund will provide, and in final salary schemes sometimes less.

**22.4**  The CETV values the benefits as at the date of the valuation (if the member is still in active service, then it values the benefits as if the member left service on the date of the valuation). Thus, in a final salary scheme, it is the value of the pension as payable from retirement age, any automatic tax-free cash lump sum also payable, any widow's or widower's pension or other dependant's pension (eg children's pensions). Put simply, each possible future payment is multiplied by the probability of the payment being made (eg for the member's pension, the probability of the member still being alive) and discounted to the current date. Any lump sum payable on death in service is not included (as it is assumed that the member leaves and is therefore no longer in service); neither are options that are exercisable that are not considered

---

[1]    See **22.35**.

valuable (eg the option to convert a pension to a lump sum, whilst attractive, does not usually add value to the pension), nor any benefits that are contingent on the member remaining in service (such as the option to take benefits early by remaining in service). Likewise all future accrual of pension rights is excluded, as well as the value that would be gained if pensionable salary were to rise faster than inflation in future; once again, this is because it is assumed that the member is leaving service at the date of the calculation of the CETV. There is no CETV for the basic state pension, but the additional state pensions (formerly known as SERPS) can be valued in the same way and the value can be obtained by submitting Form BR20 to The Pension Service.

**22.5**  The CETV has a statutory basis. Section 25D(2)(e) of the Matrimonial Causes Act 1973 and s 30 of the Welfare Reform and Pensions Act 1999 make provision for the making of regulations dealing with the calculation and verification of benefits under a pension arrangement. Regulation 3 of the Divorce etc (Pensions) Regulations 2000[2] provides that for the purposes of the court's functions in connection with the exercise of any of its powers under Part II of the Matrimonial Causes Act 1973, benefits under a pension arrangement shall be calculated and verified in the manner set out in reg 3 of the Pensions on Divorce etc (Provision of Information) Regulations 2000.

**22.6**  The Divorce etc (Pensions) Regulations 2000 also provide that the benefits under a pension scheme are required to be valued at a date to be specified by the court (being not earlier than one year before the date of the petition and not later than the date on which the court is exercising its power). In specifying a date for valuation, the court is entitled to have regard to the date specified in any information provided by the person responsible for the pension arrangement. It is not uncommon to see directions made at FDA failing to specify a date for valuation of the pension rights. It is sensible to set out the date of valuation in the court order, even if the date is that contained within the information provided by the person responsible for the pension arrangement. Taking this step will ensure that the parties and the court are reminded to make certain that valuations are not stale by the time of final hearing.[3]

**22.7**  It is submitted that determining the value of a member's pension rights is ultimately a matter for the court. In determining that value, the court may have regard to information furnished by the person responsible for the pension arrangement.[4] In many cases the CETV provided by the person responsible for the pension arrangement is accepted without question by the court.

**22.8**  The Pensions on Divorce etc (Provision of Information) Regulations 2000[5] oblige a person responsible for a pension arrangement to provide, amongst other information, a valuation of pension rights or benefits upon request. It is worth noting that the other information required to be provided

---

[2]     SI 2000/1123.
[3]     Divorce etc (Pensions) Regulations 2000, reg 3.
[4]     Divorce etc (Pensions) Regulations 2000, reg 3(1)(b).
[5]     SI 2000/1048.

includes a statement summarising the ways in which the valuation is calculated.[6] This is of course an essential piece of information if it is sought to contest the value of the CETV. It is also worth noting that reg 2 of the Information Regulations sets time limits within which the relevant information is to be provided. Where a request contains a statement that the information is required for the purposes of an application for financial relief under Part II of the Matrimonial Causes Act 1973, the information is to be provided within 6 weeks of receipt of the request. The information can be compelled to be provided within a shorter period by court order. Paragraph 3 of the Information Regulations sets out the provisions for the calculation and verification of pension benefits.

**22.9** The value is determined by the court, but the CETV is calculated by the scheme. Once the value has been determined by the court, any pension sharing order is made by ordering a percentage value of the CETV to be transferred between the parties.[7] Once an order is made, it is served on the scheme and the CETV is then re-calculated by the scheme and the re-calculated CETV is used to implement the share.[8] As will be seen below, there are circumstances where the CETV will not be a fair or realistic value of a party's benefits under a pension scheme. Where expert actuarial evidence is called to establish the 'fair value' of the pension, the court will assess what percentage of the 'fair value' of the pension is to be transferred and then express this figure as a percentage of the CETV. The most common example of this is a serving policeman, where an actuarial valuation might produce a value of eg £210,000 against a CETV of £120,000. To achieve equality in this situation, the pension sharing order has to be for 87.5% (£105,000 divided by £120,000).

**22.10** The legislation says that the CETV must be re-calculated after the pension sharing order is served on the scheme. This can cause problems in that the amount transferred to the ex-spouse can be very different from the amount expected. Although it may be possible to challenge the scheme's revised CETV, the scheme is entitled to change its basis of calculation and it cannot be forced to keep to the original value.

---

6    Pensions on Divorce etc (Provision of Information) Regulations 2000, reg 2.
7    MCA 1973, s 21A.
8    Welfare Reform and Pensions Act 1999, ss 29 and 34. Note that the implementation period is 4 months, beginning with the later of the day on which the relevant order or provision takes effect and the first day on which the person responsible for the pension arrangement receives the order, the decree and the prescribed information.

# HOW IS THE CETV OF DIFFERENT TYPES OF PENSION SCHEME CALCULATED?

## Occupational money purchase schemes and other personal pensions

**22.11** For most occupational money purchase pension schemes and the majority of personal pensions where the investments are held in unit-linked funds, the CETV will simply be the value of those funds. These will be funds available for purchasing pension benefits.

**22.12** The pension benefits ultimately purchased with the pension fund will be lower in value than the value of the funds, because the pensions are provided by financial services institutions who make deductions for their charges, profit margins, commissions to advisers and other contingencies. Therefore, a fund of money in a pension is likely to purchase a lower value of pension benefits than the CETV. Additionally, when the pension is in payment, the periodical payments will be taxed. The CETV makes no deduction for the tax which will ultimately be payable on the pension in payment. It is therefore different from a *Duxbury*-type calculation, which produces a capitalised figure required to achieve the net (after tax) income.

**22.13** There are some circumstances where the CETV will be different from the true value of the benefits. This can be where there are guaranteed annuity rates available on the policy which are exercisable at a date in future and mean that the policy is more valuable than a fund of money of the same value which does not have such options available from it. Another circumstance where the CETV may not be a fair value is where the CETV has been reduced for a Market Value Adjustment Factor ('MVAF').[9] This reduces the CETV and this may not be a fair reflection of the true value, as the MVAF may not be applied at maturity of the policy.

**22.14** For some of the money purchase policies, the funds are invested in traditional 'with profits' funds. These are more complex in their investments, but once again the CETV can be considered as a fund of money to be used to purchase pension benefits in the future. Again, providers will make deductions from the funds, and therefore this is likely to purchase a lower value of pension benefits than the CETV.

**22.15** SIPPs and SSASs may pose greater problems. Such funds may contain a variety of different types of assets, including shares and real estate. Where the fund is based chiefly upon shares in listed companies or listed unit trusts, an accurate value of the fund can be readily achieved. Where such a policy contains shares in unlisted private companies it may be very difficult to provide an accurate assessment of the overall value of the fund, because the values of the shares in each company will not be readily available and could be volatile. If

---

[9] See **22.32**.

the SIPP or SSAS contains real estate which has not recently been valued, the value provided for the fund may be wildly inaccurate, and valuations of the properties concerned may need to be carried out within the ancillary relief proceedings. Similarly, where the fund holds shares in a family company, the valuation of the pension will go hand in hand with the valuation of the family company. Where, however, a SIPP contains shares in numerous unlisted companies, an accurate valuation of the fund may be wholly impossible for the purposes of the ancillary relief proceedings. Essentially, the parties will need to make the best assessment possible with the professional advice available to them. It also follows that a carefully drafted questionnaire may need to be raised in order to establish the make-up of the funds contained within the pension before sensitive and proportionate decisions are taken about the need to obtain professional valuations of the assets held by any pension fund.

## Occupational final salary pension schemes

**22.16**   The valuation of final salary schemes is significantly more difficult. The value of the pension depends not on the value of the investments in the fund, but on the value of the pension which is promised to the member upon retirement. In simple terms, the scheme promises certain payments to each member at a given point in the future. The CETV is intended to be the capital value of those payments. The method by which this is calculated is set out below, in highly simplified form.

---

*Case study:* **How the CETV of a final salary scheme is calculated**

A man of age 45 leaves a pension scheme and employer.

He has accrued a pension of £20,000 per annum payable from age 65.

The pension increases in line with inflation between leaving and age 65.

If inflation is assumed to be 80% in the 20 years between age 45 and age 65, then in the first year of retirement the member will be paid £36,000 (assuming he is still alive at that time).

If the investment assumption between now and age 65 is 6% per annum, then £11,225 is the amount required now to meet that payment. This is the 'current value' of the payment at age 65.

This amount is then reduced to reflect the probability that the member may not be alive to receive it.

The same principle is applied to all payments from the member's pension rights, such as widow's and dependant's pensions.

The CETV is effectively the sum of all the current values of all the payments multiplied by the probability that the payment will be made. ➡

---

> In practice, commutation factors are used to combine a lot of these payments.

**22.17**   The more optimistic the scheme is about the future investment return, the lower the CETV will be, because it will be assumed that a smaller capital fund will be required to provide the promised pension benefits. In a similar way, the shorter the life expectancy used in the scheme's calculations, the smaller the fund will be. Conversely, the more conservative the scheme is about the future investment return rates, or if the life expectancies of members are considered to be high, the higher the CETV will need to be to cover the required payments. It is readily apparent that the use of assumptions in relation to different variables will have a significant impact on the final CETV figure which a scheme provides to its members. As with any valuation based on assumptions as to the future, there will be a degree of disagreement between the valuers as to the appropriate figures to adopt.

**22.18**   It is also important to note that the CETV does not take into account the value of death in service benefits in an occupational scheme, because a CETV has to assume that the member leaves service on the date of calculation. The future value of these benefits may be significant. Likewise the CETV does not allow for any future increases in salary, even if those are contractually assured by the employer.

**22.19**   CETV calculations for occupational final salary schemes are prepared on non-member-specific assumptions, and therefore two members with identical earnings and identical service records with the employer will have the same CETV even though, say, one is married and the other unmarried (and therefore the spouse's pension has no real value) and one has a lower life expectancy (smokers or those in poor health or with a family history of poor health). There is a clear artificiality in the CETVs produced for two such individuals. In real terms the pension of a married individual with a long life expectancy has a greater value than that of an unmarried person with a poor life expectancy.

## Basis of calculation of the CETV of an occupational final salary scheme

**22.20**   The CETV is not a fund value and does not represent any funds that are earmarked for the member. It is the amount that would be transferred to another scheme if the member chose to transfer out. The assumption used to calculate the CETV of the benefits (the CETV calculation) is now (since October 2008) the responsibility of the scheme's trustees. This means that there is no specific guidance for them to follow, and this has in our experience led to vastly different valuation methods being used, and consequently vastly different values being supplied for very similar benefits where they are supplied from different schemes. The key actuarial assumptions are as follows:

- Assumed investment return (before retirement).

- Assumed investment return (after retirement).

- Assumed price inflation.

- Assumed pension increases.

- Mortality and life expectancy.

**22.21** There is no single 'right answer' when setting actuarial assumptions. When calculating a CETV, it is common to set the assumed investment return based on the pension trustees' usual investment strategy. If the trustees invest in a way that seeks to maximise returns (typically investing a part of the fund in equities), then the assumption for future returns will be higher. At retirement, a lower rate of return may be assumed based on the likelihood that the trustees will invest more cautiously (since they must guarantee to pay the benefit) and, as a result, the assumed rate is more in line with bond yields.

**22.22** A transfer value in a final salary scheme (not a money purchase scheme) is not intended to provide sufficient funds to replace the benefits given up, unless the member is prepared to take similar investment risks once the money is paid to the new arrangement and not incur any costs (which in practice is unlikely to be possible).

**22.23** Another reason why CETVs may be low is that many schemes have not allowed for the recently recorded improvements in life expectancy. People are living longer, which means that pensions are paid for longer and therefore have a higher value than the CETV calculations indicate.

## WHEN IS IT APPROPRIATE TO CHALLENGE THE CETV?

**22.24** This is a question to which it is difficult to give an absolute answer. The following paragraphs endeavour to provide examples of circumstances which ought to alert the practitioner to the possibility of an independent actuarial valuation being required. There may be other cases where the CETV ought to be challenged. It is important to distinguish the two essential reasons why a challenge to the use of the CETV may be necessary. The first reason will be because the CETV may not be calculated in an appropriate and accurate way. Examples of this may be where a market adjustment factor has been applied or the CETV is based on out-of-date information. Other examples of the way in which the CETV can be affected by the assumptions used in its calculation have been considered in the previous sections of this chapter. The second reason for a challenge will be where the circumstances indicate that the use of the CETV may not be the appropriate way of putting a fair or realistic value on the pension rights. Examples of this are where the pension is a public service pension or where the pension includes guaranteed annuity rates.

## INSTRUCTING AN ACTUARY

**22.25** In most cases when challenge is to be made, there will be a need for expert actuarial evidence. Permission will therefore be required if the evidence is to be adduced at a hearing. It is rare for the CETV calculated by the person responsible for the pension scheme to be challenged. As has been seen, the basis upon which the calculation is made and the assumptions used should be provided along with the valuation. In an appropriate case, an actuary can be instructed to examine the calculation and a decision made about whether the calculation is to be challenged. This is likely to be an expensive exercise and care needs to be taken to ensure that a proportionate approach is taken.

**22.26** Where the challenge to the CETV is one based on circumstances indicating that it is unlikely to be a fair valuation of pension rights, a direction should be sought at FDA for expert actuarial evidence to be obtained. The actuary should be asked whether the CETV is a fair valuation of pension rights and, if not, why not and what a fair value would be. The actuary is also likely to be invited to provide a view as to the percentage of pension sharing required to provide a certain distribution of the pension income in retirement, based on certain assumptions as to when the parties are likely to draw upon the pensions.[10] In most cases where the pensions are substantial and important to the resolution of the case, the instruction of a single joint expert will be both appropriate and proportionate. The actuarial evidence should be available by the time of the FDR.

**22.27** Identifying the circumstances where the CETV is unlikely to represent a fair valuation of pension rights without obtaining actuarial evidence in advance is not altogether an easy task. However, a number of circumstances where this might be the case are identified in the remainder of this chapter.

### Low CETVs

**22.28** Where the CETV produced by the pension fund appears to be low, the court may accept a challenge to that CETV. There is no simple rule for determining when the CETV is 'low'. One telling feature is where the actual value of the benefits promised by the pension are quite high compared to the CETV, bearing in mind that statistical averages assume that the pension is likely to be paid from retirement age to age 85 (for men) or age 87 (for women). As already discussed in the preceding parts of this chapter, there are some circumstances where the CETV is likely to be too low. Examples of the types of situation where the CETV may be unrealistically low are as follows:

---

[10]   See **22.42–22.45** as to why an actuarial view on this may be necessary.

- Cases concerning the uniformed services and some public service pensions where the member is still in service.

- Personal pension policies where there are Guaranteed Annuity Options available or Market Value Adjustment Factors applied.

- Underfunded schemes.

- Cases where the CETV is low compared to the value of the benefits promised.

- Out-of-date CETVs.

- Where the member's benefits include some 'non-shareable' pension rights.

**22.29** The matrimonial lawyer has a dilemma when considering whether to seek an independent valuation of a pension. On the one hand, the lawyer can obtain an actuarial report from an independent actuary for an opinion as to the true value of the fund and it may be that the actuary agrees with the scheme's own valuation or, even if the actuary provides a higher figure, the court may reject this evidence. The costs incurred in instructing the expert will then have been wasted. If, however, the issue is ignored, the matrimonial lawyer could be accused later of failing to consider the pensions properly. Clearly the issue must be discussed with the client so that the options are clear and an informed decision can be made. It may be that an informal discussion with an expert actuary may provide some guidance as to whether the matter may be worth pursuing further.

## Police pensions and certain other public service pensions

**22.30** Frequently, the CETV of a member's pension rights in the Police Pension Scheme greatly understates the 'true' value of the pension benefits promised to the member where the member is still in service. This happens because the legislation[11] states that the CETV of a member of a scheme still in service must be calculated as if the member left service on the date that the calculation is completed.

**22.31** If a policeman in the Police Pension Scheme leaves service before completing 25 years' service, he can only take his retirement benefits at age 60 (except in ill health). If he completes 25 years' service or more, he can retire on a full pension at a much younger age, and if he joined at age 18 (or earlier), he can retire on a full pension as young as age 48, on completion of 30 years' service. Therefore, the CETV of a member's pension rights in the Police Pension Scheme, calculated before completion of 25 years' service and whilst the member is still in active service will ignore up to 12 years' worth of pension payments that the member could receive and, indeed, will be able to receive

---

[11] Pensions on Divorce etc (Provision of Information) Regulations 2000, reg 3(4).

once he completes 25 years of service. The practical effect of this is that a 50% pension sharing order can result in the member retaining over 75% of his accrued benefits, whilst the spouse receives less than 25% of the real value of the pension benefits.

---

### *Case study: Police pension*

PC Smith joined the Police Pension Scheme on his 18th birthday.

He has completed 24 years' service.

His salary is £30,000 per annum.

Mrs Smith is 2 years younger than PC Smith.

**Based on the Police Pension Scheme calculations the CETV is £210,000.**

**The realistic value calculated by an independent actuary is £300,000.**

*If a 50% Pension Share is effected based on the scheme's CETV:*

Mrs Smith will receive a pension of **£8,800** per annum, payable from age 60 (ie not for another 20 years).

PC Smith can retire at age 48 years with the following:

•    Pension income in respect of pension rights earned before the divorce of £12,000 per annum (75% of his accrued pension).

•    Pension income in respect of pension rights earned after the divorce of £4,000 per annum.

PC Smith therefore receives a total pension income of **£16,000** per annum, payable from age 48 (14 years before Mrs Smith receives any pension benefits from the Pension Share).

*(All pensions are expressed in today's terms and future inflation has not been taken into account.)*

---

**22.32**   In such a case, if pension sharing is used, the scheme member's spouse is unlikely to receive the share of pension benefits intended by the court unless there is an actuarial valuation carried out on the pension rights. If offsetting is to be used, an appropriate valuation of the members' pension rights should also be obtained, because the CETV may provide a misleadingly low figure for the true value of the pension.

**22.33** A new Police Pension Scheme began in April 2006 and all new entrants to the service must join this scheme, which has a retirement age of 65. At present, members with any significant amount of accrued benefits are likely to be in the original scheme and therefore will not be affected by this. However, practitioners should check whether the member has transferred to the new scheme, as this will affect the 'pension credit' benefits. 'Pension credit' benefits from the new scheme will be payable at age 65; however, assurances have been given that 'pension credit' benefits where the member is still in the original scheme will remain in that scheme and be payable from age 60.

**22.34** Similar issues will arise in relation to pensions of some members of the Armed Forces Pension Schemes, the Firefighters' Pension Scheme, the NHS Pension Scheme and Prison Officers in the Principal Civil Service Pension Scheme, where the completion of a certain period of service or the attaining of a certain rank can make a pension available at a much earlier date than the normal retirement age. Once the period of service upon which the entitlement to a pension from the earlier date has been reached, however, the CETV figure is likely to be a fairer indication of the value of the pension fund.

## Market value adjustment factor

**22.35** 'Market value adjustment factors' are often made to the fund values of personal pensions where the funds are invested in what are termed 'traditional' with profits funds. The original type of policy had guaranteed values at retirement and this is reflected in the fund value. On early encashment, the full fund value does not have to be paid, and thus the CETV will not reflect the value of this element. Similarly, a market value adjustment may sometimes be applied to such a pension during a period when the market value of the investments in the fund is low. Examples of the effect that this may have in ancillary relief proceedings are shown in the case study below.

---

### *Case study (1)*

*Background*

The husband is aged 63 and has a policy which is due to mature at age 65 in 13 months' time. Disclosure has provided information from the pension provider that his policy has a fund value of £200,000 but a transfer value of £140,000.

Further investigation reveals that the difference between the two values is due to a 'market value adjustment factor' being applied to the pension owing to the fact that the investments in the 'with profits funds' are low in value at present.

The policy is due to mature and, on enquiry, it is discovered that the full amount of £200,000 will be paid upon maturity of the fund. Therefore, as long as the policy is held for a further 13 months, it will be worth ➡

£200,000. If the policy were encashed now or made part of a pension sharing order, the value transferred is only £140,000.

*Solution*

With the policy guaranteeing to pay out £200,000 in little over a year's time, then the true value of the policy should be taken as almost £200,000 and the effect of the market value adjustment ignored. It is important not to use immediate pension sharing and, if there are no other assets to use by way of offsetting the pension, the court should give serious consideration to adjourning making a pension sharing order for 13 months until the policy can pay out in full, at which point any pension sharing order would supply the wife with a percentage of the higher value.

## Case study (2)

*Background*

In this case, the husband is aged 43 and has a policy which is due to mature at age 65 in 22 years' time. Disclosure has provided information from the pension provider that his policy has a fund value of £200,000, but the transfer value is only £140,000.

Further investigation reveals that the difference between the two values is due to a 'market value adjustment factor' being applied to the pension owing to the fact that the investments in the 'with profits funds' are low in value at present.

It is discovered that the full amount without any deduction will have to be paid at maturity, but not before that date. Therefore, over the next 22 years only the reduced value is available. The point about the market being low takes on more significance now. This means that if the market shows good future growth, then the fund value will not receive the impact of that growth, as some of it will only serve to 'pay back' the previous poor years which have led to low values and the market value adjustment being applied.

*Solution*

In this case, the transfer value may be appropriate, as there is a reasonable chance of the market recovering and such recovery being fully reflected in the transfer value but not in increases in the fund value.

## Guaranteed annuity rates

**22.36** A 'guaranteed annuity rate' is an option attached to a personal pension policy whereby at the maturity date or dates the policyholder has the option to convert the funds to a pension income at an agreed rate. Guaranteed annuity rates or 'guaranteed annuity options' were in the public spotlight a great deal when Equitable Life got into financial difficulties, principally because the House of Lords ruled that Equitable Life was bound to honour the rates included in the terms of the contract.

**22.37** A policy containing guaranteed annuity rates will almost certainly be more valuable than the nominal fund value suggests. The additional value will be lost on any portion that is transferred. It is important that practitioners are aware that guaranteed annuity options are not confined to Equitable Life policies and are common throughout the industry in policies that were taken out prior to the ruling in the Equitable Life case. In addition, the standard disclosure made by pension schemes does not reveal the presence of these options. When dealing with any money purchase policies, practitioners should consider asking the pension scheme whether there are any guaranteed rates available on the policy.

---

### *Case study*

*Background*

The husband and wife are both aged 59 and intending to retire at age 60.

The wife only has state pension provision, whilst the husband has state pension provision plus two personal pension policies. Both policies have fund values of £200,000, but one (Policy A) has a guaranteed annuity option to convert to a pension at £100 per annum for every £1,000 funds, whereas Policy B does not.

*Issues for pension sharing*

Consider three different 'Pension Sharing' options:

(i)   Pension sharing on both policies 50%.

(ii)  Pension sharing 100% on Policy B and not on Policy A.

(iii) Pension sharing 100% on Policy A and not on Policy B.

Current annuity rates are £1 per annum from age 60 for every £16 for a man and for every £17 for a woman. (We ignore tax-free cash in this example.)

Under option (i): ➡

- Husband has £50,000 in Policy A, which will pay £5,000 per annum, then, if he exercises the guaranteed annuity options, plus £50,000 in Policy B, which will pay £3,125 per annum; totalling £8,125 per annum at age 60.

- Wife receives a 'pension credit' of £100,000 from which she can receive £5,880 per annum at age 60.

The combined income is therefore £14,005 per annum.

Under option (ii):

- Husband has £100,000 in Policy A, which will pay £10,000 per annum, if he exercises the guaranteed annuity rates, and none in Policy B, totalling £10,000 per annum at age 60.

- Wife receives a 'pension credit' of £100,000 from which she can receive £5,880 per annum at age 60.

This produces a combined income of £15,880 per annum.

Under option (iii):

- Husband has nothing in Policy A, but £100,000 in Policy B, which will pay £6,250 per annum, totalling £6,250 per annum at age 60.

- Wife receives a 'pension credit' of £100,000 from which she can receive £5,880 per annum at age 60.

This produces a combined income of £12,130 per annum.

*Solution*

The above example may be obvious. In practice, it is rarely that simple; the point to remember is that the guaranteed annuity options are very valuable and are personal to the original pension holder's scheme. Practitioners should recognise that these should not be shared if at all possible, as this will result in the valuable guaranteed annuity options being lost on the proportions transferred to the ex-spouse and therefore the value of the pensions available to the parties as the whole CETV will be reduced. Some form of offsetting or larger pension sharing of other pension funds (if possible) may be appropriate, or the option of continuing periodical payments to balance the parties' respective retirement incomes may be appropriate. It is possible to put a realistic value on the policy which the policyholder owns, but if pension sharing is used, there is a loss in value.

## Pensions in payment

**22.38** The regulations for pensions in payment are worded differently from those for pensions not in payment and prescribe the value to be the 'cash equivalent of benefits' (CEB). In *Martin-Dye v Martin-Dye*[12] the Court of Appeal indicated that it was not appropriate or fair in a case where one party held large pensions in payment to aggregate the transfer value of a pension in payment with the other realisable assets of the parties before dividing the whole lot. This failed to compare like with like. A pension in payment should be characterised as 'other financial resources' within s 25(2)(a) of the Matrimonial Causes Act 1973.

## Underfunded schemes

**22.39** Any occupational final salary scheme for employees outside the public sector has to have a valuation performed every 3 years where an actuary values the promises of payments it has made to members of the scheme ('liabilities') and also the funds that it has ('assets'). Where the assets are lower in value than the liabilities, the scheme is underfunded. In these circumstances, the scheme is permitted to reduce transfer values for members transferring out to reflect the poor funding level of the scheme.

**22.40** In divorce cases, full disclosure requires the scheme to disclose the full CETV and the reduced CETV in the circumstances where the CETV is being reduced. Given the levels of protection now available in relation to underfunded pensions (described at **20.46–20.49**), there is a good argument for using the full CETV as the value of the pension. If the sponsoring company remains solvent, then the member is likely to obtain the full benefits, and therefore the full CETV may be appropriate. Practitioners should consider the specific circumstances in all such cases to ensure that the appropriate figure is used and to make certain that the parties and the court understand the situation.

## Out-of-date CETVs

**22.41** Particularly in final salary schemes, CETVs can increase rapidly. It is not unusual for a CETV to increase by 30% each year. A revaluation will be particularly important where it becomes known that the member's pensionable salary has increased significantly since the last valuation. It should be noted that the rules of some final salary schemes exclude some forms of payments such as bonus payments and other sums included in the member's remuneration packet from their definition of pensionable pay. It may be that a large increase in income in one year would not have any significant impact on the Cash Equivalent Transfer Value. Where it appears that a revalued CETV is required, it should be sought, first, by agreement and, failing that, by court order. Unless there is reason to believe that the basis of calculation of the

---

[12]   [2006] EWCA Civ 681, [2006] 2 FLR 901.

CETV is itself inappropriate for one of the reasons already discussed, the updated CETV does not require an independent actuary but can be sought from the pension provider directly.

---

## Case study: CETVs calculated in relation to different types of scheme

*Background*

Consider three husbands, all aged 59 and due to retire at age 60. Each of them has a pension fund and expects to receive £25,000 per annum in retirement (we will ignore lump sums in this example).

- Husband A has a final salary scheme with his firm, a large brewery, and the trustees of the scheme are optimistic about the future and investment returns.

- Husband B is a civil servant in the Principal Civil Service Pension Scheme.

- Husband C has a money purchase fund and will need to purchase a pension on the open market.

*Issues*

Despite the fact that they are all going to receive the same income:

- Husband A has a CETV of £368,000.

- Husband B has a CETV of £515,000.

- Husband C has a CETV of £632,000.

*Solution*

Can it be right that the same benefits have such different values depending on where they come from? These examples demonstrate why practitioners need to be aware of the pitfalls of using CETVs in some cases without further scrutiny. In cases where there are a variety of pensions, actuarial evidence can prove very useful both in calculating the true values of the pensions and in ensuring that the pensions are shared in such a way that they maximise the total value of the pensions after any pension sharing is implemented.

---

# EXTERNAL TRANSFERS AND ACHIEVING EQUALITY OF INCOME

**22.42** For the great majority of company pension schemes in the private sector (ie not public services, such as the NHS, Police, Firemen and Armed Forces etc), the divorcing spouse has to take a transfer value and place it with a pension provider, eg an insurance company. This means that the spouse receives a transfer value of the proportion of the CETV stated in the pension sharing order and has to invest that, usually in a new personal pension policy.

**22.43** If a wife receives a pension sharing order for 50% of the CETV, the pension that will very often be produced from the new pension created in her name will be lower than the pension paid to the husband.

**22.44** Contributing factors as to why the ex-spouse will receive a lower pension than the member are:

- *Costs* – If a pensions provider receives £100,000, this will not buy an annuity worth this amount. This is because the pensions provider takes into account costs and profit when calculating its rates and makes charges on funds under management.

- *CETV* – The CETV on which the pension share is based may not reflect the true value of the pension benefits promised to the scheme member (see above). If an independent valuation is obtained, the scheme will still use the CETV for pension sharing, and this valuation will need to state what percentage of the scheme's CETV needs to be specified in order to achieve a genuine 50% share of the true value of the pension.

- *Life expectancy* – If the spouse is female, then women generally have a longer life expectancy than men; therefore, the cost of purchasing the equivalent benefits for a man and woman of the same age is more expensive for the woman, as she is expected to live longer.

- *Future accrual* – If the member is still a member of the pension scheme, they will keep all the pension rights accrued after the pension share.

Clearly, most of these factors will also be present in a case where a husband benefits from a pension sharing order against his wife's pension, but his shorter statistical life expectancy will counterbalance most of the other factors and may even produce a greater pension for him than the wife retains.

**22.45** Many courts are open to accepting actuarial evidence as to the percentage of pension sharing which is required to produce equality of income. The CETV value of a pension is calculated by reference to the accrued amount of income it will provide in retirement. If it is a case where equality of pension assets (in isolation) is intended, there is a strong case to be made for creating equality of the income that the pension will produce. A 50% division of the

CETV of the pensions is not going to appear fair when the effect of the order is that more pension income will be payable to one party than the other in retirement. Where the pension funds are modest, or the parties are young and therefore the pensions are payable at a considerable time in the future, it may be difficult to persuade a court that actuarial evidence is proportionate or necessary. Indeed, as a matter of fairness a request for such evidence is generally difficult to resist where the pension benefits are substantial. The capital value of a pension is essentially tied to the income it will produce upon retirement. If it is a case where equality of pension assets (in isolation) is intended, there is a strong case to be made for equal sharing of the income the pensions will produce. However, a 50% division of the fund value of the pensions is not going to appear to be fair when the effect of the order is that more pension income will be payable to one party than the other in retirement. Where the pension funds are modest, or the parties are young and therefore the pensions are payable at a considerable time in the future, it is likely to be difficult to persuade a court that actuarial evidence on this point is proportionate or necessary. Indeed, in a case where the pension funds are very small, the costs of implementing a pension sharing order may also be disproportionate to the benefit produced by the pension share.

# Part IX

# TAX IMPLICATIONS AND PLANNING

# Chapter 23

# TAX IMPLICATIONS AND PLANNING

## INTRODUCTION[1]

**23.1**  The financial ramifications of a divorce can be far-reaching for the couple concerned and unforeseen difficulties can significantly increase the cost to both parties of untangling their finances. Tax issues are a major cause of such complications and potentially one of the most significant hidden costs of divorce. An awareness of the tax considerations is essential for legal advisers in ancillary relief cases, having an impact upon both settlement negotiations and the approach that a court will take to the fair division of assets. A detailed treatment of tax issues is beyond the scope of this book. Nevertheless, this chapter provides an outline of some of the more important tax considerations that may need to be taken into account in an ancillary relief case. As will readily be appreciated, tax law is a dynamic subject and this chapter deals with tax law and practice as at 31 March 2009.

**23.2**  Reducing tax liabilities may result in more cash being available to each spouse. So it is in the interests of both to co-operate in implementing beneficial financial arrangements. Sadly, a spirit of co-operation between parties to ancillary relief proceedings is frequently in short supply. For example, one party may 'take revenge' on the other by making allegations of tax evasion to HM Revenue & Customs (HMRC). Where allegations of tax evasion are made, it is relevant to note that under the Proceeds of Crime Act 2002 and the Money Laundering Regulations 2007 professional advisers are under a duty to report suspicions of criminal activity (which includes tax fraud). However, following clarification of the law by the Court of Appeal in *Bowman v Fels*,[2] the provisions of PCA 2002, s 328 (becoming concerned in a money laundering arrangement) do not apply to solicitors and counsel engaged in the normal conduct of civil litigation. Whether that exception extends to accountants and other advisors drafted in to assist with the litigation is not entirely clear, but it seems strongly arguable that it does. Nevertheless, professional advisors must always be careful where they have a reasonable basis to suspect that a client is involved in criminal activity, lest they inadvertently become involved in money

---

[1]  References throughout this chapter to 'spouse', 'marriage' etc should be taken to include civil partners and registered civil partnerships.

[2]  [2005] 2 FLR 247. The Court of Appeal did not expressly consider the provisions of the Money Laundering Regulations 2003, SI 2003/3075 in this case and some uncertainty remains as to what reporting obligations may arise under those Regulations, although the decision in *Bowman v Fels* suggests that the normal conduct of litigation would fall outside the definitions of 'relevant business' in the 2003 Regulations and the 'regulated sector' in s 330 of PCA 2002.

laundering. Accountants need to be particularly alert to their duties under the 2002 Act, given that their involvement in a client's affairs will usually extend far beyond the normal conduct of litigation.

# INCOME TAX

## Pre-separation

**23.3** Married couples enjoy a number of tax advantages and can legally arrange their finances to minimise tax on their combined income. One step is to ensure that the personal tax allowances and the 20% tax band to which both are entitled are utilised as fully as possible. This can be done by transferring income-producing assets between them (tax-free) by making outright and unconditional gifts to split their income. The much publicised 'income shifting' legislation which was to be introduced following the taxpayers' victory in *Jones v Garnett*,[3] has been put on hold for the time being pending further consultation, so planning of this nature remains appropriate.

**23.4** Beyond this, tax-efficient vehicles are also available to both spouses, so that a husband and wife who have planned their investments sensibly may each have their own PEPs, ISAs, National Savings Certificates and Premium Bonds, as well as pension funds and other assets in their sole names. Alternatively, where one spouse has substantial earnings, it may be that assets producing taxable income are owned by the other so that higher rate tax on it is avoided.

**23.5** Income arising on assets held in joint names will be deemed to arise equally to both parties unless they have jointly elected (on a Form 17) for it to be taxed in proportion to the original cost each subscribed to acquire them. Take as an example a couple with a joint bank deposit of £10,000, of which the wife provided £7,000 and the husband £3,000 with interest arising of £500: ordinarily £250 will be taxed on each; if they elect for the beneficial ownership proportion to be used, the wife will be taxed on £350 and the husband on £150. This treatment can apply to all investments, including buy-to-let properties.

**23.6** Where one spouse was born before 6 April 1935, the couple will be entitled to a married couple's tax allowance (see Appendix 4) for all years in which they live together, including the year in which a separation takes place.

**23.7** Unsurprisingly, there are a number of existing anti-avoidance rules applying to married couples to prevent diversion of other types of income (or gains) to a spouse to avoid tax. Perhaps the most widely known example is the 'settlement' rule highlighted in *Jones v Garnett*,[4] in which HMRC sought to tax

---

[3] [2007] WLR (D) 222, UKHL 35.

[4] [2007] WLR (D) 222, UKHL 35. Broadly the settlement rule is that income arising under a settlement during the life of the settlor shall be treated for income tax purposes as the income of the settlor, unless the income arises from property in which the settlor has no interest: Income Tax (Trading and Other Income) Act 2005, s 625. The House of Lords ruled that the

dividends paid by a family company to a shareholding wife as if they were income of the husband (the husband was the main income earner for the company).

**23.8**   Married couples on high combined incomes are likely to wish to revise their income sharing arrangements to minimise the impact of the proposed 50% top rate of tax from 6 April 2010 and may also want to consider a much wider range of investments: for example, investments giving capital growth rather than income or those where income is 'rolled up'.

## Separation

**23.9**   A couple separate for tax purposes on the later of the date they:

•   separate in circumstances that will become a permanent separation;

•   were separated under a court order or deed of separation.

**23.10**   Since 1990, spouses have been taxed separately on their personal income or share of joint income. As a result, separation is unlikely to have a significant impact for income tax purposes. Most of the anti-avoidance rules for married couples will continue to apply, as the parties will remain 'connected persons' until the decree absolute is issued.

**23.11**   However, practical considerations may lead to immediate income tax concerns where both of the couple work in the family business, as it is likely that one may wish to leave it. There may also be an immediate need for more cash to finance one party setting up a new home. Extracting this from the business is likely to have a tax cost.

## Leaving a family partnership

**23.12**   When a partner leaves a partnership, that partner is treated as if he or she had ceased a sole trade – resulting in a number of tax adjustments having to be made that can significantly affect the individual's tax liability for that tax year. The income tax position of the remaining partner(s) is not affected, although there may be capital gains tax implications.

**23.13**   On leaving, tax is payable on all the profits earned to the date of leaving which have not already been taxed – this is necessary because partners are normally taxed on the profits of the partnership accounting period ending in the tax year. Where the partnership accounting year ends early in the tax year, these catch-up rules can create a 'bunching' of profits, resulting in a large tax

---

specific exemption for an outright gift to a spouse (IT(TOI)A 2005, s 626) applied, so Mr Jones was not taxable on dividends paid to his wife. The Government subsequently announced that it proposes to tackle such 'income shifting' with new legislation, although no date for it to take effect has been announced at the time of writing.

bill for the departing partner for that tax year. However, overlap relief (to account for double-counted profits in the early years of partnership) may be available to reduce the tax liability.

**23.14**   Where the partnership has previously operated on an accounting year that is the same as or close to the tax year (eg making up annual accounts to 5 April or 31 March), this is unlikely to result in a greatly increased tax charge.

## Cessation of employment in a family company

**23.15**   It may be possible to achieve some tax savings for a spouse who leaves the family company, but it is important for the company to consider the rules on termination payments. HMRC certainly views this as an area in which employers often make mistakes.

**23.16**   Payments that are 'genuinely made solely on account of redundancy' can qualify for a special treatment that effectively exempts the first £30,000 of the payment from income tax. Where a contract of employment is terminated at short or no notice, a payment made to compensate the employee for a breach of the employment contract can also qualify for this special treatment. Whether either of these two treatments is possible will depend on the precise contractual entitlements of the leaver and how his or her departure is handled by the company. Briefly, payment of more than statutory redundancy pay which is seen to be because of the employment rights is likely to be taxable.

**23.17**   HMRC is likely to examine such payments involving former spouses very carefully. For example, if there is any suggestion that a payment in lieu of notice has been agreed between the company and the employee, it will regard the payment as fully taxable.

**23.18**   Pension contributions made by an employer are not taxable on the employee in most circumstances and usually reduce the company's taxable profits. Thus, a contribution made in respect of the leaving spouse could be a tax-efficient way to extract value from the company. However, recent legislation requires pension contributions to meet the standard test for deductible business expenses – namely that they are 'wholly and exclusively for the purpose of the business'. If the pension contribution has no business purpose, this is unlikely to be a viable option. HMRC has published guidelines in respect of contributions made by family companies encouraging inspectors to consider whether the purpose of the payment is to benefit mainly the employer, before allowing such deductions. There is also a statutory lifetime allowance to consider, which is referred to below, as well as new anti-forestalling legislation.

**23.19**   The Government intends to limit the tax relief given on pension contributions made by, or on behalf of, individuals with an annual total income of £150,000 or more from 2011/12 onwards. To prevent over-funding of pensions before the tax relief rules change on 6 April 2011, a new special annual allowance charge is to be levied on certain pension contributions made by, or on behalf of, such individuals between 22 April 2009 and 6 April 2011. Specific advice from an Independent Financial Adviser should be sought if any pension contributions are envisaged as part of a divorce settlement in this period.

**23.20** Other tax-efficient methods of transferring funds from the company to the departing spouse are the repayment of any loans owed to the spouse which are currently outstanding, or the payment of a special dividend if the spouse is a shareholder (although the implications of the prospective 'income shifting' legislation may need to be considered for the future). There is currently no indication of the date from which such legislation will apply.

## After divorce

**23.21** Maintenance payments paid after separation are not taxable on the recipient, whether to the ex-spouse or the children of the marriage, but the payer will not obtain tax relief unless either ex-spouse was born prior to 6 April 1935. For the small number of couples to whom this provision is applicable, the payer can claim a tax deduction of the annual amount of the payment up to a maximum that equals the minimum amount of married couple's allowance for that tax year (for 2009/10 that amount is £2,670 and relief is given at an effective rate of 10%). To qualify, payments must be made under a court order, a written agreement, or (albeit less likely) an assessment from the Child Support Agency.

**23.22** In some circumstances it may be sensible for maintenance payments to be secured by the transfer of income-producing assets from the responsible ex-spouse to a trust, the trustees then making the regular payments. However, such arrangements have many tax consequences.

**23.23** If the trustees are to make payments to maintain children of the marriage, the transferor will retain an interest in the trust for tax purposes (whether or not the transferor is the residual beneficiary) and will be taxed on the income arising in the trust instead of the children. If the income is paid out only to maintain the other spouse, the transferor will not be taxed on the income arising, but it will be taxable on the beneficiary. Therefore, depending on the family circumstances, it may be appropriate to consider the use of several trusts.

**23.24** However, there are also potentially expensive capital gains and inheritance tax considerations arising from such trust arrangements, so this way of securing future income for one of the parties is unlikely to be the most cost-effective.

## Planning issues

**23.25** On separation, the changes in income and expenses of the parties can be considerable – a departing spouse may leave both the family home and their employment in the family business. There may be an urgent need to release capital to the outgoing spouse for the purposes of rehousing or to meet other needs. A headlong rush towards realising cash or severing all financial and business connections can have expensive tax implications and all options should be considered carefully and, where possible, cash-raising options agreed between the parties. An agreed approach to such planning may have considerable long-term benefits for both parties.

**23.26** For example, it may not be financially sensible for the departing spouse to leave a family partnership immediately. If it is possible to continue, both parties will have a continuing income and the leaving partner can choose the most tax-efficient date to cease: eg delaying departure may allow cessation tax liabilities (see above) to be spread over 2 tax years, improving the individual's cash flow.

**23.27** Conversely, an early termination of one party's employment in the family company may help to raise income where beneficial tax treatment of a termination payment is possible, and the individual can quickly take up new employment elsewhere.

**23.28** Where a director has previously made loans to the family company (eg amounts for goodwill left outstanding on earlier incorporation of the business), repayment of these, should the company be able to afford it, will be free of tax and National Insurance Contributions (NIC). Similarly, repayment of partnership capital to an ex-spouse leaving a partnership will also be free of tax and NIC.

**23.29** It should not be forgotten that a reduction in income may have the effect of increasing individual entitlement to state benefits, particularly for the party who has primary custody of any children (see below). The income which is likely from such benefits should be considered as part of the financial settlement arithmetic.

**23.30** Depending on each party's circumstances and prospects in the longer term, division of income-producing assets can minimise tax liabilities and maximise income. For example, where an ex-wife's marginal rate of tax is 40% (or 50% from 2010/11) but the ex-husband's is 20%, assets producing tax-free income may be allocated to the ex-wife, leaving more assets producing taxable income for the ex-husband. The eventual capital gains tax upon a disposal of those assets may also be reduced in this way if the assets are transferred between the parties, either before separation or in the tax year in which the separation occurred, by effective utilisation of the spouses' annual exemptions.

**23.31** Particular care is needed where one party is not domiciled in the UK for tax purposes and there are overseas assets. Depending on the individual's circumstances and the level of overseas income generated, it may be tax-efficient for these to remain with the non-domiciled party so that any income arising on them can remain outside the UK, and therefore outside the

UK tax net, unless the individual chooses to remit them to the UK (see below). However, if the divorce settlement is not to be a clean break arrangement and the party who continues to make periodic payments is not resident in the UK, this could be a risky strategy for the other party, as enforcing a maintenance agreement against the non-domiciled party on their return overseas could prove to be difficult.

## Tax and periodic payments

**23.32** A key question for the party on the lowest income, or who has primary custody of the children, will be whether to seek a clean break settlement or arrangements involving ongoing maintenance payments.

**23.33** The fact that maintenance payments are tax-free for the recipient is attractive, but are there likely to be difficulties with payment in the long term, or in negotiating increases? It may be necessary to obtain insurance to cover the payments in the event of loss of income through redundancy or illness.[5] Where one spouse has particularly high or rising earnings and relatively little capital, it may be necessary to share the excess income in a way which allows both parties to make provision for a clean break at some point in the future.[6] In such cases, the receiving spouse should be advised to take expert advice on the best means to invest for the future. The efforts taken to provide some long-term security from the excess income are likely to be scrutinised by the court at a future variation application.

**23.34** A clean break settlement has obvious attractions for divorcing spouses and will involve the transfer of valuable assets between the parties. These may end up in the hands of an individual who is not used to managing finances. It is vital that this party takes professional advice to ensure that they are managed appropriately to generate the income that is required. This income will usually be taxable and it is likely that the individual will also need expert tax advice. It should also be remembered that there may be an ultimate tax cost in realising the assets transferred, and this needs to be factored into the figures placed before the court (see 'Capital gains tax' below). The *Duxbury* tables are the main source for calculating capitalisation of maintenance, but it should not be forgotten that some, likely to be highly exceptional, cases may call for a more bespoke form of calculation of the lump sum required to capitalise future maintenance. Actuarial involvement may then be required to provide the necessary calculations.

**23.35** However, for many couples there are simply not sufficient assets available to achieve financial stability for both parties by way of capital orders without any ongoing periodic payments. In many cases, divorce arrangements which involve a combination of asset transfers and maintenance will be the most practical solution. It should not be forgotten that where some of the

---

5  See **10.9**.
6  *McFarlane v McFarlane; Parlour v Parlour* [2004] EWCA (Civ) 872, [2004] 2 FLR 893, CA and *Miller v Miller; McFarlane v McFarlane* [2006] 1 FLR 1186, HL.

assets retained by the party who continues to make periodic payments are also income-producing (such as a family business), care needs to be taken that there is not a degree of double-counting when the court comes to consider the capital value of the asset (based in most cases, at least in part, on the income it produces) and the income the party receives from that asset (which in reality is a resource arising from the asset itself).

# CAPITAL GAINS TAX

## Introduction

**23.36**  Sensible and dispassionate structuring of disposals or transfers of assets as part of divorce arrangements can significantly reduce the amount of capital gains tax payable. However, this will not be possible unless both parties understand the tax cost of all possible options. Therefore, it is vital that both carry out a thorough assessment of the assets that are owned, including full calculations of the likely tax liability on disposal or transfer. This will help them to identify the most cost-efficient option and timing for disposal or transfer of each asset. The rules can become very complex in application and in all but straightforward cases it will be necessary to seek expert calculations of the tax liabilities likely to arise.

## The basics

**23.37**  Capital gains tax is a tax charged on the disposal by a person who is resident or ordinarily resident in the UK (some temporary non-residents may also be liable) of a capital asset which has increased in value since acquisition. However, a limited number of assets are exempt from capital gains tax. A disposal for capital gains tax purposes includes a disposal by sale (at market value or below), by gift or by exchange. Losses arising on assets which have fallen in value since acquisition may be used to reduce any capital gains tax liability on gains from the disposal of other assets. This is a useful device for reducing liabilities to capital gains tax and is often neglected by the parties and their lawyers unless an accountant or tax adviser is able to identify the savings which might be possible.

**23.38**  Gains and losses on disposals of assets are calculated by deducting the original cost from the actual (or, in some cases, deemed) proceeds of sale. A number of the complex relieving rules that were allowed to build up since capital gains tax was introduced in 1965 were repealed from 6 April 2008. The loss of taper relief, indexation allowance and reference to asset values at 31 March 1982 were all balanced by a reduction in the tax rate applied to capital gains to 18%.

**23.39**  However, some complexities remain. For example, identification rules have been simplified so that all shares of the same class in the same company will form a single 'share pool', but the existing 'same day' and 30-day 'bed and breakfast rules' will continue to apply.

**23.40** For qualifying business assets, the Government responded to an outcry from business owners about the loss of business asset taper relief (which previously gave business owners the opportunity to realise business assets and suffer an effective rate of tax of only 10%) by introducing a new entrepreneurs' relief. The relief can apply to reduce the taxable gains made on disposal of qualifying assets from 6 April 2008 onwards. The relief exempts four-ninths of the capital gain arising so that it is taxed at an effective rate of 10%, rather than the flat rate of 18% now applicable to capital gains. Entrepreneurs' relief only covers the first £1m of lifetime qualifying gains per individual, but can apply to any number of disposals until the limit is reached. Therefore, the maximum tax saving that can be achieved is £80,000 per person.

**23.41** A claim for the relief may be made on gains from the disposal by an individual (or trustee) of part or all of his or her interest in a trading business – providing the qualifying tests are met. The sale of an interest in a trading business includes the sale of company shares, sole trades and interests in partnerships and limited liability partnerships. Disposals of individual assets may also qualify under very limited circumstances.

**23.42** For an unincorporated business the relief applies to the disposal of the whole or part of a trading business carried on alone or in partnership – this includes furnished holiday lettings (up to 6 April 2010), but not other property letting 'businesses'. To qualify, the individual must have owned an interest in the business for at least one year up to the date of disposal. For a sole trader to qualify, he or she must dispose of the whole of the trading business, or a part of the business that is capable of being operated as a separate trade. This will recreate the sort of problem that arose under the old retirement relief rules, as the sale of a single trading asset in isolation is unlikely to qualify for the relief.

**23.43** Entrepreneurs' relief will be available on gains arising on the disposal of shares (and securities) in a trading company (or the holding company of a trading group) provided that the individual making the disposal has been an officer or employee of that company, or another group company, and has owned at least 5% of the ordinary share capital and voting rights of the company throughout the 12-month period ending on the date of disposal. It is not necessary for the disposal to represent at least a 5% holding, nor does an individual need to dispose of all of his or her shareholding to qualify. Similarly, there are no minimum requirements regarding the number of hours worked or remuneration paid in determining if the officer or employee test is met. However, employees holding share options in an EMI scheme cannot take unexercised options into account in determining the size of their interest in the company.

**23.44** As with the old taper relief, any company with significant non-trading activities will not qualify as a trading company. However, it is only necessary to assess the company's trading status over the 12 months to the date of disposal.

**23.45**    Where divorcing spouses jointly own a small business, the availability of entrepreneurs' relief will be a significant factor in the tax liability triggered by realising assets for a settlement. Divorcing spouses with a joint interest in a business valued considerably in excess of £2m may find practical considerations outweigh the value of this relief.

**23.46**    A loss arising on the disposal of an asset can be used to reduce any chargeable capital gains in the same tax year or, if not used in this way, may be carried forward and set against gains in future years, at present without limit. Losses must be deducted from the gross gains (for gains on the sale of a business asset, any entrepreneurs' relief is deducted first) before the annual exemption is applied to reduce taxable gains further.

**23.47**    In addition, in certain circumstances it is possible for the disposer to claim relief in respect of gifts of business assets that may otherwise be chargeable – another reason why it is vital to carry out an early assessment of the tax position for each of the couple's assets.

**23.48**    After all losses and reliefs are utilised, an individual's annual capital gains exemption (£10,100 for 2009/10) is given against the net gain. Any excess is taxable at 18%. So in many cases, even though the parties may have assets in their own name that are of a similar value to those held by the other, one party may have capital losses that significantly reduce his or her liability to tax on a disposal of those assets. Sensible use of available losses should not be forgotten when the assets are being allocated between the parties.[7]

## Pre-separation

**23.49**    Gifts, sales or other transfers of assets between a husband and wife who are living together do not have capital gains tax implications and will not create either a capital gain or a capital loss. For example, if a husband gifts shares to his wife, no capital gains tax will be chargeable on the disposal and the wife will generally be treated as if she acquired the shares at the time and cost that her husband acquired them. He has, effectively, passed over any gain to his wife and its recognition is deferred until she sells the shares.

**23.50**    A gift of assets between spouses on this no gain–no loss basis can be used to reduce a married couple's overall capital gains tax liability. If one spouse would have gains arising on an asset if sold, but has used the annual capital gains tax exemption, the asset can be gifted to the spouse who has not used the annual exemption. The sale by the transferee spouse allows that person's annual exemption to be utilised. If one spouse has losses, which cannot otherwise be used, an asset can be gifted and then sold, and the loss will be deducted from the gain arising on the sale of the asset. Care should be taken to ensure that the gift to the spouse and the sale of the asset by that spouse are not

---

[7]    See Appendix 4 for current capital gains tax reliefs.

too close together, or HMRC may question whether it was a genuine gift. There should also be no obligation on the spouse to sell.

**23.51** If a couple expect to separate, it may be tax-efficient to transfer assets between them in advance so that this beneficial treatment can be obtained. Parties who are able to work together in such a planned way may find themselves saving on very large capital gains liabilities in respect of their divorce. Regrettably, it is all too rare that the parties are able to act so rationally when in the throes of marital breakdown. If transfers of business assets are contemplated, it is important to ensure that the benefit of entrepreneurs' relief is not diminished by such transfers. For example, if one spouse is employed by a trading company and holds 5% or more of the equity of the company, they are likely to qualify for entrepreneurs' relief, giving the seller the effective 10% rate on the first £1m of gains. If these are transferred to the other spouse who is not employed by the company, a subsequent disposal of the shares will not qualify for entrepreneurs' relief, so that individual will suffer tax at 18% on the gain. This 8% tax differential may reduce the attractiveness of gifting shares in the company to the other party as a means of paying maintenance out of company profits by way of dividends.

**23.52** The disposal of an individual's main residence is exempt from capital gains tax, and in most circumstances a husband and wife who are not separated can only have one main residence. If more than one home is owned, and each could be considered the main home, the couple can elect which of the homes will be treated as the main home for capital gains tax purposes. Both properties must be lived in at some point and an election must be made to HMRC within 2 years of the second or subsequent property being acquired. If no election is made, it will be a question of fact which property is the main home.

## Separation

**23.53** For capital gains tax purposes a couple will continue to be treated as husband and wife for the tax year in which they are separated, even if they are divorced in the same tax year. Therefore, if financial arrangements can be agreed and concluded within the tax year of separation, transfers of assets between the parties in that year are free of capital gains tax. Even if all the assets are to be sold to raise cash, such transfers can ensure that the annual gains exemption for each spouse can be used.

**23.54** When a separation takes place, it is likely that some assets will be split between the parties immediately so that they can live separately. If such transfers are not covered by the 'no gain–no loss' rule (see above) they may be exempt from tax in other ways. Wasting chattels (whose value declines over time) are exempt, and chattels that retain their value (paintings, jewellery etc), would usually be exempt from capital gains tax, provided they each have a value of less than £6,000.

**23.55**   After a couple have separated, they will remain 'connected persons' in subsequent tax years until the decree absolute has been granted. This can have a number of implications, but perhaps the most significant is that transfers of assets between them will be deemed to take place at market value, even though no cash or other consideration may change hands. Where assets are transferred, the acquiring spouse does not take over the disposing spouse's acquisition history for the asset. Therefore, depending on the ownership history (for example, where entrepreneurs' relief is available to the disposing spouse), it may be more tax-efficient for the asset to be sold by the disposing spouse and the net proceeds (after allowing for any tax liability triggered) to be transferred in cash.

**23.56**   If a transfer of business assets takes place between the parties, the owner may be able to claim gift relief on a transfer to the other party that takes place after the year of separation but before the decree absolute is granted (ie while the separating spouses are only 'connected persons'). The effect of a gift relief claim is to defer any capital gains tax payable on the disposal until the new owner disposes of it. The transferor, therefore, does not have to pay capital gains tax upon the transfer, but the transferee will, when the asset is disposed of, have to pay tax on the whole of the gain accrued during the time when either of the parties owned it. If both spouses have been actively involved in the business, such a claim has the advantage of preserving potential future entrepreneurs' relief for the donor spouse for a future business venture (the £1m limit for the relief is a lifetime limit), without loss of relief for the donee spouse.

**23.57**   It is sensible for calculations to be prepared to establish the capital gain that the disposer would have made, based on the market value of the asset at the date of the transfer. This has the benefit of establishing the true net value of the asset to the acquirer and will usually require independent valuation of the asset, which is best carried out as near as possible to the date of the transfer. Often the asset in question will have been independently valued for the purposes of the ancillary relief proceedings, and such a valuation may also serve for the purpose of future tax calculations. However, the impact of entrepreneurs' relief should again be considered. Once the business asset has been transferred, it will only qualify for entrepreneurs' relief for subsequent periods by reference to the relationship of the acquiring party to the asset concerned (for example, whether or not it is used by that party in his or her trade).

**23.58**   Where assets are to be transferred at market value (ie while the separating spouses are 'connected persons'), it is important to remember that the market value for capital gains tax purposes may not be straightforward. For example, the value of one spouse's 50% share of jointly owned assets will be less than half the unencumbered market value, as a discount is given to account for the rights the other owner can exercise over the asset. In contrast, the value of a pair of antique chairs may be higher if they are currently part of a set of four. Usually such matters of discounting will have been considered when the asset was valued for the purpose of the proceedings.

**23.59** Where several properties are owned by the couple jointly (perhaps in a buy-to-let partnership they operate), it is common for them to agree to take one each, resulting in a switch or transfer of ownership: where such transfers take place after the year of separation, capital gains may arise. However, where they are joint owners of the properties, HMRC will apply extra-statutory concession D26 to give a roll-over relief so that each party acquires the other half of property at the base cost of the share in the other property. Where the values of the properties are significantly different and/or cash is paid to balance the values, a reduced capital gain may still arise to the spouse disposing of his or her share of the more valuable property (because the full proceeds are not reinvested in the other property). This treatment is not possible if any of the properties transferred has been or becomes the main residence of either spouse.

**23.60** As can be seen, the effective date that an asset is transferred has a substantial impact on the capital gains tax treatment of the transactions, but the date can be dependent on how it is transferred (see 'Planning issues' below).

## After divorce

**23.61** Once a decree absolute has been granted, ex-spouses will not be 'connected persons' for capital gains tax purposes unless they continue to be business partners or retain some other connection. Therefore, it will no longer be possible to claim gift relief on transfers of business assets between spouses unless the transfer is made under a relevant court order made before the decree absolute (see below). However, this does not mean that assets being transferred can escape the market value rule: a disposal will always be regarded as taking place at open market value if HMRC establishes that any consideration given for the receipt of an asset was less than market value.

**23.62** If part of the divorce arrangements involves providing for children, it may be appropriate to consider creating trusts for them if they are aged under 18. Changes to the tax legislation on trusts introduced in the Finance Act 2006 will mean that far more trusts fall to be treated as discretionary trusts for inheritance tax (IHT) purposes (see 'Inheritance tax' below) which may add a tax cost. Whilst creating a discretionary trust can have immediate capital gains tax advantages through use of holdover relief, this is unlikely to be available in divorce situations (as the settlor's children will often be beneficiaries, or the transfer is not a 'transfer of value' for IHT purposes, as it is to provide maintenance for a former spouse).

**23.63** Deferment of gains on business assets may be possible if the asset qualifies for IHT business property relief and, therefore, would not trigger a lifetime tax liability on transfer to a discretionary trust. In addition, if the life tenant of the trust works in the business, entrepreneurs' relief may be available when it is sold by the trustees. However, such a trust may not be the best longer-term home for business assets or assets producing significant income, as there will be an income tax charge on the settlor on income arising within the trust as, via dependent children, the settlor is deemed to retain an interest in the trust assets.

## Planning issues

### *The family home*

**23.64**  The family home will be the most valuable asset to be considered in most divorce arrangements, and it is often assumed that the sale of a main residence will be exempt from capital gains tax. The qualifying conditions for the exemption are less well known. This can lead to difficulties when a home is passed from one spouse to another or sold on divorce.

**23.65**  The exemption will apply to the whole gain if the property has been a couple's main home for the whole period of ownership. If the property has not been occupied as the couple's main residence during any part of the ownership period, a proportion of any gain made on disposal may be taxable. However, there are a number of provisions which extend the period during which the couple or individual spouses are treated as occupying the property for tax purposes. Where the parties have lived in a number of properties which they still own, it will be important to consider which property or properties they wish to claim as their principal residence at each point in time, as such provisions can have very significant tax implications.

**23.66**  In the common situation that one spouse has moved out of the property when the couple separated, the 36-month exemption will be useful. This allows any individual to be treated for tax purposes as occupying a main residence throughout the last 36 months of ownership, provided he or she actually occupied the property before the actual period of absence. Provided the property is sold or transferred within 36 months of the departing spouse leaving, no taxable gain will arise to either spouse. If the sale or transfer is delayed beyond this time, the proportion of the gain charged may be relatively small and may be covered by the departing spouse's annual gain allowance.

**23.67**  For larger gains in this situation, HMRC will apply an extra-statutory concession (D6) to exempt the gain if there have been no other periods of absence from the property and the departing spouse has not yet claimed for another property to be regarded as his or her main residence. This concession will not apply if the property is to be sold under the divorce arrangements. In such a situation, it would be better for the remaining spouse to accept a transfer of the property and sell it at a subsequent date to reduce the tax cost to the departed spouse. However, relying on this concession will mean that the main residence exemption for any new home already purchased by the departing spouse will not apply for the period that the exemption is given on the former matrimonial home.

**23.68** It may be necessary for the divorce order to specify that the spouse who has primary care of children of the family is given a right to occupy the property with the children until a certain date (eg when the children reach a certain age or complete their education). Orders, which are commonly referred to as *Mesher* orders,[8] can take different forms. In some cases (a 'true' *Mesher* order) the order creates a settlement of property in the form of a trust of land giving at least the occupying spouse an interest in possession in the property while both spouses may remain the trustees of the settlement. More common in practice, however, is a transfer of the property into the name of the occupying party, subject to a charge in favour of the other party, the realisation of the charge being deferred until the *Mesher* events trigger a sale of the property. Although the term '*Mesher* order' is widely used to describe both types of arrangement, their tax implications are quite different, and this should be borne in mind.

**23.69** Where the property is placed in a trust of land in which each party is given a beneficial interest, this is a settlement which lasts as long as the *Mesher* conditions remain unsatisfied. Once one of the 'trigger events' occurs, the property is deemed to be transferred out of the trust into a new trust where the parties hold the property on bare trust for themselves. The capital gains tax consequences at various stages are set out in the table below:

|  | **Tax liability of departed spouse (whether sole or joint owner)** | **Spouse in occupation** |
| --- | --- | --- |
| *Transfer of property into the trust (ie creation of the Mesher settlement)* | Exempt if occurs within 36 months of departure from main residence. | Exempt as main residence. |
|  | If later, proportion of the gain after expiry of 36-month period (calculated at market value) is chargeable unless transferor is able to extend the exemption by reason of having claimed no principal private residence relief on any other property since separation. |  |
| *Transfer out of the trust at the specified date (ie upon one of the Mesher 'trigger events' occurring)* | Exempt provided property occupied by person with 'interest in possession' (IIP) throughout. | Exempt provided property occupied by person with IIP throughout. |
| *Sale of the property immediately on release from trust* | Exempt as above. | Exempt as above. |

---

[8]    After *Mesher v Mesher and Hall* [1980] 1 All ER 126.

| | **Tax liability of departed spouse (whether sole or joint owner)** | **Spouse in occupation** |
|---|---|---|
| *Sale of the property at a later date* | A gain may arise, depending on the growth in value since exit from the trust. | Exempt provided continued to be main residence pending sale. |

**23.70** Where the spouses are not willing to act as co-trustees, or it is felt that one should have ownership of the property, it may be decided that it is appropriate to transfer the property to the party remaining in occupation and grant the party who is not in occupation a charge which is deferred until the desired date. The party who occupies the property has full ownership of it and will face no capital gains tax consequences if it continues to be his or her main residence. The other party will face a potential capital gains tax liability on the transfer if it takes place more than 36 months after the parties separated and the value of that party's interest has increased.[9]

**23.71** The charge can be expressed as a fixed sum or a percentage of the value of the property. If a fixed sum is used, this 'debt' does not increase in value and is exempt from capital gains tax. A chargeable gain will only arise on such a fixed charge arrangement upon exchange of the ex-spouse's interest in the property for the debt, but if this takes place within 36 months of the ex-spouse leaving the property, there will be no taxable gain.

**23.72** A percentage charge is likely to be regarded by HMRC as a form of property in its own right and, unless HMRC can be persuaded that this arrangement is also a 'settlement' with similar effects to those arising under the first form of *Mesher* order, any increase in the value of the asset is potentially liable to capital gains tax. Therefore, it will have a base cost at the time it is acquired (the proportion of the value of the property represented by the percentage of the charge at the time of the order) and any increase in the value of the property will trigger a gain upon eventual disposal of the charge. Again, exchanging the ex-spouse's original share of the property for this new asset is likely to be an exempt transaction, so long as it was made within 36 months of the date of the separation.

**23.73** No stamp duty land tax (SDLT) is payable on formally documented transfers of land between spouses in connection with divorce.

## *Insurance policies*

**23.74** Where rights to insurance-based assets (bonds and policies) are transferred, a liability to capital gains tax (a 'chargeable event') may be triggered at the date of transfer. Following observations by Coleridge J in *G v G*,[10] HMRC changed its approach to charging capital gains tax upon the

---

[9]  The final 36 months does not elapse as such – it is always the last 36 months of ownership.
[10]  [2002] 2 FLR 1143.

transfer of a life policy from spouse to spouse pursuant to an ancillary relief order. The liability for capital gains tax will be based on the policy gains to date and will not include a 'disposal for consideration' to the recipient, provided the transfer is confirmed or instituted by a court order. Hence, a transfer of such a policy by reason of a court order should not normally constitute a chargeable event.

## Family business assets

**23.75** It is common for assets used in a family business to be owned personally by a couple – this can offer a number of tax advantages during marriage, but can cause particular problems on divorce. Therefore, it is vital to quickly establish financial arrangements that allow the business to continue to trade successfully. Significant disruption will reduce the realisable value of the business to both parties.

**23.76** If assets are to be transferred between the parties, it is important that, if possible, these transfers take place in the year of separation (at no gain–no loss).[11] If the transfer takes place in a later period, a capital gain may be triggered, and it could well be that entrepreneurs' relief will not be available to reduce the gain, e g if the disposing party ceased to work in the business before the date of the transfer. Similarly, roll-over relief for the gift of business assets could be proportionately reduced.

**23.77** If both parties jointly own a family company, it is likely that one spouse will wish to continue the business without the involvement of the other. Buying the other party's shares in the company will be the simplest way to achieve this, but that spouse may not have sufficient cash available. A 'buy back of own shares' by the company may be possible if it has sufficient reserves, but there are a number of formalities to be complied with (albeit not especially onerous ones) and failure to do so can have expensive tax consequences. Another alternative is a company reconstruction, which could release cash or loan notes to the leaving party.

**23.78** Whatever option is pursued, it will be important to ensure that entrepreneurs' relief is available to the selling party if a gain is to be triggered. If the couple have not previously considered their entrepreneurs' relief position (for example, if non-business assets are held in the company), it may be tax-efficient to resolve this issue and then defer any disposal for 12 months to obtain the full relief. The impact on other shareholders or business partners must also be considered.

**23.79** Where the parties run a business in partnership with each other, or in partnership with others, similar issues arise, although the options for buying out a partner may be more limited. The 'goodwill' that may exist in a partnership (the value of the business over and above the market value of its

---

[11] See **23.49–23.50** above.

assets) is, depending on the partnership agreement, often treated as an asset that should be bought from a departing partner. However, its value is notoriously difficult to assess and may decline rapidly once the partner has left, if that partner's role in the business was an integral part of the business's success.

**23.80** A quick 'buy-out' will benefit the leaver. If there is insufficient cash in the continuing partnership to buy out the leaver immediately, the sale may be accomplished by way of a loan to the continuing business. This will need to be repaid and interest will be charged at an agreed rate. However, the leaver's cash flow position should also be carefully considered, as any gain will be calculated on the full value of his or her share in the business, whether this is actually received or not.

**23.81** Where the arrangements for buying out the other party's interest in a business raise such complexities, it may be useful simply to agree terms of settlement that are conditional upon obtaining the required clearances from HMRC for the proposed transactions. Specific clearances from HMRC will have to be requested separately.[12] Once any specific clearances have been received, the order can be finalised. Such an approach may delay the final conclusion of the case, but it has the benefit of helping to avoid nasty surprises for either party in due course.

## Overseas assets

**23.82** It is not possible to cover here all the potential tax ramifications of the ending of a marriage with an individual who is resident but not domiciled in the UK. There are likely to be many pitfalls where there are overseas assets of substantial value, as, if the non-domiciled spouse is well advised, it is possible that the income and capital gains made on these will not be taxable in the UK until they are brought into, or remitted to, this country. However, the tax rules for individuals who are resident but not domiciled, or not ordinarily resident, in the UK changed substantially on 6 April 2008.

**23.83** Individuals who are resident, ordinarily resident and domiciled in the UK are taxable on their worldwide income and gains arising in a tax year – the 'arising basis'. However, for 2007/08 and earlier years, individuals who were resident but not domiciled, or not ordinarily resident, in the UK could claim for an alternative 'remittance basis' to be applied to tax their foreign income, so that it was only taxable in the UK when they remitted it here in some form. Under the new rules, from 6 April 2008 such individuals will still be able to claim the remittance basis of taxation for foreign income and chargeable gains, but claims will subject to some new conditions.

**23.84** If their unremitted foreign income and gains are less than £2,000 for a year, the remittance basis will apply automatically. Individuals who have

---

[12]    HMRC will not provide a blanket approval for a proposed arrangement.

income and gains in excess of £2,000 for a year will have to make a formal claim to obtain the benefit of the remittance basis for that year. Making a formal claim will mean that they lose their entitlement to UK personal allowances and the CGT annual exempt amount for that year.

**23.85** Where such individuals stay in the UK for a number of years, they can claim the remittance basis for the first 7 tax years of residence without a further cost. With effect from 6 April 2008, an annual £30,000 charge to use the remittance basis will apply from the start of the eighth tax year of UK residence (where the individual has been resident in the UK for 7 out of the last 9 tax years). This means that if 2008/09 is the individual's eighth year of tax residence in the UK, the charge will apply immediately and for subsequent years in which the remittance basis is claimed.

**23.86** It will be possible to claim the remittance basis for some years but not others, eg where overseas income fluctuates. However, if overseas income is built up by a non-UK domiciled individual during years in which the remittance basis is claimed and then that income is brought into the UK in a year for which the arising basis applies, a tax liability will arise on the income. This was not previously the case.

**23.87** HMRC has stated that a decision not to claim the remittance basis in a particular year will not be used as evidence of a change of domicile under general law. UK resident non-UK domiciliaries who have unremitted foreign income and gains of more than £2,000 for a year and do not claim the remittance basis, will be subject to UK tax on their worldwide income and gains (and, potentially, income and gains attributed to them under UK principles from certain trust and company structures) in the same way as resident UK domiciliaries. They will then need to complete a UK tax return on that basis.

**23.88** For many non-UK domiciled individuals, sensible arrangements will usually have been put in place to ensure that income, gains and the original capital of such offshore assets are kept separate, so that when funds are required in the UK, only clean capital is remitted here, ensuring that no UK tax liability is triggered. However, new rules on what constitutes a taxable remittance have now complicated matters, and many individuals will have been forced to change longstanding arrangements, redistribute assets, or even wind up offshore trust or company structures. For example, if both spouses are not domiciled in the UK and one spouse gives income or gains to the other, if the donee brings the money into the UK, this will trigger a remittance of income that is taxable on the donor under the new 'relevant person' rules. This could cause particular problems in the year of separation if a donee needs to fund the acquisition of a new home: bringing their own funds into the UK could trigger a tax liability for the donor spouse.

**23.89** A divorce order may cut through a couple's existing arrangements, but it may not be in the best interests of a non-domiciled party or parties to do so in a crude fashion. For example, it is important that divorce settlement arrangements protect a non-domiciled spouse from a UK tax bill on a forced remittance of gains or income through bringing overseas assets into the UK to settle liabilities under a divorce settlement. Allowing a transfer of overseas assets to an ex-spouse to take place outside the UK should, normally, avoid a remittance from the non-domiciled ex-spouse. The recipient ex-spouse can receive a higher value tax-free asset overseas and then bring it into the UK themselves without a UK tax charge arising on either party as, after divorce, the recipient will receive clean capital and there will no longer be a 'relevant person' in relation to the other spouse. Satisfying such a UK 'debt', in the form of the ancillary relief order, by way of a transfer of funds overseas should not constitute a 'constructive remittance' to the UK, although, as yet, this hypothesis does not seem to have been tested by HMRC in the courts. HMRC could, in an appropriate case, argue that, as the funds were transferred to satisfy the order of the court in the English ancillary relief proceedings, the transaction constitutes a 'constructive remittance', because otherwise taxed UK-based funds would have been used to satisfy the order.

**23.90**   However, problems will arise when funds are required to make provision for a non-UK domiciled person's child or children aged under 18. Such a child will remain a 'relevant person', so any funds brought into the UK directly or indirectly for their benefit (eg for maintenance or to pay school fees) will constitute a remittance of income or gains unless they can be funded from clean capital. Clearly, careful planning will be required so that the financing structures that are finally agreed between the parties are tax-efficient for all concerned.

**23.91**   In addition, it may not be sensible to structure ongoing maintenance payments to an ex-spouse by way of payments made offshore. In practical terms, it may prove difficult for the recipient ex-spouse to enforce them should the non-domiciled spouse leave the UK at a future date.

**23.92**   Specific advice is recommended from international tax consultants when dealing with individuals who are not domiciled or not resident in the UK for tax purposes where those individuals have substantial assets outside the jurisdiction.

### *How and when should an asset transfer take place?*

**23.93**   The effective tax date on which the transfer of an asset between the parties takes place is not necessarily the date of physical transfer. For example, where the parties create an unconditional contract under which the assets are to be transferred, the date of the contact is the effective date for tax purposes. The same principle applies to court orders: any transfers made after a court order are deemed to take place on the date of the order.

**23.94**   However, the position can be more complex for a consent order that gives effect to arrangements that the parties have already agreed and/or put in place. The problem arises because such a consent order cannot be said to form a contract – it merely confirms the already agreed, and possibly already implemented, arrangements. In such situations, HMRC will look at the actual date of any transfers of ownership of assets, if earlier, particularly where the tax liabilities may be large. If the tax amounts involved are small, the transfers are usually treated as having taken place on a date agreed by both parties.

**23.95** In summary, therefore, if there are to be transfers of assets and it is possible for them to be made in the tax year of separation, this is likely to be the least disruptive course, as they will be no gain–no loss transactions for CGT purposes (although see 'Implications and planning' below). In the case of a non-UK domiciled spouse, once the assets have been transferred, there may well be advantages in delaying the movement of these assets into the UK until after decree absolute, when the recipient ex-spouse will no longer be a 'relevant person' under the new remittance rules.

**23.96** If all asset transfers are to be made under court orders (other than consent orders), it may be appropriate to consider staggering the tax disposal dates across different tax years by agreeing several orders relating to realisation or transfer of different assets. This could help to use the disposer's capital gains tax annual allowance over several years and allow the maximum use of losses and any lower tax rate band available.

## *Implications and planning*

**23.97** Within the parameters of what is acceptable to both parties, it is important when seeking to negotiate a settlement to consider all options for selling, retaining or transferring the assets of both parties, because achieving the lowest overall tax charge may not be straightforward. For example, one spouse may have full entrepreneurs' relief available on an asset but the other (who does not) may need it to continue in business. In such circumstances, it will be tax-efficient to claim hold-over relief upon transfer and preserve his or her own lifetime limit for entrepreneurs' relief.

**23.98** Finding the answers to the following questions will help to identify the tax-efficient options available to both parties:

- What assets are owned by the parties? Identifying the business assets and residential property is particularly important.

- Which assets are exempt from CGT?

- Can assets realistically be sold or transferred and, if so, at which dates?

- What reliefs and exemptions will be available at the anticipated date of any transactions?

- If the asset is to be sold to raise cash, which party will face the lowest tax charge on a disposal? This will involve considering:
  - Which assets are standing at a gain and which at a loss?
  - Has either party any capital losses brought forward or as yet unrealised that can be set against future gains?
  - What is the marginal tax rate of each spouse?
  - What assets qualify for entrepreneurs' relief (both now and following a possible transfer)?

- Can asset swaps reduce the overall tax liability (for example, by taking advantage of business gift relief)?

- How will any transfers affect the disposer's inheritance tax position?

**23.99** Depending on the number and value of the assets involved and the planning options available, it may then be appropriate to run through a number of 'what if' scenarios to establish the optimum tax position for both parties. It is important to take into account reductions or increases in income as a result of transfers of income-yielding assets. Only by minimising the tax liabilities of both parties will the adviser help to maximise the funds available.

## INHERITANCE TAX

**23.100** There is perhaps more chance of achieving sensible planning arrangements for divorcing couples when it comes to inheritance tax (IHT), as the benefits will be felt by their children rather than each other.

**23.101** When considering the potential impact of any financial arrangements on the IHT position of each party, it is vital to try to establish the likely domicile status of each party: the tax is charged on the worldwide assets of individuals who are resident and domiciled in the UK, but only on the UK assets of individuals who are domiciled abroad. To prevent avoidance of IHT there are also rules that:

- extend IHT to the estates of individuals who were domiciled in the UK within 3 calendar years before the date of death;

- deem an individual to be domiciled in the UK (for IHT purposes) if he or she has been resident in the UK during 17 out of the 20 years immediately prior to death.

**23.102** Whilst IHT is a death tax (at 40% where the nil band is exceeded), it is possible for a lifetime charge (at 20%) to arise. For example, a transfer to a discretionary trust may trigger such a charge.

## Pre-separation

**23.103**   Transfers of assets between a husband and wife are exempt from IHT, provided either the recipient spouse is domiciled in the UK or both spouses are non-UK domiciled. Where the donor spouse is UK domiciled and the spouse receiving the asset is not, only transfers up to the value of £55,000 are exempt: transfers in excess of this sum would only be 'potentially exempt'.

**23.104**   Most transfers which are not otherwise exempt (or specifically liable to lifetime tax) will be potentially exempt transfers, meaning that if the donor survives for 7 years after making the gifts, they will fall out of account. If the donor dies within 7 years of making a gift, it will be taxed as if the asset was still in his or her estate at death, but a taper relief (see Appendix 4) will apply to reduce the IHT on each gift.

**23.105**   Where the first spouse or civil partner to die leaves his or her assets to the surviving spouse or civil partner, up to twice the nil rate band (£325,000 for 2009/10) will be available on the survivor's death after 9 October 2007. Previously, the nil rate band available on the first death was lost, as inter-spouse gifts are exempt from IHT.

**23.106**   Entitlement to a late spouse's unused nil rate band can continue after the surviving spouse remarries. However, this is only the case where the marriage is brought to an end by the death of one party. In the unlikely event that an ex-spouse leaves all his or her assets to a former spouse on death, no additional nil rate band entitlement will arise to the surviving ex-spouse, even if the individual's nil rate band was not used fully.

## Separation

**23.107**   Transfers of assets between spouses remain tax-free if made before the decree absolute is granted.

**23.108**   Business assets (eg whole businesses, buildings and land used in a business, and shares in unlisted companies, including those listed on AIM) can qualify for 100% relief from IHT on the death of the owner. There are a number of qualifying rules, but the principal ones include a minimum period of ownership and (where appropriate) usage of 2 years. If such assets are to be passed down to children or grandchildren of the marriage, it will be vital to ensure that the assets remain in the ownership of someone (either a spouse or an adult child) who will continue to use them for business purposes to preserve the relief.

## After divorce

**23.109**   There are specific exemptions for transfers made for the maintenance of the other party in a marriage (or made on the dissolution of a marriage), or for the maintenance, education or training of a child of either party up to the age of 18. The definition of a child for these purposes includes step-children and adopted children.

**23.110**   The latter exemption for children is available to all children of couples (whether or not the couples have been married), provided that the child has been in the care of the person making the transfer for 'substantial periods' before his or her eighteenth birthday. However, when children reach the age of 18, this exemption will not apply and the normal rules on potentially exempt gifts will need to be considered on the subsequent death of the donor. Therefore, no tax liability is likely to arise, provided that at the time gifts are made the recipient child is aged 11 or less. Where gifts are made to older children, specialist insurance could be considered to cover any potential IHT liability on the death of the donor within 7 years of making the gift.

**23.111**   There is also a general exemption for transfers of assets not intended to give a 'gratuitous benefit' to the recipient, and this would cover apportionments of assets under court orders, perhaps where unmarried couples have gone to court over the ownership of assets on separation.

**23.112**   Ex-spouses planning gifts to their children should also be aware that once they are divorced, any property they own is no longer 'related'; the value of related property can increase the value of a gift for IHT purposes. Combined assets (a valuable set of chairs, pictures etc) transferred between spouses before divorce can be gifted to their children after divorce at a lower value for IHT purposes.

## Planning issues

**23.113**   The main consideration will be not to interrupt any existing IHT planning arrangements the couple may already have put in place. This will not be a problem if such plans were solely executed through the wills of both parties, as they will become invalid on divorce and must be redrawn. However, other arrangements already in place to pass on assets to children will need to be considered carefully.

**23.114**   The use of trusts in IHT planning has come under much scrutiny in the past few years, with many amendments made to the tax legislation in areas where families have successfully avoided IHT liabilities. The extension of the tax treatment of discretionary trusts to most new trusts created on or after 22 March 2006 and a large number of existing trusts will mean that many families are likely to have updated their plans and put new arrangements in place by the transition deadline of 5 April 2008 (or 5 October 2008 for changes to pre-existing interest in possession trusts). It is worth noting that trusts which do not give children an absolute interest by age 18 now have tax disadvantages. Trusts that are set up as a result of a divorce are not specifically exempted from the new rules, so trusts created on divorce to provide for the maintenance of a former spouse will be treated as discretionary trusts for IHT purposes, increasing the long-term cost of such arrangements.

**23.115** Any arrangements that involve a non-UK domiciled ex-spouse receiving UK assets will bring that individual within the scope of IHT (assuming the assets are situated in the UK) and are likely to trigger a potential liability for a UK domiciled spouse making such a transfer where the value is in excess of £55,000. Again, the use of insurance may be appropriate to protect other family members from a tax cost should the donor spouse die within 7 years.

## Implications and planning

**23.116** The primary IHT implications that need to be considered will derive from the transfer of assets into or out of an ex-spouse's estate. Whilst there are a number of exemptions for the transfers that an individual will make, it is the long-term impact on the structure of the estate that will be most important.

**23.117** For example, if business assets are given away as part of a divorce settlement, the overall IHT due on an individual's estate may be higher, and new IHT plans could be required. Equally, if the spouse receiving the assets does not continue with the business, business property relief will not be available on his or her death – increasing the IHT on the recipient's estate and reducing the net assets available to any surviving children.

# OTHER ISSUES ARISING ON DIVORCE

## Family businesses

**23.118** The break-up of a marriage may cause great disruption for a family business, but the business's deadlines for submitting returns and paying taxes will not change. There are some 'reasonable excuses' allowed for missing deadlines, but these do not include divorce.

**23.119** In England, couples trading in partnership have joint liability for some taxes owing (eg PAYE and NIC), so HMRC will expect the individual who is continuing to trade to pay any amounts outstanding, leaving that party to reclaim the appropriate share from the former partner. Joint and several liability may be imposed in respect of VAT debts. Income tax on the individual's share of profits is, however, a liability of the individual partner, and HMRC may not pursue the other partners for non-payment, whatever the reason for the debt. If separated spouses are not able to resolve outstanding business issues between them, they should each appoint advisers to do so as soon as possible to protect their own interests – surcharges, penalties and interest can soon erode the remaining value in a family business.

## Child tax credits

**23.120**   The child tax credit represents a significant source of income for many families with children aged under 16 (at 1 September in the tax year of claim) or between 16 and 19 and in full-time education. The level of credit is dependent on family income and is available in the 2009/10 tax year to one-child families with incomes of up to £58,000 (or up to £66,000 if a child was born in the previous year). The limits increase for families with more children (or for children with disabilities), but any maintenance payments received by the claimant are ignored.

**23.121**   Couples who have claimed the credit must notify HMRC (within one month) if they separate and, as the credit is paid to the main carer, must also notify any change in the main carer for the child. Early notification of a fall in income (on a spouse leaving) is also sensible, as enhanced credit may be due. Failure to make timely notifications to HMRC can lead to a penalty of up to £300 for each failure.

**23.122**   A change in circumstances will lead to a reassessment of the credit entitlement, but this may lead to the discovery of a past overpayment of credit. There may then be a reduction in the future level of credit or a direct request for repayment, and such debts should be taken into account in arriving at any financial settlement.

**23.123**   From the date of separation both parties may be entitled to claim credit in respect of a child living with them (this need not be on a full-time basis). In the year of separation, credit is time-apportioned for pre- and post-separation periods and then apportioned between the parties. In subsequent years, where the ex-spouses have two or more children, it is possible (depending on the facts) for both parties to claim credit on the basis that each party is the main carer for at least one of the children – increasing the total benefit received. Working tax credits are also available to UK tax resident individuals who work at least 16 hours a week, have income within prescribed set limits and who look after one or more children. The credit is provided to either single claimants or couples. Where a couple separates and only one of them is in work, if the non-working spouse continues not to work after separation and takes custody of the children, neither will be eligible for the working tax credit. This is because neither spouse meets all of the qualifying criteria.

## Pensions

**23.124**   Pension sharing arrangements included in a divorce settlement should not trigger a tax liability until the pension comes into payment. The maximum amount (the statutory lifetime allowance) an individual may enjoy from all pension schemes (including personal and company pension schemes) is currently £1.65m, rising to £1.8m by 2010/11. Pension sharing orders may, therefore, be particularly attractive to high earners who are already 'over-pensioned'. Any amount of pension entitlement lost (or received) on divorce will reduce (or increase) the individual's pension fund. For those individuals with the funds available to rebuild their pension fund tax-efficiently in the future, or those still accruing pension entitlement through their employment, giving away part of their pension rights – rather than other assets – may be an attractive option.

Part X

# DEALING WITH ANCILLARY RELIEF IN UNCERTAIN ECONOMIC CONDITIONS

# Chapter 24

# INTRODUCTION

**24.1** History indicates that economic growth does not follow a constant and steady upward course. There are cyclical trends in economies. At their most extreme such trends fluctuate wildly between boom and bust. Usually such violent fluctuations take place within a particular sector of the economy rather than the economy as a whole. There are many examples of an economic 'bubble' of growth rapidly expanding in a particular industry and then suddenly and unexpectedly bursting. Perhaps the most recent example of this was the 'dot-com' boom of the 1990s. As well as these fluctuations in particular industries there are similar, although usually less extreme, fluctuations in the wider economy. In the globalised economies of the twenty-first century such fluctuations are not limited to a single economy, but are likely to have worldwide implications.

## THE 'CREDIT CRUNCH'

**24.2** From mid-2007 a crisis in the world's financial markets began to become apparent.[1] Major financial institutions around the world became reluctant to lend to each other. They were concerned about each other's credit-worthiness due to vast exposures to potentially bad debts, primarily debts relating to so-called 'sub-prime' mortgage lending in the United States of America. The 'securitisation' of those debts by packaging them up in complex financial instruments which were then sold between the banks made the full extent of each bank's potential liabilities virtually impossible to assess. Only as the bad debts began to unravel did the effect on the solvency of banking institutions become apparent. As the resulting 'credit crunch' deepened, the crisis of confidence spread into the wider economy, leading to credible reports of the world being on the verge of a new 'Great Depression' to rival that of the 1930s. Dramatic and unprecedented action was taken by many governments. In the

---

[1] The first signs of impending problems became apparent outside the financial services industry around April 2007 when large 'sub-prime' mortgage lenders in the United States of America began to file for bankruptcy protection. By August 2007 large investment banks such as Bear Stearns and BNP Paribas were forced to inform investors that they could not withdraw from various investment funds which were heavily involved in securitised sub-prime lending. By this stage banks had virtually ceased to lend to each other, leading to a crisis in liquidity. Various central banks around the world, including the European Central Bank began pumping funds into the market to counter the lack of liquidity. In the United Kingdom the crisis became front page news in September 2007 when the Government had to intervene to prevent the collapse of Northern Rock plc and general panic in the banking sector.

United Kingdom vast sums of public money were applied to effectively nationalise several leading banks and to inject funds into the economy.

**24.3**  The implications of these developments soon began to be felt by the parties involved in ancillary relief proceedings and by their lawyers. Despite warnings for several years by the International Monetary Fund and other commentators that the United Kingdom property market had risen in value to an unrealistic level when compared to average incomes and that personal borrowing was unsustainably high, few in the United Kingdom appeared to heed the warnings. Many families had taken on very large mortgages and considerable personal debt during the years of strong growth in the economy, particularly in the housing market. Quite rapidly, this prosperity began to unravel. Residential property prices began to fall. Sales of properties began to be more difficult to achieve as sources of mortgage lending dried up for prospective purchasers or simply became prohibitively expensive given the reluctance of the banks to release funds to each other. The value of stock market based investments fell as stock markets around the world ended their long and successful 'bull run' and turned into 'bear markets', where the desire to sell stocks and get out of the market overtook the earlier exuberance of investors. Share values began to fluctuate wildly as panic gripped the markets.

**24.4**  Against this background, parties to proceedings found it increasingly difficult to resolve their affairs. Much of the flexibility which had been available during the times of success and cheap credit disappeared. It became more difficult for a party to satisfy the other party's claims by borrowing against assets whose values were falling, or by raising funds from their struggling businesses. Bonus payments which had previously come to be expected suddenly seemed less certain. Share options which appeared to be highly beneficial became potentially worthless. The equity in properties which the parties had previously relied upon in order to discharge their debts began to prove to be illusory or, at least, significantly lower than they had expected. In due course, through 2008, the economic situation worsened and employers began to reduce their staffing levels. Several well-known and long-established businesses failed. Other employers began to reduce their workforces. In the year between April 2008 and April 2009 the official number of unemployed persons in the United Kingdom rose from about 1.6 million to 2.22 million,[2] with some forecasting that the figure would continue to rise to well over 3 million. Rates of personal and corporate insolvency rose to near unprecedented levels. Of course, what proved to be a disaster for some was an opportunity for others, and certain individuals were able to prosper or to speculate with a view to obtaining great returns in the future.

**24.5**  For more than a decade prior to the 'credit crunch', ancillary relief law had been developed through a series of high-profile cases which concerned very wealthy families. The families whose names have become well known through

---

[2]  Office for National Statistics online bulletin on 12 May 2009. By June 2009 the figure had risen to 2.435 million (ONS bulletin for 12 August 2009).

the case law were those who had been successful in accumulating very significant assets[3] or large incomes which far surpassed their essential needs.[4] Hence, the focus in the cases had been on sharing the financial fruits of the marriage, set against a mutual assumption that the future was likely to continue to be rosy. The problems of dealing with the practicalities of reducing asset values, reducing incomes and debt did not arise in those cases. The law had developed with a view to sharing a rich harvest, not in order to cope with famine.

## OUTLINE OF THIS SECTION

**24.6** This part of the book aims to provide a short guide to some of the issues which arise in cases being litigated in a period of uncertain economic conditions, where the economy is in recession. Chapter 25 provides a brief introduction to the law of insolvency and how it interacts with ancillary relief proceedings. Chapter 26 considers the difficulties in placing values on assets during periods of market volatility and economic uncertainty and considers how fair outcomes might be achieved despite such uncertainties. Chapter 27 discusses the way that the provisions of the Matrimonial Causes Act 1973 might be used in a period of economic uncertainty, including applications to vary or set aside orders which have previously been made.

---

[3]   For example, *Miller v Miller* [2006] 1 FLR 151, *Sorrell v Sorrell* [2006] 1 FLR 497 and *Charman v Charman (No 4)* [2007 1 FLR 1246.

[4]   For example, *Parlour v Parlour* [2004] 2 FLR 893 and *McFarlane v McFarlane* [2006] 1 FLR 151.

# Chapter 25

# INSOLVENCY AND ANCILLARY RELIEF

## INTRODUCTION

**25.1**  In times of economic uncertainty ancillary relief lawyers need to be alive to the warning signs of potential insolvency. Having recognised the risk of insolvency, practitioners need to be prepared to advise their client as to the manner in which insolvency impacts on the case and the steps that ought to be taken to best protect their client's interests.[1] In order to give this advice, practitioners require at least a passing familiarity with the law of insolvency and a detailed knowledge of how the courts' distributive powers under ss 23–24 of the Matrimonial Causes Act 1973 operate in relation to an insolvent spouse. As with many areas of ancillary relief practice, a multidisciplinary approach may be required in order to advance a party's case to the best effect. Careful consideration should be given to whether the case is one where specialist legal advice on insolvency is required.

**25.2**  This chapter begins with a gentle introduction to the law of personal insolvency. For a more comprehensive approach to this subject a detailed practitioner's text should be consulted.[2] Thereafter, the chapter deals with a number of areas where bankruptcy and ancillary relief practice overlap, such as annulment of bankruptcy orders, the implications of pursuing a claim for ancillary relief against a bankrupt spouse, bankruptcy and the matrimonial home, the potential consequences of the presentation of a bankruptcy petition before the making of an order in ancillary relief proceedings and the impact of a bankruptcy order where the bankruptcy petition was presented after the order for ancillary relief came into effect.

**25.3**  There are, of course, two main categories of insolvency: corporate and personal. In the context of ancillary relief proceedings, corporate insolvency will in general result in the reduction of a party's capital assets as the value of business interests and share valuations are all but extinguished. Income streams, whether by way of director's emoluments, dividends or employed income, are also curtailed. Sometimes corporate insolvency can impact on personal liability, normally in circumstances where a party has given a personal guarantee in support of lending made to a business. In general, corporate insolvency has the potential to reduce the resources of the parties available for

---

[1]  The failure to do so may result in a negligence claim: see *Burke v Chapman and Chubb* [2008] 2 FLR 1207 QBD, Plender J.

[2]  See, for example, *Muir Hunter on Personal Insolvency* (looseleaf, Thomson/Sweet & Maxwell).

distribution by the court. Corporate insolvency is considered further at **26.24–26.31**. However, as we shall see, the consequences of personal insolvency are more far-reaching than the reduction of resources quantified under s 25(2)(a) of the Matrimonial Causes Act 1973. It is for this reason that the emphasis in this chapter is firmly placed on personal insolvency.

## PERSONAL INSOLVENCY

### Individual voluntary arrangements

**25.4**   Part VIII of the Insolvency Act 1986 contains the statutory provisions dealing with the law of individual voluntary arrangements ('IVAs'). Under an IVA a debtor enters into a composition in satisfaction of his debts or a scheme of arrangements of his affairs.[3] The debtor presents a proposal that is voted upon by his creditors for a nominee to act in relation to the voluntary arrangement, either as a trustee or otherwise, for the purpose of supervising the implementation of the proposal.[4] If the creditors vote in favour of the proposal, the effect of approval is that the IVA takes effect as if made by the debtor at the meeting of creditors, and it binds every person who in accordance with the Insolvency Rules was entitled to vote at the meeting (whether or not he was present or represented at it), or would have been so entitled if he had had notice of it as if he were party to the arrangement.[5] A meeting of creditors approving an IVA may be challenged on the ground of procedural irregularity, or on the basis that the arrangement unfairly prejudices the interests of a creditor.[6]

**25.5**   A debt in family proceedings is capable of ranking for a dividend in an IVA.[7] In *JP v A Debtor*[8] it was held that a wife with the benefit of a pre-existing lump sum order was unfairly prejudiced by an IVA voted for by her husband's creditors and was entitled to set aside her husband's IVA in the absence of agreement between herself and the other creditors.

**25.6**   Where ancillary relief proceedings post-date an IVA it will be essential to obtain a copy of the implemented arrangement to see what, if any, assets have been transferred to the supervisor of the scheme. Those assets will be impressed with a trust for the benefit of the creditors in accordance with the terms of the arrangement and will not generally be amenable to distribution in the ancillary relief proceedings. Subject to the terms of the scheme it may be that any excess realised after the sale of the debtor's assets and payment of his creditors will revert back into his personal estate. Such assets may therefore be a future resource of a debtor in ancillary relief proceedings.

---

[3]   Insolvency Act 1986, s 253(1).
[4]   IA 1986, s 253(2).
[5]   IA 1986, s 260(2).
[6]   IA 1986, s 262(1).
[7]   *Re Bradley-Hole (A Bankrupt)* [1995] 2 FLR 838.
[8]   [1999] 2 BCLC 571.

**25.7** Obviously, where a spouse is subject to an IVA, serious consideration will need to be given to whether to proceed with the ancillary relief or to issue and adjourn any claims made within the proceedings pending the termination of the IVA. It is submitted that if ancillary relief proceedings are progressed against a debtor spouse subject to an IVA a direction should be sought serving the supervisor with a copy of the Form A.

## Bankruptcy

**25.8** Part IX of the Insolvency Act 1986 deals with bankruptcy. A bankruptcy petition may be presented by, amongst others, a creditor of an individual or by the individual himself.[9] A creditor's petition may only be presented if certain conditions are satisfied, including that the amount of the debt exceeds the bankruptcy level of £750, that the debt or each of the debts is a debt which the debtor appears either unable to pay or to have no reasonable prospect of being able to pay,[10] and that there is no outstanding application to set aside a statutory demand served in respect of the debt or any of the debts.[11] A debtor's petition may only be presented on the grounds that the debtor is unable to pay his debts. The petition is required to be accompanied by a statement of the debtor's affairs.[12]

**25.9** The bankruptcy of an individual against whom a bankruptcy order has been made commences on the day on which the order is made and continues until the individual is discharged from bankruptcy.[13] In the majority of cases a bankrupt is discharged from bankruptcy at the end of the period of one year beginning with the date on which the bankruptcy commences.[14] Where a bankrupt is discharged, the discharge releases him from all bankruptcy debts, although creditors may still prove in the bankruptcy for any debt from which the bankrupt is released.[15] Discharge does not, except to such extent and on such conditions as the court may direct, release the bankrupt from any bankruptcy debt which arises under any order made in family proceedings or under a maintenance assessment made under the Child Support Act 1991. 'Family proceedings' means family proceedings within the meaning of the Magistrates' Courts Act 1980 and any proceedings which would be such proceedings but for s 65(1)(ii) of that Act (variation of periodical payments), and family proceedings within the meaning of Part V of the Matrimonial and Family Proceedings Act 1984.[16]

---

[9] IA 1986, s 264.
[10] IA 1986, s 268 provides definitions of when a debtor is unable to pay a debt or have no reasonable prospect of being able to pay a debt.
[11] IA 1986, s 267(2).
[12] IA 1986, s 273.
[13] IA 1986, s 278.
[14] IA 1986, s 279.
[15] IA 1986, s 281(1).
[16] IA 1986, s 281(5) and (8). Matrimonial causes and matters are included within the definition of family proceedings by Supreme Court Act 1981, Sch 1, para 3.

# ANNULMENT OF A BANKRUPTCY ORDER

**25.10**  The court has power to annul a bankruptcy order if at any time it appears to the court that, on any grounds existing at the time the order was made, the order ought not to have been made.[17] Annulment may therefore be ordered if at the date of the bankruptcy order the bankrupt was able to pay his debts. Once it is established that a debtor had the ability to pay, the court has discretion as to whether to annul the bankruptcy. The ability of a court to annul a bankruptcy order is not well known to the general public. A devious spouse may believe that he or she will be able to frustrate a claim for ancillary relief by presenting their own bankruptcy petition. In these circumstances deviousness can be accompanied by the presentation of a petition in a fraudulent manner where the petitioning debtor fails to disclose assets, including assets located abroad.[18] Sometimes there may be evidence to suggest that the petition was a sham, such as occurred in *Couvaras v Wolf*,[19] where the third-party petitioning creditor was unlikely to have been a creditor at all, but was working in league with the husband to defeat the ancillary relief proceedings. Whatever the background circumstances leading to the presentation of the petition, evidence is still required to establish that on the date of the order the bankrupt was able to pay his debts. No doubt the circumstances behind the presentation of the petition will be but one of the factors subsequently taken into account in the exercise of the discretion to annul the order. Other factors will include whether other bona fide creditors exist who could bankrupt the debtor. The court may also look at the extent to which the purportedly insolvent estate has been administered.[20]

**25.11**  In *Paulin v Paulin*[21] the Court of Appeal confirmed that the test for whether a bankrupt was able to pay his debts at the date of the order was not the balance sheet test of insolvency (assets exceeded by liabilities) but the test for commercial insolvency, namely whether the bankrupt could meet his liabilities as and when they fell due. Where the applicant for annulment establishes that there was no balance sheet insolvency, the evidential burden shifts to the debtor to establish that there was commercial insolvency. Furthermore, rebuttable presumptions may be drawn against a debtor who prevaricates and fails to give a considered, and indeed honest, account of his affairs. The Court of Appeal also noted that any suggestion that a sliding scale of the civil standard of proof applied on an annulment application was incorrect.[22]

---

[17]  IA 1986, s 282(1).
[18]  See the facts of *F v F (Divorce: Insolvency: Annulment of Bankruptcy Order)* [1994] 1 FLR 359, Thorpe J.
[19]  [2002] 2 FLR 107.
[20]  See also IA 1986, s 282(4).
[21]  [2009] EWCA Civ 221; see particularly [40]–[41] and [49] et seq.
[22]  In *F v F (Divorce: Insolvency: Annulment of Bankruptcy Order)* [1994] 1 FLR 359 it was stated per incuriam that a high standard of proof was required on the civil standard in order to reflect the gravity of the stain on the husband's integrity. The concept of a variable standard of

**25.12** From a procedural perspective the practice has evolved of transferring the application to annul from the Bankruptcy Court to the Family Division, which then hears the ancillary relief application at the same time.[23] The official receiver and the petitioning creditor (if not the debtor spouse) should be made parties to the application, as occurred in *Couvaras v Wolf*.[24]

## ANCILLARY RELIEF AGAINST A BANKRUPT SPOUSE

**25.13** Section 283 of the Insolvency Act 1986 defines a bankrupt's estate. In broad terms, the estate comprises all property belonging to or vested in the bankrupt at the commencement of the bankruptcy, with the exclusion of items necessary for the bankrupt in his employment, business or vocation and items necessary for satisfying the basic domestic needs of the bankrupt and his family. Subject to a notice being served by a trustee in bankruptcy under s 308A, certain leases are excluded from a bankrupt's estate. Property held by the bankrupt on trust for another person is excluded from his estate. 'Property' is defined in IA 1986, s 436 to include:

> 'money, goods, things in action, land and every description of property wherever situated and also obligations and every description of interest, whether present or future or vested or contingent, arising out of, or incidental to, property.'

**25.14** As a general proposition it used to be the case that a bankrupt's rights in respect of a pension vested in his trustee as part of the estate of the bankrupt. However, since the coming into force of s 11 of the Welfare Reform and Pensions Act 1999, approved pension arrangements are now excluded from a bankrupt's estate; approved arrangements are defined in s 11(2) of the Act. Additionally, s 12(1) of the 1999 Act provides that the Secretary of State may by regulations make provision for, or in connection with, enabling rights under unapproved arrangements being likewise excluded from a bankrupt's estate. The relevant regulations are the Occupational and Personal Pension Schemes (Bankruptcy) (No 2) Regulations 2002. Most pension schemes are unlikely now to fall within a bankrupt's estate. However, careful consideration will need to be given to determine what, if any, rights do pass to a bankrupt's trustee before consideration is given to the making of pension sharing and attachment orders. Caution is also necessary in any case where a party was declared bankrupt

---

proof depending on the seriousness of the allegation was rejected by the House of Lords in *Re B (Care Proceedings: Standard of Proof)* [2008] UKHL 35, [2008] 2 FLR 141. See **2.28–2.31**.

[23] See *Couvaras v Wolf* [2002] 2 FLR 107, *F v F (Divorce: Insolvency: Annulment of Bankruptcy Order)* [1994] 1 FLR 359, *Whig v Whig* [2008] 1 FLR 453 and *Paulin v Paulin* [2009] EWCA Civ 221. Note that in *F v F (Divorce: Insolvency: Annulment of Bankruptcy Order)* an application was made under s 285 of the Insolvency Act 1986 for permission to allow the wife's claims for ancillary relief to continue on terms. See also *F v F (S Intervening) (Financial Provision: Bankruptcy: Reviewable Disposition)* [2003] 1 FLR 911 at 928, where a husband's debtor's petition was stayed and his wife's application to annul the order adjourned to the conclusion of the ancillary relief hearing.

[24] [2002] 2 FLR 107.

before the provisions of the 1999 Act and the 2002 Regulations came into force because part or all of that party's pensions as at the date of the bankruptcy order may remain vested in the trustee in bankruptcy. Finally, in respect of pension rights and bankruptcies, any excessive pension contributions made that unfairly prejudice a bankrupt's creditors can potentially be recovered by a trustee in bankruptcy under provisions contained in s 342A(2) of the Insolvency Act 1986.

**25.15**   Section 285(1) of the Insolvency Act 1986 provides that at any time when proceedings on a bankruptcy petition are pending or an individual has been adjudged bankrupt, the court may stay any action, execution or other legal process against the property or person of the debtor or, as the case may be, the bankrupt. Furthermore, any court in which proceedings are pending against any individual may, on proof that a bankruptcy petition has been presented, either stay the proceedings or allow them to continue on such terms as it thinks fit.[25] Section 285(3) of the Act provides that, after making a bankruptcy order, no person who is a creditor of the bankrupt in respect of a debt provable in the bankruptcy shall have a remedy against the property or person of the bankrupt in respect of that debt nor, before the discharge of the bankrupt, commence any action or other legal proceedings against the bankrupt, except with the leave of the court and on such terms as the court may impose. It is submitted that as long as a meaningful order for ancillary relief is available, a court is unlikely to stay ancillary relief proceedings against a bankrupt spouse. It is submitted that at the FDA a direction should be obtained to serve a trustee in bankruptcy with a copy of the Form A and each party's Form E.

**25.16**   A bankrupt's estate vests in his trustee in bankruptcy for the ultimate benefit of his creditors.[26] Subject to a number of exclusions, the trustee in bankruptcy may by notice in writing claim for the bankrupt's estate any property that has been acquired by, or devolves upon, the bankrupt since the commencement of the bankruptcy. However, property acquired after discharge may not be claimed.[27]

**25.17**   In so far as income is concerned under s 310 of the Insolvency Act 1986, the court may make an income payments order claiming for the bankrupt's estate so much of the income of the bankrupt during the period for which the order is in force as may be specified in the order. The application can only be made by the trustee before the discharge of the bankrupt. The effect of an income payments order should not be to reduce the income of the bankrupt below what appears to the court to be necessary for meeting the reasonable domestic needs of the bankrupt and his family.[28]

---

[25]   IA 1986, s 285(2).
[26]   IA 1986, s 306. The estate vests initially in the Official Receiver before the appointment of the trustee.
[27]   IA 1986, s 307.
[28]   IA 1986, s 310(2).

**25.18** If a spouse is bankrupt and there is no prospect of the annulment of the bankruptcy order, consideration needs to be given to the range of potential orders available to the ancillary relief court. In so far as financial provision is concerned, the issue is relatively straightforward. There is no automatic bar to the making of an order for periodical payments. A periodical payments order may be made in respect of a bankrupt's income, although the sums available may be diminished by any income payments order obtained by the trustee. As Millett LJ stated in *Albert v Albert*:[29]

> 'The Family Division is concerned to ascertain the amount of the bankrupt's income and to decide how much of that income should be made available to maintain the wife and child. In making its determination it must ascertain the amount of the bankrupt's income, as best as it may, on the evidence put before it. But the amount of that income will be affected by any order that the Insolvency Court has made, or may subsequently make, which has the effect of diverting the bankrupt's income in or towards payment of his creditors. The Family Division is concerned with the division of the cake, but the size of the cake is liable to be diminished by any order made by the Insolvency Court'.

**25.19** Likewise, there is no automatic prohibition on the court making an order for the payment of a lump sum. In *Hellyer v Hellyer*[30] the husband was an undischarged bankrupt at the time of the final hearing. Despite this fact, an order was made requiring him to pay the wife a lump sum of £450,000. On appeal, Aldous LJ stated:

> 'It may seem odd to order a bankrupt to pay a sum of money within 14 days when it is known that he cannot comply with the order; but I have been convinced by the submissions of Mr Munby that there is no reason in principle as to why such an order should not be made by a judge exercising his jurisdiction under s 25 of the Matrimonial Causes Act. The fact that the bankrupt cannot pay at that time is irrelevant. However, such an order should only be made when the judge has a clear picture of the assets and liabilities of the bankrupt and the expenses of the bankruptcy. It is only then he can decide that in the foreseeable future there will be assets to pay the sum ordered. That of course only applies to a money order. Nothing in the Insolvency Act or the rules suggests that such an order should not be made. I can see nothing wrong in principle in the judge making the type of order that he did.'

**25.20** As we have seen, upon the making of a bankruptcy order the bankrupt's property ultimately vests in his trustee in bankruptcy. A property adjustment order can only be made against a party to the marriage[31] and in respect of property in which the party has an interest either in possession or reversion.[32] As a consequence of the vesting provisions in respect of a bankrupt's estate, such property falling within the estate is not property to which the bankrupt spouse has an interest in either possession or reversion and cannot be the subject of a property adjustment order. As we have seen,

---

[29]   [1997] 2 FLR 791 at 794.
[30]   [1996] 2 FLR 579, CA.
[31]   Thereby excluding a property adjustment order against a trustee in bankruptcy.
[32]   Matrimonial Causes Act 1973, s 24(1)(a).

however, pension rights are unlikely to fall within a bankrupt's estate, leaving pension sharing and attachment as potentially available options for the ancillary relief court.

## BANKRUPTCY AND THE MATRIMONIAL HOME

**25.21**   Under s 283A of the Insolvency Act 1986, if the bankrupt had an interest in the former matrimonial home at the end of 3 years from the date of the bankruptcy, the interest of the bankrupt in the former matrimonial home shall cease to be comprised in the bankrupt's estate and re-vests in the bankrupt. This provision will not apply if during the 3-year period the trustee realises the bankrupt's interest or applies for an order for possession and or sale. However, if the trustee's application is dismissed, the interest shall cease to be comprised in the bankrupt's estate and vests by operation of law in the bankrupt.[33]

**25.22**   Where property is owned beneficially by joint tenants, a bankruptcy order against one of the joint tenants automatically severs the joint tenancy[34] and the bankrupt's interest passes to his trustee in bankruptcy. In the usual course the trustee will apply for an order for sale. A trustee applies for an order for sale under s 14 of the Trusts of Land and Appointment of Trustees Act 1996.[35] On such an application the provisions of s 335A of the Insolvency Act 1986 apply. Section 335A provides that on such an application the court shall make such order as it thinks just and reasonable having regard to the interests of the bankrupt's creditors, the conduct of the spouse so far as it contributed to the bankruptcy, the financial needs and resources of the spouse, the needs of any children and all circumstances of the case other than the needs of the bankrupt. However, s 335A(3) provides that where an application for sale is made after the end of the period of one year beginning with the first vesting of the bankrupt's estate in his trustee, the court shall assume, unless the circumstances of the case are exceptional,[36] that the interests of the bankrupt's creditors outweigh all other considerations. The statutory considerations one year after the vesting in the trustee are therefore heavily slanted in favour of a sale.

**25.23**   It is considered that the operation of s 335A is more a matter of insolvency law than ancillary relief and is therefore outside the parameters of this book. The same may be said about the *Avis v Turner* litigation; nevertheless, brief comment will be made. In *Avis v Turner*[37] the appeal raised a question as to the powers of the court on an application by a trustee in

---

[33]   IA 1986, s 283A(3)–(4).
[34]   *Re Pavlou* [1993] 2 FLR 751.
[35]   The trustee in bankruptcy is also entitled to seek adjustments for occupation rent by way of equitable accounting, even if the bankrupt spouse remains in occupation of the property *Byford v Butler* [2004] 1 FLR 56.
[36]   See *Re Haghighat (A Bankrupt)* [2009] 1 FLR 1271.
[37]   [2008] 1 FLR 1127, CA.

bankruptcy for an order for the sale of a former matrimonial home in which the bankrupt had an interest in circumstances where there was an existing order, made in matrimonial proceedings between the bankrupt and his former wife, that sale be postponed until the happening of specified events which had not yet occurred. In short, the husband and wife agreed a property adjustment order by consent. The order provided for the former matrimonial home to be held on trust, with the wife entitled to two-thirds of the proceeds of the property and the husband one-third. The consent order provided for sale upon the happening of a number of trigger events, none of which had occurred at the time of the trustee's application. Subsequent to the consent order, the husband was made bankrupt and his one-third interest vested in the trustee. The Court of Appeal held that, despite the terms of the consent order, the trustee in bankruptcy was entitled to apply to the court for an order for sale under s 335A of the Insolvency Act.

**25.24** In *Turner v Avis & Avis*[38] the trustee made his application to the Chancery Division for an order for sale of the property in order to realise his interest in the proceeds of sale. The trustee was granted an order for possession and sale. It was held that the terms of the consent order were common in matrimonial proceedings and did not constitute an exceptional circumstance. In some modest asset cases it may not be possible to avoid the risk of a similar outcome. Nevertheless, practitioners need to be aware of the risk when negotiating any settlements and advocating preferred orders at final hearing.

# ANCILLARY RELIEF AFTER PRESENTATION OF BANKRUPTCY PETITION BUT BEFORE BANKRUPTCY ORDER

**25.25** Section 284(1) of the Insolvency Act 1986 provides that where a person is adjudged bankrupt, any dispositions of property made by that person in the period to which the section applies is void except to the extent that it is or was made with the consent of the court or is or was subsequently ratified by the court. The section applies not only to a disposition of property but also to a payment, whether in cash or otherwise, and where any such payment is void, the person paid holds the sum paid for the bankrupt as part of his estate.[39] The period in question begins with the day of presentation of the petition for the bankruptcy order and ends with the vesting of the bankrupt's estate in his trustee.[40] No remedy exists against a bona fide purchaser without knowledge of the presentation of the petition.[41]

**25.26** There is clearly the potential for a collision between s 284 and ancillary relief proceedings in circumstances where an order for ancillary relief was

---

[38] [2009] 1 FLR 74.
[39] IA 1986, s 284(2).
[40] IA 1986, s 284(3).
[41] IA 1986, s 284(4). See also other saving provisions under s 284(5)–(6).

obtained in the period between the presentation of the bankruptcy petition and the making of a bankruptcy order. In *Re Flint*[42] a bankruptcy petition was presented against the husband prior to the court making a property adjustment order by consent in respect of the husband's interest in the former matrimonial home. It was held that the property adjustment order, whether or not made by consent, required the husband to transfer his estate and interest in the former matrimonial home. On the basis of the equitable principle of taking as being done that which ought to be done, the husband's equitable interest passed immediately to the wife upon the operation of the court order in the ancillary relief proceedings. In the circumstances, there had been a disposition of property by the bankrupt in the period between the presentation of the petition and the vesting of his estate in his trustee, and the disposition was therefore void. Moreover, on the facts of the case, the transfer would not be ratified by the court.[43]

**25.27** In *Treharne & Sand v Forrester*[44] it was argued that, since the property adjustment order was imposed on the spouse against whom the bankruptcy petition had been served and was not made by consent, there had not been a disposition subject to the provisions of s 284 of the Insolvency Act. This argument was rejected. The disposition was made by the spouse against whom the bankruptcy petition had been served on the basis that equity took as being done that which ought to be done. Lindsay J did not rule out ratification, at least to the extent to which the non-bankrupt spouse had incurred costs seeking to find the husband's assets and so far as possible to prevent their disposition, since such expenditure would have reduced the trustee's costs. However, as a general proposition, subject to ratification or approval by the court, a property adjustment order made in the period between the presentation of the petition and the vesting of the bankrupt's estate in his trustee will be void, whether made by consent or otherwise.

**25.28** Similarly, the Court of Appeal in *Mountney v Treharne*[45] held that the effect of a property adjustment order was to confer an equitable interest in property from the date of decree absolute. The recipient of a property adjustment order was analogous to a purchaser in a specifically enforceable contract for sale. Where a property adjustment order is made, provided that decree absolute is obtained prior to the presentation of a bankruptcy petition, the trustee in bankruptcy will take subject to the equitable interest of the recipient of the property adjustment order, irrespective of whether any

---

[42] [1993] 1 FLR 763, Nicholas Stewart QC sitting as a deputy judge of the High Court in the Chancery Division.

[43] In the normal course it is for the Bankruptcy Court to ratify the disposition.

[44] [2004] 1 FLR 1173 Ch D, Lindsay J.

[45] [2002] 2 FLR 930. See [77] where Parker LJ approved the legal analysis in *Re Flint* [1993] 1 FLR 763. It is worth noting that the 2005 rules reversed the law on matrimonial orders being provable in bankruptcy, and earlier authorities on this issue need to be read with this change in mind.

property has been transferred at law pursuant to the court order. Parties to ancillary relief proceedings should therefore avoid any unnecessary delays in obtaining decree absolute.

**25.29** As a consequence of s 284(2) of the Insolvency Act 1986, the payment of a lump sum pursuant to an order for ancillary relief between presentation of petition and the order for bankruptcy will be void unless ratified. However, under s 284(4) there will be no remedy against the recipient of the lump sum payment (who holds the void payment on trust for the bankrupt's estate) if payment is received before the bankruptcy order is made, the payment was in good faith, for value and without notice of the bankruptcy petition. Such a defence is therefore unlikely to be available in the context of an order made in matrimonial proceedings, where the existence of a bankruptcy petition ought to be disclosed. A similar analysis applies to an order for periodical payments.

**25.30** Under s 310(2) of the Insolvency Act 1986 a court should not make an income payments order the effect of which would be to reduce the income of the bankrupt below what appears to the court necessary for meeting the reasonable domestic needs of the bankrupt and his family. There is, therefore, an argument to be made in respect of any periodical payments ordered to be paid in ancillary relief proceedings, that ratification ought to be ordered by analogy to the application of s 310(2) of the Insolvency Act. To the extent that a lump sum is required to meet reasonable domestic needs, there is also a similar argument to be made in respect of ratification of any such disposition between presentation of the bankruptcy petition and the vesting of the estate in the trustee.[46]

## BANKRUPTCY ORDER ON BANKRUPTCY PETITION PRESENTED SUBSEQUENT TO ORDER FOR ANCILLARY RELIEF

**25.31** Where a bankruptcy petition is presented after an order in ancillary relief proceedings and bankruptcy follows, it is necessary to consider the impact of the bankruptcy order on the order for ancillary relief. An order for a lump sum and costs in ancillary relief proceedings are both provable debts.[47] They cannot be enforced outside of the bankruptcy. An order for periodical payments is not provable in the bankruptcy, and any claim for arrears can be enforced in the usual way. Furthermore, the ability to continue to receive periodical payments will be unaffected, save in so far as affected by an income payments order. On decree absolute the recipient of a property adjustment order obtains an equitable and enforceable interest in the property to be transferred. Finally, in respect of bankruptcy following an order for ancillary relief, we have seen that discharge of the bankruptcy does not bring to an end the obligation to comply with an order made in ancillary relief proceedings.

---

[46] See *Re G (Children Act 1989, Schedule 1)* [1996] 2 FLR 171.
[47] Insolvency (Amendment) Rules 2005.

**25.32**   Until the judgment in the Court of Appeal case of *Hill v Haines*,[48] it had been thought that a property adjustment order in ancillary relief proceedings which pre-dated bankruptcy was particularly vulnerable to challenge under the law relating to transactions at an undervalue. Section 339 of the Insolvency Act 1986 provides that where an individual is made bankrupt and he has at a relevant time (in the period of 5 years ending with the date of presentation of the petition) entered into a transaction with any person at an undervalue, the trustee of the bankrupt's estate may apply to the court for such order as the court thinks fit for restoring the position to what it would have been if that individual had not entered into that transaction. An individual enters into a transaction at an undervalue if he makes a gift to that person or he otherwise enters into a transaction with that person on terms that provide for him to receive no consideration, or he enters into a transaction with that person for a consideration the value of which, in money or money's worth, is significantly less than the value, in money or money's worth, of the consideration provided by the individual.[49]

**25.33**   In *Hill v Haines* the Court of Appeal held that parties to an order of the court granting some form of ancillary relief did give 'consideration' for the purposes of s 339(3)(a) of the Insolvency Act. Thereafter the court moved to determine whether consideration was given in money or money's worth. The Chancellor concluded that:

> 'If one considers the economic realities, the order of the court quantifies the value of the applicant spouse's statutory right by reference to the value of the money or property thereby ordered to be paid or transferred by the respondent spouse to the applicant. In the case of such an order, whether following contested proceedings or by way of compromise, in the absence of the usual vitiating factors of fraud, mistake or misrepresentation the one balances the other. But if any such factor is established by a trustee in bankruptcy on an application under s 339 then it will be apparent that the prima facie balance was not the true one and the transaction may be liable to be set aside.'[50]

**25.34**   The circumstances in which a challenge can now be made to an order in ancillary relief proceedings on the basis that the transaction was at an undervalue have therefore been heavily circumscribed. In *Re Jones (A Bankrupt); Ball v Jones*[51] an application by a trustee in bankruptcy was made to set aside a transaction as being at an undervalue. In that case the husband and wife entered into a consent order whereby the wife transferred the vast majority of the assets to the husband. The husband had been unwell but was to be the primary carer of the three children of the family. After the consent order was approved, it came to light that the wife had been advised not to enter into the order and that she had probably been insolvent at the time of the order. The trustee sought to set aside on the basis that there had been collusion between

---

[48]   [2008] 1 FLR 1192.
[49]   IA 1986, s 339(3).
[50]   [2008] 1 FLR 1192 at [35] per Morritt C.
[51]   [2008] 2 FLR 1969, Chief Registrar Baister, who also held that the transaction was not liable to be set aside as a preference.

the husband and the wife. The application was dismissed. The suggestion by Rix LJ in *Hill v Haines*[52] that an order could be set aside as a transaction at an undervalue where there had been collusion or dishonesty required the establishment of an agreement whereby the parties specifically colluded to defeat the interests of creditors by putting assets beyond the reach of the trustee in bankruptcy. The fact that assets were put beyond the reach of the creditors as a collateral consequence of the order was insufficient. On the facts of the case, neither the court nor the husband had been misled into making the consent order: indeed, the court knew of the existence of creditors when approving the order. None of the vitiating factors applied and the application by the trustee was dismissed.

---

[52] [2008] 1 FLR 1192.

# Chapter 26

# ASSET VALUATION DURING TIMES OF ECONOMIC INSTABILITY

**26.1** This chapter considers the particular difficulties of valuing assets in uncertain economic circumstances. There are two principal issues to consider. First, the extent to which the court needs to accept a clear value for any particular asset before carrying out its discretionary exercise under s 25 of the Matrimonial Causes Act 1973. Second, and intertwined with the first issue, consideration will be required to be given to whether the value of an asset needs to be fixed on a certain date. Thereafter, the later sections of this chapter deal with some of the most commonly encountered species of assets and the particular valuation issues which can arise with each.

## WHAT VALUE SHOULD APPEAR ON THE SCHEDULE OF ASSETS?

**26.2** It has become conventional for the parties to prepare schedules of the assets in a case. Sometimes they even manage to agree the schedule for the use of the court. Judges are now encouraged to summarise the effect of their order in tabular form, indicating the overall net effect of the division proposed.[1]

**26.3** The schedule of assets provides a 'snapshot' view of the parties' assets at the date it was prepared. Of course, it is never a perfect representation of the parties' assets at that date. Many of the assets will have been valued weeks or even months earlier. Their values will inevitably have altered since the last valuation. In normal circumstances such expected variations will not have a significant impact on the overall outcome of the case. In recent years it has been common for the parties and the courts to work from such a balance sheet of the assets and to divide up the assets based on the values shown there. Such an approach is unlikely to cause significant difficulties or unfairness in stable market conditions.

**26.4** In times of market volatility any 'snapshot' view of the parties assets can prove to be entirely arbitrary because asset values can fluctuate wildly from one

---

[1] Such a discipline being encouraged in the light of *Vaughan v Vaughan* [2008] 1 FLR 1108 and *Behzadi v Behzadi* [2008] EWCA Civ 1070, where the Court of Appeal criticised the trial judge for failing to include such a 'balance sheet' in his judgment and encouraged judges to hand down such a schedule of assets even where their judgment is given ex tempore.

day to the next. A strict attempt to fix values at a certain date can fix the parties' respective wealth in a very unfair way. Examples of this are as follows.

**26.5** Any substantial holding of shares or other freely traded financial instruments or commodities will be affected by the movements of the market. In volatile markets such movements can be large and sudden. For example, shares in banking groups slid downwards, albeit relatively steadily during the latter part of 2007 and through much of 2008. After October 2008 those share prices began to move with much greater daily uncertainty. Shares in Barclays plc were traded at prices ranging between 47.3 pence per share and 190.6 pence per share in the span of only 9 days during January 2009. They subsequently recovered to over 280 pence per share by early May 2009, an increase of some 592% from the market low in the space of only 4 months. Clearly a 'snapshot' view of the value of a substantial holding of Barclays shares on any particular day, especially during January 2009, had the potential to be very misleading.

**26.6** Whenever assets which have their investment basis in stocks and shares are held by the parties, their values will likewise be seriously affected by such movements in the markets. The most up-to-date fund values for pensions, endowments or other fund based investments may prove to be equally misleading.

**26.7** Where a private business has been valued for the proceedings, assumptions will have been made about the trading prospects of that business for the purposes of the valuation. Usually the estimate of future earnings will be based on the previous trading history. Serious changes in the economy can entirely undermine the basis of such a valuation. Likewise, market conditions will affect the choice of a multiplier or P/E ratio used for valuing a business because of reduced activity by purchasers of businesses.[2] Similarly, problems in securing bank funding can undermine an otherwise viable business, causing cash-flow difficulties which prove to be fatal for the business despite having full order books and an otherwise healthy balance sheet. Reliance on any valuations prepared before such changes have occurred will be misleading. On the other hand, a valuation prepared during economic uncertainty may adopt an unduly pessimistic attitude to the business and therefore grossly underestimate its true value moving into the future. A valuation prepared in the midst of such an uncertain economic situation is also likely to contain a great deal of guesswork on the part of the valuer.

**26.8** Values of real property become particularly difficult to predict in a downturn. If the property is to be sold there is little real problem: it will find its own value once on the market, although a sale may take longer to achieve. Where a value is required for the property because a party intends to retain it the position is much more difficult. The number of transactions which can be used as comparables for valuation purposes tend to reduce as buyers are

---

[2]   These concepts are explained at **11.203** et seq and at **26.32–26.42**.

deterred from taking on new mortgages because of their own financial worries or problems in securing loans. Many prospective buyers in a falling market will choose to bide their time to see how far the market will fall before buying a property. Any valuer will find it difficult to place a reliable value on a property in such circumstances. The parties will also find it difficult to assess when the value will cease to fall.

**26.9** These are only some of the examples of problems in forming a 'snapshot' view of the assets which are to be divided. Any formulaic approach which attempts to draw up a schedule of the assets as at the date of the hearing and divide them up in percentage terms carries a heavy risk of unfairness to one or both of the parties. Is the court required to deal with the assets in this way? The authorities discussed in the following paragraphs indicate that the court should adopt the valuations of assets as at the date of the final hearing but, in assessing the final award, a flexible approach must be taken and the potential future value of those assets must be considered, as must the reasons for the value being at that particular level at that time.[3]

**26.10** It is clear that s 25 of the Matrimonial Causes Act 1973 requires the court to form an assessment of 'the income, earning capacity, property and financial resources which each of the parties to the marriage has or is likely to have in the foreseeable future ...'. Indeed, it seems obvious that any resolution of a married couple's financial affairs requires a clear assessment and understanding of those affairs. In *Charman v Charman (No 4)*[4] the Court of Appeal suggested that s 25(2)(a) in essence sets the first stage of the court's process, namely 'computation'. The remaining parts of s 25 essentially guide the secondary stage of the process, namely 'distribution'. Logically, computation must come before distribution. The Court of Appeal indicated that the consideration to be given to the s 25(2)(a) matters should be carried out 'with whatever degree of detail is apt to the case'. Accordingly, the court is invited to approach this assessment of the parties' financial resources in a flexible and proportionate way.

**26.11** Having identified this primary task of the court in every ancillary relief case, the Court of Appeal in *Charman v Charman (No 4)* did not provide guidance as to the date upon which the parties' financial resources were to be calculated. The language of s 25(2)(a) strongly implies that the assessment should be at the date of the hearing at which the matter is being considered. This analysis is confirmed by the words of Thorpe LJ in *Cowan v Cowan*:[5]

---

[3] For example, has there been a particular contribution made by one party since separation or has one party deliberately sought to reduce the value? Furthermore, external economic factors may have affected the value of the asset.

[4] [2007] 1 FLR 1246 at [67].

[5] [2001] 2 FLR 192 at [70]. See also *Rossi v Rossi* [2007] 1 FLR 790 at [24.1].

'The assessment of assets must be at the date of trial or appeal. The language of the statute requires that. Exceptions to that rule are rare and probably confined to cases where one party has deliberately or recklessly wasted assets in anticipation of trial.'

**26.12**  Does this mean that the court must work on the basis of the values of the assets as they are at the date of the hearing, even if that value is artificially inflated or deflated by some transient external factor? The answer appears to be 'no'. Characteristically, the family courts reject such a strict or overly technical approach in favour of a more flexible one which pursues overall fairness and a realistic approach to the situation.[6] In *S v S (Ancillary Relief After Lengthy Separation)*[7] Singer J rejected an argument that the court should value the assets as at the date of separation rather than at the hearing date and held that the court 'should look at the disposition of available assets and (so far as practicable) at their value actual *or potential* as at the hearing date'[8] (emphasis added). The learned judge went on to consider the authorities and then decided that:

'the pattern and (so far as ascertainable) the value of relevant assets are to be considered at the date of the hearing rather than of the separation of the parties, without it necessarily being the case that each party is entitled to an equivalent share of the value of each category of asset by reference to values at the hearing date'.[9]

**26.13**  In *H v H*,[10] in the context of assessing where the boundary line lay between matrimonial and non-matrimonial property Charles J explained the importance of a flexible approach based on a broad assessment in each case:

'In the application of the statutory test under the MCA which looks to past events and to the future it is inevitable that the court will have regard to current values at the time it makes its award. This does not mean that such a value would identify the value of the matrimonial property to which the yardstick of equality applies with force. Further, as in *Miller*, that yardstick may not be a fair one to apply whichever date is taken for the identification and valuation of the matrimonial property.

If those assets include one that can change in value the reasons for any increase or decrease in value over a relevant period would be a factor to be taken into account. For example, the value of a property, or the shares in a public or a private company, could go up or down for a great variety of reasons and it seems to me to run counter to the objective of the MCA, its terms and the guidance of the House of Lords to seek to set tests, or formulae, as to how these changes should be taken into account in a given case (see for example Baroness Hale of Richmond at para [158] of her speech in *Miller and McFarlane*).'

---

[6]  'Fairness has a broad horizon' per Lord Nicholls of Birkenhead in *Miller v Miller; McFarlane v McFarlane* [2006] 1 FLR 1186 at [26].

[7]  [2007] 1 FLR 2120.

[8]  [2007] 1 FLR 2120 at [87].

[9]  [2007] 1 FLR 2120 at [107].

[10]  [2007] 2 FLR 548 at [54]–[55].

**26.14**   Although the dicta in *S v S* and in *H v H* were in the specific context of whether assets earned by a party after separation or whose value increased significantly in the period after the parties' separation should be shared between the parties, the stated need to look at the potential value of an asset and the reasons for why a particular asset has risen or fallen in value is, the authors submit, of great importance in the court's overall exercise of discretion. Section 25(2)(a) does not confine the court's considerations to the assets as they are at the date of the hearing but also to those a party 'is likely to have in the foreseeable future'. This is a statutory requirement to be forward-looking. It requires the court to consider what the value of assets may be in the future as well as at the present. The court is likely to take the broad long view rather than the narrow short-term view in most cases. So the court can consider whether the current value of the assets is depressed by some short-term trend or factor rather than by some fundamental problem with the quality of the asset.

**26.15**   Where the value of an asset at the time of the hearing is unusually low or high for reasons which are transient and very likely to change in the foreseeable future, the court can be encouraged to divide the assets with a view to the likely future value of that asset. This may justify a departure from otherwise equal sharing of the assets. Of course, such assessments of future prospects are very difficult and fraught with potential danger and unfairness. The court cannot predict the future with certainty.[11] It is, in most cases, difficult to provide the court with good quality evidence of how an asset may perform.[12] The court should not embark on speculation about the future. However, where there are firm grounds for making assumptions about the future value of an asset, the court is, it is submitted, entitled to make such assumptions. The risks in making such assumptions must be taken into account and, where an alternative approach is available which allows the risk to be shared, it seems that this will be preferred. In many cases fairness will dictate a *Wells v Wells* sharing of the 'copper-bottomed versus risk-laden assets'.[13]

**26.16**   Any such assumptions about asset values bouncing back to higher levels must be kept within clear limits and not allowed to become a process of trying to value assets into the future which could 'signal a descent into forensic chaos'.[14] It is only in cases where there is clear evidence of a very likely and reasonably quantifiable increase (or decrease) in the value of an asset in the foreseeable future that such an approach is likely to be considered fair. In *CR v CR*[15] Bodey J rejected the wife's attempt to place a premium on the valuation of the husband's shareholding in a company based on expert evidence of the prospect of better than average investment returns on those shares. The evidence suggested that the investments were not a 'one way bet' and could go

---

[11]   And neither can the parties. *Myerson v Myerson* [2009] EWCA Civ 282 (considered in detail below) is a salutary lesson in what can happen where a party makes assumptions about how certain assets may perform in the future.

[12]   At least, not without incurring very significant costs in relation to expert evidence.

[13]   Considered in more detail at **27.26–27.28** and **11.98**.

[14]   Per Bodey J in *CR v CR* [2008] 1 FLR 323 at [30].

[15]   [2008] 1 FLR 323.

down as well as up, so such a premium would be based on speculation. Nevertheless, the learned judge accepted that a proven likelihood of increased values in the shares might be a resource likely to be available in the foreseeable future.[16] When the evidence on this point was considered, the court was satisfied that the shares would probably rise in value but it could not quantify in any clear way the amount by which their value might increase.[17] The learned judge decided that if the wife were to have a claim over those future increases in value, that could only fairly be achieved by a *Wells v Wells* sharing because of the court's inability to quantify what the future value might be.[18] However, on the facts of that case a *Wells v Wells* sharing was undesirable for various reasons. Instead, the court preferred to adopt the current value for the shares and give the wife a further share in the other assets equivalent to 50% of the value of the shares:

> 'The current value of the shares will be divided equally (conceptually, not literally) between the parties as part of the overall division of their resources. This is because the shares go to make up the overall kitty. Whilst it is true that the wife's contributions to the welfare of the family helped place the husband in a position to acquire the shares, the proposed asset division will give her the same proportion of them (conceptually, not literally) as him. She may, for all one knows, take away her half share of the resources and deal with them successfully to produce increasing wealth of a presently unquantifiable amount, just as the husband's shares are likely (as found) to increase in value. Take, for example, the matrimonial home, which the wife is to keep. It may be that it will increase in value more dramatically (given London property prices) than, e g the husband's properties in Dubai and Cape Town, which anyway have much lower current base values. How might such a factor as that be brought into account, if the wife succeeded on her claim to a share in any future increase in the value of the husband's shares? It is difficult to see that it could be, except by tying the parties together for the future in a manner (e g by some formula) which would be complicated, disproportionate and unacceptable.
>
> In short, a line has to be drawn in terms of the current capital, with the parties being enabled as far as possible and fair to get on with their lives (financially and generally) independent of ongoing ties. I therefore reject the wife's arguments for a share in the likely future enhanced value of the husband's shares in the group.'[19]

## REAL PROPERTY VALUATIONS

**26.17**  The valuation of real estate is seldom a very precise or accurate science. Valuers rely on their experience of other property transactions in an effort to assess the value of a property. However, the situation and circumstances of two properties are rarely identical. Neither are the circumstances and motivations of any two particular sets of purchasers and vendors. Overarching all these

---

[16]    [2008] 1 FLR 323 at [31].
[17]    [2008] 1 FLR 323 at [68].
[18]    [2008] 1 FLR 323 at [89].
[19]    [2008] 1 FLR 323 at [90]–[91].

particular variations between transactions is the overall effect of market sentiment. At times of economic prosperity and ready supply of mortgage finance a bubble of rapidly rising property prices can be formed on the back of the enthusiasm of buyers to move up the property ladder before prices rise yet further. At times of economic downturn and uncertainty the process is reversed. Buyers hold back from moving into the market in the expectation that prices will fall yet further in due course.

**26.18** Where properties are to be retained by the parties, the values of those properties need to be established for the court to form a view as to the overall financial effect of the asset division being proposed. If a property is to be sold by the parties, many of the problems and uncertainties of valuation may be less acute. The property will find its own value once on the market. If it has not been sold by the time of the final hearing, the order can provide for a division of the proceeds of sale in proportionate terms.

**26.19** However, whenever the sale of the property occurs, the parties will still need to determine when an offer for the property should be accepted. The parties to ancillary relief proceedings often have different and conflicting agendas. One may be keen to see a sale of the property as soon as possible owing to the burden of servicing the mortgage falling principally on him or her. The other may be reluctant to see a sale too soon for a low price because of consequent problems on him or her being able to rehouse. In such circumstances the court may well be required to determine the fair market value of the property in the absence of agreement by the parties.

**26.20** In times of economic uncertainty particular care needs to be given to valuation evidence. Simple market appraisals by estate agents may vary very substantially due to numerous factors. Where a dispute as to valuation of a property arises it will usually be better for the parties to pay for a full valuation report on the property rather than a mere market appraisal, so long as the value of the property makes the costs of such a report proportionate. When considering such a report the focus should be on:

- Details of the comparative transactions which the valuer has relied upon. How similar are the properties? How recent was the transaction? How long were those properties on the market before sale? Is anything known about the circumstances of the vendors and purchasers in those transactions (ie is there anything to suggest that either party was under greater pressure to complete the transaction than the norm)?

- Any statistics the valuer has relied upon. If he or she has used an index of property prices, which one? How up to date is it (ie the date of the transactions used to compile the index rather than the index itself)? How specific was the index? Was it a national index or a regional index? Was it the index for property transactions for similar properties (ie semi-detached, detached, flat, new build etc) or more general?

- Assumptions the valuer may have made about the state of the market since the last index he has relied upon, ie steady prices, upward or downward trend.

Much of the information required to challenge a valuation report is now readily available on the internet.[20]

**26.21**  As discussed above, a court may be persuaded that it should take a longer-term view of the value of a property, recognising that where property is likely to be retained for a number of years there is likely to be a reasonable investment return on that asset, albeit that the level of that return cannot be assessed with precision. Such a broad brush, long view of an asset's worth to some extent obviates the need for the court to establish a precise valuation figure for it. The extent to which such an approach is fair will depend on the circumstances of the case and the relative importance of the property in the context of the assets as a whole. It should not be forgotten that in a case where the other party is leaving the marriage with a significant share of liquid capital, those funds can be reinvested in property which ought, in theory, to provide a similar investment return to the property retained by the other party.[21]

**26.22**  As with any case where the future value of an asset assumes central importance in a case, sharing the risk and benefit of that property by way of retained joint ownership or a charge in favour of one party may well prove to be the fairest outcome.

## BUSINESS VALUATIONS

**26.23**  The valuation of a business is a somewhat uncertain process at the best of times. The difficulties which arise are discussed in more detail in Chapters 11, 12 and 13. The futility of attempting to ascertain the exact value of a business has been recognised in a number of decisions in the recent past.[22] During a recession there are two key issues that a family lawyer should consider when addressing matrimonial assets that include business assets:

- the increased risk that the business is no longer a going concern and may be insolvent; and

- the volatility of business asset valuations during a period of economic uncertainty.

---

[20]  For example, house price indices are published by the large mortgage lending institutions (eg Halifax plc, now subsumed within the Lloyds Banking Group, Nationwide Building Society). Sale prices are recorded at HM Land Registry and can also be accessed through property websites such as rightmove.co.uk (although such records of transactions are usually only up to date to within a few months before the search date).

[21]  See *CR v CR* at **26.16**.

[22]  For example, *A v A* [2006] 2 FLR 115, *D v D & B Ltd* [2007] 2 FLR 653 and *H v H* [2008] EWHC 935 (Fam).

# Increased risk of insolvency

**26.24** It is worth dwelling briefly on what is meant by insolvency in the corporate sense.[23] The question of a company's inability to pay its debts may be determined by the court as a matter of fact or settled by the application of a number of presumptions, four of which[24] turn purely on the evidence, while the fifth[25] involves a judicial assessment of the position.

**26.25** There are, broadly speaking, two tests of solvency:

- first, the company must be able to pay its debts as they become due (this may be referred to as the 'cash flow test'); or

- secondly, the value of the company's assets must be greater than the value of its liabilities, taking into account its contingent and prospective liabilities (this may be referred to as the 'balance sheet test').

**26.26** The cash flow test involves a more forward-looking assessment in the sense that debts must be considered as they become due. This was emphasised by Briggs J in *Cheyne Finance plc (in receivership)*,[26] when he used the following illustrative example:

> '[A] company has £1,000 ready cash and a very valuable but very illiquid asset worth £250,000 which cannot be sold for 2 years. It has present debts of £500, but a future debt of £100,000 due in 6 months. On any commercial view the company clearly cannot pay its debts as they fall due, but it is, or would be, balance sheet solvent.'

Cheyne was a structured investment vehicle ('SIV'). It was one of the first SIVs to go into receivership as a result of the credit crunch. The receivers sought the court's directions as they had to identify whether an 'insolvency event', which was defined by reference to the cash flow test, had occurred. Section 123(1)(e) of the Insolvency Act 1986 provides that a company is deemed unable to pay its debts 'if it is proved to the satisfaction of the court that the company is unable to pay its debts as they fall due'.

**26.27** The wider implications of the *Cheyne* decision, which is the first time the court has considered this section, are that technical insolvency may be triggered earlier in some cases than might have been expected. This decision seems especially relevant during the current credit crunch when companies may have positive net assets but insufficient liquidity.

**26.28** In other words, if the company can continue to pay its present debts, but it cannot pay a known future debt, it is insolvent. So, let us consider a

---

[23] Personal insolvency is considered more broadly in Chapter 25.
[24] Insolvency Act 1986, s 123(1)(a)–(d).
[25] Insolvency Act 1986, s 123(1)(e).
[26] [2007] EWHC 2402 (Ch).

company with positive net assets but limited cash, say £100,000, which it is consuming at a rate of £50,000 per month. In one month's time it has to pay a wages bill of £60,000. Provided that on the balance of probability it will continue to spend its cash at £50,000 per month, it is insolvent now, not simply in a month's time when it no longer has the cash to pay its present debts.

**26.29** The balance sheet test is a combination of a historic and a current assessment. Any directors considering whether a company's assets are greater than its liabilities should have regard to the most recent accounts of the company and all other circumstances which they know or ought to know affect (or may affect) the value of the company's assets and liabilities. The directors may rely on valuations of assets or estimates of liabilities that are reasonable in the circumstances.

**26.30** If a family law practitioner has concerns that a business might be on the brink of insolvency and wishes to investigate further, the following documents or sources of information may assist:

- the latest management accounts – statutory accounts are often out of date by the time they are produced;

- information on all companies within a group – statutory accounts for a parent company may not consolidate the profits or losses of its subsidiaries;

- details of any new loans or extended overdraft facilities and correspondence with the company's bank;

- existence of county court judgments against the business;

- details of any resignations, redundancies or restructuring of the business;

- details of sales of divisions of the business;

- details of sales of major fixed assets;

- current budgets and business plans; and

- minutes of board meetings, if available.

**26.31** Indicators that a company's financial health is deteriorating include:

- falling turnover (after adjusting for seasonality);

- falling like-for-like sales (particularly for retailers with multiple outlets);

- loss of key customer(s) and/or contract(s);

- worsening cash position, perhaps evidenced by the use of debt factoring or invoice discounting or an increase in creditor days (ie the company is taking longer, on average, to pay it debts);

- falling staff numbers and increased redundancy costs incurred;

- sale of parts of the business to generate cash;

- the sale and lease back of property or other asset sales used to generate cash;

- revaluation of assets from cost to market value;

- losses on the sale of fixed assets (indicating that the book values are higher than actual market values);

- the cancellation of planned capital expenditure (such as the purchase of new machinery or upgrading of IT systems);

- corporate failures within the industry;

- the resignation of directors and/or auditors;

- net liabilities and/or net current liabilities;

- operating losses;

- a reduced credit rating (from agencies or evidenced by reduced credit terms from suppliers); or

- changes to the repayment terms of loans or the security given.

## Impact of recession on valuation

**26.32** Valuations at times of economic uncertainty and downturn are particularly difficult to use in ancillary relief proceedings if there is to be no sale of the business in the imminent future. Any valuation of a business proceeds on the assumption that the business is to be sold to a willing buyer as at the date of the valuation. Accordingly, the valuer will look at the state of the business itself when considering the future maintainable earnings and the state of the market for such businesses at the date of his or her valuation when determining an appropriate P/E ratio.

**26.33** Any fall in value may be attributable to the impact of the economic downturn on the business. For example, greater uncertainty over the amount of future maintainable earnings will increase the perceived risk of an investment in the business and hence decrease the theoretical value of the company. However, predicting how a particular business may fair in a downturn is inevitably very difficult.

**26.34**  Even if the business is itself unaffected by the recession, the market for business acquisitions is likely to have shrunk in correlation with reduced credit facilities available to fund such acquisitions. For any potential purchasers who have the funds to make a corporate acquisition, such circumstances create a 'buyer's market', giving purchasers a bargaining advantage when agreeing a price. The P/E ratio to be applied in valuing a business is likely to be reduced when there is an economic downturn, and even more depressed when there are difficulties in any potential purchasers being able to raise finance in order to fund the acquisition of businesses. However, such circumstances tend to be temporary and, unless forced to do so by circumstances, owners of successful businesses are unlikely to seek to sell their stakes in those businesses at times when the sale price is likely to be significantly depressed by factors which are not directly related to the health or prospects of the business itself. To adopt the valuation at a depressed value when the reality indicates that the business will only be sold once market conditions are better is plainly capable of unfairness to the party who will not be retaining the business. Although the court may not be able to predict how much the business will be worth in the future, evidence of historical transactions in that sector may assist the court in forming a view that the P/E ratio or multiplier used in valuing the business is likely to be significantly greater in the foreseeable future. This can then be taken into account in the overall division of the assets.

**26.35**  Any assessment of an appropriate P/E ratio to apply to a company depends on evidence of other similar transactions. Inevitably there is a time lag between such transactions taking place and the data becoming available. The difficulty is compounded by the reduction in such transactions during a recession. Few business owners choose to sell a business at a time when the market favours buyers over sellers. Indeed, the historically low volume of corporate transactions in private companies may well conceal the underlying fall that takes place in valuations and the 'multiples' being paid to acquire them during a recession. The FTSE 100 fell 30% in the last quarter of 2008 and, once volumes in private company sales pick up, one might expect to see this reduction in value mirrored there.

**26.36**  A full valuation of the business may be unnecessary if the business is to be sold imminently.[27] If it is agreed, or the court determines, that the parties should share the benefits and/or risks of a business by each retaining a proportion of the ownership, then, again, an exact valuation will not be

---

[27]  Although even in the case of the sale there may need to be a valuation. If the shareholding to be sold amounts to less than the entire issued share capital of the company and there are restrictions on the sale of shares and rights of pre-emption have been granted to the other shareholders in the company, it is likely that the articles of association or any shareholders' agreement will require the shareholding to be valued and offered to the existing shareholders at that valuation price.

necessary.[28] Furthermore, if the court decides to treat the business as an income stream for one party from which periodical payments will be paid to the other party (with a view to those payments possibly being capitalised at a point in the future when the business is sold) it will probably be unnecessary to precisely value the business, because it would be unfair to double count the income from the business and its capital value.[29]

**26.37** Nevertheless, unless the court is going to order a sale of the business or leave the parties with equal interests in a business enterprise, some conclusion will need to be reached as to the current value of the business and its prospects in the foreseeable future will require examination. Careful preparation of the evidence followed by well directed questioning of the expert valuer and the business owner himself or herself will be required to permit the court to form the broad assessment of the business's future prospects which is required if the outcome is to be fair to both parties.

## SHARE VALUES

**26.38** As illustrated by the example of Barclays plc shares during 2008 and 2009, at **26.5** above, movements on the financial markets can be particularly rapid and unpredictable during periods of economic uncertainty. This poses very real problems for the ancillary relief practitioner dealing with a case where significant sums are invested in shares traded on public exchanges. Any schedule of assets prepared in advance of a hearing may provide an entirely erroneous value for the shares a few days later. In some cases, even an asset schedule based on the share price on the morning of the hearing may prove to be wholly inaccurate due to market movements during the day. How is the practitioner to deal with this?

**26.39** The first and most obvious point is to ensure that the share values are checked and updated as close to the hearing as possible.

**26.40** The second, although equally important point, is to understand the inadequacies of relying on the share price on any particular day as a fair reflection of the value of those shares on a subsequent day. Published prices for shares are based on the actual trades which have taken place in relation to those shares at the time of publication. Those published online are often based on trades which took place in the last few minutes. Those published in newspapers tend to be the price at which trading in those shares closed on the last day the stock exchange was open. On either basis, the quoted share price is a figure based on historical trades. It is no guarantee as to the price at which those shares will be traded later that same day or on any subsequent day. The party who holds those shares did not sell his or her holding at that price and that sale

---

[28]  Although if this involves a transfer of shares, some reliable valuation of those shares at the date of the transaction is likely to be required for capital gains tax purposes in any event.

[29]  For example, *Smith v Smith* [2007] 2 FLR 1103.

price may not be available again. For that reason, a snapshot view of the shares based on a single day's trading may not be a fair reflection of a share's true value to the person who retains those shares.

**26.41**   It is now relatively easy to access the trading history of any publicly listed share online. This will show the history of daily trade prices for several years, including the highest and lowest price achieved for those shares in the course of each trading session. Armed with such information it may be possible to show that the price on a single day is unusually low or high and that a broader view of the shares suggests a different and more realistic value. Of course, any such analysis must also take into account the factors which have actually caused the fluctuation in the share price. If the price is particularly low because information has become available to indicate that the underlying business of the company is about to fail, that may be a reason to believe that the share price is likely to remain low. On the other hand, there may be very positive news about that company which indicates that the high share price is likely to persist. In a case where substantial shareholdings in publicly listed companies are held, it may be proportionate and useful to have expert advice on the longer term value of those shares compared to the current listed share price.

**26.42**   Thirdly, publicly listed shares are relatively easy to transfer between the parties or to sell. They are, therefore, particularly well suited to a *Wells v Wells* sharing between the parties if it proves impossible to place a fair value on them. Nevertheless, the potential capital gains tax implications of a sale or transfer of the shares may make this course unappealing to the parties,[30] and so the question of what value to attribute to the shares will need to be addressed if they are to be retained by one of the parties alone.

## OTHER INVESTMENTS

**26.43**   Many other forms of investment rely on the values of publicly traded shares. Many Individual Savings Account ('ISAs'), unit trusts and endowment policies are based on a fund which invests in the stock market or in other commodities. Such investments are usually less affected by sudden movements in the value of one single company's share price, because the investments are spread over a wide portfolio of shares or investments, thereby smoothing the effect of individual share price movements across the fund as a whole. Nevertheless, such investments are affected by the movements of the overall market. Some funds are more specialist than others and may not move in the same way, or to the same degree, as the market as a whole. So, for example, a fund with investments based mainly in the Far East may actually increase in value whilst the stock market in London falls, or vice versa. Similarly, a fund specialising in a particular sector of industry may fall in value despite the fact

---

[30]   Unless the transfer takes place in the year of separation on a 'no gain-no loss' basis – see **23.53** et seq and **23.93–23.96**.

that the stock market as a whole is rising. Once again, careful consideration of the nature of the investment and the provision of up-to-date valuations are required. It is also important to bear in mind that a 'snapshot' valuation on a single date may not provide a fair value for the asset.

## PENSIONS

**26.44** Pensions may require particular care at times of economic uncertainty. Not only are many funds based on investments on the financial markets and therefore likely to rise and fall in value in line with the markets, but there are special actuarial adjustments made in calculating the CETVs in such pensions at times when investment values are depressed. Such 'market value adjustment factors' are explained in more detail at **22.35**. The effect of such adjustments can result in considerably different results from pension sharing orders than those which the parties intended.

**26.45** Self-invested pensions in the form of SIPPs and SSASs also require care. Again, the underlying investments may have changed in value since the last valuation. Those funds where the investments are in real estate or in private companies may have had the most significant variations in value, and this needs to be taken into account.

## TAX AND WELFARE BENEFIT IMPLICATIONS

**26.46** It should not be forgotten that changes in the values of assets may have tax implications, sometimes of a beneficial nature. Calculations of capital gains tax liabilities will need to be updated in line with revised asset values. Reduced asset values may also permit the parties to carry out transfers between themselves with lower capital gains tax liabilities than would otherwise have arisen. Parties with complex business affairs may be able to use losses incurred in one business to offset profits in another, thereby minimising their overall liability to pay income tax, depending on the nature of their business structures. Accordingly, the overall effect on a party's net income may not have been as great as initial impressions indicate. It may also be that losses sustained in a particular period may be used to offset tax on profits in future years, thereby increasing net income in those years. Expert accountancy advice may well be required to explore the full implications of such arrangements.

# Chapter 27

# USING ANCILLARY RELIEF ORDERS AT TIMES OF ECONOMIC UNCERTAINTY

**27.1** This chapter endeavours to consider the ways the parties may seek to use the powers contained in the Matrimonial Causes Act 1973 to deal with some of the difficulties which arise at times of economic uncertainty. Inevitably it strays into areas of general principle and practice in ancillary relief cases which lie outside the scope of this book,[1] but it is intended as nothing more than a general summary of those general principles. For a more detailed consideration of the general principles applicable to lump sum orders, periodical payments and applications for variation of orders, reference should be made to the more general practitioner texts.

**27.2** There is an almost limitless variety of ways in which the parties may agree to resolve their affairs in a manner which is fair in all the circumstances. With some imagination and creativity the ancillary relief practitioner should be able to craft an agreement which uses a combination of the parties' agreements and undertakings and the orders made by the court to resolve the issues in a fair manner.

**27.3** This chapter does not seek to consider how the parties might seek to resolve matters by agreement because such arrangements will by their very nature be specific to the facts of the cases in which they are negotiated. Such agreements may also incorporate terms which the court could not order. The focus in this chapter is on what the court may be able to order so as to achieve a fair outcome where the parties are either unable or unwilling to enter into suitable agreements as part of the final ancillary relief order.

## OVERCOMING LIMITATIONS IN THE COURTS' STATUTORY POWERS

**27.4** Although the court in ancillary relief proceedings has wide-ranging discretion as to how it will deal with the parties' financial affairs, the powers by which it may put its decision into practical effect are limited to those orders which it is empowered to make by ss 21A–25D, 28, 29, 31 and 37 of the Matrimonial Causes Act 1973. Those powers can prove to be somewhat limited

---

[1] See **1.2–1.3**.

when the parties' affairs are complicated, and particularly so when they are entangled with liabilities to third parties.

**27.5**   In its decision in *Livesey (formerly Jenkins) v Jenkins*[2] the House of Lords was critical of careless drafting of orders which failed to recognise the limits of that which the court was able to order using its statutory powers and that which could only be achieved by the parties reaching separate contractual agreements or by undertakings to the court. Any properly drafted order should set out such agreements and undertakings in the preamble to the order before proceeding to set out the actual orders made by the court in pursuance of its statutory powers. It appears now to be quite clear that such agreements and undertakings will be enforced by the court once they have been made, even though the court could not have made orders in similar terms in the absence of agreement between the parties.[3]

**27.6**   Where an order is reached with the parties' consent, there will usually be little difficulty in recording in the preamble to the order all the matters which they have agreed and the undertakings which the parties are prepared to be bound by. But what is the position where an order is made at the end of a contested hearing with no agreement as to such matters?

**27.7**   It will be rare that the parties will not offer at least some, even if limited, undertakings to the court to achieve the outcomes which the court would not otherwise be able to order. Usually this is because they and their lawyers recognise that the court will only grant them the other relief they are seeking if they are prepared to make such concessions. Where such agreement is indicated, or an undertaking is offered, the court may accept it and record it in the preamble to the order.

**27.8**   Sometimes, however, this will not be possible. This might be because one of the parties resolutely refuses to offer the undertaking, no matter how reasonable the request that he or she co-operate may appear to be. Alternatively, the relevant party has simply disappeared or has refused to participate in the proceedings. In the latter situation there is not a great deal the court will be able to do other than to create as satisfactory an outcome by the use of its statutory powers as it can. Although it may be tempting, the court may not make an unfair or one-sided order which was plainly wrong simply to provoke a deliberately absent party into responding to the proceedings.[4] Where the stubborn party is before the court, however, it is possible that more can be achieved. The party might be persuaded to make the required concession through cross-examination or through appropriate cajoling by the court. Alternatively, the concession can be forced by making any of the relief sought by the obstructive party conditional upon that party providing the undertaking or agreement which is sought. Ultimately, if all such efforts fail, the court is limited to its statutory powers.

---

[2]   [1985] FLR 813.
[3]   See the more detailed discussion about the use of undertakings in Chapter 6.
[4]   *Hall v Hall* [2008] EWCA Civ 350, The Times, April 30.

## DEALING WITH DEBTS

**27.9**   The Matrimonial Causes Act 1973 provides the court with powers to divide and redistribute the property of the parties to the marriage. There is no power to redistribute their liabilities. Although a debt is a form of property in its own right, it is the property of the creditor rather than the debtor. A debt is a chose in action[5] belonging to the third party creditor. Although that third party would be free to assign or transfer the chose in action to another party, the court has no jurisdiction to force the third party creditor to do so within the ancillary relief proceedings.

**27.10**   So, if the wife in ancillary proceedings owes £1,000 on a credit card with X Bank plc, having spent the money reasonably for the benefit of the family as a whole, but which she is unable to pay, the court has no jurisdiction to transfer that debt to the husband. If the husband is prepared to undertake to pay that debt and to indemnify the wife in respect of it, the court may accept that undertaking and record it in the order. The legal relationship between the wife and X Bank plc will not have changed, but, in the event the husband failed to make the payments as promised, the wife would be able to claim the payments from him. Of course, if she is unable to extract the money from the husband for whatever reason, she will still be faced with the liability to X Bank Ltd.

**27.11**   Where the husband in the above example is unwilling to provide such an undertaking, the court may still deal with the matter using its powers. If there are sufficient liquid assets to do so, or there exists some clear evidence that the husband has the means to raise the funds in some other way, the court may require the husband to pay a lump sum to the wife sufficient to allow her to clear the debt. It may extract from the wife, as the price for the order, an undertaking that she will use the lump sum to discharge the debt. Alternatively, the overall provision for the wife through property adjustment orders may be adjusted to take this liability into account. Where the assets are modest and illiquid (eg all tied up in the family home which needs to be retained for the children), such an adjustment may not, of course, provide any relief from the immediate need for payment of the debt.

**27.12**   In the absence of liquid capital from which to pay such a debt, the court may make provision for servicing the debt by way of an order for periodical payments from the husband to the wife, providing for payments sufficient to discharge the loan payments as they fall due.

**27.13**   A joint loan usually creates a joint and several liability upon the debtors. In other words, the creditor is entitled to enforce the entire debt against any one of the debtors, or against all of them. If one of two joint debtors pays half the loan, he or she remains liable for the other half until it is discharged. Joint liabilities which are being paid only by one of the parties due to a refusal by the other party to contribute to the payments can be dealt with indirectly by

---

5    See Chapter 10 for a discussion about choses in action in ancillary relief proceedings.

way of a property adjustment order, lump sum or periodical payments in the same way as a debt in the name of only one of the parties (discussed in the preceding paragraph). It is even more likely that in such cases the party receiving the lump sum or periodical payments will be required by the court to undertake to use the funds to discharge the whole debt.

**27.14** Ordinarily, a court can only require the parties to the proceedings to make payments to each other. The court may not require one of the parties to make a lump sum payment or periodical payments to a third party creditor. A limited exception exists in the case of an order for the sale of an asset pursuant to MCA 1973, s 24A. By s 24A(2)(a) the court may give consequential directions to an order for sale 'requiring the making of a payment out of the proceeds of sale of the property to which the order relates'. There is nothing on the face of the statute limiting this to a payment to one of the parties to the proceedings, and so, it is submitted, the court is entitled to direct a payment to a third party creditor from the sale proceeds. Indeed, it appears to be this power which is commonly utilised to direct that the sale proceeds are first used to discharge the mortgage and the sale costs of the property before being distributed to the parties.

**27.15** Where the debts exceed the parties' assets and their ability to service them from their income, it may well be that they simply have to face up to the realities of insolvency. The impact of personal insolvency in an ancillary relief case is considered in Chapter 25.

## DELAYING MAKING THE CLAIM

**27.16** Where much of the family wealth is held by one of the parties, it may be that the other party may wish to delay making any claim for ancillary relief at a time when asset values are depressed. The party with the wealth may, on the other hand, wish to progress the ancillary relief applications as quickly as possible so as to reap any perceived benefit from the depressed asset values. Such simplistic strategies may not, in fact, achieve their intended goal for a number of reasons:

- First, the future is inherently unpredictable. Delaying an application in the hope that asset values may rise, or rushing an application before they rise, may prove to be a terrible mistake if asset values continue to fall further and for longer than anyone had predicted. There is also the risk of any number of other events occurring in the meantime which may affect the outcome of an ancillary relief application.

- Although one party may try to exploit the reduced asset values to achieve what is perceived as a 'cheaper' settlement, the structure of the settlement may actually prove to be less palatable to that party than what might have been achieved at a time when the asset values are higher. It may be that the lack of liquid capital in the form of property and assets will frustrate attempts at a clean break or place a greater emphasis on ongoing periodical payments than might be achieved with greater asset values.

- A unilateral decision by one party to delay making an application may cause the court to approach matters differently when the application is finally made than it would have done had the application been made closer to the time when the parties separated. First, the very fact that there has been delay in making an application might be held against the applicant, particularly if the only reason for the delay is perceived to be that party's attempt to obtain a perceived tactical or financial advantage.[6] Secondly, there is the risk that increases in the values of assets in the period of delay may be held to be non-matrimonial property to which the applicant has a reduced entitlement to share.[7] Alternatively, there is a risk that property acquired by one party during that period by way of an unexpected windfall, such as an inheritance or lottery win, will be taken into account and shared with the other party.

**27.17**   Overall, therefore, tactical delays in applications based on expectations about asset values rising and falling require considerable thought and should not be approached on the basis of any simplistic assumptions. The considerations applied to ancillary relief applications are very wide-ranging and constantly developing. It is very difficult to predict how a court might deal with an ancillary relief application which has been delayed, because the court's decision will depend on the circumstances at that time and no one can predict what all those circumstances will be.

## DEFERRING A SALE OR LUMP SUM

**27.18**   An obvious way of avoiding the worst effects of depressed asset values is to delay a sale of the asset in question until market conditions improve. This option will only be available in those cases where there are no pressing claims which require an immediate liquidation of assets. Where this option is adopted, it is likely to be by the agreement of the parties. The court may also adopt this approach, but, whatever date for a deferred sale is chosen, this has a degree of arbitrariness about it which suggests speculation on the court's part. In the absence of agreement the court may well simply order an immediate sale but provide for the parties to agree a later sale date if they so wish.

**27.19**   The payment of a lump sum might also be deferred in order to permit the paying party to have the freedom to liquidate assets at a time when market conditions are more favourable. Whether such an approach is fair and, if so, the appropriate length of the deferral of the sale, will depend on all the circumstances of the case. In most cases, however, the parties must be realistic about what can be achieved in a shorter period in any event. If the lump sum is

---

6    *Rossi v Rossi* [2007] 1 FLR 790.
7    See the discussion as to property acquired post-separation in Chapters 16 and 17.

to be realised by way of borrowing, the constraints on lending during a recessionary period need to be borne in mind. Where assets are to be sold to fund a lump sum, consideration needs to be given to the reduced activity in the market and the longer periods it may take to achieve a sale at a fair price. In some cases the act of selling a very large holding of shares by one party may have the effect of reducing the price of the shares, and in such cases a structured phasing of the sale of the assets and payment of the lump sum needs to be considered.

**27.20**   It is also important to note that there are powers of variation granted to the court in relation to lump sums payable by instalments and orders for the sale of property (considered further below).

## ADJOURNING A CLAIM FOR A LUMP SUM, PROPERTY ADJUSTMENT OR PENSION ORDER

**27.21**   The court does have jurisdiction to adjourn any of the parties' claims where justice demands this course. It is, however, an exceptional step in most cases, because it is inconsistent with achieving a complete severance of the parties' mutual financial ties as soon as possible. Applications for lump sums have been adjourned in cases where there was a likelihood of an asset becoming available in the foreseeable future, usually either a retirement gratuity or an inheritance. Such cases have been considered in Chapter 18. It would be extremely unusual for applications to be adjourned simply to await an increase in property values. However, where the parties agree such an approach by agreement, there is no reason, as a matter of principle, why the court should not approve that course.

**27.22**   In one particular situation an adjournment of an application for a pension sharing order might be required in order to achieve fairness. This is where a market valuation reduction factor has been temporarily applied to the calculation of the CETV of a pension.[8] To implement a pension sharing order against such a reduced CETV could result in unfairness. Simply adjusting the pension sharing percentage to take this into account may also prove to be unfair in the event that the MVR factor continued to be applied to the remaining pension for longer than anticipated. Adjournment of a claim even in these circumstances would remain very unusual if not agreed by both parties. It would be very difficult to determine how long the adjournment should be for. There would also be a potential unfairness if contributions continued to be made to the pension during the period of the adjournment. However, where the pension values are very significant compared to the other assets and so long as the other assets have been divided without taking the pension into account, an adjournment may be justified as the only means by which a fair outcome can be reached.

---

[8]   See **22.35** for an explanation of the effect of this.

## LUMP SUM BY INSTALMENTS

**27.23**   Economic downturns make raising capital by borrowing or by selling assets more difficult. A lump sum payable by instalments pursuant to MCA 1973, s 23(3(c) is a classic means by which difficulties in liquidating assets are resolved.[9] This technique is frequently used where one party wishes to retain a business but lacks the access to sufficient funds to make an immediate outright lump sum payment to compensate the other party in respect of the value of this asset. It has the benefit of spreading the period over which the funds must be found. It also often suits the receiving party, because, unlike a claim to periodical payments, the liability to pay the lump sum will survive the payee's remarriage and will also remain due from the payer's estate in the event of death.

**27.24**   Such arrangements also carry risks which the parties must understand before they enter into them:

- From the payer's point of view, the risk lies in the fact that the lump sum will be quantified at the date of the hearing based on the values of the assets at that date as the court can best establish them. So the risk attached to future changes in asset values crystallises and attaches itself entirely to the payer. If, in due course, the value of the payer's share of the assets collapses, he or she will continue to remain liable for the lump sum payment, subject only to the court's residual power to vary the order (as to which, see below).

- From the payee's point of view, although there is the apparent certainty of having a defined amount of capital to come in the future, this must be set in proper context. First, there is the risk that the payer's circumstances may change in the future so as to make him unable to satisfy the remaining instalments (although this risk can be reduced to a considerable extent by obtaining sufficient security for the unpaid parts of the lump sum). Secondly, there is the risk that the lump sum may, in due course, be varied by the court. Variation of such an order is considered further below.

## DISCOUNTING OR ENHANCING AN ASSET SHARE IN VIEW OF FUTURE PROSPECTS

**27.25**   The courts are well accustomed to taking a pragmatic and broad view of the assets before they are divided. This includes looking at the financial resources which a party is likely to have in the foreseeable future as well as those held at the time of the hearing. Accordingly, where there is good reason to believe that the values of assets held by one party will change in the foreseeable future, that future value can justify a reduction or increase in the share of the

---

9   For example, *R v R (Lump Sum Repayments)* [2004] 1 FLR 928.

assets to be taken by the other party. Nevertheless, the court must be careful not to enter into the realms of speculation when making such assumptions. Even the parties to litigation often fail to fully appreciate the prospects of their asset values not following the course they expect. Lessons should be learned from the period spanning 2007 and the early part of 2008, when few people foresaw the full extent of the consequences of the 'credit crunch'.[10] Whilst speculation as to the future is unwise, small adjustments for future prospects are quite commonly made by the court and the parties. Where the adjustment needs to be more significant, it seem more likely that fairness will demand a *Wells v Wells* type sharing of the assets (see below) unless there is solid evidence upon which the assumption about future values can be based. There is a further discussion on this topic in the context of asset valuation in Chapter 26.

## *WELLS V WELLS* SHARING

**27.26**   In *Wells v Wells*[11] the Court of Appeal highlighted the iniquities which could arise in any case where one party took the relatively risk-free and liquid 'copper-bottomed assets', typically the family savings and the family home, whilst the other retained the 'illiquid and risk-laden assets'. Sometimes these distinctions are referred to as 'the apples and pears argument'.[12] In practice, the points made in the Court of Appeal's decision in *Wells v Wells* has resulted in two approaches being adopted. The first, the purest approach, is the adoption of a '*Wells v Wells* sharing' of the assets, where similar categories of assets are shared between the parties in similar proportions, so that the benefit and risk in each category is also shared between the parties. The second approach, less pure in its form but nevertheless useful and regularly adopted, is to recognise the differing practical values of different categories of assets, so that the overall division of the assets takes into account the greater risk or illiquidity of the assets retained by one of the parties. When this approach is adopted, one party may take a larger share of all the assets than the other, based on their paper values, in an effort fairly to reflect the greater illiquidity and risk attaching to those assets.

**27.27**   The use of the *Wells v Wells* approach is considered in more detail in Chapter 11.

**27.28**   The 'credit crunch' has starkly revealed how one party can benefit whilst the other suffers if the assets are divided in a way which does not share the copper-bottomed assets and the illiquid and risk-laden assets proportionately between the parties. In *Myerson v Myerson*[13] the husband agreed to a division of assets of some £25m. The result was that he retained 57% of the assets and his wife 43%. The husband's share was largely made up of his

---

[10]   For a stark example of an experienced and successful businessman making just such a misjudgement see *Myerson v Myerson* [2009] EWCA Civ 282.
[11]   [2002] 2 FLR 97.
[12]   *D v D & B Ltd* [2007] EWHC 278 (Fam) at [94].
[13]   [2009] EWCA Civ 282.

shareholding in his company, valued at about £15m. He agreed to pay the wife a lump sum of £9.5m. The lump sum was to be paid by a first instalment of £7m and four further equal instalments of £625,000 over the 4 succeeding years. He paid the first instalment by April 2008. During the rest of 2008 the value of the husband's shares in the company collapsed from a high shortly before the order was made of over £3.00 per share to only 27.5 pence per share by March 2009. The effect of this was utterly to distort the effect of the order. Instead of achieving the 57% to 43% division anticipated in March 2008, the fall in the value of the shares meant that, once the lump sum was paid in full, the husband's share of the assets would reduce to minus 5.2% whilst the wife's rose to 105.2%. Clearly, this outcome could have been avoided had the husband sought to share the assets in the purer *Wells v Wells* manner referred to above. He had chosen to gamble on his shares increasing in value in the future, but the gamble had failed. His subsequent attempts to escape the consequences of this arrangement are discussed further below.

## THE FLEXIBILITY OF PERIODICAL PAYMENTS ORDERS

**27.29**   The risks of one party retaining a business whilst the other retains the 'copper-bottomed' assets have been illustrated in the previous section of this chapter. Very often such an unbalanced allocation of the copper-bottomed and risky assets stems from the eagerness of the parties to achieve a clean break from each other. The party who would be liable to maintain the other party in the future is likely to have to raise a considerable amount of cash to provide the other party with a *Duxbury* fund from which the income needs can be met. Unless the liquid assets available to the parties are a large proportion of the total assets available to them, the pursuit of a clean break in this way is likely to result in one party taking on a much larger share of the risk-laden assets and, very often, also a considerable amount of debt, which will need to be serviced.

**27.30**   While the economy grows rapidly, such settlements appear to be fair and have obvious attractions for both parties. The party who would otherwise receive periodical payments has the security of a *Duxbury* fund and a predictable income. The other party is free to work and accumulate assets without fear of further proceedings seeking a share in the income so generated. The 'credit crunch' and resulting economic hardship for many households has revealed the shortcomings of such an approach. The clean break approach involving a capitalisation of future periodical payments is based on a fundamental assumption that the paying party will continue to work into the future and earn an income sufficient to make periodical payments at that level. As soon as that party's business fails or he or she becomes unemployed, that fundamental assumption is undermined. Even if the level of income merely falls by a significant amount, the clean break order can quickly look rather one-sided and unfair. This has been seen most dramatically by those who have been employed in the banking and financial services industries, where bonuses, which were often multiples of basic salary and very substantial, came to be regarded as virtually assured during the years leading up to 2008. The downturn in the financial services industries from late 2007 onwards saw such bonuses reduce, both as a result of reduced profits and because of wider public pressure on institutions to reign in what was popularly perceived to be excessive remuneration. Any clean break order which assumed that such income would continue on the paying party's part becomes increasingly unfair the longer the levels of remuneration remain depressed.

**27.31** The other side of this particular coin is that during an economic downturn, the party who is likely to be liable to pay periodical payments may seek to capitalise the other party's claims for a sum based on much lower levels of remuneration. Of course, this assumes that levels of remuneration will remain depressed or reduced for a considerable period. Quite simply, in most cases, no one is able to predict what the future might hold and there is a risk of unfairness if levels of remuneration rise rapidly quite soon after a clean break has been agreed on the basis of overly pessimistic predictions of future income.

**27.32** Such considerations illustrate the inherent fairness and flexibility of an ongoing periodical payments order. Periodical payments may be varied as often as circumstances and fairness require. They can adapt to increases and reductions in earnings and to changes in the circumstances of the receiving party. In the case of high incomes, the surplus income can be shared in a way which allows some capital to be accrued by each party with a view to financial independence being achieved at some point in the future.[14] Where one party owns a business, which is a classic illiquid risk-laden asset, and earns a significant income from that business, the future performance of that business (including the risk of it failing) can be shared between the parties by regarding the business as a source of income rather than an asset with capital value. The income generated by the business can be shared through periodical payments.[15] In the future, should the capital value of the business be released through a sale, the periodical payments can be capitalised by the payment of a lump sum in exchange for a clean break.

**27.33** Although the parties to a failed marriage usually prefer the certainty of a clean break order, because of the very uncertainty and unpredictability of a periodical payments order, the future is itself uncertain and unpredictable and a periodical payments order permits the court to react to events fairly rather than attempting to predict what the future may hold. In many cases, therefore, the court will prefer the flexibility offered by a periodical payments order rather than the somewhat speculative attempt to predict the future and achieve a clean break by way of a capitalisation of maintenance claims. A continuing periodical payments order is particularly likely where the assets are not

---

[14]    As illustrated by *McFarlane v McFarlane; Parlour v Parlour* [2004] 2 FLR 893 (see also [2006] 1 FLR 1186). Mrs McFarlane subsequently successfully applied to increase her periodical payments following an increase in Mr McFarlane's remuneration: see [2009] EWHC 891.

[15]    Suggested as an option in *D v D & B Ltd* [2007] EWHC 278 (Fam) at [104].

particularly large but one party's income is significant and that income is not generated from the parties' assets, such as a family business, but from employment.

**27.34** However, where a clean break can be achieved by way of a division of the assets which distributes the benefits and risks of the financial fruits of the marriage fairly, a clean break remains an outcome which the parties and the court can, and should, strive to achieve. Section 25A(1) of the Matrimonial Causes Act 1973 specifically requires the court to terminate the parties' financial obligations to each other as soon after the grant of the decree as the court considers just and reasonable. In reality, such an outcome is most likely in those cases where the assets are very substantial and in cases where one party's income is generated from the capital assets, classically where the income comes from a family-owned business.[16]

# VARYING PERIODICAL PAYMENTS ORDERS

**27.35** Periodical payments orders are, by their very nature, the most flexible form of ancillary relief order. A periodical payments order can be varied as often as required by changes in circumstances. The advantages of such orders are obvious when the future prospects for the parties and their incomes are unclear, as discussed above.

**27.36** The court's power to vary a periodical payments order is very broad. The court has the power to 'vary or discharge the order or to suspend any provision thereof temporarily and to revive the operation of the provision so suspended'.[17] The court may backdate the variation to the date of the application, or may direct that the variation should take effect at some later date.[18] The factors the court is to consider are specified in s 31(7) of the Matrimonial Causes Act 1973 and can be broken down as follows:

- The court must have regard to all the circumstances of the case.

- First consideration must be given to the welfare while a minor of any child of the family who has not attained the age of 18.

- The circumstances of the case include any change in any of the matters to which the court was required to have regard when making the order to which the application relates.

- The court should consider whether it is appropriate to limit the duration of further periodical payments for such period as will be sufficient to

---

[16] In such a case the court must be careful not to double-count the value of the business as a capital asset and the income from that asset. In reality the asset's capital value reflects its income-producing potential. See *V v V (Financial Relief)* [2005] 2 FLR 697.

[17] MCA 1973, s 31(1).

[18] MCA 1973, s 31(10).

enable the party in whose favour the order was made to adjust without undue hardship to the termination of those payments.

The court is empowered to make further lump sum, property adjustment or pension sharing orders to achieve this last aim of bringing about a clean break between the parties, if this is possible.[19]

**27.37** It is clear from the reported cases that the court must approach the question of periodical payments on the variation application de novo.[20] The variation of the order will depend on what is reasonable in all the circumstances at the time of the variation application being heard. It is not simply a matter of using the existing order as a starting point and making adjustments to it in accordance with changes in the circumstances since the order was made. It follows that a reduction in the paying party's income will not automatically justify a downward variation in the level of periodical payments. The court will have to take into account all the circumstances of the case, including the circumstances of the party benefiting from the periodical payments order. The court will also apply the legal principles which prevail at the time of the variation application and not those which applied when the original order was made. For example, on hearing the variation application the court may assess the receiving party's entitlement to periodical payments more generously than the court which made the original order did, particularly if the original order was made prior to the elucidation of the compensation principle in *Miller v Miller; McFarlane v McFarlane*.[21] So the periodical payments order may be left unvaried, or even increased, notwithstanding a fall in income.

**27.38** During a period of recession or economic uncertainty the most likely reason for making an application for variation of a periodical payments order will be a reduction in the income of either the paying party or the receiving party. A paying party whose income reduces is likely to seek a downward variation of the order. A receiving party whose income falls is likely to seek an upward variation in an effort to make ends meet. This reduction may be the result of unemployment, loss of overtime, loss of bonus payments or, in the case of a self-employed person or a person paid based on performance or by way of commission, a reduction in turnover. The court is likely to look very critically at all the circumstances of the case before making a variation of the order. Clearly, the facts of each case will be different and the individual circumstances will determine the outcome, but there are a few general considerations to bear in mind, as follows.

**27.39** The reasons for the reduction in income will need to be very carefully considered. The court will wish to be clear that the party seeking the variation has not engineered the reduction in income in order to obtain the variation to the order.

---

[19] MCA 1973, s 31(7A)–(7G).
[20] *Lewis v Lewis* [1977] 1 WLR 409, *Flavell v Flavell* [1997] 1 FLR 353.
[21] [2006] 1 FLR 1186. For examples of this see *Lauder v Lauder* [2007] 2 FLR 802 and *VB v JP* [2008] 1 FLR 742.

**27.40**   Similarly, the court looks to earning capacity as well as actual earnings. Accordingly, the court will wish to be satisfied that all reasonable efforts have been made to increase the income. Where such efforts, if made, are likely to produce an income, the court is likely to deem that income to be available. The court will also look to any social security benefits which are available to either party.

**27.41**   The court must look at the circumstances of the receiving party as well as those of the paying party. It may be that the receiving party's own conduct has been unreasonable and that this is a more significant factor than the paying party's ability to make the payments.[22] On the other hand, the needs of a child of the family to remain appropriately housed and provided for may be determinative of the application.

**27.42**   The likely duration of the reduction in income is important. If the reduction is likely to be short-lived, it is unlikely that the court will exercise its power of variation. Where the paying party has a naturally fluctuating income, which is very common with the self-employed, the court will expect there to be lean years and fat years. An average income over the course of several years will most probably have been adopted in setting the original rate of periodical payments in such a case. So the court may say that the paying party will have to be prepared to suffer a degree of financial pain in the lean years, just as he or she will have benefited from a surplus of income in the fat years. In such a case the paying party may need to prove that the reduction in income is likely to persist for a lengthier period in order to justify a reduction in periodical payments.

**27.43**   The court is likely to scrutinise carefully the parties' outgoings and lifestyles. Where the available income has been reduced, the court will look at the extent to which each party has a surplus of disposable income on luxuries or pleasure which is capable of being used for the payment of living costs or periodical payments. Where the parties each have similar outgoings but the periodical payments amount to less than half of the paying party's income, it is likely that there will be greater scope for economies to be made by the paying party than by the receiving party. On the other hand, where the capital was divided between the parties unequally, it may well be that the party who makes the periodical payments may have higher fixed costs in terms of rent and mortgage costs than the receiving party, with the effect that the scope for making economies in the budget is greater for the receiving party.

**27.44**   It may be that the income needs of the parties may have to be met out of capital reserves or by borrowing. Although the court must be careful on a variation application not to reopen capital claims,[23] the court does look to the reality of the situation[24] and, if one party is having to borrow or draw on

---

[22]   For example, *North v North* [2008] 1 FLR 158.
[23]   *Pearce v Pearce* [2003] 3 FCR 178.
[24]   'The ecclesiastical courts showed a degree of practical wisdom ... They were not misled by appearances ... they looked at the realities ... The court not only ascertained what monies the

capital to meet his or her income needs, the court may require the other to do the same in order to satisfy a periodical payments order. Thus, a court need not vary a periodical payments order when there is no income from which to pay it if, in all the circumstances of the case, it is fair that the parties' income needs are met from capital.

**27.45**　The court is also likely to explore whether there are any non-income earning assets held by the parties which could be used to provide an income. So the court may require unnecessary or unproductive assets to be sold in order to provide an investment fund which will produce an income. By this means either party could be deemed to have a notional *Duxbury* fund from which an income is produced.

## VARYING CAPITAL ORDERS

**27.46**　Section 31 of MCA 1973 sets out the types of order which the court may seek to vary, discharge or suspend. That list includes at s 31(2):

> '(d)　any order made by virtue of section 23(3)(c) or 27(7)(b) above (provision for payment of a lump sum by instalments);
> (dd)　any deferred order made by virtue of section 23(1)(c) (lump sums) which includes provision made by virtue of—
> 　　(i)　section 25B(4), or
> 　　(ii)　section 25C,
> 　　(provision in respect of pension rights);
> 　　…
> (f)　any order made under section 24A(1) above for the sale of property;
> (g)　a pension sharing order under section 24B above which is made at a time before the decree has been made absolute.'

These provisions make it clear that a variation may be sought of a lump sum order by instalments, a deferred lump sum order from a pension by way of a pension attachment order, an order for sale and, only in the limited circumstances where decree absolute has not been granted, a pension sharing order. Despite these powers of variation being available, the courts have chosen to exercise them sparingly.

**27.47**　It is an established principle that capital orders made as part of an ancillary relief order are almost always meant to be once and for all orders which are not capable of being subsequently varied. Periodical payments orders are more readily variable in line with variations in income and outgoings which occur from time to time. However, there is no doubt that Parliament has left a limited residual discretion to vary only three types of capital order:

---

husband had, but what monies he could have if he liked, and the term "faculties" describes the capacity and ability of the respondent to provide maintenance': *N v N* (1928) 44 TLR 324 at 327 per Lord Merrivale P.

(i)   deferred lump sums by way of pension earmarking or attachment;

(ii)  lump sums ordered to be paid by instalments; and

(iii) a pension sharing order, but only at a time before the decree is made absolute.

To date there appears to be no reported case where a court has been asked to consider the variation of a pension lump sum earmarking or attachment order. There have, however, been a number of cases where the court has been asked to use the power to vary a lump sum payable by instalments.

## Lump sum orders payable by instalments

**27.48**   In *Tilley v Tilley*[25] the Court of Appeal held that the court could use the power of variation to suspend the remaining instalments due under an order for payment of a lump sum by instalments. However, the use of the power of variation actually to alter the lump sum which was to be paid was not used by the court, and it seems that the court considered that there would need to be something truly exceptional about the case to permit that to be done.

**27.49**   In *Penrose v Penrose*[26] Balcombe LJ said:

> 'Mr Blair has conceded that the way the order is framed makes it an instalment order and the decision of this court in *Tilley v Tilley* (1979) 10 Fam Law 89 makes it clear that there is jurisdiction to suspend the remaining instalments due under a lump sum instalment order. So the jurisdiction to vary does exist. Whether the husband could make out a case which would satisfy the judge at first instance that there is a case for exercising that jurisdiction, I express no opinion. Clearly it is a jurisdiction to be exercised with caution.'

The last sentence of Balcombe LJ's words underlines the exceptional nature of the court exercising this power of variation.

**27.50**   In *Westbury v Sampson*[27] the Court of Appeal looked at the scope of the power to vary an order for the payment of a lump sum by instalments. The case concerned a claim for negligence by a husband against the solicitor who acted in his ancillary relief proceedings. The husband had agreed to accept an order whereby his wife was to pay him £2,500 very quickly and then £40,000 within 6 months, failing which her property was to be sold and the £40,000 paid from the sale proceeds. The order was made on the understanding that the equity in the property was in the region of £118,000. The wife did not make the second payment and the house was sold, realising a net sum of only £18,000. The wife successfully applied to vary the order so that she only had to pay

---

[25]   (1979) 10 Fam Law 89.
[26]   [1994] 2 FLR 621.
[27]   [2002] 1 FLR 166.

£22,500 in total.[28] The husband sued his solicitor for failing to advise him of the risk that such a variation might happen. In dismissing the husband's appeal from the dismissal of his negligence action against the solicitor, Bodey J accepted that the variation of the amount of the award was within the court's jurisdiction but such a variation was a quite exceptional event (which is why the solicitor had not been negligent in failing to bring the possibility of such a variation to the husband's attention):

> 'Judging by the text books, the propriety of such an order varying the overall quantum of such an order would appear to be in some doubt; but in my judgment, the cases of *Tilley v Tilley* (1980) 10 Fam Law 89 and *Penrose v Penrose* [1994] 2 FLR 621 make it clear that the jurisdiction created by s 31(1) of the Matrimonial Causes Act 1973 (below) not only empowers the court to re-timetable/adjust the amounts of individual instalments, but also to vary, suspend or discharge the principal sum itself, provided always that this latter power is used particularly sparingly, given the importance of finality in matters of capital provision.'

Again, the last words of this passage underline the exceptional nature of the circumstances which would permit the exercise of this power.

**27.51** At the time of writing, the husband in the case of *Myerson v Myerson*[29] seeks to vary the order for payment of a lump sum by instalments made by consent. It is expected that his application will be heard in July 2009 and is likely to provide a high-profile opportunity for the courts to set out the appropriate approach to these powers. Whilst hearing Mr Myerson's appeal from the refusal to set aside the original order in his case, the Court of Appeal was careful to say little about his variation application. Thorpe LJ limited himself to noting that the broad discretion to vary existed and, subject to the exercise of the judicial discretion, the judge had the power 'to rewrite that part of the consent order'.[30] Despite the apparent encouragement in *Myerson v Myerson* to use the power of variation in preference to an appeal out of time on *Barder* grounds,[31] in *Horne v Horne*[32] Thorpe LJ pointed out that the court would apply a stringent approach to such a variation application, likening it to a *Barder* appeal.

## Earmarked pension lump sum orders

**27.52** It is likely that the same principles which govern the variation of lump sums by instalments will also govern any attempt to vary a deferred pension lump sum attachment order, although, as yet, there is no reported authority dealing with such an application.

---

[28]   This decision has not been reported, but it provides evidence to suggest that this power of variation has been used successfully, at least in the lower courts.

[29]   [2009] EWCA Civ 282.

[30]   [2009] EWCA Civ 282 at [36].

[31]   See **27.55** et seq.

[32]   [2009] EWCA Civ 487.

## Orders for sale

**27.53**   MCA 1973, s 31(2)(f) provides the court with power to vary an order for sale made pursuant to s 24A(1). On the basis that s 24A(2) indicates that consequential or supplementary provisions may be included in an order for sale made pursuant to s 24A(1), such provisions constitute part of the order for sale and may also be varied. This power of variation is useful in the event that the court needs to specify a different sale price for the property or to deal with some other practical aspect of the sale. Such variations of the consequential provisions attached to an order for sale are used quite routinely as part of the implementation of orders.

**27.54**   The absence of any qualification to this power of variation, discharge or suspension does suggest that the court has the power to vary the date when a sale should occur (ie to delay a sale or to bring forward a deferred sale). Similarly, the court appears to have the power to completely discharge an order for sale or to suspend such an order. As already discussed in the context of variation of lump sums, the courts are generally reluctant to alter the effect of orders dealing with the division of capital. Indeed, in *Omielan v Omielan*[33] the Court of Appeal interpreted s 31(2)(f) narrowly:

> 'Section 24A is a purely procedural section inserted into the statute to clarify or expand the court's power of implementation and enforcement. Any power to vary such a procedural enactment must be construed to be equally limited to matters of enforcement, implementation and procedure. In other words s 31(2)(f) gives the court jurisdiction to revisit the territory of the ancillary order under s 24A but not the territory of the primary order under s 24 which it supports.'

In other words, an application to vary an order for sale which has the effect of altering the nature of the capital provision intended by the original order will not be permitted. However, an application which permits a party a little more time to raise a lump sum payment in order to avoid a sale may be permitted, so long as the effect of the original order is not altered.[34]

## RE-OPENING EARLIER ORDERS – *BARDER* EVENTS

**27.55**   To what extent can a radical change in economic conditions justify the reopening of an order? In *Barder v Caluori*[35] the House of Lords set out the grounds upon which a court may exercise its discretion to grant permission to appeal out of time on the basis of an unforeseen supervening event:

> 'The first condition is that new events have occurred since the making of the order which invalidate the basis, or fundamental assumption, upon which the order was made, so that, if leave to appeal out of time were to be given, the appeal would be

---

[33]   [1996] 2 FLR 306 at 312.
[34]   See *Swindale v Forder (Forder intervening)* [2007] 1 FLR 1905.
[35]   [1988] AC 20.

certain, or very likely, to succeed. The second condition is that the new events should have occurred within a relatively short time of the order having been made. While the length of time cannot be laid down precisely, I should regard it as extremely unlikely that it could be as much as a year, and that in most cases it will be no more than a few months. The third condition is that the application for leave to appeal out of time should be made reasonably promptly in the circumstances of the case. To these three conditions, which can be seen from the authorities as requiring to be satisfied, I would add a fourth, which it does not appear has needed to be considered so far, but which it may be necessary to consider in future cases. That fourth condition is that the grant of leave to appeal out of time should not prejudice third parties who have acquired, in good faith and for valuable consideration, interests in property which is the subject matter of the relevant order.'[36]

**27.56** This test has been applied in a number of reported cases based on a variety of new events which were claimed to undermine the basis of the order. Of particular relevance to periods of economic uncertainty are those cases where the value of an asset has changed after the order was made. The approach to such changes in the values of assets was considered by Hale J, as she then was, in *Cornick v Cornick*.[37] The learned judge identified three separate categories of case where the value of an asset had changed:[38]

'(1)   An asset which was taken into account and correctly valued at the date of the hearing changes value within a relatively short time owing to natural processes of price fluctuation. The court should not then manipulate the power to grant leave to appeal out of time to provide a disguised power of variation which Parliament has quite obviously and deliberately declined to enact.

(2)   A wrong value was put upon that asset at the hearing, which had it been known about at the time would have led to a different order. Provided that it is not the fault of the person alleging the mistake, it is open to the court to give leave for the matter to be reopened. Although falling within the *Barder* principle, it is more akin to the misrepresentation or non-disclosure cases than to *Barder* itself.

(3)   Something unforeseen and unforeseeable had happened since the date of the hearing which has altered the value of the assets so dramatically as to bring about a substantial change in the balance of assets brought about by the order. Then, provided that the other three conditions are fulfilled, the *Barder* principle may apply. However, the circumstances in which this can happen are very few and far between. The case law, taken as a whole, does not suggest that the natural processes of price fluctuation, whether in houses, shares or any other property, and however dramatic, fall within this principle.'

**27.57** In *Myerson v Myerson*[39] the husband sought to appeal an order out of time on the basis of a catastrophic collapse in the value of his shareholding in a company which he had chosen to retain as the bulk of his share of the

---

[36]   [1988] AC 20 at 43 per Lord Brandon of Oakbrook.
[37]   [1994] 2 FLR 530.
[38]   [1994] 2 FLR 530 at 536.
[39]   [2009] EWCA Civ 282. See **27.28** for the facts of this case.

matrimonial assets. He sought to argue that the financial crisis which gripped the developed world during 2008 had been an unforeseen event falling within the *Barder* principles. The Court of Appeal dismissed his application for permission to appeal out of time. Thorpe LJ approved and applied the dicta of Hale J in *Cornick v Cornick* and endorsed the arguments advanced on behalf of Mrs Myerson that (i) the history of the market value of Mr Myerson's shares showed that it was highly volatile and had fluctuated significantly even before the 'credit crunch', (ii) Mr Myerson held a senior position in the company and had been well placed to form a view as to the company's prospects at the time he entered into the consent order, and (iii) Mr Myerson had chosen to retain his shares, and the risks and potential benefits which went with them, rather than adopt a *Wells v Wells* sharing of the assets with his wife. A fourth argument also appears to have carried weight with the court, that being that Mr Myerson still had the opportunity to relieve himself of the perceived unfairness through his parallel application to vary the order for a lump sum by instalments, and there was no need for the Court of Appeal to reopen the matter by way of an appeal.[40]

**27.58** It appears clear from the cases of *Cornick v Cornick* and *Myerson v Myerson* that it will prove extremely difficult for a party to reopen an order on a *Barder* basis where the values of assets have altered as a result of changes in the market, no matter how dramatic those changes may have been.[41] This underlines the importance of parties considering some of the alternative options for spreading the risks between them, as discussed earlier in this chapter, particularly the division of assets on a *Well v Wells* basis or by using a flexible order such as a periodical payments order.

---

[40]  Which application was waiting to be heard at the time of writing.
[41]  The Court of Appeal has confirmed this stringent approach by refusing to reopen orders in *Horne v Horne* [2009] EWCA Civ 487 (a case concerning a significant fall in the value of a business retained by the husband) and *Walkden v Walkden* [2009] EWCA Civ 627 (where there had been a significant increase in the value of an asset after the making of the final order).

# Appendix 1

# COMPANIES (TABLES A TO F) REGULATIONS 1985, SI 1985/805[1]

### TABLE A
### REGULATIONS FOR MANAGEMENT OF
### A COMPANY LIMITED BY SHARES

**Interpretation**

1 In these regulations—

'the Act' means the Companies Act 1985 including any statutory modification or re-enactment thereof for the time being in force.

'the articles' means the articles of the company.

'clear days' in relation to the period of a notice means that period excluding the day when the notice is given or deemed to be given and the day for which it is given or on which it is to take effect.

['communication' means the same as in the Electronic Communications Act 2000,

'electronic communication' means the same as in the Electronic Communications Act 2000][2]

'executed' includes any mode of execution.

'office' means the registered office of the company.

'the holder' in relation to shares means the member whose name is entered in the register of members as the holder of the shares.

'the seal' means the common seal of the company.

'secretary' means the secretary of the company or any other person appointed to perform the duties of the secretary of the company, including a joint, assistant or deputy secretary.

'the United Kingdom' means Great Britain and Northern Ireland.

---

[1]   Made under: Companies Act 1985, ss 3 and 8.
[2]   Definitions 'communication', 'electronic communication' inserted: Companies Act 1985 (Electronic Communications) Order 2000, SI 2000/3373, art 32(1), Sch 1, para 1, with effect from 22 December 2000.

Unless the context otherwise requires, words or expressions contained in these regulations bear the same meaning as in the Act but excluding any statutory modification thereof not in force when these regulations become binding on the company.

**Share Capital**

2 Subject to the provisions of the Act and without prejudice to any rights attached to any existing shares, any share may be issued with such rights or restrictions as the company may by ordinary resolution determine.

3 Subject to the provisions of the Act, shares may be issued which are to be redeemed or are to be liable to be redeemed at the option of the company or the holder on such terms and in such manner as may be provided by the articles.

4 The company may exercise the powers of paying commissions conferred by the Act. Subject to the [provisions][3] of the Act, any such commission may be satisfied by the payment of cash or by the allotment of fully or partly paid shares or partly in one way and partly in the other.

5 Except as required by law, no person shall be recognised by the company as holding any share upon any trust and (except as otherwise provided by the articles or by law) the company shall not be bound by or recognise any interest in any share except an absolute right to the entirety thereof in the holder.

**Share Certificates**

6 Every member, upon becoming the holder of any shares, shall be entitled without payment to one certificate for all the shares of each class held by him (and, upon transferring a part of his holding of shares of any class, to a certificate for the balance of such holding) or several certificates each for one or more of his shares upon payment for every certificate after the first of such reasonable sum as the directors may determine. Every certificate shall be sealed with the seal and shall specify the number, class and distinguishing numbers (if any) of the shares to which it relates and the amount or respective amounts paid up thereon. The company shall not be bound to issue more than one certificate for shares held jointly by several persons and delivery of a certificate to one joint holder shall be a sufficient delivery to all of them.

7 If a share certificate is defaced, worn-out, lost or destroyed, it may be renewed on such terms (if any) as to evidence and indemnity and payment of the expenses reasonably incurred by the company in investigating evidence as the directors may determine but otherwise free of charge, and (in the case of defacement or wearing-out) on delivery up of the old certificate.

**Lien**

8 The company shall have a first and paramount lien on every share (not being a fully paid share) for all moneys (whether presently payable or not) payable at

---

[3]     Word substituted: Companies (Tables A to F) (Amendment) Regulations 1985, SI 1985/1052, with effect from 1 August 1985.

a fixed time or called in respect of that share. The directors may at any time declare any share to be wholly or in part exempt from the provisions of this regulation. The company's lien on a share shall extend to any amount payable in respect of it.

9 The company may sell in such manner as the directors determine any shares on which the company has a lien if a sum in respect of which the lien exists is presently payable and is not paid within fourteen clear days after notice has been given to the holder of the share or to the person entitled to it in consequence of the death or bankruptcy of the holder, demanding payment and stating that if the notice is not complied with the shares may be sold.

10 To give effect to a sale the directors may authorise some person to execute an instrument of transfer of the shares sold to, or in accordance with the directions of, the purchaser. The title of the transferee to the shares shall not be affected by any irregularity in or invalidity of the proceedings in reference to the sale.

11 The net proceeds of the sale, after payment of the costs, shall be applied in payment of so much of the sum for which the lien exists as is presently payable, and any residue shall (upon surrender to the company for cancellation of the certificate for the shares sold and subject to a like lien for any moneys not presently payable as existed upon the shares before the sale) be paid to the person entitled to the shares at the date of the sale.

**Calls on Shares and Forfeiture**

12 Subject to the terms of allotment, the directors may make calls upon the members in respect of any moneys unpaid on their shares (whether in respect of nominal value or premium) and each member shall (subject to receiving at least fourteen clear days' notice specifying when and where payment is to be made) pay to the company as required by the notice the amount called on his shares. A call may be required to be paid by instalments. A call may, before receipt by the company of any sum due thereunder, be revoked in whole or part and payment of a call may be postponed in whole or part. A person upon whom a call is made shall remain liable for calls made upon him notwithstanding the subsequent transfer of the shares in respect whereof the call was made.

13 A call shall be deemed to have been made at the time when the resolution of the directors authorising the call was passed.

14 The joint holders of a share shall be jointly and severally liable to pay all calls in respect thereof.

15 If a call remains unpaid after it has become due and payable the person from whom it is due and payable shall pay interest on the amount unpaid from the day it became due and payable until it is paid at the rate fixed by the terms of allotment of the share or in the notice of the call or, if no rate is fixed, at the appropriate rate (as defined by the Act) but the directors may waive payment of the interest wholly or in part.

16 An amount payable in respect of a share on allotment or at any fixed date, whether in respect of nominal value or premium or as an instalment of a call, shall be deemed to be a call and if it is not paid the provisions of the articles shall apply as if that amount had become due and payable by virtue of a call.

17 Subject to the terms of allotment, the directors may make arrangements on the issue of shares for a difference between the holders in the amounts and times of payment of calls on their shares.

18 If a call remains unpaid after it has become due and payable the directors may give to the person from whom it is due not less than fourteen clear days' notice requiring payment of the amount unpaid together with any interest which may have accrued. The notice shall name the place where payment is to be made and shall state that if the notice is not complied with the shares in respect of which the call was made will be liable to be forfeited.

19 If the notice is not complied with any share in respect of which it was given may, before the payment required by the notice has been made, be forfeited by a resolution of the directors and the forfeiture shall include all dividends or other moneys payable in respect of the forfeited shares and not paid before the forfeiture.

20 Subject to the provisions of the Act, a forfeited share may be sold, re-allotted or otherwise disposed of on such terms and in such manner as the directors determine either to the person who was before the forfeiture the holder or to any other person and at any time before sale, re-allotment or other disposition, the forfeiture may be cancelled on such terms as the directors think fit. Where for the purposes of its disposal a forfeited share is to be transferred to any person the directors may authorise some person to execute an instrument of transfer of the share to that person.

21 A person any of whose shares have been forfeited shall cease to be a member in respect of them and shall surrender to the company for cancellation the certificate for the shares forfeited but shall remain liable to the company for all moneys which at the date of forfeiture were presently payable by him to the company in respect of those shares with interest at the rate at which interest was payable on those moneys before the forfeiture or, if no interest was so payable, at the appropriate rate (as defined in the Act) from the date of forfeiture until payment but the directors may waive payment wholly or in part or enforce payment without any allowance for the value of the shares at the time of forfeiture or for any consideration received on their disposal.

22 A statutory declaration by a director or the secretary that a share has been forfeited on a specified date shall be conclusive evidence of the facts stated in it as against all persons claiming to be entitled to the share and the declaration shall (subject to the execution of an instrument of transfer if necessary) constitute a good title to the share and the person to whom the share is disposed of shall not be bound to see to the application of the consideration, if any, nor shall his title to the share be affected by any irregularity in or invalidity of the proceedings in reference to the forfeiture or disposal of the share.

**Transfer of Shares**

23 The instrument of transfer of a share may be in any usual form or in any other form which the directors may approve and shall be executed by or on behalf of the transferor and, unless the share is fully paid, by or on behalf of the transferee.

24 The directors may refuse to register the transfer of a share which is not fully paid to a person of whom they do not approve and they may refuse to register the transfer of a share on which the company has alien. They may also refuse to register a transfer unless—

   (a)   it is lodged at the office or at such other places as the directors may appoint and is accompanied by the certificate for the shares to which it relates and such other evidence as the directors may reasonably require to show the right of the transferor to make the transfer;

   (b)   it is in respect of only one class of shares; and

   (c)   it is in favour of not more than four transferees.

25 If the directors refuse to register a transfer of a share, they shall within two months after the date on which the transfer was lodged with the company send to the transferee notice of the refusal.

26 The registration of transfers of shares or of transfers of any class of shares may be suspended at such times and for such periods (not exceeding thirty days in any year) as the directors may determine.

27 No fee shall be charged for the registration of any instrument of transfer or other document relating to or affecting the title to any share.

28 The company shall be entitled to retain any instrument of transfer which is registered, but any instrument of transfer which the directors refuse to register shall be returned to the person lodging it when notice of the refusal is given.

**Transmission of Shares**

29 If a member dies the survivor or survivors where he was a joint holder, and his personal representatives where he was a sole holder or the only survivor of joint holders, shall be the only persons recognised by the company as having any title to his interest; but nothing herein contained shall release the estate of a deceased member from any liability in respect of any share which had been jointly held by him.

30 A person becoming entitled to a share in consequence of the death or bankruptcy of a member may, upon such evidence being produced as the directors may properly require, elect either to become the holder of the share or to have some person nominated by him registered as the transferee. If he elects to become the holder he shall give notice to the company to that effect. If he elects to have another person registered he shall execute an instrument of transfer of the share to that person. All the articles relating to the transfer of shares shall apply to the notice or instrument of transfer as if it were an instrument of transfer executed by the member and the death or bankruptcy of the member had not occurred.

31 A person becoming entitled to a share in consequence of the death or bankruptcy of a member shall have the rights to which he would be entitled if he were the holder of the share, except that he shall not, before being registered as the holder of the share, be entitled in respect of it to attend or vote at any meeting of the company or at any separate meeting of the holders of any class of shares in the company.

**Alteration of Share Capital**

32 The company may by ordinary resolution—

(a) increase its share capital by new shares of such amount as the resolution prescribes;

(b) consolidate and divide all or any of its share capital into shares of larger amount than its existing shares;

(c) subject to the provisions of the Act, sub-divide its shares, or any of them, into shares of smaller amount and the resolution may determine that, as between the shares resulting from the sub-division, any of them may have any preference or advantage as compared with the others; and

(d) cancel shares which, at the date of the passing of the resolution, have not been taken or agreed to be taken by any person and diminish the amount of its share capital by the amount of the shares so cancelled.

33 Whenever as a result of a consolidation of shares any members would become entitled to fractions of a share, the directors may, on behalf of those members, sell the shares representing the fractions for the best price reasonably obtainable to any person (including, subject to the provisions of the Act, the company) and distribute the net proceeds of sale in due proportion among those members, and the directors may authorise some person to execute an instrument of transfer of the shares to, or in accordance with the directions of, the purchaser. The transferee shall not be bound to see to the application of the purchase money nor shall his title to the shares be affected by any irregularity in or invalidity of the proceedings in reference to the sale.

34 Subject to the provisions of the Act, the company may by special resolution reduce its share capital, any capital redemption reserve and any share premium account in any way.

**Purchase of Own Shares**

35 Subject to the provisions of the Act, the company may purchase its own shares (including any redeemable shares) and, if it is a private company, make a payment in respect of the redemption or purchase of its own shares otherwise than out of distributable profits of the company or the proceeds of a fresh issue of shares.

**General Meetings**

36 All general meetings other than annual general meetings shall be called extraordinary general meetings.

37  The directors may call general meetings and, on the requisition of members pursuant to the provisions of the Act, shall forthwith proceed to convene an extraordinary general meeting for a date not later than eight weeks after receipt of the requisition. If there are not within the United Kingdom sufficient directors to call a general meeting, any director or any member of the company may call a general meeting.

## Notice of General Meetings

38  An annual general meeting and an extraordinary general meeting called for the passing of a special resolution or a resolution appointing a person as a director shall be called by at least twenty-one clear days' notice. All other extraordinary general meetings shall be called by at least fourteen clear days' notice but a general meeting may be called by shorter notice if it is so agreed—

(a)  in the case of an annual general meeting, by all the members entitled to attend and vote thereat; and

(b)  in the case of any other meeting by a majority in number of the members having a right to attend and vote being a majority together holding not less than ninety-five per cent. in nominal value of the shares giving that right.

The notice shall specify the time and place of the meeting and the general nature of the business to be transacted and, in the case of an annual general meeting, shall specify the meeting as such.

Subject to the provisions of the articles and to any restrictions imposed on any shares, the notice shall be given to all the members, to all persons entitled to a share in consequence of the death or bankruptcy of a member and to the directors and auditors.

39  The accidental omission to give notice of a meeting to, or the non-receipt of notice of a meeting by, any person entitled to receive notice shall not invalidate the proceedings at that meeting.

## Proceedings at General Meetings

40  No business shall be transacted at any meeting unless a quorum is present. Two persons entitled to vote upon the business to be transacted, each being a member or a proxy for a member or a duly authorised representative of a corporation, shall be a quorum.

41  If such a quorum is not present within half an hour from the time appointed for the meeting, or if during a meeting such a quorum ceases to be present, the meeting shall stand adjourned to the same day in the next week at the same time and place or [to][4] such time and place as the directors may determine.

---

4     Word substituted: Companies (Tables A to F) (Amendment) Regulations 1985, SI 1985/1052, with effect from 1 August 1985.

42 The chairman, if any, of the board of directors or in his absence some other director nominated by the directors shall preside as chairman of the meeting, but if neither the chairman nor such other director (if any) be present within fifteen minutes after the time appointed for holding the meeting and willing to act, the directors present shall elect one of their number to be chairman and, if there is only one director present and willing to act, he shall be chairman.

43 If no director is willing to act as chairman, or if no director is present within fifteen minutes after the time appointed for holding the meeting, the members present and entitled to vote shall choose one of their number to be chairman.

44 A director shall, notwithstanding that he is not a member, be entitled to attend and speak at any general meeting and at any separate meeting of the holders of any class of shares in the company.

45 The chairman may, with the consent of a meeting at which a quorum is present (and shall if so directed by the meeting), adjourn the meeting from time to time and from place to place, but no business shall be transacted at an adjourned meeting other than business which might properly have been transacted at the meeting had the adjournment not taken place. When a meeting is adjourned for fourteen days or more, at least seven clear days' notice shall be given specifying the time and place of the adjourned meeting and the general nature of the business to be transacted. Otherwise it shall not be necessary to give any such notice.

46 A resolution put to the vote of a meeting shall be decided on a show of hands unless before, or on the declaration of the result of, the show of hands a poll is duly demanded. Subject to the provisions of the Act, a poll may be demanded—

(a)   by the chairman; or
(b)   by at least two members having the right to vote at the meeting; or
(c)   by a member or members representing not less than one-tenth of the total voting rights of all the members having the right to vote at the meeting; or
(d)   by a member or members holding shares conferring a right to vote at the meeting being shares on which an aggregate sum has been paid up equal to not less than one-tenth of the total sum paid up on all the shares conferring that right;

and a demand by a person as proxy for a member shall be the same as a demand by the member.

47 Unless a poll is duly demanded a declaration by the chairman that a resolution has been carried or carried unanimously, or by a particular majority, or lost, or not carried by a particular majority and an entry to that effect in the minutes of the meeting shall be conclusive evidence of the fact without proof of the number or proportion of the votes recorded in favour of or against the resolution.

48 The demand for a poll may, before the poll is taken, be withdrawn but only with the consent of the chairman and a demand so withdrawn shall not be taken to have invalidated the result of a show of hands declared before the demand was made.

49 A poll shall be taken as the chairman directs and he may appoint scrutineers (who need not be members) and fix a time and place for declaring the result of the poll. The result of the poll shall be deemed to be the resolution of the meeting at which the poll was demanded.

50 In the case of an equality of votes, whether on a show of hands or on a poll, the chairman shall be entitled to a casting vote in addition to any other vote he may have.

51 A poll demanded on the election of a chairman or on a question of adjournment shall be taken forthwith. A poll demanded on any other question shall be taken either forthwith or at such time and place as the chairman directs not being more than thirty days after the poll is demanded. The demand for a poll shall not prevent the continuance of a meeting for the transaction of any business other than the question on which the poll was demanded. If a poll is demanded before the declaration of the result of a show of hands and the demand is duly withdrawn, the meeting shall continue as if the demand had not been made.

52 No notice need be given of a poll not taken forthwith if the time and place at which it is to be taken are announced at the meeting at which it is demanded. In any other case at least seven clear days' notice shall be given specifying the time and place at which the poll is to be taken.

53 A resolution in writing executed by or on behalf of each member who would have been entitled to vote upon it if it had been proposed at a general meeting at which he was present shall be as effectual as if it had been passed as a general meeting duly convened and held and may consist of several instruments in the like form each executed by or on behalf of one or more members.

**Votes of Members**

54 Subject to any rights or restrictions attached to any shares, on a show of hands every member who (being an individual) is present in person or (being a corporation) is present by a duly authorised representative, not being himself a member entitled to vote, shall have one vote and on a poll every member shall have one vote for every share of which he is the holder.

55 In the case of joint holders the vote of the senior who tenders a vote, whether in person or by proxy, shall be accepted to the exclusion of the votes of the other joint holders; and seniority shall be determined by the order in which the names of the holders stand in the register of members.

56 A member in respect of whom an order has been made by any court having jurisdiction (whether in the United Kingdom or elsewhere) in matters concerning mental disorder may vote, whether on a show of hands or on a poll,

by his receiver, curator bonis or other person authorised in that behalf appointed by that court, and any such receiver, curator bonis or other person may, on a poll, vote by proxy. Evidence to the satisfaction of the directors of the authority of the person claiming to exercise the right to vote shall be deposited at the office, or at such other place as is specified in accordance with the articles for the deposit of instruments of proxy, not less than 48 hours before the time appointed for holding the meeting or adjourned meeting at which the right to vote is to be exercised and in default the right to vote shall not be exercisable.

57 No member shall vote at any general meeting or at any separate meeting of the holders of any class of shares in the company, either in person or by proxy, in respect of any share held by him unless all moneys presently payable by him in respect of that share have been paid.

58 No objection shall be raised to the qualification of any voter except at the meeting or adjourned meeting at which the vote objected to is tendered, and every vote not disallowed at the meeting shall be valid. Any objection made in due time shall be referred to the chairman whose decision shall be final and conclusive.

59 On a poll votes may be given either personally or by proxy. A member may appoint more than one proxy to attend on the same occasion.

60 [The appointment of][5] a proxy shall be ...[6] executed by or on behalf of the appointor and shall be in the following form (or in a form as near thereto as circumstances allow or in any other form which is usual or which the directors may approve)—

'            PLC/Limited

I/We,                , of                , being a member/members of the above-named company, hereby appoint                of                , or failing him,                of                , as my/our proxy to vote in my/our name[s] and on my/our behalf at the annual/extraordinary general meeting of the company to be held on                19     , and at any adjournment thereof.

Signed on 19     .'

61 Where it is desired to afford members an opportunity of instructing the proxy how he shall act the [appointment of][7] a proxy shall be in the following form (or in a form as near thereto as circumstances allow or in any other form which is usual or which the directors may approve)—

'            PLC/Limited

---

[5]   Words substituted: Companies Act 1985 (Electronic Communications) Order 2000, SI 2000/3373, art 32(1), Sch 1, para 2, with effect from 22 December 2000.

[6]   Words revoked: Companies Act 1985 (Electronic Communications) Order 2000, SI 2000/3373, art 32(1), Sch 1, para 2, with effect from 22 December 2000.

[7]   Words substituted: Companies Act 1985 (Electronic Communications) Order 2000, SI 2000/3373, art 32(1), Sch 1, para 3, with effect from 22 December 2000.

I/We,            , of            , being a member/members of the above-named company, hereby appoint            of            , or failing him,            of            , as my/our proxy to vote in my/our name[s] and on my/our behalf at the annual/extraordinary general meeting of the company, to be held on            19    , and at any adjournment thereof.

This form is to be used in respect of the resolutions mentioned below as follows:

Resolution No.1 *for *against
Resolution No.2 *for *against.

*Strike out whichever is not desired.

Unless otherwise instructed, the proxy may vote as he thinks fit or abstain from voting.

Signed this        day of 19    .'

62 [The appointment of][8] a proxy and any authority under which it is executed or a copy of such authority certified notarially or in some other way approved by the directors may—

(a)   [in the case of an instrument in writing][9] be deposited at the office or at such other place within the United Kingdom as is specified in the notice convening the meeting or in any instrument of proxy sent out by the company in relation to the meeting not less than 48 hours before the time for holding the meeting or adjourned meeting at which the person named in the instrument proposes to vote; or

[(aa)   in the case of an appointment contained in an electronic communication, where an address has been specified for the purpose of receiving electronic communications—

(i)    in the notice convening the meeting, or

(ii)   in any instrument of proxy sent out by the company in relation to the meeting, or

(iii)  in any invitation contained in an electronic communication to appoint a proxy issued by the company in relation to the meeting,

be received at such address not less than 48 hours before the time for holding the meeting or adjourned meeting at which the person named in the appointment proposes to vote;][10]

---

[8]    Words substituted: Companies Act 1985 (Electronic Communications) Order 2000, SI 2000/3373, art 32(1), Sch 1, para 4(1), (2), with effect from 22 December 2000.

[9]    Words inserted: Companies Act 1985 (Electronic Communications) Order 2000, SI 2000/3373, art 32(1), Sch 1, para 4(1), (3), with effect from 22 December 2000.

[10]   Subparagraph inserted: Companies Act 1985 (Electronic Communications) Order 2000, SI 2000/3373, art 32(1), Sch 1, para 4(1), (4), with effect from 22 December 2000.

(b)     in the case of a poll taken more than 48 hours after it is demanded, be deposited [or received][11] as aforesaid after the poll has been demanded and not less than 24 hours before the time appointed for the taking of the poll; or

(c)     where the poll is not taken forthwith but is taken not more than 48 hours after it was demanded, be delivered at the meeting at which the poll was demanded to the chairman or to the secretary or to any director;

[and an appointment of proxy which is not deposited, delivered or received][12] in a manner so permitted shall be invalid. [In this regulation and the next, 'address', in relation to electronic communications, includes any number or address used for the purposes of such communications.][13]

63 A vote given or poll demanded by proxy or by the duly authorised representative of a corporation shall be valid notwithstanding the previous determination of the authority of the person voting or demanding a poll unless notice of the determination was received by the company at the office or at such other place at which the instrument of proxy was duly deposited [or, where the appointment of the proxy was contained in an electronic communication, at the address at which such appointment was duly received][14] before the commencement of the meeting or adjourned meeting at which the vote is given or the poll demanded or (in the case of a poll taken otherwise than on the same day as the meeting or adjourned meeting) the time appointed for taking the poll.

## Number of Directors

64 Unless otherwise determined by ordinary resolution, the number of directors (other than alternate directors) shall not be subject to any maximum but shall be not less than two.

## Alternate Directors

65 Any director (other than an alternate director) may appoint any other director, or any other person approved by resolution of the directors and willing to act, to be an alternate director and may remove from office an alternate director so appointed by him.

66 An alternate director shall be entitled to receive notice of all meetings of directors and of all meetings of committees of directors of which his appointor is a member, to attend and vote at any such meeting at which the director appointing him is not personally present, and generally to perform all the

---

[11]   Words inserted: Companies Act 1985 (Electronic Communications) Order 2000, SI 2000/3373, art 32(1), Sch 1, para 4(1), (5), with effect from 22 December 2000.

[12]   Words substituted: Companies Act 1985 (Electronic Communications) Order 2000, SI 2000/3373, art 32(1), Sch 1, para 4(1), (6), with effect from 22 December 2000.

[13]   Words inserted: Companies Act 1985 (Electronic Communications) Order 2000, SI 2000/3373, art 32(1), Sch 1, para 4(1), (7), with effect from 22 December 2000.

[14]   Words inserted: Companies Act 1985 (Electronic Communications) Order 2000, SI 2000/3373, art 32(1), Sch 1, para 5, with effect from 22 December 2000.

functions of his appointor as a director in his absence but shall not be entitled to receive any remuneration from the company for his services as an alternate director. But it shall not be necessary to give notice of such a meeting to an alternate director who is absent from the United Kingdom.

67  An alternate director shall cease to be an alternate director if his appointor ceases to be a director; but, if a director retires by rotation or otherwise but is reappointed or deemed to have been reappointed at the meeting at which he retires, any appointment of an alternate director made by him which was in force immediately prior to his retirement shall continue after his reappointment.

68  Any appointment or removal of an alternate director shall be by notice to the company signed by the director making or revoking the appointment or in any other manner approved by the directors.

69  Save as otherwise provided in the articles, an alternate director shall be deemed for all purposes to be a director and shall alone be responsible for his own acts and defaults and he shall not be deemed to be the agent of the director appointing him.

**Powers of Directors**

70  Subject to the provisions of the Act, the memorandum and the articles and to any directions given by special resolution, the business of the company shall be managed by the directors who may exercise all the powers of the company. No alteration of the memorandum or articles and no such direction shall invalidate any prior act of the directors which would have been valid if that alteration had not been made or that direction had not been given. The powers given by this regulation shall not be limited by any special power given to the directors by the articles and a meeting of directors at which a quorum is present may exercise all powers exercisable by the directors.

71  The directors may, by power of attorney or otherwise, appoint any person to be the agent of the company for such purposes and on such conditions as they determine, including authority for the agent to delegate all or any of his powers.

**Delegation of Directors' Powers**

72  The directors may delegate any of their powers to any committee consisting of one or more directors. They may also delegate to any managing director or any director holding any other executive office such of their powers as they consider desirable to be exercised by him. Any such delegation may be made subject to any conditions the directors may impose, and either collaterally with or to the exclusion of their own powers and may be revoked or altered. Subject to any such conditions, the proceedings of a committee with two or more members shall be governed by the articles regulating the proceedings of directors so far as they are capable of applying.

**Appointment and Retirement of Directors**

73 At the first annual general meeting all the directors shall retire from office, and at every subsequent annual general meeting one-third of the directors who are subject to retirement by rotation or, if their number is not three or a multiple of three, the number nearest to one-third shall retire from office; but, if there is only one director who is subject to retirement by rotation, he shall retire.

74 Subject to the provisions of the Act, the directors to retire by rotation shall be those who have been longest in office since their last appointment or reappointment, but as between persons who became or were last reappointed directors on the same day those to retire shall (unless they otherwise agree among themselves) be determined by lot.

75 If the company, at the meeting at which a director retires by rotation, does not fill the vacancy the retiring director shall, if willing to act, be deemed to have been reappointed unless at the meeting it is resolved not to fill the vacancy or unless a resolution for the reappointment of the directors is put to the meeting and lost.

76 No person other than a director retiring by rotation shall be appointed or reappointed a director at any general meeting unless—

(a)    he is recommended by the directors; or

(b)    not less than fourteen nor more than thirty-five clear days before the date appointed for the meeting, notice executed by a member qualified to vote at the meeting has been given to the company of the intention to propose that person for appointment or reappointment stating the particulars which would, if he were so appointed or reappointed, be required to be included in the company's register of directors together with notice executed by that person of his willingness to be appointed or reappointed.

77 Not less than seven nor more than twenty-eight clear days before the date appointed for holding a general meeting notice shall be given to all who are entitled to receive notice of the meeting of any person (other than a director retiring by rotation at the meeting) who is recommended by the directors for appointment or reappointment as a director at the meeting or in respect of whom notice has been duly given to the company of the intention to propose him at the meeting for appointment or reappointment as a director. The notice shall give the particulars of that person which would, if he were so appointed or reappointed, be required to be included in the company's register of directors.

78 Subject as aforesaid, the company may by ordinary resolution appoint a person who is willing to act to be a director either to fill a vacancy or as an additional director and may also determine the rotation in which any additional directors are to retire.

79 The directors may appoint a person who is willing to act to be a director, either to fill a vacancy or as an additional director, provided that the

appointment does not cause the number of directors to exceed any number fixed by or in accordance with the articles as the maximum number of directors. A director so appointed shall hold office only until the next following annual general meeting and shall not be taken into account in determining the directors who are to retire by rotation at the meeting. If not reappointed at such annual general meeting, he shall vacate office at the conclusion thereof.

80 Subject as aforesaid, a director who retires at an annual general meeting may, if willing to act, be reappointed. If he is not reappointed, he shall retain office until the meeting appoints someone in his place, or if it does not do so, until the end of the meeting.

## Disqualification and Removal of Directors

81 The office of a director shall be vacated if—

(a) he ceases to be a director by virtue of any provision of the Act or he becomes prohibited by law from being a director; or

(b) he becomes bankrupt or makes any arrangement or composition with his creditors generally; or

(c) he is, or may be, suffering from mental disorder and either—

(i) he is admitted to hospital in pursuance of an application for admission for treatment under the Mental Health Act 1983 or, in Scotland, an application for admission under the Mental Health (Scotland) Act 1960, or

(ii) an order is made by a court having jurisdiction (whether in the United Kingdom or elsewhere) in matters concerning mental disorder for his detention or for the appointment of a receiver, curator bonis or other person to exercise powers with respect to his property or affairs; or

(d) he resigns his office by notice to the company; or

(e) he shall for more than six consecutive months have been absent without permission of the directors from meetings of directors held during that period and the directors resolve that his office be vacated.

## Remuneration of Directors

82 The directors shall be entitled to such remuneration as the company may by ordinary resolution determine and, unless the resolution provides otherwise, the remuneration shall be deemed to accrue from day to day.

## Directors' Expenses

83 The directors may be paid all travelling, hotel and other expenses properly incurred by them in connection with their attendance at meetings of directors or committees of directors or general meetings or separate meetings of the holders of any class of shares or of debentures of the company or otherwise in connection with the discharge of their duties.

## Directors' Appointments and Interests

84 Subject to the provisions of the Act, the directors may appoint one or more of their number to the office of managing director or to any other executive office under the company and may enter into an agreement or arrangement with any director for his employment by the company or for the provision by him of any services outside the scope of the ordinary duties of a director. Any such appointment, agreement or arrangement may be made upon such terms as the directors determine and they may remunerate any such director for his services as they think fit. Any appointment of a director to an executive office shall terminate if he ceases to be a director but without prejudice to any claim to damages for breach of the contract of service between the director and the company. A managing director and a director holding any other executive office shall not be subject to retirement by rotation.

85 Subject to the provisions of the Act, and provided that he has disclosed to the directors the nature and extent of any material interests of his, a director notwithstanding his office—

(a) may be a party to, or otherwise interested in, any transaction or arrangement with the company or in which the company is otherwise interested;

(b) may be a director or other officer of, or employed by, or a party to any transaction or arrangement with, or otherwise interested in, any body corporate promoted by the company or in which the company is otherwise interested; and

(c) shall not, by reason of his office, be accountable to the company for any benefit which he derives from any such office or employment or from any such transaction or arrangement or from any interest in any such body corporate and no such transaction or arrangement shall be liable to be avoided on the ground of any such interest or benefit.

86 For the purposes of regulation 85—

(a) a general notice given to the directors that a director is to be regarded as having an interest of the nature and extent specified in the notice in any transaction or arrangement in which a specified person or class of persons is interested shall be deemed to be a disclosure that the director has an interest in any such transaction of the nature and extent so specified; and

(b) an interest of which a director has no knowledge and of which it is unreasonable to expect him to have knowledge shall not be treated as an interest of his.

## Directors' Gratuities and Pensions

87 The directors may provide benefits, whether by the payment of gratuities or pensions or by insurance or otherwise, for any director who has held but no longer holds any executive office or employment with the company or with any body corporate which is or has been a subsidiary of the company or a predecessor in business of the company or of any such subsidiary, and for any

member of his family (including a spouse and a former spouse) or any person who is or was dependent on him, and may (as well before as after he ceases to hold such office or employment) contribute to any fund and pay premiums for the purchase or provision of any such benefit.

### Proceedings of Directors

88 Subject to the provisions of the articles, the directors may regulate their proceedings as they think fit. A director may, and the secretary at the request of a director shall, call a meeting of the directors. It shall not be necessary to give notice of a meeting to a director who is absent from the United Kingdom. Questions arising at a meeting shall be decided by a majority of votes. In the case of an equality of votes, the chairman shall have a second or casting vote. A director who is also an alternate director shall be entitled in the absence of his appointor to a separate vote on behalf of his appointor in addition to his own vote.

89 The quorum for the transaction of the business of the directors may be fixed by the directors and unless so fixed at any other number shall be two. A person who holds office only as an alternate director shall, if his appointor is not present, be counted in the quorum.

90 The continuing directors or a sole continuing director may act notwithstanding any vacancies in their number, but, if the number of directors is less than the number fixed as the quorum, the continuing directors or director may act only for the purpose of filling vacancies or of calling a general meeting.

91 The directors may appoint one of their number to be the chairman of the board of directors and may at any time remove him from that office. Unless he is unwilling to do so, the director so appointed shall preside at every meeting of directors at which he is present. But if there is no director holding that office, or if the director holding it is unwilling to preside or is not present within five minutes after the time appointed for the meeting, the directors present may appoint one of their number to be chairman of the meeting.

92 All acts done by a meeting of directors, or of a committee of directors, or by a person acting as a director shall, notwithstanding that it be afterwards discovered that there was a defect in the appointment of any director or that any of them were disqualified from holding office, or had vacated office, or were not entitled to vote, be as valid as if every such person had been duly appointed and was qualified and had continued to be a director and had been entitled to vote.

93 A resolution in writing signed by all the directors entitled to receive notice of a meeting of directors or of a committee of directors shall be as valid and effectual as if it had been passed at a meeting of directors or (as the case may be) a committee of directors duly convened and held and may consist of several documents in the like form each signed by one or more directors; but a resolution signed by an alternate director need not also be signed by his

appointor and, if it is signed by a director who has appointed an alternate director, it need not be signed by the alternate director in that capacity.

94 Save as otherwise provided by the articles, a director shall not vote at a meeting of directors or of a committee of directors on any resolution concerning a matter in which he has, directly or indirectly, an interest or duty which is material and which conflicts or may conflict with the interests of the company unless his interest or duty arises only because the case falls within one or more of the following paragraphs—

(a) the resolution relates to the giving to him of a guarantee, security, or indemnity in respect of money lent to, or an obligation incurred by him for the benefit of, the company or any of its subsidiaries;

(b) the resolution relates to the giving to a third party of a guarantee, security, or indemnity in respect of an obligation of the company or any of its subsidiaries for which the director has assumed responsibility in whole or part and whether alone or jointly with others under a guarantee or indemnity or by the giving of security;

(c) his interest arises by virtue of his subscribing or agreeing to subscribe for any shares, debentures or other securities of the company or any of its subsidiaries, or by virtue of his being, or intending to become, a participant in the underwriting or sub-underwriting of an offer of any such shares, debentures, or other securities by the company or any of its subsidiaries for subscription, purchase or exchange;

(d) the resolution relates in any way to a retirement benefits scheme which has been approved, or is conditional upon approval, by the Board of Inland Revenue for taxation purposes.

For the purposes of this regulation, an interest of a person who is, for any purpose of the Act (excluding any statutory modification thereof not in force when this regulation becomes binding on the company), connected with a director shall be treated as an interest of the director and, in relation to an alternate director without prejudice to any interest which the alternate director has otherwise.

95 A director shall not be counted in the quorum present at a meeting in relation to a resolution on which he is not entitled to vote.

96 The company may by ordinary resolution suspend or relax to any extent, either generally or in respect of any particular matter, any provision of the articles prohibiting a director from voting at a meeting of directors or of a committee of directors.

97 Where proposals are under consideration concerning the appointment of two or more directors to offices or employments with the company or any body corporate in which the company is interested the proposals may be divided and considered in relation to each director separately and (provided he is not for another reason precluded from voting) each of the directors concerned shall be entitled to vote and be counted in the quorum in respect of each resolution except that concerning his own appointment.

98  If a question arises at a meeting of directors or of a committee of directors as to the right of a director to vote, the question may, before the conclusion of the meeting, be referred to the chairman of the meeting and his ruling in relation to any director other than himself shall be final and conclusive.

## Secretary

99  Subject to the provisions of the Act, the secretary shall be appointed by the directors for such term, at such remuneration and upon such conditions as they may think fit; and any secretary so appointed may be removed by them.

## Minutes

100  The directors shall cause minutes to be made in books kept for the purpose—

(a)   of all appointments of officers made by the directors; and
(b)   of all proceedings at the meetings of the company, of the holders of any class of shares in the company, and of the directors, and of committees of directors, including the names of the directors present at each such meeting.

## The Seal

101  The seal shall only be used by the authority of the directors or of a committee of directors authorised by the directors. The directors may determine who shall sign any instrument to which the seal is affixed and unless otherwise so determined it shall be signed by a director and by the secretary or by a second director.

## Dividends

102  Subject to the provisions of the Act, the company may by ordinary resolution declare dividends in accordance with the respective rights of the members, but no dividend shall exceed the amount recommended by the directors.

103  Subject to the provisions of the Act, the directors may pay interim dividends if it appears to them that they are justified by the profits of the company available for distribution. If the share capital is divided into different classes, the directors may pay interim dividends on shares which confer deferred or non-preferred rights with regard to dividend as well as on shares which confer preferential rights with regard to dividend, but no interim dividend shall be paid on shares carrying deferred or non-preferred rights if, at the time of payment, any preferential dividend is in arrears. The directors may also pay at intervals settled by them any dividend payable at a fixed rate if it appears to them that the profits available for distribution justify the payment. Provided the directors act in good faith they shall not incur any liability to the holders of shares conferring preferred rights for any loss they may suffer by the lawful payment of an interim dividend on any shares having deferred or non-preferred rights.

104 Except as otherwise provided by the rights attached to shares, all dividends shall be declared and paid according to the amounts paid up on the shares on which the dividend is paid. All dividends shall be apportioned and paid proportionately to the amounts paid up on the shares during any portion or portions of the period in respect of which the dividend is paid; but, if any share is issued on terms providing that it shall rank for dividend as from a particular date, that share shall rank for dividend accordingly.

105 A general meeting declaring a dividend may, upon the recommendation of the directors, direct that it shall be satisfied wholly or partly by the distribution of assets and, where any difficulty arises in regard to the distribution, the directors may settle the same and in particular may issue fractional certificates and fix the value for distribution of any assets and may determine that cash shall be paid to any member upon the footing of the value so fixed in order to adjust the rights of members and may vest any assets in trustees.

106 Any dividend or other moneys payable in respect of a share may be paid by cheque sent by post to the registered address of the person entitled or, if two or more persons are the holders of the share or are jointly entitled to it by reason of the death or bankruptcy of the holder, to the registered address of that one of those persons who is first named in the register of members or to such person and to such address as the person or persons entitled may in writing direct. Every cheque shall be made payable to the order of the person or persons entitled or to such other person as the person or persons entitled may in writing direct and payment of the cheque shall be a good discharge to the company. Any joint holder or other person jointly entitled to a share as aforesaid may give receipts for any dividend or other moneys payable in respect of the share.

107 No dividend or other moneys payable in respect of a share shall bear interest against the company unless otherwise provided by the rights attached to the share.

108 Any dividend which has remained unclaimed for twelve years from the date when it became due for payment shall, if the directors so resolve, be forfeited and cease to remain owing by the company.

**Accounts**

109 No member shall (as such) have any right of inspecting any accounting records or other book or document of the company except as conferred by statute or authorised by the directors or by ordinary resolution of the company.

**Capitalisation of Profits**

110 The directors may with the authority of an ordinary resolution of the company—

    (a)    subject as hereinafter provided, resolve to capitalise any undivided profits of the company not required for paying any preferential dividend (whether or not they are available for distribution) or any sum standing to the credit of the company's share premium account or capital redemption reserve;

(b)    appropriate the sum resolved to be capitalised to the members who would have been entitled to it if it were distributed by way of dividend and in the same proportions and apply such sum on their behalf either in or towards paying up the amounts, if any, for the time being unpaid on any shares held by them respectively, or in paying up in full unissued shares or debentures of the company of a nominal amount equal to that sum, and allot the shares or debentures credited as fully paid to those members, or as they may direct, in those proportions, or partly in one way and partly in the other: but the share premium account, the capital redemption reserve, and any profits which are not available for distribution may, for the purposes of this regulation, only be applied in paying up unissued shares to be allotted to members credited as fully paid;

(c)    make such provision by the issue of fractional certificates or by payment in cash or otherwise as they determine in the case of shares or debentures becoming distributable under this regulation in fractions; and

(d)    authorise any person to enter on behalf of all the members concerned into an agreement with the company providing for the allotment to them respectively, credited as fully paid, of any shares or debentures to which they are entitled upon such capitalisation, any agreement made under such authority being binding on all such members.

## Notices

[111 Any notice to be given to or by any person pursuant to the articles (other than a notice calling a meeting of the directors) shall be in writing or shall be given using electronic communications to an address for the time being notified for that purpose to the person giving the notice.

In this regulation, 'address', in relation to electronic communications, includes any number or address used for the purposes of such communications.][15]

112 The company may give any notice to a member either personally or by sending it by post in a prepaid envelope addressed to the member at his registered address or by leaving it at that address [or by giving it using electronic communications to an address for the time being notified to the company by the member][16]. In the case of joint holders of a share, all notices shall be given to the joint holder whose name stands first in the register of members in respect of the joint holding and notice so given shall be sufficient notice to all the joint holders. A member whose registered address is not within the United Kingdom and who gives to the company an address within the

---

[15]   Regulation substituted: Companies Act 1985 (Electronic Communications) Order 2000, SI 2000/3373, art 32(1), Sch 1, para 6, with effect from 22 December 2000.

[16]   Words inserted: Companies Act 1985 (Electronic Communications) Order 2000, SI 2000/3373, art 32(1), Sch 1, para 7(a), with effect from 22 December 2000.

United Kingdom at which notices may be given to him[, or an address to which notices may be sent using electronic communications,][17] shall be entitled to have notices given to him at that address, but otherwise no such member shall be entitled to receive any notice from the company.

[In this regulation and the next, 'address', in relation to electronic communications, includes any number or address used for the purposes of such communications.][18]

113 A member present, either in person or by proxy, at any meeting of the company or of the holders of any class of shares in the company shall be deemed to have received notice of the meeting and, where requisite, of the purposes for which it was called.

114 Every person who becomes entitled to a share shall be bound by any notice in respect of that share which, before his name is entered in the register of members, has been duly given to a person from whom he derives his title.

115 Proof that an envelope containing a notice was properly addressed, prepaid and posted shall be conclusive evidence that the notice was given. [Proof that a notice contained in an electronic communication was sent in accordance with guidance issued by the Institute of Chartered Secretaries and Administrators shall be conclusive evidence that the notice was given.][19] A notice shall, ...[20], be deemed to be given at the expiration of 48 hours after the envelope containing it was posted [or, in the case of a notice contained in an electronic communication, at the expiration of 48 hours after the time it was sent.][21]

116 A notice may be given by the company to the persons entitled to a share in consequence of the death or bankruptcy of a member by sending or delivering it, in any manner authorised by the articles for the giving of notice to a member, addressed to them by name, or by the title of representatives of the deceased, or trustee of the bankrupt or by any like description at the address, if any, within the United Kingdom supplied for that purpose by the persons claiming to be so entitled. Until such an address has been supplied, a notice may be given in any manner in which it might have been given if the death or bankruptcy had not occurred.

### Winding Up

117 If the company is wound up, the liquidator may, with the sanction of an extraordinary resolution of the company and any other sanction required by

---

[17] Words inserted: Companies Act 1985 (Electronic Communications) Order 2000, SI 2000/3373, art 32(1), Sch 1, para 7(b), with effect from 22 December 2000.

[18] Words inserted: Companies Act 1985 (Electronic Communications) Order 2000, SI 2000/3373, art 32(1), Sch 1, para 7(c), with effect from 22 December 2000.

[19] Words inserted: Companies Act 1985 (Electronic Communications) Order 2000, SI 2000/3373, art 32(1), Sch 1, para 8(1), (2), with effect from 22 December 2000.

[20] Words revoked: Companies (Tables A to F) (Amendment) Regulations 1985, SI 1985/1052, with effect from 1 August 1985.

[21] Words inserted: Companies Act 1985 (Electronic Communications) Order 2000, SI 2000/3373, art 32(1), Sch 1, para 8(1), (3), with effect from 22 December 2000.

the Act, divide among the members in specie the whole or any part of the assets of the company and may, for that purpose, value any assets and determine how the division shall be carried out as between the members or different classes of members. The liquidator may, with the like sanction, vest the whole or any part of the assets in trustees upon such trusts for the benefit of the members as he with the like sanction determines, but no member shall be compelled to accept any assets upon which there is a liability.

**Indemnity**

118 Subject to the provisions of the Act but without prejudice to any indemnity to which a director may otherwise be entitled, every director or other officer or auditor of the company shall be indemnified out of the assets of the company against any liability incurred by him in defending any proceedings, whether civil or criminal, in which judgment is given in his favour or in which he is acquitted or in connection with an application in which relief is granted to him by the court from liability for negligence, default, breach of duty or breach of trust in relation to the affairs of the company.

# Appendix 2

# FINANCIAL MEASURES AND STATISTICS

## TURNOVER AND TRADING HISTORY

- Sales give an indication of the scale and complexity of the operation.

- Are they increasing, decreasing or stable? Get as many years' accounts as possible and remember the 'current' year will already be out of date by the time the accounts are published.

- The detailed trading account or management accounts may analyse sales into categories (although they are not publicly available).

- The directors' report or the operating and financial review may give narrative explanation of any change in trends and forecasts for the future. Websites and trade journals may also state the aims and objectives of the company.

## PROFITS, PROFIT MARGINS AND EXPENSE RATIOS

- Is the company making a gross profit? The gross margin is affected by the sales volumes, the sales price and the level of direct costs.

- Calculate the gross profit margin (gross profit / turnover × 100%). Has it changed in recent years?

- Is the company making an operating profit?

- Calculate the return on sales (operating profit margin) (operating profit / turnover × 100%). Has it changed in recent years?

- Compare margins to other companies in the industry if possible.

- Calculate the expense ratios:
  (1) distribution costs / sales;
  (2) administration costs / sales.
     Have they changed?

- Consider employee productivity (calculate sales per employee = employee costs / sales). In an efficient company, 'sales per employee' grows faster than 'sales'. Compare this with competitors in the industry to reveal relative efficiency and productivity.

## DIVIDENDS

- Has the company paid dividends in recent years?

- Do dividend levels correspond to levels of profit after tax (ie increasing in more profitable years) or are they a similar level each year, regardless of profits? In an owner-managed business, dividends could be returns for services as a director (in lieu of salary), rather than shareholder returns. Look at directors' remuneration and compare with others in the industry. If it seems low, but dividends are high, treat them as remuneration for management services rather than returns on equity.

- Calculate dividend cover (profit after tax / dividend).

## NET ASSETS (LIABILITIES), NET CURRENT ASSETS (LIABILITIES)

- Does the company have net current liabilities (ie cannot pay debts as they fall due)? If so, it is balance sheet insolvent. It is likely to be in financial difficulty and reliant on working capital management (to pay its creditors more strongly than it collects its debts), or reliant on lenders to allow it to continue trading or to require shareholders to inject capital.

- Does the company have net assets or net liabilities? Net liabilities can indicate financial difficulty, but not always. If the company has net current assets but overall net liabilities it might continue to trade in the short term, as it can meet its short-term liabilities.

## LIQUIDITY RATIOS AND CASH

- Liquidity is the company's ability to pay its debts as they fall due. Most companies use short term sources of finance, such as a bank overdraft and trade creditors, but in order to continue trading it is essential that the company retains the confidence of these lenders. Two ratios are commonly used to analyse liquidity:
  - (1) Current ratio [(current assets / current liabilities (that is, creditors falling due within one year)]. This indicates the extent to which the claims of short-term creditors are covered by assets which are

expected to be turned into cash within one year. If current assets exceed current liabilities, liquidity should not be a problem.

(2)  Quick ratio (Current assets excluding stock / current liabilities). This ratio acknowledges that stock is the most difficult asset to turn into cash and the most likely to incur a loss on disposal. However, this ratio can be meaningless to compare year on year, so also take into account the cash flow statement.

•  The cash flow statement shows us how much cash is generated during the year from the 'core' business via 'the net cash inflow (or outflow) from operating activities'.

•  It is also possible to identify the amount of cash invested in fixed assets during the year from the cash flow statement. Significant capital expenditure may indicate a long term investment to improve future profitability, possibly at the expense of short term profitability.

•  Consider the total amount of cash and overdraft held by the company. Is it cash-rich? Is the cash position improving or deteriorating?

•  Is there an overall cash inflow or outflow?

•  Ideally it would be useful to know the 'headroom' the company has, ie how much more it could borrow. If you cannot get this information from the company, look at interest cover. That is calculated as 'Operating profit / interest payable'. It measures how many times over the company is able to meet its interest obligations. Lenders (typically banks) will not lend unless they expect the company to pay the interest on time for as long as required and then repay the principal. Depending on the relative risk aversion of the lender, loans are typically made with interest cover ranging from 1.5 (a risk-loving lender) to 5.0 (a risk-averse lender).

## FIXED ASSETS

•  Does the company own significant fixed assets? Land and buildings represent important collateral and are often the key to raising cash.

•  Were there any additions or disposals in the year? Were they at a consistent level with previous years?

•  If there were any revaluations during the year, were they based on professional valuations or the directors' opinion? Why did the directors decide to revalue at this point in time?

# EBITDA

EBITDA (Earnings before Interest, Taxes, Depreciation, and Amortisation) is an indicator of a company's financial performance. EBITDA can be used to analyse the profitability between companies and industries, because it eliminates the effects of financing and accounting decisions. It is particularly useful in industries with expensive assets that have to be written down over long periods of time.

# CAPITAL RATIOS

- These can be used to get an overall idea of working capital management within the company.

- Calculate fixed asset productivity (sales / fixed assets) and compare to prior years. This shows the ratio of sales to fixed assets.

- Calculate working capital productivity (sales / current assets) and compare to prior years. This shows the ratio of sales to current assets.

- Debtor days (trade debtors / sales × 365) show the average length of time before the company collects its debts. Have there been any changes in debtor days over the years? Consider if the company offers a prompt payment discount to customers and compare debtor days to other companies in the industry.

- Creditor days (trade creditors / purchases[1] × 365) show the average length of time before the company pays its suppliers. Have there been any changes over the years? If the company is paying sooner, it could be to get better prices. If paying later, it could be due to cash flow difficulties. Compare creditor days to other companies in the industry.

- Are stock levels rising year on year?

- Are goods being held in stock longer? Calculate stock days (finished stock / cost of sales × 365) and compare to prior years and to other companies in the industry. High stock levels tie up capital in stock, incur high storage costs and increase the risk of obsolescence.

---

[1]   Purchases with cost of sales.

# FUNDING STRUCTURE AND GEARING (DEBT AND EQUITY)

Gearing (the debt to equity ratio) considers the relationship between the proportion of capital employed that is borrowed and that which is provided by shareholders' funds. A company is 'highly geared' if it relies on borrowing for a significant part of its capital. The debt to equity ratio (expressed as a percentage) is calculated as 'Borrowed funds / (net assets – intangibles) × 100%'.

# RETURN ON CAPITAL EMPLOYED ('ROCE')

This is the prime ratio for measuring the profitability and the efficiency of a company. It is calculated as:

(profits before tax + interest on borrowings) / (share capital + reserves + all borrowings [this includes loans, corporation tax creditor and the overdraft less cash on deposit] + minority interests + deferred liabilities – intangibles).

Directors aim to maximise the cash generated from the money invested in the business and hence a high ROCE is desirable. Potential investors will compare ROCE to the interest they would receive from a bank. Compare the ROCE with other companies in the industry and look at the trend over several years. ROCE can decline even if profits are increasing.

# Appendix 3

# CALCULATING FINANCIAL RATIOS

| Called | Broad description | Features | Risks |
|---|---|---|---|
| **Creditor days** | Number of days' cost of sales (excluding payroll) which payables (creditors) represent. | Average creditors x 365 (if a year) / purchases. | VAT effect. |
| **Current ratio** *or* **Working capital ratio** | Ratio showing the number of times current assets exceed current liabilities. | Current assets / current liabilities. | Crude – affected by method of valuing stock and WIP. |
| **Debtor days** | Number of days' sales which receivables (trade debtors) represent. | Average debtors x 365 (if a year) / sales. | VAT effect. |
| **Debtor turnover** | Ratio of sales to debtors. | Sales / average debtors. | VAT effect. |
| **Dividend cover** | Ratio showing the number of times a dividend can be paid out of a year's earnings. | Profits divided by dividend. | |
| **Dividend yield** | Measure of historical dividend return against share price. | | High yield may reflect risk or anticipated reduction in dividend. |
| **EPS** | Earnings per share (pence). | Profit after tax / average number of shares in issue. | Definition of earnings. Differential categories of shares. |
| **Fixed asset ratio** | Indicates level of activity. | Sales/ total fixed assets. | Depreciation will reduce fixed assets and may flatter the trend. |

| Called | Broad description | Features | Risks |
|---|---|---|---|
| **Gearing** | Ratio of debt finance to equity. | Debt finance / equity capital. Classification between the two may not be simple. | High gearing produces fast returns when conditions are favourable. The reverse when tough. |
| **GP%** | Ratio of gross profit to sales. | Gross profit / sales. | Gross margin percentage is a variant of this, although similar. |
| **Interest cover** | Ratio showing the number of times interest can be paid out of a year's operating profit. | Operating profit divided by interest cost. | |
| **IRR** | Internal rate of return. | Net income as an annual percentage rate earned on an investment. | Can be highly subjective. |
| **Liquidity** | How readily assets are converted to cash. Or how readily shares may be traded. | May be cash and near cash divided by sums due for payment in near future. | |
| **Net profit %** | Ratio of net profit to sales. | Net profit / sales. | |
| **P/E** | Price expressed as the number of years' earnings. | (Market) price of a share / earnings per share. | Effect of anticipated news not yet adjusted in the earnings. |
| **Quick ratio** *or* **Acid-test ratio** | Cash and debtors divided by current creditors and bank overdraft. | | This measure excludes stock and WIP from assets. |
| **ROCE** | Return on capital employed (percent). | Profit after tax / Average capital employed x 100. | Definition of profit. Definition of capital employed. |

| Called | Broad description | Features | Risks |
|---|---|---|---|
| **ROI** | Return on investment (percent). | Profit / assets x 100. | Definition of profit. Definition of assets. |
| **Stock turnover** | Ratio of the two – may be turned the other way up and expressed as days. | Cost of sales / average stock. | Blunt measure – variances between product lines or areas of operation. |

# Appendix 4

# TAX RATES, LIMITS AND RELIEFS

## INCOME TAX

### Income tax allowances 2009/10

| | |
|---|---|
| Personal allowance (age under 65) | £6,475 |
| Personal allowance (age 65–74) | £9,490 |
| Personal allowance (age 75 and over) | £9,640 |
| Married couple's allowance[1] (age 75 and over) | £6,965 |
| Married couple's allowance[1] – minimum amount | £2,670 |
| Income limit for age-related allowances | £22,900 |

[1]   Given at the rate of 10%.

### Income tax bands 2009/10

| | | |
|---|---|---|
| Basic rate | 20% | £0–£37,400 |
| Higher rate | 40% | Over £37,400 |

## CAPITAL GAINS TAX

### Exempt assets

The following are wholly exempt from capital gains tax:

- wasting chattels (eg private motor cars, yachts etc);

- savings certificates and similar non-marketable securities;

- gilt-edged securities (eg Treasury stock);

- qualifying corporate bonds;

- cash (although foreign currency held as an investment is not exempt);

- pension and annuity rights.

## Exempt disposals

Some gains arising from the disposal of certain assets are exempt from capital gains tax in particular circumstances; examples of assets which may qualify are:

- main residence;

- non-wasting chattels (valued at less than £6,000);

- debts (disposal by original creditor or his or her personal representative or legatee);

- policies of insurance/life assurance (if sold by original owner);

- SAYE terminal bonuses;

- decorations for valour (if sold by original owner);

- foreign currency for personal use abroad;

- compensation for personal injury.

## Capital gains 2009/10

| | |
|---|---|
| *Rate of tax* | 18% |
| *Annual allowance* | |
| Individuals | £10,100 |
| Trusts | £5,050[2] |

[2] Divided by the number of trusts set up by the same settlor, subject to a minimum allowance of £505 per trust.

## INHERITANCE TAX

## Exempt gifts

| Type of gift | Date given | Limits |
|---|---|---|
| Between husband & wife | Any time | None (£55,000 limit if donee is not UK domiciled, but donor is) |
| To charity | Any time | None |
| Lump sum paid out by pension scheme | On death only | None |

| Type of gift | Date given | Limits |
|---|---|---|
| Annual exemption | Per tax year | £3,000 plus any unused balance from the previous tax year only. |
| Small gifts | Per tax year | Up to a total value of £250 per person, for any number of people. |
| Marriage gifts | On marriage | Parents can give £5,000 each, grandparents £2,500 each, others £1,000 each. |
| Regular gifts | During lifetime | Gift must be funded from income, not from savings. |
| Any gift to an individual not covered above | During lifetime | Exempt unless donor dies within 7 years of making the gift (see below). Gift must be made without 'strings attached'. |

## Inheritance tax rates

|  |  | 2008/09 | 2009/10 |
|---|---|---|---|
| Nil band |  | £312,000 | £325,000 |
| Death tax | 40% | Excess | Excess |
| Lifetime tax | 20% | Excess | Excess |

## Taper relief

Where tax is charged on death on any gift made within 7 years of death, taper relief may apply as follows:

| Years before death | 0–3 | 3–4 | 4–5 | 5–6 | 6–7 |
|---|---|---|---|---|---|
| Percentage taxable on death | 100 | 80 | 60 | 40 | 20 |

## CORPORATION TAX BANDS

| | | |
|---|---|---|
| Small companies rate | 21% | 0–£300,000 |
| Marginal relief | 29.75%[3] | £300,001–£1,500,000 |
| Main rate | 28% | £1,500,000 or more |

[3] Effective rate.

# Appendix 5

# FAMILY PROCEEDINGS RULES 1991,
# SI 1991/1247

\*\*\*\*

### 2.51B Application of ancillary relief rules

(1) The procedures set out in rules 2.51D to 2.71 ('the ancillary relief rules') apply to –

> (*a*)   any ancillary relief application,
> (*b*)   any application under section 10(2) of the Act of 1973, and
> (*c*)   any application under section 48(2) of the Act of 2004.

(2) In the ancillary relief rules, unless the context otherwise requires:

> 'applicant' means the party applying for ancillary relief;
> 'respondent' means the respondent to the application for ancillary relief;
> 'FDR appointment' means a Financial Dispute Resolution appointment in accordance with rule 2.61E.

**Amendments**—Inserted by SI 1999/3491; amended by SI 2005/2922; SI 2006/352.

\*\*\*\*

### 2.51D The overriding objective

(1) The ancillary relief rules are a procedural code with the overriding objective of enabling the court to deal with cases justly.

(2) Dealing with a case justly includes, so far as is practicable –

> (*a*)   ensuring that the parties are on an equal footing;
> (*b*)   saving expense;
> (*c*)   dealing with the case in ways which are proportionate –
> >  (i)    to the amount of money involved;
> >  (ii)   to the importance of the case;
> >  (iii)  to the complexity of the issues; and
> >  (iv)   to the financial position of each party;
> (*d*)   ensuring that it is dealt with expeditiously and fairly; and
> (*e*)   allotting to it an appropriate share of the court's resources, while taking into account the need to allot resources to other cases.

(3) The court must seek to give effect to the overriding objective when it –

> (*a*)   exercises any power given to it by the ancillary relief rules; or
> (*b*)   interprets any rule.

(4) The parties are required to help the court to further the overriding objective.

(5) The court must further the overriding objective by actively managing cases.

(6) Active case management includes –

(a)    encouraging the parties to co-operate with each other in the conduct of the proceedings;

(b)    encouraging the parties to settle their disputes through mediation, where appropriate;

(c)    identifying the issues at an early date;

(d)    regulating the extent of disclosure of documents and expert evidence so that they are proportionate to the issues in question;

(e)    helping the parties to settle the whole or part of the case;

(f)    fixing timetables or otherwise controlling the progress of the case;

(g)    making use of technology; and

(h)    giving directions to ensure that the trial of a case proceeds quickly and efficiently.

**Amendments**—Inserted by SI 1999/3491; amended by SI 2005/2922.

### 2.52  Right to be heard on ancillary questions

A respondent may be heard on any question of ancillary relief without filing an answer and whether or not he has returned to the court office an acknowledgement of service stating his wish to be heard on that question.

### 2.53  Application by petitioner or respondent for ancillary relief

(1) Any application by a petitioner, or by a respondent who files an answer claiming relief, for –

(a)    an order for maintenance pending suit,

(aa)   an order for maintenance pending outcome of proceedings,

(b)    a financial provision order,

(c)    a property adjustment order,

(d)    a pension sharing order

shall be made in the petition or answer, as the case may be.

(2) Notwithstanding anything in paragraph (1), an application for ancillary relief which should have been made in the petition or answer may be made subsequently –

(a)    by leave of the court, either by notice in Form A or at the trial, or

(b)    where the parties are agreed upon the terms of the proposed order, without leave by notice in Form A.

(3) An application by a petitioner or respondent for ancillary relief, not being an application which is required to be made in the petition or answer, shall be made by notice in Form A.

**Amendments**—SI 1999/3491; SI 2000/2267; SI 2005/2922.

**2.54 Application by parent, guardian etc for ancillary relief in respect of children**

(1) Any of the following persons, namely –

(*a*)   a parent or guardian of any child of the family,

(*b*)   any person in whose favour a residence order has been made with respect to a child of the family, and any applicant for such an order,

(*c*)   any other person who is entitled to apply for a residence order with respect to a child,

(*d*)   a local authority, where an order has been made under section 31(1)(*a*) of the Act of 1989 placing a child in its care,

(*e*)   the Official Solicitor, if appointed the guardian ad litem of a child of the family under rule 9.5, and

(*f*)   a child of the family who has been given leave to intervene in the cause for the purpose of applying for ancillary relief,

may apply for an order for ancillary relief as respects that child by notice in Form A.

(2) In this rule 'residence order' has the meaning assigned to it by section 8(1) of the Act of 1989.

**Amendments**—SI 1999/3491; SI 2005/2922.

**2.55, 2.56**

(*revoked*)

**2.57 Children to be separately represented on certain applications**

(1) Where an application is made to the High Court or a designated county court for an order for a variation of settlement, the court shall, unless it is satisfied that the proposed variation does not adversely affect the rights or interests of any children concerned, direct that the children be separately represented on the application, either by a solicitor or by a solicitor and counsel, and may appoint the Official Solicitor or other fit person to be guardian ad litem of the children for the purpose of the application.

(2) On any other application for ancillary relief the court may give such a direction or make such appointment as it is empowered to give or make by paragraph (1).

(3) Before a person other than the Official Solicitor is appointed guardian ad litem under this rule there shall be filed a certificate by the solicitor acting for the children that the person proposed as guardian has no interest in the matter adverse to that of the children and that he is a proper person to be such guardian.

**Amendments**—SI 2005/2922.

**2.58**

(*revoked*)

### 2.59 Evidence on application for property adjustment or avoidance of disposition order

(1) (*revoked*)

(2) Where an application for a property adjustment order or an avoidance of disposition order relates to land, the notice in Form A shall identify the land and –

    (*a*)    state whether the title to the land is registered or unregistered and, if registered, the Land Registry title number; and

    (*b*)    give particulars, so far as known to the applicant, of any mortgage of the land or any interest therein.

(3) Copies of Form A and of Form E completed by the applicant, shall be served on the following persons as well as on the respondent to the application, that is to say –

    (*a*)    in the case of an application for an order for a variation of settlement, the trustees of the settlement and the settlor if living;

    (*b*)    in the case of an application for an avoidance of disposition order, the person in whose favour the disposition is alleged to have been made;

and such other persons, if any, as the district judge may direct.

(4) In the case of an application to which paragraph (2) refers, a copy of Form A shall be served on any mortgagee of whom particulars are given pursuant to that paragraph; any person so served may apply to the court in writing, within 14 days after service, for a copy of the applicant's Form E.

(5) Any person who –

    (*a*)    is served with copies of Forms A and E pursuant to paragraph (3), or

    (*b*)    receives a copy of Form E following an application made in accordance with paragraph (4),

may, within 14 days after service or receipt, as the case may be, file a statement in answer.

(6) A statement filed under paragraph (5) shall be sworn to be true.

Amendments—SI 1992/456; SI 1999/3491.

### 2.60 Service of statement in answer

(1) Where a form or other document filed with the court contains an allegation of adultery or of an improper association with a named person ('the named person'), the court may direct that the party who filed the relevant form or document serve a copy of all or part of that form or document on the named person, together with Form F.

(2) If the court makes a direction under paragraph (1), the named person may file a statement in answer to the allegations.

(3) A statement under paragraph (2) shall be sworn to be true.

(4) Rule 2.37(3) shall apply to a person served under paragraph (1) as it applies to a co-respondent.

**Amendments**—Substituted by SI 1999/3491.

### 2.61 Information on application for consent order for financial relief

(1) Subject to paragraphs (2) and (3), there shall be lodged with every application for a consent order under any of sections 23, 24 or 24A of the Act of 1973, or Parts 1, 2 and 3 of Schedule 5 to the Act of 2004, two copies of a draft of the order in the terms sought, one of which shall be indorsed with a statement signed by the respondent to the application signifying his agreement, and a statement of information (which may be made in more than one document) which shall include –

- (*a*)   the duration of the marriage or civil partnership, as the case may be, the age of each party and of any minor or dependent child of the family;
- (*b*)   an estimate in summary form of the approximate amount of value or the capital resources and net income of each party and of any minor child of the family;
- (*c*)   what arrangements are intended for the accommodation of each of the parties and any minor child of the family;
- (*d*)   whether either party has subsequently married or formed a civil partnership or has any present intention to do so or to cohabit with another person;
- (*dd*)   where the order includes provision to be made under section 25B or 25C of the Act of 1973 or under paragraphs 25 or 26 of Schedule 5 to the Act of 2004, a statement confirming that the person responsible for the pension arrangement in question has been served with the documents required by rule 2.70(11) and that no objection to such an order has been made by that person within 21 days from such service;
- (*e*)   where the terms of the order provide for a transfer of property, a statement confirming that any mortgagee of that property has been served with notice of the application and that no objection to such a transfer has been made by the mortgagee within 14 days from such service; and
- (*f*)   any other especially significant matters.

(2) Where an application is made for a consent order varying an order for periodical payments paragraph (1) shall be sufficiently complied with if the statement of information required to be lodged with the application includes only the information in respect of net income mentioned in paragraph (1)(*b*) (and, where appropriate, a statement under paragraph (1)(*dd*)), and an application for a consent order for interim periodical payments pending the determination of an application for ancillary relief may be made in like manner.

(3) Where all or any of the parties attend the hearing of an application for financial relief the court may dispense with the lodging of a statement of information in accordance with paragraph (1) and give directions for the

information which would otherwise be required to be given in such a statement to be given in such a manner as it sees fit.

Amendments—SI 1996/1674; SI 2000/2267; SI 2003/2839; SI 2005/2922; SI 2006/2080.

### 2.61A  Application for ancillary relief

(1) A notice of intention to proceed with an application for ancillary relief made in the petition or answer or an application for ancillary relief must be made by notice in Form A.

(2)  The notice must be filed:

(*a*)  if the case is pending in a designated county court, in that court; or
(*b*)  if the case is pending in the High Court, in the registry in which it is proceeding.

(3) Where the applicant requests an order for ancillary relief that includes provision to be made by virtue of section 24B, 25B or 25C of the Act of 1973 or under paragraphs 15, 25 or 26 of Schedule 5 to the Act of 2004 the terms of the order requested must be specified in the notice in Form A.

(4)  Upon the filing of Form A the court must:

(*a*)  fix a first appointment not less than 12 weeks and not more than 16 weeks after the date of the filing of the notice and give notice of that date;
(*b*)  serve a copy on the respondent within 4 days of the date of the filing of the notice.

(5) The date fixed under paragraph (4) for the first appointment, or for any subsequent appointment, must not be cancelled except with the court's permission and, if cancelled, the court must immediately fix a new date.

Amendments—Inserted by SI 1999/3491; amended by SI 2000/2267; SI 2005/2922.

### 2.61B  Procedure before the first appointment

(1)  Both parties must, at the same time, exchange with each other, and each file with the court, a statement in Form E, which –

(*a*)  is signed by the party who made the statement;
(*b*)  is sworn to be true, and
(*c*)  contains the information and has attached to it the documents required by that Form.

(2) Form E must be exchanged and filed not less than 35 days before the date of the first appointment.

(3)  Form E must have attached to it:

(*a*)  any documents required by Form E;
(*b*)  any other documents necessary to explain or clarify any of the information contained in Form E; and

(*c*)   any documents furnished to the party producing the form by a person responsible for a pension arrangement, either following a request under rule 2.70(2) or as part of a 'relevant valuation' as defined in rule 2.70(4); and

(*d*)   any notification or other document referred to in paragraphs (2), (4) or (5) of rule 2.70A which has been received by the party producing the form.

(4) Form E must have no documents attached to it other than the documents referred to in paragraph (3).

(5) Where a party was unavoidably prevented from sending any document required by Form E, that party must at the earliest opportunity:

(*a*)   serve copies of that document on the other party, and

(*b*)   file a copy of that document with the court, together with a statement explaining the failure to send it with Form E.

(6) No disclosure or inspection of documents may be requested or given between the filing of the application for ancillary relief and the first appointment, except –

(*a*)   copies sent with Form E, or in accordance with paragraph (5); or

(*b*)   in accordance with paragraph (7).

(7) At least 14 days before the hearing of the first appointment, each party must file with the court and serve on the other party –

(*a*)   a concise statement of the issues between the parties;

(*b*)   a chronology;

(*c*)   a questionnaire setting out by reference to the concise statement of issues any further information and documents requested from the other party or a statement that no information and documents are required;

(*d*)   a notice in Form G stating whether that party will be in a position at the first appointment to proceed on that occasion to a FDR appointment.

(8) (*revoked*)

(9) At least 14 days before the hearing of the first appointment, the applicant must file with the court and serve on the respondent, confirmation of the names of all persons served in accordance with rule 2.59(3) and (4), and that there are no other persons who must be served in accordance with those paragraphs.

**Amendments**—Inserted by SI 1999/3491; amended by SI 2000/2267; SI 2006/2080.

### 2.61C  Expert evidence

CPR rules 35.1 to 35.14 relating to expert evidence (with appropriate modifications), except CPR rules 35.5(2) and 35.8(4)(*b*), apply to all ancillary relief proceedings.

**Amendments**—Inserted by SI 1999/3491.

### 2.61D  The first appointment

(1)  The first appointment must be conducted with the objective of defining the issues and saving costs.

(2)  At the first appointment the district judge –

(*a*)  must determine –
　　(i)  the extent to which any questions seeking information under rule 2.61B must be answered, and
　　(ii)  what documents requested under rule 2.61B must be produced, and give directions for the production of such further documents as may be necessary;

(*b*)  must give directions about –
　　(i)  the valuation of assets (including, where appropriate, the joint instruction of joint experts);
　　(ii)  obtaining and exchanging expert evidence, if required; and
　　(iii)  evidence to be adduced by each party and, where appropriate, about further chronologies or schedules to be filed by each party;

(*c*)  must, unless he decides that a referral is not appropriate in the circumstances, direct that the case be referred to a FDR appointment;

(*d*)  must, where he decides that a referral to a FDR appointment is not appropriate, direct one or more of the following:
　　(i)  that a further directions appointment be fixed;
　　(ii)  that an appointment be fixed for the making of an interim order;
　　(iii)  that the case be fixed for final hearing and, where that direction is given, the district judge must determine the judicial level at which the case should be heard;
　　(iv)  that the case be adjourned for out-of-court mediation or private negotiation or, in exceptional circumstances, generally;

(*e*)  in considering whether to make a costs order under rule 2.71(4), must have particular regard to the extent to which each party has complied with the requirement to send documents with Form E; and

(*f*)  may –
　　(i)  make an interim order where an application for it has been made in accordance with rule 2.69F returnable at the first appointment;
　　(ii)  having regard to the contents of Form G filed by the parties, treat the appointment (or part of it) as a FDR appointment to which rule 2.61E applies;
　　(iii)  in a matrimonial cause, in a case where an order for ancillary relief is requested that includes provision to be made under section 24B, 25B or 25C of the Act 1973, direct any party with pension rights to file and serve a Pension Inquiry Form (Form P), completed in full or in part as the court may direct;
　　(iv)  in a civil partnership cause, in a case where an order for ancillary relief is requested that includes provision to be made under paragraphs 15, 25 or 26 of Schedule 5 to the Act of 2004, direct

any civil partner with pension rights to file and serve a Pension Inquiry Form (Form P), completed in full or in part as the court may direct.

(3) After the first appointment, a party is not entitled to production of any further documents except in accordance with directions given under paragraph (2)(*a*) above or with the permission of the court.

(4) At any stage:

    (*a*)    a party may apply for further directions or a FDR appointment;

    (*b*)    the court may give further directions or direct that the parties attend a FDR appointment.

(5) Both parties must personally attend the first appointment unless the court orders otherwise.

**Amendments**—Inserted by SI 1999/3491; amended by SI 2003/184; SI 2005/2922; SI 2006/352.

## 2.61E  The FDR appointment

(1) The FDR appointment must be treated as a meeting held for the purposes of discussion and negotiation and paragraphs (2) to (9) apply.

(2) The district judge or judge hearing the FDR appointment must have no further involvement with the application, other than to conduct any further FDR appointment or to make a consent order or a further directions order.

(3) Not later than 7 days before the FDR appointment, the applicant must file with the court details of all offers and proposals, and responses to them.

(4) Paragraph (3) includes any offers, proposals or responses made wholly or partly without prejudice, but paragraph (3) does not make any material admissible as evidence if, but for that paragraph, it would not be admissible.

(5) At the conclusion of the FDR appointment, any documents filed under paragraph (3), and any filed documents referring to them, must, at the request of the party who filed them, be returned to him and not retained on the court file.

(6) Parties attending the FDR appointment must use their best endeavours to reach agreement on the matters in issue between them.

(7) The FDR appointment may be adjourned from time to time.

(8) At the conclusion of the FDR appointment, the court may make an appropriate consent order, but otherwise must give directions for the future course of the proceedings, including, where appropriate, the filing of evidence and fixing a final hearing date.

(9) Both parties must personally attend the FDR appointment unless the court orders otherwise.

**Amendments**—Inserted by SI 1999/3491.

**2.61F Costs**

(1) Subject to paragraph (2), at every hearing or appointment each party must produce to the court an estimate in Form H of the costs incurred by him up to the date of that hearing or appointment.

(2) Not less than 14 days before the date fixed for the final hearing of an application for ancillary relief, each party must (unless the court directs otherwise) file with the court and serve on each other party a statement in Form H1 giving full particulars of all costs in respect of the proceedings which he has incurred or expects to incur, to enable the court to take account of the parties' liabilities for costs when deciding what order (if any) to make for ancillary relief.

**Amendments**—Inserted by SI 1999/3491; amended by SI 2006/352.

**2.62 Investigation by district judge of application for ancillary relief**

(1) (*revoked*)

(2) An application for an avoidance of disposition order shall, if practicable, be heard at the same time as any related application for financial relief.

(3) (*revoked*)

(4) At the hearing of an application for ancillary relief the district judge shall, subject to rules 2.64, 2.65 and 10.10 investigate the allegations made in support of and in answer to the application, and may take evidence orally and may at any stage of the proceedings, whether before or during the hearing, order the attendance of any person for the purpose of being examined or cross-examined and order the disclosure and inspection of any document or require further statements.

(4A) A statement filed under paragraph (4) shall be sworn to be true.

(5), (6) (*revoked*)

(7) Any party may apply to the court for an order that any person do attend an appointment (an 'inspection appointment') before the court and produce any documents to be specified or described in the order, the inspection of which appears to the court to be necessary for disposing fairly of the application for ancillary relief or for saving costs.

(8) No person shall be compelled by an order under paragraph (7) to produce any document at an inspection appointment which he could not be compelled to produce at the hearing of the application for ancillary relief.

(9) The court shall permit any person attending an inspection appointment pursuant to an order under paragraph (7) above to be represented at the appointment.

**Amendments**—SI 1999/3491.

**2.63**

(*revoked*)

## 2.64 Order on application for ancillary relief

(1) Subject to rule 2.65 the district judge shall, after completing his investigation under rule 2.62, make such order as he thinks just.

(2) Pending the final determination of the application, and subject to rule 2.69F, the district judge may make an interim order upon such terms as he thinks just.

(3) RSC Order 31, rule 1 (power to order sale of land) shall apply to applications for ancillary relief as it applies to causes and matters in the Chancery Division.

**Amendments**—SI 1999/3491.

## 2.65 Reference of application to judge

The district judge may at any time refer an application for ancillary relief, or any question arising thereon, to a judge for his decision.

## 2.66 Arrangements for hearing of application etc by judge

(1) Where an application for ancillary relief or any question arising thereon has been referred or adjourned to a judge, the proper officer shall fix a date, time and place for the hearing of the application or the consideration of the question and give notice thereof to all parties.

(2) The hearing or consideration shall, unless the court otherwise directs, take place in chambers.

(3) In a matrimonial cause, where the application is proceeding in a divorce county court which is not a court of trial or is pending in the High Court and proceedings in a district registry which is not in a divorce town, the hearing or consideration shall take place at such court of trial or divorce town as in the opinion of the district judge is the nearest or most convenient.

For the purposes of this paragraph the Royal Courts of Justice shall be treated as a divorce town.

(3A) In a civil partnership cause, where an application is proceeding in a civil partnership proceedings county court which is not a court of trial or pending in the High Court and proceeding in a district registry which is not in a dissolution town, the hearing or consideration shall take place at such court of trial or dissolution town as in the opinion of the district judge is the nearest or most convenient.

For the purposes of this paragraph the Royal Courts of Justice shall be treated as a dissolution town.

(4) In respect of any application referred to him under this rule, a judge shall have the same powers to make directions as a district judge has under these rules.

Amendments—SI 1999/3491; SI 2005/2922.

### 2.67 Request for periodical payments order at same rate as order for maintenance pending suit or outcome of proceedings

(1) Where at or after the date of a decree nisi of divorce or nullity of marriage or a conditional order of dissolution or nullity of civil partnership an order for maintenance pending suit or outcome of proceedings, as the case may be, is in force, the party in whose favour the order was made may, if he has made an application for an order for periodical payments for himself in his petition or answer, as the case may be, request the district judge in writing to make such an order (in this rule referred to as a 'corresponding order') providing for payments at the same rate as those provided for by the order for maintenance pending suit or outcome of proceedings.

(2) Where such a request is made, the proper officer shall serve on the other spouse or civil partner, as the case may be, a notice in Form I requiring him, if he objects to the making of a corresponding order, to give notice to that effect to the court and to the applicant within 14 days after service of the notice on Form I.

(3) If the other spouse or civil partner does not give notice of objection within the time aforesaid, the district judge may make a corresponding order without further notice to that spouse or civil partner and without requiring the attendance of the applicant or his solicitor, and shall in that case serve a copy of the order on the applicant as well as on the other spouse or civil partner, as the case may be.

Amendments—SI 1999/3491; SI 2005/2922.

### 2.68 Application for order under section 37(2)(*a*) of Act of 1973 or paragraph 74(2) of Schedule 5 to Act of 2004

(1) An application under section 37(2)(*a*) of the Act of 1973 or paragraph 74(2) of Schedule 5 to the Act of 2004 for an order restraining any person from attempting to defeat a claim for financial provision or otherwise for protecting the claim may be made to the district judge.

(2) Rules 2.65 and 2.66 shall apply, with the necessary modifications, to the application as if it were an application for ancillary relief.

Amendments—SI 2005/2922.

### 2.69–2.69D

*(revoked)*

## 2.69E  Open proposals

(1) Not less than 14 days before the date fixed for the final hearing of an application for ancillary relief, the applicant must (unless the court directs otherwise) file with the court and serve on the respondent an open statement which sets out concise details, including the amounts involved, of the orders which he proposes to ask the court to make.

(2) Not more than 7 days after service of a statement under paragraph (1), the respondent must file with the court and serve on the applicant an open statement which sets out concise details, including the amounts involved, of the orders which he proposes to ask the court to make.

**Amendments**—Inserted by SI 1999/3491.

## 2.69F  Application for interim orders

(1) A party may apply at any stage of the proceedings for an order for maintenance pending suit or outcome of proceedings, as the case may be, interim periodical payments or an interim variation order.

(2) An application for such an order must be made by notice of application and the date fixed for the hearing of the application must be not less than 14 days after the date the notice of application is issued.

(3) The applicant shall forthwith serve the respondent with a copy of the notice of application.

(4) Where an application is made before a party has filed Form E, that party must file with the application and serve on the other party, a draft of the order requested and a short sworn statement explaining why the order is necessary and giving the necessary information about his means.

(5) Not less than 7 days before the date fixed for the hearing, the respondent must file with the court and serve on the other party, a short sworn statement about his means, unless he has already filed Form E.

(6) A party may apply for any other form of interim order at any stage of the proceedings with or without notice.

(7) Where an application referred to in paragraph (6) is made with notice, the provisions of paragraphs (1) to (5) apply to it.

(8) Where an application referred to in paragraph (6) is made without notice, the provisions of paragraph (1) apply to it.

**Amendments**—Inserted by SI 1999/3491; amended by SI 2005/2922.

## 2.70  Pensions

(1) This rule applies where an application for ancillary relief has been made, or notice of intention to proceed with the application has been given, in Form A, or an application has been made in Form B, and the applicant or respondent has or is likely to have any benefits under a pension arrangement.

(2) When the court fixes a first appointment as required by rule 2.61A(4)(*a*),

(*a*)　　in a matrimonial cause, the party with pension rights, and
(*b*)　　in a civil partnership cause, the civil partner with pension rights,

shall within 7 days after receiving notification of the date of that appointment, request the person responsible for each pension arrangement under which he has or is likely to have benefits to furnish the information referred to in regulation 2(2) of the Pensions on Divorce etc (Provision of Information) Regulations 2000.

(3) Within 7 days of receiving information under paragraph (2) the party with pension rights or civil partner with pension rights, as the case may be, shall send a copy of it to the other party or civil partner, together with the name and address of the person responsible for each pension arrangement.

(4) A request under paragraph (2) above need not be made where the party with pension rights or the civil partner with pension rights is in possession of, or has requested, a relevant valuation of the pension rights or benefits accrued under the pension arrangement in question.

(5) In this rule, a relevant valuation means a valuation of pension rights or benefits as at a date not more than twelve months earlier than the date fixed for the first appointment which has been furnished or requested for the purposes of any of the following provisions –

(*a*)　　the Pensions on Divorce etc (Provision of Information) Regulations 2000;
(*b*)　　regulation 5 of and Schedule 2 to the Occupational Pension Schemes (Disclosure of Information) Regulations 1996 and regulation 11 of and Schedule 1 to the Occupational Pension Schemes (Transfer Value) Regulations 1996;
(*c*)　　section 93A or 94(1)(*a*) or (*aa*) of the Pension Schemes Act 1993;
(*d*)　　section 94(1)(*b*) of the Pension Schemes Act 1993 or paragraph 2(*a*) (or, where applicable, 2(*b*)) of Schedule 2 to the Personal Pension Schemes (Disclosure of Information) Regulations 1987.

(6) Upon making or giving notice of intention to proceed with an application for ancillary relief which includes a request for a pension sharing order, or upon adding a request for such an order to an existing application for ancillary relief, the applicant shall send to the person responsible for the pension arrangement concerned a copy of Form A.

(7) Upon making or giving notice of intention to proceed with an application for ancillary relief which includes an application for a pension attachment order, or upon adding a request for such an order to an existing application for ancillary relief, the applicant shall send to the person responsible for the pension arrangement concerned –

(*a*)　　a copy of Form A;

(*b*)    an address to which any notice which the person responsible is required to serve on the applicant under the Divorce etc (Pensions) Regulations 2000 or the Dissolution etc (Pensions) Regulations 2005, as the case may be, is to be sent;

(*c*)    an address to which any payment which the person responsible is required to make to the applicant is to be sent; and

(*d*)    where the address in sub-paragraph (*c*) is that of a bank, a building society or the Department of National Savings, sufficient details to enable payment to be made into the account of the applicant.

(8) A person responsible for a pension arrangement on whom a copy of a notice under paragraph (7) is served may, within 21 days after service, require the party or civil partner with the pension rights, as the case may be, to provide him with a copy of section 2.13 of his Form E; and that party or civil partner must then provide that person with the copy of that section of the statement within the time limited for filing it by rule 2.61B(2), or 21 days after being required to do so, whichever is the later.

(9) A person responsible for a pension arrangement who receives a copy of section 2.13 of Form E as required pursuant to paragraph (8) may within 21 days after receipt send to the court, the applicant and the respondent a statement in answer.

(10) A person responsible for a pension arrangement who files a statement in answer pursuant to paragraph (9) shall be entitled to be represented at the first appointment, and the court must within 4 days of the date of filing of the statement in answer give the person notice of the date of the first appointment.

(11) Where the parties have agreed on the terms of an order and the agreement includes a pension attachment order, then unless service has already been effected under paragraph (7), they shall serve on the person responsible for the pension arrangement concerned –

(*a*)    the notice of application for a consent order under rule 2.61(1);

(*b*)    a draft of the proposed order under rule 2.61(1), complying with paragraph (13) below; and

(*c*)    the particulars set out in sub-paragraphs (*b*), (*c*) and (*d*) of paragraph (7) above.

(12) No consent order under paragraph (11) shall be made unless either –

(*a*)    the person responsible has not made any objection within 21 days after the service on him of such notice; or

(*b*)    the court has considered any such objection

and for the purpose of considering any objection the court may make such direction as it sees fit for the person responsible to attend before it or to furnish written details of his objection.

(13) An order for ancillary relief, whether by consent or not, which includes a pension sharing order or a pension attachment order, shall –

(a)   in the body of the order, state that there is to be provision by way of pension sharing or pension attachment in accordance with the annex or annexes to the order; and

(b)   be accompanied by an annex in Form P1 (Pension Sharing annex) or Form P2 (Pension Attachment annex) as the case may require; and if provision is made in relation to more than one pension arrangement there shall be one annex for each pension arrangement.

(16) A court which makes, varies or discharges a pension sharing order or a pension attachment order, shall send, or direct one of the parties to send, to the person responsible for the pension arrangement concerned –

(a)   a copy of –
   (i)   in a matrimonial cause, the decree of divorce, nullity of marriage or judicial separation; or
   (ii)   in a civil partnership cause, the conditional order of dissolution, nullity of civil partnership or the order of separation;

(b)   in the case of –
   (i)   divorce or nullity of marriage, a copy of the certificate under rule 2.51 that the decree has been made absolute; or
   (ii)   dissolution or nullity of civil partnership, a copy of the order making the conditional order final under rule 2.51A; and

(c)   a copy of that order, or as the case may be of the order varying or discharging that order, including any annex to that order relating to that pension arrangement but no other annex to that order.

(17) The documents referred to in paragraph (16) shall be sent –

(a)   in a matrimonial cause, within 7 days after –
   (i)   the making of the relevant pension sharing or pension attachment order; or
   (ii)   the decree absolute of divorce or nullity or decree of judicial separation,
   whichever is the later; and

(b)   in a civil partnership cause, within 7 days after –
   (i)   the making of the relevant pension sharing or pension attachment order; or
   (ii)   the final order of dissolution or nullity or order of separation,
   whichever is the later.

(18) In this rule –

(a)   in a matrimonial cause, all words and phrases defined in sections 25D(3) and (4) of the Act of 1973 have the meanings assigned by those subsections;

(ab)   in a civil partnership cause, all words and phrases defined in paragraphs 16(4) to (5) and 29 of Schedule 5 to the Act of 2004 have the meanings assigned by those paragraphs;

(b)   all words and phrases defined in section 46 of the Welfare Reform and Pensions Act 1999 have the meanings assigned by that section;

(c)   'pension sharing order' means –

(i) in a matrimonial cause, an order making provision under section 24B of the Act of 1973; and

(ii) in a civil partnership cause, an order making provision under paragraph 15 of Schedule 5 to the Act of 2004; and

(d) 'pension attachment order' means –

(i) in a matrimonial cause, an order making provision under section 25B or 25C of the Act of 1973; and

(ii) in a civil partnership cause, an order making provision under paragraph 25 and paragraph 26 of Schedule 5 to the Act of 2004.

**Amendments**—Substituted by SI 2000/2267; amended by SI 2001/821; SI 2003/184; SI 2005/2922.

### 2.70A Pension Protection Fund

(1) This rule applies where –

(a) rule 2.70 applies; and

(b) the party with pension rights or the civil partner with pension rights ("the member") receives or has received notification in compliance with the Pension Protection Fund (Provision of Information) Regulations 2005 ("the 2005 Regulations") –

(i) from the person responsible for the pension arrangement, that there is an assessment period in relation to the pension arrangement; or

(ii) from the Board that it has assumed responsibility for the pension arrangement or part of it.

(2) If the person responsible for the pension arrangement notifies or has notified the member that there is an assessment period in relation to the pension arrangement, the member must send to the other party or civil partner –

(a) a copy of the notification; and

(b) a copy of the valuation summary,

in accordance with paragraph (3).

(3) The member must send the documents referred to in paragraph (2) –

(a) if available, when he sends the information received under rule 2.70(2); or

(b) otherwise, within 7 days of receipt.

(4) If –

(a) the pension arrangement is in an assessment period; and

(b) the Board notifies the member that it has assumed responsibility for the pension arrangement, or part of it,

the member must –

(i) send a copy of the notification to the other party or civil partner within 7 days of receipt; and

(ii) comply with paragraph (5).

(5) Where paragraph (4) applies, the member must –

    (*a*)    within 7 days of receipt of the notification, request the Board in writing to provide a forecast of his compensation entitlement as described in the 2005 Regulations; and

    (*b*)    send a copy of the forecast of his compensation entitlement to the other party or civil partner within 7 days of receipt.

(6) In this rule –

    (*a*)    in a matrimonial cause, all words and phrases defined in section 25E(9) of the Act of 1973 have the meanings assigned by that subsection;

    (*b*)    in a civil partnership cause, all words and phrases defined in paragraph 37 of Schedule 5 to the Act of 2004 have the meanings assigned by that paragraph; and

    (*c*)    "valuation summary" has the meaning assigned to it by the 2005 Regulations.

(7) Paragraph (18) of rule 2.70 shall apply to this rule as it applies to rule 2.70.

**Amendments**—Inserted by SI 2006/2080.

## 2.71 Costs orders

(1) CPR rule 44.3(1) to (5) shall not apply to ancillary relief proceedings.

(2) CPR rule 44.3(6) to (9) apply to an order made under this rule as they apply to an order made under CPR rule 44.3.

(3) In this rule 'costs' has the same meaning as in CPR rule 43.2(1)(*a*) and includes the costs payable by a client to his solicitor.

(4)

    (*a*)    The general rule in ancillary relief proceedings is that the court will not make an order requiring one party to pay the costs of another party; but

    (*b*)    the court may make such an order at any stage of the proceedings where it considers it appropriate to do so because of the conduct of a party in relation to the proceedings (whether before or during them).

(5) In deciding what order (if any) to make under paragraph (4)(*b*), the court must have regard to –

    (*a*)    any failure by a party to comply with these Rules, any order of the court or any practice direction which the court considers relevant;

    (*b*)    any open offer to settle made by a party;

    (*c*)    whether it was reasonable for a party to raise, pursue or contest a particular allegation or issue;

    (*d*)    the manner in which a party has pursued or responded to the application or a particular allegation or issue;

    (*e*)    any other aspect of a party's conduct in relation to the proceedings which the court considers relevant; and

    (*f*)    the financial effect on the parties of any costs order.

(6) No offer to settle which is not an open offer to settle shall be admissible at any stage of the proceedings, except as provided by rule 2.61E.

**Amendments**—Inserted by SI 2006/352.

\*\*\*\*

# Appendix 6

# MATRIMONIAL CAUSES ACT 1973

\*\*\*\*

## PART II
## FINANCIAL RELIEF FOR PARTIES TO MARRIAGE
## AND CHILDREN OF FAMILY

*Financial provision and property adjustment orders*

### 21 Financial provision and property adjustment orders

(1) The financial provision orders for the purposes of this Act are the orders for periodical or lump sum provision available (subject to the provisions of this Act) under section 23 below for the purpose of adjusting the financial position of the parties to a marriage and any children of the family in connection with proceedings for divorce, nullity of marriage or judicial separation and under section 27(6) below on proof of neglect by one party to a marriage to provide, or to make a proper contribution towards, reasonable maintenance for the other or a child of the family, that is to say –

(*a*) any order for periodical payments in favour of a party to a marriage under section 23(1)(*a*) or 27(6)(*a*) or in favour of a child of the family under section 23(1)(*d*), (2) or (4) or 27(6)(*d*);

(*b*) any order for secured periodical payments in favour of a party to a marriage under section 23(1)(*b*) or 27(6)(*b*) or in favour of a child of the family under section 23(1)(*e*), (2) or (4) or 27(6)(*e*); and

(*c*) any order for lump sum provision in favour of a party to a marriage under section 23(1)(*c*) or 27(6)(*c*) or in favour of a child of the family under section 23(1)(*f*), (2) or (4) or 27(6)(*f*);

and references in this Act (except in paragraphs 17(1) and 23 of Schedule 1 below) to periodical payments orders, secured periodical payments orders, and orders for the payment of a lump sum are references to all or some of the financial provision orders requiring the sort of financial provision in question according as the context of each reference may require.

(2) The property adjustment orders for the purposes of this Act are the orders dealing with property rights available (subject to the provisions of this Act) under section 24 below for the purpose of adjusting the financial position of the parties to a marriage and any children of the family on or after the grant of a decree of divorce, nullity of marriage or judicial separation, that is to say –

(*a*) any order under subsection (1)(*a*) of that section for a transfer of property;

(b) any order under subsection (1)(*b*) of that section for a settlement of property; and

(c) any order under subsection (1)(*c*) or (*d*) of that section for a variation of settlement.

## 21A Pension sharing orders

(1) For the purposes of this Act, a pension sharing order is an order which –

(a) provides that one party's –
(i) shareable rights under a specified pension arrangement, or
(ii) shareable state scheme rights,
be subject to pension sharing for the benefit of the other party, and

(b) specifies the percentage value to be transferred.

(2) In subsection (1) above –

(a) the reference to shareable rights under a pension arrangement is to rights in relation to which pension sharing is available under Chapter I of Part IV of the Welfare Reform and Pensions Act 1999, or under corresponding Northern Ireland legislation,

(b) the reference to shareable state scheme rights is to rights in relation to which pension sharing is available under Chapter II of Part IV of the Welfare Reform and Pensions Act 1999, or under corresponding Northern Ireland legislation, and

(c) 'party' means a party to a marriage.

**Amendments**—Inserted by Welfare Reform and Pensions Act 1999, s 19, Sch 3, para 2.

*Ancillary relief in connection with divorce proceedings etc*

## 22 Maintenance pending suit

On a petition for divorce, nullity of marriage or judicial separation, the court may make an order for maintenance pending suit, that is to say, an order requiring either party to the marriage to make to the other such periodical payments for his or her maintenance and for such term, being a term beginning not earlier than the date of the presentation of the petition and ending with the date of the determination of the suit, as the court thinks reasonable.

## 23 Financial provision orders in connection with divorce proceedings etc

(1) On granting a decree of divorce, a decree of nullity of marriage or a decree of judicial separation or at any time thereafter (whether, in the case of a decree of divorce or of nullity of marriage, before or after the decree is made absolute), the court may make any one or more of the following orders, that is to say –

(a) an order that either party to the marriage shall make to the other such periodical payments, for such term, as may be specified in the order;

(b) an order that either party to the marriage shall secure to the other to the satisfaction of the court such periodical payments, for such term, as may be so specified;

(c)    an order that either party to the marriage shall pay to the other such lump sum or sums as may be so specified;

(d)    an order that a party to the marriage shall make to such person as may be specified in the order for the benefit of a child of the family, or to such a child, such periodical payments, for such term, as may be so specified;

(e)    an order that a party to the marriage shall secure to such person as may be so specified for the benefit of such a child, or to such a child, to the satisfaction of the court, such periodical payments, for such term, as may be so specified;

(f)    an order that a party to the marriage shall pay to such person as may be so specified for the benefit of such a child, or to such a child, such lump sum as may be so specified;

subject, however, in the case of an order under paragraph (d), (e) or (f) above, to the restrictions imposed by section 29(1) and (3) below on the making of financial provision orders in favour of children who have attained the age of eighteen.

(2) The court may also, subject to those restrictions, make any one or more of the orders mentioned in subsection (1)(d), (e) and (f) above –

(a)    in any proceedings for divorce, nullity of marriage or judicial separation, before granting a decree; and

(b)    where any such proceedings are dismissed after the beginning of the trial, either forthwith or within a reasonable period after the dismissal.

(3) Without prejudice to the generality of subsection (1)(c) or (f) above –

(a)    an order under this section that a party to a marriage shall pay a lump sum to the other party may be made for the purpose of enabling that other party to meet any liabilities or expenses reasonably incurred by him or her in maintaining himself or herself or any child of the family before making an application for an order under this section in his or her favour;

(b)    an order under this section for the payment of a lump sum to or for the benefit of a child of the family may be made for the purpose of enabling any liabilities or expenses reasonably incurred by or for the benefit of that child before the making of an application for an order under this section in his favour to be met; and

(c)    an order under this section for the payment of a lump sum may provide for the payment of that sum by instalments of such amount as may be specified in the order and may require the payment of the instalments to be secured to the satisfaction of the court.

(4) The power of the court under subsection (1) or (2)(a) above to make an order in favour of a child of the family shall be exercisable from time to time; and where the court makes an order in favour of a child under subsection (2)(b) above, it may from time to time, subject to the restrictions mentioned in subsection (1) above, make a further order in his favour of any of the kinds mentioned in subsection (1)(d), (e) or (f) above.

(5) Without prejudice to the power to give a direction under section 30 below for the settlement of an instrument by conveyancing counsel, where an order is made under subsection (1)(*a*), (*b*) or (*c*) above on or after granting a decree of divorce or nullity of marriage, neither the order nor any settlement made in pursuance of the order shall take effect unless the decree has been made absolute.

(6) Where the court –

(*a*)    makes an order under this section for the payment of a lump sum; and
(*b*)    directs –

(i)    that payment of that sum or any part of it shall be deferred; or
(ii)    that the sum or any part of it shall be paid by instalments,

the court may order that the amount deferred or the instalments shall carry interest at such rate as may be specified by the order from such date, not earlier than the date of the order, as may be so specified, until the date when payment of it is due.

**Amendments**—Administration of Justice Act 1982, s 16.

## 24  Property adjustment orders in connection with divorce proceedings etc

(1) On granting a decree of divorce, a decree of nullity of marriage or a decree of judicial separation or at any time thereafter (whether, in the case of a decree of divorce or of nullity of marriage, before or after the decree is made absolute), the court may make any one or more of the following orders, that is to say –

(*a*)    an order that a party to the marriage shall transfer to the other party, to any child of the family or to such person as may be specified in the order for the benefit of such a child such property as may be so specified, being property to which the first-mentioned party is entitled, either in possession or reversion;

(*b*)    an order that a settlement of such property as may be so specified, being property to which a party to the marriage is so entitled, be made to the satisfaction of the court for the benefit of the other party to the marriage and of the children of the family or either or any of them;

(*c*)    an order varying for the benefit of the parties to the marriage and of the children of the family or either or any of them any ante-nuptial or post-nuptial settlement (including such a settlement made by will or codicil) made on the parties to the marriage, other than one in the form of a pension arrangement (within the meaning of section 25D below);

(*d*)    an order extinguishing or reducing the interest of either of the parties to the marriage under any such settlement, other than one in the form of a pension arrangement (within the meaning of section 25D below);

subject, however, in the case of an order under paragraph (*a*) above, to the restrictions imposed by section 29(1) and (3) below on the making of orders for a transfer of property in favour of children who have attained the age of eighteen.

(2) The court may make an order under subsection (1)(*c*) above notwithstanding that there are no children of the family.

(3) Without prejudice to the power to give a direction under section 30 below for the settlement of an instrument by conveyancing counsel, where an order is made under this section on or after granting a decree of divorce or nullity of marriage, neither the order nor any settlement made in pursuance of the order shall take effect unless the decree has been made absolute.

**Amendments**—Welfare Reform and Pensions Act 1999, s 19, Sch 3, para 3.

## 24A Orders for sale of property

(1) Where the court makes under section 23 or 24 of this Act a secured periodical payments order, an order for the payment of a lump sum or a property adjustment order, then, on making that order or at any time thereafter, the court may make a further order for the sale of such property as may be specified in the order, being property in which or in the proceeds of sale of which either or both of the parties to the marriage has or have a beneficial interest, either in possession or reversion.

(2) Any order made under subsection (1) above may contain such consequential or supplementary provisions as the court thinks fit and, without prejudice to the generality of the foregoing provision, may include –

   (*a*)  provision requiring the making of a payment out of the proceeds of sale of the property to which the order relates, and

   (*b*)  provision requiring any such property to be offered for sale to a person, or class of persons, specified in the order.

(3) Where an order is made under subsection (1) above on or after the grant of a decree of divorce or nullity of marriage, the order shall not take effect unless the decree has been made absolute.

(4) Where an order is made under subsection (1) above, the court may direct that the order, or such provision thereof as the court may specify, shall not take effect until the occurrence of an event specified by the court or the expiration of a period so specified.

(5) Where an order under subsection (1) above contains a provision requiring the proceeds of sale of the property to which the order relates to be used to secure periodical payments to a party to the marriage, the order shall cease to have effect on the death or re-marriage of, or formation of a civil partnership by, that person.

(6) Where a party to a marriage has a beneficial interest in any property, or in the proceeds of sale thereof, and some other person who is not a party to the marriage also has a beneficial interest in that property or in the proceeds of sale thereof, then, before deciding whether to make an order under this section in relation to that property, it shall be the duty of the court to give that other person an opportunity to make representations with respect to the order; and

any representations made by that other person shall be included among the circumstances to which the court is required to have regard under section 25(1) below.

**Amendments**—Inserted by Matrimonial Homes and Property Act 1981, s 7; amended by Matrimonial and Family Proceedings Act 1984, s 46(1), Sch 1, para 11; Civil Partnership Act 2004, s 261(1), Sch 27, para 42.

### 24B Pension sharing orders in connection with divorce proceedings etc

(1) On granting a decree of divorce or a decree of nullity of marriage or at any time thereafter (whether before or after the decree is made absolute), the court may, on an application made under this section, make one or more pension sharing orders in relation to the marriage.

(2) A pension sharing order under this section is not to take effect unless the decree on or after which it is made has been made absolute.

(3) A pension sharing order under this section may not be made in relation to a pension arrangement which –

(*a*)   is the subject of a pension sharing order in relation to the marriage, or
(*b*)   has been the subject of pension sharing between the parties to the marriage.

(4) A pension sharing order under this section may not be made in relation to shareable state scheme rights if –

(*a*)   such rights are the subject of a pension sharing order in relation to the marriage, or
(*b*)   such rights have been the subject of pension sharing between the parties to the marriage.

(5) A pension sharing order under this section may not be made in relation to the rights of a person under a pension arrangement if there is in force a requirement imposed by virtue of section 25B or 25C below which relates to benefits or future benefits to which he is entitled under the pension arrangement.

**Amendments**—Inserted by Welfare Reform and Pensions Act 1999, s 19, Sch 3, para 4.

### 24C Pension sharing orders: duty to stay

(1) No pension sharing order may be made so as to take effect before the end of such period after the making of the order as may be prescribed by regulations made by the Lord Chancellor.

(2) The power to make regulations under this section shall be exercisable by statutory instrument which shall be subject to annulment in pursuance of a resolution of either House of Parliament.

**Amendments**—Inserted by Welfare Reform and Pensions Act 1999, s 19, Sch 3, para 4.

**24D Pension sharing orders: apportionment of charges**

If a pension sharing order relates to rights under a pension arrangement, the court may include in the order provision about the apportionment between the parties of any charge under section 41 of the Welfare Reform and Pensions Act 1999 (charges in respect of pension sharing costs), or under corresponding Northern Ireland legislation.

**Amendments**—Inserted by Welfare Reform and Pensions Act 1999, s 19, Sch 3, para 4.

**25 Matters to which court is to have regard in deciding how to exercise its powers under ss 23, 24 and 24A**

(1) It shall be the duty of the court in deciding whether to exercise its powers under section 23, 24, 24A or 24B above and, if so, in what manner, to have regard to all the circumstances of the case, first consideration being given to the welfare while a minor of any child of the family who has not attained the age of eighteen.

(2) As regards the exercise of the powers of the court under section 23(1)(*a*), (*b*) or (*c*), 24, 24A or 24B above in relation to a party to the marriage, the court shall in particular have regard to the following matters –

(*a*)  the income, earning capacity, property and other financial resources which each of the parties to the marriage has or is likely to have in the foreseeable future, including in the case of earning capacity any increase in that capacity which it would in the opinion of the court be reasonable to expect a party to the marriage to take steps to acquire;

(*b*)  the financial needs, obligations and responsibilities which each of the parties to the marriage has or is likely to have in the foreseeable future;

(*c*)  the standard of living enjoyed by the family before the breakdown of the marriage;

(*d*)  the age of each party to the marriage and the duration of the marriage;

(*e*)  any physical or mental disability of either of the parties to the marriage;

(*f*)  the contributions which each of the parties has made or is likely in the foreseeable future to make to the welfare of the family, including any contribution by looking after the home or caring for the family;

(*g*)  the conduct of each of the parties, if that conduct is such that it would in the opinion of the court be inequitable to disregard it;

(*h*)  in the case of proceedings for divorce or nullity of marriage, the value to each of the parties to the marriage of any benefit which, by reason of the dissolution or annulment of the marriage, that party will lose the chance of acquiring.

(3) As regards the exercise of the powers of the court under section 23(1)(*d*), (*e*) or (*f*), (2) or (4), 24 or 24A above in relation to a child of the family, the court shall in particular have regard to the following matters –

(*a*)  the financial needs of the child;

(b)    the income, earning capacity (if any), property and other financial resources of the child;

(c)    any physical or mental disability of the child;

(d)    the manner in which he was being and in which the parties to the marriage expected him to be educated or trained;

(e)    the considerations mentioned in relation to the parties to the marriage in paragraphs (a), (b), (c) and (e) of subsection (2) above.

(4) As regards the exercise of the powers of the court under section 23(1)(d), (e) or (f), (2) or (4), 24 or 24A above against a party to a marriage in favour of a child of the family who is not the child of that party, the court shall also have regard –

(a)    to whether that party assumed any responsibility for the child's maintenance, and, if so, to the extent to which, and the basis upon which, that party assumed such responsibility and to the length of time for which that party discharged such responsibility;

(b)    to whether in assuming and discharging such responsibility that party did so knowing that the child was not his or her own;

(c)    to the liability of any other person to maintain the child.

**Amendments**—Matrimonial and Family Proceedings Act 1984, s 3; Pensions Act 1995, s 166; Welfare Reform and Pensions Act 1999, s 19, Sch 3, para 5.

### 25A Exercise of court's powers in favour of party to marriage on decree of divorce or nullity of marriage

(1) Where on or after the grant of a decree of divorce or nullity of marriage the court decides to exercise its powers under section 23(1)(a), (b) or (c), 24, 24A or 24B above in favour of a party to the marriage, it shall be the duty of the court to consider whether it would be appropriate so to exercise those powers that the financial obligations of each party towards the other will be terminated as soon after the grant of the decree as the court considers just and reasonable.

(2) Where the court decides in such a case to make a periodical payments or secured periodical payments order in favour of a party to the marriage, the court shall in particular consider whether it would be appropriate to require those payments to be made or secured only for such term as would in the opinion of the court be sufficient to enable the party in whose favour the order is made to adjust without undue hardship to the termination of his or her financial dependence on the other party.

(3) Where on or after the grant of a decree of divorce or nullity of marriage an application is made by a party to the marriage for a periodical payments or secured periodical payments order in his or her favour, then, if the court considers that no continuing obligation should be imposed on either party to make or secure periodical payments in favour of the other, the court may dismiss the application with a direction that the applicant shall not be entitled to make any future application in relation to that marriage for an order under section 23(1)(a) or (b) above.

**Amendments**—Inserted by Matrimonial and Family Proceedings Act 1984, s 3; amended by Welfare Reform and Pensions Act 1999, s 19, Sch 3, para 6.

## 25B Pensions

(1) The matters to which the court is to have regard under section 25(2) above include –

    (*a*)    in the case of paragraph (*a*), any benefits under a pension arrangement which a party to the marriage has or is likely to have, and

    (*b*)    in the case of paragraph (*h*), any benefits under a pension arrangement which, by reason of the dissolution or annulment of the marriage, a party to the marriage will lose the chance of acquiring,

and, accordingly, in relation to benefits under a pension arrangement, section 25(2)(*a*) above shall have effect as if 'in the foreseeable future' were omitted.

(2) (*repealed*)

(3) The following provisions apply where, having regard to any benefits under a pension arrangement, the court determines to make an order under section 23 above.

(4) To the extent to which the order is made having regard to any benefits under a pension arrangement, the order may require the person responsible for the pension arrangement in question, if at any time any payment in respect of any benefits under the arrangement becomes due to the party with pension rights, to make a payment for the benefit of the other party.

(5) The order must express the amount of any payment required to be made by virtue of subsection (4) above as a percentage of the payment which becomes due to the party with pension rights.

(6) Any such payment by the person responsible for the arrangement –

    (*a*)    shall discharge so much of his liability to the party with pension rights as corresponds to the amount of the payment, and

    (*b*)    shall be treated for all purposes as a payment made by the party with pension rights in or towards the discharge of his liability under the order.

(7) Where the party with pension rights has a right of commutation under the arrangement, the order may require him to exercise it to any extent; and this section applies to any payment due in consequence of commutation in pursuance of the order as it applies to other payments in respect of benefits under the arrangement.

(7A) The power conferred by subsection (7) above may not be exercised for the purpose of commuting a benefit payable to the party with pension rights to a benefit payable to the other party.

(7B) The power conferred by subsection (4) or (7) above may not be exercised in relation to a pension arrangement which –

(a) is the subject of a pension sharing order in relation to the marriage, or
(b) has been the subject of pension sharing between the parties to the marriage.

(7C) In subsection (1) above, references to benefits under a pension arrangement include any benefits by way of pension, whether under a pension arrangement or not.

**Amendments**—Inserted by Pensions Act 1995, s 166; amended by Welfare Reform and Pensions Act 1999, ss 21, 88, Sch 4, para 1, Sch 13, Pt II.

### 25C  Pensions: lump sums

(1) The power of the court under section 23 above to order a party to a marriage to pay a lump sum to the other party includes, where the benefits which the party with pension rights has or is likely to have under a pension arrangement include any lump sum payable in respect of his death, power to make any of the following provision by the order.

(2) The court may –

(a) if the person responsible for the pension arrangement in question has power to determine the person to whom the sum, or any part of it, is to be paid, require him to pay the whole or part of that sum, when it becomes due, to the other party,

(b) if the party with pension rights has power to nominate the person to whom the sum, or any part of it, is to be paid, require the party with pension rights to nominate the other party in respect of the whole or part of that sum,

(c) in any other case, require the person responsible for the pension arrangement in question to pay the whole or part of that sum, when it becomes due, for the benefit of the other party instead of to the person to whom, apart from the order, it would be paid.

(3) Any payment by the person responsible for the pension arrangement under an order made under section 23 above by virtue of this section shall discharge so much of his liability in respect of the party with pension rights as corresponds to the amount of the payment.

(4) The powers conferred by this section may not be exercised in relation to a pension arrangement which –

(a) is the subject of a pension sharing order in relation to the marriage, or
(b) has been the subject of pension sharing between the parties to the marriage.

**Amendments**—Inserted by Pensions Act 1995, s 166; amended by Welfare Reform and Pensions Act 1999, s 21, Sch 4, para 2.

### 25D  Pensions: supplementary

(1) Where –

(a)    an order made under section 23 above by virtue of section 25B or 25C above imposes any requirement on the person responsible for a pension arrangement ('the first arrangement') and the party with pension rights acquires rights under another pension arrangement ('the new arrangement') which are derived (directly or indirectly) from the whole of his rights under the first arrangement, and

(b)    the person responsible for the new arrangement has been given notice in accordance with regulations made by the Lord Chancellor,

the order shall have effect as if it had been made instead in respect of the person responsible for the new arrangement.

(2) The Lord Chancellor may by regulations –

(a)    in relation to any provision of sections 25B or 25C above which authorises the court making an order under section 23 above to require the person responsible for a pension arrangement to make a payment for the benefit of the other party, make provision as to the person to whom, and the terms on which, the payment is to be made,

(ab)   make, in relation to payment under a mistaken belief as to the continuation in force of a provision included by virtue of section 25B or 25C above in an order under section 23 above, provision about the rights or liabilities of the payer, the payee or the person to whom the payment was due,

(b)    require notices to be given in respect of changes of circumstances relevant to such orders which include provision made by virtue of sections 25B and 25C above,

(ba)   make provision for the person responsible for a pension arrangement to be discharged in prescribed circumstances from a requirement imposed by virtue of section 25B or 25C above,

*(c), (d)  (repealed)*

(e)    make provision about calculation and verification in relation to the valuation of –

(i)    benefits under a pension arrangement, or

(ii)   shareable state scheme rights,

for the purposes of the court's functions in connection with the exercise of any of its powers under this Part of this Act.

(2A) Regulations under subsection (2)(e) above may include –

(a)    provision for calculation or verification in accordance with guidance from time to time prepared by a prescribed person, and

(b)    provision by reference to regulations under section 30 or 49(4) of the Welfare Reform and Pensions Act 1999.

(2B) Regulations under subsection (2) above may make different provision for different cases.

(2C) Power to make regulations under this section shall be exercisable by statutory instrument which shall be subject to annulment in pursuance of a resolution of either House of Parliament.

(3) In this section and sections 25B and 25C above –

'occupational pension scheme' has the same meaning as in the Pension Schemes Act 1993;

'the party with pension rights' means the party to the marriage who has or is likely to have benefits under a pension arrangement and 'the other party' means the other party to the marriage;

'pension arrangement' means –

(*a*)   an occupational pension scheme,

(*b*)   a personal pension scheme,

(*c*)   a retirement annuity contract,

(*d*)   an annuity or insurance policy purchased, or transferred, for the purpose of giving effect to rights under an occupational pension scheme or a personal pension scheme, and

(*e*)   an annuity purchased, or entered into, for the purpose of discharging liability in respect of a pension credit under section 29(1)(*b*) of the Welfare Reform and Pensions Act 1999 or under corresponding Northern Ireland legislation;

'personal pension scheme' has the same meaning as in the Pension Schemes Act 1993;

'prescribed' means prescribed by regulations;

'retirement annuity contract' means a contract or scheme approved under Chapter III of Part XIV of the Income and Corporation Taxes Act 1988;

'shareable state scheme rights' has the same meaning as in section 21A(1) above; and

'trustees or managers', in relation to an occupational pension scheme or a personal pension scheme, means –

(*a*)   in the case of a scheme established under a trust, the trustees of the scheme, and

(*b*)   in any other case, the managers of the scheme.

(4) In this section and sections 25B and 25C above, references to the person responsible for a pension arrangement are –

(*a*)   in the case of an occupational pension scheme or a personal pension scheme, to the trustees or managers of the scheme,

(*b*)   in the case of a retirement annuity contract or an annuity falling within paragraph (*d*) or (*e*) of the definition of 'pension arrangement' above, the provider of the annuity, and

(*c*)   in the case of an insurance policy falling within paragraph (*d*) of the definition of that expression, the insurer.

**Amendments**—Inserted by Pensions Act 1995, s 166; amended by Welfare Reform and Pensions Act 1999, ss 21, 88, Sch 4, para 3, Sch 13, Pt II.

### 25E  The Pension Protection Fund

(1) The matters to which the court is to have regard under section 25(2) include –

(*a*)   in the case of paragraph (*a*), any PPF compensation to which a party to the marriage is or is likely to be entitled, and

(*b*)   in the case of paragraph (*h*), any PPF compensation which, by reason of the dissolution or annulment of the marriage, a party to the marriage will lose the chance of acquiring entitlement to,

and, accordingly, in relation to PPF compensation, section 25(2)(*a*) shall have effect as if 'in the foreseeable future' were omitted.

(2) Subsection (3) applies in relation to an order under section 23 so far as it includes provision made by virtue of section 25B(4) which –

(*a*)   imposed requirements on the trustees or managers of an occupational pension scheme for which the Board has assumed responsibility in accordance with Chapter 3 of Part 2 of the Pensions Act 2004 (pension protection) or any provision in force in Northern Ireland corresponding to that Chapter, and

(*b*)   was made before the trustees or managers of the scheme received the transfer notice in relation to the scheme.

(3) The order is to have effect from the time when the trustees or managers of the scheme receive the transfer notice –

(*a*)   as if, except in prescribed descriptions of case –
  (i)    references in the order to the trustees or managers of the scheme were references to the Board, and
  (ii)   references in the order to any pension or lump sum to which the party with pension rights is or may become entitled under the scheme were references to any PPF compensation to which that person is or may become entitled in respect of the pension or lump sum, and

(*b*)   subject to such other modifications as may be prescribed.

(4) Subsection (5) applies to an order under section 23 if –

(*a*)   it includes provision made by virtue of section 25B(7) which requires the party with pension rights to exercise his right of commutation under an occupational pension scheme to any extent, and

(*b*)   before the requirement is complied with the Board has assumed responsibility for the scheme as mentioned in subsection (2)(*a*).

(5) From the time the trustees or managers of the scheme receive the transfer notice, the order is to have effect with such modifications as may be prescribed.

(6) Regulations may modify section 25C as it applies in relation to an occupational pension scheme at any time when there is an assessment period in relation to the scheme.

(7) Where the court makes a pension sharing order in respect of a person's shareable rights under an occupational pension scheme, or an order which includes provision made by virtue of section 25B(4) or (7) in relation to such a scheme, the Board subsequently assuming responsibility for the scheme as mentioned in subsection (2)(*a*) does not affect –

(*a*)    the powers of the court under section 31 to vary or discharge the order or to suspend or revive any provision of it, or

(*b*)    on an appeal, the powers of the appeal court to affirm, reinstate, set aside or vary the order.

(8) Regulations may make such consequential modifications of any provision of, or made by virtue of, this Part as appear to the Lord Chancellor necessary or expedient to give effect to the provisions of this section.

(9) In this section –

'assessment period' means an assessment period within the meaning of Part 2 of the Pensions Act 2004 (pension protection) (see sections 132 and 159 of that Act) or an equivalent period under any provision in force in Northern Ireland corresponding to that Part;

'the Board' means the Board of the Pension Protection Fund;

'occupational pension scheme' has the same meaning as in the Pension Schemes Act 1993;

'prescribed' means prescribed by regulations;

'PPF compensation' means compensation payable under Chapter 3 of Part 2 of the Pensions Act 2004 (pension protection) or any provision in force in Northern Ireland corresponding to that Chapter;

'regulations' means regulations made by the Lord Chancellor;

'shareable rights' are rights in relation to which pension sharing is available under Chapter 1 of Part 4 of the Welfare Reform and Pensions Act 1999 or any provision in force in Northern Ireland corresponding to that Chapter;

'transfer notice' has the same meaning as in section 160 of the Pensions Act 2004 or any corresponding provision in force in Northern Ireland.

(10) Any power to make regulations under this section is exercisable by statutory instrument, which shall be subject to annulment in pursuance of a resolution of either House of Parliament.

**Amendments**—Inserted by Pensions Act 2004, Sch 12, para 3.

## 26 Commencement of proceedings for ancillary relief etc

(1) Where a petition for divorce, nullity of marriage or judicial separation has been presented, then, subject to subsection (2) below, proceedings for maintenance pending suit under section 22 above, for a financial provision order under section 23 above, or for a property adjustment order may be begun, subject to and in accordance with rules of court, at any time after the presentation of the petition.

(2) Rules of court may provide, in such cases as may be prescribed by the rules –

(*a*)    that applications for any such relief as is mentioned in subsection (1) above shall be made in the petition or answer; and

(*b*)    that applications for any such relief which are not so made, or are not made until after the expiration of such period following the presentation of the petition or filing of the answer as may be so prescribed, shall be made only with the leave of the court.

*Financial provision in case of neglect to maintain*

## 27 Financial provision orders etc in case of neglect by party to marriage to maintain other party or child of the family

(1) Either party to a marriage may apply to the court for an order under this section on the ground that the other party to the marriage (in this section referred to as the respondent) –

(*a*)   has failed to provide reasonable maintenance for the applicant, or

(*b*)   has failed to provide, or to make a proper contribution towards, reasonable maintenance for any child of the family.

(2) The court shall not entertain an application under this section unless –

(*a*)   the applicant or the respondent is domiciled in England and Wales on the date of the application; or

(*b*)   the applicant has been habitually resident there throughout the period of one year ending with that date; or

(*c*)   the respondent is resident there on that date.

(3) Where an application under this section is made on the ground mentioned in subsection (1)(*a*) above, then, in deciding –

(*a*)   whether the respondent has failed to provide reasonable maintenance for the applicant, and

(*b*)   what order, if any, to make under this section in favour of the applicant,

the court shall have regard to all the circumstances of the case including the matters mentioned in section 25(2) above, and where an application is also made under this section in respect of a child of the family who has not attained the age of eighteen, first consideration shall be given to the welfare of the child while a minor.

(3A) Where an application under this section is made on the ground mentioned in subsection (1)(*b*) above then, in deciding –

(*a*)   whether the respondent has failed to provide, or to make a proper contribution towards, reasonable maintenance for the child of the family to whom the application relates, and

(*b*)   what order, if any, to make under this section in favour of the child,

the court shall have regard to all the circumstances of the case including the matters mentioned in section 25(3)(*a*) to (*e*) above, and where the child of the family to whom the application relates is not the child of the respondent, including also the matters mentioned in section 25(4) above.

(3B) In relation to an application under this section on the ground mentioned in subsection (1)(*a*) above, section 25(2)(*c*) above shall have effect as if for the reference therein to the breakdown of the marriage there were substituted a reference to the failure to provide reasonable maintenance for the applicant, and in relation to an application under this section on the ground mentioned in subsection (1)(*b*) above, section 25(2)(*c*) above (as it applies by virtue of section 25(3)(*e*) above) shall have effect as if for the reference therein to the breakdown of the marriage there were substituted a reference to the failure to provide, or to make a proper contribution towards, reasonable maintenance for the child of the family to whom the application relates.

(4) (*repealed*)

(5) Where on an application under this section it appears to the court that the applicant or any child of the family to whom the application relates is in immediate need of financial assistance, but it is not yet possible to determine what order, if any, should be made on the application, the court may make an interim order for maintenance, that is to say, an order requiring the respondent to make to the applicant until the determination of the application such periodical payments as the court thinks reasonable.

(6) Where on an application under this section the applicant satisfies the court of any ground mentioned in subsection (1) above, the court may make any one or more of the following orders, that is to say –

> (*a*) an order that the respondent shall make to the applicant such periodical payments, for such term, as may be specified in the order;
> (*b*) an order that the respondent shall secure to the applicant, to the satisfaction of the court, such periodical payments, for such term, as may be so specified;
> (*c*) an order that the respondent shall pay to the applicant such lump sum as may be so specified;
> (*d*) an order that the respondent shall make to such person as may be specified in the order for the benefit of the child to whom the application relates, or to that child, such periodical payments, for such term, as may be so specified;
> (*e*) an order that the respondent shall secure to such person as may be so specified for the benefit of that child, or to that child, to the satisfaction of the court, such periodical payments, for such term, as may be so specified;
> (*f*) an order that the respondent shall pay to such person as may be so specified for the benefit of that child, or to that child, such lump sum as may be so specified;

subject, however, in the case of an order under paragraph (*d*), (*e*) or (*f*) above, to the restrictions imposed by section 29(1) and (3) below on the making of financial provision orders in favour of children who have attained the age of eighteen.

(6A) An application for the variation under section 31 of this Act of a periodical payments order or secured periodical payments order made under this section in favour of a child may, if the child has attained the age of sixteen, be made by the child himself.

(6B) Where a periodical payments order made in favour of a child under this section ceases to have effect on the date on which the child attains the age of sixteen or at any time after that date but before or on the date on which he attains the age of eighteen, then, if at any time before he attains the age of twenty-one an application is made by the child for an order under this subsection, the court shall have power by order to revive the first-mentioned order from such date as the court may specify, not being earlier than the date of the making of the application, and to exercise its powers under section 31 of this Act in relation to any order so revived.

(7) Without prejudice to the generality of subsection (6)(*c*) or (*f*) above, an order under this section for the payment of a lump sum –

(*a*) may be made for the purpose of enabling any liabilities or expenses reasonably incurred in maintaining the applicant or any child of the family to whom the application relates before the making of the application to be met;

(*b*) may provide for the payment of that sum by instalments of such amount as may be specified in the order and may require the payment of the instalments to be secured to the satisfaction of the court.

(8) (*repealed*)

**Amendments**—Domicile and Matrimonial Proceedings Act 1973, s 6(1); Domestic Proceedings and Magistrates' Courts Act 1978, ss 63, 89(2)(*b*), Sch 3; Matrimonial and Family Proceedings Act 1984, ss 4, 46(1), Sch 1, para 12; Family Law Reform Act 1987, s 33(1), Sch 2, para 52.

*Additional provisions with respect to financial provision and property adjustment orders*

## 28 Duration of continuing financial provision orders in favour of party to marriage, and effect of remarriage or formation of civil partnership

(1) Subject in the case of an order made on or after the grant of a decree of a divorce or nullity of marriage to the provisions of sections 25A(2) above and 31(7) below, the term to be specified in a periodical payments or secured periodical payments order in favour of a party to a marriage shall be such term as the court thinks fit, except that the term shall not begin before or extend beyond the following limits, that is to say –

(*a*) in the case of a periodical payments order, the term shall begin not earlier than the date of the making of an application for the order, and shall be so defined as not to extend beyond the death of either of the parties to the marriage or, where the order is made on or after the grant of a decree of divorce or nullity of marriage, the remarriage, or formation of a civil partnership by, of the party in whose favour the order is made; and

(*b*) in the case of a secured periodical payments order, the term shall begin not earlier than the date of the making of an application for the order, and shall be so defined as not to extend beyond the death or, where the order is made on or after the grant of such a decree, the remarriage, or formation of a civil partnership by, of the party in whose favour the order is made.

(1A) Where a periodical payments or secured periodical payments order in favour of a party to a marriage is made on or after the grant of a decree of divorce or nullity of marriage, the court may direct that that party shall not be entitled to apply under section 31 below for the extension of the term specified in the order.

(2) Where a periodical payments or secured periodical payments order in favour of a party to a marriage is made otherwise than on or after the grant of a decree of divorce or nullity of marriage, and the marriage in question is subsequently dissolved or annulled but the order continues in force, the order shall, notwithstanding anything in it, cease to have effect on the remarriage of, or formation of a civil partnership by, that party, except in relation to any arrears due under it on the date of the remarriage or formation of the civil partnership.

(3) If after the grant of a decree dissolving or annulling a marriage either party to that marriage remarries whether at any time before or after the commencement of this Act or forms a civil partnership, that party shall not be entitled to apply, by reference to the grant of that decree, for a financial provision order in his or her favour, or for a property adjustment order, against the other party to that marriage.

**Amendments**—Matrimonial and Family Proceedings Act 1984, s 5, Civil Partnership Act 2004, s 261(1), Sch 27, para 43(1)-(5).

## 29 Duration of continuing financial provision orders in favour of children, and age limit on making certain orders in their favour

(1) Subject to subsection (3) below, no financial provision order and no order for a transfer of property under section 24(1)(*a*) above shall be made in favour of a child who has attained the age of eighteen.

(2) The term to be specified in a periodical payments or secured periodical payments order in favour of a child may begin with the date of the making of an application for the order in question or any later date or a date ascertained in accordance with subsection (5) or (6) below but –

  (*a*)  shall not in the first instance extend beyond the date of the birthday of the child next following his attaining the upper limit of the compulsory school age (construed in accordance with section 8 of the Education Act 1996) unless the court considers that in the circumstances of the case the welfare of the child requires that it should extend to a later date; and

  (*b*)  shall not in any event, subject to subsection (3) below, extend beyond the date of the child's eighteenth birthday.

(3) Subsection (1) above, and paragraph (*b*) of subsection (2), shall not apply in the case of a child, if it appears to the court that –

(*a*)   the child is, or will be, or if an order were made without complying with either or both of those provisions would be, receiving instruction at an educational establishment or undergoing training for a trade, profession or vocation, whether or not he is also, or will also be, in gainful employment; or

(*b*)   there are special circumstances which justify the making of an order without complying with either or both of those provisions.

(4) Any periodical payments order in favour of a child shall, notwithstanding anything in the order, cease to have effect on the death of the person liable to make payments under the order, except in relation to any arrears due under the order on the date of the death.

(5) Where –

(*a*)   a maintenance calculation ('the current calculation') is in force with respect to a child; and

(*b*)   an application is made under Part II of this Act for a periodical payments or secured periodical payments order in favour of that child –
(i)   in accordance with section 8 of the Child Support Act 1991, and
(ii)   before the end of the period of 6 months beginning with the making of the current calculation,

the term to be specified in any such order made on that application may be expressed to begin on, or at any time after, the earliest permitted date.

(6) For the purposes of subsection (5) above, 'the earliest permitted date' is whichever is the later of –

(*a*)   the date 6 months before the application is made; or

(*b*)   the date on which the current calculation took effect or, where successive maintenance calculations have been continuously in force with respect to a child, on which the first of those calculations took effect.

(7) Where –

(*a*)   a maintenance calculation ceases to have effect by or under any provision of the Child Support Act 1991; and

(*b*)   an application is made, before the end of the period of 6 months beginning with the relevant date, for a periodical payments or secured periodical payments order in favour of a child with respect to whom that maintenance calculation was in force immediately before it ceased to have effect,

the term to be specified in any such order made on that application may begin with the date on which that maintenance calculation ceased to have effect, or any later date.

(8) In subsection (7)(*b*) above, –

(*a*)   where the maintenance calculation ceased to have effect, the relevant date is the date on which it so ceased (*b*)    (*repealed*)

Amendments—Matrimonial and Family Proceedings Act 1984, s 5; SI 1993/623; Education Act 1996, s 582(1), Sch 37, para 136; Child Support, Pensions and Social Security Act 2000, ss 26, 85, Sch 3, para 3, Sch 9.

## 30 Direction for settlement of instrument for securing payments or effecting property adjustment

Where the court decides to make a financial provision order requiring any payments to be secured or a property adjustment order –

(*a*)    it may direct that the matter be referred to one of the conveyancing counsel of the court for him to settle a proper instrument to be executed by all necessary parties; and

(*b*)    where the order is to be made in proceedings for divorce, nullity of marriage or judicial separation it may, if it thinks fit, defer the grant of the decree in question until the instrument has been duly executed.

*Variation, discharge and enforcement of certain orders etc*

## 31 Variation, discharge etc of certain orders for financial relief

(1) Where the court has made an order to which this section applies, then, subject to the provisions of this section and of section 28(1A) above, the court shall have power to vary or discharge the order or to suspend any provision thereof temporarily and to revive the operation of any provision so suspended.

(2) This section applies to the following orders, that is to say –

(*a*)    any order for maintenance pending suit and any interim order for maintenance;

(*b*)    any periodical payments order;

(*c*)    any secured periodical payments order;

(*d*)    any order made by virtue of section 23(3)(*c*) or 27(7)(*b*) above (provision for payment of a lump sum by instalments);

(*dd*)    any deferred order made by virtue of section 23(1)(*c*) (lump sums) which includes provision made by virtue of –
(i)    section 25B(4), or
(ii)    section 25C,
(provision in respect of pension rights);

(*e*)    any order for a settlement of property under section 24(1)(*b*) or for a variation of settlement under section 24(1)(*c*) or (*d*) above, being an order made on or after the grant of a decree of judicial separation;

(*f*)    any order made under section 24A(1) above for the sale of property.

(*g*)    a pension sharing order under section 24B above which is made at a time before the decree has been made absolute.

(2A) Where the court has made an order referred to in subsection (2)(*a*), (*b*) or (*c*) above, then, subject to the provisions of this section, the court shall have power to remit the payment of any arrears due under the order or of any part thereof.

(2B) Where the court has made an order referred to in subsection (2)(*dd*)(ii) above, this section shall cease to apply to the order on the death of either of the parties to the marriage.

(3) The powers exercisable by the court under this section in relation to an order shall be exercisable also in relation to any instrument executed in pursuance of the order.

(4) The court shall not exercise the powers conferred by this section in relation to an order for a settlement under section 24(1)(*b*) or for a variation of settlement under section 24(1)(*c*) or (*d*) above except on an application made in proceedings –

(*a*)   for the rescission of the decree of judicial separation by reference to which the order was made, or

(*b*)   for the dissolution of the marriage in question.

(4A) In relation to an order which falls within paragraph (*g*) of subsection (2) above ('the subsection (2) order') –

(*a*)   the powers conferred by this section may be exercised –

(i)    only on an application made before the subsection (2) order has or, but for paragraph (*b*) below, would have taken effect; and

(ii)   only if, at the time when the application is made, the decree has not been made absolute; and

(*b*)   an application made in accordance with paragraph (*a*) above prevents the subsection (2) order from taking effect before the application has been dealt with.

(4B) No variation of a pension sharing order shall be made so as to take effect before the decree is made absolute.

(4C) The variation of a pension sharing order prevents the order taking effect before the end of such period after the making of the variation as may be prescribed by regulations made by the Lord Chancellor.

(5) Subject to subsections (7A) to (7G) below and without prejudice to any power exercisable by virtue of subsection (2)(*d*), (*dd*), (*e*) or (*g*) above or otherwise than by virtue of this section, no property adjustment order or pension sharing order shall be made on an application for the variation of a periodical payments or secured periodical payments order made (whether in favour of a party to a marriage or in favour of a child of the family) under section 23 above, and no order for the payment of a lump sum shall be made on an application for the variation of a periodical payments or secured periodical payments order in favour of a party to a marriage (whether made under section 23 or under section 27 above).

(6) Where the person liable to make payments under a secured periodical payments order has died, an application under this section relating to that order (and to any order made under section 24A(1) above which requires the proceeds of sale of property to be used for securing those payments) may be made by the person entitled to payments under the periodical payments order or by the personal representatives of the deceased person, but no such

application shall, except with the permission of the court, be made after the end of the period of 6 months from the date on which representation in regard to the estate of that person is first taken out.

(7) In exercising the powers conferred by this section the court shall have regard to all the circumstances of the case, first consideration being given to the welfare while a minor of any child of the family who has not attained the age of eighteen, and the circumstances of the case shall include any change in any of the matters to which the court was required to have regard when making the order to which the application relates, and –

(*a*)    in the case of a periodical payments or secured periodical payments order made on or after the grant of a decree of divorce or nullity of marriage, the court shall consider whether in all the circumstances and after having regard to any such change it would be appropriate to vary the order so that payments under the order are required to be made or secured only for such further period as will in the opinion of the court be sufficient (in the light of any proposed exercise by the court, where the marriage has been dissolved, of its powers under subsection (7B) below) to enable the party in whose favour the order was made to adjust without undue hardship to the termination of those payments;

(*b*)    in a case where the party against whom the order was made has died, the circumstances of the case shall also include the changed circumstances resulting from his or her death.

(7A) Subsection (7B) below applies where, after the dissolution of a marriage, the court –

(*a*)    discharges a periodical payments order or secured periodical payments order made in favour of a party to the marriage; or

(*b*)    varies such an order so that payments under the order are required to be made or secured only for such further period as is determined by the court.

(7B) The court has power, in addition to any power it has apart from this subsection, to make supplemental provision consisting of any of –

(*a*)    an order for the payment of a lump sum in favour of a party to the marriage;

(*b*)    one or more property adjustment orders in favour of a party to the marriage;

(*ba*)  one or more pension sharing orders;

(*c*)    a direction that the party in whose favour the original order discharged or varied was made is not entitled to make any further application for –

(i)     a periodical payments or secured periodical payments order, or

(ii)    an extension of the period to which the original order is limited by any variation made by the court.

(7C) An order for the payment of a lump sum made under subsection (7B) above may –

(*a*)    provide for the payment of that sum by instalments of such amount as may be specified in the order; and

(*b*)    require the payment of the instalments to be secured to the satisfaction of the court.

(7D) Section 23(6) above applies where the court makes an order for the payment of a lump sum under subsection (7B) above as it applies where the court makes such an order under section 23 above.

(7E) If under subsection (7B) above the court makes more than one property adjustment order in favour of the same party to the marriage, each of those orders must fall within a different paragraph of section 21(2) above.

(7F) Sections 24A and 30 above apply where the court makes a property adjustment order under subsection (7B) above as they apply where it makes such an order under section 24 above.

(7G) Subsections (3) to (5) of section 24B above apply in relation to a pension sharing order under subsection (7B) above as they apply in relation to a pension sharing order under that section.

(8) The personal representatives of a deceased person against whom a secured periodical payments order was made shall not be liable for having distributed any part of the estate of the deceased after the expiration of the period of 6 months referred to in subsection (6) above on the ground that they ought to have taken into account the possibility that the court might permit an application under this section to be made after that period by the person entitled to payments under the order; but this subsection shall not prejudice any power to recover any part of the estate so distributed arising by virtue of the making of an order in pursuance of this section.

(9) In considering for the purposes of subsection (6) above the question when representation was first taken out, a grant limited to settled land or to trust property shall be left out of account and a grant limited to real estate or to personal estate shall be left out of account unless a grant limited to the remainder of the estate has previously been made or is made at the same time.

(10) Where the court, in exercise of its powers under this section, decides to vary or discharge a periodical payments or secured periodical payments order, then, subject to section 28(1) and (2) above, the court shall have power to direct that the variation or discharge shall not take effect until the expiration of such period as may be specified in the order.

(11) Where –

(*a*)    a periodical payments or secured periodical payments order in favour of more than one child ('the order') is in force;

(*b*)    the order requires payments specified in it to be made to or for the benefit of more than one child without apportioning those payments between them;

(*c*)    a maintenance calculation ('the calculation') is made with respect to one or more, but not all, of the children with respect to whom those payments are to be made; and (*d*)    an application is made, before the end of the period of 6 months beginning with the date on which the assessment was made, for the variation or discharge of the order,

the court may, in exercise of its powers under this section to vary or discharge the order, direct that the variation or discharge shall take effect from the date on which the calculation took effect or any later date.

(12) Where –

(*a*)    an order ('the child order') of a kind prescribed for the purposes of section 10(1) of the Child Support Act 1991 is affected by a maintenance calculation;

(*b*)    on the date on which the child order became so affected there was in force a periodical payments or secured periodical payments order ('the spousal order') in favour of a party to a marriage having the care of the child in whose favour the child order was made; and

(*c*)    an application is made, before the end of the period of 6 months beginning with the date on which the maintenance calculation was made, for the spousal order to be varied or discharged,

the court may, in exercise of its powers under this section to vary or discharge the spousal order, direct that the variation or discharge shall take effect from the date on which the child order became so affected or any later date.

(13) For the purposes of subsection (12) above, an order is affected if it ceases to have effect or is modified by or under section 10 of the Child Support Act 1991.

(14) Subsections (11) and (12) above are without prejudice to any other power of the court to direct that the variation of discharge of an order under this section shall take effect from a date earlier than that on which the order for variation or discharge was made.

(15) The power to make regulations under subsection (4C) above shall be exercisable by statutory instrument which shall be subject to annulment in pursuance of a resolution of either House of Parliament.

**Amendments**—Matrimonial Homes and Property Act 1981, s 8(2); Administration of Justice Act 1982, s 51; Matrimonial and Family Proceedings Act 1984, s 6; SI 1993/623; Pensions Act 1995, s 166; Family Law Act 1996, Sch 8, para 16(5)(*a*), (6)(*b*), (7) (as modified by SI 1998/2572); Welfare Reform and Pensions Act 1999, s 19, Sch 3, para 7; Child Support, Pensions and Social Security Act 2000, s 26, Sch 3, para 3.

## 32 Payment of certain arrears unenforceable without the leave of the court

(1) A person shall not be entitled to enforce through the High Court or any county court the payment of any arrears due under an order for maintenance pending suit, an interim order for maintenance or any financial provision order without the leave of that court if those arrears became due more than twelve months before proceedings to enforce the payment of them are begun.

(2) The court hearing an application for the grant of leave under this section may refuse leave, or may grant leave subject to such restrictions and conditions

(including conditions as to the allowing of time for payment or the making of payment by instalments) as that court thinks proper, or may remit the payment of the arrears or of any part thereof.

(3) An application for the grant of leave under this section shall be made in such manner as may be prescribed by rules of court.

### 33 Orders for repayment in certain cases of sums paid under certain orders

(1) Where on an application made under this section in relation to an order to which this section applies it appears to the court that by reason of –

(*a*) a change in the circumstances of the person entitled to, or liable to make, payments under the order since the order was made, or

(*b*) the changed circumstances resulting from the death of the person so liable,

the amount received by the person entitled to payments under the order in respect of a period after those circumstances changed or after the death of the person liable to make payments under the order, as the case may be, exceeds the amount which the person so liable or his or her personal representatives should have been required to pay, the court may order the respondent to the application to pay to the applicant such sum, not exceeding the amount of the excess, as the court thinks just.

(2) This section applies to the following orders, that is to say –

(*a*) any order for maintenance pending suit and any interim order for maintenance;

(*b*) any periodical payments order; and

(*c*) any secured periodical payments order.

(3) An application under this section may be made by the person liable to make payments under an order to which this section applies or his or her personal representatives and may be made against the person entitled to payments under the order or her or his personal representatives.

(4) An application under this section may be made in proceedings in the High Court or a county court for –

(*a*) the variation or discharge of the order to which this section applies, or

(*b*) leave to enforce, or the enforcement of, the payment of arrears under that order;

but when not made in such proceedings shall be made to a county court, and accordingly references in this section to the court are references to the High Court or a county court, as the circumstances require.

(5) The jurisdiction conferred on a county court by this section shall be exercisable notwithstanding that by reason of the amount claimed in the application the jurisdiction would not but for this subsection be exercisable by a county court.

(6) An order under this section for the payment of any sum may provide for the payment of that sum by instalments of such amount as may be specified in the order.

*Consent orders*

### 33A  Consent orders for financial provision on property adjustment

(1) Notwithstanding anything in the preceding provisions of this Part of this Act, on an application for a consent order for financial relief the court may, unless it has reason to think that there are other circumstances into which it ought to inquire, make an order in the terms agreed on the basis only of the prescribed information furnished with the application.

(2) Subsection (1) above applies to an application for a consent order varying or discharging an order for financial relief as it applies to an application for an order for financial relief.

(3) In this section –

'consent order', in relation to an application for an order, means an order in the terms applied for to which the respondent agrees;
'order for financial relief' means an order under any of sections 23, 24, 24A, 24B or 27 above; and
'prescribed' means prescribed by rules of court.

**Amendments**—Inserted by Matrimonial and Family Proceedings Act 1984, s 7; amended by Welfare Reform and Pensions Act 1999, s 19, Sch 3, para 8.

*Maintenance agreements*

### 34  Validity of maintenance agreements

(1) If a maintenance agreement includes a provision purporting to restrict any right to apply to a court for an order containing financial arrangements, then –

(*a*)  that provision shall be void; but
(*b*)  any other financial arrangements contained in the agreement shall not thereby be rendered void or unenforceable and shall, unless they are void or unenforceable for any other reason (and subject to sections 35 and 36 below), be binding on the parties to the agreement.

(2) In this section and in section 35 below –

'maintenance agreement' means any agreement in writing made, whether before or after the commencement of this Act, between the parties to a marriage, being –
(*a*)  an agreement containing financial arrangements, whether made during the continuance or after the dissolution or annulment of the marriage; or
(*b*)  a separation agreement which contains no financial arrangements in a case where no other agreement in writing between the same parties contains such arrangements;

'financial arrangements' means provisions governing the rights and liabilities towards one another when living separately of the parties to a marriage (including a marriage which has been dissolved or annulled) in respect of the making or securing of payments or the disposition or use of any property, including such rights and liabilities with respect to the maintenance or education of any child, whether or not a child of the family.

### 35 Alteration of agreements by court during lives of parties

(1) Where a maintenance agreement is for the time being subsisting and each of the parties to the agreement is for the time being either domiciled or resident in England and Wales, then, subject to subsection (3) below, either party may apply to the court or to a magistrates' court for an order under this section.

(2) If the court to which the application is made is satisfied either –

(*a*)   that by reason of a change in the circumstances in the light of which any financial arrangements contained in the agreement were made or, as the case may be, financial arrangements were omitted from it (including a change foreseen by the parties when making the agreement), the agreement should be altered so as to make different, or, as the case may be, so as to contain, financial arrangements, or

(*b*)   that the agreement does not contain proper financial arrangements with respect to any child of the family,

then subject to subsections (3), (4) and (5) below, that court may by order make such alterations in the agreement –

(i)   by varying or revoking any financial arrangements contained in it, or

(ii)   by inserting in it financial arrangements for the benefit of one of the parties to the agreement or of a child of the family,

as may appear to that court to be just having regard to all the circumstances, including, if relevant, the matters mentioned in section 25(4) above; and the agreement shall have effect thereafter as if any alteration made by the order had been made by agreement between the parties and for valuable consideration.

(3) A magistrates' court shall not entertain an application under subsection (1) above unless both the parties to the agreement are resident in England and Wales and the court acts in, or is authorised by the Lord Chancellor to act for, a local justice area in which at least one of the parties is resident, and shall not have power to make any order on such an application except –

(*a*)   in a case where the agreement includes no provision for periodical payments by either of the parties, an order inserting provision for the making by one of the parties of periodical payments for the maintenance of the other party or for the maintenance of any child of the family;

(*b*)   in a case where the agreement includes provision for the making by one of the parties of periodical payments, an order increasing or reducing the rate of, or terminating, any of those payments.

(4) Where a court decides to alter, by order under this section, an agreement by inserting provision for the making or securing by one of the parties to the agreement of periodical payments for the maintenance of the other party or by increasing the rate of the periodical payments which the agreement provides shall be made by one of the parties for the maintenance of the other, the term for which the payments or, as the case may be, the additional payments attributable to the increase are to be made under the agreement as altered by the order shall be such term as the court may specify, subject to the following limits, that is to say –

    (*a*)    where the payments will not be secured, the term shall be so defined as not to extend beyond the death of either of the parties to the agreement or the remarriage of, or formation of a civil partnership by, the party to whom the payments are to be made;

    (*b*)    where the payments will be secured, the term shall be so defined as not to extend beyond the death or remarriage of, or formation of a civil partnership by, that party.

(5) Where a court decides to alter, by order under this section, an agreement by inserting provision for the making or securing by one of the parties to the agreement of periodical payments for the maintenance of a child of the family or by increasing the rate of the periodical payments which the agreement provides shall be made or secured by one of the parties for the maintenance of such a child, then, in deciding the term for which under the agreement as altered by the order the payments, or as the case may be, the additional payments attributable to the increase are to be made or secured for the benefit of the child, the court shall apply the provisions of section 29(2) and (3) above as to age limits as if the order in question were a periodical payments or secured periodical payments order in favour of the child.

(6) For the avoidance of doubt it is hereby declared that nothing in this section or in section 34 above affects any power of a court before which any proceedings between the parties to a maintenance agreement are brought under any other enactment (including a provision of this Act) to make an order containing financial arrangements or any right of either party to apply for such an order in such proceedings.

**Amendments**—Matrimonial and Family Proceedings Act 1984, s 46(1), Sch 1, para 13; Justices of the Peace Act 1997, s 73(2), Sch 5, para 14; Access to Justice Act 1999, s 106, Sch 15; Civil Partnership Act 2004, s 261(1), Sch 27, para 44; Courts Act 2003, Sch 8, para 169.

## 36 Alteration of agreements by court after death of one party

(1) Where a maintenance agreement within the meaning of section 34 above provides for the continuation of payments under the agreement after the death of one of the parties and that party dies domiciled in England and Wales, the surviving party or the personal representatives of the deceased party may, subject to subsections (2) and (3) below, apply to the High Court or a county court for an order under section 35 above.

(2) An application under this section shall not, except with the permission of the High Court or a county court, be made after the end of the period of 6 months from the date on which representation in regard to the estate of the deceased is first taken out.

(3) A county court shall not entertain an application under this section, or an application for permission to make an application under this section, unless it would have jurisdiction by virtue of section 22 of the Inheritance (Provision for Family and Dependants) Act 1975 (which confers jurisdiction on county courts in proceedings under that Act if the value of the property mentioned in that section does not exceed £5,000 or such larger sum as may be fixed by order of the Lord Chancellor) to hear and determine proceedings for an order under section 2 of that Act in relation to the deceased's estate.

(4) If a maintenance agreement is altered by a court on an application made in pursuance of subsection (1) above, the like consequences shall ensue as if the alteration had been made immediately before the death by agreement between the parties and for valuable consideration.

(5) The provisions of this section shall not render the personal representatives of the deceased liable for having distributed any part of the estate of the deceased after the expiration of the period of 6 months referred to in subsection (2) above on the ground that they ought to have taken into account the possibility that a court might permit an application by virtue of this section to be made by the surviving party after that period; but this subsection shall not prejudice any power to recover any part of the estate so distributed arising by virtue of the making of an order in pursuance of this section.

(6) Section 31(9) above shall apply for the purposes of subsection (2) above as it applies for the purposes of subsection (6) of section 31.

(7) Subsection (3) of section 22 of the Inheritance (Provision for Family and Dependants) Act 1975 (which enables rules of court to provide for the transfer from a county court to the High Court or from the High court to a county court of proceedings for an order under section 2 of that Act) and paragraphs (*a*) and (*b*) of subsection (4) of that section (provisions relating to proceedings commenced in county court before coming into force of order of the Lord Chancellor under that section) shall apply in relation to proceedings consisting of any such application as is referred to in subsection (3) above as they apply in relation to proceedings for an order under section 2 of that Act.

**Amendments**—Inheritance (Provision for Family and Dependants) Act 1975, s 26(1).

*Miscellaneous and supplemental*

### 37 Avoidance of transactions intended to prevent or reduce financial relief

(1) For the purposes of this section 'financial relief' means relief under any of the provisions of sections 22, 23, 24, 24B, 27, 31 (except subsection (6)) and 35 above, and any reference in this section to defeating a person's claim for financial relief is a reference to preventing financial relief from being granted to that person, or to that person for the benefit of a child of the family, or

reducing the amount of any financial relief which might be so granted, or frustrating or impeding the enforcement of any order which might be or has been made at his instance under any of those provisions.

(2) Where proceedings for financial relief are brought by one person against another, the court may, on the application of the first-mentioned person –

(*a*)   if it is satisfied that the other party to the proceedings is, with the intention of defeating the claim for financial relief, about to make any disposition or to transfer out of the jurisdiction or otherwise deal with any property, make such order as it thinks fit for restraining the other party from so doing or otherwise for protecting the claim;

(*b*)   if it is satisfied that the other party has, with that intention, made a reviewable disposition and that if the disposition were set aside financial relief or different financial relief would be granted to the applicant, make an order setting aside the disposition;

(*c*)   if it is satisfied, in a case where an order has been obtained under any of the provisions mentioned in subsection (1) above by the applicant against the other party, that the other party has, with that intention, made a reviewable disposition, make an order setting aside the disposition;

and an application for the purposes of paragraph (*b*) above shall be made in the proceedings for the financial relief in question.

(3) Where the court makes an order under subsection (2)(*b*) or (*c*) above setting aside a disposition it shall give such consequential directions as it thinks fit for giving effect to the order (including directions requiring the making of any payments or the disposal of any property).

(4) Any disposition made by the other party to the proceedings for financial relief in question (whether before or after the commencement of those proceedings) is a reviewable disposition for the purposes of subsection (2)(*b*) and (*c*) above unless it was made for valuable consideration (other than marriage) to a person who, at the time of the disposition, acted in relation to it in good faith and without notice of any intention on the part of the other party to defeat the applicant's claim for financial relief.

(5) Where an application is made under this section with respect to a disposition which took place less than three years before the date of the application or with respect to a disposition or other dealing with property which is about to take place and the court is satisfied –

(*a*)   in a case falling within subsection (2)(*a*) or (*b*) above, that the disposition or other dealing would (apart from this section) have the consequence, or

(*b*)   in a case falling within subsection (2)(*c*) above, that the disposition has had the consequence,

of defeating the applicant's claim for financial relief, it shall be presumed, unless the contrary is shown, that the person who disposed of or is about to dispose of or deal with the property did so or, as the case may be, is about to do so, with the intention of defeating the applicant's claim for financial relief.

(6) In this section 'disposition' does not include any provision contained in a will or codicil but, with that exception, includes any conveyance, assurance or gift of property of any description, whether made by an instrument or otherwise.

(7) This section does not apply to a disposition made before 1 January 1968.

**Amendments**—Welfare Reform and Pensions Act 1999, s 19, Sch 3, para 9.

## 38 Orders for repayment in certain cases of sums paid after cessation of order by reason of remarriage or formation of civil partnership

(1) Where –

    (*a*)    a periodical payments or secured periodical payments order in favour of a party to a marriage (hereafter in this section referred to as 'a payments order') has ceased to have effect by reason of the remarriage of, or formation of a civil partnership by, that party, and

    (*b*)    the person liable to make payments under the order or his or her personal representatives made payments in accordance with it in respect of a period after the date of the remarriage or formation of the civil partnership in the mistaken belief that the order was still subsisting,

the person so liable or his or her personal representatives shall not be entitled to bring proceedings in respect of a cause of action arising out of the circumstances mentioned in paragraphs (*a*) and (*b*) above against the person entitled to payments under the order or her or his personal representatives, but may instead make an application against that person or her or his personal representatives under this section.

(2) On an application under this section the court may order the respondent to pay to the applicant a sum equal to the amount of the payments made in respect of the period mentioned in subsection (1)(*b*) above or, if it appears to the court that it would be unjust to make that order, it may either order the respondent to pay to the applicant such lesser sum as it thinks fit or dismiss the application.

(3) An application under this section may be made in proceedings in the High Court or a county court for leave to enforce, or the enforcement of, payment of arrears under the order in question, but when not made in such proceedings shall be made to a county court; and accordingly references in this section to the court are references to the High Court or a county court, as the circumstances require.

(4) The jurisdiction conferred on a county court by this section shall be exercisable notwithstanding that by reason of the amount claimed in the application the jurisdiction would not but for this subsection be exercisable by a county court.

(5) An order under this section for the payment of any sum may provide for the payment of that sum by instalments of such amount as may be specified in the order.

(6) The designated officer for a magistrates' court to whom any payments under a payments order are required to be made, and the collecting officer under an attachment of earnings order made to secure payments under a payments order, shall not be liable –

(a)   in the case of the designated officer, for any act done by him in pursuance of the payments order after the date on which that order ceased to have effect by reason of the remarriage of, or formation of a civil partnership by, the person entitled to payments under it, and

(b)   in the case of the collecting officer, for any act done by him after that date in accordance with any enactment or rule of court specifying how payments made to him in compliance with the attachment of earnings order are to be dealt with,

if, but only if, the act was one which he would have been under a duty to do had the payments order not so ceased to have effect and the act was done before notice in writing of the fact that the person so entitled had remarried or formed a civil partnership was given to him by or on behalf of that person, the person liable to make payments under the payments order or the personal representatives of either of those persons.

(7)   In this section 'collecting officer', in relation to an attachment of earnings order, means the officer of the High Court, the district judge of a county court or the designated officer for a magistrates' court to whom a person makes payments in compliance with the order.

**Amendments**—Access to Justice Act 1999, s 90, Sch 13, para 82; Civil Partnership Act 2004, s 261(1), Sch 27, para 43(1)–(4); Courts Act 2003, Sch 8, para 170.

### 39 Settlement etc made in compliance with a property adjustment order may be avoided on bankruptcy of settlor

The fact that a settlement or transfer of property had to be made in order to comply with a property adjustment order shall not prevent that settlement or transfer from being a transaction in respect of which an order may be made under section 339 or 340 of the Insolvency Act 1986 (transfers at an undervalue and preferences).

**Amendments**—Insolvency Act 1985, s 235(1), Sch 8, para 23; Insolvency Act 1986, s 439(2), Sch 14.

### 40 Payments etc under order made in favour of person suffering from mental disorder

(1) Where the court makes an order under this Part of this Act requiring payments (including a lump sum payment) to be made, or property to be transferred, to a party to a marriage and the court is satisfied that the person in whose favour the order is made [("P") lacks capacity (within the meaning of the Mental Capacity Act 2005) in relation to the provisions of the order] then,

subject to any order, direction or authority made or given in relation to [P under that Act], the court may order the payments to be made, or as the case may be, the property to be transferred, to such person ("D") as it may direct.

(2) In carrying out any functions of his in relation to an order made under subsection (1), D must act in P's best interests (within the meaning of that Act).

**Amendments**—Mental Capacity Act 2005, s 67 (1), Sch 6, para 19.

### 40A Appeals relating to pension sharing orders which have taken effect

(1) Subsections (2) and (3) below apply where an appeal against a pension sharing order is begun on or after the day on which the order takes effect.

(2) If the pension sharing order relates to a person's rights under a pension arrangement, the appeal court may not set aside or vary the order if the person responsible for the pension arrangement has acted to his detriment in reliance on the taking effect of the order.

(3) If the pension sharing order relates to a person's shareable state scheme rights, the appeal court may not set aside or vary the order if the Secretary of State has acted to his detriment in reliance on the taking effect of the order.

(4) In determining for the purposes of subsection (2) or (3) above whether a person has acted to his detriment in reliance on the taking effect of the order, the appeal court may disregard any detriment which in its opinion is insignificant.

(5) Where subsection (2) or (3) above applies, the appeal court may make such further orders (including one or more pension sharing orders) as it thinks fit for the purpose of putting the parties in the position it considers appropriate.

(6) Section 24C above only applies to a pension sharing order under this section if the decision of the appeal court can itself be the subject of an appeal.

(7) In subsection (2) above, the reference to the person responsible for the pension arrangement is to be read in accordance with section 25D(4) above.

**Amendments**—Inserted by Welfare Reform and Pensions Act 1999, s 19, Sch 3, para 10.

# Appendix 7

## DIVORCE ETC (PENSIONS) REGULATIONS 2000, SI 2000/1123

### 1  Citation, commencement and transitional provisions

(1) These Regulations may be cited as the Divorce etc (Pensions) Regulations 2000 and shall come into force on 1 December 2000.

(2) These Regulations shall apply to any proceedings for divorce, judicial separation or nullity of marriage commenced on or after 1 December 2000, and any such proceedings commenced before that date shall be treated as if these Regulations had not come into force.

### 2  Interpretation

In these Regulations –

  (a)   a reference to a section by number alone means the section so numbered in the Matrimonial Causes Act 1973;
  (b)   'the 1984 Act' means the Matrimonial and Family Proceedings Act 1984;
  (c)   expressions defined in sections 21A and 25D(3) have the meanings assigned by those sections;
  (d)   every reference to a rule by number alone means the rule so numbered in the Family Proceedings Rules 1991.

### 3  Valuation

(1) For the purposes of the court's functions in connection with the exercise of any of its powers under Part II of the Matrimonial Causes Act 1973, benefits under a pension arrangement shall be calculated and verified in the manner set out in regulation 3 of the Pensions on Divorce etc (Provision of Information) Regulations 2000, and –

  (a)   the benefits shall be valued as at a date to be specified by the court (being not earlier than one year before the date of the petition and not later than the date on which the court is exercising its power);
  (b)   in determining that value the court may have regard to information furnished by the person responsible for the pension arrangement pursuant to any of the provisions set out in paragraph (2); and
  (c)   in specifying a date under sub-paragraph (a) above the court may have regard to the date specified in any information furnished as mentioned in sub-paragraph (b) above.

(2) The relevant provisions for the purposes of paragraph (1)(b) above are –

(a)  the Pensions on Divorce etc (Provision of Information) Regulations 2000;

(b)  regulation 5 of and Schedule 2 to the Occupational Pension Schemes (Disclosure of Information) Regulations 1996 and regulation 11 of and Schedule 1 to the Occupational Pension Schemes (Transfer Value) Regulations 1996;

(c)  section 93A or 94(1)(a) or (aa) of the Pension Schemes Act 1993;

(d)  section 94(1)(b) of the Pension Schemes Act 1993 or paragraph 2(a) (or, where applicable, 2(b)) of Schedule 2 to the Personal Pension Schemes (Disclosure of Information) Regulations 1987.

## 4 Pension attachment: notices

(1) This regulation applies in the circumstances set out in section 25D(1)(a) (transfers of pension rights).

(2) Where this regulation applies, the person responsible for the first arrangement shall give notice in accordance with the following paragraphs of this regulation to –

(a)  the person responsible for the new arrangement, and

(b)  the other party.

(3) The notice to the person responsible for the new arrangement shall include copies of the following documents –

(a)  every order made under section 23 imposing any requirement on the person responsible for the first arrangement in relation to the rights transferred;

(b)  any order varying such an order;

(c)  all information or particulars which the other party has been required to supply under any provision of rule 2.70 for the purpose of enabling the person responsible for the first arrangement –

    (i)  to provide information, documents or representations to the court to enable it to decide what if any requirement should be imposed on that person; or

    (ii)  to comply with any order imposing such a requirement;

(d)  any notice given by the other party to the person responsible for the first arrangement under regulation 6;

(e)  where the pension rights under the first arrangement were derived wholly or partly from rights held under a previous pension arrangement, any notice given to the person responsible for the previous arrangement under paragraph (2) of this regulation on the occasion of that acquisition of rights.

(4) The notice to the other party shall contain the following particulars –

(a)  the fact that the pension rights have been transferred;

(b)  the date on which the transfer takes effect;

(c)  the name and address of the person responsible for the new arrangement;

(*d*) the fact that the order made under section 23 is to have effect as if it had been made in respect of the person responsible for the new arrangement.

(5) Both notices shall be given –

(*a*) within the period provided by section 99 of the Pension Schemes Act 1993 for the person responsible for the first arrangement to carry out what the member requires; and

(*b*) before the expiry of 21 days after the person responsible for the first arrangement has made all required payments to the person responsible for the new arrangement.

## 5 Pension attachment: reduction in benefits

(1) This regulation applies where –

(*a*) an order under section 23 or under section 17 of the 1984 Act has been made by virtue of section 25B or 25C imposing any requirement on the person responsible for a pension arrangement;

(*b*) an event has occurred which is likely to result in a significant reduction in the benefits payable under the arrangement, other than:

    (i) the transfer from the arrangement off all the rights of the party with pension rights in the circumstances set out in section 25D(1)(*a*), or

    (ii) a reduction in the value of assets held for the purposes of the arrangement by reason of a change in interest rates or other market conditions.

(2) Where this regulation applies, the person responsible for the arrangement shall, within 14 days of the occurrence of the event mentioned in paragraph (1)(*b*), give notice to the other party of –

(*a*) that event;

(*b*) the likely extent of the reduction in the benefits payable under the arrangement.

(3) Where the event mentioned in paragraph (1)(*b*) consists of a transfer of some but not all of the rights of the party with pension rights from the arrangement, the person responsible for the first arrangement shall, within 14 days of the transfer, give notice to the other party of the name and address of the person responsible for any pension arrangement under which the party with pension rights has acquired rights as a result of that event.

## 6 Pension attachment: change of circumstances

(1) This regulation applies where –

(*a*) an order under section 23 or under section 17 of the 1984 Act has been made by virtue of section 25B or 25C imposing any requirement on the person responsible for a pension arrangement; and

(*b*) any of the events set out in paragraph (2) has occurred.

(2) Those events are –

    (*a*)    any of the particulars supplied by the other party under rule 2.70 for any purpose mentioned in regulation 4(3)(*c*) has ceased to be accurate; or

    (*b*)    by reason of the remarriage of the other party, or his having formed a subsequent civil partnership, or otherwise, the order has ceased to have effect.

(3) Where this regulation applies, the other party shall, within 14 days of the event, give notice of it to the person responsible for the pension arrangement.

(4) Where, because of the inaccuracy of the particulars supplied by the other party under rule 2.70 or because the other party has failed to give notice of their having ceased to be accurate, it is not reasonably practicable for the person responsible for the pension arrangement to make a payment to the other party as required by the order:

    (*a*)    it may instead make that payment to the party with pension rights, and

    (*b*)    it shall then be discharged of liability to the other party to the extent of that payment.

(5) Where an event set out in paragraph (2)(*b*) has occurred and, because the other party has failed to give notice in accordance with paragraph (3), the person responsible for the pension arrangement makes a payment to the other party as required by the order –

    (*a*)    its liability to the party with pension rights shall be discharged to the extent of that payment, and

    (*b*)    the other party shall, within 14 days of the payment being made, make a payment to the party with pension rights to the extent of that payment.

**Amendments**—SI 2005/2114, art 2(1), Sch 1, para 8.

### 7 Pension attachment: transfer of rights

(1) This regulation applies where –

    (*a*)    a transfer of rights has taken place in the circumstances set out in section 25D(1)(*a*);

    (*b*)    notice has been given in accordance with regulation 4(2)(*a*) and (*b*);

    (*c*)    any of the events set out in regulation 6(2) has occurred; and

    (*d*)    the other party has not, before receiving notice under regulation 4(2)(*b*), given notice of that event to the person responsible for the first arrangement under regulation 6(3).

(2) Where this regulation applies, the other party shall, within 14 days of the event, give notice of it to the person responsible for the new arrangement.

(3) Where, because of the inaccuracy of the particulars supplied by the other party under rule 2.70 for any purpose mentioned in regulation 4(3)(*c*) or because the other party has failed to give notice of their having ceased to be

accurate, it is not reasonably practicable for the person responsible for the new arrangement to make a payment to the other party as required by the order –

(*a*)   it may instead make that payment to the party with pension rights, and

(*b*)   it shall then be discharged of liability to the other party to the extent of that payment.

(4) Subject to paragraph (5), where this regulation applies and the other party, within one year from the transfer, gives to the person responsible for the first arrangement notice of the event set out in regulation 6(2) in purported compliance with regulation 7(2), the person responsible for the first arrangement shall –

(*a*)   send that notice to the person responsible for the new arrangement, and

(*b*)   give the other party a second notice under regulation 4(2)(*b*);

and the other party shall be deemed to have given notice under regulation 7(2) to the person responsible for the new arrangement.

(5) Upon complying with paragraph (4) above, the person responsible for the first arrangement shall be discharged from any further obligation under regulation 4 or 7(4), whether in relation to the event in question or any further event set out in regulation 6(2) which may be notified to it by the other party.

## 8 Service

A notice under regulation 4, 5, 6 or 7 may be sent by fax or by ordinary first class post to the last known address of the intended recipient and shall be deemed to have been received on the seventh day after the day on which it was sent.

## 9 Pension sharing order not to take effect pending appeal

(1) No pension sharing order under section 24B or variation of a pension sharing order under section 31 shall take effect earlier than 7 days after the end of the period for filing notice of appeal against the order.

(2) The filing of a notice of appeal within the time allowed for doing so prevents the order taking effect before the appeal has been dealt with.

\*\*\*\*

# Appendix 8

# PENSIONS ON DIVORCE ETC (PROVISION OF INFORMATION) REGULATIONS 2000, SI 2000/1048

## 1 Citation, commencement and interpretation

(1) These Regulations may be cited as the Pensions on Divorce etc (Provision of Information) Regulations 2000 and shall come into force on 1 December 2000.

(2) In these Regulations –

'the 1993 Act' means the Pension Schemes Act 1993;
'the 1995 Act' means the Pensions Act 1995;
'the 1999 Act' means the Welfare Reform and Pensions Act 1999;
'the Charging Regulations' means the Pensions on Divorce etc (Charging) Regulations 2000;
'the Implementation and Discharge of Liability Regulations' means the Pension Sharing (Implementation and Discharge of Liability) Regulations 2000;
'the Valuation Regulations' means the Pension Sharing (Valuation) Regulations 2000;
'active member' has the meaning given by section 124(1) of the 1995 Act;
'day' means any day other than –
  (*a*) Christmas Day or Good Friday; or
  (*b*) a bank holiday, that is to say, a day which is, or is to be observed as, a bank holiday or a holiday under Schedule 1 to the Banking and Financial Dealings Act 1971;

'deferred member' has the meaning given by section 124(1) of the 1995 Act;
'implementation period' has the meaning given by section 34(1) of the 1999 Act;
'member' means a person who has rights to future benefits, or has rights to benefits payable, under a pension arrangement;
'money purchase benefits' has the meaning given by section 181(1) of the 1993 Act;
'normal benefit age' has the meaning given by section 101B of the 1993 Act;
'normal pension age' has the meaning given in section 180 of the 1993 Act (normal pension age);
'notice of discharge of liability' means a notice issued to the member and his former spouse or former civil partner by the person responsible for a pension arrangement when that person has discharged his liability in respect of a pension credit in accordance with Schedule 5 to the 1999 Act;

'notice of implementation' means a notice issued by the person responsible for a pension arrangement to the member and his former spouse or former civil partner at the beginning of the implementation period notifying them of the day on which the implementation period for the pension credit begins;

'occupational pension scheme' has the meaning given by section 1 of the 1993 Act;

'the party with pension rights' and 'the other party' have the meanings given by section 25D(3) of the Matrimonial Causes Act 1997;

'pension arrangement' has the meaning given in section 46(1) of the 1999 Act;

'pension credit' means a credit under section 29(1)(*b*) of the 1999 Act;

'pension credit benefit' means the benefits payable under a pension arrangement or a qualifying arrangement to or in respect of a person by virtue of rights under the arrangement in question which are attributable (directly or indirectly) to a pension credit;

'pension credit rights' means rights to future benefits under a pension arrangement or a qualifying arrangement which are attributable (directly or indirectly) to a pension credit;

'pension sharing order or provision' means an order or provision which is mentioned in section 28(1) of the 1999 Act;

'pensionable service' has the meaning given by section 124(1) of the 1995 Act;

'person responsible for a pension arrangement' has the meaning given by section 46(2) of the 1999 Act;

'personal pension scheme' has the meaning given by section 1 of the 1993 Act;

'qualifying arrangement' has the meaning given by paragraph 6 of Schedule 5 to the 1999 Act;

'retirement annuity contract' means a contract or scheme which is to be treated as becoming a registered pension scheme under 153(9) of the Finance Act 2004 in accordance with paragraph 1(1)(f) of Schedule 36 to that Act;

'salary related occupational pension scheme' has the meaning given by regulation 1A of the Transfer Values Regulations;

'transfer day' has the meaning given by section 29(8) of the 1999 Act;

'the Transfer Values Regulations' means the Occupational Pension Schemes (Transfer Values) Regulations 1996;

'transferee' has the meaning given by section 29(8) of the 1999 Act;

'transferor' has the meaning given by section 29(8) of the 1999 Act;

'trustees or managers' has the meaning given by section 46(1) of the 1999 Act.

**Amendments**—SI 2000/2691; SI 2005/2877; SI 2006/744; SI 2008/1050; SI 2009/615.

## 2 Basic information about pensions and divorce or dissolution of a civil partnership

(1) The requirements imposed on a person responsible for a pension arrangement for the purposes of section 23(1)(*a*) of the 1999 Act (supply of pension information in connection with divorce etc) are that he shall furnish –

    (*a*)    on request from a member, the information referred to in paragraphs (2) and (3)(*b*) to (*f*);

    (*b*)    on request from the spouse or civil partner of a member, the information referred to in paragraph (3); or

    (*c*)    pursuant to an order of the court, the information referred to in paragraph (2), (3) or (4),

to the member, the spouse or civil partner of the member, or, as the case may be, to the court.

(2) The information in this paragraph is a valuation of pension rights or benefits accrued under that member's pension arrangement.

(3) The information in this paragraph is –

    (*a*)    a statement that on request from the member, or pursuant to an order of the court, a valuation of pension rights or benefits accrued under that member's pension arrangement, will be provided to the member, or, as the case may be, to the court;

    (*b*)    a statement summarising the way in which the valuation referred to in paragraph (2) and sub-paragraph (*a*) is calculated;

    (*c*)    the pension benefits which are included in a valuation referred to in paragraph (2) and sub-paragraph (*a*);

    (*d*)    whether the person responsible for the pension arrangement offers membership to a person entitled to a pension credit, and if so, the types of benefits available to pension credit members under that arrangement;

    (*e*)    whether the person responsible for the pension arrangements intends to discharge his liability for a pension credit other than by offering membership to a person entitled to a pension credit; and

    (*f*)    the schedule of charges which the person responsible for the pension arrangement will levy in accordance with regulation 2(2) of the Charging Regulations (general requirements as to charges).

(4) The information in this paragraph is any other information relevant to any power with respect to the matters specified in section 23(1)(*a*) of the 1999 Act and which is not specified in Schedule 1 or 2 to the Occupational Pension Schemes (Disclosure of Information) Regulations 1996 (basic information about the scheme and information to be made available to individuals), or in Schedule 1 or 2 to the Personal Pension Schemes (Disclosure of Information) Regulations 1987 (basic information about the scheme and information to be made available to individuals), in a case where either of those Regulations applies.

(5) Where the member's request for, or the court order for the provision of, information includes a request for, or an order for the provision of, a valuation under paragraph (2), the person responsible for the pension arrangement shall furnish all the information requested, or ordered, to the member –

(*a*)   within 3 months beginning with the date the person responsible for the pension arrangement receives that request or order for the provision of the information;

(*b*)   within 6 weeks beginning with the date the person responsible for the pension arrangement receives the request, or order, for the provision of the information, if the member has notified that person on the date of the request or order that the information is needed in connection with proceedings commenced under any of the provisions referred to in section 23(1)(*a*) of the 1999 Act; or

(*c*)   within such shorter period specified by the court in an order requiring the person responsible for the pension arrangement to provide a valuation in accordance with paragraph (2).

(6)  Where –

(*a*)   the member's request for, or the court order for the provision of, information does not include a request or an order for a valuation under paragraph (2); or

(*b*)   the member's spouse or civil partner requests the information specified in paragraph (3),

the person responsible for the pension arrangement shall furnish that information to the member, his spouse, civil partner, or the court, as the case may be, within one month beginning with the date that person responsible for the pension arrangement receives the request for, or the court order for the provision of, the information.

(7)  At the same time as furnishing the information referred to in paragraph (1), the person responsible for a pension arrangement may furnish the information specified in regulation 4(2) (provision of information in response to a notification that a pension sharing order or provision may be made).

Amendments—SI 2005/2877.

### 3 Information about pensions and divorce and dissolution of a civil partnership: valuation of pension benefits

(1) Where an application for financial relief under any of the provisions referred to in section 23(*a*)(i), (i*a*),(iii) or (iv) of the 1999 Act (supply of pension information in connection with domestic and overseas divorce etc in England and Wales and corresponding Northern Ireland powers) has been made or is in contemplation, the valuation of benefits under a pension arrangement shall be calculated and verified for the purposes of regulation 2 of these Regulations in accordance with –

(*a*)   paragraph (3), if the person with pension rights is a deferred member of an occupational pension scheme;

(*b*)   paragraph (4), if the person with pension rights is an active member of an occupational pension scheme;

(*c*)   paragraphs (5) and (6), if –

   (i)   the person with pension rights is a member of a personal pension scheme; or

   (ii)   those pension rights are contained in a retirement annuity contract; or

(*d*)   paragraphs (7) and (8), if –

   (i)   the pension of the person with pension rights is in payment;

   (ii)   the rights of the person with pension rights are contained in an annuity contract other than a retirement annuity contract; or

   (iii)   the rights of the person with pension rights are contained in a deferred annuity contract other than a retirement annuity contract; or

   (iv)   the pension of the person with pension rights is not in payment and the person has attained normal pension age.

(2) Where an application for financial provision under any of the provisions referred to in section 23(1)(*a*)(ii) of the 1999 Act (corresponding Scottish powers) has been made, or is in contemplation, the valuation of benefits under a pension arrangement shall be calculated and verified for the purposes of regulation 2 of these Regulations in accordance with regulation 3 of the Divorce etc (Pensions) (Scotland) Regulations 2000 (valuation).

(3) Where the person with pension rights is a deferred member of an occupational pension scheme, the value of the benefits which he has under that scheme shall be taken to be –

(*a*)   in the case of an occupational pension scheme other than a salary related scheme, the cash equivalent to which he acquired a right under section 94(1)(*a*) of the 1993 Act (right to cash equivalent) on the termination of his pensionable service, calculated on the assumption that he has made an application under section 95 of that Act (ways of taking right to cash equivalent) on the date on which the request for the valuation was received; or

(*b*)   in the case of a salary related occupational pension scheme, the guaranteed cash equivalent to which he would have acquired a right under section 94(1)(*aa*) of the 1993 Act if he had made an application under section 95(1) of that Act, calculated on the assumption that he has made such an application on the date on which the request for the valuation was received.

(4) Where the person with pension rights is an active member of an occupational pension scheme, the valuation of the benefits which he has accrued under that scheme shall be calculated and verified –

(*a*)   on the assumption that the member had made a request for an estimate of the cash equivalent that would be available to him were his pensionable service to terminate on the date on which the request for the valuation was received; and

(b)    in accordance with regulation 11 of and Schedule 1 to the Transfer Values Regulations (disclosure).

(5) Where the person with pension rights is a member of a personal pension scheme, or those rights are contained in a retirement annuity contract, the value of the benefits which he has under that scheme or contract shall be taken to be the cash equivalent to which he would have acquired a right under section 94(1)(b) of the 1993 Act, if he had made an application under section 95(1) of that Act on the date on which the request for the valuation was received.

(6) In relation to a personal pension scheme which is comprised in a retirement annuity contract made before 4th January 1988, paragraph (5) shall apply as if such a scheme were not excluded from the scope of Chapter IV of Part IV of the 1993 Act by section 93(1)(b) of that Act (scope of Chapter IV).

(7) Cash equivalents are to be calculated and verified in accordance with regulations 7 to 7C and 7E(1) to (3) of the Transfer Values Regulations as appropriate.

(8) But when calculating and verifying a cash equivalent in accordance with those regulations –

(a)    references to "trustees" must be read as references to "person responsible for the pension arrangement";
(b)    where the person with pension rights is a pensioner member on the date on which the request for the valuation is received, the value of his pension must be calculated and verified in accordance with regulations 7 to 7E of the Transfer Values Regulations as appropriate;
(c)    where the person is over normal pension age but not in receipt of a pension –
   (i)    the value of his pension must be calculated and verified in accordance with regulations 7 to 7E of the Transfer Values Regulations as appropriate; and
   (ii)   the person responsible for the pension arrangement must assume that the pension came into payment on the date on which the request for the valuation was received; and
(d)    the date by reference to which the cash equivalent is to be calculated and verified is to be the date on which the request for the valuation was received.

(9) (*revoked*).

(10) Where paragraph (3), (4) or (7) has effect by reference to provisions of Chapter IV of Part IV of the 1993 Act, section 93(1)(a)(i) of that Act (scope of Chapter IV) shall apply to those provisions as if the words 'at least one year' had been omitted from section 93(1)(a)(i).

**Amendments**—SI 2005/2877; SI 2007/0060; SI 2008/1050.

**4 Provision of information in response to a notification that a pension sharing order or provision may be made**

(1) A person responsible for a pension arrangement shall furnish the information specified in paragraph (2) to the member or to the court, as the case may be –

    (*a*)    within 21 days beginning with the date that the person responsible for the pension arrangement received the notification that a pension sharing order or provision may be made; or

    (*b*)    if the court has specified a date which is outside the 21 days referred to in sub-paragraph (*a*), by that date.

(2) The information referred to in paragraph (1) is –

    (*a*)    the full name of the pension arrangement and address to which any order or provision referred to in section 28(1) of the 1999 Act (activation of pension sharing) should be sent;

    (*b*)    in the case of an occupational pension scheme, whether the scheme is winding up, and, if so, –

        (i)    the date on which the winding up commenced; and

        (ii)    the name and address of the trustees who are dealing with the winding up;

    (*c*)    in the case of an occupational pension scheme, whether a cash equivalent of the member's pension rights, if calculated on the date the notification referred to in paragraph (1)(a) was received by the trustees or managers of that scheme, would be reduced in accordance with the provisions of paragraphs 2, 3 and 12 of Schedule 1A to the Transfer Values Regulations (reductions in initial cash equivalents;

    (*d*)    whether the person responsible for the pension arrangement is aware that the member's rights under the pension arrangement are subject to any, and if so, to specify which, of the following

        (i)    any order or provision specified in section 28(1) of the 1999 Act;

        (ii)    an order under section 23 of the Matrimonial Causes Act 1973 (financial provision orders in connection with divorce etc.), so far as it includes provision made by virtue of section 25B or 25C of that Act (powers to include provisions about pensions);

        (iii)    an order under section 12A(2) or (3) of the Family Law (Scotland) Act 1985 (powers in relation to pensions lump sums when making a capital sum order) which relates to benefits or future benefits to which the member is entitled under the pension arrangement;

        (iv)    an order under Article 25 of the Matrimonial Causes (Northern Ireland) Order 1978, so far as it includes provision made by virtue of Article 27B or 27C of that Order (Northern Ireland powers corresponding to those mentioned in paragraph (2)(*d*)(ii));

        (v)    a forfeiture order;

        (vi)    a bankruptcy order;

(vii) an award of sequestration on a member's estate or the making of the appointment on his estate of a judicial factor under section 41 of the Solicitors (Scotland) Act 1980 (appointment of judicial factor);

(*e*) whether the member's rights under the pension arrangement include rights specified in regulation 2 of the Valuation Regulations (rights under a pension arrangement which are not shareable);

(*f*) if the person responsible for the pension arrangement has not at an earlier stage provided the following information, whether that person requires the charges specified in regulation 3 (charges recoverable in respect of the provision of basic information), 5 (charges in respect of pension sharing activity), or 6 (additional amounts recoverable in respect of pension sharing activity) of the Charging Regulations to be paid before the commencement of the implementation period, and if so –

(i) whether that person requires those charges to be paid in full; or
(ii) the proportion of those charges which he requires to be paid;

(*g*) whether the person responsible for the pension arrangement may levy additional charges specified in regulation 6 of the Charging Regulations, and if so, the scale of the additional charges which are likely to be made;

(*h*) whether the member is a trustee of the pension arrangement;

(*i*) whether the person responsible for the pension arrangement may request information about the member's state of health from the member if a pension sharing order or provision were to be made;

(j) (*revoked*)

(*k*) whether the person responsible for the pension arrangement requires information additional to that specified in regulation 5 (information required by the person responsible for the pension arrangement before the implementation period may begin) in order to implement the pension sharing order or provision.

Amendments—SI 2000/2691; SI 2003/1727; SI 2008/1050.

## 5 Information required by the person responsible for the pension arrangement before the implementation period may begin

The information prescribed for the purposes of section 34(1)(*b*) of the 1999 Act (information relating to the transferor and the transferee which the person responsible for the pension arrangement must receive) is –

(*a*) in relation to the transferor –
(i) all names by which the transferor has been known;
(ii) date of birth;
(iii) address;
(iv) National Insurance number;
(v) the name of the pension arrangement to which the pension sharing order or provision relates; and
(vi) the transferor's membership or policy number in that pension arrangement;

(*b*)   in relation to the transferee –
  (i)   all names by which the transferee has been known;
  (ii)   date of birth;
  (iii)   address;
  (iv)   National Insurance number; and
  (v)   if the transferee is a member of the pension arrangement from which the pension credit is derived, his membership or policy number in that pension arrangement;
(*c*)   where the transferee has given his consent in accordance with paragraph 1(3)(*c*), 3(3)(*c*) or 4(2)(*c*) of Schedule 5 to the 1999 Act (mode of discharge of liability for a pension credit) to the payment of the pension credit to the person responsible for a qualifying arrangement –
  (i)   the full name of that qualifying arrangement;
  (ii)   its address;
  (iii)   if known, the transferee's membership number or policy number in that arrangement; and
  (iv)   the name or title, business address, business telephone number, and, where available, the business facsimile number and electronic mail address of a person who may be contacted in respect of the discharge of liability for the pension credit;
(*d*)   where the rights from which the pension credit is derived are held in an occupational pension scheme which is being wound up, whether the transferee has given an indication whether he wishes to transfer his pension credit rights which may have been reduced in accordance with the provisions of regulation 16(1) of the Implementation and Discharge of Liability Regulations (adjustments to the amount of the pension credit – occupational pension schemes which are underfunded on the valuation day) to a qualifying arrangement; and
(*e*)   any information requested by the person responsible for the pension arrangement in accordance with regulation 4(2)(i) or (*k*).

## 6 Provision of information after the death of the person entitled to the pension credit before liability in respect of the pension credit has been discharged

(1) Where the person entitled to the pension credit dies before the person responsible for the pension arrangement has discharged his liability in respect of the pension credit, the person responsible for the pension arrangement shall, within 21 days of the date of receipt of the notification of the death of the person entitled to the pension credit, notify in writing any person whom the person responsible for the pension arrangement considers should be notified of the matters specified in paragraph (2) –

(*a*)   the person whom the person entitled to the pension credit nominated pursuant to regulation 4(2)(*j*) to receive pension credit benefit; and
(*b*)   any other person whom the person responsible for the pension arrangement considers should be notified,

of the matters specified in paragraph (2).

(2) The matters specified in this paragraph are –

   (a)  how the person responsible for the pension arrangement intends to discharge his liability in respect of the pension credit;
   (b)  whether the person responsible for the pension arrangement intends to recover charges from the person nominated to receive pension credit benefits, in accordance with regulations 2 to 9 of the Charging Regulations, and if so, a copy of the schedule of charges issued to the parties to pension sharing in accordance with regulation 2(2)(b) of the Charging Regulations (general requirements as to charges); and
   (c)  a list of any further information which the person responsible for the pension arrangement requires in order to discharge his liability in respect of the pension credit.

Amendments—SI 2000/2691.

### 7 Provision of information after receiving a pension sharing order or provision

(1) A person responsible for a pension arrangement who is in receipt of a pension sharing order or provision relating to that arrangement shall provide in writing to the transferor and transferee, or, where regulation 6(1) applies, to the person other than the person entitled to the pension credit referred to in regulation 6 of the Implementation and Discharge of Liability Regulations (discharge of liability in respect of a pension credit following the death of the person entitled to the pension credit), as the case may be –

   (a)  a notice in accordance with the provisions of regulation 7(1) of the Charging Regulations (charges in respect of pension sharing activity – postponement of implementation period);
   (b)  a list of information relating to the transferor or the transferee, or, where regulation 6(1) applies, the person other than the person entitled to the pension credit referred to in regulation 6 of the Implementation and Discharge of Liability Regulations, as the case may be, which –
      (i)   has been requested in accordance with regulation 4(2)(i) and (k), or, where appropriate, 6(2)(c), or should have been provided in accordance with regulation 5;
      (ii)  the person responsible for the pension arrangement considers he needs in order to begin to implement the pension sharing order or provision; and
      (iii) remains outstanding;
   (c)  a notice of implementation; or
   (d)  a statement by the person responsible for the pension arrangement explaining why he is unable to implement the pension sharing order or agreement.

(2) The information specified in paragraph (1) shall be furnished in accordance with that paragraph within 21 days beginning with –

   (a)  in the case of sub-paragraph (a), (b) or (d) of that paragraph, the day on which the person responsible for the pension arrangement receives the pension sharing order or provision; or (*b*)   in the case of sub-paragraph (*c*) of that paragraph, the later of the days specified in section 34(1)(*a*) and (*b*) of the 1999 Act (implementation period).

**8 Provision of information after the implementation of a pension sharing order or provision**

(1) The person responsible for the pension arrangement shall issue a notice of discharge of liability to the transferor and the transferee, or, as the case may be, the person entitled to the pension credit by virtue of regulation 6 of the Implementation and Discharge of Liability Regulations no later than the end of the period of 21 days beginning with the day on which the discharge of liability in respect of the pension credit is completed.

(2) In the case of a transferor whose pension is not in payment, the notice of discharge of liability shall include the following details –

(*a*)   the value of the transferor's accrued rights as determined by reference to the cash equivalent value of those rights calculated and verified in accordance with regulation 3 of the Valuation Regulations (calculation and verification of cash equivalents for the purposes of the creation of pension debits and credits);

(*b*)   the value of the pension debit;

(*c*)   any amount deducted from the value of the pension rights in accordance with regulation 9(2)(*c*) of the Charging Regulations (charges in respect of pension sharing activity – method of recovery);

(*d*)   the value of the transferor's rights after the amounts referred to in sub-paragraphs (*b*) and (*c*) have been deducted; and

(*e*)   the transfer day.

(3) In the case of a transferor whose pension is in payment, the notice of discharge of liability shall include the following details –

(*a*)   the value of the transferor's benefits under the pension arrangement as determined by reference to the cash equivalent value of those rights calculated and verified in accordance with regulation 3 of the Valuation Regulations;

(*b*)   the value of the pension debit;

(*c*)   the amount of the pension which was in payment before liability in respect of the pension credit was discharged;

(*d*)   the amount of pension which is payable following the deduction of the pension debit from the transferor's pension benefits;

(*e*)   the transfer day;

(*f*)   if the person responsible for the pension arrangement intends to recover charges, the amount of any unpaid charges –

(i)   not prohibited by regulation 2 of the Charging Regulations (general requirements as to charges); and

(ii)   specified in regulations 3 and 6 of those Regulations;

(*g*)   how the person responsible for the pension arrangement will recover the charges referred to in sub-paragraph (*f*), including –

(i) whether the method of recovery specified in regulation 9(2)(*d*) of the Charging Regulations will be used;

(ii) the date when payment of those charges in whole or in part is required; and

(iii) the sum which will be payable by the transferor, or which will be deducted from his pension benefits, on that date.

(4) In the case of a transferee –

(*a*) whose pension is not in payment; and

(*b*) who will become a member of the pension arrangement from which the pension credit rights were derived,

the notice of discharge of liability to the transferee shall include the following details –

(i) the value of the pension credit;

(ii) any amount deducted from the value of the pension credit in accordance with regulation 9(2)(*b*) of the Charging Regulations;

(iii) the value of the pension credit after the amount referred to in sub-paragraph (*b*)(ii) has been deducted;

(iv) the transfer day;

(v) any periodical charges the person responsible for the pension arrangement intends to make, including how and when those charges will be recovered from the transferee; and

(vi) information concerning membership of the pension arrangement which is relevant to the transferee as a pension credit member.

(5) In the case of a transferee who is transferring his pension credit rights out of the pension arrangement from which those rights were derived, the notice of discharge of liability to the transferee shall include the following details –

(*a*) the value of the pension credit;

(*b*) any amount deducted from the value of the pension credit in accordance with regulation 9(2)(*b*) of the Charging Regulations;

(*c*) the value of the pension credit after the amount referred to in sub-paragraph (*b*) has been deducted;

(*d*) the transfer day; and

(*e*) details of the pension arrangement, including its name, address, reference number, telephone number, and, where available, the business facsimile number and electronic mail address, to which the pension credit has been transferred.

(6) In the case of a transferee, who has reached normal benefit age on the transfer day, and in respect of whose pension credit liability has been discharged in accordance with paragraph 1(2), 2(2), 3(2) or 4(4) of Schedule 5 to the 1999 Act (pension credits: mode of discharge – funded pension schemes, unfunded public service pension schemes, other unfunded pension schemes, or other pension arrangements), the notice of discharge of liability to the transferee shall include the following details –

(*a*)   the amount of pension credit benefit which is to be paid to the transferee;

(*b*)   the date when the pension credit benefit is to be paid to the transferee;

(*c*)   the transfer day;

(*d*)   if the person responsible for the pension arrangement intends to recover charges, the amount of any unpaid charges –

    (i)   not prohibited by regulation 2 of the Charging Regulations; and

    (ii)   specified in regulations 3 and 6 of those Regulations; and

(*e*)   how the person responsible for the pension arrangement will recover the charges referred to in sub-paragraph (*d*), including –

    (i)   whether the method of recovery specified in regulation 9(2)(*e*) of the Charging Regulations will be used;

    (ii)   the date when payment of those charges in whole or in part is required; and

    (iii)   the sum which will be payable by the transferee, or which will be deducted from his pension credit benefits, on that date.

(7) In the case of a person entitled to the pension credit by virtue of regulation 6 of the Implementation and Discharge of Liability Regulations, the notice of discharge of liability shall include the following details –

(*a*)   the value of the pension credit rights as determined in accordance with regulation 10 of the Implementation and Discharge of Liability Regulations (calculation of the value of appropriate rights);

(*b*)   any amount deducted from the value of the pension credit in accordance with regulation 9(2)(*b*) of the Charging Regulations;

(*c*)   the value of the pension credit;

(*d*)   the transfer day; and

(*e*)   any periodical charges the person responsible for the pension arrangement intends to make, including how and when those charges will be recovered from the payments made to the person entitled to the pension credit by virtue of regulation 6 of the Implementation and Discharge of Liability Regulations.

## 9 Penalties

Where any trustee or manager of an occupational pension scheme fails, without reasonable excuse, to comply with any requirement imposed under regulation 6, 7 or 8, the Regulatory Authority may by notice in writing require that trustee or manager to pay within 28 days from the date of its imposition, a penalty which shall not exceed –

(*a*)   £200 in the case of an individual, and

(*b*)   £1,000 in any other case.

Amendments—SI 2009/615.

## 10 Provision of information after receipt of an earmarking order

(1) The person responsible for the pension arrangement shall, within 21 days beginning with the day that he receives –

(a)    an order under section 23 of the Matrimonial Causes Act 1973, so far as it includes provision made by virtue of section 25B or 25C of that Act (powers to include provision about pensions);

(b)    an order under section 12A(2) or (3) of the Family Law (Scotland) Act 1985; or

(c)    an order under Article 25 of the Matrimonial Causes (Northern Ireland) Order 1978, so far as it includes provision made by virtue of Article 27B or 27C of that Order (Northern Ireland powers corresponding to those mentioned in sub-paragraph (a)),

issue to the party with pension rights and the other party a notice which includes the information specified in paragraphs (2) and (5), or (3), (4) and (5), as the case may be.

(2) Where an order referred to in paragraph (1)(a), (b) or (c) is made in respect of the pension rights or benefits of a party with pension rights whose pension is not in payment, the notice issued by the person responsible for a pension arrangement to the party with pension rights and the other party shall include a list of the circumstances in respect of any changes of which the party with pension rights or the other party must notify the person responsible for the pension arrangement.

(3) Where an order referred to in paragraph (1)(a) or (c) is made in respect of the pension rights or benefits of a party with pension rights whose pension is in payment, the notice issued by the person responsible for a pension arrangement to the party with pension rights and the other party shall include –

(a)    the value of the pension rights or benefits of the party with pension rights;

(b)    the amount of the pension of the party with pension rights after the order has been implemented;

(c)    the first date when a payment pursuant to the order is to be made; and

(d)    a list of the circumstances, in respect of any changes of which the party with pension rights or the other party must notify the person responsible for the pension arrangement.

(4) Where an order referred to in paragraph (1)(a) or (c) is made in respect of the pension rights of a party with pension rights whose pension is in payment, the notice issued by the person responsible for a pension arrangement to the party with pension rights shall, in addition to the items specified in paragraph (3), include –

(a)    the amount of the pension of the party with pension rights which is currently in payment; and

(b)    the amount of pension which will be payable to the party with pension rights after the order has been implemented.

(5) Where an order referred to in paragraph (1)(a), (b) or (c) is made the notice issued by the person responsible for a pension arrangement to the party with pension rights and the other party shall include –

(a)    the amount of any charges which remain unpaid by –

(i)    the party with pension rights; or

(ii)    the other party,

in respect of the provision by the person responsible for the pension arrangement of information about pensions and divorce or dissolution of a civil partnership pursuant to regulation 3 of the Charging Regulations, and in respect of complying with an order referred to in paragraph (1)(*a*), (*b*) or (*c*); and

(*b*)    information as to the manner in which the person responsible for the pension arrangement will recover the charges referred to in sub-paragraph (*a*), including –

    (i)    the date when payment of those charges in whole or in part is required;

    (ii)    the sum which will be payable by the party with pension rights or the other party, as the case may be; and

    (iii)    whether the sum will be deducted from payments of pension to the party with pension rights, or, as the case may be, from payments to be made to the other party pursuant to an order referred to in paragraph (1)(*a*), (*b*) or (*c*).

**Amendments**—SI 2005/2877.

# Appendix 9

# SHARING OF STATE SCHEME RIGHTS (PROVISION OF INFORMATION AND VALUATION) (NO 2) REGULATIONS 2000, SI 2000/2914

**1 Citation, commencement and interpretation**

(1) These Regulations may be cited as the Sharing of State Scheme Rights (Provision of Information and Valuation) (No 2) Regulations 2000 and shall come into force on 1 December 2000.

(2) In these Regulations –

'the 1992 Act' means the Social Security Contributions and Benefits Act 1992;
'the 1999 Act' means the Welfare Reform and Pensions Act 1999;
'shareable state scheme rights' has the meaning given by section 47(2) of the 1999 Act.

**2 Basic information about the sharing of state scheme rights and divorce or the dissolution of a civil partnership**

(1) The requirements imposed on the Secretary of State for the purposes of section 23(1)(*a*) of the 1999 Act (supply of pension information in connection with divorce etc) are that he shall furnish –

(*a*) the information specified in paragraphs (2) and (3) –
  (i) to a person who has shareable state scheme rights on request from that person; or
  (ii) to the court, pursuant to an order of the court; or
(*b*) the information specified in paragraph (3) to the spouse or civil partner of a person who has shareable state scheme rights, on request from that spouse or civil partner.

(2) The information specified in this paragraph is a valuation of the person's shareable state scheme rights.

(3) The information in this paragraph is an explanation of –

(*a*) the state scheme rights which are shareable;
(*b*) how a pension sharing order or provision will affect a person's shareable state scheme rights; and

(*c*) how a pension sharing order or provision in respect of a person's shareable state scheme rights will result in the spouse or civil partner of the person who has shareable state scheme rights becoming entitled to a shared additional pension.

(4) The Secretary of State shall furnish the information specified in paragraphs (2) and (3) to the court or, as the case may be, to the person who has shareable state scheme rights within –

(*a*) 3 months beginning with the date the Secretary of State receives the request or, as the case may be, the order for the provision of that information;

(*b*) 6 weeks beginning with the date the Secretary of State receives the request or, as the case may be, the order for the provision of the information, if the person who has shareable state scheme rights has notified the Secretary of State on the date of the request or order that the information is needed in connection with proceedings commenced under any of the provisions referred to in section 23(1)(*a*) of the 1999 Act; or

(*c*) such shorter period specified by the court in an order requiring the Secretary of State to provide a valuation in accordance with paragraph (2).

(5) Where –

(*a*) the request made by the person with shareable state scheme rights for, or the court order requiring, the provision of information does not include a request or, as the case may be, an order for a valuation under paragraph (2); or

(*b*) the spouse or civil partner of the person with shareable state scheme rights requests the information specified in paragraph (3),

the Secretary of State shall furnish that information to the person who has shareable state scheme rights, his spouse, civil partner, or the court, as the case may be, within one month beginning with the date the Secretary of State receives the request or the court order for the provision of that information.

Amendments—SI 2005/2877.

### 3 Information about the sharing of state scheme rights and divorce or dissolution of a civil partnership: valuation of shareable state scheme rights

Where an application for financial relief or financial provision under any of the provisions referred to in section 23(1)(*a*) of the 1999 Act has been made or is in contemplation, the valuation of shareable state scheme rights shall be calculated and verified for the purposes of regulation 2(2) of these Regulations in such manner as may be approved by or on behalf of the Government Actuary.

Amendments—SI 2005/2877.

**4 Calculation and verification of cash equivalents for the purposes of the creation of state scheme pension debits and credits**

For the purposes of –

(*a*)   section 49 of the 1999 Act (creation of state scheme pension debits and credits);

(*b*)   section 45B of the 1992 Act (reduction of additional pension in Category A retirement pension: pension sharing);

(*c*)   section 55A of the 1992 Act (shared additional pension); and

(*d*)   section 55B of the 1992 Act (reduction of shared additional pension: pension sharing),

cash equivalents shall be calculated and verified in such manner as may be approved by or on behalf of the Government Actuary.

**5 Revocation**

The Sharing of State Scheme Rights (Provision of Information and Valuation) Regulations 2000 are revoked.

# Appendix 10

# USEFUL INFORMATION TO REQUEST WHEN PREPARING A BUSINESS VALUATION

## 1   History of the business, including:

- Date established.

- Period of ownership.

- Details of previous ownership, if applicable.

- Brief details of the main activities over its history together with the reasons for any significant changes in activity.

## 2   Detailed description of activities, including:

- Details of all key products and services provided together with the percentage of total sales each main category represents.

- Current capacity of business using existing resources, current utilisation of resources and potential for increasing capacity, including an estimate of any additional costs in terms of personnel, trading assets or other resources required to do so.

- Inter-company/inter-business relationships if any (including full company names and registration numbers) and reasons therefore, together with brief details of inter-company transactions for the last 3 years, if these are not disclosed in the accounting information.

- Details of relevant certifications etc, eg ISO 9001, ISO 14001.

## 3   Markets and marketing

- Brief details on the overall structure of the market in which the business operates, main sectors, main players.

- Details of recent trends in the market.

- Geographical features of the market.

- A strengths, weaknesses, opportunities and threats analysis for the business, in bullet point format.

- Summary of key competitive advantages.

- Details of main competitors, including names, size etc.

- Details of marketing activities, including website address, names of relevant trade journals, resources, branding and routes to market.

- Copies of any promotional literature, press cuttings etc.

## 4 Copies of the last three years' detailed accounts and the most recent management accounts, including:

- A summary of the turnover in terms of volume and value by product by month for the last 24 months up to the date of the latest management or annual accounts supplied.

- A brief narrative on any significant trends in the results in relation to the performance of the business or changes in the market, together with reasons for variances in the normal overhead costs.

- A note of any costs or income that would not be expected to be repeated in future years so that profits can be adjusted accordingly to show the sustainable profit trend. For example, exceptional legal costs or one off costs.

- Analysis, and description where necessary, of all assets or liabilities not separately identified in the latest balance sheet (e g accruals / prepayments other debtors or creditors).

## 5 Current and future prospects, including:

- Valuation of forward order position and details on the average lead time between placing an order and delivery of products.

- Any Business Plans or financial projections (including future capital expenditure requirements).

- Details of the assumptions used to prepare the projections.

# 6   Trading relationships, including:

- Annual turnover for the top 10 customers (disclosing the individual balances) for the last financial year and a copy of the latest aged sales ledger (or at least the total ageing profile) ideally reconciled to the management accounts.

- Details of customer profile, levels of recurring work.

- Comments of the level of bad debts over the last 3 years.

- Annual purchases for the top 10 suppliers (disclosing individual balances) for the last financial year and a copy of the latest aged purchase ledger (or at least the total ageing profile) ideally reconciled to the management accounts.

- Summary details of major customer or supplier contracts.

- General terms of trade with suppliers and customers, if not included in above, including any special payment arrangements.

# 7   Borrowings and security, including:

- Details of all bank loans, HP agreements and finance leases.

- Details of any security provided in respect of the above.

- A copy of the latest Facility Letter(s) and any other correspondence with the bank(s) in the past 12 months.

# 8   Directors and employees, including:

- Summary of all employees, including directors analysed by function (eg admin, production etc) to include age / length of service / pension payments and benefits / service agreements / whether full time or part time / salary details / qualifications / membership of unions / normal hours worked.

- A brief narrative on how the business is managed and the levels of responsibility of the key members of the management team (an organisation chart would be helpful).

- Details of additional staff that may be desirable in the short to medium term to develop the business.

## 9    Business assets, including:

- Summary of fixed assets by category and details of the cost of replacement (net of VAT) for any assets that may require replacement in the next 3 years and, where individual assets exceed £10,000, these are identified separately.

- Premises details, including facilities (square footage, security features and any recent modernisation) and summary details of any leases.

- Copies of latest buildings valuation, if any.

- A summary of the key categories of stock and the basis of valuation and provisioning.

## 10   Tax returns

- Corporation Tax returns and computations.

- Directors' (and other relevant parties') tax returns.

- Directors' (and other relevant parties') P11Ds.

- VAT returns.

## 11   Other

- Full details of management information systems, including list of hardware and software.

- Details of all operating leases for plant and ongoing maintenance contracts.

- Details of all intellectual property held or being applied for.

- Details of all licences held or being applied for in connection with business activities.

- Details of any significant legal claims or ongoing disputes, including HMRC enquiries.

- Brief details of any significant insurance claims (>£50,000) in the last 6 years and also any employee claims against the business.

- Details of any other contingent liabilities, such as environmental, health and safety issues.

- Copy of the Memorandum and Articles of Association and any Shareholders' Agreements, together with a brief summary of the key rights of individual classes of shareholders with regard to receipt of dividends and voting powers.

- Details of any other significant matters that may impact on the business.

# Appendix 11

# Draft Letter of Instruction to a Forensic Accountant

Divide & Conquer LLP
14, Aington Lane,
Paington,
Devon
TQ2 0AC

Your ref:

Our ref:    ABC.DE.0123.Smith

Mr David Liddell
PKF
DX 7120780
BIRMINGHAM 29

27 September 2009

Dear Sir

**Our client: George Smith**

We represent Mr George Smith, the Respondent husband in respect of family proceedings currently being heard before Westminster County Court (case number MMM0PQ567).

Mrs Lauren Smith, the Applicant, is represented by Messrs Weare Divorce Lawyers, solicitors, of Wenting Chambers, 3 Donald Street, Cambridge C02 7RKO telephone: 01383 515 000 and fax: 01383 515 001 (ref: XYZ.VW.1098. lsmith).

Both parties attended Court before District Judge Smart at the First Appointment Hearing on 2 September 2009. District Judge Smart ordered the parties to instruct a forensic accountant to deal with some rather complex issues in terms of the husband's businesses. Both parties need to agree on a forensic accountant by 16 October 2009 and it is in this regard we are writing to you.

A letter of instruction is to be despatched to the agreed forensic account by 24 October 2009 and a report will need to be filed by 4pm on 6 December 2009.

The report will need to cover the following issues:

(i)    The current market value of two companies – Treasury Investment Management Limited ('TIM Ltd') and Number 10 Fund Management Plc ('NTFM Plc').

(ii)    The value of the Respondent's 75% shareholding in TIM Ltd.

(iii)    The value of the parties' respective shareholdings in NTFM Plc.

(iv)    The value of the parties' combined shareholdings in NTFM Plc.

(v)    The value of the combined shareholdings of the parties and the Smith Trust Settlement.

(vi)    The value of the Respondent's shareholdings in these companies and/or such companies in which he had a shareholding as at 2 May 1997 (the date of co-habitation).

(vi)    The ways in which the value in the parties' shareholdings could be realised and the tax consequences of so doing.

(vii)    The ability to raise capital from the companies and the tax consequences of so doing.

(viii)    The maximum income (gross and net) that the Respondent could draw out of the companies by way of salary, bonus, dividend and/or commissions, now and in the foreseeable future.

(ix)    The tax consequences of a transfer and/or sale of each parties' shareholdings.

(x)    The tax consequences of a transfer by the Applicant to the Respondent of her estate and interest in Freshden Hall.

(xi)    The tax consequences of a sale of Freshden Hall.

In order to assist you in determining if you are able to assist in the preparation of the above report, we enclose our client's Form E financial statement.

If both parties agree upon your instruction, you will be instructed as a single joint expert and in this respect we enclose a copy of the Civil Procedure Rules part 35 Direction for your ease of reference. We are sure that we would not need to remind you that if you instructed on this matter, your primary duty will be to the Court.

We would be grateful if you could by return:

1.  Provide a copy of your Curriculum Vitae;

2.  State what form of internal licensing you have from your firm or from ICAEW to undertake assignments as expert witness involving companies which are FSA regulated;

3.  Estimates of the costs of:
    a.  your report;
    b.  answering questions from the parties – here an hourly rate will do, as you will not know how long this will take;
    c.  attending Court for one day, if the matter goes to a final contested hearing and either party of the Court wishes to ask you questions; and
    d.  the whole exercise – a range will do.

As you are instructed as a single joint expert, both parties will be equally responsible for your reasonable fees.

When responding to this letter, would you ensure that Messrs Weare Divorce Lawyers are copied into all correspondence.

Please do not hesitate to contact me on 020 666 9999 or Messrs Weare Divorce Lawyers on 01383 515 000 with regards to any further information that you may require on the above.

I look forward to hearing from you.

Yours faithfully


Oliver Patrick

Family Law Partner
Divide & Conquer LLP

Direct Dial: 020 666 9009
Direct Fax: 020 666 9991
E-mail:oliverpatrick@D&C.com

c.c.  Mr Thomas Louis, Weare Divorce Lawyers.

# INDEX

References are to paragraph numbers.